Human Nature
and the
Evolution of Society

Human Nature
and the
Evolution of Society

STEPHEN K. SANDERSON

WESTVIEW
PRESS

A Member of the Perseus Books Group

Westview Press was founded in 1975 in Boulder, Colorado, by notable publisher and intellectual Fred Praeger. Westview Press continues to publish scholarly titles and high-quality undergraduate- and graduate-level textbooks in core social science disciplines. With books developed, written, and edited with the needs of serious nonfiction readers, professors, and students in mind, Westview Press honors its long history of publishing books that matter.

Find us on the World Wide Web at www.westviewpress.com.
Every effort has been made to secure required permissions for all text, images, maps, and other art reprinted in this volume.

Westview Press books are available at special discounts for bulk purchases in the United States by corporations, institutions, and other organizations. For more information, please contact the Special Markets Department at the Perseus Books Group, 2300 Chestnut Street, Suite 200, Philadelphia, PA 19103, or call (800) 810-4145, ext. 5000, or e-mail special.markets@ perseusbooks.com.

Library of Congress Cataloging-in-Publication Data
Sanderson, Stephen K.
    Human nature and the evolution of society / Stephen K. Sanderson.
        pages cm
    Includes bibliographical references and index.
    ISBN 978-0-8133-4936-7 (pbk.)—ISBN 978-0-8133-4937-4 (e-book) 1. Social evolution. 2. Human evolution. 3. Human behavior. I. Title.

HM626.S357 2014
303.4—dc23
                                                                2013036926

10 9 8 7 6 5 4 3 2 1

CONTENTS

Preface ix
Notes on Dating xiii

1 Theoretical Foundations **1**

Darwinian Social Science Redux, 1
Darwinian Foundations, 3
Sociobiology and Evolutionary Psychology, 5
Qualifiers, 8
The Contents of Human Nature, 11
Conclusion, 12
Summary, 13
Questions for Discussion, 16
References and Notes, 16

2 Beginnings **19**

African Genesis, African Exodus, 20
Big Brains, 24
The Language Instinct, 27
The Cultural Big Bang, 32
Conclusion, 34
Summary, 35
Questions for Discussion, 37
References and Notes, 38

3 Getting a Living **41**

To Hunt and to Gather, 41
Ancient Affluence?, 46
First Agriculture, 49
Tillers of the Soil, 53
Herders of Beasts, 59
Merchants and Traders, 60

Capitalists Small and Large, 63
Capitalists by Nature?, 68
Conclusion, 69
Summary, 70
Questions for Discussion, 73
References and Notes, 74

4 Foodways   77

What's for Dinner?, 77
Sweets and Meats, 81
Strategic Foraging, 83
Sacred Cows and Abominable Pigs, 87
The Milky Way, 92
Summary, 100
Questions for Discussion, 103
References and Notes, 104

5 Finding Mates   107

Incest Avoidance and the Incest Taboo, 108
Sexual Selection, 115
Strategic Sex, 119
Mate Choice, 126
Dominant Males Litter the Landscape, 141
The Straight and the Gay, 144
Summary, 152
Questions for Discussion, 154
References and Notes, 155

6 Family and Marriage   161

Kith and Kin, 162
Father's Kin or Mother's?, 164
One Wife or Many?, 170
One Husband or Many?, 175
Summary, 181
Questions for Discussion, 183
References and Notes, 184

7 Parenthood   187

Maternal Instincts, 188
A Child's-Eye View, 192
Many Children or Few?, 195

Sons or Daughters?, 200
Infanticidal Deeds, 205
Summary, 209
Questions for Discussion, 212
References and Notes, 213

8 Gender   215

Gender Everywhere, 216
Learning About Gender, 224
Gender Economies, 225
Men, Women, and Work, 229
Conclusion, 238
Summary, 239
Questions for Discussion, 241
References and Notes, 242

9 Status and Wealth   245

Status Striving, 245
Status Striving Unleashed, 248
Status and Wealth in Modern Times, 254
Status Striving Run Amok, 256
Conclusion, 259
Summary, 260
Questions for Discussion, 261
References and Notes, 262

10 Power and Politics   265

Struggling for Power, 266
Societies Without Bosses, 269
Chiefs on the Horizon, 271
Kings, Emperors, and Oriental Despots, 274
Conclusion, 281
Summary, 282
Questions for Discussion, 284
References and Notes, 285

11 Violence   287

Murder, He Wrote, 287
Getting in Touch with Our Inner Chimp, 296
Killing Enemies: The Small Scale, 298
Killing Enemies: The Large Scale, 305

Summary, 310
Questions for Discussion, 312
References and Notes, 313

12 Race and Ethnicity   317

The Origins of Races, 317
Racism Then and Now, 324
Ethnic Primordialism, 330
Summary, 334
Questions for Discussion, 336
References and Notes, 337

13 Religion   339

Spirits, Gods, and Ritual Specialists, 339
Shamans and Healers, 341
Many Gods or One?, 343
Why Are People Religious?, 344
Religion in Its Socioecological Context, 347
The New Atheism, 349
Summary, 350
Questions for Discussion, 352
References and Notes, 353

14 Arts   355

What Are the Arts?, 355
Visual Art, 358
Literature, 364
Music, 369
Conclusion, 374
Summary, 375
Questions for Discussion, 377
References and Notes, 378

Epilogue: Evolution and Existence   381

Bibliography   387
Technical Terms   427
Index   433

PREFACE

For much of the twentieth century, especially after the 1930s, social science was dominated by explanations of human behavior that gave primary (and sometimes overwhelming) emphasis to the causal role of the social and cultural environment. Social scientists embraced the view of the seventeenth-century English philosopher John Locke, who claimed that the human mind was a tabula rasa, or "blank slate," on which society wrote its "script." Human behavior was therefore principally determined by the social and cultural circumstances in which people live. This is the prevailing view still today. Indeed, the Harvard psychologist Steven Pinker calls it "the official view."

But in the 1970s and 1980s an intellectual revolution began. Some social scientists, mostly anthropologists and psychologists (and a handful of sociologists), returned to the general theory of life adumbrated by Charles Darwin more than a century before. Darwin is, of course, best known for his theory of evolution by natural selection, and he focused mostly on animals. But he also thought that humans evolved from earlier animals—primates, principally the great apes—and he thought that the human mind was much more than a blank slate. It contained numerous features that were evolutionary products and continued to shape behavior. His most important book on humans was *The Expression of the Emotions in Man and Animals*, in which he argued that human emotions and their expression, principally in the human face, were universals that were innate.

The new maverick social scientists thought that Darwinian thinking held one of the keys to explaining many features of human behavior and social life. The new approaches were called, first, sociobiology, and then later evolutionary psychology. In time a major intellectual organization was formed, the Human Behavior and Evolution Society, or HBES. The evolutionary analysis of behavior was becoming a significant force. New specialized journals were founded and textbooks started to be written, sure signs that Darwinian social science was becoming institutionalized.

This book is a new contribution to the list. There are several excellent textbooks, but most of them concentrate heavily on theoretical principles and are highly technical. There is nothing wrong with this—in fact, such books are much needed—but

ix

it is not the only way to do it. This book, intended both for students and the general reader, is different in several important ways. First, it is less technical and lighter on theory. The first chapter outlines the most basic principles of Darwinian social science, but only to the extent that they are necessary to understand what follows. Second, an effort has been made to choose topics that are highly appealing to students and general readers and to present them in lively, engaging, and highly accessible prose. Finally, it expands the coverage by adding topics that are either underemphasized in existing texts or ignored altogether. I refer in particular to the subjects of language origins, subsistence strategies, human foodways and dietary practices, gender roles and relations, race and ethnicity, religion, and the arts. The book concludes by asking whether evolutionary theory can shed any light on the perennial question of the meaning of human existence. Just to give a sample of specific topics, the book explores

- ✓ The origins of language
- ✓ Why humans invented agriculture
- ✓ Economic exchange and capitalism
- ✓ Innate tastes
- ✓ Which humans drink milk and why
- ✓ Why some men have many wives
- ✓ Why some women have many husbands
- ✓ Where there is an incest taboo
- ✓ Why men and women seek different qualities in mates
- ✓ Why some people are gay rather than straight
- ✓ Whether there is a maternal instinct
- ✓ Why infanticide occurs
- ✓ The biology of gender
- ✓ Why status strivings exist and sometimes run amok
- ✓ Why people seek power
- ✓ Why people sometimes kill each other and why it is most often men who do so
- ✓ Why war is so common
- ✓ Whether there are biological races
- ✓ Whether racism is modern or ancient
- ✓ Why ethnic groups are frequently in conflict
- ✓ Why people are religious
- ✓ Why some religions have many gods and others only one
- ✓ Why atheism is on the rise
- ✓ Why people like art, music, and stories
- ✓ Why there is something rather than nothing, and why humans are part of the something

Some critics say that evolutionary arguments are mostly "just-so stories," or made-up explanations that are provocative and interesting but are not supported by real evidence. But in fact there is a good deal of evidence, and in this book I have taken care to present some of the most important evidence for specific evolutionary claims. In the bibliography the many books that contain this evidence, and the specialized journals in which hundreds if not thousands of research articles have appeared, can be found.

To test evolutionary theories empirically it is necessary to study behavior in the full range of human societies that have ever existed. You can't just study Americans or Westerners in general, or just people in any modern society east or west. You also have to look at behavior among people who live by hunting and gathering, by one or another type of agriculture, by animal herding, or by some combination of these. A historical perspective is necessary as well. What were people doing in ancient Egypt, ancient Rome, medieval Europe, or traditional China and India? And you need to explore human action in all of the major regions of the world, where some people live in grasslands, atop tall mountains, in deserts, in tropical rain forests, in hot, humid climates or bitterly cold ones, and so on. This sort of comparative and historical perspective is essential for understanding the similarities and differences in human behavior everywhere. It is essential to understand what thoughts and behaviors may be universal, what may be common but not universal, and what may be rare or not exist at all. No general principles of human behavior and human society can be developed without collecting these sorts of data.

I started out in sociology, but even as a graduate student I knew that a comparative perspective is crucial. The sociologists whose work I respected most were doing comparative research with a heavy dose of anthropology. After my PhD, I felt increasingly attracted to anthropology. Although I am officially a member of a sociology department, I am equally comfortable in both fields and, I believe, equally knowledgeable of both. I feel that this gives me something of an advantage because it allows me to grasp the many details of behavior in the entire range of human societies.

I have presented many of the ideas contained in this book in several courses I have taught over many years. I have always found the vast majority of students to be very receptive to them. (There are of course dissenters and those who can't quite decide.) They have often said that it seems patently obvious that there should be such a thing as human nature, and they have been puzzled that many social scientists wish to deny this. In any event, you read the book and you decide.

As aids to the reader, each chapter contains a summary of the main points and a list of questions that you should be able to answer after reading the chapter. If you struggle to answer these questions, you had better go back and have another look. At the end of the book is a short list of technical terms and their definitions. These are boldfaced in the text.

I am indebted to many people who have contributed to my understanding of the ideas developed in this book, but they are far too numerous to thank individually. I would inevitably leave someone out, and then feelings would be hurt. The people who contributed most to the book's development once a first draft was finished were the reviewers solicited by the publisher: Jennie R. Brown, Franklin Pierce University; Jack David Eller, Community College of Denver; William F. McKibbin, University of Michigan–Flint; Benjamin Grant Purzycki, University of British Columbia; and Andreas Wilke, Clarkson University. I also owe a large debt of gratitude to my editor at Westview Press, Leanne Silverman. She resurrected my book proposal after the previous editor departed and it got buried, said she liked it, and solicited reviews of the book's first draft and another set of reviews of the second draft. This is my twelfth book, but I have never had an editor who got so directly involved. Leanne requested several revisions of some material, important clarifications and additions, and the removal of dubious assertions. She has undoubtedly improved the book greatly and has truly earned the title of editor. She made me work hard, but it has been a delight working with her.

STEPHEN K. SANDERSON
Riverside, California

NOTES ON DATING

- Dates for human evolution prior to a million years ago are given in Mya. Thus 4 Mya = 4 million years ago. Dates more recent than one million years ago are given as Kya, or thousand years ago. Thus 350 Kya = 350,000 years ago.
- Prehistoric dates refer to societies known archaeologically and without any written records. They are given in number of years ago (e.g., 8,000 years ago) or in Kya if the date is very old (e.g., 45 Kya = 45,000 years ago).
- Historical dates refer to earlier societies known primarily through the work of historians relying on written records. Historical dates are given in BCE (before the common era) and CE (common era). These dates are now widely used in place of the traditional BC and AD. Dates for historical societies that are relatively recent are given in terms of the century, for example, tenth century CE, or the precise year if known and relevant.

ARTIST'S CARICATURE OF CHARLES DARWIN   Darwin was the greatest biologist of all time. His theories of natural and sexual selection have had enormous impact on evolutionary biology, biological anthropology, sociobiology, evolutionary psychology, and several other academic disciplines.

(Courtesy of the Archives, California Institute of Technology)

Theoretical Foundations

Darwinian Social Science Redux

Anthropologists and sociologists have spent about a century and a half trying to figure out the principles governing the operation of human society. Success has been rather modest, especially when compared to our bigger cousins in the physical and natural sciences, but some progress has nonetheless been made. There are several reasons why progress has not been greater, but one stands out above all the others: the failure to take seriously the notion that there is such a thing as human nature and that this nature plays a major role in human action. Anthropologists and sociologists have for many decades operated under one or another version of what has come to be called the **Standard Social Science Model**,* or **SSSM**.[1] This model assumes that behavior is determined almost entirely by various features of the social and cultural environment. Actually, the SSSM is a broad umbrella term encompassing a variety of approaches that vary in some of their details. The best known version of the SSSM was set forth early in the twentieth century by the anthropologist Franz Boas and has been carried forward by anthropologists and sociologists down to the present day.[2] The idea is that what separates humans from all other animals is **culture**, or the sum total of learned traditions, beliefs, values, and norms that people have created and acquired as members of a particular society. Culture was made possible by the evolution of the large and highly complex human brain, but once the capacity for culture emerged culture overrode human biology as the principal determinant of human behavior and social life.

Other versions of the SSSM include what might be called **role theory** and, more recently, **social constructionism**. Beginning in the 1930s the celebrated sociologist Talcott Parsons formulated the idea that social roles were central elements of social life.[3] Roles were scripts designed by society that prescribed certain courses of action

---

*Terms in boldface are given more extensive definition in the Technical Terms section that appears after the bibliography. Italics are used only for emphasis.

as appropriate or inappropriate. Through a process of **socialization**—direct teaching of juniors by their elders, as well as imitation of elders by juniors—people learned what was expected of them and acted accordingly. (Or, if they failed to act accordingly, they were subjected to sanctions designed to bring them back into line.) This kind of perspective gained wide traction in sociology and is still a major theme even today. Social constructionism is a reaction against what are called **essentialist** explanations of behavior. These are explanations that rely on the idea that certain social categories, such as gender or race, have "essential" characteristics that make them what they are. Essential characteristics are those that are a kind of defining essence of a category. For social constructionists, there are no defining essences. Social categories are cultural inventions or "constructions" created by particular groups of people at particular times. For the constructionists, an essence would be a type of biological essence, and this they reject emphatically. Social constructionism is probably the one version of the SSSM that denies the importance of human biology completely.

Things were not always this way. In the early years of social science, the late nineteenth and early twentieth centuries, a Darwinian evolutionary perspective was often employed. In sociology the leading Darwinian was a Finn by the name of Edward Westermarck. Westermarck wrote a series of books, the most important of which were a fat three-volume work on the history of human marriage and an equally fat two-volume work on the origin of the human moral sense.[4] Westermarck's contemporaries considered him to be one of the leading sociologists of the day and, indeed, we now know that he was far, far ahead of his time. Unfortunately, Westermarck's star began to fade in the 1920s, and by the time of his death in 1939 his ideas had passed out of favor. The reason is that the tide had turned against Darwinian social science, with its emphasis on an evolved human nature, and sharply toward social and cultural explanations. Darwinism became a dead letter in social science for half a century, and the SSSM stole the show. If such a thing as a biologically determined human nature even existed, social scientists thought, it had to be of minor importance.

Why did things change in this way? The intellectual historian Carl Degler has argued persuasively that the reason was not new research or the discovery of new facts.[5] At this time there was a great debate between "hereditarians" and "environmentalists." Existing research could have been interpreted in a convincing way from either perspective. The most defensible interpretation would have emphasized the complex interplay of the genetic or biological and the social or cultural. And, indeed, some scholars drew this conclusion. Degler contends that the tide turned because of a new emerging ideology and social philosophy of *egalitarianism*. A new emphasis was being placed on social equality, and the new egalitarians fervently promoted this goal. Even some hereditarians got swept up in the tide and changed sides. Emphasis on heredity and individual differences, it was thought, undermined the quest for equality, whereas an emphasis on the role of the social and cultural environment promoted it. And thus the SSSM prevailed.

Nevertheless, important developments in theoretical biology in the 1960s and 1970s, especially in evolutionary biology, provided a basis for reconsidering biology's relevance for human behavior. Major theoretical innovations by such eminent scholars as William Hamilton, Robert Trivers, and John Maynard Smith laid new foundations for the study of animal behavior, and human applications were quickly envisioned.[6] As a result, Darwinism reawakened in social science in the 1970s and 1980s, being revived by people calling themselves sociobiologists or evolutionary psychologists.[7] As Westermarck had done three-quarters of a century earlier, they used as their starting point the Darwinian theory of evolution by natural selection to understand the most fundamental features of human social behavior and social organization. This has led to a quantum leap in our understanding of how human social life works.

Darwinian Foundations

Before outlining the basic assumptions and principles of the new Darwinian social science, we first need to understand their general Darwinian foundations. Charles Darwin wrote his great book, *On the Origin of Species*, in 1859. His ideas have been modified and updated over the past century and a half, but most of the core ideas remain intact. He was not the first to introduce the idea of evolution as a way of explaining the wide diversity of species, but he introduced the mechanism that could explain how the evolutionary process worked. This mechanism is known as **natural selection**, and it is one of the simplest processes in nature. Here is how it works. In any population of organisms there are always more offspring produced than there are resources to support. Not all can survive and prosper. A "struggle for existence" is therefore going on all of the time, and organisms are unequally endowed for success in this struggle. Those organisms that have the characteristics that are most useful in adapting to a particular environment will have both a survival and a reproductive advantage. Being more likely to survive, they are also more likely to reproduce and thus leave copies of their **genes** in future generations. (Darwin didn't know about genes, the science of genetics not yet having been developed, but he knew that organisms had traits that were passed on through reproduction, and that this was very important.)

Evolution by natural selection is a two-step process. It starts with variation, which we today know as genetic variation. There is always variation within any population of organisms. This variation arises through both genetic recombination (sexual reproduction) and, most importantly, through mutations, or small changes in single genes. Mutations provide the raw material essential for evolution to occur. Most mutations are harmful and often lethal. They may kill the organism outright, or prevent it from surviving to reproductive age. Some mutations are neutral in their effects, and a few are beneficial, which means that they contribute to survival and reproduction.

The second step is a selection process in which beneficial genes are favored and harmful genes are disfavored. Organisms with beneficial mutations are more likely than those with harmful mutations to survive and reproduce, and thus to pass their beneficial mutations to offspring, who in turn pass them along to their offspring, and so on. Harmful mutations get weeded out as a result of the earlier death and low reproductive rates of organisms containing them. Over very long periods of time, the large-scale accumulation of beneficial or favorable mutations produces changes in populations of organisms, and it is these changes that we call evolution.

Because the mechanism by which evolution occurs is natural selection, it is "nature" that is doing the selecting. By nature we mean the environments in which organisms live. Darwin and modern-day evolutionists have stressed that natural selection is an *adaptive* process, or one that fits organisms to their environments. Let's take a simple example. Imagine a species of organisms called wuzzies, small mammals which have fur that is rather thin. Imagine also that the warm environment in which the wuzzies have been living has been getting colder and that the wuzzies do not have enough fur to protect them from the changing conditions. They start to die off. But a genetic mutation for thicker fur happens to arise in one of the wuzzies, and this mutation gives it a survival and reproductive advantage. It is a beneficial mutation. This wuzzy mates and passes its beneficial mutant gene along to the next generation. Many of its furrier offspring have the same advantage with the same reproductive results. Eventually, thin-furred wuzzies are replaced by thick-furred wuzzies. This is an evolutionary event, but on a rather small scale. Over millions or tens of millions of years much more evolution is possible. The evolving wuzzies may eventually give rise to new species, much like themselves in some ways but also distinct.

For natural selection to occur, organisms must do more than survive. They must also *reproduce*. This is the only way copies of their genes can remain in the gene pool and be passed along to descendants. An organism's success, or **fitness**, is measured in terms of its degree of **reproductive success**. The fittest organisms are those that leave the most offspring and thus the greatest number of genes in future generations. This is the precise meaning of fitness, and in fact is the *only* meaning of fitness. In evolutionary terms, fitness cannot be measured or assessed in any other way.

A variation on the concept of fitness known as **inclusive fitness** was developed in the 1960s and 1970s.[8] You can measure any organism's inclusive fitness by counting its number of descendents, but you can also do it by enumerating its relatives in the same generation. Parents share half of their genes with offspring, but these offspring also share half of their genes with each other. Therefore, it came to be recognized that an organism can promote its genetic representation in a population by showing favoritism toward siblings, and also to some extent toward cousins. You can promote your inclusive fitness by producing offspring, but if you have brothers and sisters you can also do it by helping them reproduce. Favoring kin in this way is often called **kin selection**. The sum total of the copies of your genes in present and descendant generations is your inclusive fitness. It is this idea of inclusive fitness that became the conceptual foundation of what was to be called sociobiology and later evolutionary psychology.

Virtually all anthropologists and sociologists readily agree that evolution has occurred, and that natural selection is the principal mechanism responsible for it.[9] They do not doubt that it is this process that produced humans from their prehuman ancestors. But most balk at the claim that natural selection applies to human *behavior* as well as to human anatomy and physiology. They say no, it doesn't apply to behavior. But this book says yes. You are not being asked to accept this on faith, and evidence will be provided to support this claim. But that will take time and thus has to be postponed to later discussions. Indeed, that is mostly what this book is about.

If human behavior evolved just as the human body did, and if evolution is an adaptive process, then it stands to reason that many features of human behavior must be adaptive. As mentioned previously, this means that there must be something called human nature, which is the sum total of these adaptive behavioral tendencies. (More precisely, human nature is the sum total of the *brain mechanisms* that, in interaction with environmental contingencies, generate adaptive behaviors.) From a Darwinian point of view, the task is therefore to figure out what this human nature is like and how it evolved. What is inside the organism that drives its behavior? In this book we will figure that out and apply it to understand how people throughout the world behave and how societies work.

Sociobiology and Evolutionary Psychology

The term **sociobiology** came into general use in 1975 when the Harvard University biologist Edward O. Wilson published a huge book entitled *Sociobiology: The New Synthesis*.[10] Most of it was about animal behavior, but the final chapter was about humans. Some social scientists paid close attention to that chapter and began to use some of its ideas. A decade later several anthropologists and psychologists started to think in Darwinian terms and introduced a very similar approach that they called **evolutionary psychology**. In the most general sense, sociobiologists and evolutionary psychologists seek to understand the biological foundations of human behavior and social life. More precisely, they argue that the human brain evolved to adapt itself to both the challenges of nature and the challenges imposed by interacting with other people. Humans' evolved species-specific nature interacted with the natural and social environments to shape particular social behaviors and modes of social life.

Some say that evolutionary psychology is basically just a new name for sociobiology. E. O. Wilson, for example, has said that they are the same thing. Evolutionary psychologists see it differently, sometimes very differently. But first we need to consider where the representatives of the two approaches agree. Both agree that human nature evolved in what is called the **Environment of Evolutionary Adaptedness (EEA)**, more often called the **ancestral environment**. This is the environment that existed prior to 10,000 years ago when humans everywhere subsisted by hunting and gathering and most often lived in relatively small bands or camps. Both approaches also agree that human nature evolved as a package of traits that were adaptive in solving the most important problems of human living. Human nature, in other words, consists of a package of **evolutionary adaptations**. In Darwinian terms, a trait is an evolutionary adaptation if it directs behavior that promotes the survival and reproductive success of any organism with the trait.

As for the differences, there are two principal bones of contention. Although agreeing with the evolutionary psychologists that human nature evolved in the ancestral environment, sociobiologists generally assume that what was adaptive back then continues to be adaptive today despite major changes in the nature of social life. Sociobiologists try to infer the content of human nature by looking at the consequences of any given behavior, especially its reproductive consequences. They try to assess whether any given behavior is fitness promoting, regardless of the type of society or environment in which people are living.

Evolutionary psychologists, by contrast, insist that what was adaptive in earlier environments may not be adaptive in novel modern environments. This has an important methodological implication. Evolutionary psychologists suggest that it is of no use to evaluate the reproductive consequences of a behavior in modern environments because a novel environment often deflects behavior in different directions. It doesn't matter whether or not a behavior maximizes reproductive success in modern environments because "the key issue is not whether or not a given phenotypic feature influences reproductive success, but rather whether **differential reproductive success** *historically influenced* the form of the phenotypic feature."[11] (A phenotypic feature is the outward expression of a gene or set of genes. Brown eyes, for example, are phenotypic. The underlying genetic structure is the genotype. A person with brown eyes may carry two genes for brown eyes, or one for brown and another for blue. The brown/brown and brown/blue combinations are genotypic features.) Rather than trying to measure reproductive success in modern environments (or in any society other than the ancestral environment), we should instead be looking for evidence of **adaptive design** in brain mechanisms.

A second difference between the two approaches is evolutionary psychologists' emphasis on the *modular* nature of the brain. They contend that the brain is not a general purpose mechanism, as is claimed by most anthropologists and sociologists (adherents of some version of the SSSM), but an organ that contains a large number of highly specialized mechanisms, usually known as **domain-specific mechanisms**. Each domain-specific mechanism carries out a highly specialized task. These tasks would be things like being alert to predators, sizing up whether someone is a friend or an enemy, or evaluating the reproductive value of a potential mate. Evolutionary psychologists provide several reasons why the brain must be modular.[12] First, the adaptive problems confronted by our ancestors were not general but very specific. An all-purpose brain would be too clumsy and inefficient to solve these problems, and a clumsy and inefficient brain would do a very poor job of promoting survival and reproductive success. Organisms with a general purpose brain would have been at a severe competitive disadvantage and would likely have been extinguished long ago. They would have become no one's ancestors. As John Tooby and Leda Cosmides suggest, "Many adaptive problems that humans routinely solve are simply not solvable by any known general problem-solving strategy, as demonstrated by [such things as] formal solvability analyses on language acquisition."[13]

In addition, because a great deal of (reproductively) successful behavior depends on highly variable environmental conditions requiring behavioral flexibility, such flexibility requires highly specialized brain mechanisms. As Donald Symons points out, "Extreme behavioral plasticity implies extreme mental complexity and stability; that is, an elaborate human nature. Behavioral plasticity for its own sake would be worse than useless, random variation suicide. During the course of evolutionary history the more plastic hominid behavior became the more complex the neural machinery must have become to channel this plasticity into adaptive action."[14]

Finally, there is an important analogy between the brain and the body. The body is not a highly general structure, but rather a complex composite of many highly specialized organs, tissues, and cells, each with a specific function. The heart just pumps blood, the kidneys just filter blood, and so on. The intestines don't process food, pump blood, and take in oxygenated air all at the same time. They just extract nutrients from food and eliminate what cannot be processed. Therefore, since the body directs survival through specialization, the brain must direct behavior through specialization.

The evolutionary psychologists' emphasis on the modular brain seems right, but their point about eschewing the study of reproductive success in modern environments is problematic. So is their idea that the objective should be to find evidence of adaptive design. This is indeed the ideal approach, but it is a great challenge. It is easy to see that the eye reveals evidence of complex adaptive design, but much more difficult to find adaptive design in the mental modules that direct behavior. One way would be to actually locate a brain module and study its design in microscopic detail. But no one has yet found such a module. The existence of brain modules therefore has to be *inferred*. But how? The evolutionary biologist Richard Alexander points out that design cannot be studied except by reference to behavior. "One studies behavioral and other outcomes, judges their reproductive significance, . . . and then infers the underlying physiological and morphological designs. Information about psychological and physiological mechanisms can be gained only by observing ultimate expressions of the phenotype."[15]

Moreover, it is likely that most evolutionary adaptations that arose ancestrally continue to promote adaptive behavior in the modern world. After all, if we say that history has unfolded to produce a series of different types of societies, and if

Darwinian adaptationist assumptions are correct, then later and newer societies should have been built within the framework of those adaptations.[16] It seems highly unlikely that modern societies radically inconsistent with deep human motivations would ever have evolved. (Social experiments attempting to establish radically different communities or societies almost always fail because they are designed in ways that are completely at odds with natural human inclinations.) In modern societies people still favor kin over non-kin, strive for status, and seek high-quality mates, just as they did in the ancestral environment.

Of course, there is no denying that *some* behaviors that were once adaptive will not be adaptive in the modern context. For example, in earlier times everyone sought to reproduce, but in modern times some people choose to remain childless. We therefore need to be sensitive to the evolutionary psychologists' point. However, if we study the reproductive consequences of certain behaviors in modern environments and find that many people are not maximizing their reproductive success, then an important opportunity is presented. We can ask why they are failing to do this, which will give us additional information about underlying psychological mechanisms.[17] As another example, we find that men in all societies seek to mate with many women, a variety of women, and young women. This is just as true in modern times as it was in earlier times. In modern times men are not seeking to produce more offspring by way of mating with many young women, but it is easy to conclude that *they are still acting in accordance with an evolved adaptation that would be reproductively adaptive in the absence of modern contraception.*

A sensible conclusion may be to split the difference between sociobiologists and evolutionary psychologists. The evolutionary psychologists' point about novel environments must be taken seriously, but it seems unwise to completely eschew the study of reproductive success in modern societies. Splitting the difference may seem like having our cake and eating it too, but in this case I think it is justifiable because the approaches are complementary rather than competing. As for terminology, this book uses the term "evolutionary psychology" because it is widely preferred and strongly established. But since sociobiologists and evolutionary psychologists are united in their commitment to Darwinian principles, the term **Darwinian** is also useful and appropriate. Thus one can speak of evolutionary psychological explanations, but also of **Darwinian evolutionary** explanations. In this book the terms are considered equivalent.[18]

Qualifiers

There are several important qualifications to what has been said thus far. Perhaps most importantly, it is crucial to stress that sociobiology and evolutionary psychology are not forms of **biological determinism**, a charge often made by critics. Biological determinism, a viewpoint that hardly anyone has ever advocated, assumes that human behavior is entirely or almost entirely the product of human biology.

The evolved adaptations of the human brain are anything but rigid instincts and do not operate in a vacuum. They operate within a context and the specifics of this context play an important role in determining how they are expressed. A good name for this is **socioecological context**, which is the total set of environmental conditions to which people must adjust or adapt. Socioecological context includes the natural or physical environment, as well as the economic, political, social, and cultural environments, indeed all of the external contingencies that constrain and enable people. Most adaptations are *facultative* in nature. A **facultative adaptation** is one in which individuals assess the socioecological contexts in which they live and adjust their behavior accordingly in order to achieve the objectives that the adaptation is designed for. Sometimes maximizing reproductive success means having numerous children. This might be the case, for example, if infant mortality is high and a substantial number of children are expected to die before they reach reproductive age. But in other contexts maximizing reproductive success can best be done by having fewer children and investing more resources in each. This might be the best strategy when most children are expected to survive to adulthood.

And, as evolutionary psychologists stress, socioecological context can compromise adaptations by deflecting them. This has led the sociologist Joseph Lopreato to formulate what he calls the **modified maximization principle**.[19] This principle speaks to the idea that human nature consists of more than just one thing. People have many goals, and these goals frequently conflict with each other. For example, some people in affluent societies are so concerned with gratifying hedonistic desires that they find children a nuisance and choose not to have any. Consider also mother-infant bonding. Much evidence suggests that mothers and infants are biologically predisposed to bond to each other, but in some instances bonding may be weak or may fail completely. Some women show no interest in becoming mothers because they are pursuing goals that conflict with motherhood. Or, even though people have strong religious propensities, in modern societies in which science plays a major role some people may become persuaded that religious ideas are false and give up religious beliefs and practices altogether. There are many atheists in modern industrialized societies, but they would have been few and far between in past societies.

It is also necessary to distinguish between the conscious and the unconscious origins of behavior. People usually have a very limited understanding of what drives their behavior. If they understood their behavior, there would be no need for social scientists, let alone clinical psychologists or psychiatrists. We could just ask people why they did this or that, and they would tell us. Freud stressed that much human behavior is driven by unconscious motives. Although his overall understanding of these motives has left much to be desired, and has therefore been abandoned by all but a very small number of faithful adherents, he did get that part right. Do people know that in seeking status or promoting their children's well-being they are trying to promote the representation of their genes in the gene pool? Not likely. And if we told them that is what they were doing, most would probably look at us with utter consternation or laugh us out of the room. So none of the mechanisms driving behavior necessarily depend on any conscious understanding on people's part.

Finally, there is an important distinction between the **proximate** and the **ultimate causes** of behavior. Proximate causes are immediate things, often consciously recognized, that induce us to act in a certain way. Humans, for example, like sweet foods. If you are served apple strudel and you like the taste, a proximate explanation of your liking for apple strudel is straightforward: apple strudel is sweet and you, like most people, like sweet things. But another question remains: why do most people like sweets? To answer that question is to provide an explanation in terms of ultimate causes. Darwinian thinking provides us with a two-step ultimate explanation. Step one says that eating a lot of sweet foods in the ancestral environment contributed to survival, good health, and by extension reproductive success. Step two says that evolution crafted the human brain to like sweet things so people will eat more of them and thus be healthier and leave more progeny. And we can say that this explanation is very likely correct. A large part of the human diet in ancestral environments was highly nutritious fruit, and fruit is sweet. And thus the human brain evolved to like sweet foods.

Or take a college student in a classroom sitting next to an attractive young woman. He gets to know her and, unsurprisingly, feels sexual interest. Why does he want sex with this particular woman? At the proximate level, the cause of his behavior is simply that he, like almost all men, finds women who are attractive, young, and well proportioned very desirable. But what would be the ultimate cause of his behavior? The answer is that young, attractive women with certain kinds of body shapes tend to be healthier, have greater fecundity (the ability to conceive), and give birth to healthier offspring than older, less attractive women with body shapes that display lower fecundity. Evolution has sculpted men's brains for such preferences because of the payoff in reproductive success. Like the ultimate explanation of the human fondness for sweet foods, this is a Darwinian evolutionary explanation—it identifies the ultimate causes underlying human motivation and behavior.

Similarly, consider a woman who chooses a physician or a lawyer as her mate rather than a starving artist. We can understand the logic underlying her preference as one for a man with status and resources. Identifying her preference in these terms is a proximate explanation for her choice of a mate. But there is still the question why this woman (and many other women) have such a preference. Why does she prefer a man with status and resources to a man without them (above and beyond the obvious creature comforts that status and resources can provide)? Answering this question requires an understanding of the brain mechanisms that make choosing men with status and resources reproductively adaptive. To identify these mechanisms, which constitute evolved adaptations, is to provide an ultimate explanation that, once again, is a type of Darwinian evolutionary explanation.[20]

The Contents of Human Nature

If our subject is **human nature**, what then does it consist of? What is inside the organism? The following may be suggested as the most important features.[21]

- Humans are self-interested organisms in the sense that they give priority to their own interests over those of others. Being *self-interested* is not the same as being *selfish*. Giving priority to your own interests—being self-interested—cannot be equated with being inconsiderate of others, refusing to share or cooperate, and so on—in other words, being selfish. The promotion of self-interest often involves behavior that is highly cooperative and helpful to others, and thus not really selfish at all.
- Humans are highly sexed and the vast majority prefer heterosexual sex. Powerful sex drives increase the desire to mate and reproduce. People of each sex seek the most favorable mates, which are the ones who will provide their offspring with the best genes. In the mating game, males give priority to females who are young and sexually attractive, whereas females give priority to males who demonstrate that they can be good resource providers.
- Humans are designed to favor kin over non-kin because they share genes in common with kin. Because people can promote the representation of their genes in the gene pool through both their own reproduction and by helping relatives be reproductively successful, kin will be favored over non-kin and close kin over more distant kin. Kinship and the family therefore rest on a natural foundation.
- The most important kinship bond is the parent-child bond, especially the mother-child bond. Appropriate parental behavior is essential for people to promote the representation of their genes. But what constitutes appropriate parental behavior—the most adaptive parental behavior—depends on the kinds of environmental conditions people face. Parental behavior is highly contingent on circumstances.
- Because there are two sexes that contribute in different ways to reproduction, all societies are naturally sexually differentiated. And because sex is related to gender, individuals everywhere have a strong sense of gender identity, which is the most fundamental of all human identities.
- Humans are naturally competitive, and they compete most vigorously for status and resources. Status or social rank is useful and often necessary for acquiring resources and attracting good mates. Although there is natural variation among individuals in the strength of the desire for status and resources, this desire is found in nearly all people in all societies. It is fundamental to how people interact and to how every society is structured.

- Closely tied to status and resource seeking is power seeking. In general, people desire to control situations and influence others, which in many instances takes the form of dominating them in coercive ways. The innate desire to influence, control, or dominate allows humans to try to structure situations so they can gain advantages or benefits for themselves. However, as in the case of status and resource seeking, there is variation in the extent to which particular individuals seek power or influence.

- People not only compete; they also cooperate. They are strongly attached to their fellow humans and feel such natural emotions as affection, sympathy, love, and friendship. They cannot develop normally without social bonds, and they find these bonds necessary to a fulfilling life. The cooperation that makes society possible rests, like competition, on a natural foundation. Nevertheless, people are most likely to cooperate when others can benefit them, or when the failure to cooperate is disadvantageous or injurious. In all known societies, cooperation is most likely to occur among kin, somewhat less likely to occur among friends and close acquaintances, and least likely to be found among distant acquaintances or strangers.

- People are primed for complex learning, which may take one of two principal forms. One form is the direct teaching of juniors by elders. The other involves imitating what others are saying or doing. Most learning likely occurs in the second way; humans are extraordinarily imitative animals. Humans are primed to learn because, given the very wide range of natural and social environments to which they must adapt, learning is essential to human survival and reproduction.[22]

- People everywhere strongly identify with others who share the same culture and language. Ethnic identification arose in ancestral environments because it was adaptive in promoting the interests of the members of groups engaged in competition with other groups.

- Humans have an innate propensity for religious understanding and experience. Religion has many functions, but most importantly it offers people comfort and security, release from anxiety, and the like. People who are more religious tend to be healthier, to live longer, and to leave more offspring than less religious people.

Conclusion

Does evolutionary psychology have all the answers? Can it replace traditional anthropology and sociology? Certainly not. It is not necessary to throw all of standard anthropology and sociology out, because these fields have produced many insights. Although evolutionary psychologists include socioecological context in their explanations, they often do not go far enough. But socioecological context is the stock and trade of traditional anthropology and sociology. We can draw on many of the insights of these fields and combine them with evolutionary psychology to produce more thorough and complete explanations.

Moreover, there are numerous features of social life that have at best a tenuous connection to human biology. If we want to understand why societies have evolved over time as they have—the subject of Chapter 3—human nature may be relevant, but it is only part of the story. Other factors apart from human nature are critical. (In Chapter 3 we will see what these factors are.) And if we want to understand such things as rebellions or revolutions, biology is of almost no help at all. And then take religion. If humans have a biological propensity for religious experience, this alone will hardly tell us why some societies have shamans, why some have priesthoods and others don't, why some practice animal sacrifice and others forbid it, or why some have many small gods and others just one big one. Obviously the entire social, cultural, economic, and political environments in which people find themselves are crucial in understanding the many different forms of religion, and in fact the different forms that all other human institutions take.

SUMMARY

1. Anthropology and sociology have had only limited success because for nearly a century they have largely rejected the notion of human nature and have consequently failed to inquire into the biological foundations of behavior and society. In the late nineteenth and early twentieth centuries human nature was taken seriously, but this concept dwindled in significance and all but disappeared after the 1930s. The social sciences came to be dominated by the so-called Standard Social Science Model, or SSSM. The SSSM exists in various guises, but all versions emphasize that human behavior is predominantly a social and cultural creation.

2. The triumph of the SSSM was largely the result of the triumph of a new social philosophy and ideology of egalitarianism rather than of new facts. However, new developments in theoretical biology in the 1960s and 1970s paved the way for a revival of the human nature concept and a major theoretical shift in the thinking of some social scientists.

3. In the 1970s and 1980s it came to be seen that the most useful way of thinking about human nature is by using key concepts from Darwinian evolutionary biology. Darwinian approaches use the concept of natural selection to explain not only animal (including human) anatomy and physiology but also behavior. Natural selection is the process whereby organisms compete with each other for survival and mates, with those having the genes that are most adaptive in particular environments out-surviving and out-reproducing those with genes that are less adaptive or non-adaptive.

4. For evolution to occur there must be genetic variation within animal and human populations. One of the main sources of variation is genetic mutation. Most mutations are harmful or neutral in their effects, but some are beneficial. When environments change, beneficial mutations will be favored and will spread throughout the gene pool by way of the greater survival and reproductive success of the organisms containing the beneficial genes.

5. The basic currency of adaptation is reproductive success. Organisms can promote the representation of their genes in the gene pool by mating and leaving offspring, but also by favoring relatives who themselves will be better able to leave more offspring. Favoring relatives and helping them reproduce is known as kin selection. Kin selection leads to inclusive fitness, which is the total representation of an organism's genes in the gene pool.

6. These principles apply to humans just as they apply to other animals. In the past forty years two approaches have emerged that use evolutionary principles to understand human behavior. The first, sociobiology, emerged in the 1970s, whereas the second, evolutionary psychology, emerged in the late 1980s. Both approaches seek to understand how a species-specific human nature evolved to promote human survival and reproductive success.

7. Human nature consists of evolutionary adaptations contained in the brain. Sociobiologists and evolutionary psychologists seek to understand the nature of these adaptations. There is debate concerning how similar or different sociobiology and evolutionary psychology are. Both agree that these adaptations arose in the human ancestral environment, which was the period prior to 10,000 years ago in which humans lived in small groups devoted to hunting and gathering. Sociobiologists seek to identify an evolutionary adaptation for a particular behavior by looking to see if that behavior promotes inclusive fitness. Evolutionary psychologists contend that this is a misleading strategy because a behavior that promoted inclusive fitness in the ancestral environment may not do so in modern environments, which are highly novel. Therefore they do not seek to measure reproductive success but look for evidence of adaptive design in the brain.

8. This book takes no strong position on the disagreement between sociobiologists and evolutionary psychologists. It is true that some behaviors that were adaptive in ancestral environments may no longer be adaptive in modern environments, but the issue should be addressed on a case-by-case basis. It is likely that many evolutionary adaptations will continue to be adaptive in modern contexts. The most important point is that sociobiology and evolutionary psychology are far more similar than different. They are united in their emphasis on an evolved human nature as the foundation of much behavior, and as such should be seen as partners rather than competitors. They are Darwinian evolutionary approaches.

9. Evolutionary psychologists stress that the brain is not a general purpose organ; instead, it consists of many highly specialized modules that are domain specific. A module may be specialized for assessing the reproductive value of a potential mate. That is all it does. Or a module may be specialized for rapid language learning. The argument in favor of domain-specific modules is based on the recognition that a general purpose brain would be too clumsy and inefficient to allow people to cope with the various and sundry challenges of human life.

10. Darwinian evolutionary approaches are not forms of biological determinism. They stress that all of the evolutionary adaptations of the brain operate within a socioecological context, or a total set of characteristics of the natural and social environments. Evolutionary adaptations are highly sensitive to this context and adjust themselves to it. For example, people's decisions about how many children to have are highly dependent on several features of the human environment.

11. An important evolutionary principle is the so-called modified maximization principle: people generally strive to maximize reproductive success, but under some circumstances this goal may be deflected by competing goals. In modern societies, for example, some people focus so intensely on their careers that they choose not to have children, fearing that parenthood would interfere with their ability to do their job.

12. Darwinian theory distinguishes between the proximate and the ultimate causes of behavior. Proximate causes are immediate or direct and include such things as natural human preferences (whether conscious or unconscious) and sex hormones. If we explain the human desire for wealth by saying that wealth brings pleasure, we have given a proximate explanation of the desire for wealth. But there is still the question why wealth brings pleasure. If we say that the brain evolved in ancestral environments to associate wealth with pleasure because wealth contributed to reproductive success, then we have given an ultimate explanation of the desire for wealth.

13. Human nature has many dimensions, but the most important are : (a) humans are self-interested organisms who favor their own interests over the interests of others; (b) humans are highly sexed and generally prefer heterosexual sex; (c) humans favor kin over non-kin and close kin over more distant kin; (d) humans are primed for optimal parental behavior; (e) humans are naturally competitive and compete most vigorously for status, resources, and dominance; (f) humans cooperate as well as compete and have natural emotions such as affection, sympathy, love, and friendship; (g) humans are primed to learn because adaptive behavior requires an understanding of socioecological context; (h) humans have an innate propensity for religious understanding and experience; (i) human males and females have a natural sense of gender identity; and (j) humans strongly identify with co-ethnics, or those with whom they share a common culture and language.

QUESTIONS FOR DISCUSSION

✓ What is the Standard Social Science Model, or SSSM, and how has it affected social scientists' receptivity to Darwinian thinking? What are some of the different versions of the SSSM?

✓ Why did the SSSM triumph in the early twentieth century?

✓ What led the late-twentieth-century challenge to the dominance of the SSSM?

✓ Darwinian thinking assumes that human nature is a product of evolution by natural selection. Explain how natural selection works. What key concepts are necessary to explain this process?

✓ Explain the concepts of adaptation and fitness. How is fitness measured in Darwinian terms?

✓ What does it mean to call something an evolutionary adaptation?

✓ What are the similarities and differences between sociobiology and evolutionary psychology as Darwinian approaches to human behavior? Is it necessary to choose one over the other?

✓ What does it mean to say that the brain is not a general purpose organ but consists of a wide range of domain-specific mechanisms? Why do evolutionary psychologists emphasize domain specificity?

✓ What are kin selection and inclusive fitness as evolutionary processes?

✓ What is socioecological context and why is it important to Darwinian social science?

✓ What is the so-called maximization principle? Why is it qualified by calling it the modified maximization principle?

✓ What is the difference between proximate and ultimate causes? Which type of cause is emphasized in Darwinian approaches?

✓ What is meant by human nature? Describe some of its most important dimensions.

References and Notes

1. Tooby and Cosmides 1992.
2. See reprinted articles in Boas 1940.
3. Parsons 1937.
4. Westermarck 1906–1908, 1922a, b, c.
5. Degler 1991.

6. Hamilton 1964; Trivers 1971, 1972, 1974; Maynard Smith 1964, 1974, 1978; cf. Chagnon 2013.

7. E. O. Wilson 1975; Van den Berghe 1978; Daly and Wilson 1978; Chagnon and Irons 1979; Lopreato 1984, 1989; Badcock 1991; Barkow, Cosmides, and Tooby 1992; Nielsen 1994; Betzig 1997; Crawford and Krebs 1998; Lopreato and Crippen 1999; Cronk, Chagnon, and Irons 2000; Segerstråle 2000; Pinker 1997, 2002; Gaulin and McBurney 2003; Buss 2007; Cartwright 2008.

8. Hamilton 1964; Maynard Smith 1964; Alexander 1974.

9. Darwin actually identified another mechanism of evolution that he called *sexual selection*. Discussion of this mechanism is taken up in Chapter 5.

10. E. O. Wilson 1975.

11. Symons 1989, p. 137; emphasis added.

12. Thornhill and Palmer 2000; Tooby and Cosmides 1992.

13. Tooby and Cosmides 1992, p. 111.

14. Symons 1987, p. 127; quoted in Thornhill and Palmer 2000.

15. Alexander 1990, p. 247.

16. Turke 1990, p. 316.

17. Turke 1990.

18. Some evolutionary social scientists use the term *human behavioral ecology* (HBE). Behavioral ecologists study how behavioral variation both within and between societies is the result of evolved mental adaptations interacting with specific features of the ecological environment. Whether this is a distinct approach or simply another name for sociobiology remains unclear. Irons and Cronk 2000 point out that the work of some contemporary scholars who call themselves human behavioral ecologists is based on the same theoretical principles as those calling themselves human sociobiologists. Hames 2001 provides a brief sketch of HBE and some of its major research findings. E. A. Smith 2000 and Winterhalder and Smith 2000 provide a similar sketch, but also explicitly compare HBE and evolutionary psychology. They suggest that it is most productive to see these as complementary rather than competing approaches even though some of their assumptions differ. HBE has proved to be especially useful in the study of dietary practices and is used in the analysis of foodways in Chapter 4.

19. Lopreato 1984, 1989.

20. It is worth pointing out that not all proximate causes involve people's preferences, whether conscious or unconscious (many preferences are unconscious). A proximate cause of the higher levels of aggressiveness found in males relative to females is the male hormone testosterone. There are many such proximate causes of many behaviors.

21. A partially overlapping but much longer list is found in Arnhart 1998.

22. A good discussion of the importance of imitative learning can be found in Boyd and Richerson 1985.

2

Beginnings

Humans are distinguished from all other animal species in a variety of ways, but in particular by large and extremely powerful brains, by the ability to create and learn language and engage in rapidly articulated speech, and by having abstract culture. Humans are most closely related genetically to chimpanzees, and the two species shared a common ancestor some 5–6 million years ago. Modern chimpanzees, which evolved along their own separate line, never developed language or abstract culture or brains anywhere near the size and complexity of the modern human brain.

This chapter tells the story of human evolution after the chimpanzee-human split. Species of humans after that split, previously called hominids, are now known as *hominins*.[1] We will trace the overall transition from one hominin species to another and look at the major changes that occurred, especially in bodies and brains and in the ability to make and use tools. At some point in the development of the brain, humans acquired the capacity for language. When this occurred is still poorly understood. It could have been as recently as 50,000 years ago, as some would have it, but in all likelihood it was earlier, possibly 200,000 years ago, or perhaps even hundreds of thousands of years before then. Whenever language emerged, it is very unlikely that it arose all of a sudden. In all probability language developed gradually over a long period of time and was increasingly perfected. In any event, we will explore the nature of language and explain why it is a safe bet that there is a "language instinct."

Human culture has many components. Material, or technological, culture consists of tools, techniques, and information that people use to make a living and fight wars. Culture also includes socially patterned ways of thinking and acting that the members of a community or society have developed and that persist into subsequent generations, whether by direct teaching or processes of imitation. For most of human history and prehistory, cultures were simple and only started to become highly developed about 50,000 years ago, when a sort of "cultural big bang" was initiated. Culture at this level required complex language and a capacity for highly abstract thought. We will consider the nature of this development at the end of the chapter.

African Genesis, African Exodus

Humans were born in Africa and left it for elsewhere at least three times. Although the first fossils thought to be human were discovered in the nineteenth century, it has been mostly in the past forty years that major discoveries have been made and a much more complete understanding of human evolution has been achieved.

The oldest hominins, known as the australopithecines, first appear in the fossil record around 4–4.5 million years ago (Mya), their remains having been discovered in southern Africa. The australopithecines are identified as humans rather than apes primarily because of their way of getting around and the shape of their dentition. Apes are quadrupeds and have a predominantly pronograde ("hunched over") posture. They walk on all four limbs, usually on their knuckles. The australopithecines, by contrast, had a largely orthograde (upright) posture and were bipedal—they walked only on their legs.[2]

As for teeth and jaws, apes have an elongated, U-shaped dental arcade, whereas the australopithecine arcade was less elongated and had a softly rounded, more V-like shape. In addition, the australopithecine canine teeth were a lot smaller and their molars much larger. Smaller canines suggest a lower level of aggression, and the larger molars indicate a diet consisting primarily of tough plant foods, probably nuts, seeds, and hard fruits. Molars are grinding teeth and large ones are useful for masticating these plants into a digestible form.[3]

The australopithecines were small creatures. Males stood less than five feet tall and weighed about a hundred pounds, whereas females stood barely three and a half feet tall and weighed only about sixty-five pounds. They were not very smart by modern standards. The braincase of modern humans averages about 1,350 cubic centimeters (cc's), but *Australopithecus* had a tiny braincase by comparison. Fossils show that its size varied from 380 to 540 cc's, with an average of about 450.[4]

Artists have tried to reconstruct the appearance of the australopithecine face and, if this reconstruction is reasonably accurate, anyone looking at it would almost certainly say, "this is an ape" (the name *Australopithecus* means "southern ape"). And there are other apelike characteristics: a prominently prognathic (projecting rather than straight) face, an apelike nose and ribcage, and long arms. It is likely that *Australopithecus* was not fully bipedal and did a lot of climbing. In the words of the biological anthropologist Richard Klein, "The australopiths were essentially bipedal apes, who still spent considerable time feeding, sleeping, or avoiding predation in trees."[5]

Some australopithecines may have survived until about a million years ago, but a new hominin species evolved well before this time: *Homo habilis*, meaning "handy man." It is more clearly a hominin. *H. habilis* fossils were first found in the Olduvai Gorge region of eastern Africa, with other fossils being discovered somewhat later in the Lake Turkana region. The various fossils are dated between 2.3 and 1.8 Mya. The differences between *H. habilis* and *Australopithecus* were not pronounced but are important nonetheless. *H. habilis* was less apelike, probably fully bipedal, and somewhat more intelligent, with a cranial capacity in the range of 510–750 cc's. *H. habilis* ate meat and was likely the first hominin to use tools. Fossil remains have been found in association with a variety of stone tools, which were specialized primarily for hammering, butchering carcasses, and scraping hides. Interestingly, *H. habilis* was slightly smaller than *Australopithecus*. Males stood just over four feet and weighed about eighty pounds, whereas females were closer to three feet and seventy pounds.[6]

Next in the evolutionary line is *Homo erectus*, whose fossilized remains begin to show up in the archaeological record some 1.8 Mya. With *H. erectus* we see a large increase in size, with males at about 5 feet 9 and 145 pounds, and females 5 feet 2 and 125 pounds. This shows a reduction in sexual dimorphism—differences in size between the sexes—compared to *H. habilis* and especially to *Australopithecus*. *H. erectus* had a robust build with heavy bones and a large supraorbital (brow) ridge. There was a pronounced increase in brain size, with some fossilized crania measuring 1,000 cc's or slightly larger. A bigger brain allowed *H. erectus* to make better and more specialized tools. *H. erectus* was likely a big game hunter for whom meat was a major part of the diet. *H. erectus* may have been relatively hairless and, if so, probably developed dark skin as a protection against the high levels of ultraviolet radiation that occur in Africa.[7]

H. erectus was the first hominin to leave Africa, doing so at least a million years ago and possibly as early as 1.5 Mya. *H. erectus* fossils have been found in China and Java, some dated to about 800,000 years ago (800 Kya). *H. erectus* may have continued to evolve in east Asia and have been present as recently as 50 Kya, eventually being displaced by in-migrating modern humans.[8]

We are now on the cusp of the Neanderthals, the best-known prehistoric humans to both biological anthropologists and the public at large. Neanderthal remains were the first hominin fossils to be discovered (in 1859 in the Neander valley of Germany, for which they were named), and they are by far the most numerous and complete of all prehistoric human fossils. More recently fossils similar to those of the Neanderthals have been discovered, the best known of which belong to *Homo heidelbergensis*, so named because they were discovered near Heidelberg, Germany. *H. heidelbergensis* probably originated in Africa and later migrated to Europe, eventually evolving into the Neanderthals between about 600 and 400 Kya. Heidelbergers who stayed in Africa later evolved into modern *Homo sapiens*, but that is getting ahead of the story.[9]

The Neanderthals inhabited a wide territory extending from western Asia through most of Europe. They were ruggedly built and heavily muscled, with thick chests, broad trunks, large heads and faces, and short limbs. These are features signifying adaptation to very cold climates, and the climate throughout their range was indeed extremely cold during most of their time on earth. The Neanderthals had improved greatly on the tool kit of earlier hominins, with many more highly specialized and much more efficient tools. They also hunted large game with spears, such as wooly mammoth, wild horses and cattle, and deer. They were probably the first hominins to wear clothing. And their intelligence approximated that of modern humans, with braincases averaging about 1,435 cc's.[10]

Until recently the Neanderthals were thought to be directly ancestral to modern humans and were therefore classified as *Homo sapiens neanderthalensis*, a subspecies of *Homo sapiens*. But we now know that the Neanderthals were an evolutionary dead end, and so they have been assigned to their own species, *Homo neanderthalensis*. The Neanderthals became extinct between about 25 and 30 Kya, and the extinction was rapid. What happened? It is now fairly certain that the Neanderthals had to cope with waves of modern humans entering their territories from Africa and that they simply could not compete on level terms with the moderns. Modern humans were smarter, technologically superior, and better hunters. After they appeared, Neanderthal numbers began to dwindle and within perhaps 10,000 years they had disappeared. They were driven to extinction by the new arrivals. As Richard Klein tells us:

> It is not difficult to understand why the Neanderthals failed to survive. The archaeological record shows that in virtually every detectable aspect—artifacts, site modification, ability to adapt to extreme environments, subsistence, and so forth—the Neanderthals lagged their modern successors, and their more primitive behavior limited their ability to compete for game and other shared resources.[11]

These newcomers were *anatomically modern humans*, who belong to the same species as present-day humans, *Homo sapiens*. Anatomically modern humans evolved in Africa (Ethiopia) sometime around 200 Kya and some groups migrated out of Africa approximately 50–60 Kya. Actually, "migration" is not quite the right word, since modern humans were not necessarily trying to leave Africa and settle in a new region. In all likelihood they were simply dispersing their settlements little by little until they found themselves somewhere else. In any event, they would eventually fill up the entire habitable world.[12]

The exodus is thought to have proceeded through a narrow corridor between northeast Africa and southwest Asia. From Asia groups moved in several directions. Some traveled east through central Asia and then into China. Others moved through the Indian subcontinent and eventually to southeast Asia. From there some populations ended up in Indonesia, Papua New Guinea, and Australia. Some may also have turned north from southeast Asia and entered China from that direction. Northeast Siberia was eventually occupied, and from there some of the Siberians crossed the Bering land bridge into Alaska and gradually occupied North and South America, previously home to no hominin species. There was also, of course, a major

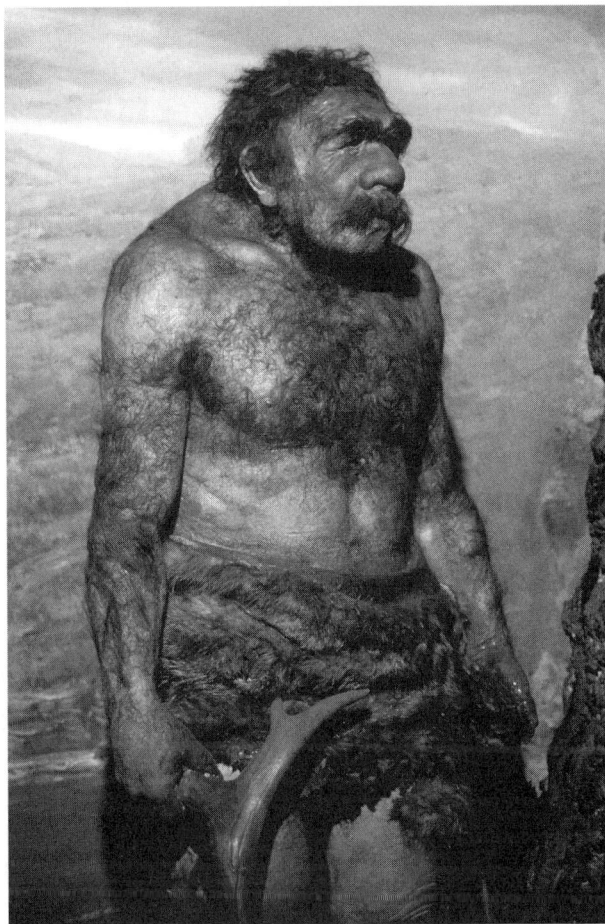

FIGURE 2.1 NEANDERTHAL MAN Based on evidence from skeletal remains, a Neanderthal man might have looked something like this. Note the robust body, large head, and forward projecting face.

(Tom McHugh. Reproduced by permission of Getty Images.)

expansion from southwest Asia to the north and west through western Asia and on into eastern and western Europe, the land of the Neanderthals. This particular expansion and its consequences is the best understood.[13]

As for when modern humans arrived in these various regions, estimates vary, but it was probably after 40 Kya in the Asian regions and Australia, and perhaps after about 35 Kya in Europe. The northeast Siberians crossed into Alaska probably between 15 and 20 Kya and moved rapidly throughout the Americas. They are thought to have arrived at the tip of South America by 10 Kya.

What was happening in eastern Asia is not well understood. One view is that *H. erectus* populations evolved over hundreds of thousands of years into a more advanced form of *H. erectus,* and that later *H. erectus* evolved into anatomically modern humans in this region without being replaced by modern humans migrating from elsewhere (central or southeast Asia). On the other hand, some hold that the later *H. erectus* populations were replaced by in-migrating modern humans.[14]

The overall theory that modern humans evolved in Africa and eventually left that continent to populate the rest of the world is known as the "Out of Africa" theory. Thirty years ago it was basically a hypothesis advocated by a minority of biological anthropologists, but enough evidence has now accumulated for it to have gained wide acceptance. Most biological anthropologists think that this theory, or something very much like it, is a good description of what happened.[15]

Big Brains

The human brain tripled in size in the evolution from *Australopithecus* to anatomically modern humans, from about 450 cc's to approximately 1,350. However, increasing brain size alone does not tell the whole story and can be somewhat misleading. What is critical is the *encephalization quotient* (EQ), which expresses the ratio of brain size to body size.[16] Richard Klein calculates that the hominin EQ increased from approximately 2.5 in *Australopithecus* to 5.3 in modern humans. *H. habilis* is estimated to have had an EQ of 3.6, late *H. erectus* and *H. heidelbergensis* 4.0, and the Neanderthals 4.8. Note that the Neanderthal EQ is lower than that for modern humans even though the Neanderthals had greater brain volume, which is why we can say confidently that modern humans are "brainier."[17] (Chimpanzees, incidentally, have an EQ of 2.0, which makes them a smart animal species but not nearly as smart as the least intelligent early humans.)

Clearly intelligence has been strongly selected for in human evolution, and thus it must have conferred a large adaptive advantage. This is especially true when we consider that the human brain is extremely costly in energetic terms. It makes up only about 2–3 percent of body weight but uses 20 percent of the energy (calories) the average human consumes. But what was this advantage? For many decades it has been widely assumed that nature imposed the main challenges hominin species faced. Humans had to get enough food to survive and then process it into edible form. This meant understanding where and how the best plants grew, what animals could be pursued and killed most efficiently, and how to obtain sufficient shelter and protection from the elements. Moreover, because environments change over time, one needs to know how to deal with such changes so that one's family or tribe doesn't go extinct. A powerful brain is an extremely useful thing to have in meeting these challenges.

Of critical importance in coping with the demands of nature throughout human evolution was the invention of tools. The australopithecines did not make tools.

Tools only appear in the prehistoric record with the transition to the genus *Homo*, and they were gradually improved over time. Anatomically modern humans were much more technologically sophisticated than *H. habilis* or *H. erectus* (and somewhat more sophisticated than the Neanderthals). Krist Vaesen has delineated the cognitive abilities that were necessary for inventing and improving tools.[18] These include good hand-eye coordination, fine motor control, inferential causal reasoning, an ability to conceptualize a particular tool as having a specialized function rather than a range of possible functions, foresight and planning, the ability to monitor whether one's actions are leading to the goal being sought, imitative learning, social intelligence (especially the ability to read the intentions of others), and, for the more sophisticated forms of tool construction and use, language. Thus tool making and cognitive ability go hand in hand.

This argument, sometimes known as the *ecological hypothesis*, seems sensible enough and, indeed, may seem so obvious that it hardly needs to be stated. No doubt coping with nature's demands is an important part of the story of hominin brain evolution. But more recently a different theory has emerged, the so-called *social brain hypothesis*.[19] Advocates of this hypothesis contend that most of the increase in brain size was not for the purpose of negotiating the environment but rather for negotiating *other people*. Humans seek not only to survive and to live as well as possible, but also to acquire social status and mates, who are vitally important to reproductive success. Because everyone in a community is attempting to achieve many of the same things, social competition ensues. Collaboration with other people is usually needed for success in this competition, and therefore it is important to understand the intentions of others. Is this person an ally or an enemy? Is he going to help me achieve status and acquire a good mate, or is he going to thwart me in my efforts so he can advance his own position? In the words of Mark Flinn, David Geary, and Carol Ward, humans had to deal with a "mental chess game" in which life centered around being able to predict "future moves of a social competitor-cooperator, and [formulate] appropriate countermoves, amplified by networks of multiple relationships, shifting coalitions, and deception."[20] The stage was set for a process of runaway selection or an evolutionary arms race[21] "whereby the more cognitively, socially, and behaviorally sophisticated individuals are able to outmaneuver and manipulate other individuals."[22]

One of the most important dimensions of human cognition is what is known as Theory of Mind (ToM). This involves the ability to understand the minds of other individuals, especially to know what their goals and intentions are. For example, ToM allows a person to understand the following: "Mary thinks that John believes that Jill is romantically interested in Roger but not in him." The earliest hominins may have had a ToM, but it would have been poorly developed compared to the highly sophisticated ToM possessed by modern humans.[23] We know that the principal part of the brain that expanded in human evolution was the neocortex. Evidence suggests that the regions of the neocortex that grew proportionately larger over time were those associated with attention, spatial competencies, a sense of body position, visual perception, speech perception, and, in particular, behavioral control, executive functions, highly developed self-awareness, social problem solving, ability to recall personal interactions, and an ability to mentally project oneself into the future ("mental time travel").[24]

In general, these cognitive skills are less useful for hunting or coping with changing environments than they are for forging alliances with people who can advance one's interests, and in successfully engaging competitors.[25] Often the most successful individuals are those who are good at using deceptive tactics, and it has been shown that those who are most skilled in the use of such tactics are people who are not truly aware they are using them.[26] A critical human cognitive skill is the ability to read human facial expressions. Many people who attempt to deceive by lying are not very good at it because their facial expression or tone of voice gives them away. But deceivers who are not really conscious of their lying and manipulative behavior are able to maintain facial expressions and tones of voice that suggest they are being truthful. In such individuals the brain is somehow capable of compartmentalizing these thoughts and behaviors so they do not come into contact. They mislead, prevaricate, and lie without realizing they are doing so; they actually believe what they are saying. In short, the best deceivers are self-deceivers.[27]

Both of these hypotheses have been subjected to empirical scrutiny. A study by Jessica Ash and Gordon Gallup tests the ecological hypothesis that growing brain size was largely due to increasingly successful adaptation to the demands of nature and survival. Ash and Gallup used a sample of 109 fossilized hominin skulls drawn from the main representatives of the genus *Homo*. Working from the assumption that survival is more difficult in colder climates at higher latitudes, the authors found a very strong **correlation coefficient** between brain volume and temperature—bigger brains at lower temperatures—and a weaker but still strong correlation between brain volume and latitude—bigger brains at higher latitudes. These findings seem to support the ecological hypothesis.[28]

However, Ash and Gallup's study fails to consider the variables making up the social brain hypothesis and to control for their effects. In other words, they do not test the competing hypotheses against each other. Such a test has been carried out by Drew Bailey and David Geary. They concede that at least some of brain evolution has been the result of increasing skills at negotiating nature, but contend nonetheless that it was increasing social competition and social competence that was the main driving force. Their study used 175 hominin crania spanning the period between 1.9 Mya and 10 Kya. Like Ash and Gallup, they included a measure of temperature to assess the ecological hypothesis, but also included a measure of temperature variation, since environmental changes create selective pressure for higher intelligence. To assess the social brain hypothesis, the authors used a proxy measure of population density, reasoning that in larger, denser populations the number of interactions is greater and thus people are forced to cooperate and compete with more individuals. They used a multivariate statistical analysis in which the independent effect of each variable could be determined. Their results showed that population density was a much better predictor of cranial capacity than either temperature or temperature variation. The authors therefore concluded that increasing brain size throughout human evolution has been determined mainly by social competition.[29]

Yet, as an old adage says, "Correlation is not causation." Two variables can be highly correlated, but it is often difficult to determine what is causing what. To demonstrate causation, a researcher must show that the cause precedes the effect in time. Experimental psychologists can do this by the way they set up their experiments, but in biological anthropology such experiments are virtually impossible. Consequently Bailey and Geary cannot actually demonstrate that increasing population density is causing increasing brain size. It is just as plausible to argue that because hominins with bigger brains have both better survival chances and higher levels of reproductive success, greater population densities will be an *effect* rather than a cause of bigger brains.

Obviously the matter cannot be settled without additional research. A provisional conclusion might simply be that increases in cranial capacity have been driven by both the demands of subsistence *and* those of social cooperation and competition. Those who like definitive conclusions may find this disappointing. But most of the time uncertainty is the normal condition in all of the sciences. Caution is often the wisest choice, since many a hypothesis considered strongly supported has been disconfirmed by later research.

The Language Instinct

Language is a human monopoly. Only humans can invent and use symbols that arbitrarily represent the physical and biological world, other people, one's inner feelings and intentions, and so on, and combine these symbols into larger systems of representation that have syntax—word order and sentence structure—and grammatical rules. But not so fast, some investigators say. The capacity for language also exists among some of humans' primate relatives.

Beginning in the 1960s some psychologists tried to teach the rudiments of language to apes, chimpanzees in particular, and these experiments picked up steam in the 1970s and 1980s as enthusiasm for them grew. A central figure in this research, Sue Savage-Rumbaugh of Emory University in Atlanta, taught two young male chimps named Sherman and Austin a system of symbolic communication requiring them to make responses on a computerized keyboard. However, Savage-Rumbaugh's greatest success was with the bonobo (pygmy chimpanzee) Kanzi. Kanzi was able to go far beyond Sherman and Austin; he could use symbols at an earlier age than his predecessors, and he was much more likely to make spontaneous rather than prompted or imitated utterances. Astonishingly, Kanzi showed an apparent capacity to understand spoken English. Among other things, he could respond accurately to spoken requests and even seemed to understand conversations between people that did not involve him.[30]

Kanzi's achievements are very impressive, and bonobos in general are often regarded as the most intelligent creatures on earth next to humans, thus making them even smarter than our closest biological relative, the common chimpanzee *Pan troglodytes*. However, greater scrutiny revealed that Kanzi was not using true language but what the linguist Derek Bickerton has called *protolanguage*. Protolanguage is characteristic of four categories of speakers: apes trained to use symbols, children under the age of two, adults deprived of language use in their early years, and speakers of pidgin languages. Protolanguage allows for the communication of arbitrarily represented meanings, but it lacks two critical features of true language: grammatical rules and syntax. Also, neither Kanzi nor any other ape has produced protolanguage spontaneously. The capacity is there but remains totally unrealized in the absence of human intervention.[31]

So it appears that language is a unique human trait after all. But where did it come from? How did we acquire it? Some of the best recent thinking has come from the Harvard cognitive and evolutionary psychologist (and psycholinguist) Steven Pinker, who contends that language is almost certainly a biological adaptation that evolved by natural selection.[32] Pinker points out that, compared to protolanguage or the even more-primitive sign systems of animals other than primates, language is an extremely efficient mode of communication and thus extraordinarily useful. Any gene predisposing toward language use would thus confer enormous survival advantage on its bearer. Our hunting and gathering ancestors, it is now clear, had detailed knowledge of their environment, especially the life cycles and behavior of plants and animals. Since this hard-won knowledge would have taken many generations to acquire, any communication system that could transmit it reliably would be enormously useful. As Pinker wryly remarks, "It makes a difference whether a far-off region is reached by taking the trail that is in front of the large tree or the trail that the large tree is in front of. It makes a difference whether that region has animals that you can eat or animals that can eat you. It makes a difference whether it has fruit that is ripe or fruit that was ripe or fruit that will be ripe. It makes a difference whether you can get there if you walk for three days or whether you can get there and walk for three days."[33]

If language is an evolutionary adaptation, then it must be innate. Or the capacity to produce it must be innate, since the particular content of any language is obviously a social product. No one is born knowing how to speak French, Tamil, or Mandarin Chinese. But everyone is born knowing how to imitate the sounds, meanings, and combinations of sounds and meanings used by those who already speak and understand the language to which young children are exposed. Darwin recognized as much when he commented that language involves "an instinctive tendency to acquire an art."

If you remain unconvinced that humans possess a language instinct, consider the following:[34]

- Children acquire language with remarkable speed in all societies and cultures beginning at about the same age: eighteen to twenty-four months.
- What children acquire is an ability to create an infinite number of phrases and sentences they have never heard before. The vast majority of sentences a person utters or understands is a brand new combination of words. Therefore the brain must contain a recipe or program capable of building an unlimited set of sentences out of a finite list of words.
- When very young children say things like "We holded the rabbits" or "John goed to town," it cannot be a simple act of imitation by a brain with no biasing tendencies because no adult or older child says such a thing; rather, it is a child's use of a grammatical rule in English—add "-ed" to form the past tense of verbs—that obviously does not apply to every verb.
- The three-year-old is a grammatical genius, obeying rules far more often than flouting them. Since children are notoriously incompetent at many other activities, the basic organization of grammar must be wired into the child's brain.
- The same basic design features of language are found everywhere.
- There is a critical period for language learning, coming in the first six years of life; language learning is more difficult after this age, and notoriously more difficult for adults.
- When children learn to speak a language, they learn not only vocabulary, grammar, and syntax, but also *pronunciation*. Anyone learning a foreign language in late adolescence or adulthood knows how difficult it can be to pronounce foreign words accurately, and many never acquire accurate pronunciation. Languages contain *phonemes*—elementary sound units that get combined into words. Native speakers of Chinese and Japanese have difficulty distinguishing between *r* and *l,* so that "lots of luck" sometimes comes out "rots of ruck" and "Cleveland Clinic" "Creverand Crinic." The French have trouble pronouncing the *th* sound in English. "This" often comes out "zees." In Dutch, there is a kind of *v* sound that is not quite the same as the English *v,* but not exactly the English *f* sound either. It seems to be somewhere between a *v* and an *f.* English speakers trying to pronounce a Dutch word beginning in *v* are frequently corrected by their Dutch interlocutors. Most children learn to pronounce words correctly by imitating the sounds they hear, not by direct instruction. And in order to pronounce words correctly, they must know how to position their lips and tongue to make the sound. That is rarely taught, except, perhaps, in the case of speech impediments or adults taking instruction in foreign languages. Children must therefore possess an innate tendency to

know how to position their mouth, tongue, and lips in order to reproduce the sounds they are hearing.

- Then there is the related matter of *accent*. Accents are acquired almost entirely unconsciously. It is again a question of knowing how to imitate what one hears or thinks they hear. Accents are virtually never taught. One picks them up automatically. New Englanders drop many of their final r's, which are known as postvocalic r's. They say, "I pawked my caw in Hawvawd Yawd." In parts of the American South, *I* often comes out as *Ah*, as in "Ah see what y'all mean." Like pronunciation, accent is a matter of positioning lips and tongue in certain ways. Children seem to know automatically how to do this without anyone telling them how. It has to be part of a language instinct and carried out in an unconscious way by child speakers.

But many linguists who accept the innateness of language still resist the idea that it is an evolved adaptation. The world's most famous linguist, Noam Chomsky, was the first to argue that the human brain contains an innate language processing device, but he has explicitly denied that language evolved by means of natural selection, or even that it is adaptive. Chomsky contends that language is nothing more than a by-product of other cognitive functions, especially those associated with the expansion in brain size and complexity.[35] Rather startlingly, Chomsky even claims that the main function of language is not communication; rather, it is an aid to internalized thought.

But this is belied by almost everything we know about language. For example, language is crucial to social interaction: gossiping, informing others of one's intentions, misleading others about one's intentions, and so on. The ability to mislead often requires considerable subtlety and sophistication in the use of language.[36] Along Chomskyan lines, Massimo Piatelli-Palmarini says that language cannot be an adaptation because it could be both better than it is and different than it is.[37] But no evolutionary argument assumes that any adaptation is perfect, and indeed the vast majority of adaptations are not.[38] The human pelvis is an evolutionary compromise between bipedal locomotion and the successful birth of infants; it is far from perfect because the pelvic opening is so narrow that infants and their mothers often died during the birth process prior to the development of modern medicine. Moreover, the peacock's tail is a compromise between attracting mates and escaping predators. If the tail is too small and lacking in color, fewer mates are acquired, and if it is too large and elaborate the peacock is more likely to be eaten. And of course almost any adaptation could be different than it is, since there are different adaptations everywhere in nature that have the same or a very similar function.[39] Bats, for example, fly with membranes attached to their forelimbs, whereas birds fly with wings made up of feathers.

The best way to determine whether a trait is an evolutionary adaptation is to look for evidence of complex design. The vertebrate eye has such complex design that there can be no doubt that it is an adaptation whose functional benefits are obvious. Pinker and Paul Bloom suggest that language also reveals evidence of complex design and that such design can only be explained in adaptationist terms. They discuss many of the features of language that reveal complex design, but consider just the following:

> Major phrasal categories (noun phrase, verb phrase, etc.) start off with a major lexical item, the "head," and allow it to be combined with specific kinds of affixes and phrases. The resulting conglomerate is then used to refer to entities in our mental models of the world. Thus a noun like dog does not itself describe anything but it can combine with articles and other parts of speech to make noun phrases, such as those dogs, my dog, and the dog that bit me, and it is these noun phrases that are used to describe things. Similarly, a verb like hit is made into a verb phrase by marking it for tense and aspect and adding an object, thus enabling it to describe an event. In general, words encode abstract general categories and only by contributing to the structure of major phrasal categories can they describe particular things, events, states, locations, and properties. This mechanism enables the language-user to refer to an unlimited range of specific entities while possessing only a finite number of lexical items.[40]

If this seems complicated, that's because it is! (If you don't get it, do not fret; the point is *not* to get it, at least not completely!) It is difficult to imagine that something this complicated—something consisting of all of these elements, properties, and their complex combinations—can simply be a by-product or side effect of something else.[41]

If there is a language instinct, then we should find evidence of it in the genes. Recently such evidence has been discovered. In the early 1990s scientists became aware of a family, which came to be called KE, half of whose members suffered from a severe form of language impairment, known generally as verbal dyspraxia. The affected individuals were unable to speak intelligibly, had difficulty processing words according to grammatical rules, understanding complex sentences, and moving the lower part of the face.[42] A search for a genetic basis of the disorder resulted in the identification of a mutation in a single gene, FOXP2.[43] Genetic testing of the KE family showed that all of the affected individuals possessed the mutated version of the gene, compared to none of the unaffected individuals.[44] Later several other geneticists did genetic screening of three members of another family who had been diagnosed with a type of verbal dyspraxia, two siblings and their mother. They found a mutation at another location within the FOXP2 gene. All three individuals displayed speech difficulties closely resembling those of the affected members of the KE family.[45]

FOXP2 is a regulatory gene that affects the expression of numerous other genes. A slightly different version of FOXP2 has been found in chimpanzees, and the human version of the gene differs from the chimp version by only two amino acids. Wolfgang Enard and colleagues suggest that one or both of the two changes in the gene after the evolutionary separation of chimps and humans may have been critical for the development of human speech. The research team has attempted to determine when the human FOXP2 gene became fixed in human populations and estimate that it was sometime within the past 200,000 years. They point out that this is approximately the time of the transition to anatomically modern humans, and that their expansion may have been due to the development of a spoken language that was more proficient than any earlier language.[46]

These recent findings have generated great excitement among geneticists and cognitive scientists, who see them as "opening a molecular window into speech and language."[47] The discovery of the role of FOXP2 in language also has implications for the debate over whether language is an adaptation or a by-product. Pinker and Ray Jackendoff point out that the sequencing of the gene shows "that the normal version of the gene is universal in the human population, that it diverged from the primate homologue subsequent to the evolutionary split between humans and chimpanzees, and that it was a target of natural selection rather than a product of genetic drift or other stochastic [probabilistic] evolutionary processes."[48] They add that the findings "support the notion that language evolved piecemeal in the human lineage under the influence of natural selection, with the selected genes having pleiotropic effects [effects on many other genes] that incrementally improved multiple components."[49]

The Cultural Big Bang

The discovery and analysis of the FOXP2 gene also has potential implications for the development of human culture. The period from about 35 Kya until 15 Kya, the Upper Paleolithic, was a time of dramatic changes, the so-called Upper Paleolithic cultural revolution. The most important new developments were:[50]

- Improved hunting tools, such as spear throwers, bows and arrows, and boomerangs
- Systematic use of grinding and pounding tools
- The use of bone, antler, and ivory for tools and ritual objects
- First evidence of fishing
- Exchange networks involving stone and other raw materials transported over scores or hundreds of miles
- Distinct spatial organization of habitations (e.g., kitchen areas, butchering spaces, sleeping areas, and discard zones)
- First appearance of art, especially paintings in caves, rock shelters, and exposed rocky surfaces

- First appearance of body decoration and ornamentation, such as beads and pendants, made from such materials as teeth, ivory, marine shells, and ostrich egg shells
- First evidence of ceremony and ritual, especially as expressed in human burials

Anthropologists have given special emphasis to the last three items. In the late nineteenth century elaborate paintings were discovered in caves in France and Spain, especially at Lascaux, Niaux, and Altamira. The drawings mostly depicted large game animals, especially wild horses, reindeer, bison, and mammoth, along with hunters and spears. Originally these paintings were dated to between 11 and 16 Kya, but more sophisticated dating techniques show that some of the paintings are 20,000 to 27,000 years old.[51]

In 1994 there was a more spectacular discovery. A team of French spelunkers were exploring a cave that was unusually large and deep and found what amounted to a primitive art gallery. There were elaborate paintings of about 260 animals, many of them bears, mammoths, lions, and rhinoceroses. There were four galleries stretching approximately 1,600 feet. The artists had also made engravings, geometric patterns, and stenciled hand prints. The cave was named Chauvet Cave in honor of the search team's leader, Jean-Marie Chauvet, and the art has been dated to between 31 and 32 Kya. This makes it the earliest known art of the Upper Paleolithic.[52]

Upper Paleolithic art has not been limited to cave paintings. The peoples of this period also produced items for personal use, such as figurines made from ivory or teeth along with beads and pendants. Some figurines had exaggerated breasts and buttocks and may have functioned as fertility symbols. One figurine, found in southwestern Germany, had the body of a man and the head of a lion. Such figurines may have been totemic representations of kinship groups. Others may have been symbols of spirits or deities. Beads and pendants made of ivory, soft stone, or animal (sometimes human) teeth—objects of personal decoration—have also been found, some dating to as early as 32,000 years ago.[53]

The Neanderthals buried their dead, but many Upper Paleolithic graves are much more elaborate and suggest the idea of an afterlife. These graves indicate burial rituals because they contain various art objects and artifacts. Some graves contain pierced seashells and animal teeth, along with dense concentrations of ocher. A grave located in Russia was especially elaborate. There were two child skeletons, likely one of each sex. The male was surrounded by 4,903 beads, 250 perforated arctic fox canines, and several figurines and pendants. The female was surrounded by 5,374 beads along with numerous artifacts made of ivory or antlers.[54]

Although anatomically modern humans may go back as far as 200,000 years, the period beginning around 50,000 years ago, when humans began to disperse out of Africa, is said to mark the beginning of *behaviorally* modern humans. After this time humans rapidly developed a previously unknown capacity for abstract thought. What accounts for the sudden and dramatic change? A variety of expla-nations have been proposed, most of which focus on new social relations leading to population growth and an increasing need to innovate.[55] However, these expla-nations cannot tell us why the change was, in archaeological terms, so rapid and dramatic. In addition, population growth seems to have occurred after the changes had already begun, not before.[56]

Alternatively, Richard Klein suggests what he calls a "neural hypothesis." He be-lieves that there was a fortuitous genetic mutation leading to a quantum leap in the area of the brain that governs abstract thought. Klein surmises that the mutation in question occurred in the FOXP2 gene. This mutation led to the development of fully modern, rapidly articulated speech, a prerequisite for the kind of abstract thought represented by the art and artifacts of the Upper Paleolithic. Indeed, lan-guage would have been a critical development since, as Klein expresses it, "modern humans probably need fully modern language to ask the hypothetical 'what if' ques-tions that underlie the modern capacity for innovation. Archaeological evidence for this capacity burgeons after 50 Kya, and its appearance could explain why human fitness—the ability to survive and reproduce—increased simultaneously."[57]

This hypothesis is plausible, but evidence to support it is far from definitive. For one thing, we do not know when the mutation in FOXP2 occurred, and it may well have been much earlier than 50,000 years ago. If the mutation occurred much earlier, then FOXP2 cannot logically be the candidate gene in Klein's argu-ment. However, Klein's overall argument stands if we can identify one or more other genes affecting human cognition. This is an ongoing process that may take many years to sort out.

Be that as it may, Klein contends that the period after 50,000 years ago marks the "dawn of human culture."[58] This may be overstating the point since culture includes tools and techniques, and humans have been making and using tools for some 2 million years. Consequently asserting that culture was literally invented at this point is awkward. What occurred was a big leap in the capacity for abstract and symbolic culture—a sort of "big bang" of human culture.[59]

Conclusion

We have seen that after about 50,000 years ago humans had become both anatom-ically and behaviorally modern. But they were still living by hunting and gathering until about 10,000 or 11,000 years ago, when we see the first stirrings of agricul-ture in the archaeological record. From this point on human societies and cultures started down a path of rapid—on an archaeological scale, very rapid—economic evolution. In the next chapter we will explore the nature of the hunting and gath-ering mode of life and the evolution of new and increasingly intensive modes of getting a living.

SUMMARY

1. The human lineage split from the chimpanzee lineage around 5–6 million years ago. The first members of the human lineage, known as australopithecines, were small apelike creatures with small brains. They would have looked more like apes than humans, but are classified as human because of their humanlike dentition and because they had an upright posture and walked on two feet.

2. The australopithecines lived until about a million years ago but around 1.8 to 2.3 Mya gave rise to another human species known as *Homo habilis*. *H. habilis* was somewhat larger and had a larger brain. It may have been the first human species to use tools.

3. Next in the evolutionary line was *Homo erectus*, who shows up in the archaeological record about 1.8 Mya. *H. erectus* was larger than *H. habilis* and had a much larger brain. *H. erectus* made better and more-specialized tools and was likely a big game hunter. *H. erectus* was the first human species to leave Africa, probably sometime between 1 and 1.5 Mya. *H. erectus* fossils have been found in China and Java, and *H. erectus* may have continued to evolve in east Asia until as recently as 50 Kya.

4. The best-known prehistoric humans are the Neanderthals, fossils of which were first discovered in 1859 in Germany. More recently similar fossils have been discovered and classified as *Homo heidelbergensis*. *H. heidelbergensis* likely originated in Africa and migrated to Europe, where it evolved into the Neanderthals between about 600 and 400 Kya. The Neanderthals lived throughout a wide stretch of territory from Europe to western Asia. During most of the time the Neanderthals lived the climate was extremely cold, and their bodies were adapted to this climate. They were ruggedly built, heavily muscled humans with stocky bodies and large brains. And the tools they used were more complex than those of earlier species.

5. So-called anatomically modern humans evolved in Africa sometime after 200 Kya. They were members of the same species as ourselves, *Homo sapiens*. About 50 to 60 Kya they left Africa and eventually occupied most of the other habitable regions of the world. In Europe anatomically modern humans encountered the Neanderthals, perhaps around 40 Kya. By 30 Kya the Neanderthals had disappeared, probably driven to extinction by modern humans, who would have had superior intelligence, superior technology, and possibly other adaptive advantages. This interpretation of recent human evolution is known as the Out of Africa theory.

6. One of the most important developments in the long stretch of human evolution is the increase in brain size. The australopithecines had small brains averaging only about 450 cc's. By the time of *H. erectus* the brain had grown to about 1,000 cc's, and

H. sapiens has an average brain size of about 1,350 cc's. A more accurate indicator of the brain's intellectual capacity is the encephalization quotient (EQ), which is the ratio of brain size to body size. The australopithecines had an EQ of about 2.5, late *H. erectus* and *H. heidelbergensis* about 4.0, the Neanderthals 4.8, and *H. sapiens* around 5.3.

7. There has obviously been strong selection for greater brain capacity in human evolution because of its adaptive advantages. The traditional view is that brain power increased in order to permit humans to deal more effectively with the challenges of nature—obtaining food, building shelters, and so on. A more recent theory, the social brain hypothesis, contends that the main adaptive value of greater intelligence was to allow humans to negotiate the social environment—the challenges of dealing with other humans. Both theories have empirical support, and therefore both may be partially true.

8. Humans are unique in having language. It was once thought that language is entirely learned, but in the 1960s the idea arose that there is an innate language acquisition device that all humans share. This idea is strongly supported by the fact that young children everywhere acquire their local language rapidly and at about the same age. Only later was it argued that such a device was an evolutionary adaptation. The adaptationist argument is strongly supported by the extraordinary usefulness of language for coping with both the natural and social environments. Many features of language suggest that it is the product of complex design, which is further evidence of adaptive evolution.

9. The adaptationist position is also supported by the discovery of genetic mutations that severely impair the use of language in affected individuals. The main gene in question is known as FOXP2. Genetic analysis shows that the normal version of the gene is found in all human populations and that it very likely has been the target of strong selection.

10. There is still strong resistance to the adaptationist position. Some claim that language is a by-product of selection for other cognitive capacities. It has even been claimed that communication is not the main function of language. Instead, language is an aid to internalized thought.

11. Archaeologists call the period between 35 and 15 Kya the Upper Paleolithic. This period is marked, especially in Europe, by several major cultural innovations. These include improved hunting tools; first evidence of fishing; use of grinding and pounding tools; use of bone, antler, and ivory for tools and ritual objects; transport of raw materials over long distances; distinct spatial organization of habitats; first appearance of art;

and first indications of ceremony and ritual. One of the most striking innovations was paintings on the walls of caves in France and Spain that demonstrate remarkable skill.

12. The Upper Paleolithic represents what can be called a "cultural big bang." During this period humans seem to have undergone a kind of quantum leap in the capacity for symbolic thought, which allowed them to become behaviorally as well as anatomically modern. There is debate over the causes of these changes. One hypothesis is that there was a favorable mutation in the FOXP2 gene that led to the development of fully modern, rapidly articulated speech. This is an intriguing idea, but evidential support is still rather thin.

QUESTIONS FOR DISCUSSION

✓ How did the course of human evolution proceed over the past 4 million years? What were the major hominin species and how did they differ?

✓ What changed during the long course of human evolution?

✓ What happened to the Neanderthals and why did it happen?

✓ What is the difference between anatomically and behaviorally modern humans?

✓ How does the Out of Africa theory explain modern human origins?

✓ Why did the human brain become so large and complex over the course of human evolution? Discuss competing answers to this question and the evidence that can be used to adjudicate them.

✓ Do apes have language? Explain.

✓ Is language an evolutionary adaptation or just a by-product of other cognitive adaptations? Explain why you take one side or the other.

✓ Why may the FOXP2 gene provide a window into the biological basis of language, as some cognitive scientists have argued?

✓ What were the most important changes in culture and social life that occurred after about 50,000 years ago?

✓ In what sense do the changes referred to above constitute a kind of "big bang" in human social and cultural development?

✓ If there was a cultural big bang, what might have caused it?

References and Notes

1. The term "hominid" is now used to include chimpanzees and gorillas, leaving hominin to identify humans exclusively, both living and extinct. Unfortunately, the change in terminology revolves around an esoteric taxonomic debate and has led to confusion. But this need not detain us here. For further discussion, see www.madsci.org/posts/archives/Apr2003/1050350684.Ev.r.html.

2. Johanson and White 1979; Nelson and Jurmain 1985; Klein 2009.

3. Johanson and White 1979; Nelson and Jurmain 1985; Klein 2009.

4. Johanson and White 1979; Nelson and Jurmain 1985; Klein 2009.

5. Klein 2009, p. 275.

6. Klein 2009.

7. Klein 2009.

8. Klein 2009.

9. Stringer and Andrews 2005.

10. Stringer and Andrews 2005; Klein 2009.

11. Klein 2009, p. 586.

12. Wade 2006; Klein 2009.

13. Stringer and Andrews 2005; Klein 2009; Trinkaus 2005.

14. Klein 2009.

15. Stringer and Andrews 1988; Cann 1987; Cann, Stoneking, and Wilson 1987; Stringer and McKie 1996; Stringer 2012.

16. Klein 2009.

17. Klein 2009.

18. Vaesen 2012.

19. Alexander 1989; Dunbar 1998, 2003; Dunbar and Shultz 2007; Flinn, Geary, and Ward 2005; Gowlett, Gamble, and Dunbar 2012.

20. Flinn, Geary, and Ward 2005.

21. In an evolutionary arms race, interactions between organisms cause changes, sometimes very rapid, in each. For example, if a cheetah somehow becomes faster at chasing down an antelope, then there is selective pressure on antelope to run faster. The antelope who are naturally faster will survive at the expense of the slower ones. But as antelope become faster, there is selective pressure on cheetahs to become faster, and so on. In the human case, deceitful individuals create selective pressure for their competitors to become better at detecting deceit, which then creates selective pressure for the deceivers to become even better at deception, and so on. Evolutionary arms races of various types are widespread in nature and in human societies.

22. Flinn, Geary, and Ward 2005, p. 15.

23. For nearly four decades there has been extensive debate over whether chimpanzees have a theory of mind. So far the debate has not been resolved. See Penn and Povinelli 2007; Call and Tomasello 2008 for recent contributions.

24. Flinn, Geary, and Ward 2005.

25. Flinn, Geary, and Ward 2005.

26. Trivers 2011; Von Hippel and Trivers 2011.

27. D. L. Smith 2004; Trivers 2011; Von Hippel and Trivers 2011.

28. Ash and Gallup 2007.

29. Bailey and Geary 2009.

30. Savage-Rumbaugh 1986; Savage-Rumbaugh, Rumbaugh, and McDonald 1985.

31. Bickerton 1990.

32. Pinker 1994. See also Pinker and Bloom 1990; Pinker and Jackendoff 2005; and Jackendoff and Pinker 2005.

33. Pinker 1994, pp. 367–368.

34. Partially based on Pinker 1994.

35. Chomsky 1965, 1988. See also Piatelli-Palmarini 1989; Pinker and Bloom 1990.

36. Pinker and Bloom 1990.

37. Piatelli-Palmarini 1989.

38. Pinker and Bloom 1990.

39. Pinker and Bloom 1990.

40. Pinker and Bloom 1990, p. 712.

41. The disagreement between Chomsky and other nonadaptationists on the one hand and the adaptationists on the other continues to this day and has been the subject of much recent debate. See Hauser, Chomsky, and Fitch 2002; Pinker and Jackendoff 2005; Jackendoff and Pinker 2005; and Fitch, Hauser, and Chomsky 2005. A recent article by Evans and Levinson 2009 goes off in its own direction by challenging some of the views of all of these scholars. There are numerous debates among linguists and cognitive scientists about many dimensions of language apart from the adaptation by-product debate.

42. MacAndrew 2003; Carroll 2005.

43. Lai et al. 2001; Marcus and Fisher 2003.

44. MacAndrew 2003; Carroll 2005.

45. MacDermot et al. 2005.

46. Enard et al. 2002.

47. Fisher and Scharff 2009.

48. Pinker and Jackendoff 2005, p. 218.

49. Pinker and Jackendoff 2005, p. 218.

50. Klein 2009; Bar-Josef 2002.

51. Klein 2009.

52. Klein and Edgar 2002.

53. Klein 2009.

54. Klein 2009.

55. R. White 1992, 1993; Bar-Josef 1998, 2002. All as summarized in Klein 2009; Klein and Edgar 2002.

56. Klein 2009; Klein and Edgar 2002.

57. Klein 2009, p. 650.

58. Klein and Edgar 2002.

59. The idea that a cultural "big bang" was associated with the emergence of behaviorally modern humans is not accepted by everyone. In a major article, Sally McBrearty and Alison Brooks (2000) challenge this notion. They contend that there was no abrupt transformation in Europe. Rather, most of the cultural traits said to be new were found in Africa tens of thousands of years earlier. The authors claim that there was no actual revolution, but a gradual shift toward behavioral modernity that began in Africa long before *Homo sapiens* left there. For responses to McBrearty and Brooks, see Klein 2009; Klein and Edgar 2002.

3

Getting a Living

The two most fundamental things humans must do is obtain a living from nature and find mates and reproduce. They lose in the struggle for existence in the ultimate way if they don't succeed at these things. This chapter discusses the first of these. Humans have been able to make a living in a variety of ways, but four have been most prominent. The simplest is hunting, fishing, and gathering plant foods. This can be a fairly easy way to make a living when resources are plentiful. But if resources are scarce, it is a difficult way because more time must be devoted to foraging efforts. Cultivating the soil—planting crops, tending them, and harvesting them—is another way of making a living. There is a wide range of cultivating practices. At one end people may tend only small gardens using simple hand tools, whereas at the other end they may cultivate large fields using plows and draft animals. Some communities and societies live in areas that are too dry for cultivation, and as a result they concentrate on herding animals and living off animal products. These subsistence strategies are not necessarily mutually exclusive. Agriculturalists, or at least the simplest ones, often do some hunting and gathering, and animal herders often practice some agriculture. Occasionally all three are combined.

A fourth way to get a living is by making goods and selling them. Throughout history few have done this, but in the past five hundred years it has become increasingly important. The most developed version of this is called capitalism. In Europe beginning around the sixteenth century societies based mainly on farming became increasingly commercialized, and commercialization intensified over time and more and more people made a living from it. Late in the eighteenth century capitalist societies began to industrialize; increasing numbers of people moved off the land into cities and worked in factories. Urban and industrial life gradually replaced agrarian life. Life began to revolve around producing goods and selling them in markets.

To Hunt and to Gather

Until about ten or eleven thousand years ago, humans all over the earth lived by hunting wild animals and gathering wild plants, tubers, nuts, and fruits. Large animals were favored, which usually required cooperative hunts, but many smaller animals were sought as well. In environments on or near rivers, lakes, or other large bodies of water, fishing provided a goodly share of animal protein.

Although a number of prehistoric hunter-gatherer societies have now been described by archaeologists,[1] most of what we know about the hunting and gathering way of life is based on ethnographic accounts, or descriptions of fieldwork carried out by cultural anthropologists spending many months or even years living with these groups. The most intensively studied hunter-gatherers are the !Kung[2] of the Kalahari desert in southern Africa; the Mbuti, a group occupying the Ituri rain forest in equatorial eastern Africa; the Hadza, a group living in Tanzania; the Inuit of the arctic (formerly known as Eskimos); the Aché, rain forest hunter-gatherers of Paraguay; and various aboriginal Australian groups, such as the Tiwi and Aranda.[3]

Most hunter-gatherers live in small bands of a few dozen people who carry on a nomadic existence, although a few live in permanent or semipermanent villages. There is a great deal of variation in how frequently foragers move their camps. For example, the Yurok of the northwest coast of North America and the Vedda of Sri Lanka moved only about twice a year, whereas the Yuqui and Aché of South America move more than fifty times a year. There is also a lot of variation in how far people move. The Mirrngadja and Anbarra of Australia move only about a dozen miles a year, whereas the Crow and Blackfoot tribes of North America each moved over five hundred miles a year.[4]

Most foraging bands are economically self-sufficient, although they are usually connected by language, a common culture, and marriage ties into a much larger tribal unit that may number in the hundreds or thousands. Tools are crude and simple: spears, bows and arrows, nets, and traps used in hunting, as well as digging sticks used for plant collecting. Hunter-gatherers live basically from hand to mouth, consuming food as they go and seldom storing it for later consumption.

How do hunter-gatherers divide their time between hunting and gathering and what are the respective contributions of animal protein and plants to the diet? For a very long time it was taken for granted that meat was primary, and thus the phrase "man the hunter" became popular. But this view was challenged in the 1960s by the anthropologist Richard Lee,[5] who estimated that contemporary hunter-gatherers, except for those living at very high latitudes, derived about two-thirds of their diet from gathered foods of all sorts, a figure he thought would have applied to prehistoric hunter-gatherers as well. This view became popular and some anthropologists began to call these foraging groups "gatherer-hunters."[6] Since most gatherers are women, a book was even written with the title *Woman the Gatherer*.[7] But Lee's revisionist picture proved false because the evidence on which he drew was much too selective; Lee did not have an adequate sample of hunter-gatherer societies. Another problem was that Lee classified the collection of shellfish as gathering. Counting it as fishing makes more sense, since the food is animal protein.[8]

Carol Ember revised the revisionists. Ember's study was based on all of the

FIGURE 3.1   Two !Kung Families out Foraging, Botswana
(IrvenDeVore/Anthro-Photo)

hunter-gatherer societies (181) available in the ***Ethnographic Atlas***, a compendium of 1,267 nonindustrial societies originally assembled by the anthropologist George Peter Murdock.[9] She found that the original view was correct: hunting plays a bigger role than gathering in about two-thirds of hunter-gatherer societies. Going on to look at the actual number of calories contributed by animal protein compared to plant matter, including fishing together with hunting, Ember found that animal proteins contributed more than half of the total calories people were consuming in nearly 80 percent of the societies.[10]

Yet Ember's study suffers from the fact that most of the hunter-gatherer societies in the Atlas represent one region of the world, North America. Fortunately, more recent and more extensive data are available. I have been able to analyze foraging patterns in a large sample of over 339 hunter-gatherer societies put together through the prodigious efforts of the late archaeologist Lewis Binford.[11] These societies represent all of the major regions of the world where hunter-gatherers have been found in the past two centuries. Results show that gathered foods contribute 35 percent of the diet, hunted foods 33 percent, and fishing 33 percent. Animal proteins therefore contribute about 66 percent of the diet, and thus predominate over plant foods by a nearly 2:1 ratio. It therefore turns out that, despite the limitations of her sample, Ember was basically right anyway.

However, the proportion of animal to plant foods varies enormously from one part of the world to another, and the critical factor is climate: gathering is prominent at low

TABLE 3.1   Foraging Patterns by Latitude

Latitude	Percent Gathering	Percent Hunting	Percent Fishing	Percent Hunting + Fishing
0–15'(47)	56.6	20.3	23.1	43.4
16–30'(61)	54.6	28.8	16.7	45.4
31–45'(114)	41.5	33.2	25.4	58.5
46–60'(79)	11.1	39.4	49.5	88.9
61' and higher (38)	2.3	42.1	55.7	97.7

Source: Lewis R. Binford, *Constructing Frames of Reference: An Analytical Method for Archaeological Theory Building Using Hunter-Gatherer and Environmental Data Sets* (Berkeley: University of California Press, 2001). The number of societies is indicated in parentheses.

latitudes and declines in direct proportion to increasing latitude. Table 3.1 shows the relationship between latitude and the relative proportions of animal protein and plant foods in the diet. As can be seen, among foragers living at low to moderate latitudes (0–30°), gathering provides slightly more than half of the diet. Foragers living at 31–45 degrees latitude rely somewhat more on hunting and fishing (59 percent), and at latitudes above 45 degrees there is a pronounced shift. At the 46–60 degree range, which mostly includes peoples living in the subarctic and continental midlatitude regions of North America and Asia, foods obtained from hunting and fishing make up nearly 90 percent of the diet, and in the arctic regions above 60 degrees they make up about 98 percent. Edible plants are widely available at low to moderate latitudes and become less available as latitude increases. In subarctic and arctic regions, they are extremely scarce and available for only a small part of the year.[12]

Who hunts and who gathers? Virtually without exception, men are the hunters and women the gatherers. In 90 percent or more of hunter-gatherer societies, it is *only* men who hunt. In the rest both sexes hunt, although women never hunt big game, and there are no known societies in which women do all of the hunting.[13] There are several reasons why men overwhelmingly monopolize hunting. One is that men are stronger and generally have better spatial skills. This makes it easier for them to track animals over long distances and bring down big game. Since the objective is to get the maximum amount of animal protein for one's own family (and to some extent for the entire band) it makes much more sense to put most hunting in the hands of men.

But to explain why men hunt far more than women, the question can be posed in a different way: why don't *women* hunt? The answer involves the most crucial activity in which women engage—infant and child care. In all societies, hunter-gatherer societies in particular, the vast majority of child care is done by mothers rather than fathers. Infants go everywhere with their mothers, who usually breast-feed them on demand and sometimes for three, four, or even five years. Women's maternal responsibilities are incompatible with most hunting, but quite compatible with gathering. Women's hunting can also expose children to danger when they must accompany their mothers on hunting expeditions, so this is another good reason to make men the principal hunters.[14]

Women among the Agta of the Philippines were reported to do more hunting than usual. Although this may have been the case in earlier times, contemporary Agta claim not to remember women ever hunting. However, the Agta benefited from having numerous alloparents, or women who look after a mother's children when she is otherwise occupied. Moreover, many female hunters were either sterile or in their postreproductive years, and women's hunting was usually carried out close to home, allowing them to return quickly to their children. Anecdotal evidence also suggests that Agta women seldom or never hunted when they were pregnant or lactating.[15]

So everyone benefits when men concentrate on hunting and women on gathering. People eat better and children have higher survival rates. But there is an interesting aspect of male hunting that has only recently been recognized: some men in a band, sometimes most men, do not hunt, or if they do they are not very good at it. Hunting is a highly skilled, demanding activity that can take boys one or two decades to learn effectively, and some never become successful hunters. Often a few able-bodied men provide most of the meat. These highly skilled hunters enjoy certain benefits not available to poor hunters. Women prefer skilled hunters; among the Aché, men trade meat for sex, and women commonly refuse sex to men not bringing them meat. Meat brings men not only more sex but higher status and therefore better mates—mates with greater reproductive potential—and sometimes more mates. These things are the royal road to greater reproductive success.[16]

The French anthropologist Alain Testart has drawn a very important distinction between hunter-gatherers who store food and those who do not.[17] Although nonstoring hunter-gatherers predominate, hunter-gatherers who store food are probably more common than previously realized, and in any event differ in important respects from nonstorers. Storing hunter-gatherers are more likely to be sedentary rather than nomadic, to have larger populations and higher population densities, and to have greater social complexity. Such societies seem to have been relatively common in the last few millennia before the development of agriculture (around 15,000 to 10,000 years ago),[18] and probably represented hunter-gatherers on the verge of developing an agricultural economy.

A recently studied archaeological case is the Chumash, who for several thousand years lived along the coastline of what is now Santa Barbara, California, and on four islands near the coast. They subsisted on marine resources, terrestrial mammals such

as deer, and highly abundant acorns. Large villages were the norm, as was a much
higher level of social and political complexity than is normal for hunter-gatherers.[19]
The best-known ethnographic cases of hunter-gatherers who store food are a number of Indian tribes occupying the northwest coast of North America, in particular
the Kwakiutl. They lived in a bountiful environment teeming with fish (especially
salmon), game, and plant foods. This allowed them to collect food far in excess of
mere subsistence levels and to live in villages containing hundreds of people.

Ancient Affluence?

For many years social scientists depicted hunter-gatherers quite negatively. It was
widely believed that they led a precarious and difficult life. People had to work hard
and long just to eke out a bare existence, and sometimes they could not even achieve
that. Life was often miserable. If only they knew about agriculture, things would
have been much better for them.

But there followed a swift sea-change in this view. It began with a famous
conference on hunter-gatherer societies held in 1966. (This conference launched
hunter-gatherer studies as a major research endeavor within anthropology.) One of
the papers that emerged from the conference, "The Original Affluent Society," was
published by the eminent cultural anthropologist Marshall Sahlins, then at Columbia University and now at the University of Chicago. By calling hunter-gatherers
affluent, Sahlins did not mean that they were rich and enjoyed abundant material
possessions, which would be an absurd claim to make. That is affluence in the modern sense. What Sahlins meant was that hunter-gatherers have very limited needs
and wants that can be satisfied with minimal effort. Sahlins provided examples of
a few existing hunter-gatherer societies to support his claim, but these counted
mainly as illustrations rather than the comprehensive evidence that was needed to
test his theory.[20]

Other research evidence bearing on Sahlins's thesis was soon uncovered, however, and new studies were undertaken. The Canadian anthropologist Richard Lee,
who spent many years studying the !Kung and became their leading anthropological expert, pointed out that their environment, even though a desert, provided a
wide variety of resources, many of them of high quality. Mongongo trees grew in
their habitat, and the highly nutritious nuts they produced didn't even have to be
picked. They fell to the ground and were so numerous that thousands rotted every
year. The !Kung could also rely on more than eighty other species of edible plants
and, according to Lee, could never even eat them all.[21] Another anthropologist,
James Woodburn, reported that his group, the Hadza of Tanzania, had abundant
game.[22] Both anthropologists concluded that their respective societies were able to
meet their basic subsistence needs, and then some.

The other question that had to be answered to evaluate the Sahlins thesis was,
How long do hunter-gatherers have to work to obtain the levels of subsistence they

enjoy? To answer this question, anthropologists turned to the few existing studies that contained information on the workload, and also began to conduct new research that measured and recorded what kinds of work people did and how long they spent doing it. Sahlins pointed to existing studies of the subsistence activities of some Australian hunter-gatherers and found that they did not work very hard, that hunting and collecting were intermittent activities, and that considerable leisure time was available. In new research meticulously calculating !Kung food-getting activities over more than a month, Lee found that the average adult hunter spent only about seventeen hours a week hunting.[23] Woodburn did not collect precise data on actual work rates among the Hadza, but his impression was that they obtained enough food without working very long or very hard. It was also his impression that the Hadza worked even less than their agricultural neighbors.[24]

Some other studies were not as encouraging and, as it turns out, should have been given more attention than they were at the time. John Yellen noted that Lee's data on the !Kung were selective because they were collected only during the dry season of the year. Yellen therefore calculated work rates during the !Kung wet season and found that they worked many more hours than just the seventeen per week reported by Lee.[25] More recently, Robert Kelly has presented data on the workload in eleven hunter-gatherer societies in five different world regions which show that the average amount of time both men and women spend foraging is about twenty-eight hours a week.[26]

However, if we calculate the total subsistence effort in these same eleven societies by adding in the amount of time people spend at such tasks as manufacturing and repairing tools and processing food, then people were working about forty-six hours a week. This is only slightly less than the members of modern industrial societies work if we add the time they spend in such activities as getting to and from work, shopping for food, cooking, and household maintenance.[27] In addition, a team of anthropologists from the University of New Mexico and University of Utah found that men among the Aché spend perhaps forty to fifty hours a week hunting.[28] Two of these same anthropologists also report that the Alyawarra of central Australia spend anywhere from two to five times as many hours foraging as the !Kung.[29]

But the story gets worse. David Kaplan has reassessed the entire affluence thesis and concludes that it does not hold up well. Kaplan first looked at the workload. He points out that even if we accept Lee's figures for the !Kung, they not only have to forage but also to butcher animals, process plants and nuts, obtain water and firewood, cook the food, manufacture and maintain tools, clean up after themselves, and periodically move to new locations and build new huts. He estimates that when the time spent in these activities is added to direct foraging time, !Kung women work about forty hours a week and men about forty-five hours. Using Yellen's figures for the !Kung workload during the wet season, these figures expand to about fifty and fifty-five hours, respectively. Moreover, much of what Sahlins and others have referred to as leisure time is not really leisure time at all. In dry, hot environments it is often very unpleasant to forage during the day (and too risky as well) since exposure to especially hot conditions may lead to dehydration, sunstroke, and other health threats. The !Kung are obviously aware of these hazards, and usually wait out the heat of the day, foraging either earlier or later. This is enforced idleness, not leisure. In addition, when resources are especially scarce, people may not spend much time foraging because there is very little to obtain. This too is enforced idleness.[30]

What then of the quality of the diet? Again we see a very different picture from that presented by Sahlins, Lee, and Woodburn. Kaplan notes that numerous biomedical researchers have suggested that the !Kung diet is not only nutritionally inadequate but often results in semistarvation.[31] Many !Kung have a stunted stature, the result of caloric insufficiency. Lorna Marshall, one of the first anthropologists to study the !Kung, reported at the very time that Sahlins formulated his affluence thesis that the !Kung were excessively thin and were constantly anxious about food; others have also reported excessive thinness and food anxiety.[32] Another problem for the !Kung is periodic resource failure. Drought often leads to the failure of mongongo trees to produce nuts, which, since the !Kung rely heavily on this food source, is a very serious problem.[33]

However, it is important not to overemphasize the difficulties faced by the !Kung when evaluating the adequacy of the hunter-gatherer diet. The !Kung attempt to survive in a very marginal environment that presents many difficulties. Many hunter-gatherers inhabit, or at least have inhabited in the past, favorable environments with abundant plant and animal foods. Many groups are found in tropical or subtropical regions where heavy rains can be expected during certain seasons and where the risk of resource failure is, presumably, lower. It remains for some especially enterprising anthropologist to do the labor-intensive work necessary to find out about the adequacy of subsistence in a wider range of foraging groups.

This qualification aside, let us return to the critique. Kaplan points out that even beyond whatever dietary inadequacies any particular hunting and gathering group may experience, these are hardly the only miserable conditions they face. In virtually all foraging groups, rates of infant and child mortality are extremely high, with nearly half of all children dying by age five, and there is great susceptibility to infectious diseases. Moreover, hunter-gatherers are legendary for harassing and browbeating each other to share food. There are many accusations of stinginess, and people thought to be stingy are mocked and often ostracized.

Then there is the question of "wants" as opposed to "needs." One of Sahlins's main points was that hunter-gatherer wants, like those of many nonindustrial peoples, are very limited. But how does Sahlins know this, Kaplan asks, since he presents no actual evidence for his claim. Kaplan concludes that Sahlins is relying on a mere assumption based largely on his dislike of modern capitalist society and his desire to romanticize the original form of human society. His claim is ideological rather than scientific. Kaplan zeroes in on this, pointing out that the main reason the affluent society thesis caught on so quickly was because it resonated strongly with many anthropologists in the special decade of the 1960s, when capitalist society was under attack from many quarters.[34]

The notion that hunter-gatherers have limited wants is contradicted by a great deal of evidence. They enthusiastically adopt such modern conveniences as CD players, VCRs, televisions, cassette recorders, shotguns and rifles, and even cars and trucks when these things become available. (Of course, the foragers have to be in a position to use these things. Televisions have to be plugged in, for example. This means that foragers can only adopt them if they are in sufficient contact with societies with the technology to make them usable. Foragers isolated from such populations could not adopt them. Still, they could adopt, and often do adopt, shotguns and rifles, as well as such things as steel machetes and aluminum pots and pans.) All of these things make life easier and more interesting. The Yanomama of the Amazon rain forest, who subsist primarily by plant cultivation, desire steel axes and machetes as well as all kinds of cooking utensils because they too make life easier (steel axes vastly reduce the amount of time and energy it takes to cut down trees and large shrubs).[35] Virtually all nonindustrial populations have a great interest in modern technology.

A reasonable conclusion would be that hunting and gathering was most often a difficult way to live. Resources were often scarce and in most groups periods of hunger or even near starvation were common. But did things improve with the transition to agricultural societies? We will see.

First Agriculture

Between 10,000 and 11,500 years ago the first steps toward agriculture were taken in a transformation known as the Neolithic Revolution. Agriculture originated in a part of southwest Asia known as the Fertile Crescent. Its center is located between the Tigris and Euphrates rivers in what was then called Mesopotamia (and now Iraq). It is often said to include adjacent parts of Anatolia (Turkey), as well as the eastern Mediterranean region that comprises the present-day countries of Syria, Lebanon, Jordan, and Israel. Sometimes the Nile Valley is also included.[36] Foraging peoples who had lived there for many years exploited wild grains for much of their subsistence and gradually learned to domesticate them. The principal grains were wheat, barley, and rye, but legumes such as peas, lentils, and chickpeas were also domesticated and cultivated. A number of animal species were domesticated at the same time, sheep and goats in particular, but also cattle and pigs.[37]

As people became more dependent on domesticates, life became increasingly sedentary and small villages or towns, usually containing mud-brick houses, were built. Technologically, polished stone axes began to be used, along with sickles for harvesting. Planting was done with digging sticks or wooden hoes (plows were several thousand years into the future). Pottery, although not unknown in foraging societies, became much more common, both for storing food and for eating such cereal-based foods as porridges and gruels.[38]

After perhaps two thousand years, these first farmers began to migrate to both southern and northern Europe to the west, to parts of central Asia to the east, and to Egypt and adjacent regions of North Africa to the south. In these regions they encountered hunter-gatherer populations. For a while agriculturalists lived side by side with these foraging groups, who did not adopt agriculture immediately and in some cases strongly resisted it. In time, though, most hunter-gatherer communities took up agriculture, although usually not all at once. The entire complex of domesticated plants and animals appeared in Greece by 9,000 years ago and along the northern Mediterranean about a thousand years later. After about 7,400 years ago agriculturalists began to move farther north to the Danube Valley, and on past the Alps to the Rhineland and the Paris basin. Agriculturalists also moved into Scandinavia and the British Isles, but not until around 5,500 years ago. Hunter-gatherers were not always happy to see the new arrivals, and there must have been more than the occasional skirmish.[39]

Occupation of parts of central Asia by agriculturalists from southwest Asia, especially the Caucasus and what is now Turkmenistan, is observed by 9,000–8,000 years ago. Again we see the full complex of southwest Asian domesticates. Agricultural populations also moved into Egypt and the Indian subcontinent. In the subcontinent we see a greater variety of crops. Cereals and legumes were brought in from southwest Asia, but rice came in from China. African sorghum and legumes were also introduced, but later.[40]

China was a second region of independent agricultural development. Here agriculture is first observed in the basins of the Yellow and Yangzi rivers in northern and central China around 8,500 years ago. Several crops were domesticated, especially rice, two varieties of millet, and soybeans. The main domesticated animals were pigs, cattle, sheep, goats, and water buffalo. Archaeologists have discovered the remains of houses with sunken floors, between which were storage pits. Technology included polished stone axes, stone or shell knives for reaping, and pestles and mortars for grinding grain. Remains of pigs, chickens, and dogs have also been unearthed. By around 7,000 years ago both the Yangzi and Yellow basins contained numerous agricultural settlements. By 5,000 years ago rice cultivation had spread as far south as Taiwan and Guangdong, and taro and yams were cultivated in southern China.[41]

Agriculture arrived in southeast Asia from China around 5,500 years ago or perhaps slightly later. Agricultural communities containing pottery, polished stone axes, spindle whorls, and domesticated yams, taro, rice, cattle, pigs, and dogs moved "down a north-south axis from Southern China through Mainland Southeast Asia toward the Malay Peninsula, and through Taiwan and the Philippines toward Indonesia," gradually replacing resident hunter-gatherer populations as they moved.[42]

Various islands in the Pacific Ocean were eventually occupied, although considerably later.

In these times the Old and New Worlds were unknown to each other, and thus the development of agriculture in the New World was an entirely independent process. There were several major subregions of New World agriculture: South America, mostly Andean Ecuador, Peru, Bolivia, and northern Chile; Mesoamerica, mainly Mexico, Honduras, and El Salvador; the American Southwest; and the eastern woodlands of North America centering around the drainage basins of the Mississippi River. In the southern regions the main domesticate was maize, whose wild ancestor is thought to have been a plant known as *teosinte*. The date for domestication is uncertain, but it was probably around 7,000–6,000 years ago. Maize was the only staple for the entirety of New World agriculture, although minor crops such as squash, beans, chili peppers, and gourds were domesticated. Maize arrived in the American Southwest from Mesoamerica around 4,000 years ago, but did not appear in the eastern woodlands until around 1,500 years ago (500 CE).[43]

Unlike the Old World, the New World had no large animals suitable for domestication. In the Andean region there were llamas and alpacas, but they were used as pack animals more than as food sources. Turkeys and guinea pigs were also domesticated. Because of this ecological difference, sedentary village communities appeared much later in the New World. Hunting continued to be the main source of meat.[44]

Several important features of the agricultural transition command our attention. It was worldwide, occurred independently in at least four regions of the world (southwest Asia, China, Andean South America plus Mesoamerica, and the eastern woodlands of North America), and took place in a remarkably short time considered within an archaeological time frame. Most of the transitions were made, or at least begun, in the 4,500-year span between 11,500 and 7,000 years ago. This is not much more than the blink of an eye in archaeological terms, since humans of one species or another have been around for over 4 million years (more than 2 million for the genus *Homo*) and anatomically modern humans for about 200,000. These facts are crucial to understanding why the transition to agriculture was made.

Many years ago it was thought that agriculture was "invented" in the Fertile Crescent and then diffused to the other world regions. Some unknown genius finally "cracked the code" of how domestication and cultivation could be achieved, and the "idea" was so compelling that it spread far and wide. Today we know this is wrong. Implicit in this theory was the notion that people who are aware of agriculture will automatically adopt it. In fact, there are many examples of hunter-gatherers living in close proximity to agricultural communities who show no interest in becoming agriculturalists themselves.[45] They may borrow various things from them, but their mode of subsistence is not necessarily one of them.

In fact, hunter-gatherers often resist adopting agriculture in the absence of some compelling need. Several reasons have been suggested for this resistance. The archaeologist Mark Cohen believes that ancient hunter-gatherers had probably long understood how to domesticate plants and animals, but refused to put this knowledge to use for thousands of years because they thought that the costs of agriculture outweighed the benefits.[46] On average, agricultural peoples work harder and longer than hunter-gatherers, and ancient hunter-gatherers may have sensed this or observed it directly in their agricultural neighbors. People prefer not to work harder or longer than necessary to meet their basic needs.

Foraging peoples may also have seen that agriculture carried risk. As foragers they could go get the plants and animals they wanted and consume them forthwith. But cultivating is different because there is no immediate return on work invested. Crops are planted in hopes that in a few months they will mature into an abundant harvest. But there is no guarantee. What if the rains don't come and the crops fail, or there is too much rain and the crops rot? These are serious matters. Why take chances if you don't have to?[47]

However counterintuitive it may seem to those of us in the modern world, hunter-gatherers often *like* hunting and gathering. People usually become habituated to their way of life and are reluctant to give it up without a good reason. After all, the Inuit of Greenland and Alaska, despite their forbidding environment, have chosen to remain there. And Scandinavians who immigrated to the United States in the nineteenth century moved to cold northern states like Minnesota and Wisconsin because the climate was familiar. They didn't head south to Florida or west to California and their warm climates.

Evidence from paleopathological studies— studies looking for signs of disease in ancient bones and teeth—indicates that all over the world some 30,000 years ago foragers seemed to have been better nourished than people living in more recent agricultural societies. Compared to later agricultural populations, ancient hunter-gatherers showed less evidence of infection and chronic malnutrition, less biological stress that would have disrupted childhood growth, and fewer dental cavities and less oral disease. People in early hunter-gatherer populations also seemed to live just as long as the members of later agricultural communities.[48]

If, then, ancient hunter-gatherers were reasonably well nourished and knew how to plant crops but avoided doing so for any number of reasons, what finally compelled some of them to cross the threshold to the agricultural way of life? Cohen argues that it was a "food crisis" due to growing population. Hunter-gatherer groups in several regions of the world finally outgrew the capacity of their environments to sustain them. When this occurred, they were forced to start producing their own food in order to prevent the food crisis from getting worse. They became willing to work harder and longer because they now had something to gain from it and the costs of not doing so were becoming too great.[49]

One of the most important features of Cohen's theory is that it is designed to explain the *worldwide* transition to agriculture and its independent development in at least four regions of the world. As Cohen has argued, this worldwide character is of such striking significance that only a general theory that explains the whole process can hope to succeed. "Such widespread common events require relatively simple common core events and causes. To argue otherwise defies the odds of coincidence given the enormously widespread complex sequences of events occurring in parallel but independently in so many regions of the world."[50]

But Cohen's theory is not the whole story. There is also a crucial ecological ingredient. Paleoclimatic research shows that between about 20,000 and 11,500 years ago climates were colder and drier than they are today. In addition, there was a great deal of climatic variability over time "such that major swings of temperature and moisture supply could have taken place literally on decadal scales."[51] As the Australian archaeologist Peter Bellwood points out, these circumstances would have made attempts to domesticate and cultivate plants virtually impossible. But beginning around 11,500 years ago, there was an overall warming trend that was accompanied by increased rainfall and fewer climate swings. The new conditions made agriculture possible.[52]

And yet just because agriculture became possible it need not have developed unless there was some compelling need. Ecological change *enabled* agriculture, but was not a direct cause of it. Here is where population pressure comes back into the picture as the cause of the set of events that ecological change made possible.[53] People could now successfully plant and they had good reason to do so. They needed more food to satisfy larger populations.

Tillers of the Soil

Ethnography supplements archaeology. The agricultural societies discussed above are those known from archaeological research. But ethnographers—anthropologists who live for a time with "their tribe" and describe its way of life—have provided us with a large amount of information about how small-scale agricultural societies work. A useful distinction is often drawn between agriculture and *horticulture*—the cultivation of gardens using simple hand tools. Agriculture, in the narrow sense, is the cultivation of fields, which are usually larger plots of land that have been mostly or entirely denuded of trees and shrubs. Anthropologists usually call these societies *intensive agricultural societies*, whereas sociologists more commonly call them *agrarian societies*.

In horticultural systems of cultivation, there is by definition some fallowing of land. It may be extensive, so that most available land at any one time may not be used. Among horticultural societies that are fortunate to have a great deal of land suitable for cultivation, most of it will likely be fallow at any given time. A garden plot may be cultivated for a year or two and then left to go fallow for perhaps ten or twenty years.

Many horticulturalists known today live in tropical forests and have to cut down trees in order to make gardens. They may be preparing a new garden or bringing an old garden back into cultivation, with only brush or small trees to clear away.

This method of garden preparation is known as *slash-and-burn* for the simple reason that vegetation is cut down (slashed) and then burned off. The ashes make a decent fertilizer, and then crops—usually root crops like yams, manioc, tubers, and so on—can be planted amid the ashes with simple digging sticks. This is usually women's work. When the crops mature, they are harvested, and this too is most often women's work. For these reasons, horticultural societies are sometimes called *female-farming societies*.[54]

Horticulturalists with abundant land leave much of it fallow because cultivating the soil with the slash-and-burn method rapidly depletes its nutrients. In a couple of years its yields start to decline, but soil fertility can be restored with long-term fallowing. However, other horticultural societies are not so fortunate. Their land is less abundant either because they have greater population densities, live on small islands, or some such thing. The population-to-land ratio is higher, and people do not have the luxury of lengthy fallowing. The fallow period is shortened to perhaps as little as five years and in some instances is eliminated altogether, resulting in permanent or near-permanent cultivation. At that point something must be done to prevent soil fertility from plunging too low, such as adding fertilizer.

Horticulturalists live in villages containing anywhere from fifty to, say, five hundred people. The Yanomama are one such group, several thousand of which live in small villages in the rain forests of Venezuela and Brazil. They cultivate plantains as their staple crop, which they make into a variety of dishes. They have no domesticated animals and rely on hunting for meat, mainly wild pigs, monkeys, and several species of birds. The Yanomama are long-fallow cultivators who spend a good deal of time clearing forest land, but some groups do a lot of gathering. They may abandon their gardens for part of the year and go trekking through the forest collecting what they can.[55]

Oceania, a vast chain of mostly small islands in the Pacific Ocean bounded by New Guinea in the west, Tahiti in the east, and Hawaii in the northeast, is also one of the best places to find horticulturalists. Oceania is divided into three main regions: Melanesia, Micronesia, and Polynesia. Melanesia (dark islands) includes the large island of New Guinea, as well as smaller islands to the east and southeast, such as the Solomons and Trobriands. Most of Micronesia (little islands) is north of Melanesia and includes the Marshall, Mariana, and Gilbert islands, among others. Polynesia (many islands) is east of Melanesia and Micronesia and extends over a large region of the Pacific from north to south. Its best-known islands are Hawaii, Samoa, Tahiti, and Tonga. The societies inhabiting these islands have been extensively studied for more than a century and so we know quite a bit about them. They span the entire range from short-fallowers to long-fallowers and even permanent cultivators. Some of them retain aboriginal practices to this day, although they are scarcely as pristine as they were a century or two ago.

The Kapauku of west New Guinea are a horticultural group whose subsistence practices were carefully studied by the anthropologist Leopold Pospisil in the 1950s.

They live in the highlands some 5,000 feet above sea level. The habitat is a tropical rain forest, although there is some secondary forest and grassland. The Kapauku use slashing and burning to cultivate the mountain slopes. The forest is cut down and burned off by men, sometimes aided by women, who then take over the planting and harvesting. They carry sweet potato shoots and plant them in shallow holes in the ashes that they dig with simple digging sticks. Sweet potatoes make up about 90 percent of cultivated food. On valley floors there are no trees, only grassland and a few shrubs. This land is prepared by burning; crops include sugar cane, taro, gourds, and native beans, among others. A more intensive method of cultivation is employed on the valley floors. A type of spade is used to turn over the soil to make rectangular beds surrounded by drainage ditches. After a crop is harvested more fertilizer is placed on the bed and then covered with mud. This maintains soil fertility and permits almost continuous cultivation. These gardens are the most productive. Unlike the Yanomama, the Kapauku have domesticated animals. Pigs are prized possessions that not only provide meat but are important status symbols.[56]

In Polynesia cultivation ranged from relatively simple, nonintensive methods to methods that were extremely intensive. The Tahitians used relatively intensive methods. They terraced hillsides, diverted streams to provide irrigation in drier areas, and enriched the soil in a variety of ways. Domesticated plants, brought originally from Indonesia, included breadfruit trees, taro, yams, sweet potatoes, bananas, plantains, and some sugar cane. Animal protein came partly from fish. Fishing equipment included nets, poisons, harpoons, and hooks and lines. Domesticated pigs and chickens also provided animal protein.[57]

The most intensive methods of cultivation anywhere in Oceania were found in Hawaii. Here there was not only short-fallow cultivation but fully permanent cultivation of some plots of land. There were complex irrigation networks and elaborate terraced slopes. These methods were necessary to support large populations, and the Hawaiian islands had the largest and densest populations of any Polynesian societies. In addition, much of the land was owned by powerful chiefs, who expected the cultivators to produce not only enough for their own subsistence, but also enough for the subsistence of the chiefs themselves. This required that cultivation be even more intensive.[58]

Intensive agricultural or agrarian societies are those in which land is more or less permanently cultivated, with no fallow period at all. In contrast to horticultural societies, men usually do the majority of the field work for several reasons. The work is long and hard. During the busiest seasons farmers work from sunup to sundown. It is difficult for women to be heavily involved in farming because they have important child care and domestic responsibilities. Taking infants and small children into the fields can pose serious dangers; they can be stepped on and killed by oxen or horses, for example. Because most agricultural work is men's work, agrarian societies have been called *male-farming* societies.[59]

Many agrarian societies have adopted the plow, which seems to have been used some 4,000 years ago in the early civilizations of the Old World (there were never any plows in the New World), although it may have been invented as early as 6,000 years ago.[60] The first plows, known as scratch plows or ards, were basically just pointed sticks equipped with a handle. They were initially made entirely of wood, although in time a metal tip was added. Scratch plows were fairly primitive by later standards. They did little more than cut a shallow furrow for seeds. Weeds were cut but remained on the surface. The Greeks and Romans used scratch plows, as have most agrarian societies until recent times.[61]

The first major innovation in the plow did not come until some two millennia later. The Han Chinese in the late first millennium BCE invented the moldboard plow, which had a sideboard and curved metal plates attached to the plowshare. It was superior in several ways: it cut deeper furrows, turned over the soil, and buried the cut weeds. It enabled a farmer to plow in a single operation, since the scratch plow required cross-plowing. Because scratch plows were light, they were often pulled by people, especially in societies where there were no draft animals. Moldboard plows were much heavier and required animal power.[62]

By the early Middle Ages (or perhaps somewhat earlier) moldboard plows were used in northern Europe. The soils in these regions were much heavier and wetter than soils elsewhere, and required a heavy moldboard plow to till them effectively. Strong animal power was also needed. A team of oxen was used for centuries, and eventually horses became widely used.[63]

Why do some agrarian societies use the plow whereas others do not? There are three basic reasons. First, plows are much more likely to be adopted where population densities are very high, especially in excess of a hundred persons per square mile. Second, because high population densities on average require the fallow period to be greatly reduced or even eliminated, plows are much more commonly found in short-fallow rather than long-fallow societies. Finally, and most importantly, whether or not plows are introduced depends on the types of crops that are being cultivated. Some crops are "plow-negative," which means that they require only small to moderate amounts of land to produce an adequate amount of food. Plow-negative crops are also relatively easy and efficient to cultivate. These crops include maize, root crops such as yams, tree crops, and some types of millet. Maize can be cultivated, for example, by simply making small holes in the ground and depositing seeds in them, for which a simple digging stick will suffice. Similarly, millet does not require extensive land cultivation because its seeds do not require furrows or deep holes in order to sprout.[64]

"Plow-positive" crops, by contrast, require large amounts of land and heavy land preparation. Here we find such familiar staples as wheat, barley, and rye. In large-scale societies with high population densities, these crops can only be made to yield enough calories if plows are the primary cultivating instrument. In the case of one of the world's most important staples, rice, the method of cultivation depends on the type of rice. Wet rice is a plow-positive crop, but dry rice can be cultivated without plows.[65]

Farmers in agrarian societies are usually known as peasants. Medieval England was a peasant society. English peasants lived in small villages containing one or two hundred persons who spent most of their lives doing farmwork. Often teams of peasants worked cooperatively. Some peasants farmed the land in a "two-field" fashion. They would work in one field one year while allowing the other to remain fallow; then the next year they would reverse the process. Other peasants farmed the land using a "three-field" system. One field would be planted in the autumn with wheat or possibly rye; another would be planted with oats or barley the following spring; in the meantime, the third field would lie fallow. The next year the fallow field would be sown with wheat, the first field with oats or barley, and the second field would remain fallow, and so on. This system of crop rotation was designed to keep soil fertility as high as possible.[66]

Peasants applied animal manure to the soil to aid its fertility, but getting enough manure was a constant struggle. Peasants seldom had enough animals to produce all the manure they needed. Fodder—food for livestock, such as hay and straw—to produce a sufficient quantity of manure was also in short supply. So peasants did the best they could under difficult conditions, and this meant that they sometimes worked marl or lime into the ground as an additional fertilizer.[67] In addition, in numerous peasant societies farmers would apply human waste, generally known as "night soil." As unpleasant as it seems, night soil was widely used in ancient Greece, Japan, China, and many other earlier societies, and is still used today in many developing countries. Of course, by applying their own waste as a fertilizer people entailed the risk of disease, but in general seemed to prefer that to the risk of severe hunger or even starvation.

Peasants kept numerous animals, both as draft animals and as food sources. Oxen and cows pulled plows and provided both meat and milk. Sheep were kept for their wool and for food. Pigs were also kept. They were of no use for plowing or milking—you simply cannot use pigs as traction animals and they give very little milk—but they were excellent food sources. Pigs can be fed efficiently, put on weight quickly, and are easily prepared for slaughter.[68]

Throughout Europe the climate was wet enough to support rainfall agriculture. But in many other regions of the world, especially large areas of Asia, there was not enough rainfall for agriculture to be productive. In the arid or semiarid zones of China, India, Mesopotamia, and Egypt, for example, complex irrigation works had to be constructed to bring river water to distant areas.[69] These often enormous undertakings required a great deal of manpower. Irrigation agriculture is the most intensive form of agriculture observed in nonindustrial societies.

The earliest agriculturalists were essentially horticulturalists who used digging sticks and simple hoes and started out with nonintensive forms of cultivation. In open areas grass would be burned off to help in garden preparation, but many early cultivators lived in forested regions and had to cut down and burn trees. In time these early cultivators had to adopt more intensive methods.

Just as population pressure is a crucial piece of the puzzle in understanding the first agricultural transitions, it is highly relevant in explaining why agriculture has been steadily intensified over thousands of years. The main elements of this intensification have been shortening the fallow period, bringing more land under cultivation, using poorer soils previously avoided, terracing and irrigating, and adopting new modes of technology, such as metal hoes, plows, improved methods of fertilization, and crop rotation.

The earliest version of the population pressure argument for agricultural intensification was presented by Ester Boserup, a Danish economist, in 1965. Her work had a revolutionary impact on our thinking about agricultural change. Boserup argued, against the standard wisdom of the day, that people have no inherent desire to advance their level of technology. What people really want is to make a decent living by the simplest and easiest means possible. Their natural inclinations are to meet their subsistence needs by minimizing time and effort. Since adopting new technologies usually results in people having to work harder and longer, they will not switch to new methods unless special conditions compel them to do so, and the most common condition is the pressure of increasingly dense populations. As the number of mouths to be fed increases, a point is eventually reached at which people begin to deplete their resources and suffer a significant drop in their standard of living. It is at this point that people will start to intensify production. They adopt new forms of technology and work harder and longer in order to produce more food to feed more people.[70]

One of the most intriguing pieces of evidence Boserup presented to support her argument was that decreases in population density have often been followed by an actual *regression* in cultivation techniques. For example, in recent centuries some areas of South America experienced population declines resulting from new diseases introduced by encroaching Europeans, and the indigenous societies of these regions reverted to less intensive cultivation techniques. Likewise, in the twentieth century farmers in Tanzania, Vietnam, Sri Lanka, and India adopted less intensive agricultural methods when they were resettled by their governments to less populated regions and given more land to use. This was true even when the purpose of the resettlement was to spread more intensive methods to the areas of immigration.[71]

We also find relatively unintensive methods of cultivation in places where they would be least expected. Nineteenth-century Sweden was on the cusp of becoming an industrial society, but there was an enormous amount of land and population densities were very low. This gave farmers in the most thinly populated regions the luxury of slash-and-burn cultivation with hand tools, and they took advantage of it. Labor time was significantly reduced compared to plowing the land with draft animals, the traditional practice throughout the rest of Europe.

Peter Bellwood has noted that resource stress due to population pressure seemed to be present in some of the earliest agricultural communities not long after agriculture first developed. When more land must be put under cultivation and used more intensively, deforestation and other forms of environmental degradation result. Bellwood points to evidence in the archaeological record of sites growing to large size and then shrinking or disappearing altogether, which he interprets as reliable indicators of resource shortfall.[72]

Herders of Beasts

In the most arid regions of the world agriculture is difficult or impossible. People make a living by tending animal herds rather than growing crops. It is not completely clear exactly when this subsistence practice—herding or pastoralism—first emerged. There is evidence that early in prehistory—perhaps 8,000 years ago—some groups in the Middle East seemed to depend heavily on domesticated animals.[73] However, true pastoralism—exclusive or near-exclusive dependence on animal herds, with little or no agriculture—may be a more recent phenomenon, dating only from approximately 3,700 years ago.[74]

Pastoralists tend their animal herds—usually sheep, goats, cattle, horses, and camels—year round and usually move seasonally in search of pasture. Some pastoral groups depend on a single animal species, but most herd several species. A few pastoralists practice no agriculture at all, obtaining agricultural products by trading for them with agricultural neighbors. The majority of pastoral groups practice some agriculture, but this is always (by definition) secondary to their herding activities.[75] Agriculture is usually disdained as a very poor way to make a living, and people who practice agriculture full-time are often held in contempt.

Pastoralists live and travel in small groups of, at most, a few hundred members. Most of the diet is provided by milk, although this is often processed into butter and cheese. Sometimes blood is drawn and mixed with the milk. The mixture might be drunk, but sometimes it is roasted to form a sort of cake. Meat does not provide the bulk of the diet, since animals are capital investments. If people eat them, then their numbers become depleted. Occasionally a healthy animal is butchered, but most meat comes from animals that die naturally.

Thomas Barfield has identified five main geographical zones where pastoral nomadism is common:[76]

1. *Africa just south of the Sahara, running from west to east, and from north to south in east Africa.* Here cattle are the most prominent animal, although sheep and goats may also be herded. Some of the best-studied groups in this region are the Dinka, Maasai, and Nuer. The Nuer, most of whose economic activity centers around cattle herding, live mostly in the Sudan in east Africa. Like most pastoralists, they disdain cultivation and esteem herding and caring for

their animals as the best way to live. Cattle are cherished possessions that con-stitute the main form of wealth. They are pampered—talked to, petted, their horns decorated with ribbons, and so on. Milk is the main food, being drunk fresh, combined with millet into a type of porridge, and made into cheese.[77]

2. *The Saharan and Arabian deserts.* Pastoralists of this region, mostly Bedouin Arabs, typically specialize in just one animal, the dromedary (one-humped) camel, which provides both food and transport. The form of pastoralism practiced here is extreme not only because it is based on a single species but also because people must travel long distances to find enough pasture for their animal herds.

3. *Central Eurasia, north of the Saharan and Arabian deserts, through the pla-teaus of Turkey and Iran and farther east.* Pastoralists living in this region herd sheep, goats, camels, donkeys, and horses. Some of the best-known groups are the Turkmen, the central Asian Arabs of Afghanistan, and the Qashqa'i and Basseri of Iran. The Basseri live in the dry steppes and mountains of southern Iran. They move about with their animal herds, mostly sheep and goats, and live in tents. Milk obtained from these animals is processed into sour milk and cheese, and lambs are sometimes slaughtered for meat.[78]

4. *The Asian steppe, running from the Black Sea to Mongolia.* Horse-riding pasto-ralists have long predominated in this region. Horses are not only ridden but used for food as well. Sheep, goats, cattle, and Bactrian (two-humped) camels are also herded. Today these groups are most commonly found in Kazakh-stan, Uzbekistan, and Xinjiang, China. The most famous groups of this region are historical. These include the Xiongnu of the northern steppes of ancient China, the Uighur of northwest Mongolia, and the Zunghar in the area where Russia, Mongolia, and China meet. The Mongols lived in the Mongolian steppe adjacent to China and created a massive empire in the thirteenth cen-tury.

5. *The Tibetan plateau and neighboring mountain regions.* Groups in this region live at extremely high altitudes where there are vast grasslands suitable for grazing animals, especially sheep, goats, and yaks. The yak is uniquely adapt-ed to high altitudes and extreme cold, and is used for its milk, meat, and hair, as well as for transport. Some groups also herd a yak/cattle hybrid known as a *dzo*. The Drokba are a well-known group from this region.

Merchants and Traders

In the types of societies we have been considering, producing goods and selling them played little or no role in economic life. Getting a living by producing goods could not exist until humans created *markets*—economic institutions with rules and procedures for buying and selling. When did markets come about? This cannot be pinpointed exactly but we know that they existed in some advanced horticultural societies. The Aztecs of central Mexico, for example, had fairly elaborate markets when the first Spaniards encountered them in the early sixteenth century. Large markets existed in cities throughout the Aztec empire, connected to each other and to the Aztec capital, Tenochtitlán, by a system of traveling merchants known as *pochtecah*. A huge market located in a suburb of Tenochtitlán took place every fifth day. Potential buyers came to this market from miles around to buy the many and varied goods that were offered: gold, silver, jewels, clothing, chocolate, tobacco, hides, footwear, slaves, fruits and vegetables, salt, honey, tools, pottery, household furnishings, and many other items.[79]

In the Old World, markets were present at least 5,000 years ago and very likely one or two thousand years earlier. The earliest civilizations in Mesopotamia, Egypt, and China certainly had markets. Markets require merchants, who are economic specialists in buying and selling. They can sell goods locally, but often they move them over considerable distances to offer them for sale in other markets. This can be a very lucrative strategy, because a merchant may be able to buy a product cheaply in one market and sell it in a distant market where people are willing to pay more. Markets also require craftsmen or artisans. After all, someone has to make the goods that merchants sell, and merchants usually don't make these goods themselves.

In agrarian societies in which merchants have plied their trade over the past few thousand years, they have comprised only around 5 percent of the population. This is because agrarian societies were made up largely of numerous peasants and a few landlords. Some peasants owned their own land, but many did not. And even if they did, what they could do with their land and its products was usually controlled by the tiny landlord class. Most landlords were very well-off, and many were extremely rich. Much of their wealth came from the labor of the peasants they controlled. But landlords usually had great influence over government, and governments in these societies continually engaged in wars of conquest with other societies. This was another major source of the landlord class's wealth. Landlords didn't acquire their wealth by making or selling goods, but by exploiting peasants and reaping the benefits of the conquest of foreign lands.[80]

So landlords pretty much ran the show, and the way in which they gained their wealth caused them to disdain merchants, who were usually held to be money-grubbers who dealt in the dirty business of commerce. (There were differences in the level of disdain shown to merchants. In Europe, for example, merchants held a somewhat higher status than in China and India.) So why didn't landlords use their influence over government to crush the merchants and get them out of the way? Because merchants had things that landlords and other nobles wanted regardless of how the merchants acquired them. So merchants had to be tolerated and sometimes encouraged.

Some societies in the ancient world supported a great deal of mercantile and trading activity, such as the Phoenicians of the eastern Mediterranean in the late second millennium and early first millennium BCE. The Phoenicians, who called themselves Canaanites, had no real agricultural sector and were almost entirely spe-cialized for commerce.[81] Here merchants ruled the roost. But this situation was very unusual. And so with a few exceptions, for thousands of years merchants' small numbers and low status meant that they had little influence over economic life. And yet merchants refused to give up trying to increase their influence. They kept plunging ahead despite the obstacles.

With merchants go both trade networks and cities. If we look back to about 2000 BCE, we see small trade networks and very few cities of any real size. In 2250 BCE trade was mostly local and regional. Agrarian civilizations in Mesopotamia and Egypt were linked by trade, but that was about as far as things went. Over the next two thousand years trade underwent a dramatic expansion. By 200 BCE world trade had expanded west to encompass Greece and Rome and much of western Europe, south to incorporate the Arabian peninsula and parts of northeast Africa, north to incorporate central Asia, and east and southeast to take in all of the Indian sub-continent and much of China—the famous Silk Road. As the name suggests, silk from China was the most highly desired commodity traded, but there were nu-merous other trade goods: gold and other precious metals, precious stones, ivory, furs, ceramics, bronze objects, jade, lacquer, glass, iron, and even exotic animals and plants.[82] By 600 CE a trade network encompassing nearly all of the Old World had formed, with all of China and southeast Asia now included, along with most of Europe. Only northern and northeast Europe, Russia, Siberia, and sub-Saharan Af-rica were left out. By 1500 CE world trade had extended into most of these regions.[83]

The expansion of trade networks was directly paralleled by major increases in the number and size of large cities. In 2250 BCE there were only eight cities in the world with populations greater than 30,000, but by 430 BCE there were more than fifty, the largest of which, Babylon, had some 200,000 inhabitants. After a decline in cities following the fall of Rome, this urbanization process accelerated once again. By 1000 CE there were seventy cities with populations between 40,000 and 450,000, and by 1500 CE there were more than seventy-five cities with populations ranging from 45,000 to 670,000 inhabitants.[84]

It has often been assumed that in ancient economies the kind of rational organi-zation of business enterprise found in modern economies was largely absent. Prices were not set by market forces of supply and demand, but rather by a kind of negoti-ating or haggling.[85] Moreover, it was thought that merchants were often casual about their business and were not necessarily concerned with maximizing profits.[86] But recent research has put these ideas to rest. Studies conducted by a number of his-torians show that in ancient economies there were frequently large-scale markets, including price-setting markets regulated by supply and demand; extensive use of money as a medium of exchange; private warehouses stocked with goods; merchant middlemen; extensive investment in capital goods; professional moneylenders who gave interest-bearing loans to merchants; sophisticated credit systems; and a strong desire to maximize profits and accumulate them over the long term.[87]

Merchants were still second-class citizens and economic inferiors but were gaining numbers and influence. The world was gradually becoming more commercialized. Beginning a few hundred years ago the influence of landlords and aristocrats was in decline and merchants were finally beginning to gain the upper hand. How did this happen?

Capitalists Small and Large

The European Middle Ages began after the fall of Rome and continued until the fifteenth century, lasting a millennium. It has long been assumed that little of interest was happening during this time, which is the reason the name "Dark Ages" was applied to this period. But in fact quite a bit was happening, and much of it was pretty interesting.

On the economic front, commercial activity was growing stronger, especially in Europe. By the so-called Late Middle Ages, roughly between the twelfth and fifteenth centuries, the most vibrant activity was in the northwest, primarily in what is now Belgium, and in southern Europe, especially the Italian city-states. The northwest was part of a large trading area that covered the Mediterranean, Portugal, France, England, the Rhineland, and the Hanseatic League.[88] The Hanseatic League was a trading association of merchants who operated from England to the Baltic Sea. In the south a vigorous form of capitalism developed in such Italian city-states as Florence, Genoa, and Venice.[89] Banking became well developed, and merchants were greatly admired and respected. Many Italian business practices provided the basis for the spread of capitalism to other parts of Europe. Double-entry bookkeeping, marine insurance, and commercial law were invented by the Italians, who were the only ones to use them until the sixteenth century.[90]

The Italian city-states were overwhelmingly devoted to foreign trade, but some of them had a surprising amount of industry and manufacturing.[91] Textile manufacturing was especially important, and in some cases was highly mechanized. For example, "in Florence in 1338 there were said to be as many as two hundred workshops engaged in cloth manufacture, employing a total of thirty thousand workmen or about a quarter of the whole occupied population of the city."[92]

By the sixteenth century, the center of capitalist activity had begun to shift from Italy to northwest Europe, first to Antwerp and then later to the Netherlands, England, and France, and capitalism came to be associated with large territorial states rather than small city-states.[93] In the seventeenth century these large states vigorously promoted capitalism in the form of mercantilism, as governments granted monopolies to trading companies so that the companies could benefit from trade between European nations and the overseas colonies they were establishing.[94]

The great mercantilist trading companies of the seventeenth century were created in the Netherlands, England, and France. In 1602 the Dutch East India Company was formed and quickly acquired a monopoly on trade with India. Each year the company brought between 10 and 12 million florins worth of goods into Europe. Domestically the Netherlands established important processing industries, such as wool and linen processing; diamond cutting; and dyeing, weaving, and silk spinning.[95] In 1600 the English East India Company was established and within fifteen years the company had created more than twenty trading posts in India, several islands in the Indian Ocean, Indonesia, and Japan. Between 1610 and 1640 England's foreign trade increased by ten times. English kings "distributed privileges and monopolies, regulated and organized the control of manufactures, prohibited the export of wool, and raised taxes on imported French and Dutch fabrics; Acts of Parliament went so far as to make obligatory the use of woolen cloth for mourning clothes."[96]

Mercantilist policies were also prominent in France. The trading companies were regarded as the armies of the king, the manufactures of France as his reserves. The king's economic minister supervised the establishment and operation of some four hundred manufactures. There were large companies with branches in several provinces, especially in mining, metallurgy, and woolen goods. Government policies were devoted to iron working, paper making, armaments, woolen and linen fabrics, tapestries, porcelain, and glassware.[97]

A surprising amount of capitalism also developed in Japan at about the same time. During its Tokugawa period (1600–1868), Japan saw widespread commercialization of agriculture, increasing flight of peasants into the towns and cities, large-scale urbanization, increased economic monetization, and the beginning of the factory system.[98]

What accounts for this great capitalist spurt? It was a complex process involving several different factors and predisposing conditions. The most important predisposing condition was a long-term process of world commercialization that had begun more than four millennia earlier. Because of the low status of merchants in earlier societies, and the domination of economic life by landlords and other nobles, capitalist practices could only develop slowly and fitfully. But by the later Middle Ages a kind of "critical mass" had been reached in which capitalist activity began to spread more rapidly. As commercialization advanced, many landlords suffered declining fortunes and became capitalists themselves, hiring workers to produce agricultural commodities that could be sold in markets. After thousands of years of limited mercantile activity, capitalists were finally getting themselves ensconced at the top.

But why did the capitalist spurt occur in certain places rather than others? The main actors—the Italian city-states, Antwerp, England, the Netherlands, and France (especially northern France)—were favorably situated for a "great leap forward." The Italian city-states were located on or right near the water, which gave them a tremendous advantage as traders. They could concentrate overwhelmingly on maritime rather than overland trade, which allowed more goods to be traded over larger distances. The city-states also had small governments that encouraged capitalist activity—indeed, directly participated in it. Much the same was true of the bigger countries of northwest Europe. They too were located right near water or, in the case of Britain, completely surrounded by it. This gave them the same advantage that the Italian city-states had, the opportunity to concentrate on maritime trade.

Another clear advantage for Europe was the situation of its towns in relation to governments and landlords. European towns differed in several crucial respects from the towns of other civilizations, such as China or the ancient Greek and Roman world. The merchants and craftsmen of these towns held a socially inferior position, as they did in almost all agrarian civilizations. The ideals of the landlord classes and of rural life dominated and submerged the ideas of the urban classes. The towns of late medieval Europe, on the other hand, enjoyed considerably more economic and social independence. Their autonomy was signified by the fact that they were separated from the countryside by walls and gates. They had a legal independence too; persons passing through a city's gates became subject to its own laws. The towns were culturally distinct from the countryside as well. Townsmen rejected the values of the rural world and developed their own.[99]

Finally, European societies were much smaller than Asian ones like China and India. Not only was Europe filled with numerous societies, but the societies that we today call Italy or Germany did not yet exist. There was no "Italy," but several hundred independent city-states throughout the Italian peninsula. Nor was there a "Germany" but rather several dozen free cities and numerous bishoprics, duchies, and principalities. The number of states within the boundaries of Europe may have totaled close to five hundred.[100] Europe was thus a large continent filled with many small to medium-size states, and these states *competed with each other*. This competition was economic, political, and military, and it was a major spur to capitalist development. Asia had a system of interlinked states—Japan, China, Korea, Vietnam, Laos, and Thailand—but these states did not compete with each other in the way that European states did, which meant that an important capitalist dynamic was missing.[101]

Japan was something of an exception in that it was the only Asian society to become capitalistic. It had the same basic advantages as Europe, especially England. Like England, Japan was a group of islands close to a very large mainland. It also had a decentralized type of government that contrasted with the big Asian bureaucratic states. As in Europe, this meant that towns and merchants had more economic freedom.[102]

In recent years some scholars have tried to make the case that Asia had just as much capitalism, if not more, than Europe.[103] They claim that it was actually ahead of Europe in the eighteenth century. But this is not quite true. There was a great deal of market activity in China, but this activity was different from what went on in Europe. Europe had *private* capitalists who were remarkably free from state interference, whereas in Asia there was no truly private, or at least autonomous, capitalist class. Europe thus had a *capitalist* economy, whereas Asia had only a *market* economy. As expressed by Giovanni Arrighi, "The capitalist character of market-based development is not determined by the presence of capitalist institutions and dispositions but by the relation of state power to capital. Add as many capitalists as you like to a market economy, but unless the state has been subordinated to their class interest, the market economy remains non-capitalist."[104] Arrighi contends that Japan also had a market rather than a capitalist economy, but that is disputable.

So over several millennia we have gone from small-time to big-time capitalists. But something even larger was on the horizon. This was the Industrial Revolution, a dramatic transformation of a technology resting heavily on human labor and animal power into one characterized by machines.[105] Along with this came the transition from reliance on agricultural production to a reliance on the manufacture of goods for sale in the context of a factory system. The Industrial Revolution created new and profound changes in the economic structure of society, bringing new methods of production and dramatic changes in how labor was organized.

The Industrial Revolution began in England during the second half of the eighteenth century. This initial phase of industrialization was characterized by the great expansion of the textile industry and by major developments in iron manufacturing and coal mining. The textile industry, especially the manufacture of cotton cloth, was advanced through the invention of such machines as the spinning jenny, the water frame, the power loom, and the cotton gin. The growth of textile manufacturing spurred the development of the factory system. The invention of the steam engine was important because it was used to power the heavy machinery housed in the textile mills. The iron industry also expanded, as iron was increasingly in demand for the manufacture of steam engines and machine tools.[106]

Industrial technology developed in several other parts of Europe during the nineteenth century, especially in Belgium, France, and Germany. The United States began to emerge as a major industrial society in the 1830s. Textile factories grew up and spread across New England, the heartland of early industrialization. There were also important developments in machine building and printing. The development of railroads in the 1850s and 1860s was an extremely important part of American industrialization, especially as they expanded westward and allowed the opening up of the American frontier.[107]

A new mode of economic production was being created, *industrial capitalism.* Its establishment on a major scale required the reorganization of the workforce into the factory system, and the factory became the basic unit of economic production. But obviously industrialization did not end with these developments. In the middle of the nineteenth century, further technological innovations emerged and existing technologies were elaborated and applied to capitalist production on a wider scale. The steam engine came to be applied to transportation, being used to create the first steam railway. It was also applied to navigation with the invention of the steamboat. And railroads became an extremely important part of capitalist investment.[108] By the turn of the twentieth century, the automobile, electrical, and petroleum industries were becoming important features of economic life, and by World War II the aviation, aluminum, and electronics industries were achieving major economic significance. Recent years have witnessed such notable technological developments as the harnessing of nuclear energy and the massive development of electronic gadgets of innumerable types, such as personal computers and smartphones.[109]

What was behind the Industrial Revolution? Why did it happen? Some scholars have seen it as rooted in population pressure.[110] They see industrialization as simply another technological advance that, like earlier technological advances such as the emergence of agriculture or the invention of the plow, was rooted in the desire to stave off declining living standards created by the growth of numbers. It is unlikely, though, that industrialization can be explained by demographic expansion. The Industrial Revolution was a technological change far different from the technological changes of earlier eras.

A better explanation is that the Industrial Revolution was the predictable outcome of evolving capitalism.[111] By the middle of the eighteenth century, Britain had become the world's dominant capitalist power. It had expanded its import and export markets throughout the capitalist system and had acquired enormous wealth. This wealth was essential as capital used in financing factories and machinery, and thus Britain was in a uniquely favorable financial position to pursue industrial development. As the historian Peter Stearns has noted, "Considerable investment funds were required—the new machines were expensive, far costlier than any manufacturing equipment previously devised, even in the very small factories that characterized much early industry."[112] The other industrializing nations were the most advanced capitalist societies of the day with the wealth and resources needed for industrialization.

Although wealth was necessary for capitalist societies to industrialize, there also had to be an incentive, a reason why industrialization was beneficial. The incentive was greater profits. Industrialization permitted increasing productivity and lowered costs, which in turn allowed for the expansion of existing domestic and foreign markets and the creation of new ones. The result was the increasing accumulation of capital on a grand scale. Industrialization made it possible for capitalism to expand from big capitalism to mega capitalism.

The Industrial Revolution was an economic and technological revolution, but it was socially revolutionary as well. Rural societies became increasingly urbanized as the workforce was radically reshaped. Societies in which peasants and other farmers made up the largest segment of society turned into societies in which factory workers, and then later office workers, constituted the bulk of the labor force. Basic social institutions were transformed, some of them radically. The new kind of society that formed during this time is what we call *industrial society*. But is it still industrial society? In recent decades social scientists of all stripes have argued that we now live in a *postindustrial* rather than an industrial society. This is a type of society in which the service sector has expanded at the expense of manufacturing and a "knowledge class"—consisting of such workers as scientists, health care professionals, government officials, artists, and intellectuals—has gained increasing influence.[113] This contention has much to recommend it, but it falls beyond the bounds of the current discussion.

Capitalists by Nature?

The great eighteenth-century Scottish economist Adam Smith, one of the founders of modern economics, famously proclaimed that humans "have a natural tendency to truck, barter, and exchange." He also declared that "it is not from the benevolence of the butcher, the brewer, or the baker that we expect our dinner, but from their regard to their own interest." If Smith is right—that people are bartering and exchanging for their own personal benefit—is capitalism, then, a product of human nature? After all, Smith's thinking on this matter might be regarded as a special case of Darwinian thinking applied to the economic sphere.

It's a tricky question when formulated this way, and certainly too simplistic. Since capitalism in a highly developed form has appeared only recently in human history, it would appear that the answer must clearly be no. But this is also an oversimplification. Obviously capitalism requires preconditions, many of them, and most of these preconditions have not been present throughout human history. Can we say then that capitalist economic relations lie dormant in human nature and develop when the preconditions appear? When the question is framed in this way, many scholars say that the answer is yes.

The evolutionary psychologists Leda Cosmides and John Tooby have argued that the human brain is equipped with a highly specialized set of algorithms for social exchange that provides the biological basis for our economic and social institutions. However, this same set of algorithms leads to very different results in different socio-ecological contexts. As Cosmides and Tooby put it, "Wherever human beings live, their cultural forms and social life are infused with social exchange relations. . . . Such relations appear in an enormous range of different guises, both simple and highly elaborated, implicit and explicit, deferred and simultaneous, practical and symbolic. The magnitude, variety, and complexity of our social exchange relations are among the most distinctive features of human social life, and differentiate us strongly from all other animal species."[114]

The evidence strongly supports this argument because in all societies we find people doing these things. The most basic form of human exchange is reciprocity. To reciprocate is to return favor for favor. This can be done in a highly generalized and unstated way in the sense that there is no explicitly acknowledged agreement between the parties. There is no time limit for repayment, nor is there any indication how repayment should be made. Although reciprocity of this nature is found in all societies, it is pervasive in small-scale societies. Most often it occurs among close kin or intimate acquaintances who have a history with each other and thus have developed trust.

A different form of reciprocity works more along the lines of tit for tat. In this case people are obligated to provide equivalent and sometimes immediate repayment. People deliberately and openly calculate what they are giving each other and formally state how repayment is to be made. Reciprocity of this sort, which is usually known as balanced reciprocity, is more apt to occur among people who are only moderately acquainted or not acquainted at all. Economic markets involve balanced reciprocity—the Nissan dealer gives me the Altima and I give him the $25,000—as do legal contracts. More simply, balanced reciprocity is a matter of people making agreements and sticking by them.

Modern capitalism is the most advanced form of reciprocal exchange known to human history. Given enough time and sufficiently large and dense populations, capitalism was more or less the inevitable outcome of the natural human tendency to truck, barter, and exchange.

Conclusion

In life there are two main forms of evolution, the biological and the social (often called the cultural). The term **social evolution** is sometimes used to refer to changes over the short run, such as decades,[115] but we use it here to refer to changes occurring over thousands of years. This chapter has been primarily about social rather than **biological evolution**. Some scholars have argued that the same basic theoretical principles can be used to explain both forms.[116] It is true that "fitter"—better adapted—social structures have generally replaced "less fit" structures over the course of time, but this is true only in a general sense, and the meaning of "fitness" here is quite different from its meaning in evolutionary biology. The guiding forces of Darwinian biological evolution are genetic variation and differential reproductive success. But the guiding forces of social evolution are different. They are primarily the material conditions of social life that are essential to human survival and well-being—ecological, demographic, technological, and economic forces.[117] Social structures are "fit" to the extent that people are able to meet their basic needs and wants as these are shaped by human nature interacting with socioecological conditions.

Throughout the course of social evolution social structures have invariably suffered periodic declines in fitness as environments changed and especially as population grew and made the existing structure no longer workable under the new conditions. Shifts to new and more adaptive modes of production became necessary, and thus hunting and gathering gave way to horticulture, horticulture to more intensive agriculture, and so on. Technology advanced. Along the way people used their natural tendencies for reciprocity to barter, then to exchange using money, and then to exchange over wider and wider parts of the world. Eventually capitalism was born and the technological possibilities inherent in it continued, and have continued, to transform it to the point where we are today. Although Marxists and other social critics would certainly dispute the point, capitalism is perhaps the most "fit" social structure that has yet existed. The main line of evidence in support of this contention is that capitalism has promoted survival, health, longevity, and the various other goals imbedded in human nature—not least that of reproductive success—better than any previously existing economic system.[118] But capitalism is not some sort of final system because there is no such thing as a final system. Nor is it necessarily the best of all possible systems because we cannot know what future systems will look like. It is simply what we have reached at this point in the human adventure.

SUMMARY

1. Until about 11,000 years ago, people everywhere made their living exclusively by hunting and gathering. Some hunter-gatherer groups survive today. They live in small bands of a few dozen people and move frequently as resources in one area become depleted. Men do most of the hunting, women most of the gathering. Gathered foods provide more than half of the diet in groups that live at low latitudes, whereas food obtained from hunting or fishing becomes increasingly important as people live at higher and higher latitudes. Most hunter-gatherers do not store food, but those that do tend to live in societies with larger and denser populations and distinctions of social rank.

2. Several decades ago hunter-gatherers were depicted as leading a difficult and precarious life in which people could barely eke out a living. In the 1960s there was a shift toward seeing hunter-gatherers as a kind of "original affluent society," or one in which people were able to meet their basic needs with minimal effort. At first some studies seemed to support this notion, but more recent work challenges it. In many hunter-gatherer societies people work much longer than the affluent society thesis suggests. In others people have difficulty meeting their basic calorie and nutritional needs and experience periods of starvation. It is likely that there is a great deal of variation based on the kinds of environments in which particular groups live. Hunter-gatherers do much better in more favorable environments than in unfavorable ones.

3. The first agricultural communities began to develop in southwest Asia sometime between 11,500 and 10,000 years ago. People were cultivating grains and had domesticated animals such as sheep, goats, and pigs. They started to live in sedentary villages. After about 2,000 years, people from these communities began to migrate into Europe, central Asia, and Egypt, taking their domesticated plants and animals with them. Agriculture had reached central Asia by about 8,000 to 9,000 years ago. It did not reach northern Europe until about 5,500 years ago.

4. China was an area of independent agricultural development beginning around 8,500 years ago in north and central China and 6,000 years ago in south China. Agriculture had reached southeast Asia by about 5,500 years ago. Rice was a main crop, and pigs and cattle had been domesticated.

5. Agriculture developed in the New World on an entirely independent basis. There were independent developments in the regions of Andean South America and Mesoamerica (about 7,000 to 6,000 years ago) and the eastern woodlands of North America (around 1,500 years ago). Agriculture was carried to the American Southwest some 4,000 years ago. Maize was one of the principal domesticates. In the New World there were no large animals suitable for domestication and thus sedentary village life did not appear until long after cultivation began.

6. The question of why agriculture arose when and where it did has been one of the most important questions in anthropology. The fact that it developed independently in at least four major regions of the world is highly suggestive. One popular theory is that as hunter-gatherer populations became larger and denser in all of these regions, getting enough food grew increasingly difficult, necessitating a switch to cultivation. The matter of timing is also important. Between about 20,000 and 11,500 years ago climates were cold and dry and there were major and rapid swings in temperature and moisture. Developing agriculture under these circumstances would have been difficult if not impossible. But after 11,500 years ago there was a warming trend and fewer sharp climatic swings, and cultivating crops became possible.

7. Anthropologists and historians have studied many different types of farming methods. The simplest form of farming is horticulture, which is the cultivation of small gardens using hand tools. Horticulturalists with abundant land usually cultivate a plot for short periods and then fallow it for long periods. Where land is less abundant and populations larger and denser, it becomes necessary to shorten the fallow period and try to wrest more from the land.

8. Where population densities are very high, people shift from horticulture to more intensive forms of agriculture. Land is cultivated more or less permanently. The most intensive form of agriculture involves the plow and draft animals. Several kinds of crops, such as maize or root crops, can be cultivated without plowing the land first. But other crops, such as wheat, barley, and rye, can only produce enough calories for very large populations if the land is plowed before seeding. Plowing is difficult and demanding work and people prefer not to adopt it if enough food can be produced by continuing to rely on hand tools.

9. The evolution of modes of subsistence throughout human history has occurred primarily as a response to larger and denser populations. Increasingly intensive subsistence

practices have evolved as more food needed to be produced to feed more mouths. Population growth and resulting population pressure also degrades the environment, and this makes the production of enough food even more difficult.

10. In some regions of the world climates are too dry for effective cultivation. People in these regions often adopt pastoralism, or animal herding, as the primary mode of subsistence. The most commonly herded animals are sheep, goats, cattle, horses, and camels, which are driven from pasture to pasture, sometimes over long distances. Pastoralism has been found in east Africa, the Saharan and Arabian deserts, parts of central Asia, the arid steppes of northern Asia, and the Tibetan plateau.

11. Another major way to get a living is to manufacture goods and sell them in markets. Craftsmen make the goods that merchants buy and then resell. The earliest markets probably arose around 5,000 years ago, but they played a small role in economic life. Over several thousand years mercantile activity slowly expanded. Landlords dominated agrarian societies and in most instances disdained merchants. Four thousand years ago trade was mostly local and regional, but within two thousand years it had expanded to encompass a region extending all the way from Rome to China. Since merchants operate in cities, as trade expanded cities grew more numerous and much larger.

12. Between the twelfth and fifteenth century CE the world had become much more commercialized, especially in Europe. The world was slowly becoming capitalist. Italian city-states, Venice in particular, were almost entirely specialized for trade. By the sixteenth century the center of capitalist activity shifted from Italy to northwest Europe, especially the Netherlands, England, and northern France. Europe began to dominate the world economically.

13. Europe was favored over the rest of the world for several reasons. The leading capitalist countries were located on large bodies of water that facilitated maritime trade, a more efficient and profitable form of trade than overland trade. Europe also had towns with remarkable economic freedom. Compared to other parts of the world, governments and landlords interfered less with European towns. In addition, Europe was filled with numerous countries that were small and that vigorously competed with each other economically. This competition intensified capitalist development.

14. By the eighteenth century capitalist activity had built up to such an extent that it facilitated a major technological and economic revolution known as the Industrial Revolution. Manufacturing became increasingly central to economic life, and rural life increasingly gave way to life in cities. Industrialization required great wealth to finance the new machines and factories that housed them. But the machines and factories produced far greater wealth for those who owned and operated them, which is the major reason they were developed in the first place.

15. A basic feature of human nature is the desire for social exchange. In the economic realm, the simplest form of exchange is reciprocity, or returning like for like. This may occur in a highly generalized way so that giving and taking occur in implicit ways without any specific rules. Alternatively, there may be formal rules in terms of what is exchanged and under what circumstances. This form of exchange, known as balanced reciprocity, is the basis for economic markets. People use balanced reciprocity for individual benefit; each has something the other wants. It was probably inevitable that the human tendency for exchange for individual benefit would evolve into modern capitalism, given enough time and enough people.

16. In addition to biological evolution there is social evolution, but the two forms of evolution operate according to different principles. Biological evolution is all about genetic variation and reproductive success. Social evolution is a matter of old social structures being replaced by new ones as the result of environmental changes, population growth, developing technology, and new economic opportunities. Most social evolution leads to "fitter" social structures, at least in the sense that had people clung to the older and increasingly inadequate structures they would eventually have gone extinct, or at least their numbers would have declined precipitously.

QUESTIONS FOR DISCUSSION

✓ What is the relationship between the latitudes at which hunter-gatherer groups live and the proportion of the diet that is made up of hunting, fishing, and gathering, and why?

✓ In hunter-gatherer societies, who hunts and who gathers, and why?

✓ Most hunter-gatherers don't store food, but some do. Why should this be?

✓ In the 1960s the original affluent society thesis challenged the prevailing wisdom concerning hunter-gatherers. What was the nature of this challenge? Discuss.

✓ What evidence was first presented in defense of the affluence thesis?

✓ How has the affluence thesis fared in light of more recent research?

✓ When and where did agriculture first develop? What plants and animals were domesticated?

✓ What are some of the reasons why some hunter-gatherer societies adopt agriculture when exposed to it, whereas others resist it?

✓ What is the significance of the observation that agriculture developed independently in at least four major regions of the world?

✓ What are the likely reasons why agriculture developed when and where it did? Indeed, why did it develop at all?

✓ Explain the differences between horticulture and intensive agriculture as different modes of cultivating the land. For what reasons might horticulturalists adopt intensive agriculture?

✓ Were people in early agricultural communities better nourished and healthier than their hunter-gatherer predecessors? Explain.

✓ Some intensive agriculturalists use plows, whereas others don't. Under what conditions do plows become useful or necessary?

✓ What is pastoralism as a mode of economic life and where is it most likely to be found?

✓ When did buying and selling begin in earlier times?

✓ Trace the progress of buying and selling throughout history.

✓ What was the attitude of landlords to merchants in historical societies, and what impact did this have on how people made a living?

✓ What is capitalism as a mode of economic life? When did the first capitalist societies develop?

✓ Discuss some of the reasons why capitalism first developed in Western Europe.

✓ How and why did capitalism industrialize?

✓ What is an industrial society?

✓ Is capitalism part of human nature? Discuss.

✓ How are biological and social evolution similar and different? Discuss.

References and Notes

1. Binford 2001; Lee and Daly 1999.
2. The !Kung are one of many related groups who speak unique "click" languages. Linguists signify these clicks by using exclamation points, slashes, and other non-alphabetic characters. One type of click (the ! click) is made by putting the tongue against the roof of the mouth and then "popping" it.
3. Lee and Daly 1999. Marlowe 2010 is the most comprehensive work on the Hadza to date.
4. Binford 2001.
5. Lee 1968.
6. Kelly 1995.
7. Dahlberg 1981.
8. Ember 1978.
9. Murdock 1967.
10. Ember 1978.
11. Binford 2001.

12. Calculations based on data in Binford 2001.
13. Gurven and Hill 2009.
14. Gurven and Hill 2009.
15. Gurven and Hill 2009.
16. Gurven and Hill 2009.
17. Testart 1982, 1988.
18. M. N. Cohen 1985.
19. Kennett 2005.
20. Sahlins 1968, 1972.
21. Lee 1968.
22. Woodburn 1968.
23. Lee 1968.
24. Woodburn 1968.
25. Yellen 1977.
26. Kelly 1995.
27. Kelly 1995.
28. Hill, Kaplan, Hawkes, and Hurtado 1985.
29. O'Connell and Hawkes 1981; D. Kaplan 2000.
30. D. Kaplan 2000.
31. Truswell and Hansen 1976, as discussed in D. Kaplan 2000; D. Kaplan 2000.
32. Marshall 1968; Howell 1986. Both as discussed in D. Kaplan 2000.
33. Speth 1990; Wilmsen 1982; Wiessner 1982. All as discussed in D. Kaplan 2000.
34. D. Kaplan 2000.
35. Chagnon 2013.
36. Bellwood 2005.
37. Wenke 1999; Bellwood 2005; Fagan 2009.
38. Wenke 1999; Bellwood 2005; Fagan 2009.
39. Bellwood 2005.
40. Phillipson 1985; Bellwood 2005; Fagan 2009; Milisauskas 2010.
41. Chang 1986; Bellwood 2005.
42. Bellwood 2005, p. 130; M. N. Cohen 1977; Fagan 2009.
43. MacNeish 1978; Fiedel 1992; Bellwood 2005; Fagan 2009.
44. M. Harris 1977; Bellwood 2005.
45. Bellwood 2005.
46. M. N. Cohen 1977.
47. M. N. Cohen 2009.
48. Cohen and Armelagos 1984; Cohen 1989.
49. M. N. Cohen 1977.
50. M. N. Cohen 2009, p. 591.
51. Bellwood 2005, p. 20.
52. Bellwood 2005; Bettinger, Richerson, and Boyd 2009.
53. M. N. Cohen 2009.
54. Boserup 1970.
55. Chagnon 1983.
56. Pospisil 1963.
57. Service 1963.
58. Kirch 1984; Johnson and Earle 2000.
59. Boserup 1970.
60. Pryor 1985; Smil 1994.
61. Smil 1994.
62. Smil 1994.
63. Derry and Williams 1961; L. White Jr. 1962.
64. Pryor 1985.
65. Pryor 1985.

66. Bennett 1937.

67. Bennett 1937.

68. Bennett 1937.

69. Wittfogel 1957.

70. Boserup 1965. See also R. Wilkinson 1973; M. Harris 1977.

71. Boserup 1965.

72. Bellwood 2005.

73. Hole 1977; Cribb 1991.

74. Sahlins 1968; Cribb 1991; Barfield 1993. Frachetti 2012 dates the origins of mobile pastoral societies throughout the vast region of the Eurasian steppes to at least four thousand years ago.

75. Salzman 2004.

76. Barfield 1993.

77. Evans-Pritchard 1940; Service 1963; Mair 1974.

78. Barth 1961.

79. Beals and Hoijer 1971; Hassig 1985.

80. Snooks 1996, 1997.

81. Aubet 1993.

82. Wild 1992.

83. D. Wilkinson 1992, 1993.

84. Chandler 1987; D. Wilkinson 1992, 1993.

85. Sjoberg 1960.

86. Polanyi 1957; Dalton 1969.

87. Kohl 1987; Silver 1995.

88. Braudel 1984.

89. J. Cohen 1980.

90. J. Cohen 1980.

91. J. Cohen 1980.

92. Dobb 1963.

93. Braudel 1984.

94. Beaud 1983.

95. Beaud 1983.

96. Beaud 1983, pp. 28–29.

97. Beaud 1983.

98. Sanderson 1994.

99. Cipolla 1993.

100. Tilly 1990.

101. Arrighi 2007.

102. Sanderson 1994.

103. Frank 1998; Pomeranz 2000.

104. Arrighi 2007, pp. 331–332.

105. Landes 1969.

106. Landes 1969.

107. Stearns 1993.

108. Dobb 1963.

109. Lenski 1970.

110. R. Wilkinson 1973; Boserup 1981.

111. Wallerstein 1989.

112. Stearns 1993, p. 34.

113. Bell 1973.

114. Cosmides and Tooby 1992, p. 206.

115. Boyd and Richerson 1985, 2005.

116. Runciman 2009.

117. Harris 1977, 1979; Sanderson 1995.

118. Fogel 2004.

4

Foodways

People obviously need to eat to survive. But what to eat? That is the question. And what not to eat? All over the world people have food preferences and in almost every society food aversions or outright prohibitions. This chapter examines how natural selection has contributed to the formation of human foodways. The branch of evolutionary biology known as *behavioral ecology* has been particularly useful in addressing this issue. Behavioral ecology developed several decades ago primarily as a means of understanding animal foraging behavior. Later it was applied to humans and then came to be called **human behavioral ecology** (HBE).[1] HBE is a close cousin of both sociobiology and evolutionary psychology, but it focuses on behavioral *variations* (in this case variations in food seeking) and how these are shaped by ecological circumstances (specifically, the *ecological* part of socioecology). HBE's most fundamental premise is that human food preferences are guided by cost-benefit decisions. Humans wish to maximize the calories they can obtain from food sources while minimizing the amount of time and energy they must expend in getting them. They are inclined to choose foods that generate the best cost-benefit ratios. Choosing such foods leads to the best diets and thus to the highest rates of survival and reproductive success.

In this chapter we apply the principles of HBE to a number of foodways, such as why humans everywhere have a strong liking for meat and sweet foods, why most humans don't eat dogs and cats, why Hindus ban eating the cow, and why both Jews and Muslims abhor the pig. We will also consider foraging strategies, examining how people arrive at decisions concerning the combination of plants and animals that they make fundamental to their diet. Finally, we will see why only a minority of the world's peoples drink milk and how the capacity to digest milk evolved by natural selection in conjunction with the cultural evolution of dairying.

What's for Dinner?

In the preindustrial era, before the modern world economy made transporting food across the globe relatively easy, people would tend to eat foods that were most readily available in their environment. During the early Neolithic people domesticated and ate sheep, goats, and cattle because the wild forms existed where they lived. They also domesticated and ate wheat, barley, rye, and rice because the undomesticated forms were there as well. In Japan there is a strong preference for seafood of every conceivable type; the Japanese also like seaweed. This is no surprise considering that Japan comprises a set of islands completely surrounded by water. In the Amazon rain forest there are no cattle because there are no grasslands suitable for them. Game is not especially abundant, but there are wild forest-dwelling pigs, birds, and monkeys, so people spend a lot of time capturing and eating them. And so it goes.

But just because an animal happens to be in the neighborhood doesn't mean it will be eaten. In India cattle were eaten for thousands of years, but at some point their flesh became forbidden. In Israel and other parts of the Middle East, pigs were eaten for a long time but eventually Jews decided they were unclean and should therefore be avoided. After the rise of Islam, Muslims too decided that the pig should never be eaten.

Let's look at a sampling of food habits. In the early years of the United States, between approximately 1750 and 1850, pigs were widely raised and pork was considered special. This was because most of the US population lived east of the Mississippi River, and most of the land was forested. Pigs are forest creatures. They prefer cool temperatures and are very successful at rooting for acorns and other items widely available on the forest floor. But after about 1850 several things changed. More people began to move west of the Mississippi, and the vast grasslands of the American plains opened up to cattle raising. Cattle were at first raised primarily in Texas, and then in such plains states as Kansas and Nebraska. In the early days of cattle raising cowboys drove the animals to slaughterhouses in Omaha, Kansas City, and Chicago. The drives were long and hard and inevitably some cattle died. Getting them to slaughterhouses became cheaper and more efficient once railroads were available to transport cattle en masse. After refrigeration was invented, processed meat could be shipped in refrigerated boxcars to distant markets. Beef now became widely available and people already liked its taste. They consumed beef roasts and big steaks with gusto. And why not? Beef was good food, full of protein and all kinds of nutrients. And so what began to happen is that pork declined as a proportion of the diet and was increasingly replaced by beef. Of course, plenty of pork was still being produced and consumed, as it is today, but beef had taken over the number one spot as the most desirable meat.[2]

In some parts of the world dogs have been regularly eaten, but in other places dog flesh has been considered extremely repugnant. Dogs were domesticated at least 10,000 years ago, but as sentry animals rather than a food source. They are still used in many parts of the world for that purpose, and increasingly as pets in more-developed countries. The major dog-eating regions of the world have been China and southeast Asia. The Chinese raised dogs for food for millennia, even selling dog carcasses in markets. In his book *Unmentionable Cuisine*, Calvin Schwabe describes how to make a kind of "puppy ham." He also provides some Chinese doggie recipes. One dish, "stir-fried dog," is made by deep-frying puppy chunks and mixing them with green onions, garlic, ginger, bean curd, soy sauce, and black beans.[3]

Dogs have also been eaten by various groups in Vietnam, Burma, Thailand, Indonesia, and the Philippines. Southeast Asians apparently carried the practice to the islands of Oceania. There are reports of dog eating in Morocco and Algeria, as well as in parts of sub-Saharan Africa. Dogs may have been eaten occasionally in ancient Rome, but there was very little dog consumption in Eurasia.[4]

Whether or not dogs are eaten depends on what other animals are available as a source of protein and what other uses dogs may have. Societies and cultures in which dogs are commonly eaten tend to have a limited supply of other suitable animals. China has long had domesticated pigs, but they have often been in short supply. Dogs can be inexpensive to keep because they scavenge for food, and the Chinese didn't really need dogs for other purposes. Why not eat them if meat is otherwise scarce? The Maori of New Zealand ate dogs, but they had no other domesticated animals. In Mexico in pre-Columbian times dogs were eaten, but there were no large animals that could be hunted or domesticated. In societies in which dogs play a very important role in hunting and trapping, dog eating is often regarded with horror.[5]

No one has ever reported dog raising on a par with cattle or pig raising. Who has ever heard of large-scale dog farms or slaughterhouses in modern developed countries? No one. But why not? The answer is not difficult to come by. Compared to cattle, pigs, or sheep, dogs don't have a lot of flesh on their bones. Moreover, since they are carnivores, dogs naturally compete with other animals. A large-scale dog industry would have to be paralleled by cattle, pig, horse, or chicken industries devoted to feeding dogs as well as humans. In all dog-eating societies, dogs were able to scavenge for their food.[6]

So people in modern industrial societies, and most others for that matter, don't eat dogs and are generally repelled at the thought of gulping them down and then gnawing on their bones. Even more repellant in the industrialized world is the thought of eating insects. Most Americans feel intense disgust at insect eating. But from a global perspective, Americans are unusual; insects have been eaten in many societies without revulsion. A wide range of peoples have shown a fondness for ants, termites, crickets, grasshoppers, locusts, beetles, and moth larvae and pupae. In tropical rain forests insects are often a staple protein. The Yanomama, for example, eat a wide range of insects, as well as other small crawling invertebrates. They have a special liking for tarantulas, which can be roasted and then cracked open to get at the surprising amount of flesh. Even the members of large-scale civilizations have eaten insects. The Chinese ate stinkbugs, cockroaches, giant water beetles, and even fly maggots. Southeast Asians had similar tastes. Europeans once ate insects. Aristotle claimed that cicadas taste best in the nymph stage, and that male adult cicadas taste better than the females (although if the females were full of eggs, then they were tastier).[7]

Why are insects so widely eaten? Because they, especially the larger ones, are a good source of protein and nutrients. Insects are most likely to be a significant part of the diet in societies living in jungles and forests. Such environments are often deficient in large game animals, especially large herbivores like cattle, sheep, and goats. As noted above, the Yanomama eat wild pigs, monkeys, and birds, but monkeys and birds have small amounts of flesh and sometimes are difficult to come by. Insect eating under such conditions makes a good deal of sense, at least when large, juicy insects are relatively abundant.[8]

Another interesting dietary practice involves adding spices to food. Food is more highly spiced among peoples who live in regions of low latitude and high temperature. Anyone who has sampled many of the world's cuisines knows that Thai or Indian food is very spicy, whereas food in England or Sweden is relatively bland. Chinese food can be either bland or spicy, depending on the region. In Sichuan province in the south it is spicy, but in more northerly regions it tends to be blander.

It was once thought that because spicy food causes sweating, people in hot climates eat it to cool off. But there is now a better explanation. Paul Sherman and his colleagues have shown that spices have important antimicrobial functions. Meat spoils quickly in hot climates, especially when there is no artificial refrigeration. The hotter the climate, the more likely meat dishes will contain a combination of spices, as well as the spices that have the greatest antimicrobial effect (the four most antimicrobial spices are onions, garlic, allspice, and oregano). Sherman's argument is reinforced by data showing that spices are more likely to be added to meat than vegetables, since meat is more likely to spoil, and spoil quickly, than vegetables.[9]

Of course, explaining how a particular cuisine got started is one thing and why it persists is another. People naturally prefer those things they have traditionally eaten, and thus spicy food can continue to be preferred simply because people have learned to like the taste. Thais or Indians who leave home to live in countries at higher latitudes or who have access to refrigeration still prefer spicy foods, even if there is no longer any biological reason to keep using spicy recipes.

How do people acquire their tastes and distastes *at an individual level*? Elizabeth Cashdan, an anthropologist at the University of Utah, has proposed that there is a sensitive or critical period for the acquisition of food tastes.[10] Children under two years of age will tend to eat most things their mothers feed them. After age two, they become much more resistant to eating novel foods and much more apt to react with disgust to some of these foods. Cashdan concludes that "sensitive period learning probably evolved as an adaptation to the high costs associated with eating toxic and unwholesome substances."[11] The basic idea is that over time the members of a society will have figured out the best and safest foods to eat, and these are the foods that a mother will feed to her child of six months to two years. Since novel foods carry a greater risk than familiar foods of being unsafe, a child will tend to develop a resistance to novel ones once the sensitive period has passed. This enhances the probability of child survival. Natural selection should have crafted things so that people are cautious about novel foods, even at a very young age.[12]

Sweets and Meats

Although human tastes and likes and dislikes are to a large extent learned, there are at least two food preferences that appear to have a strong innate basis: the desire for sweet food and the desire for meat. Two lines of evidence support this claim. One is that people in all societies, even societies in the very distant prehistoric past, consume these things on a regular basis. The other is that both animal proteins and foods that have a high sugar content provide substantial nutritional benefits not easily obtained from other foods.[13]

In the ancestral environment highly nutritious fruits with a high sugar content constituted a major part of the human diet. This was probably not something that originated with humans, since our closest living relative, the chimpanzee, also consumes a lot of sweet fruit. It is therefore likely that we inherited the desire for fruit from our nonhuman primate ancestors. The strong human liking for sweet things is suggested not only by its universality, but also by the eagerness with which people in societies without a sugar tradition eat (or drink) sweet substances introduced from the outside.

Beginning around 1500, many European societies set up large-scale slave plantations in the New World devoted heavily to the production of sugar cane. These enterprises were extremely profitable because processed sugar was in great demand in Europe for sweetening coffee and tea. Sugar was also added to the newly discovered cacao bean to make a sweeter type of chocolate, which became extremely popular and eventually spread throughout much of the world.[14] In the early twentieth century various companies began to experiment with the production of sweetened carbonated drinks, and in time Coca-Cola and Seven-Up were produced and mass-marketed to a very receptive audience. And of course, there were many spin-offs, such as Pepsi-Cola, Dr. Pepper, Mountain Dew, and numerous others. The soft drink industry has now spread all over the world. Enormous quantities of these drinks are consumed, and individual serving sizes keep getting bigger and bigger.

What then of the strong preference for animal protein? What evidence is there to suggest that this preference is innate rather than socially learned? There is in fact a great deal. Meat plays a very important role in the eating habits of people in all societies, and a meal that does not include meat is considered incomplete. Many horticultural tribes hold elaborate feasts, and meat is the focal point. In a wide range of societies people distinguish between two kinds of hunger—general hunger and "meat hunger," often having a separate word for the latter.[15] Among the Bemba of Zambia, for example, the word *ubukashya* refers to a craving for meat.[16] The Hadza hunter-gatherers of Tanzania eat mostly plant foods, but this is because meat is relatively scarce. "For them, meat is the preferred food and, when there is not enough of it to please them, they claim to be suffering from hunger even though, in fact, they may be very well fed."[17] Among the Miskito Indians of Central America, people think constantly of meat. They "characterize good times as ones having an abundance of meat, and bad times as ones when meat is lacking. Without meat, women may even refuse to prepare food, or they do so without enthusiasm."[18]

Why should the strong desire for meat have been selected for in the long course of human evolution? The answer involves the special nutritional qualities that meat provides. For one thing, meat is a much better source of protein than plant foods. Many plant foods provide important amino acids, but these can be obtained far more efficiently from meat. As the esteemed anthropologist Marvin Harris has shown, in order to obtain all of the amino acids that meat provides one would have to consume many plant foods in combination at the same meal, something extremely difficult for any human population.[19]

Animal protein has many other nutritional advantages. Meat provides such essential minerals as iron and zinc, as well as vitamins, such as B_{12}, that are difficult to obtain from other foods. It is also a major source of fats that are very important in the diets of nonindustrial peoples. Moreover, meat provides these nutrients in an easily digested form and is nutrient dense, which means that people can get their basic daily allowances of protein, fat, iron, and zinc, along with other nutrients, by eating much smaller amounts of meat relative to plant foods. For instance, a single ounce of cooked lean meat provides eight grams of protein, the same amount as four slices of enriched bread or four medium-size potatoes.[20]

Some readers will no doubt object to this line of analysis, claiming that the existence of vegetarians indicates that the desire for meat is learned rather than innate. They can point to the emphasis placed on vegetarianism in some religions, like Hinduism, Jainism, and Buddhism, as well as to an increase in the number of vegetarians in the modern world. Even if individuals and groups throughout history have been vegetarian, however, vegetarianism has never existed at the level of an entire society. And where large numbers of people have followed religious prescriptions in favor of vegetarianism, these prescriptions likely came into existence because most members of the societies in which the religions were practiced did not have enough land to raise animals for food. When land is extremely scarce, all of it must be devoted to raising cereals and other plant foods, along with animals whose primary function is to pull plows. Under these circumstances, meat becomes a luxury that people cannot afford, and thus the religious celebration of vegetarianism makes a virtue of necessity.[21]

Another objection is that meat eating, especially the consumption of red meat, is actually unhealthy and therefore could not possibly be a part of our human biological heritage. But, like the first objection, this claim is misplaced as well. What is actually unhealthy is eating *too much* meat. In the contemporary United States people consume enormous numbers of Big Macs and mountains of French fries cooked in animal fat, and many of us spend a great deal of time firing up the patio barbecue for grilling big steaks. One can always carry a good thing to excess, and this is certainly happening in American society today. Various social and cultural conditions are capable of taking human adaptations and intensifying and elaborating them in maladaptive ways, and overeating meat is one of many examples.

Strategic Foraging

Hunting and gathering can be hard and onerous work, and peoples who depend on this method of food production have to make careful and wise decisions about what to hunt and what to gather. In the 1970s and 1980s an elegant theoretical model known as *optimal foraging theory* (OFT) was developed as a means of understanding this decision-making process.[22] This was the most important specific theory within the more general approach of human behavioral ecology. In line with HBE, OFT assumes that natural selection has designed humans to forage in such a way that they maximize the resources needed for individual survival and reproductive success. This means maximizing their rate of energy return relative to the amount of time they spend foraging.

The first thing foragers have to decide is what particular territory or patch of land they will try to exploit. Once the territory has been selected, they then move through it looking closely for the edible plants and animals they expect to find. This process is their *search time*. Once a food source is found and judged to be worth taking, it has to be acquired, which means tracking and killing it in the case of animals or digging it up or cutting it down in the case of plants. This is the foragers' *handling* or *processing time*. Actually, there is a bit more involved in the handling time, because the food has to be taken back to camp and, in most instances, processed so it is ready to be eaten. An animal needs to be skinned and butchered, a plant might need to be ground or pounded, and so on.

Skilled hunter-gatherers who have lived a long time in a given habitat develop a very good sense of what items are available and what the search and handling costs are of acquiring them. They are well aware of the so-called *opportunity costs* involved in foraging: time spent searching for a particular food source means that less time is available for obtaining other possible food sources, which might have to be bypassed altogether. Foragers learn to rank food items along a continuum or hierarchy of utility; they can achieve an optimal diet by collecting food items in an order of descending rank so that the expected energy return is maximized for every unit of foraging time. If a newly encountered food item yields a rate of return equal to or higher than the average rate that foragers are currently experiencing, it will be collected, but if it leads to a lower rate of return then it will be ignored.

It is essential to note that foragers' decisions to include a particular food item in their diet are not made in terms of that item's availability, but rather in terms of the availability of a higher-ranked item. For example, hunters among the Hadza pay more attention to large game animals than to small game, often completely ignoring the latter, even though small game is more abundant. Armed with this knowledge, several anthropologists wanted to see if this hunting strategy fit OFT. They asked Hadza hunters if they would agree to concentrate for a short time hunting only small game. The hunters obliged. When the outcomes were tallied up at the end of the experiment, they showed that the average energy return per unit of hunting time was significantly lower for small game than they had already been shown to be for large game. Hadza hunters thus seemed to be making hunting decisions in the manner predicted by OFT.[23] They knew what they were doing.

The Hadza are only one of many foraging societies that have been studied with OFT in hand. Other studies have been conducted on the Cree of North America, the Alyawara of Australia, the Machiguenga of Peru, the Aché of Paraguay, the arctic Inuit, and the Yanomama of the Amazon rain forest.[24] Most of these studies show that OFT is a good match to reality. One of the most thorough studies was conducted among the Aché by Kristen Hawkes, Kim Hill, and James O'Connell.[25] These anthropologists devoted more than sixty days to following the Aché on several foraging expeditions, taking careful note of what the Aché procured and how much time they spent obtaining and processing it. Their results showed that Aché foraging closely followed the predictions made by the theory. The Aché had developed a rank ordering of plants and animals that the researchers were able to systematize as shown in Table 4.1.

What the table means is essentially this: if on a foraging expedition the Aché took only collared peccaries and deer and then decided to stop, they would receive an average rate of return for both items combined of 148 calories per forager per hour. However, if they continued and took a coati as well, their average rate of return for all three resources combined would increase to 405 calories per hour. Likewise, if they also took the third-ranked resource, snake, their average rate of return for all four resources combined would improve to 546 calories per hour. The Aché are best off if they take all eight resources, because this gives them an average return for all of the resources of 783 calories per hour. They will stop collecting a resource only when it reduces the average rate of return for all resources combined. Hawkes, Hill, and O'Connell note that high-ranked resources never drop out of the Aché diet, whereas low-ranked resources move in and out according to the extent to which they or other low-ranked resources are encountered.[26]

At this point readers may wonder whether foragers can actually make such precise calculations of how to rank plants and animals, as well as such complex decisions about what food sources to take and what to ignore. Of course they can't. No Aché forager could ever say to another, "Look, we have a peccary, a deer, and a coati, and that gives us an average return of 405 calories for every hour we have been foraging in this area. But let's not stop here. Maybe we will see a snake, and capturing it would increase our average return to 546 calories. Then, if we see a bunch of oranges, our average return would go up to 625 calories." Foragers could not pos-

TABLE 4.1   Rank Ordering of Caloric Returns from Plants and Animals Among the Aché

Resource	Calories yielded per hour	Rank	Average cal./hr. after resource added
Collared peccary	65,000	1	
Deer	27,300	1	148
Coati	6,964	2	405
Snake	5,882	3	546
Oranges	5,071	4	625
Bird	4,769	5	632
Honey	3,266	6	660
White-lipped peccary	2,746	7	783

Source: Kristen Hawkes, Kim Hill, and James F. O'Connell, "Why hunters gather: Optimal foraging and the Aché of eastern Paraguay," *American Ethnologist* 9 (1982):379–398.

sibly produce such precise information for many reasons: they do not know what a calorie is, would not know how to measure one if they did, probably do not have an arithmetic system allowing them to make such calculations, and so on. (Anthropologists can do this because they come from a science-based society and can spend a great deal of time calculating the results once the foraging is finished.) But foragers do have a generalized knowledge, built up over many generations of foraging and compiled into a stock of folk wisdom, that certain kinds of resources take such and such a length of time to obtain and yield such and such a quantity of desirable food. They also have a sense of how particular combinations of items fit together on any given foraging trip in terms of maximizing overall foraging efficiency.

OFT is an ideal model of how people would behave if they had perfect knowledge of everything in their environment, as well as every essential tool they needed to make precise calculations of the time they are investing and the end results they are obtaining. No pattern of behavior can possibly fit this model perfectly, or any other ideal model for that matter. The model is there to give as close an approximation as possible to how foragers obtain food.

Why should humans be optimal foragers? Why don't they just go into the bush, kill the first animal they see and eat it, pull up any tuber or pick any fruit and sit down and eat it, and then relax and take a nap. The answer is that such a strategy would be far from calorically optimal. Foragers employing such a strategy wouldn't survive very long, certainly not long enough to mate and leave copies of their genes in future generations. Any forager who behaved this way would never have become anyone's ancestor. In the matter at hand, natural selection selects for optimal efficiency in procuring resources because any other foraging strategy would be at a selective disadvantage.

It is important not to give the impression that OFT is the whole story. It is not. Several features of foraging behavior are difficult to explain in terms of a pure optimal foraging model. Because people everywhere have a strong preference for animal protein and fat, they will often pass up plant foods that yield a high rate of energy return in favor of game or fish that yield a lower rate. For example, the Yaminahua hunter-gatherers of Peru concentrate on three major food sources during their dry season: bananas, caiman (a type of alligator), and various species of fish. If they passed up fish, they would be better off in terms of energy return—that is, adding fish lowers it.[27] Likewise, when men among the Hiwi of Venezuela are hunting, they ignore high-yield tubers in order to continue to hunt, even though successful hunting will actually decrease their energy return by nearly two-thirds.[28] And among nearly all horticultural societies in South America, men spend more time attempting to procure game and fish even though they can get higher rates of energy return from cultivating plants.[29]

Nonetheless, favoring lower-yield animal protein and fat over higher-yield plant matter qualifies rather than overturns OFT and thus is not a genuine exception. Although animal protein and fat may yield less energy, as we saw earlier they have certain nutritional advantages over plant foods that make it rational to favor meat over plants. Besides, people have a very powerful desire to eat animal protein and fat, which is the proximate cause of their bias in favor of animal products.

But there appear to be at least two genuine exceptions to OFT. Hunters in a number of societies sometimes pass up certain kinds of game that yield a very high energy return in order to concentrate on game with a much lower return. Why would they do this? Because people have motives other than eating the best they can for the least amount of effort. One of these, found especially among men, is a motive to achieve high status. The anthropologist Richard Sosis of the University of Connecticut found that men on the island of Ifaluk in Micronesia spend a great deal of time torch fishing for dog-toothed tuna even though the rate of return from dog-toothed tuna is much lower than the rate yielded by yellow fin tuna.[30] Sosis discovered that torch fishing was the type of fishing most widely observed by women, and that through successful torch fishing men seemed to be advertising themselves as high-quality mates.

Similarly, Eric Alden Smith and Rebecca Bliege Bird studied turtle hunting among the Meriam of Torres Strait, Australia.[31] Turtle hunting requires a great deal of time and effort, but during turtle feasts men receive no material compensation for the turtles they distribute, not even a portion of their own catch. Only a small number of men hunt turtles, with just three in this particular study accounting for more than a third of the nominations for good turtle hunters. The researchers concluded that demonstrated skill at turtle hunting is the primary means by which men advertise leadership skills, and that the main benefit they receive is high social status. A related study of the Meriam found that when men engage in spear fishing they bypass the abundant shellfish swimming all around them.[32] The shellfish are easy to collect and provide a significantly higher energy return than the fish obtained from spearing. But spear fishing confers status whereas shellfish collecting does not.

The other exception is unsurprising. Some foods simply taste better to people and the tastier ones may be chosen even if they provide a lower energy return than less tasty ones. Just as the flavor of meat is a major consideration for modern consumers, it stands to reason that people in other kinds of societies would also take flavor into account. In one study of the Mayangna and Miskito of Nicaragua, hunters were asked to rank-order seventeen wild game species in terms of both importance in the diet and flavor.[33] As expected, the importance of a species was highly correlated with its amount of harvested biomass. And yet importance was also highly correlated with flavor.[34] It is likely that this result can be generalized to other societies, and that everywhere people strive to eat what they like.

Sacred Cows and Abominable Pigs

It has long been known to Westerners that the Hindus of India worship the cow and consider eating it a sacrilegious act. The taboo on slaughtering and eating cattle is interesting for several reasons. The most prominent is that it seems to occur only in Hinduism, or at least in India. Cattle were domesticated nearly 10,000 years ago and have been eaten all over the world for thousands of years, and they are still the most common animal raised for food. Of 837 societies in the *Ethnographic Atlas* that have domesticated animals, 447 (53 percent) have bovines (mostly cattle, but some water buffalo and yaks) as their principal animal. These figures compare to 179 (21 percent) for sheep and goats, and to 113 (14 percent) for pigs.

For many centuries Hindus have regarded the cow as sacred, but cattle have also been highly regarded in many other societies and religions throughout human history. For millennia in Near Eastern societies cattle were held in such high regard that they were often deified. In the Zoroastrian religion of ancient Iran, cattle were thought of as "clean and holy" and as important forms of wealth, and references were made to the "holy cattle-breeding man."[35] In Mesopotamia and surrounding areas the bull was regarded as a deity or as a companion of deities.[36] And yet cattle were often important objects of ritual sacrifice and beef was widely eaten.

Throughout much of North Africa cattle have been prominent in both agricultural and pastoral societies. The Fulani of Nigeria possess millions of cattle and they are the main source of wealth and prestige. In east and south Africa cattle-keeping populations have been numerous, and among pastoralists, in particular, cattle were the central element of social life. The Maasai, for example, despise people who do not live by cattle tending, and the Nuer express contempt for people who have few or no cattle. Groups like these are extremely proud of their cattle and show them great affection.[37] Yet, although cattle-keeping pastoralists love their cattle, they show no reluctance to eat them at the occasional sacrificial feast or when they die of natural causes.

So this makes the Hindu ban on eating the cow all the more puzzling. Most peoples who keep and esteem cattle also eat them, but Indian Hindus, who keep and esteem cattle, do not. Why not? Most Westerners and other beef-eating peoples have long thought that the Hindu taboo makes no logical sense. It is an irrational and inexplicable religious belief that is one of the reasons why there is so much poverty in the Indian subcontinent. Millions of cattle are going to waste.

In the 1950s Marvin Harris began to study the cow taboo and continued to develop and extend his research findings and theoretical conclusions for years. Harris came to the conclusion that the cow-love complex was not irrational or inexplicable at all. In fact, it was a very rational and sensible response to the ecological and economic circumstances in which Indian peasant farmers have found themselves for more than a thousand years.[38]

Harris discovered that the cow—in this case the zebu cow, not quite the same animal familiar to most of us—performs vital economic functions that can only be performed by living cattle. Cattle dung provides essential fertilizer for fields and when allowed to harden, it makes a good cooking fuel (a necessary one when other sources of fuel are scarce). Some farmers also use it as a flooring material for their houses. When it dries it makes the floor very hard and easy to sweep.[39]

In its most useful role, the cow functions as a traction animal for plowing fields. Because most Indian farmers cannot afford tractors, the cow is vital to subsistence. Can the cow do anything else? Well, yes, the females can be milked, although the extent to which milk can contribute to the diet depends on how many cows a family has, which in many cases is very few. And, of course, cows can be eaten if they die a natural death.

But slaughtering cattle would be disastrous. Indian farmers have very few cattle, and consuming them would mean that soon there would be none at all. No flooring material. No fuel. No fertilizer. No plowing. This would spell the end of the farm and the farmers. Without any means of subsistence, farmers would have little option but to leave their farms and move into the already extremely overcrowded cities, a very unappealing way to live. Best to hang on to one's cattle and keep them breathing, eating, plowing, and fertilizing.[40]

But what if a drought comes, the crops fail, and people are faced with starvation? Can they hold out until the rains come again? Perhaps, and perhaps not. They may be miserable with hunger. They look at their cattle (who themselves are growing thinner every day). Maybe we should take the risk and eat them, they reason, or we ourselves will die. The temptation increases as hunger increases. Harris contends that, faced with this great temptation, Hindus had to find a way to cope with it, and their solution was to define the cow as a sacred animal that had to be protected from harm. They therefore made it an unholy and unthinkable act to kill and consume it.[41]

A sense of historical perspective can be very helpful. Throughout much of Indian history cattle were regularly eaten and there was nothing considered particularly sacred about them. Brahman priests sacrificed and consumed cattle for hundreds of years, and it may not have been until sometime around 700 CE that the cow-love complex developed into its now familiar form. Under what conditions would priests have stopped sacrificing cattle in favor of protecting them? Harris suggests that the answer involves a growing population and a declining standard of living. As populations became denser, land grew increasingly scarce and farms got smaller. Animals had to be fed from the land and thus increasingly competed with humans. It became more and more costly for farmers to raise animals for food, and so they gradually had to be eliminated. All, that is, but one. The cow could not be removed because of its necessity in pulling the plow as well as the other benefits it provided. And because of the temptation to eat it, the religious taboo arose.[42]

Like cattle, pigs have been a favorite source of meat in many societies throughout much of the world. The ancient Greeks and Romans sacrificed pigs to their deities and associated pigs with crop fertility, as did the Celtic, Germanic, Slavic, and Baltic peoples. Pigs have been kept, sacrificed, and eaten by many tribal peoples in India. For thousands of years in China the pig was the most important animal raised for food, and in southeast Asia the pig has also been predominant. Peoples from southeast Asia who colonized Oceania took pigs along with them, and the pig is the most important domesticated animal throughout this region. In Melanesia huge feasts are held in which hundreds of pigs may be butchered and eaten. In this chain of islands pigs bring great prestige to a man, and men are therefore highly motivated to accumulate them. In Papua New Guinea women fondle and pet pigs as they are being fed, and among many Oceanic peoples lactating mothers actually breast-feed piglets.[43]

Pigs thrive best in relatively cool environments where there is a lot of shade. As noted earlier, in the eastern woodlands of the United States pigs have been raised for food since colonial times. The part of the world where pigs are *not* raised for food, and where they are most often considered unclean animals, is the broad expanse of land that includes the Middle East, North Africa, and parts of central Asia. The dominant religions in this part of the world, Judaism and Islam, both consider the pig unclean. Yet they are the only religions with strong prohibitions against pig eating. No other religion singles out the pig as an animal unfit for human consumption. Even Christianity, which arose in the same general region as Judaism and Islam and was greatly influenced by the former, does not scorn the pig. Indeed, on one of the two major religious holidays of Western Christianity, Easter, ham is often the meat of choice for family gatherings. Since all other religions have shown no aversion to eating pork, why have Jews and Muslims regarded it with such revulsion?

The most common answer to this question is that the pig *really is* an unclean animal: it wallows in mud, garbage, and its own excrement, and is a carrier of disease. Yet this explanation is unsatisfactory. Pigs are not particularly dirty animals when they live in habitats for which they are well suited. Since pigs cannot sweat, they are better adapted to environments where the temperature does not get too hot. In dry, hot environments, pigs have difficulty keeping cool, and therefore they wallow in mud in order to cool their bodies. As for the claim that pigs transmit such diseases as trichinosis, this is true, but other farm animals, including the cow, also carry diseases that are harmful to human health.[44]

As in the case of the Indian sacred cow, Harris has made a special study of the pig taboo, concentrating on the Jewish version. Harris believes that the taboo originated among the ancient Israelites because of the natural environment in which they lived. Pigs were among the first domesticated animals in the Middle East, and the predecessors of the Hebrews and numerous other contemporaneous Middle Eastern peoples raised pigs for food. At this time, perhaps around 4,000 years ago and earlier, there was enough woodland to raise pigs effectively. But this was a situation that did not last because of the environmental impact of growing populations. When the Hebrews arrived in Palestine around 1300 BCE, they settled on previously uncultivated land and began cutting down woodlands and building irrigated terraces. Pigs can be relatively inexpensive to raise if there is enough woodland to allow them to eat what grows there, such as truffles, beechnuts, acorns, and other things that grow wild on the forest floor. But with less and less woodland, pigs increasingly had to be fed grains as dietary supplements, making them directly competitive with humans, and artificial shade and moisture had to be provided. Moreover, increasing population densities made land suitable for pig raising increasingly scarce, thus making pigs even more costly.[45]

If pigs were ecologically and economically costly, yet continued to be a tempting source of meat, what could the Israelites do to combat the problem? The solution, Harris argues, was to forbid the raising and consumption of pigs entirely, and the best way to make such a prohibition stick would be to establish it as a matter of divine interdiction: make it a religious taboo.[46]

But this was not the same kind of taboo as the Hindu taboo on eating the cow. The Hindu taboo was a "positive" taboo: the cow is good and needs to be kept alive, so don't eat it. But the Jewish taboo on the pig was a "negative" taboo: the pig was bad because it was too costly to raise for food and had no other useful functions. Pigs cannot pull plows, wagons, or carts, and they cannot be milked. You cannot ride a pig as you would a horse, donkey, or camel. The pig had become not only useless but dangerous, and therefore it came to be redefined as a dirty, disease-carrying animal.

This theory's plausibility is enhanced when we remember that the Hebrews shared the pig taboo with many of their neighbors. Even the Egyptians, mortal enemies of the Israelites, forbade the eating of pork. Other civilizations of the time, such as the Mesopotamians and Babylonians, also prohibited the pig, although like

the ancestors of the Hebrews they once ate it. Like the Hebrews, they were pig rais-
ers who later came to abominate the animal, and for the same reasons: a shrinkage
of woodlands and the growing costs of raising pigs.[47]

With the rise of Islam in the seventh century CE, abominating the pig became part
of yet another major religious tradition. Islam arose in some of the hottest and driest
regions on earth that were still habitable. But here there are some interesting variations in how the pig is regarded. Most cultures into which Islam has spread avoid the
pig, but some Muslims eat it, although often surreptitiously. Some Berbers in Muslim
Morocco, for example, raise pigs, although they deny to outsiders that they have pigs,
hiding them when visitors arrive.[48] Can it be mere coincidence that these Berbers
live in a forested region of the Atlas Mountains and are able to let their pigs forage in
the forests during the day, bringing them back out of the forest only after sundown?[49]

But just because the cow and pig taboos have plausible ecological and economic
explanations, we cannot assume that all food taboos result from such factors. Surely
many of them do not. The Old Testament refers to many other tabooed creatures. In
addition to pigs, forbidden flesh included that of camels, hares, rock badgers, crustaceans, mollusks, sharks, and twenty-four species of birds (e.g., vultures, hawks,
owls, ostriches). Anything that crawled on its belly was prohibited, as were winged
swarming things, lizards, and rodents. And one could not consume the products
of forbidden animals, such as camel's milk or vulture's eggs.[50] Why should camels
be prohibited for ecological reasons since they are exceptionally well suited to hot
and dry environments and are eaten by many Middle Eastern peoples, Muslims
included? And why does the Old Testament prohibit so many other creatures? The
answers to these questions are by no means clear. Many food taboos may have no
rational basis other than as a marker of group identity, a way to distinguish your
own group from others, and this may be what is at work with at least some of the
Old Testament taboos.

There are some additional considerations. In a comprehensive study of seventy-
eight band and tribal societies, Daniel Fessler and Carlos Navarette show that meat
is the food that is most commonly tabooed.[51] In all of these societies combined,
there were 235 meat taboos, but only 9 vegetable taboos, 14 fruit taboos, and a
smattering of taboos involving dairy products, sweets, sour foods, spicy foods, and
starches. The authors suggest that the overwhelming predominance of meat taboos
can be attributed to the fact that meat often contains pathogens such as bacteria and
protozoans. This makes it more likely to be an object of disgust. Some plant foods
are toxic, but people quickly learn which ones are and avoid them. But detecting the
presence of pathogens in meat is trickier; sometimes meat may contain pathogens
and sometimes not. And some types of meat are more likely to contain pathogens
than others.

Fessler and Navarette probably have an important point to make, but their argument is only part of the story. Both cattle and pigs carry pathogens, and yet cattle
are a source of taboo in only one religion and pigs in only one part of the world.

Everywhere else they are eaten. Their theory needs further testing, especially on a society by society basis. One would need to look at the details of specific cases.

There is also an important distinction to be drawn between why a taboo originated many years ago and why it continues to be followed. Among modern Jews, who have become a predominantly urban people, the ban on pork has no ecological or economic necessity. Observant Jews continue to avoid pork and to follow all of the other Jewish dietary rules because these practices are an integral part of their religious identity. Likewise, most Muslims living in parts of the world where pigs can easily be raised still object to pigs and pork, often clashing with indigenous non-Muslims who eat pork. In the case of traditional Hindu farmers who don't own tractors and can't afford artificial fertilizers, there are still good reasons to avoid eating beef. But the tens of millions of Hindus who live in large Indian cities or have left India for other parts of the world have no economic reason to avoid beef, yet many continue to do so for religious reasons. The sacred cow is an important marker of Hindu group identity, just as the abominable pig is for devout Jews and Muslims.

The Milky Way

Milk, the best of foods. Or so it is claimed in television commercials, on billboards, and other modes of advertising. The claim is both true and false. For many people, including the Americans and other Westerners who are the targets of advertising, milk is indeed a good food, nourishing and containing important vitamins and nutrients. But most of the world does not drink milk, or at least not very much. In China and Southeast Asia, only a handful of people drink milk, and milk is often regarded as repugnant. For thousands of years there has been a strong aversion to it in this part of the world. Some peoples in these regions believe that milk is unclean and impure. In some instances it is thought to be a body excretion similar to urine, and some strongly dislike the taste and smell, sometimes even vomiting after smelling it.[52] A Burmese man said to an interviewer, "Our people just don't like milk—the smell. Just the idea of drinking all that white stuff coming from a cow. They just don't like it."[53] And throughout most of Africa, milk is consumed in a minority of societies, and in African nonmilking societies the reaction to milk is often similar to the reaction of Asians.

The human reaction to milk depends on one principal factor: whether or not people can digest it. Milk contains an important sugar, lactose, which can only be digested if a person's intestinal tract contains the enzyme lactase. Infants throughout the world have lactase, which allows them to digest their mother's milk as well as milk from cattle or goats. But most people lose their lactase by the time they reach adolescence or adulthood. In fact, until several thousand years ago, nearly every person alive on earth lost their lactase, and thus their ability to digest milk, after a certain age.

When people no longer have lactase, they can become very ill after drinking milk. They develop severe gastrointestinal discomfort: bloating, diarrhea, and so on. If these symptoms are severe and persistent, death may even ensue. Who, then, would drink milk if it had such unpleasant effects? But people who retain their lactase throughout life can reap the benefits milk has to offer. Who are these people and how did they get that way?

We call people who can digest milk *lactose absorbers* and those who cannot *lactose malabsorbers*. The distribution of these people throughout the world is shown in Table 4.2. Clearly the absorbers are heavily concentrated in Western and Northern Europe. The overwhelming majority of people in this region are absorbers (average: 90 percent). Notice also that these are the very same people who are the world leaders in milk consumption. And, crucially as we will see, they live at very high latitudes.

Most people in the rest of the world are malabsorbers, although in some societies there are both absorbers and malabsorbers. In the two hunter-gatherer and three African agricultural societies shown in the table, most people are malabsorbers (average: 89.5 percent), and an almost identical figure (89 percent) is found for the four East and Southeast Asian societies. But the three African pastoral societies in the table contain mostly absorbers (average: 95 percent).

The situation is more complex for peoples living around the Mediterranean. Two groups contain a substantial percentage of absorbers, whereas the other three have only a small minority of absorbers. The situation is also complicated for East Indians, Americans, and residents of the United Kingdom. India exhibits a wide range of variation on the absorber-malabsorber continuum. In the United States, most whites are absorbers, Mexican Americans are about equally divided between absorbers and malabsorbers, the majority of blacks are malabsorbers, and almost all Native Americans are malabsorbers. In the UK, nearly all whites are absorbers, but most East Indians and Afro-Caribbeans are malabsorbers.

There is a close connection between the ability to digest lactose and the presence of a dairying economy that produces large quantities of fresh milk. The two, lactose absorption and dairying, appear to have evolved together, a process known as **co-evolution** (the simultaneous evolution of genes and cultural practices). But how, precisely, did this happen? It is not certain exactly when dairying was first practiced, but it was probably at least 5,000 years ago, and possibly as long as 8,000 years ago, in Mesopotamia and Egypt.[54] From Egypt some stock raising peoples would have eventually moved south into parts of east and then west Africa. As seen earlier, the first farmers in the Fertile Crescent migrated into Mediterranean Europe around 8,500 years ago and eventually reached northern Europe between 5,500 and 6,000 years ago. Naturally they took their domesticated animals along with them. They may already have been practicing dairying by the time they reached northern Europe, but if not it would have been established soon afterward.[55]

A dairying economy would not be able to develop in the absence of at least some people who could tolerate milk and milk products. In ancient times, even though most people were lactose intolerant, a few were not. As the first steps toward a dairying economy were taken, those with the rare **allele** for lactose absorption would

TABLE 4.2   World Distribution of Lactose Absorbers and Malabsorbers by Latitude and Level of Milk Consumption

Society	Percent of Population Lactose Absorbers	Latitude	Milk Consumption (liters per person per year)
Hunter-gatherers			
Greenland Inuit	15.1	69 N	0
!Kung	2.5	20 S	0
African agricultural tribes			
Yoruba	9	6 N	4.5
Bantu of Zaire	2	4 S	0.2
Hausa	24	12 N	4.5
African pastoralists			
Hima	91	1 S	NA
Congo Tutsi	100	4 S	NA
Rwandan Tutsi	93	2 S	NA
Dairying peoples of North Africa and Mediterranean			
Israeli Jews	41	32 N	204 (40% processed into cheese)
Jordanian Arabs	23	32 N	16 (54% processed into cheese)
Egyptian Fellahin	7	30 N	49 (55% processed into cheese)
Greeks	52.1	38 N	181 (49% processed into cheese)
Greek Cypriots	28	35 N	141 (56% processed into cheese)
India			
Mohajirs	80	25 N	NA
Bombay	56	19 N	NA
Hyderabad	39	17 N	NA
East and Southeast Asian Peoples			
Japanese	27	40 N	43
Chinese	15	42 N	3
Taiwanese	0	24 N	16
Thai	2	15 N	30
Malays in Singapore	0	1 N	NA

(Continues on facing page)

(Table 4.2 continued)

Society	Percent of Population Lactose Absorbers	Latitude	Milk Consumption (liters per person per year)
Dairying peoples of Northern Europe			
Swedes	98	59 N	393
Finns	85	60 N	678
Germans	86	52 N	390
Dutch	86	52 N	828
Czechs	91	49 N	392
French	93	49 N	580
Others			
U.S. whites	85		NA
U.S. blacks	38 (range = 23–76)		NA
U.S. Native Americans	5		NA
U.S. Mexican-Americans	47		NA
U.K. whites	95		NA
U.K. East Indians	25		NA
U.K. Afro-Caribbeans	10		NA

Source: Gabrielle Bloom and Paul W. Sherman, "Dairying barriers affect the distribution of lactose malabsorption," *Evolution and Human Behavior* 26 (2005): 301e1–301e33; William H. Durham, *Coevolution: Genes, Culture, and Human Diversity* (Stanford, CA: Stanford University Press, 1991); Dallas M. Swallow, "Genetics of lactase persistence and lactose intolerance," *Annual Review of Genetics* 37 (2003): 197–219.

have been at a selective advantage. They could drink milk and reap its benefits, and their genes could gradually spread throughout the population. More lactose absorbers in the population would allow further development of dairying, which in turn would produce more absorbers. In essence, dairying and genes for lactose absorption would have spread hand in hand, each ratcheting the other up over time.[56]

But now we come to a crucial part of the story. Since most of the world's peoples don't drink milk, they obviously do not need it to survive or maintain good health. East and Southeast Asians today enjoy long lives without ever getting near a glass of milk. Therefore, the contribution of milk to the diet must be more specific than overall health. We now have a good idea of what that contribution is. In 1973 two geneticists, Gebhard Flatz and Hans Rotthauwe, argued that the most important quality of milk is its contribution to the body's ability to absorb calcium.[57] We know that vitamin D plays an important role in calcium absorption, and this vitamin can be synthesized by the ultraviolet radiation present in ordinary sunlight. But the key ingredient in milk, lactose, can also facilitate calcium absorption by acting like a vitamin D supplement.[58]

Peoples who live at lower latitudes with sunny climates, the vast majority of whom drink little or no milk, get plenty of vitamin D by means of sunlight, and therefore do not need lactose in order to get enough calcium. But people living at higher latitudes are in a different situation. In Europe, especially northern Europe, winter can be long and overcast, and even during the warmer months many days are cloudy and rainy. This is true of countries on the North Sea in particular—the British Isles, Germany, northern France, Belgium, and the Netherlands. And the situation is even more marked in Scandinavia, where many winter days are extremely short and there is no sunlight at all. Northern latitude peoples are therefore at much greater risk of bone diseases caused by calcium deficiency, such as rickets and osteomalacia, than people at mid to low latitudes.[59]

But there is, or was, a saving grace. When sunlight is scarce, lactose can become a substitute. Enter dairying. European peoples must have developed an increasingly intensive dairying economy as they moved into the more temperate parts of the continent. Lactose consumption and digestion was a major cultural adaptation to a biological need. But something else was occurring at the same time—lightening of the skin. We know that dark skin provides protection against the harmful effects of ultraviolet radiation. The people with the darkest skin live on or very near the equator, where ultraviolet radiation is greatest. As people moved farther north, the skin gradually lightened in direct proportion to the latitudes that people reached and the levels of ultraviolet radiation they were receiving.[60]

Lighter skin exposes people to the harmful effects of ultraviolet radiation. These include not only skin cancer but damage to sweat glands and thus the disruption of thermoregulation.[61] But if skin got lighter the farther north people lived, light skin must have conferred some adaptive advantage to counteract its potential costs. What might this advantage have been? The answer is a greater ability to absorb meager levels of sunlight than is possible with darker skin, and thus another means of synthesizing the vitamin D needed for calcium absorption. What in effect was happening was not a two-pronged but a three-pronged form of co-evolution. There were genetic changes in the ability to absorb lactose, genetic changes in skin color, and cultural changes in the direction of increased reliance on dairying. William Durham raises the interesting question as to whether skin depigmentation may have been sufficient by itself to overcome the problem of vitamin D deficiency. His answer is no; the increased ability to absorb lactose was also needed for good health.[62] Marvin Harris agrees, commenting that "the doubly exceptional combination of fair skin and lactase sufficiency is not a coincidence."[63] In other words, the risk to health or life in northern latitudes was great enough to require more than one mode of biological adaptation.

But there are several things yet to be explained. Of the two hunter-gatherer cases in Table 4.2, the Greenland Inuit are especially interesting because they live at one of the most extreme latitudes on earth and yet are mostly malabsorbers. However, this is unsurprising when we see that they drink no milk because they live too far north for dairying to be possible. But with no dairy animals, an environment with very little sunlight, and skin darker than normal for such a high latitude people, how did they avoid severe bone disease, which apparently occurred only rarely? The answer is that they consumed enormous quantities of fish oil, which is at least as good as sunlight and high levels of lactose in preventing rickets and osteomalacia.[64]

As for the !Kung, their rate of absorption is extremely low because, like all hunting and gathering peoples at all latitudes, they do not practice dairying and therefore consume no milk. And the three African agricultural tribes, the Yoruba, Zairean Bantu, and Hausa, are mostly malabsorbers because, like the Inuit and the !Kung, they have no dairying. None of these groups has ever been under any selection pressure to develop dairying because they are low latitude peoples with ample sunlight.

But then why do the extremely low latitude Ugandan Hima and the Tutsi of Congo and Rwanda have levels of lactose absorption that are even higher than those of Europeans? The reason is that these are pastoral populations whose major source of subsistence is milk and milk products. Thus they, like European dairy farmers, were under strong selection pressure to develop lactase sufficiency and eventually did. Yet unlike Europeans, they did not need lactose for calcium absorption because they had plenty of ultraviolet radiation. They simply needed to be able to digest lactose because it was a major component of most of what they were consuming.[65]

What then of East and Southeast Asian populations? In this part of the world, intensive agriculture has been practiced for thousands of years but mostly without use of the plow. Without plows people did not need draft animals, and thus it was not necessary to keep a large number of cows for breeding oxen. A dairying economy therefore never developed, nor did Asians have any real need for one. As Harris has pointed out with respect to China, "A considerable portion of the Chinese diet has long consisted of various cabbages, varieties of lettuce, spinach, and other dark green, leafy vegetables,"[66] adding that such vegetables are a good source of calcium. Another major Chinese crop was soybeans, also an excellent source of calcium. A second reason why dairying was never necessary in the main East Asian societies of China, Japan, and Korea was a relative abundance of sunny days that provided enough ultraviolet radiation for synthesizing vitamin D.[67] The Chinese, Japanese, and Koreans all have somewhat darker skin than Europeans.[68] Farther south, in Southeast Asia, there is even more sunshine and more ultraviolet radiation, and the skin is darker still.[69]

But the case of Japan is somewhat less clear. There are more Japanese lactose absorbers (about 27 percent) than Chinese absorbers (15 percent in mainland China, 0 in Taiwan). Milk and ice cream are sold in ample quantities in Japanese grocery stores, and there are ice cream shops. You can also get ice cream desserts in many restaurants. It turns out that the Japanese had begun to adopt dairying around the time Buddhism was introduced into the country, approximately the sixth century CE.[70] This may explain why Japan has more lactose absorbers than its neighbors. The still relatively low rate of absorbers may be because dairying began much later in Japan than in Europe.

There has been little to no dairying in Southeast Asia; only 2 percent of the Thai, for example, are absorbers. Many peoples in this part of the world have a strong aversion to milk, as in the case of the Burmese mentioned earlier. The Khmer of Cambodia have been described as regarding milk with an "invincible repugnance." And in Laos the Lao were contemptuous of the French colonists' liking for milk. The Lao did not make any use of milk, nor did other Laotian groups, such as the Meo, Khmu, and Lamet. Nor did Malays use milk (0 percent absorbers among Malays in Singapore), at least not traditionally. One early Western visitor reported that the Malays had an "unholy aversion to milk."[71]

Although not shown in the table, there are a number of East Asian populations in addition to Japan that have practiced dairying. The vast majority of these are Tibetan and Mongol groups living on China's borders. Mongols have for many centuries been pastoralists highly dependent on the horse for both riding and milking. Tibetans practice a mixture of agriculture and animal herding, and their primary animal is the yak. And yet all of these groups are predominantly malabsorbers (available figures suggest 6–13 percent absorbers).[72] But they process most of their milk into other products. The Mongols consume a fermented milk drink known as *kumiss*, and also make cheese, curds, and yogurt. The Tibetans process milk in similar ways.[73] This processing removes most of the lactose, and thus these products can be consumed by malabsorbers without gastrointestinal discomfort.

East Indians have a higher percentage of lactose absorbers than their neighbors to the east and southeast. There is a great deal of variation in the degree of lactose absorption throughout the Indian subcontinent.[74] In general, there are more absorbers in northern India and more malabsorbers in the south.[75] The Mohajirs, with an 80 percent absorber rate, are a northern Indian people who migrated into Pakistan at the time of independence from Britain and the separation of India and Pakistan. Both Bombay and Hyderabad have lower percentages of absorbers and are located in southern India. Indians have used plows for thousands of years, and thus have needed traction animals, mostly cattle, to pull them. And cows were often milked. But plows and traction animals have been more common in the north where the main crop has been wheat. Wheat is a grain that normally requires a great deal of land preparation, and this is best carried out by plowing.[76] In the more southern parts of India, rice has been the main crop and can often be efficiently cultivated without plows and traction animals. Dairying has therefore been more common in the north, where lactose absorption rates are higher.

The Manipuri in the Himalayan region of extreme eastern India are interesting because they practice dairying whereas their neighbors do not. The Manipuri are sedentary farmers who use ox-drawn plows, but the hill tribes that surround them are horticulturalists using hand tools. The Manipuri also have horses, water buf-falo, and cattle, but none of their neighbors keep these animals.[77] Unfortunately, the extent to which the Manipuri are lactose absorbers is unknown, but a reasonable prediction is that many are.

The five societies in the circum-Mediterranean region constitute another set of unusual cases. Two of the societies, Israel and mainland Greece, have intermediate levels of absorption, whereas the other three have low levels. But note that although these societies have well-developed dairying economies, approximately half of the milk they produce is processed into cheese. As noted above, this removes most of the lactose.

Finally, there are the various ethnic groups in the United States and the United Kingdom. White Americans are mostly absorbers because they are descended quite recently from European populations. Black Americans, however, are recent descen-dants of African tribes. Africans brought to America as slaves came mostly from west Africa, but from a variety of tribal populations. Most of these tribes were ag-riculturalists, but some were pastoralists. Blacks are on average malabsorbers, but their level of malabsorption is not as high as that for Asians or for strictly agricultural African tribes. American blacks are substantially interbred with whites (an average of about 25–30 percent white genetic admixture), which has no doubt increased the representation of genes for lactose absorption in the black population. Native Americans, who are overwhelmingly malabsorbers, are another interesting case, but not difficult to explain. They are descended from Siberian populations of extreme northeast Asia, and thus have a genetic heritage of malabsorption. And nowhere in the New World did indigenous Indian populations ever practice dairying, except perhaps for a small amount of milking of llamas in Peru. Mexican Americans are a mixed group, with about equal proportions of absorbers and malabsorbers. The majority of them are mestizos, or persons of mixed European (Spanish) and Cen-tral American Indian descent.[78] In the United Kingdom we find similar diversity among ethnic groups. Most British whites are absorbers, but only about 25 percent of immigrants from the Indian subcontinent and 10 percent of Afro-Caribbeans are absorbers.[79] The low numbers for these two groups are understandable in terms of the arguments made above.

Considerable progress has been made recently in unraveling the genetics of lac-tose absorption and malabsorption. Some years ago a gene known as LCT was discovered to be involved in lactase absorption.[80] More recently, research by Sarah Tishkoff and her team has identified a particular allele of this gene, T-13910, that is strongly associated with lactose absorption in Europeans; it evolved between 2,000 and 20,000 years ago. It is a Mendelian dominant allele. However, the allele was found to be present in less than 14 percent of individuals in west African pas-toral societies and was entirely absent among east African pastoralists. An analy-sis of 470 east African individuals from 43 different pastoral populations located in Kenya, Tanzania, and Sudan has identified three different alleles that are associated with lactose absorption: C-14010, G-13907, and G-13915. The C-14010 allele was found in 39 percent of individuals in Nilo-Saharan populations in Tanzania, 46 percent of individuals from Afro-Asiatic populations in Tanzania, and 32 percent of individuals from Nilo-Saharan groups in Kenya. The other two alleles were found at much lower frequencies. G-13907 was found in 21 percent of Afro-Asiatic Beja individuals and only 5 percent of Afro-Asiatic Kenyans. G-13915 was found in only 12 percent of Afro-Asiatic Beja individuals and only 9 percent of Afro-Asiatic Kenyans.[81] The researchers conclude "that at least two, and probably four or more, distinct causal variants associated with lactase persistence (T-13910 in Europeans and C-14010, G-13907, and G-13915 in Africans) have evolved independently in European and African populations owing to convergent evolution in response to a strong selective force, adult milk consumption."[82] However, there are obviously other alleles for lactose absorption in the African populations, since the three alleles identified are found in less than half (in some cases much less than half) of individuals who are lactose absorbers. Undoubtedly continuing research will identify some of these alleles.

SUMMARY

1. In all societies people have food preferences, but there are also foods they avoid. They find them disgusting or place a taboo on eating them. Pigs are widely consumed all over the world, but Judaism and Islam forbid pork. Among Hindus the cow is sacred but cattle are otherwise eaten wherever they can be suitably raised. In modern societies people are repulsed by the thought of eating dogs, but dogs have been eaten in some places, such as China and Southeast Asia. The thought of eating insects may be even more repellant to Westerners, but insects have been eaten in many societies. Milk drinking is common throughout Europe and in some African pastoral societies, but in many societies people find it repugnant.

2. The branch of evolutionary biology known as behavioral ecology provides a useful way of thinking about food choices. Human behavioral ecologists assume that humans make food decisions on the basis of maximizing the benefits and minimizing the costs of using the plant and animal resources found in their habitats. Some animals are too costly to raise in certain environments. Pigs, for example, do not thrive in hot environments with little shade because they cannot effectively cool their bodies. They are naturally adapted to woodland environments where there is shade and where they can forage on the forest floor. People in the former kind of environment will tend to avoid pigs, whereas people in the latter will likely find them quite palatable.

3. Humans have an innate taste for animal protein and sweet food as a result of ancient evolutionary adaptations. In nearly all societies meat is the most highly valued food. The reason is that it is an efficient source of calories, nutrients, and amino acids. Sweet foods are high on the list because in the ancestral environment sweet fruits made up a major part of the diet. The brain evolved to prefer sweetness.

4. Optimal foraging theory says that natural selection has designed humans to forage in a way that maximizes caloric returns for the minimum investment of time and energy. Based on long experience, foragers develop a rank ordering of potential food sources and capture the most highly ranked sources they encounter. Many hunter-gatherers pay more attention to large game than to small, sometimes even ignoring the latter even though it is abundant. This is because large game yields more energy per unit of foraging time. On foraging expeditions, people will capture additional food sources if they yield a rate of energy return equal to or higher than the average rate of return they are experiencing. Optimal foraging theory has been subjected to numerous tests, and many support it. Optimal foraging theory is, however, an incomplete theory and there are a number of foraging habits that it cannot explain.

5. Cattle are widely eaten throughout the world, but Hindus regard the cow as sacred and forbid eating it. This has often been regarded as an irrational taboo, but research shows that cattle have provided many important benefits for Hindu farmers that would disappear if cattle were killed and eaten. The most important benefits are pulling plows and providing manure for fertilizer.

6. Pigs are also widely eaten, but tabooed by Jews and Muslims. This taboo is often explained in religious terms, but pigs are very costly to raise in the hot, dry environments in which these religions originated. Pigs were costly but tempting, and to remove the temptation a religious taboo was created. Pigs thrive in cooler, wetter, and shadier environments, especially woodlands. When pigs are found in such environments they are usually consumed with gusto.

7. Many food taboos have yet to be explained. The Old Testament forbids camels, crustaceans, sharks, many bird species, winged insects, and rodents, among many other animals. No one has yet been able to determine why these prohibitions existed several thousand years ago.

8. There is an important distinction between the origins of a food taboo and its persistence over time. Devout Jews and Muslims will avoid eating pork even when they live in places where raising pigs is not costly and pork is widely available. Once established, taboos can be maintained for religious and cultural reasons, and as markers of group identity.

9. Although milk is a highly nutritious food, most people in the world today cannot drink it because they cannot digest it. This is because as adults they lack the enzyme lactase, which is necessary to digest lactose, the sugar in milk. Nearly everyone has lactase as infants and young children, but most people lose it in adolescence or adulthood.

10. As the first farmers migrated into Europe around 8,500 years ago, the domesticated animals they took with them included cattle. They may already have begun to practice some dairying, but by the time they reached northern Europe 5,500 years ago, dairying had probably become a widespread practice. This means that they were consuming milk and thus digesting it. Natural selection had to be operating on those few individuals who retained lactase and could digest milk, and genes for lactase persistence would have spread throughout the gene pool. Most Europeans became lactose absorbers, and today Europe is the largest region of the world where milk is widely consumed.

11. Milk was an important food for Europeans, especially northern Europeans, because they were living in a climate with many rainy days and limited sunlight. Sunlight activates vitamin D in the body, which helps it absorb calcium, and calcium is essential for healthy bones and teeth. With limited sunlight, European populations were under pressure to develop another means of calcium absorption, and this was found in milk. Lactose acts like a vitamin D supplement in helping the body to absorb calcium.

12. A dairying industry and genes for lactose absorption co-evolved, one socially and the other biologically. The same type of co-evolutionary process has occurred in African pastoral populations highly dependent on milk and milk products. These populations needed to be able to digest lactose, and thus natural selection operated on their genes as well. Because they lived in hot and sunny climates, these populations did not require milk for vitamin D synthesis. But as milk was a major food, people evolved from lactose malabsorbers into lactose absorbers.

13. Dairying never developed in most east and southeast Asian populations, and today most people in these regions are lactose intolerant. In some parts of Asia milk is regarded with disgust. Dairying was never necessary because these populations had enough sunlight and green, leafy vegetables to supply adequate amounts of calcium.

14. Geneticists have begun to identify some of the genes involved in lactose absorption. It appears that alleles for lactose absorption in Europeans are different from those in Africans. These alleles evolved independently in the two regions through a process known as convergent evolution.

QUESTIONS FOR DISCUSSION

✓ How do people decide what foods to eat and what foods to avoid?

✓ People throughout most of the world don't eat dogs and feel repulsed by the thought. Yet in some societies dogs have been eaten. Why would most people avoid dogs but some people think it is perfectly fine to eat them? Discuss.

✓ Where in the world have people eaten insects? Why do contemporary Westerners find insect eating repugnant?

✓ Some food is very spicy, other food is very bland. The lower the latitudes at which people live, the more spicy the food is likely to be. Why is this?

✓ How do people acquire food likings and disgusts at an individual level, and why?

✓ What are some innate human tastes, and why should we have them?

✓ What is optimal foraging theory? How successful is it in explaining foraging patterns? Discuss.

✓ Are there any exceptions to optimal foraging theory—any facts inconsistent with it? Explain.

✓ Cattle are eaten all over the world, yet Hindus consider the cow holy and ban eating it. Is this food taboo the result of some sort of irrational religious belief, or does the taboo arise from practical considerations? Discuss.

✓ Why should Jews and Muslims abominate the pig when no other religion prohibits it and pigs are widely eaten throughout the world?

✓ In most societies people do not consume milk and often find it disgusting. In what parts of the world is milk most likely to be consumed and why?

✓ A leading theory of milk consumption is that it co-evolved with the development of a dairying economy. Discuss this theory.

✓ What are some of the benefits conferred by consuming milk?

✓ In many societies adolescents and adults lack the enzyme lactase and thus cannot digest milk. Yet in some of these same societies people keep animals that can be milked and actually do milk them. How would you explain this?

✓ What does it mean to say that alleles for lactose absorption are products of convergent evolution?

References and Notes

1. Smith and Winterhalder 1992a, 1992b; E. A. Smith 2000; Winterhalder and Smith 2000; Hames 2001.

2. E. B. Ross 1980.

3. Schwabe 1979; discussed in Simoons 1994.

4. Simoons 1994.

5. Harris 1985.

6. Harris 1985.

7. Harris 1985.

8. Harris 1985.

9. Billing and Sherman 1998; Sherman and Hash 2001.

10. Cashdan 1994.

11. Cashdan 1994, p. 287.

12. See also Rozin et al. 1986.

13. Harris 1987; Rozin 1987.

14. Mintz 1985.

15. Harris 1985; Simoons 1994.

16. Simoons 1994.

17. Simoons 1994, p. 5.

18. Simoons 1994, p. 5.

19. Harris 1985; Abrams 1987.

20. Lieberman 1987.

21. Harris 1977.

22. Winterhalder and Smith 1981; E. A. Smith 1983; Hawkes, Hill, and O'Connell 1982; Hawkes and O'Connell 1985; Winterhalder 1987; Kaplan and Hill 1992; Kelly 1995. See Winterhalder and Smith 2000 for a summary of the status of optimal foraging theory after twenty-five years of research.

23. Kelly 1995.

24. Studies summarized in E. A. Smith 1983; Kaplan and Hill 1992. For individual studies see Winterhalder 1981; O'Connell and Hawkes 1981; Keegan 1986; Hawkes, Hill, and O'Connell 1982; E. A. Smith 1991; and Hames and Vickers 1982.

25. Hawkes, Hill, and O'Connell 1982.

26. Hawkes, Hill, and O'Connell 1982. In their original article the authors list sixteen resources and their rank order. Only eight are given here for illustrative purposes.

27. Hill and Kaplan 1989; Hill 1988.

28. Hill 1988.

29. Beckerman 1989; Hames 1988. Studies summarized in Kaplan and Hill 1992.

30. Sosis 2000.

31. Smith and Bliege Bird 2000.

32. Bliege Bird, Smith, and Bird 2001.

33. Koster et al. 2010. See also Koster 2008.

34. Correlation coefficients: importance X harvested biomass = .716; importance X flavor = .772. The amount of harvested biomass yielded by a species was also correlated with flavor ratings, but only modestly at .367.

35. Simoons 1994.

36. Simoons 1994.

37. Simoons 1994.

38. Harris 1966, 1977, 1985.

39. Harris 1966, 1977, 1985.

40. Harris 1966, 1977, 1985.

41. Harris 1966, 1977, 1985.

42. Harris 1966, 1977, 1985.

43. Simoons 1994; Harris 1974.

44. Harris 1974, 1977.

45. Harris 1985.

46. Harris 1966, 1977, 1985.

47. Harris 1977.

48. Coon 1951; Harris 1985.

49. Harris 1985.

50. Robinson 2000.

51. Fessler and Navarette 2003.

52. Simoons 1970, 1980.

53. Simoons 1970, p. 552.

54. Simoons 1971.

55. Durham 1991.

56. Durham 1991.

57. Flatz and Rotthauwe 1973, as discussed in Durham 1991.

58. Durham 1991.

59. Harris 1985; Durham 1991.

60. The correlations between latitude, ultraviolet radiation, and skin color are extremely high. Coefficients: latitude X skin color = -.937, ultraviolet radiation X skin color = .922. These correlations are nearly perfect.

61. Jablonski and Chaplin 2000, p. 61.

62. Durham 1991.

63. Harris 1985, p. 143.

64. Durham 1991.

65. Durham 1991.

66. Harris 1985, p. 151.

67. Harris 1985.

68. A reliable skin color scale was developed by Biasutti 1967. The scale ranges from 1 (lightest) to 8 (darkest). Most Europeans rate a 1, whereas East Asians rate a 2.

69. On the Biasutti scale southeast Asians range from 3.67 (Thailand) to 5.00 (Cambodia).

70. Fujimoto 2003.

71. Simoons 1970.

72. Simoons 1970; Bloom and Sherman 2005.

73. Simoons 1970.

74. Bloom and Sherman 2005.

75. Swallow and Hollox 2000.

76. Pryor 1985.

77. Simoons 1970.

78. Swallow 2003.

79. Swallow 2003.

80. Swallow 2003.

81. Tishkoff et al. 2007.

82. Tishkoff et al. 2007, pp. 37–38. See also Wooding 2007.

5

Finding Mates

There are two dimensions of human mating: choosing a mate merely for sex or choosing one for a committed, long-term relationship. The two overlap, of course, and in many instances the former is a prelude to the latter. This chapter discusses mating in both senses. We begin with a discussion of incest avoidance. Most anthropologists and sociologists think there is no reason why family members cannot be sexually attracted to one another, and therefore society must impose a taboo to prevent incest from happening. Others disagree, holding that there is a kind of innate disinclination for sex within the family that is triggered by certain socioecological conditions. We will examine these two views and decide which is more consistent with the evidence.

Then we will see how Darwin's concept of sexual selection can be used to understand the different sexual strategies employed by males and females. We will show, among other things, that the male sex drive is more urgent than the female's; that males have more interest than females in multiple partners and sexual variety; that males are more interested in looking at the bodies of the opposite sex than females are; and that, although both sexes exhibit jealousy, it takes different forms in the sexes. This leads us to what males and females are looking for in long-term mates, as distinguished from casual sex partners. We will review research that shows that males display a keen interest in female physical attractiveness, and that attractiveness has been selected for in human evolution because it correlates with genetic fitness. We will also examine research evidence showing that males prefer younger females, and that males everywhere prefer a particular type of female body shape represented by a narrow waist and wide hips. As for female choice, females also value physical attractiveness, but not as strongly as males do. They give greatest emphasis to a man's status and resources, which are usually observable, but women are also attracted to certain male body scents that are known to be correlated with social dominance and masculinity.

In the final two sections of the chapter we consider, first, the relationship between male dominance and reproductive success, showing that these are highly correlated in all societies. Then we turn to sexual orientation, focusing on homosexuality and its likely causes. Is homosexuality a "choice," as many assert, or is it somehow hard-wired into the brains of gay individuals, as many others contend?

Incest Avoidance and the Incest Taboo

The most fundamental fact about family relations in every society is that they are never to include sexual relations or marriage, which is to say they should not be incestuous. You want to have sex or get married? Go find those things with some-one in another family. There is an important distinction between incest *avoidance* and an incest *taboo*. Incest avoidance is simply the absence of sexual relations and marriage between members of a family unit, at a minimum between parents and children and brothers and sisters. In societies in which people live in extended fam-ily households, the avoidance usually includes cousins as well. An incest taboo exists when a society actively prohibits incestuous relations. Many societies extend the taboo beyond the first cousin range so that even distant cousins may be forbidden. In most societies the incest taboo is extremely strong, with a feeling of revulsion or even horror at the very thought of the act. Incest happens occasionally, but if it is discovered people are shocked and it is often severely punished. There are a handful of exceptions to these patterns, but they are only partial exceptions and occur under very special circumstances.[1] The cases are not sufficient to say that the avoidance and the taboo are not human universals.

Explanations

What accounts for the universality of incest avoidance and the incest taboo? Early anthropological and sociological explanations relied on Sigmund Freud's famous assertion that there is strong sexual attraction within the family. A boy secretly lusts for his mother, a girl for her father. Father and son therefore become sexual rivals for the wife-mother, mother and daughter for the husband-father. Since these rival-ries are extremely dangerous to family cohesion, they have to be overcome, which occurs, Freud suggested, by the boy identifying with his father and the girl with her mother. They admire them and want to be like them. Identification leads sons and daughters to repudiate their sexual attraction to the opposite sex parent.

The idea of sexual attraction within the family was taken for granted by most social scientists when they began to offer explanations for the incest taboo. In the 1940s, Kingsley Davis developed what can be called the role confusion theory.[2] Ev-ery family member has several roles to play, and they must be consistent or com-patible. A man is thus a father and a husband, a woman a mother and a wife. A son may also be a brother, and in wider family networks he is also a grandson, a cousin, and so on. Davis asked what might disrupt or confuse these roles so as to put them in conflict. His answer was incest, especially if it produced offspring. In his own words, "Should children be born [of an incestuous union] the confusion of statuses would be phenomenal. The incestuous child of a father-daughter union, for example, would be a brother of his own mother, i.e., the son of his own sister; a stepson of his own grandmother; possibly a brother of his own uncle; and certainly a grandson of his own father. This confusion of generations would be contrary to the authority relations so essential to the fulfillment of parental duties."[3]

Davis thought that incestuous relations within the family would lead to its ultimate breakdown. Moreover, since the family is a linchpin of society—essential to its cohesion—if family members mated then they would not depend on other families for mates and families would therefore tend to become isolated. The integration of the larger society would be threatened.

The social cohesion argument in one form or another is standard anthropological and sociological thinking on the subject. The problem with this argument is that it is not based on actual evidence showing that incest would have these kinds of consequences. This is simply assumed, never demonstrated. Moreover, in some human societies people have developed extraordinarily complex webs of kinship that take all kinds of relationships into account, so there is no reason, in principle at least, why roles could not be suitably redefined and reassigned when incest occurs. But the most fatal flaw in the cohesion theory is that it rests on an untenable assumption: family members are sexually attracted to each other. The evidence, to be reviewed shortly, strongly suggests otherwise.

The best alternative to this kind of explanation is one of the very first theories ever developed, a type of Darwinian theory formulated by Edward Westermarck in 1889 and published in his book *The History of Human Marriage* in 1891.[4] It turns out to be the theory for which there is now the most compelling evidence. Westermarck's argument was simple and straightforward: children of opposite sex reared in close contact with each other in early childhood will develop a sexual indifference or even a strong aversion to each other. Either there is no attraction, or the thought of sexual relations is repugnant.

As noted in Chapter 1, Westermarck was the very first sociologist to use Darwinian principles in ways that are now very similar to modern-day sociobiologists or evolutionary psychologists. As a Darwinian, Westermarck reasoned that because the offspring of incestuous unions tend to have above-average levels of deformity and disease, such unions had to have been selected against in the evolutionary past. The brain had to have evolved a mechanism that would trigger disinterest or aversion, and thus sexual avoidance, under certain environmental conditions. The most common condition would be close contact early in life, because the parties in most instances would be sister and brother. But Westermarck said that the brain cannot distinguish actual siblings from stepsiblings or unrelated children. All that matters is that the children, whatever their ancestry, are in close contact from a very early point.

Evidence Supporting Westermarck: Inbreeding Depression

People in many societies have long observed that incestuous unions, when they occur, tend to produce less healthy offspring. There is a good deal of scientific evidence

to support these observations. Eva Seemanova studied the offspring of 161 incestuous unions in Czechoslovakia between 1933 and 1970. She found that these offspring
were much more likely to have genetic abnormalities and suffer premature death
than a control group of the offspring of unrelated individuals, a phenomenon known
as *inbreeding depression*. Forty-two percent of the offspring of parents who were related by one-half of their genes (parent-child or brother-sister unions) suffered from
these difficulties compared to only 7 percent of children from the control group. The
level of inbreeding depression declined as relatedness declined; the rate of depression for offspring of sexual partners related by one-fourth of their genes (usually
uncle-niece unions) was 25 percent, and for offspring related by one-eighth of their
genes (first cousin unions) the rate was about 13 percent.[5]

Recently Alan Bittles and James Neel carried out research on a much larger
number of populations. This may be the most comprehensive study of inbreeding
depression ever undertaken.[6] Bittles and Neel examined the genetic effects of first
cousin marriages in thirty-eight populations in seven different countries (India, Pakistan, Japan, Kuwait, Nigeria, Brazil, and France) and found that the offspring of
these marriages had an average excess mortality of 4.4 percent. In a separate analysis
Saggar and Bittles estimated the likelihood that offspring of individuals related by
one-quarter or one-half of their genes would carry two copies of a deleterious recessive gene.[7] Their estimates were 8–10 percent for the offspring of uncle-niece and
half-sibling matings (related by one-quarter of their genes), and a much larger 30
percent for parent-child or brother-sister matings (related by one-half).

These numbers initially appear considerably lower than those obtained by Seemanova but in fact are similar. Seemanova found a rate of abnormality or premature
death of 7 percent in her control group of offspring from nonincestuous unions.
When this number is subtracted from Seemanova's other numbers, her true inbreeding depression numbers are 35 percent excess abnormality or premature death
for offspring of parents related by one-half, 18 percent excess for offspring of parents
related by one-fourth, and 6 percent excess for offspring of parents related by one-
eighth. The Bittles-Neel findings and Saggar-Bittles estimates show less inbreeding
depression than Seemanova's findings, but not much less. Actually, they may not
be lower at all, since Bittles and Neel were considering only mortality and Saggar
and Bittles only lethal recessive genes. Inbreeding depression also includes morbid-
ity—disease and malformation—and when this is added to mortality the inbreeding
depression levels for all of the studies should be about the same.

Evidence Supporting Westermarck: Natural Experiments

Westermarck's theory was given serious consideration when it was first formulated,
but critics thought it was difficult to evaluate empirically. But several decades after
Westermarck died, testing the theory became possible due to an extraordinary discovery concerning mating patterns in Israeli kibbutzim. The kibbutzim (singular:
kibbutz) were communal settlements established in Israel early in the twentieth cen-

tury by Jews who were radical Marxists. The new settlements were devoted to abolishing traditional gender roles, eliminating the nuclear family, and establishing a highly egalitarian community. To abolish the nuclear family, children were removed from their parents at birth and reared by teams of nurses in communal nurseries. Here they received their upbringing and education, and their parents had limited contact with them.

In the late 1950s, it was discovered that members of the same kevutza—the peer group in which children were reared and educated—almost never married.[8] Joseph Shepher, an Israeli sociologist and himself a former kibbutznik, followed up on this discovery with an extensive study.[9] In examining records of 2,769 marriages occurring in many different kibbutzim, he found that only fourteen took place between members of the same kevutza, a stunning 99.5 percent rate of outmarriage. And these fourteen exceptions turned out to be very instructive in their own right. In seven of the marriages the couple joined the same kevutza between the ages of four and eight, and in five of the marriages they joined between the ages of ten and fifteen. In one case the couple was together at birth but separated between the ages of two and six, and in the one remaining marriage the couple was never in the same kevutza (thus apparently misclassified).

To explain this striking pattern, Shepher went back to Westermarck's old theory. Somehow kevutza associates, most of whom were genetically unrelated and who (except brothers and sisters) were actually encouraged to marry (there was no incest taboo within a kevutza), felt no attraction for each other. Or at least this is what they told Shepher when he asked them about their feelings. A common response was, "We feel like brother and sister."

Thus Westermarck's "familiarity breeds aversion" theory gained new life. Other supporting research evidence appeared at about the same time. Stanford University anthropologist Arthur Wolf had been studying Chinese marriage patterns by looking at records from the first half of the twentieth century. On Taiwan there were two principal forms of marriage. The more common one was a traditional arranged marriage in which the bride and groom met on the day of their wedding. The other involved a family's adopting a daughter into their family who was destined to be her stepbrother's future wife. This was known as *sim-pua*, "little daughter-in-law," marriage. The daughter was usually an infant, and her brother was usually slightly older. They grew up together and played just like regular siblings. But what happened when they married? The marriage records Wolf examined showed a well-above-average rate of infidelity and divorce, and a well-below-average rate of childbearing, than the more traditional marriages. Wolf learned that the couples would often fiercely resist sexual intercourse. It was frequently necessary for the parents to force them into their bedroom on their wedding night kicking and screaming, and to unlock the door only after they had consummated the marriage.[10]

Like Shepher, Wolf turned to Westermarck's theory to explain this pattern of sexual aversion. He studied the marriage records very thoroughly to see whether there might be some sort of critical period for the acquisition of an incest aversion. He found that the first three years seemed to be the most important. Couples who were together from birth to age three were much more likely to experience aversion as adults than couples who made contact after that age. The older the couples were when they first met the less aversive they were, and those who did not meet until age ten or older usually experienced no aversion at all.[11]

Two other "natural experiments" have come to light in support of Westermarck. Justine McCabe studied a type of marriage in Lebanon in which cousins who belong to the same lineage (extended kin group) married. These lineages were residential groups, and thus cousins would have had extensive social contact early in life. Throughout the world, marriage between lineage mates is usually regarded as incestuous and therefore prohibited; people are required to choose mates from other lineages. As predicted by Westermarck's theory, McCabe found the same pattern for the Lebanese that Wolf found for the Taiwanese: frequent and often strong sexual aversion as exhibited by much higher divorce rates and lower rates of childbearing.[12]

Most recently, Daniel Fessler, an anthropologist at UCLA, discovered a fourth case, the Karo Batak of Indonesia. In their concept of the ideal form of marriage, a boy marries a cousin who is his father's sister's daughter (from the girl's perspective, her husband would be her mother's brother's son). Parents encourage this type of marriage for what appear to be economic and political reasons. But despite such encouragement the cousins, known locally as *impal*, seldom marry (the figure is about 4 percent). The cousins say they do not marry because they are not sexually or romantically attracted and "feel like siblings." As you may already have concluded, the majority of *impal* grow up in close contact from early childhood.[13]

Additional Evidence

There are several other lines of evidence consistent with the Darwinian explanation rather than the traditional social cohesion theory. One is the widespread avoidance of incest among many other animal species. Among primates, for example, inbreeding avoidance occurs primarily through the dispersal of males from their own groups; they leave the groups into which they were born and enter other groups, mating with females there. For example, in a long-term study of olive baboons at Gombe National Park in Tanzania, every one of eighty-nine males dispersed into other groups after reaching adulthood, whereas every female remained in her group.[14] Chimpanzees are different in that it is the females rather than the males who disperse. Nevertheless, the point still holds: primates are mating with individuals outside their own group. As argued earlier, if a behavior pattern that is virtually universal in humans is also widely found in our prehuman ancestors, there is a strong presumptive case that we have inherited that tendency from those ancestors. Look to the animals![15]

Another very interesting line of evidence involves siblings who have been separated at birth or in very early childhood and then reunited in late adolescence or adulthood. One of the first systematic studies of incest was carried out by S. Kirson

Weinberg. Among his subjects were six sibling pairs separated in early childhood. Upon being reunited much later in life, they all experienced mutual attraction and developed sexual and romantic relationships. Three of the couples married.[16] Many other similar cases have been found, with one study suggesting that half or more of separated siblings who reunite later in life become sexually and romantically involved.[17] A number of fictional works include siblings who meet for the first time as adults and develop sexually charged relationships. Because good novelists usually have penetrating insights into the complexities, subtleties, and ironies of human relationships, these characters are very likely based on the real behavior of real people.[18] And thus we see once again that it is familiarity bred from long-term proximity and interaction rather than relatedness that inhibits attraction.

One-Generation Versus Two-Generation Inhibitions

Several questions remain to be answered. One involves a possible omission in Westermarck's theory. The theory is formulated in terms of contact between siblings without specific reference to parents and offspring, who obviously cannot have had contact with each other in early childhood. However, Westermarck does refer to the "normal want of sexual intercourse between persons who have been living closely together from the childhood *of one or both of them.*"[19] This statement is crucial because, since parents and offspring are just as closely related as siblings (by one-half of their genes), offspring of a union between parent and child should display the same degree of inbreeding depression as the offspring of siblings. Indeed, the evidence reviewed earlier indicates that this is the case. Therefore, natural selection should have selected against parent-child attraction as much as against sibling attraction. Arthur Wolf recognizes this problem, commenting that parents "are somehow inhibited by association with their children. But how?"[20] It also follows that children should be inhibited by association with their parents. But again, how?

What we know of father-daughter incest, which is the most common type, is that the father is almost always the perpetrator and the daughter the victim. She is coerced and regards the act as extremely unpleasant not so much because it is coercive, but because she is very likely to be strongly aversive to sex with her father, period. Her inhibition follows from the logic of Westermarck's theory because she starts her relationship with her father from birth. Her inhibition therefore develops in essentially the same manner as the brother-sister aversion. How then does the inhibition of the *father* work itself out, since he is an adult when he first encounters his daughter? Unfortunately, the answer to this question remains to be determined.

Why Incest?

A second question involves explaining why incest does sometimes occur. Why isn't everyone inhibited? A persuasive answer has been supplied by Mark Erickson, a psychiatrist who has worked extensively with incest victims. After many years of listening to these victims discuss their family dynamics, Erickson came to realize that the common thread running through his patients' lives was severe family dysfunction. Based on this evidence, Erickson drew a crucial distinction between two types of intimate bonding, what he called *familial bonding* and *sexual bonding*. The idea of familial bonding derives from the English psychologist John Bowlby, who argued that under normal circumstances a natural attachment forms between parent and child. This attachment has evolved by natural selection because it is necessary for the child's protection and well-being.[21] The attachment goes in both directions: parent to child and child to parent. In contrast, sexual bonding develops between husbands and wives or lovers. It is charged with a very different type of emotional intensity than familial bonding. Natural selection has seen to it that these two types of bonding oppose each other. That is, if a person forms a familial bond with a relative, a sexual bond is extremely unlikely to develop. The familial bond is a caretaking bond, and a caretaking relationship is incompatible with a sexual relationship.

The main type of dysfunction Erickson discovered in his incest victims was an absence of nurturance, in other words, an absence of the familial or caretaking bond. The family dysfunction usually occurs in both the incest victim's own immediate family and in the prior family of the perpetrator. As Erickson explains it, "Parents who had insecure attachments in their childhood are usually less responsive to offspring, who in turn become insecurely attached. It is important to recall that the early childhood experience of incestuous fathers, mothers, and siblings is marked by neglect, abandonment, and physical and sexual abuse. These are the conditions that lead to insecure attachment."[22] With the critically important familial bond undeveloped or underdeveloped, the door is left open to sexual bonding from the point of view of the parent.

Various studies support Erickson's overall argument. A study by Flores, Mattos, and Salzano examined thirty-nine cases of incest in São Paulo, Brazil.[23] Seven were brother-sister incest, twenty-five father-daughter incest, six father-stepdaughter incest, and one son-mother incest. The authors conducted detailed interviews with the victims and some of their family members and found that the most important contributing factors were extreme violence within the family environment, mental illness in the aggressor, and social interaction difficulties within the family. Another study compared two kinds of sex offenders, sibling-incest sex offenders (N = 32) and nonsibling sex offenders (N = 28).[24] It was found that difficulties of individual functioning, as assessed by low self-esteem, depression, hostility, aggressiveness, and lack of popularity did not differentiate between the two groups. It was difficulties in family functioning that made a difference. Compared to the nonincest offenders, the incest offenders came from families with significantly higher levels of physical punishment, parental rejection, marital discord, and negative family atmosphere, and a significantly lower level of family satisfaction.

Avoidance Versus Taboo
Finally, if incest is rare because people naturally find it uninteresting or repugnant,

why do nearly all societies have strong incest taboos? Moreover, why are these ta-boos often extended to people from different villages who have very little contact? One possible answer to the first question is that, because not everyone is disinclined toward incest, a taboo is needed to prevent its occasional occurrence. Another pos-sible answer, perhaps more compelling, is that because most people find the thought of incest repugnant in terms of their own behavior, they generalize this feeling of repugnance toward the act when engaged in by others and thus feel a desire to pun-ish it. It comes to be seen as morally wrong.[25] This idea was first suggested by Wes-termarck.[26] Here an analogy with cannibalism may be appropriate. Although it has been practiced in some societies, cannibalism generally is not seen, and most people feel a repugnance toward it that may be at least as strong as the feeling against in-cest. Even when cases of cannibalism come to light in which people under extreme conditions eat the bodies of compatriots who have already died so that they them-selves may live, there is still a sense of uneasiness. It is not surprising that people are inclined to punish acts they regard with repugnance bordering on shock or horror.

Regarding the second question, in many societies people seem to recognize that when close relatives mate the result is above-average numbers of unhealthy offspring. In small-scale societies sisters are often exchanged as wives between dif-ferent kin groups. If the Eagle Clan exchanges with the Hawk Clan, there will be first-cousin marriages between the clans; such marriages have been found in about a third of the world's small-scale societies. But if the groups notice over time negative biological consequences of cousin marriages, they are likely to develop a taboo so that these maladaptive consequences can be avoided.[27]

In this respect, an examination of 752 societies from the *Ethnographic Atlas* shows that 62 percent forbid marriage between all first cousins, and almost half of these extend the taboo to all second cousins. However, there are very few taboos beyond the second-cousin range.[28] We know that beyond this range the rate of inbreeding depression is very low; genetic abnormalities are no more likely to occur than in the offspring of unrelated individuals. It appears that in the majority of societies people figure these things out and adjust the scope of their incest prohibitions accordingly.

Sexual Selection

In addition to his concept of natural selection, Darwin identified another form of selection that he called **sexual selection**. Natural selection operates on the ability of an organism to find food and protection from the elements, and thus to survive. But sexual selection is selection for traits that help organisms find mates.

Darwin identified two types of sexual selection, which he called *male combat* and *female choice*. Both will be highly familiar to any reader. In male combat, males fight for access to females, and sexual selection has equipped them with features that are necessary to win. The champions par excellence are members of the pinniped family: seals, sea lions, and walruses. Among many walruses and sea lions, there is marked sexual dimorphism, with males much larger than females.[29] Among southern elephant seals, for example, males weigh nearly eight times as much as females, and often much more than many subordinate males.[30] Larger males win more fights and gain access to more females. Southern elephant seals have been observed to have "harems" as large as 100 females, with an average harem size of 48. In northern fur seals, males are six times larger than females, with an average harem size of 40 and a maximum observed size of 153. Sexual dimorphism and harem size are very highly correlated. Harp seals are monogamous and males and females are the same size. Likewise, in another monogamous species, the common seal, males are only slightly larger than females.[31] Size matters![32]

Male combat is also the form that sexual selection has taken in ungulates, such as deer, elk, and antelope. Males of these species use antlers for fighting, with those having the largest antlers generally winning more battles and getting more of the females. Body size matters too. Saiga antelope males are 14 percent larger than females and have an average harem size of twelve and a maximum observed size of twenty-six. By contrast, the Kirk's dik-dik is monogamous, and males and females are of equal size.[33]

Among nonhuman primates, the same pattern is evident. Male gorillas are twice the size of females; they have an average harem size of five and a maximum observed size of nine. In Patas monkeys males are also about twice the size of females, and males have an average harem size of eight and a maximum size of seventeen. In the monogamous dusky titi, there is no size dimorphism. The same is true of monogamous Mentawai gibbons (where males are slightly smaller than females).[34]

Sexual selection has operated differently in birds, taking the form of female choice. Here the critical features are bright colors and elaborate plumage instead of antlers, tusks, and body size. It is the males that are colorful and plumed, with the females being rather drab. The classic example is the peacock. Peacocks have elaborate, colorful tails, which attract females. But since there is always variation in any species or population of animals, some peacocks have more elaborate tails than others. The more elaborate the tail, the more the females (the peahens) like them.

In their mating rituals, leks (groups) of peacocks fan out their tails and strut around while the peahens watch the action. Observational studies show that the peahens usually visit at least two or three peacocks and end up choosing those with the most elaborate tails.[35] Tails vary in a number of features, but especially in train length and the number of eyespots on the tail. The peahens prefer peacocks with longer trains, but they appear to put more emphasis on the number of eyespots. In an interesting experiment, the experimenters cut off part of the trains of some peacocks and found that the peahens strongly preferred the peacocks with their tails intact. They also removed a few of the eyespots on the tails of some males and found that those males were less successful in mating (even removing just 5 of 150 eyespots made a difference). In summarizing the results, the experimenters found a very high correlation (0.72) between the number of eyespots on a male's tail and the number of females he mated with.[36]

Because the chosen peacocks end up mating with more peahens (unlike many bird species, peafowl are polygynous) than their less finely feathered male competitors, they leave more copies of their genes—including the genes for beautiful tails (among their male offspring) and the preference for beautiful tails (among their female offspring)—in future generations.

Almost as interesting are bowerbirds, natives of Australia. Male bowerbirds spend hours and sometimes days building elaborate structures known as bowers, which can be up to five feet high and ten feet long. They use sticks to build the bowers and then decorate them elaborately, using flowers, berries, and even bottle caps and tinfoil.[37] They also like to find colorful objects for decoration. Satin bowerbirds collect a lot of blue feathers and place them around their bowers. Another species, spotted bowerbirds, makes extensive use of a type of green berry. In a fascinating experiment, decorations were removed from completed bowers and then sixty objects, including the green berry, were placed near the birds to see what they would choose. They chose mostly the green berries, which they carried back to their bowers. Do the blue feathers and green berries do their intended job and attract females? Indeed they do, and in large numbers. The larger the number of feathers and berries decorating the bowers, the greater the number of females who show up for mating.[38]

Why do females prefer beautiful colors and elaborate plumage? For decades the widely accepted explanation was that devised by the famous evolutionary geneticist Sir Ronald Fisher in 1915. Focusing on the peacock, he contended that the female preference for elaborate tails was essentially arbitrary. They just preferred them and that was that. And as peahens mated more often with the brighter peacocks, genes for elaborate plumage were passed on to their offspring, thus producing a lot of colorful sons. The end result was what Fisher called "runaway selection," a process in which a preference becomes rapidly established in a population (i.e., "runs away").

More recently, however, the idea that elaborate tails don't signal anything in particular about the peacock has been shown to be wrong. Evidence has now accumulated to show that, in fact, it is the "fittest" peacocks who grow the best tails. Amotz and Avishag Zahavi summarize the present state of knowledge. They note that, in a peacock's display,

> The male holds his tail upright and spread out—which demands considerable effort. From time to time he shakes his tail vigorously; this requires yet more effort and produces a remarkable rattle. The "eye" patterns of the peacock's tail, the glisten of his feathers, the crown on his head, all add up to a symphony of shape, color, and sound. . . .
>
> Each aspect of the display seems to convey specific, reliable information about a particular feature of the male. The long tail feathers are

grown over a period of several months, during a time of year when food is scarce. Unhealthy birds arrest the process, so a male who displays a set of perfect tail feathers advertises that he has been in good health and has managed to find food even during molt season.

The long, heavy, brightly colored tail also attests to the owner's strength and skill, for he has succeeded in avoiding predators despite such a burden.[39]

The relationship between natural and sexual section is an important feature of Darwinian evolutionary theory. In many cases, the two forms of selection operate antagonistically so that sexual selection impairs natural selection. The tails of the most elegant peacocks, for example, are very heavy and hamper the birds' mobility, thus increasing their vulnerability to predators. In essence, natural and sexual selection converge on a kind of compromise: sexual selection must be strong enough so that its net fitness (reproductive) benefits exceed the costs imposed by natural selection. Some sort of balancing mechanism has to be at work. The same sort of thing is happening in the tungara frogs of South America. The males have inflatable vocal sacs that they use to sing to females for hours on end. However, their elaborate serenades attract not only females but the bloodsucking flies and bats that prey on them.[40]

Is sexual selection at work in humans? Indeed, there is every indication that it is. According to Robert Trivers, there are at least two dimensions to any species' reproductive strategy: *parental investment* and *mating effort*.[41] Parental investment is the amount of time and effort that is put into caring for offspring, and there is always a trade-off between this type of investment and mating investment, which is the amount of time and effort put into acquiring mates.

The balance between parental investment and mating effort varies by sex and species. In highly polygynous species—those in which males have many mates—males emphasize mating and invest relatively little in parental care, which is primarily the business of the female. In such species, there is much sexual dimorphism, with males being bigger, more aggressive, and usually highly dominant over females. Polygynous species are also prone to mate guarding, with males vigorously seeking to limit females' access to other males. The walruses and sea lions obviously fit in here.[42]

In monogamous species, such as most birds, both males and females tend to invest equally in parental care, and there are smaller differences between the sexes in mating effort than there are in polygynous species (males don't fight to the death but strut around and fan out their plumage, sing at night, and so on). There is little or no size dimorphism and minimal male dominance. Males and females mate for life and work cooperatively to raise their broods.[43]

Most animal species are polygynous rather than monogamous and moderately to highly dimorphic. We humans are a moderately polygynous, moderately dimorphic species. Males are larger but not a great deal larger. Males have more testosterone, are more aggressive, and tend to be dominant over females. But we don't come close to elephant seals.

In the next two sections we consider the implications of these features of our species' nature for sexual and mating strategies, and then in later chapters for marriage, family life, and gender relations.

Strategic Sex

Sociosexuality

Differences in sexuality between men and women are the product of sexual selection. In humans, sexual selection has been fully at work for tens of thousands of years shaping men's and women's sexual emotions and behaviors. What are the most fundamental differences between male and female sexuality? How "sexy" is each sex, and what mating strategies do the respective sexes use?

On average, it is the male of the species who has a more urgent and persistent interest in sex; he is more eager to mate, more desirous of multiple partners, more interested in casual sex, and more likely to separate sex from love. Men are much more likely to show interest in mating with someone they have never met or have known only briefly. Two imaginative and widely cited studies conducted by Clark and Hatfield had student volunteers from an experimental social psychology class approach strangers on the campus of Florida State University and ask them three questions. In the first study four male volunteers approached forty-eight female students at five different campus locations and asked them if they were willing to go on a date, go back to their apartment, or have sex (each question was prefaced by a statement to the effect "I have been noticing you around and find you very attractive"). Fifty-six percent of the women agreed to a date, but only 6 percent were willing to go back to the interviewer's apartment and none were willing to have sex. At the same time five female volunteers asked forty-eight male students the same three questions. Here the results were dramatically different. Fifty percent of the men agreed to go on a date, but 69 percent agreed to go to the interviewer's apartment and a whopping 75 percent were willing to have sex that very day.[44]

A follow-up study was conducted using the very same research design. The results were almost identical. Fifty percent of women agreed to a date, but not one would agree to go back to the apartment or to have sex. For the men, 50 percent agreed to a date, 69 percent to go back to the apartment, and another 69 percent to have sex.[45] A similar study conducted in Austria a few years later found that only 6 percent of women invited to have sex with a total stranger were willing to accept the offer.[46] The most recent study, by Hald and Høgh-Olesen, included 389 subjects (216 women and 173 men) from the four largest cities in Denmark. Twenty-one experimental confederates (10 men and 11 women) who were psychology students at Aarhus University approached the subjects on a university campus or at a centrally located park or pedestrian area and asked them the same three questions that were asked in the previous studies. The differences between male and female subjects on the date question were not particularly large (30 percent of men consented compared to 20 percent of women), although for the "go back to my apartment" question the difference was somewhat larger (22 percent of men consented compared to 8 percent of women). But, as in the previous studies, there was a very large male-female difference on the consent to sex question. Here 38 percent of men consented compared to only 2 percent of women.[47]

The authors were also interested in the role of certain conditions in determining subjects' answers. Relationship status mattered a great deal. Fewer subjects of both sexes who were in a romantic relationship were willing to have sex, although here again there was a male-female difference, with 18 percent of men willing to have sex compared to only 4 percent of women. For subjects not in a relationship, the male-female gap was extremely large; 59 percent of the men consented to sex compared to none of the women. Regardless of relationship status, women were somewhat more likely to consent to sex if the male confederate was especially attractive, but attractiveness of the confederate did not play a role for men.

One potential objection that might be raised against the results of these studies is that women were extremely reluctant to agree to sex or to go back to a man's apartment because they felt a sense of danger.[48] Men, after all, are more dangerous than women, as women are certainly aware. One recent study attempted to test for a danger effect and found that a sense of danger was of marginal significance.[49] Moreover, Hald and Høgh-Olesen point out that 21 percent of the women in their sample who were not in a relationship agreed to go to the man's apartment even though none would agree to sex. The authors believe that this essentially neutralizes the danger argument because the sense of danger for a woman should be just as great for agreeing to go to a man's apartment as for consenting to sex.

In the early 1990s two evolutionary psychologists designed an index they called the Sociosexual Orientation Inventory, or SOI.[50] The SOI is intended to measure an orientation toward unrestricted versus restricted sexuality. Unrestricted sexuality involves an interest in sex outside of marriage or a committed relationship, a high degree of sexual fantasizing, and a strong interest in casual sex. Restricted sexuality involves more interest in monogamous relationships, in long-term courtships, and in a high level of relationship commitment. The higher someone's score on the SOI, the more that person is oriented toward unrestricted sex.

An extremely comprehensive study looking at gender differences in SOI scores was carried out in 2000 by David Schmitt of Bradley University and a bevy of research assistants.[51] There were over 14,000 subjects from forty-eight nations representing every region of the world: three countries from North America, four from South America, eight from Western Europe, eleven from Eastern Europe, five from Southern Europe, four from North Africa and the Middle East, four from East Asia, two from South and Southeast Asia, four from sub-Saharan Africa, and three from

Oceania. For all forty-eight countries combined, the average SOI score for males was 46.7 and for females 27.3. The average SOI score for the United States was 48.0 for males and 29.2 for females, extremely close to the overall average. Some individual countries revealed much larger discrepancies. In Bolivia males scored 61.5 and females 21.9, in Bangladesh the respective scores were 31.1 and 11.8, in Morocco the scores were 65.6 and 20.1, in the Philippines they were 51.2 and 18.0, and in Turkey men scored 54.1 and women 21.7. In every nation men's SOI score exceeded women's, usually by a wide margin.[52]

But Schmitt also found an important role for socioecological context, especially the status of women. The five societies with large gender disparities mentioned above are all ones in which the status of women is relatively low. Schmitt looked at the relationship between the male-female discrepancy and an index of gender empowerment, finding a high correlation.[53] In societies with higher gender empowerment scores, the male-female discrepancy was smaller. For example, in Finland, where women have higher status than in almost every other society in the world, the male SOI score was 64.0 and the female score 41.6. In Germany the male score was 46.4, the female score 34.4. In Switzerland the scores were 45.3 and 34.3, and in Latvia they were 49.4 and 41.7.[54] Women have a higher status in Europe than in any other world region, and they appear to respond to their higher status by expressing their sexuality more freely.

As we will see later, males in all societies wish to control female sexuality. However, they are more successful in some societies than in others. Where women's status is low, men have more power to place restrictions on women's sexual behavior than where women's status is high. In modern societies, the status of women is higher than ever before in human history, and it is here that the male-female SOI discrepancy tends to be smallest.

Multiple Partners

A massive amount of research, as well as observational and anecdotal evidence, indicates that males have a stronger, perhaps much stronger, desire for multiple sex partners and sexual variety than females. The SOI contains two questions designed to assess these interests, but Schmitt carried out a separate study to look at them in greater detail. This study used the same set of subjects, but in this case fifty-two nations and more than 16,000 subjects were available for analysis. Subjects were asked a variety of questions. One concerned the number of sexual partners they desired for both short-term and long-term mating. Men indicated a desire for an average of 2.63 partners within the next six months compared to 0.99 for women. For average number of desired partners within the next year, the male-female discrepancy was greater, 3.36 for men and 1.18 for women. The discrepancy increased as the period of time increased. Within the next five years men desired an average of 5.64 partners, women 1.95. For the next twenty years, men wanted 6.40 partners, women 2.34. In essence, men desire almost three times as many partners as women.

Schmitt also tabulated the percentage of men and women who reported wanting more than one sex partner at any time. The overall average was 27 percent for men and 7 percent for women. The difference was much larger for subjects who were strongly seeking multiple partners only for short-term mating. For these subjects, 54 percent of men and only 19 percent of women indicated a strong desire for multiple short-term mates.[55]

Despite lower SOI scores, women of course do have sexual affairs—what evolutionary psychologists like to call *extrapair copulations*—and to a greater extent than is often imagined. Nevertheless, they are still less likely to have an extrapair copulation than men, as well as less likely to have many. Moreover, there is an important gender difference in the conscious motivation for extrapair relationships. Men, it seems, are looking mainly for sex, whereas women are much more likely to value an extrapair relationship *as a relationship* and to use sex as a means of establishing and cementing it. Women often seek extrapair liaisons because of dissatisfaction with their committed romantic relationships.[56]

However, in recent years it has been learned that women are more likely to engage in extrapair copulations during their fertile period, and these copulations do have a sexual and not just a romantic element. During their fertile periods women appear to show a preference for men who display indicators of high genetic quality. If women who mate with high quality men become pregnant, they may acquire better genes for future offspring than they are able to obtain with their current mates.[57]

Visual Sexual Stimuli

Although not studied by Schmitt, we know from a huge amount of evidence that men everywhere appear to be much more aroused by visual sexual stimuli than women. In Western societies the male market for pornography is enormous, but the female market is so small as to be virtually nonexistent. Today there are countless pornographic magazines, videos, and Internet sites; it is overwhelmingly men who are looking at this pornography. Many of the men who view pornography are married or have steady girlfriends, but their continued interest in porn indicates that they never outgrow their desire to look at women's bodies, as many different bodies as possible. Only a tiny fraction of women express any interest in pornography.[58] In the 1970s a pornographic magazine showing naked male bodies, *Playgirl*, was launched to a female market. However, very few women bought it, and 95 percent of its patrons turned out to be gay men. This was the only way the magazine was able to avoid shutting down its presses.

Pornography is hardly limited to Western industrial societies. Indeed, it is found in societies of every type and is likely a cultural universal. And it is strikingly similar in content wherever it is found. As Catherine Salmon points out,

> The utopian male fantasy realm depicted in pornography . . . has remained essentially unchanged through time and space. Pornographic

works survive from many ancient cultures, from ancient Greek vase paintings to the wall paintings of Pompeii brothels to Renaissance sculptures. They differ little in their essential nature or design from modern pornographic magazines or movies.[59]

It is sometimes argued that women in fact do like looking at naked male bodies as long as they are filmed or otherwise depicted in ways different from the depiction of naked female bodies in male-oriented pornography. Women often enjoy "soft pornography," such as films depicting couples making love. However, it is the love making that interests women, not the naked male body in and of itself.

What is the evolutionary logic underlying the male interest in pornography? Because it is obviously a product of the male desire for multiple partners, it can be argued that the more naked female bodies men look at, the more sexually aroused they will become and the more partners they will seek out. This will then increase their reproductive success. This would be an ultimate explanation in terms of how selection operated in the ancestral environment. Of course, in modern environments evolutionary adaptations may no longer be (or may not always be) adaptive. Men just like to look at the naked bodies of women whether they do anything about it or not. In this regard, men might be using pornography as a type of compromise between their own sexual desires and their desire to maintain commitment to their long-term partners. This would make pornography a kind of outlet or safety valve. Obviously this is a proximate rather than an ultimate explanation.

Sexual Jealousy

Then there is the related matter of sexual jealousy. According to the evolutionary psychologist David Buss, men not only place an extremely high value on fidelity in their wives or girlfriends, but rate infidelity as the least desirable characteristic in a mate. His research shows that unfaithfulness is more upsetting to men than any other emotional pain women can inflict on them.[60] From the standpoint of a man's reproductive success, one of the worst things that can happen to him is to be *cuckolded* by his mate—to be led by her to believe that her offspring fathered by another man are really his. If a man has been cuckolded and doesn't know it, he ends up promoting the other man's reproductive success and undermining his own. For men, cuckoldry is bad. Very bad. To combat it males have evolved techniques of protecting their mates from encroachments by other males. Sexual jealousy is the first line of defense.[61]

The sexual jealousy found among males everywhere is a sure indication that males regard females as possessions. Throughout the world's societies there is remarkable consistency in the view that sexual intercourse between a married woman and someone who is not her husband is a violation; the victim is the husband, who is entitled to compensation. Many societies punish adulterous women severely. A jealous rage is expected in many societies as the result of this offense against a husband. Adultery by a wife is perhaps the single-most common reason for divorce throughout the world, and the leading cause of male aggression against women.[62]

A number of scholars and social and political commentators have insisted that there are societies in which jealousy is not found and where both sexes are allowed a great deal of sexual freedom outside marriage.[63] However, careful scrutiny of these claims shows that they almost always fail to hold up.[64] Many of the societies that have been said to permit adultery tend to do so only under very restrictive circumstances. In nearly every society that has been characterized as unusually sexually permissive, men were actually found not only to restrict the sexual freedom of their wives but to use or threaten violence in doing so. In the 1960s the idea emerged that sexual jealousy was just a "hang-up" of people in modern societies. People should practice "free love." But this idea was utterly fanciful and disappeared within a decade. Some people still promote free love and engage in it themselves, but they are only a tiny segment of any population. And many who have tried it have found that it didn't work out as expected, and they soon abandoned it. Sexual jealousy of husbands toward wives is an extremely powerful, hard-wired emotion and almost certainly a human universal.

What then of female jealousy? Men's jealousy appears to be stronger, and it seems to be easier for a wife to forgive her husband than for him to forgive her. Indeed, women in many societies are reconciled to the adulterous affairs of their husbands. Nevertheless, there is plenty of female jealousy, and it is just as much an evolutionary adaptation as male jealousy. Philandering men can impose high costs on their wives or lovers. An unfaithful man may leave his wife for another woman, and thus the wife loses the resources her husband has been providing for her and her offspring. In the ancestral environment, women were often critically dependent on such male provisioning.[65]

Several studies have shown important and highly predictable sex differences in jealousy. One study found that 60 percent of the males reported more distress over sexual infidelity than over their mates' emotional attachment to a rival. By contrast, only 17 percent of women indicated they would be more distressed over sexual rather than romantic infidelity, and an extremely large 83 percent indicated they would be more upset over their mates' emotional attachment to someone else.[66] Another study found even greater sex differences. Of the males, 73 percent said they would be more upset over sexual infidelity, but only 4 percent of the females said this would be more upsetting. A huge 96 percent of females expressed far more distress over emotional infidelity compared to only 27 percent of males.[67] Although these results pertain to American subjects, very similar results have been reported from studies in China, Korea, Japan, Germany, the Netherlands, and Sweden.[68]

At least two studies have measured men's and women's physiological arousal to imagined sexual and emotional infidelity. In the first, men showed much more arousal (agitation) with respect to sexual infidelity, whereas women showed just the opposite—more agitation with respect to emotional infidelity—and this difference was large.[69] In the second study, subjects were measured for several indicators of emotional response, and there were very large sex differences in so-called surface electromyographic activity (EMG). Males showed a pronounced elevation in EMG in response to an experimenter's instruction to imagine a partner engaged in sexual intercourse with another man, but there was no EMG increase when they were asked to imagine emotional infidelity. Females showed a large increase in EMG when told to think about a partner's emotional infidelity, but no increase when considering a partner's sexual unfaithfulness.[70]

However, studies such as these (there are many more) have been criticized on two grounds. One is methodological. The charge is made that many studies have not measured emotional reactions in an appropriate way, and thus the results are subject to doubt. The second criticism is that most of the studies assess only responses to hypothetical infidelities, not responses to actual infidelities. Therefore, Brad Sagarin and several colleagues reanalyzed forty studies designed to evaluate these criticisms. They found that the type of measurement scale did not affect the outcome. They also compared studies that assessed hypothetical infidelities to those that assessed actual infidelities. Once again, there were no significant differences between the studies. The results were essentially the same regardless of the type of infidelity being studied.[71]

Men are concerned with acquiring and controlling mates and preventing other men from inseminating them. This is why they find sexual infidelity more disturbing than emotional infidelity. Women, on the other hand, are more upset by emotional infidelity because they seek mates who will be reliable providers. Emotional attachment or bonding is what solidifies such a relationship, and so women will be more concerned about anything that threatens the emotional bond.

Evolved Sexual Strategies

All of the findings discussed above are highly consistent with a Darwinian view of sex differences in mating strategies. Greater male sociosexuality is an evolutionary adaptation that promotes male reproductive success. Greater sexual urgency, more interest in short-term mating and anonymous sex, a greater desire for multiple partners, more sexual fantasies, more interest in pornography, and so on lead to more sex and more potential inseminations. From the female side of the aisle, women's brains have been selected for a more cautious and discriminating approach to sex because, as we will see, they are primarily looking for males who will be reliable providers for, and strong protectors of, them and their children.[72] There is no evolutionary advantage to a female to have a very large number of sexual partners, or to be visually aroused by the sight of naked males. No matter how many males she may mate with, a woman can produce only a very small number of offspring in her lifetime.

Schmitt's findings are extremely important because they show that men and women adopt different evolutionarily predictable mating strategies in every society studied. Not one of the fifty-two societies Schmitt studied displayed a male-female difference inconsistent with a Darwinian view of human sexuality. And the finding that people adjust their mating strategies to socioecological context is also very much in line with Darwinian expectations. Humans have basic biological predispositions that are expressed in different ways as the context changes.

But it is crucial to separate proximate from ultimate causes. The male desire for more sex and the female desire for more intimacy in extrapair copulations are proximate causes of their behavior, but these causes must have evolutionary foundations. What men and women consciously seek and what their evolved brains are telling them to seek are two different things. Even though the evolutionary advantage to men for extrapair copulations is greater reproductive success, you may be thinking that in modern societies the last thing men want is for their extrapair mates to become pregnant; such an outcome can complicate their lives enormously. Surely, then, modern men cannot be seeking extrapair sex in order to increase their number of offspring. This is undeniably true, but the human brain evolved in ancestral environments, not modern ones, and modern and ancestral environments differ in important ways. In ancestral environments in which contraception was frequently unreliable and marriages or mating partnerships often broke up easily, it may not have been especially problematic for a man to impregnate his extrapair mates. Indeed, in terms of pure reproductive success, it was advantageous.

More to the point, however, is that men are not seeking extrapair copulations *in any society* because of a conscious desire to leave more offspring. What they are seeking is *sexual pleasure*, which is the proximate cause of their behavior. This desire for pleasure is an evolutionary adaptation whose ultimate cause is its reproductive advantages in typical human societies. The same kind of logic holds for women. Even though women may experience increased sexual desire and be more likely to seek extrapair copulations during their fertile periods, they seldom have a conscious desire to be impregnated by their extrapair mates. An extrapair pregnancy will complicate a woman's life at least as much as a man's. But, again, what people want or do not want is on the surface level. This is important, of course, but evolutionarily speaking what really counts is what is going on at the unconscious level deep inside the brain. The human brain did not evolve to figure itself out. If it did, there would be little need for anthropologists, psychologists, and sociologists.

Mate Choice

In humans both forms of sexual selection, male combat and female choice, are operating, but there is something else as well: *male choice*. Because human males are attracted to the physical and sexual ornaments of females, humans are the odd man out among species.[73] In the vast majority of species in which choice is more important than combat, it is the male that possesses ornaments and the female that chooses. Of course, this does not eliminate female choice in humans; it simply creates two sets of choices instead of one. On what basis do men and women make their choices? What are men and women looking for in the opposite sex?

Male Choice: Attractiveness

It should hardly come as a surprise to anyone that for males female attractiveness plays a major role in mate choice. Other things being equal, men seek the most beautiful and sexually attractive women. Research has shown that the most beautiful women are those whose facial dimensions are in every respect average. The most beautiful women have the entire combination of average noses, ears, mouths, lips, chins, foreheads, and so on. (The one exception is cheek bones. Women with high cheek bones are judged more attractive than women with average cheek bones.) Women are judged less attractive to the extent that these facial dimensions depart from the average, and especially if they are highly exaggerated. Thus women whose eyes are set too far apart or too close together, who have unusually large noses or unusually small ones, whose chins jut out, or whose ears stick out will be judged less attractive. Even the departure from average of a single facial dimension results in a loss of perceived beauty. Facial symmetry is another important dimension of judgments of attractiveness. Women with more symmetrical faces are deemed more attractive than women with less symmetrical faces.[74]

Many modern social critics contend that the male preference for highly attractive women is not an innate male desire but a product of modern Western culture. In her book *The Beauty Myth*, Naomi Wolf goes so far as to say that the emphasis on beauty is a modern social construction designed to reinforce male domination.[75] It is frequently claimed that the emphasis on female beauty has nothing to do with male biology but rather images promoted by the mass media. Both men and women learn from the media that these qualities are extremely important and thus come to value them. The media are simply imposing their own standards on the rest of the population.

These arguments are fatally flawed for several reasons. In terms of the proposed role of the media, the argument begs the question as to why the media would have adopted a cultural standard of beauty in the first place. The media are not some sort of institution existing outside the framework of the societies in which they perform their work. The real story is that the media reflect standards that already exist in society.[76] For media to be successful, they have to be in touch with the kinds of symbols and images people like. Beautiful women are common in the media because people, including other women, naturally like looking at beautiful women.

The claim that the emphasis on beauty is unique to modern Western culture is, fortunately, empirically testable. To show that it is false—and indeed it is—researchers have presented evidence showing that the preference for beauty is widespread in the world's societies and possibly even universal. There have been numerous studies, but one of the most comprehensive and informative has been carried out by Jonathan Gottschall and a large team of research assistants. Their study examined the content of folktales from the entire range of nonindustrial societies representing all of the major regions of the world.[77] Ninety collections of folktales were examined totaling over 16,000 single-spaced pages and more than 8 million words.

Gottschall's group first calculated the number of references to the attractiveness of female versus male characters. For all world regions taken together, there were twice as many references to the attractiveness of female characters than to the attractiveness of male characters. However, the researchers considered this figure a substantial underestimate of the importance given to female attractiveness because there were three times as many male characters as female characters. For this reason they multiplied the two numbers (2 and 3) in order to ascertain the relative likelihood that female characters would be described as attractive compared to male characters (assuming an equal number of characters of each sex). For the entire sample this number is 6, which can be expressed as the ratio 6:1—female characters are six times as likely to be described as attractive as male characters. The corresponding likelihood ratios for the other world regions are shown in Table 5.1. As can be seen, for the separate regions the ratios vary from 3.9 to 8.8. Female beauty is most strongly emphasized in Europe (with a ratio of 8.8), but aboriginal Australia and Japan are just barely behind (ratios of 8.7 and 8.5, respectively), and Oceania and the Middle East not far behind them (ratios of 7.5 and 7.4, respectively). And it makes little difference whether the folktales come from small-scale bands and tribes or large-scale agrarian societies. All emphasize female beauty to about the same extent.[78] It is therefore not just in modern Western societies that attractiveness in a female is considered important. Attractiveness is obviously important in every type of society in every part of the world.

But if female beauty matters throughout the world, why does it matter? It seems that there is a significant correlation between beauty and genetic quality, what is often called "good genes." Research shows that deviations from facial averageness may be indicators of chromosomal abnormalities, congenital deformities, and various diseases.[79] Fluctuating asymmetry—random departures from bilateral symmetry—has been shown to be predictive of poor skin condition, back pain, breast cancer, neurocognitive performance, such mental disorders as depression and schizophrenia and, perhaps most importantly, parasite infestation.[80] Symmetrical faces are correlated with resistance to parasites that cause various infectious diseases, such as rabies, plague, hantavirus, Dengue fever, measles, cholera, and malaria.[81] High levels of facial averageness and symmetry are difficult to achieve in women who have low resistance to parasites. (The same holds for men. As the discussion of female choice later in this chapter shows, men with low parasite resistance also have difficulty achieving facial averageness and symmetry.) Thus men in effect have evolved to prefer average and highly symmetrical faces because in doing so they are choosing women in very good health, or what is sometimes called "superior condition."[82] (This is akin to the large, beautiful tails of peacocks.) Condition, in turn, predicts high levels of female fecundity (the ability of a woman to conceive) and greater

TABLE 5.1 References to Female and Male Attractiveness in World Folktales

Region	Ratio
All	6.0
Hunter-Gatherers and Horticulturalists	5.5
Agrarian Societies	7.1
Europe	8.8
Aboriginal Australia	8.7
Japan	8.5
Oceania	7.5
Middle East	7.4
Northwest Coast Indians	5.9
Africa	5.8
Arctic Coast	4.9
North American Indians	4.8
South American Indians	4.7
Maya Indians	4.0
India	3.9

Source: Jonathan Gottschall et al., "The 'beauty myth' is no myth: Emphasis on male-female attractiveness in world folktales," *Human Nature* 19 (2008):174–188.

reproductive success for the male who chooses such a mate (and, of course, for the female mate herself).

And recent research bears out this prediction. Lena Pflüger and colleagues studied seventy-six post-menopausal women in a rural community in Austria. One hundred and twenty-five male students from the University of Vienna rated photographs of the women for their level of attractiveness when they were in young adulthood (19–23 years of age). The researchers found a sizable correlation between a woman's attractiveness rating and the number of pregnancies she had had in her lifetime.[83] Objective measures of the women's degree of facial symmetry were also substantially correlated with their number of lifetime pregnancies.

Male Choice: Youth

Males everywhere show a strong desire for younger females. Evidence from many nonindustrial societies shows that as men get older the age gap between them and their mates increases.[84] On the island of Poro, for example, the age gap between the youngest husbands and their mates was less than one year, whereas the gap between the oldest husbands and their mates was nearly twenty-one years.[85] David

Buss conducted a massive study of over 10,000 individuals from thirty-seven so-cieties and cultures.[86] The study's subjects were located on six different continents, came from both rural and urban areas, and represented a wide range of socio-economic levels. Buss found that in every society men showed a preference for younger mates, and that they took on younger and younger mates whenever they were able to do so. He also found that the age gap between men and their wives or lovers was larger in societies with higher levels of male power.[87] The more power men have relative to women the easier it is for men to realize their preferences.

This desire for younger females is without doubt an evolved mating strategy. Younger females are more likely to become pregnant and to produce strong, healthy offspring. They also have a longer reproductive period ahead of them than do older women, and thus men who mate with younger women can produce more off-spring.[88] A well-known study of 774 Hungarian males found that males who chose younger mates had significantly more surviving children than those who chose older mates.[89] Other studies show similar results.

The preference for younger women is also indicated by studies of what biolo-gists call *neoteny*, or the retention of juvenile characteristics in adults. Everyone knows that infants and small children are cute, which is attributable to relatively large eyes, a short distance from mouth to chin, a small nose, and full lips. Many women partially retain these characteristics as they mature into adolescence and adulthood, and there seems to be a strong male attraction to such traits. A study in the 1990s examined the faces of ten leading female models whose pictures had been displayed on the covers of *Cosmopolitan* and *Glamour* magazines. Measure-ments of facial features were made and entered into a computer. A software program designed to estimate the models' ages based only on these features indicated that they were approximately seven years old! When the study was repeated using male models, no facial neoteny was found, and the computer predicted the models to be approximately their actual ages.[90] It is perhaps important to add that modern men are not attracted to seven-year-old girls. They are attracted to women *some of whose features* resemble those of seven-year-olds.

Women are acutely aware of the male preference for youth and go to consider-able effort to make themselves appear young, especially as they age. In Western soci-eties there is a multibillion dollar cosmetics industry that provides women with the means to do so. Geoffrey Miller highlights some of the most important cosmetics women use, how they use them, and what they use them for:[91]

- Eye size, whiteness, and contrast start to decline around age twenty-five, and women use eyeliner, mascara, and brow pencils to make their eyes look larger. (Large eyes are a neotenous feature.)
- The fullness and redness of the lips decline after about twenty-five, so women use lip color, lip gloss, and lip plumper to make their lips appear fuller and brighter. (Full, red lips are neotenous and also good fertility indicators.)

- Women's cheekbones usually shrink as they age, and they use blush to highlight cheekbones and make them appear the same size. (Men are highly attracted to women with prominent cheekbones, which appear to signal femininity.)
- The thickness and glossiness of the hair decline with age, and so women use products that increase hair volume and enhance glossiness. (Thick, glossy hair signals youth.)

Critics of the claim that the male preference for youth is an evolutionary adaptation contend, just as they do in the case of the preference for beauty, that the emphasis on youth is a Western cultural phenomenon, again promoted by the mass media. But women in societies and cultures all over the world are well aware of the effects of aging on men's attraction to them, and use cosmetic ingredients similar to modern Western ingredients to try to maintain a youthful appearance. As Geoffrey Miller points out,

> Cosmetic choices are much less culturally arbitrary than they appear at first glance. Ancient Egyptians may have used kohl rather than liquid eyeliner to increase apparent eye size, red ochre rather than blush to increase cheek redness, and mesdemet (ground copper and lead ore) rather than foundation to make their complexions look more uniform. Yet in each case, they sought to increase rather than decrease the facial cues of estrogenization, youthful sexual maturity, and fertility. Across cultures, people have used different cosmetic ingredients, pigments, colors, and bases, and different cosmetic application methods, styles, and patterns. Yet I cannot find any cases in which cosmetics have been widely used by women in a culture to give an impression of small, jaundiced eyes, pale thin lips, or wrinkled, pockmarked skin.[92]

The average Western woman may well use more youth-enhancing cosmetics than the average woman in earlier societies (although not necessarily more than elite women of the past). But this is merely a modern cultural amplification of an innate desire.

Male Choice: Body Shape

Devendra Singh and his colleagues have carried out a variety of fascinating studies in which they show that the most important dimension of the attractiveness of the female body is the ratio of the waist (at its smallest point) to the hips (at their widest point). In Singh's original study, twelve line drawings were made of women who varied by both waist-to-hip ratio (WHR) and body weight. There were four drawings for each of three body weight categories, normal weight, underweight, and overweight. For each weight category, WHR varied from .70 to 1.0. All of the drawings can be seen in Figure 5.1. The authors showed the drawings to 106 white and Hispanic male undergraduate students who were asked to rate them in terms of attractiveness, sexiness, and health. Drawings N7, U7, and N8 were rated highest, drawings O8, O9, and O10 lowest. Drawing N7 was far and away the top choice. In each weight category, the lower the WHR the higher the rating. Approximately 70 percent of the subjects preferred a .70 WHR, and 20 percent a .80 WHR. In sum, the findings show that men use both WHR and body weight as indicators of female attractiveness, sexiness, and health, but WHR is more important than body weight.[93]

In a second part of the study, Singh sought to determine whether older men would rate female body attractiveness in the same way as the college undergraduates. Here eighty-nine white men between the ages of twenty-five and eighty-five, representing a wide range of educational backgrounds and socioeconomic statuses, were asked to judge the drawings. The results were extremely similar. As in the case of the eighteen- to twenty-two-year-old undergraduates, older men strongly preferred drawing N7 and, in general, rated drawings with lower WHR more favorably than drawings with higher WHR.

What explains the strong male preference for women with low WHR? In Darwinian terms, low WHR is an excellent indicator of female reproductive status and overall health.[94] Girls with a lower WHR show earlier pubertal endocrine activity, and in adult women lower WHR is associated with a lower incidence of such diseases as diabetes, high blood pressure, heart attack, stroke, menstrual irregularity, elevated plasma triglycerides, and ovarian and breast cancer. Married women with a higher WHR have more difficulty getting pregnant and give birth to their first child at a later age.[95] As women age, their WHR increases, and after menopause women's WHR approximates that of men. Singh suggests that human males the world over are descended from ancestral males who maximized their reproductive success by mating with low-WHR females.[96]

The male preference for females with a low WHR is widespread and probably universal. Studies have been conducted in a wide range of societies with supportive results, including the United States, England, Germany, New Zealand, India, Indonesia, Hong Kong, Papua New Guinea, Samoa, Guinea-Bissau, and Cameroon.[97] Moreover, one ingenious study collected evidence on female attractiveness as depicted in 286 sculptures from ancient India, Egypt, Greece, and Africa, finding an average female WHR of about .70.[98] The same study also reported that poetry from the European Middle Ages emphasized small waists, and that Chinese and Indian poetry both in earlier times and today gives much more emphasis to waist size than to breasts, thighs, and legs.

But there are some apparently contradictory findings. A study of American undergraduates by Tassinary and Hansen reported that men judged drawings with higher WHRs to be more attractive than those with lower WHRs.[99] However, in this study the authors used different line drawings than those designed by Singh and used in all previous research. In their new drawings, Tassinary and Hansen confounded WHR with both hip size and perceived body weight, which caused

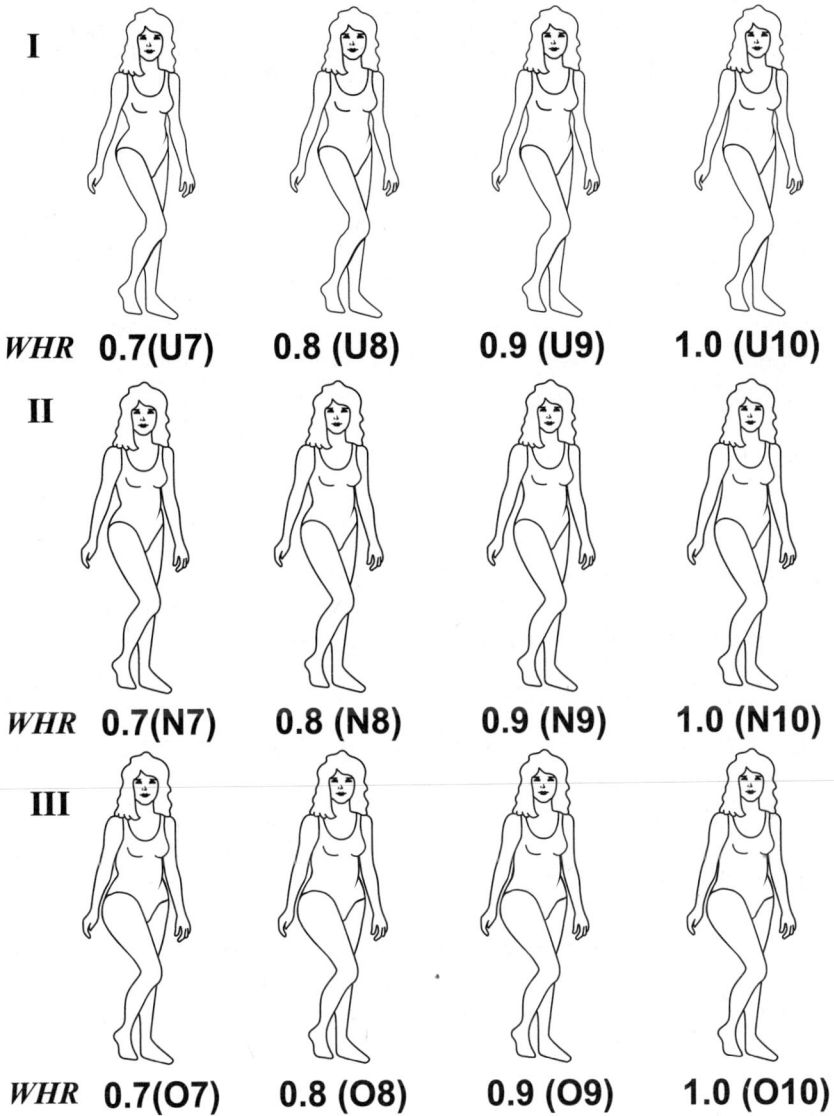

FIGURE 5.1 Waist-to-Hip Ratios and Body Weight

Source: Devendra Singh, "Adaptive significance of female physical attractiveness: Role of waist-to-hip ratio," *Journal of Personality and Social Psychology* 65 (1993):293–307. © American Psychological Association.

drawings with low WHRs to be judged as much as twenty pounds heavier and fourteen years older than drawings with high WHRs.[100] Since American men judge younger and thinner women to be more attractive than older and heavier women, it is unsurprising that they would judge the drawings with lower WHRs more negatively. When Tassinary and Hansen's drawings were properly corrected, men judged WHRs of about .70 to be more attractive.[101]

Some studies of forager and horticultural societies have found a male preference for WHRs higher than .70, sometimes considerably higher.[102] However, small-scale subsistence societies differ from modern societies in that body fat is an important indicator of mate value, primarily because such societies often suffer from periodic food shortages. And body fat is positively correlated with WHR: more body fat means a higher WHR. In his research on the Shiwiar, a foraging-horticultural society in the Ecuadorian rain forest, Lawrence Sugiyama found that men assess attractiveness and reproductive value according to both WHR and body fat. Shiwiar men give more positive ratings to women with higher WHRs. But because body fat and WHR are positively correlated, Sugiyama adjusted the drawings shown to Shiwiar men for the amount of body fat. When they viewed the adjusted drawings, men preferred lower WHRs more than twice as often as higher WHRs.[103] The proper conclusion seems to be that Shiwiar men prefer lower WHRs, *other things being equal.*

A study of the Hadza found that men preferred WHRs in the .90–1.00 range.[104] In this study, as in all others, WHR was measured and depicted frontally. But because Hadza women have unusually protruding buttocks, the evolutionary scientists Marlowe, Apicella, and Reed considered it more appropriate to depict their WHRs in profile. New drawings were made and shown to forty-seven Hadza men (drawings for five different WHRs are shown in Figure 5.2A). The men not only preferred a low WHR, but a ratio considerably lower than .70. When rating female attractiveness, more Hadza men (33 percent) chose a .60 ratio than any other. A .65 ratio was chosen by 20 percent of Hadza men, and an extremely low ratio of .55 by 17 percent. The authors also asked a group of ninety-four American men to rate the same drawings (slightly altered for skin color, hair color, and hair style; see Figure 5.2B). They found that 54 percent of the men preferred a .65 ratio, 20 percent a .60 ratio, and another 20 percent a .70 ratio.[105]

Clearly, then, Hadza men are not an exception. Indeed, they prefer a remarkably low profile WHR. Moreover, American men prefer a lower ratio than .70 when WHR is depicted in profile. In addition to low WHR, males in general prefer females with high lordosis—protrusion or curvature of the buttocks. Lordosis is more easily detected in profile WHRs than in frontal WHRs, so Marlowe and colleagues' drawings also depicted women's degree of lordosis.[106]

Bear in mind also that average body shapes vary from one type of society to another. Among the Shiwiar and Hadza, the average woman's WHR is higher than it is for women in modern societies. The normal WHR range for Shiwiar women is .81 to 1.02, whereas for Western women it is .68 to .80. Sugiyama and Marlowe both

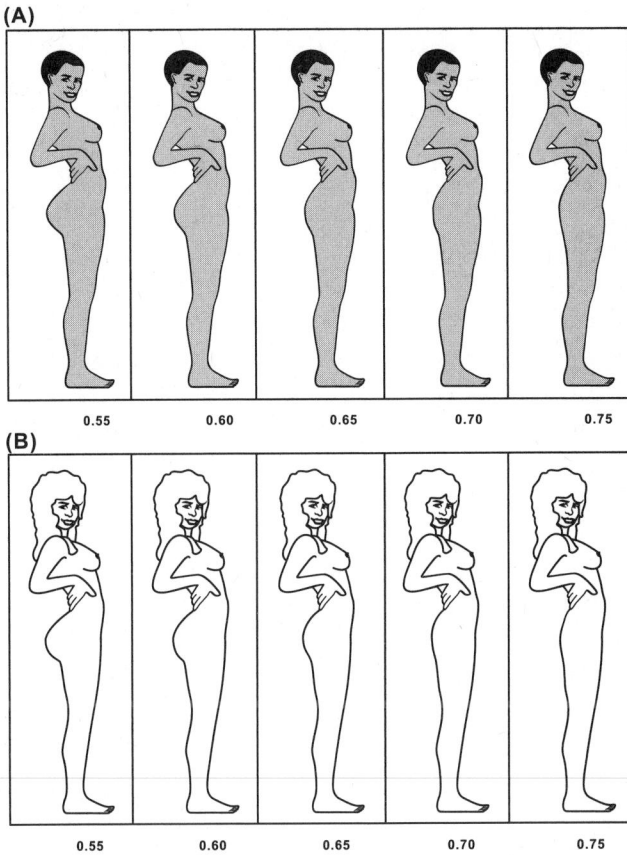

FIGURE 5.2 Five Waist-to-Hip Ratios in Profile for Two Populations

Source: Frank W. Marlowe, Coren Apicella, and Dorian Reed, "Men's preferences for women's profile waist-to-hip ratio in two societies," *Evolution and Human Behavior* 26 (2005):458–468. © Elsevier Publishing Co., Ltd. Reprinted by permission of the publisher.

make the point that studies of WHR must take into account these local variations because cues for good mates are environmentally sensitive. Marlowe et al. took buttock protrusion into account for the Hadza by looking at profile WHR; Sugiyama took body fat into account for the Shiwiar.

Research on the Machiguenga, a South American tribe, shows that men who have had little or no contact with Westerners prefer higher WHRs, but those who have frequently interacted with Westerners prefer lower WHRs.[107] Why should this be? It seems that men exposed to Western women notice that their average WHR is lower than the average WHR for Machiguenga women. Males may therefore be judging mate value in terms of the population averages that are familiar to them, which may function as good cues to mate value.

In 2010 Perilloux, Webster, and Gaulin looked at judgments of female body attractiveness made by 140 American male undergraduates, who were shown photographs of nude women from the back.[108] In addition to WHR, the authors looked at the effects of fluctuating asymmetry (FA) and body mass index (BMI, the ratio of height to weight). As noted earlier, research has shown that symmetrical faces are judged more attractive because FA is an indicator of poor genetic condition. Previous research also shows that high BMI is judged less attractive (as Singh found). Like low FA, low BMI is also a cue to health, at least in modern societies. The authors found that all three variables were highly negatively correlated with attractiveness ratings, meaning that low WHR, low FA, and low BMI were judged much more attractive. And there was a strong interaction effect between WHR and FA. Men rated women who had both low WHR and low FA 8.68 (on a 10-point scale), but rated women with both high WHR and high FA only 3.14. Men gave in-between ratings when one of the variables was low and the other high.

Low female WHR and high lordosis are part of a complex of traits known as *female fat deposition*. Females have both gynoid and android fat, or "female fat" and "male fat." Android fat is deposited in the trunk and abdomen, whereas gynoid fat is stored in the thighs, hips, buttocks, and breasts. As girls reach puberty large amounts of gynoid fat are deposited in these areas of their bodies. Gynoid fat is necessary to support reproduction. Men are attracted to breasts and buttocks just as they are to faces. Small breasts tend to be disfavored, as do excessively large ones that sag. Round, firm buttocks are considered highly attractive, whereas flatter or excessively large and fatty buttocks are not.[109] In what is probably the only study (or at least the first study) to look at the waist size–breast size combination, Jasieńska and colleagues found that women who had both low WHR and large breasts were about two to three times as likely as women with other combinations to get pregnant, as assessed by the levels of specific hormones influencing the likelihood of conception.[110] Here at last we seem to have an explanation for the male fascination with large breasts! And an explanation for attraction to buttocks too.

It is important not to give the impression that male judgments of female bodies are simply a matter of how the male brain is wired. Here, as elsewhere, socioecological context matters.[111] Yet although cultural differences in standards of attractiveness can be found, they cannot take just any form. Other things being equal, no standards should be found that directly undermine female efforts to attract males and male efforts to mate with females of high reproductive value. For example, in most nonindustrial societies and as recently as the nineteenth century in Western societies, plumpness in a female was regarded more favorably than it is today. Go look at paintings by, for example, Dutch masters of the sixteenth, seventeenth, and eighteenth centuries. Where nude or seminude females are depicted, they are almost always much plumper than women are depicted today. We live in a world in which thinness rather than plumpness is more highly valued.

But this change is not just an arbitrary cultural shift; even here innate predispositions are clearly at work. Plumpness was highly valued in a society in which food was much scarcer than it is today. It was mostly people of higher status who were plump because they had much more food to eat, and it was the lower classes who were apt to be thin. Now it is those of lower status who tend to be heavier and those of higher status who are more likely to be thin. And whereas plumpness was once a sign of good health, good health is now signified by thinness (although not excessive thinness). The change is understandable in terms of both an innate status psychology—once everyone had enough food to be plump, "the rich began to distinguish themselves through thinness"—and an innate male sexual psychology—desire most those women who are the healthiest.[112]

Female Choice: Status and Resources

In selecting mates men have been highly motivated to find numerous mates and to find mates who are the most reproductively valuable.[113] We have already seen these motivations playing themselves out in men's desire for casual sex, for physically attractive females with a certain type of body shape, for young females, and for mates with a sufficiently strong commitment such that they are unlikely to engage in cuckoldry. What then of female choice? What do women seek in a mate?

Buss and Schmitt indicate that women's mating strategies have focused on solving several main adaptive problems. The most important of these include:[114]

- Finding men who are *able* to invest resources in them and their children
- Finding men who are *willing* to invest resources in them and their children
- Finding men who display signs of commitment to a long-term relationship
- Finding men who are capable of protecting them from harm, especially as the result of aggression directed against them by other men

With respect to the first two adaptive problems, research has shown again and again that women give primary emphasis to a man's status and resources. In Buss's study of thirty-seven societies referred to earlier, women were found to be about twice as likely as men to give importance to a partner's economic resources, and women were more desirous than men of a high-status partner. As Buss notes, "Social status is a universal cue to the control of resources. Along with status come better food, more abundant territory, and superior health care."[115] Women shun men, he says, who can be easily dominated by other men or do not command the respect of the group. Interestingly, women who themselves have high status and considerable economic resources do not relax their desire for high-status and resource-rich men. Indeed, evidence suggests that such women still prefer men who have more status and resources than they do.[116]

In a study of forty-two college women, Buss and Schmitt gave the participants a list of male characteristics and asked them to evaluate them as desirable or undesirable as both short-term and long-term mates.[117] Women rated as especially desirable the traits "good financial prospects," "likely to succeed in a profession," and "a reliable future career." They rated as especially undesirable "unable to support you financially," "financially poor," "lacks ambition," and "uneducated." Women rated the negative traits as substantially more undesirable when considering long-term versus short-term mating.

In an especially interesting study, Kenrick, Sadalla, Groth, and Trost attempted to determine the degree of selectivity in the mate choice of women compared to men.[118] They asked a sample of ninety-three college students to indicate the minimum criteria they would accept in a mate. Each student was asked to rate a particular trait in terms of a percentile from 0 to 100. The results are shown in Table 5.2. What do they mean? Basically, that women are much choosier than men, especially when it comes to status and resources, and that they become even choosier the more intimate or committed the relationship. Looking just at marriage, the college women indicated that they would not accept a man unless he was at least as powerful as 45 percent of all men, and that they would not accept a man unless he fell in the top third of men with a good earning capacity or was a college graduate. As can be seen, men were considerably less fussy. All respondents were even fussier with respect to a potential mate having an exciting personality, being friendly, or being kind and understanding. But here the male-female differences in most instances were either small or negligible.

A limitation of these studies is that the subjects were all from modern or modernizing societies and most were college students. As in the case of men's emphasis on female attractiveness, to determine whether women's mate preferences are widespread or universal it is necessary to examine a wider range of societies. In a study by Gottschall and colleagues, 658 traditional folktales from every world region and every type of nonindustrial society were analyzed, along with 240 works of Western literature. In both the folktales and Western literature, female characters were more likely than male characters to emphasize status and wealth. In the folktales, 26 percent of females but only 9 percent of males emphasized the importance of status and wealth in a mate. In bands and tribes 34 percent of female and 9 percent of male characters stressed status and wealth, and in agrarian states the respective numbers were 21 and 8. The pattern was much the same in every major world region. In the Western stories, 31 percent of female characters compared to 21 percent of male characters stressed status and wealth.[119] The results, then, were highly consistent with the earlier findings and suggest that status and wealth are reliable indicators of widespread female mate choices.

In Buss's study it was also found that women generally prefer men who are older than they, on average men who are about three and a half years older. This, of course, is the converse of men's preference for youth.[120] It makes sense in evo-

TABLE 5.2   Minimum Standards of Acceptability in a Mate

Characteristic	Gender	Dating	Sexual Relations	Exclusive Dating	Marriage
Powerful	F	33	35	42	45
	M	21	20	27	28
Good earning	F	45	49	61	67
capacity	M	24	20	37	42
College	F	37	40	59	67
graduate	M	25	21	32	38
Exciting	F	42	55	59	70
personality	M	46	47	63	67
Friendly	F	55	59	63	65
	M	47	49	59	66
Kind and	F	45	63	67	72
understanding	M	45	48	65	71

Source: Douglas T. Kenrick, Edward K. Sadalla, Gary Groth, and Melanie R. Trost, "Evolution, traits, and the stages of human courtship: Qualifying the parental investment model," *Journal of Personality* 58 (1990):97–116. Numbers are percentages, which are rounded.

lutionary terms because older men are more emotionally and economically stable and more likely to be good providers. In all societies it takes time for men to gain status and accumulate resources. Other qualities that women seek in men are ambitiousness, which Buss found was much more highly regarded by women than by men; intelligence, because more-intelligent men are on average better providers of resources;[121] and size, strength, and physical prowess, qualities that obviously relate closely to resource-providing abilities.

Female Choice: Attractiveness, Love, Commitment, and Protection

Although women rate men's status and resources more highly than their physical attractiveness, they do regard male attractiveness as important and judge average and symmetrical faces as the most attractive.[122] As in the case of attractive women, attractive men tend to have higher genetic quality—superior condition—in terms of the health conditions discussed earlier. In choosing attractive men, women are choosing "better genes" for their offspring. However, there are three deviations from facial symmetry that women regard as particularly attractive: cheek bones, jaw size, and chin size. Like men, women prefer prominent cheek bones in members of the opposite sex. But unlike men, they prefer a certain exaggeration of the jaw and the chin—"square jaws" and "strong chins." These traits are secondary sex characteristics controlled by testosterone. They signal masculinity, a trait highly desired by women.[123] Top male models usually exhibit all three traits.

In this regard, a number of studies have focused on women's responses to male characteristics during the fertile and nonfertile phases of their ovulatory cycle. Much sexual attraction for both sexes involves scents—pheromones—that males and females give off but without conscious awareness. Certain scents, however, may be detectible. Experiments have been conducted in which women in their fertile phase smelled T-shirts worn for two days by different men. They tended to prefer the T-shirts of men with greater facial and vocal masculinity, body muscularity, and sexual attractiveness.[124]

Female attraction to highly masculine men makes evolutionary sense because such men, especially those who are tall, muscular, and strong, are likely to be good protectors of women against aggression from other males or other dangers. Women also strongly desire men who show reliable signs of commitment because such men are willing to invest resources in them and their children. Enter love. Both men and women value being loved by their mates, but women seem to place more emphasis on being loved. Being loved by her mate is perhaps the most reliable sign that he has made a long-term commitment to her.

These desires are neatly combined in what might be regarded as the female counterpart to male pornography: the romance novel. This literary device began to take shape in the seventeenth and eighteenth centuries as romantic love was rapidly becoming the principal basis for marriage.[125] Today the book market is flooded with romance novels, many of which have been translated into dozens of languages throughout the world. They are almost exclusively read by women and are of virtually no interest to men. The romance novel is extraordinarily appealing to women because it incorporates the major themes of female mate choice we have been discussing. Catherine Salmon comments that "the core of a romance novel's plot is a love story in which the heroine overcomes all obstacles to find and win the heart of one man, her true love."[126] And the heroine's true love, the hero, is almost invariably portrayed in the same way in novel after novel. Salmon has shown that the

> essential characteristics of the hero of a successful romance novel have to do primarily with his physical appearance, physical and social competence, and intense love for the heroine. . . . The heroes of successful romance novels may or may not be rich, aristocratic, or well-educated, but they consistently possess characteristics that would have made them highly desirable mates over the course of human evolutionary history; they are tall, strong, handsome, healthy, intelligent, confident, competent men whose love for the heroine ensures that she and her children will reap the benefits of these qualities.[127]

Salmon explains that the ideal man in a romance novel is little like the gentle, sensitive, "new age" type of man. Rather, he is much more like the character of Maximus as played by Russell Crowe in *Gladiator*, a movie that drew an especially large female audience. In the movie, the fictional character of Maximus is portrayed as a rugged, fierce gladiator in ancient Rome who displayed a deep love for his wife and children and a strong desire to protect them from harm.

Dominant Males Litter the Landscape

Human females all over the world prefer socially dominant males, and throughout the animal world we find the same pattern. Dominant males therefore have better mating prospects than males of lower rank. They will have more opportunities to mate with the most-desirable females, as well as with more females. It is therefore to be expected that dominant males will, on average, leave more offspring than males lower in the status hierarchy. And this is what we find.

Hundreds of studies show a close correlation between male dominance and reproductive success in a wide range of animal species. These studies assess reproductive success primarily in terms of the number of copulations, the number of copulations with estrous females, or the number of offspring sired. In one exhaustive review of these studies, 93 percent reported a positive relationship between male dominance and reproductive success for nonprimates, and 83 percent a positive relationship for primates.[128] One study of a group of wild savannah baboons found that a single male sired 81 percent of the offspring born during a four-year span. Before he became the alpha male and after he lost his dominant position, he fathered only 20 percent of the offspring. Research on three groups of wild long-tailed macaques showed that the dominant male fathered between 52 and 92 percent of the offspring, whereas the low-ranking males combined sired only between 2 and 9 percent of the offspring.[129]

Abundant evidence shows that male social status and reproductive success are closely linked in humans as well. High-status males have been found to have more offspring, often many more, than lower status males in such diverse societies as the Yomut Turkmen, rural Trinidad, the Ifalukese of the western Pacific, sixteenth-century Portugal, and nineteenth-century England, Sweden, and Germany.[130] Indeed, there are at least a hundred carefully studied societies showing that high male status and reproductive success are closely associated.[131] Some of the most painstaking research has been conducted by the anthropologist Napoleon Chagnon among the Yanomama. The most dominant male among the Yanomama is known as a *unokai*, or a man who has killed at least one other man (some *unokais* have killed many men). In calculating reproductive success among nearly 400 Yanomama men, Chagnon found that 137 *unokais* had a total of 673 offspring, or 4.91 per man. By contrast, 243 non-*unokais* had a total of 380 offspring, or only 1.59 per man. The imbalance between *unokais* and non-*unokais* was greatest in the 20–24 age group, and as men got older the reproductive gap between *unokais* and non-*unokais* narrowed. Nevertheless, even in the oldest group, those 41 and older, the *unokais* averaged some 7 offspring per man, whereas the non-*unokais* averaged just over 4 per man.[132] In Darwinian terms, where even very small differences have important long-term outcomes, these differences in reproductive success are extremely large.

The anthropologist Laura Betzig has carried out studies of the levels of reproductive success reported for powerful men in the Old Testament. Throughout the Old Testament, Betzig notes, we find statement after statement indicating that powerful men "have sex with more wives and concubines; they have sex with more slaves; they have more sex with other men's women; and they father many children."[133] David had eight wives, ten concubines, and twenty children; Rehoboam eighteen wives, sixty concubines, and eighty-seven children; and Abijah fourteen wives and thirty-eight offspring. The number of wives and concubines for Gideon, Jair, Ibzan, and Abdon is not reported, but they are said to have had, respectively, seventy-two, thirty, thirty, and forty children.[134]

In the Old Testament God tells his people to "be fruitful and multiply." Indeed, they followed his advice, especially the most powerful. But many men were unable to reproduce at all. As Betzig comments, "For every prestigious man with a harem, many other men went without women. Some were turned into eunuchs, some died on the battlefield, and some became slaves. But most men simply were unable to acquire the basic resources to obtain women and successfully raise children."[135] "Armies were composed mostly of young, unmarried men," she adds, "millions of whom, according to Scripture, died in battle and failed to successfully reproduce."[136]

Perhaps the most astonishing example of the link between male dominance and reproductive success comes from a study by Tatiana Zerjal and colleagues.[137] The authors looked at more than thirty-two genetic markers of 2,123 men living throughout a large swath of Asia stretching from central Asia to the Pacific Ocean. They found a distinctive cluster of genes on the Y chromosome (the male chromosome) that was represented in sixteen different populations within this region and included approximately 8 percent of the region's total male population. They estimated that the most recent common ancestor of these males lived in Mongolia a thousand years ago. Based on historical evidence, they concluded that this ancestor was likely Chinggis Khan, the ferocious leader of the Mongols in the twelfth and thirteenth centuries. Chinggis was probably the most dominant male who ever lived and his sexual exploits knew no bounds. Because the Mongols had the largest empire known to history (see Chapter 10), it is likely that this genetic cluster was spread by conquest. The cluster is found in some 0.5 percent of the world's male population, or about 16 million men, all of whom can trace their genetic ancestry to Chinggis and his male relatives. Reproductive success indeed!

It is often argued that in modern industrial societies the relationship between status and reproductive success has been reversed. Higher status men in modern societies are said to have fewer children, on average, than men of lower status. However, caution is in order. Daniel Pérusse distributed questionnaires to 3,000 students at two French-speaking universities in Montréal, Canada, nearly half of which were completed and returned. He found that although higher status males in his sample did not have greater reproductive success than lower status males, the higher status males did have *much more sex*, or what Pérusse calls "potential conceptions." Pérusse concludes that these findings still support the general argument linking social status and reproductive success, because higher status men in industrial societies would be having more offspring than lower status men if it were not for modern contraception and legal prohibitions on having more than one wife.[138] Males have evolved to think more about how much sex they are having than about how many offspring. Although more sex has led to more offspring in nearly all societies throughout human history, technology can change that.

Even then, sociologists Pierre van den Berghe and Joseph Whitmeyer have directly challenged the claim that the relationship between social status and reproductive success is reversed in industrial societies. They point to evidence showing that this has not occurred in Japan; that a German census for 1981 showed that the fertility of wives increased along with their husbands' income; and that in the United States in both 1960 and 1970 the childlessness of wives decreased as their husbands' income increased. Moreover, when higher status men remarry they are more likely than lower status men to wed younger, more fertile women, and thus to produce more offspring by second or third wives.[139] This can easily be observed by anyone who is paying attention. In the movie *It's Complicated*, starring Alec Baldwin, Meryl Streep, and Steve Martin, several of the characters (including Baldwin's character) are late-middle-aged high-powered men who have divorced their first wives and married much younger women. Even though these men have adolescent or adult children, they are still electing to have at least one more child with the younger wife.

Two recent studies support van den Berghe and Whitmeyer. The first, conducted by psychologist Jason Weeden and colleagues, used a large sample of men from the general US population, along with a smaller sample of Harvard University alumni. The authors showed that men who earned higher incomes had higher levels of reproductive success than men who earned less. The differences were not large, but they pointed in a positive rather than a negative direction.[140] The second study, by Martin Fieder and Susanne Huber, drew on the Wisconsin Longitudinal Study of 4,491 men and 5,326 women. This was a survey conducted between 1990 and 1993 of a random sample of 1957 Wisconsin high school graduates. The subjects were therefore between fifty and fifty-three years of age at the time of the survey. The authors showed that high-status men had more offspring than low-status men, but that high-status women had fewer offspring than low-status women. More specifically, it was found that men who worked in supervisory positions averaged 3.0 offspring compared to 2.8 offspring for men working in nonsupervisory positions. Women who worked in supervisory positions averaged 2.95 offspring, whereas women in nonsupervisory positions averaged 3.05 offspring.[141] Once again the offspring differential between higher-status and lower-status men was small but pointed in the expected direction.

The Straight and the Gay

The vast majority of people in all societies are heterosexual, and thus most sex is heterosexual. Nevertheless, homosexuality is widely found, although probably not universal. In some societies when people have homosexual behavior described to them by outsiders and are asked if such a thing is found in their society, they react with extreme puzzlement, wondering why anyone would think of doing that.

There is an important distinction between homosexual *behavior* and *homosexuals*. Some people who are not homosexual by orientation nevertheless engage in homosexual acts occasionally. Given ample opportunities for heterosexual sex, they will stick to that and may only turn to homosexual behavior when heterosexual outlets, for one reason or another, become unavailable or extremely limited. This kind of homosexual activity is known as *situational* or *substitutional* homosexuality. The most familiar example is homosexual behavior in prisons, which are strictly sex segregated and provide no heterosexual outlets. (Some now provide for occasional visitation by members of the opposite sex.) It has also been known to occur among sailors spending long periods of time at sea and among boys in all-male boarding schools. Homosexuals—gay men and women—practice *preferential* homosexuality. They engage exclusively (or almost exclusively) in homosexual activity because they are sexually attracted to members of their own sex and find heterosexuality unsatisfying.

Situational Homosexuality

One of the most interesting cases of situational homosexuality was found in ancient Greece in the time of such great philosophers as Plato, Socrates, and Aristotle. The Greeks developed the world's first educational system devoted to the rigorous exploration of ideas about nature, society, and politics. It was nothing like modern mass education, being based on one-to-one relationships between a master tutor and a pupil. This relationship in time often evolved into a sexual relationship between the two (all tutors and pupils were males). The main sexual activity was something called intercrural intercourse; approaching his pupil from the front, the tutor placed his penis between the pupil's legs and ejaculated. Anal intercourse was also practiced, although fellatio (mouth-genital contact) was frowned on. In time the tutor and pupil would often express love for each other and exchange love letters. The relationship became idealized, and it was thought to enhance the boy's masculinity and potential for military valor.[142]

The tutor-pupil sexual relationship was carried on primarily while the pupil was still a boy or an early adolescent. As he grew into later adolescence, the relationship ended. Usually the tutor moved on as well, eventually marrying and having a family.

So the tutors were heterosexual men who, apparently, were substituting homosexual acts for heterosexual ones because of the relative unavailability of women. Greece was a highly patriarchal society and women of the citizen class, of which the tutors were a part, were secluded so that sexual access to them was more or less impossible before marriage (virginity was demanded). Marriage was late, so male citizens did not have heterosexual outlets until long after they reached puberty and developed strong sexual desires. Because the tutors were already engaged in relationships with young boys, they could be opportunistic and develop their educational relationships into sexual ones.[143]

It is sometimes assumed that Greek society as a whole approved of this homosexual activity, but in fact the parents of the boys often objected strenuously. Moreover, preferential homosexuality was highly disdained throughout Greek society, including by the tutors themselves. A tutor who did not give up his love affairs with his pupils and move on to marriage and family life was regarded most unfavorably.[144]

A number of other ancient civilizations practiced a similar form of situational homosexuality. Japan was one of these, as was China. Like the Greeks, the Chinese had developed one of the first educational systems devoted to more than just literacy and numeracy, and this system was intertwined with a form of man-boy homosexuality.[145] The Romans also developed it. In the earliest days of the Roman Republic, sex between an adult male and a free-born boy was frowned on, although a man could have sex with slave boys. Later, the Romans became more relaxed about such matters and many men took up relationships with free-born boys. Romans, like Greeks, strongly disdained preferential homosexuality; men who took the receptive position in anal intercourse with other men were held in particular contempt. But even this changed in time. Receptive intercourse became increasingly common, and male prostitutes emerged.[146]

Many small-scale societies have also had man-boy homosexual practices. Well-known cases include the Siwans and Zande of Africa and the Etoro of New Guinea. The Etoro are one of a number of societies sharing the very unusual view that sex with women is "debilitating." It is thought to drain men of their energy and hamper their effectiveness as warriors. As a result they proscribe it for as many as 260 days out of each year, and on these days sexual relations with young boys are common. The sexes among the Etoro sleep separately, the men and boys in men's houses and the women and girls in women's houses. The sleeping arrangements between men and boys thus provide a golden opportunity for sexual activity. Young boys fellate men, and men anally penetrate boys.[147] A related group, the Sambia, have an extraordinary preoccupation with semen. Young boys are introduced to fellatio by practicing sucking on flutes. Once they have learned their "craft," they begin fellating older boys. When they themselves become the older boys, they are fellated in turn by the younger ones. As a boy turns into a man, he gives up this practice and takes up heterosexual relations.[148]

Why are young boys so commonly preferred as partners for men? Since this is situational homosexuality, the men naturally desire a female, but females are often scarce as sex partners. The best substitute would be someone who looks most like a female. Young boys, especially prepubescent boys, fit the bill best because they have little body hair, have not yet developed low voices, and are soft and smooth to the touch. In sex the world over people have their preferred partners. When these partners are unavailable, people will turn to the next best thing. The sex drive, especially the male drive, is extremely powerful and vigorously seeks an outlet. Masturbation is one outlet, but it becomes tedious after a while and people, being the intensely social animals that they are, like nice warm bodies to cuddle with. Some men will even accept the bodies of *animals* as sex objects. This practice, known as bestiality, is found most often in rural areas for the obvious reason that animals are common there. No one knows how many people may engage in this practice. Alfred Kinsey, in his celebrated study of human sexual behavior conducted in the 1940s, found that about 8 percent of the people he interviewed admitted to sex with animals. However, this figure is undoubtedly inflated. Kinsey's subjects were not a random sample of Americans but volunteers, and volunteers for such a project would most likely be sexually driven individuals whose sexual appetites are unusually large.[149]

Preferential Homosexuality and Its Causes

What then of preferential homosexuality? Here we obviously have something quite different. One thing we know is that it is found among only a small fraction of modern populations. Kinsey gave an estimate of 10 percent of the population, but this figure is unreliable because of Kinsey's reliance on volunteers rather than a random sample.[150] More recent estimates using large random samples are much lower. Edward Laumann and colleagues in a large sample of US adults found that 3.7 percent of their male and 1.7 percent of their female respondents reported homosexual or bisexual attraction.[151] Other studies report very similar numbers. This is the case not only for the United States,[152] but also for societies as different as the Netherlands, Brazil, Peru, and Thailand.[153]

Numerous scholars, including some Darwinians, regard preferential homosexuality as a puzzle;[154] it cannot be an evolved adaptation, they say, because it is obviously nonreproductive and thus would promote no one's inclusive fitness. Since it is reproductively maladaptive in the extreme, why does it exist at all? One answer is simply to acknowledge that not all behavioral traits are adaptations; there are always genetic mutations that make some people different. Another possibility is that homosexuality is not a biological phenomenon at all, but rather a socially determined condition. Those who advocate this view are the social constructionists referred to in Chapter 1.

The social constructionists regard sexuality as malleable to such an extent that nearly anything is possible. Humans may have some sort of primordial sex drive, but this drive is neutral in terms of its target. There is no reason why a man's target could not be other men, a woman's target other women. Society creates "social scripts" that envelop individuals and guide them in one direction or another. In the words of prominent social constructionist Ken Plummer, "Sexuality has no meaning other than that given to it in social situations. Thus the forms and the contents of sexual meanings are another cultural variable, and why certain meanings are learnt and not others is problematic."[155] Another social constructionist, Steven Seidman, says that we "are born with bodies, but it is society that determines which parts of the body and which pleasures and acts are sexual."[156]

Social constructionists are usually quite vague in telling us exactly what it is that society does to determine sexual feelings and behaviors, or why one "social script" operates in one situation and other scripts in other situations. But one fashionable idea is that sex is really about power. Just as there are dominant social norms in every society, there are also dominant sexual norms, and in modern societies these norms strongly incline toward what has lately been called "heteronormativity." What this essentially boils down to is the idea that heterosexuals have seized social power, and they use this power to impose their own sexual preferences on others. They define heterosexuality as good and proper, homosexuality as bad and improper, and younger generations are socialized into these norms, which have percolated throughout the culture.[157]

This argument is about as badly flawed as an argument possibly could be. Natural selection could never have been indifferent to an organism's sexual orientation since any sexually reproducing species whose members were not biologically wired for heterosexuality would quickly go extinct in the struggle for survival. The key to both natural selection and sexual selection is sex, and sex with partners of the opposite sex. Moreover, an extreme embarrassment for social constructionists is human sexual anatomy. What are penises designed to do? Insert themselves into vaginas, ejaculate, and inseminate females, the evolutionary significance of which is patently obvious. Men do not become pregnant and give birth to offspring through their penises or anuses. And if most people are heterosexual simply because they have been culturally conditioned by a heterosexual power elite imposing its sexual will from above, this obviously begs the question as to why all societies are "heteronormative" rather than "homonormative." And how could a sexual "elite" "seize power" in the first place? It is extremely difficult to understand how that would work.

These are only some of the objections that can be made against the social constructionist view, but they suffice to make the point that sexual orientation cannot be understood as a cultural whim. The most logical alternative to social constructionism is some type of biological perspective, and a great deal of research and theorizing has now been done to suggest that sexual orientation may be largely imprinted on the brain. Sociologists Lee Ellis and Ashley Ames have reviewed much of the research on the biological roots of homosexuality and formulated their own biological theory. This theory assumes that human sexual orientation develops in the same basic way as in all mammals, which is during the period of fetal development when the brain is being "sexed." In humans, neurological development takes place between the middle of the second and the end of the fifth month of gestation, and the "sexing" of the brain is part of this neurological development. Ellis and Ames contend that a homosexual orientation develops when the fetal brain receives an excess of hormones of the opposite sex. If an anatomically male fetus's developing brain is embalmed in too much estrogen and other female hormones, the outcome is a homosexual male; if, by contrast, an anatomically female fetus's brain is embalmed in too much testosterone and other male hormones, the outcome is a female homosexual. Of course, the actual process will undoubtedly turn out to be more complex, but one gets the general idea.[158]

A claim for biological causation requires locating, at least eventually, the mechanism whereby the proposed causal forces do their work. In the 1990s Simon LeVay, a neuroscientist at the Salk Institute in San Diego, and himself an openly gay man, studied the brains of a small sample of gay men who had died from AIDS, along with the brains of some presumably heterosexual men and a few women. In dissecting their brains, LeVay concentrated on the hypothalamus, a part of the brain that is associated with primal urges such as hunger, thirst, and sex. He discovered that a particular region of the hypothalamus of the gay men, known as INAH3, was much smaller than normal, being only about one-third to one-half the size of INAH3 in the brains of heterosexual men; and the INAH3 of heterosexual females was close to the size of INAH3 in the homosexual males. Later, it was found that INAH3 in homosexual females was about twice the size of INAH3 in heterosexual females, and thus approximately the same size as INAH3 in heterosexual males. A reasonable conclusion is that homosexual males have a "feminized" INAH3, whereas homosexual females have a "masculinized" INAH3.[159]

It has long been known that homosexual behavior occurs frequently in many animal species, not only in mammals but in some birds. Studies have been carried out on rats in which females are injected with testosterone. These females proceed to behave more like males, including mounting other females. Relatedly, researchers at Brigham Young University examined the brains of six male rats that would not mount females. Their brains were dissected and, lo and behold, a portion of the hypothalamus was shown to be abnormal for their sex—it was only about half the size found in rats that did mount females. In an earlier study, a geneticist at Yale University discovered that some of his male *Drosophila*, fruit flies widely used in biological studies, seemed to be "courting" other males. A mutant gene was suspected, and it was eventually discovered. Researchers studying sheep in Idaho noticed that some of the rams avoided mounting ewes, but they did mount and actually anally penetrate other rams. The rams' brains were studied and found to be different in an important way from those of the other rams.[160]

Discovering that other animal species behave very similarly to humans in certain important respects is usually regarded as providing a strong presumption that the behaviors in question have a biological foundation. After all, while animals learn much of their behavior, they cannot "socially construct" anything according to a set of "scripts." The mammalian brain is highly similar across all species, and thus the behavior of mammals is often a very good basis for making inferences about the causes of human behavior.

Around the time LeVay was doing his research, human geneticists began a series of studies to determine if homosexuality was heritable. Early studies, using identical and fraternal twins, suggested that homosexuality has considerable heritability. A study by Bailey and Pillard found that when one twin was gay his identical twin was gay 52 percent of the time, but the number for fraternal twins was only 22 percent.[161] Similar numbers were obtained by Fred Whitam, 65 and 29 percent.[162] In a study of female twins by Bailey and Pillard along with two other colleagues, the numbers obtained were 48 and 16 percent.[163] In a review of eight studies by Scott Hershberger, six of the studies reported similar differences between identical and fraternal twins.[164] More recent twin studies have estimated heritability for females and males separately. A study of nearly 2,000 Australian twins reported heritability coefficients of between 50 and 60 percent for females and 30 to 40 percent for males.[165] A study by Katarina Alanko and colleagues of over 3,000 Finnish twins estimated heritability for women at 45 percent and for men at 50 percent.[166]

In a widely discussed study by Dean Hamer of the National Cancer Institute in Bethesda, Maryland, a region of the X chromosome known as Xq28 was identified as a possible location for a "gay gene."[167] Other researchers, including members of Hamer's own research team, have followed up on Hamer's interesting finding. One study replicated it, another did not, and a third achieved partial replication. In this last study Xq28 was shown not to have as strong a link to homosexual orientation as found by Hamer but, interestingly, the study did identify several other chromosomal locations 8p12, 7q36, and 10q26—to be highly suggestive of a link to homosexual orientation.[168] The researchers found the 7q36 region especially interesting because one of the genes in this chromosomal segment has been shown to be necessary for the development of the so-called hypothalamic suprachiasmatic nucleus in mice, and an enlarged suprachiasmatic nucleus has been found in some homosexual men.[169] This returns us to the very interesting territory of the hypothalamus. However, the search for specific genes that bear on a gay sexual orientation is still in its very early stages. Evidence for the location of such genes at this point is only suggestive.[170]

Several other lines of evidence suggest a major role for biology in sexual orientation. LeVay contends that sexual orientation is closely intertwined with other gendered traits, and that the two develop in the prenatal brain as parts of an overall "package."[171] This assertion is strongly supported by numerous studies showing that homosexual adults frequently exhibit so-called gender nonconforming or gender atypical behavior (GAB) early in life. Male homosexuals were likely as children to display effeminacy and to have female play and occupational interests (e.g., preferring girls as playmates, wanting to play with dolls rather than guns and trucks), whereas lesbians were more likely to exhibit male play and occupational interests (e.g., being tomboys, expressing less interest in motherhood and more interest in a career). Most of these studies are retrospective studies, which ask adult homosexuals to recall their gendered feelings and behavior in childhood. Bailey and Zucker reviewed forty-eight studies and determined that in most of them adult homosexuals recalled much more childhood GAB than adult heterosexuals.[172] This was especially true of males.

To what extent do these findings hold cross-culturally? Fernando Luiz Cardoso interviewed 177 homosexual, 157 bisexual, and 544 heterosexual men from Brazil, Thailand, and Turkey.[173] Homosexual men in all three countries reported much more gender nonconformity in childhood than either bisexual or heterosexual men. The differences were especially pronounced in response to the questions "cross-dressed" and "liked to do girls' tasks." Nancy Bartlett and Paul Vasey studied fifty-three men in Samoa known as *fa'afafine*.[174] This Samoan word means "in the manner of a woman" and is used to identify adult men who show strongly feminine behavior. Most *fa'afafine* recalled much more childhood GAB than a control group of twenty-seven heterosexual men and twenty-four heterosexual women. For example, with respect to the question "talked or acted like a girl," *fa'afafine* scored 4.2 on a five-point scale compared to 4.0 for the heterosexual women and only 1.4 for the heterosexual men. The pattern was the same for other questions. It is striking that *fa'afafine* displayed even more childhood femininity than heterosexual women.

Retrospective studies have been criticized on the grounds that people's memories of their childhood can be selective and thus somewhat faulty. To get around this problem, Rieger, Linsenmeier, Gygax, and Bailey designed an ingenious study in which they recruited twenty-one homosexual men, twenty homosexual women, twenty-three heterosexual men, and twenty-six heterosexual women who had retained childhood videos of themselves.[175] The researchers then recruited undergraduate students—twenty homosexual men, twenty homosexual women, twenty heterosexual men, and twenty-two heterosexual women—to watch the videos and rate the degree of gender conformity or nonconformity of the children. The raters, who did not know the adult sexual orientation of the children in the videos, regarded the pre-homosexual children as much more gender nonconformist than the pre-heterosexual children.

So-called prospective studies seek to determine the extent to which childhood GAB predicts adult homosexuality. In a widely discussed study, Richard Green studied sixty-six boys considered highly feminine, along with fifty-six other boys to serve as a control group.[176] The boys in the control group were recruited without regard to gendered characteristics. Green followed most of these boys through adolescence or into early adulthood. He found that thirty-three of the forty-four feminine boys who remained in the study became homosexual or bisexual, but not a single one of the thirty-five boys remaining in the control group became homosexual or bisexual. All became heterosexual.

Like adult homosexuality, GAB has a substantial level of heritability. Alanko and colleagues, in their study of adult Finnish homosexuals mentioned above, reported heritability estimates of childhood GAB of 51 percent for women and 29 percent for men.[177] Van Beijsterveldt, Hudziak, and Boomsma studied several thousand Dutch twins at the ages of seven and ten.[178] Gendered behavior was rated by their mothers at both of these ages. Results showed an extremely large GAB heritability of 70 percent for both sexes and both ages.

Sexual orientation strongly resists psychotherapies designed to reverse homosexuality. Such treatments are seldom practiced anymore but were common in the past—and they have almost never worked. People can clearly change such things as attitudes concerning gender or race, which are significantly influenced by cultural conditioning, but they can almost never change their sexual orientation. This fact suggests that conditioning is not operating in this case.

Finally, we observe that the percentage of homosexuals is approximately the same in all cultures, remains stable over time, and seems to be completely unaffected by the extent to which a society is tolerant or intolerant of gays.[179] If homosexuality is an individual "choice" or some sort of social construction, it would seem to be a highly self-destructive choice in any society with extreme intolerance of gays, such as the United States and Great Britain fifty or sixty years ago. Attitudes toward gays have become much more open and receptive in these and other Western countries over this period of time, but there is no evidence that there are more gay people now than there were then. Some might argue that this cannot be true, since large gay subcultures are found in such cities as San Francisco, Houston, Palm Springs, and Berlin. But this is in part a reflection of gays "coming out of the closet." In the old days, homosexuals usually tried to hide their homosexuality, but only a minority do so today. It is also due to the tendency of gays to congregate in large cities because it is much easier to find gay partners in urban than in rural environments.[180]

The various lines of evidence seem to converge on the conclusion that homosexual orientation is largely biologically rather than socially determined. The specific way (or ways) in which this works is still unclear, but it seems that a homosexual orientation results when there is an atypical "gendering" and "sexing" of the brain during prenatal development. LeVay proposes a general theory of sexual orientation, which he calls the *prenatal hormone theory*. He says that

> the most parsimonious explanation for the development of sexual orientation is this: If testosterone levels during a critical prenatal period are high, the brain is organized in such a way that the person is predisposed to become typically masculine in a variety of gendered traits, including sexual attraction to females. If testosterone levels are low during that same period, the brain is organized in such a way that the person is predisposed to become typically feminine in gendered traits, including sexual attraction to males.[181]

LeVay adds that it might not be, or at least might not always be, a matter of the amount of testosterone that is circulating in the prenatal brain. It might be a matter of how the brain responds to testosterone through its specific receptor sites. These sites may "underrespond" or "overrespond" to whatever amount of testosterone is there. But, LeVay notes, the same general process is at work regardless of the precise way in which it works. It can hardly escape notice that LeVay's theory is very similar to the theory developed by Ellis and Ames a quarter century earlier.

Is there any role for the effects of specific types of social environments, which might induce changes in the brain centers regulating sexual orientation? Possibly. But it is difficult to think of just what type of environment would produce a result as momentous as a change in a person's most fundamental trait and sense of personal identity.

SUMMARY

1. Incest avoidance is the major limiting condition in human mating. Because people are strongly disinclined to mate with close relatives, and because of strong societal prohibitions of incest, people must seek mates outside nuclear families, and often outside extended families.

2. Anthropologists and sociologists have traditionally explained the incest taboo as a cultural invention designed to maintain family cohesion. Alternatively, Westermarck's theory assumes that children in close contact in early childhood become sexually indifferent or averse to each other. Much evidence supports Westermarck's theory, including studies of inbreeding depression, mating patterns in Israeli kibbutzim, Taiwanese sim-pua marriages, Lebanese cousin marriages, and cousin marriages among the Karo Batak of Indonesia.

3. Despite incest avoidance and incest taboos, incest does sometimes occur, usually as the result of severe forms of family dysfunction that disrupt sexual and familial bonding.

4. Sexual selection is a special form of evolutionary selection that selects for the ability to attract mates rather than to survive. It is widespread in the animal world, taking the form of male combat (e.g., walruses, elk) in some species and female choice in others (e.g., birds). It applies equally to humans, but in this case male choice exists alongside female choice.

5. There are major differences between human males and females in their sexual strategies. The male sex drive is more urgent than the female's. Males are more inter-

ested in sexual variety and multiple partners and show more interest in casual and impersonal sex. These differences have been found worldwide.

6. Sexual jealousy is a powerful emotion in both sexes and exists as a means of counteracting infidelity. Most studies find that men show more jealousy with respect to sexual infidelity, whereas women are more concerned about emotional (romantic) infidelity. Men seek to control women's sexuality in order to avoid cuckoldry, or investing in offspring who have been fathered by another man.

7. In mate choice, men strongly focus on female attractiveness, an emphasis found worldwide. Female beauty is indicated by highly symmetrical faces as well as faces whose features are average. Research shows that average and symmetrical faces are correlated with good health and high fitness. Men are attracted to young women because their reproductive value is greater than that of older women. This pattern also exists throughout the world.

8. Female body shape is a major determinant of male mate choice. Many studies show that men have a strong preference for women with low waist-to-hip ratios. Women with lower ratios are in general healthier and more reproductively fit than women with higher ratios. The preference for low ratios is widely found in different societies.

9. The most important criteria determining female choice are the status and resources possessed by men. Women seek high-status and resource-endowed men because such men are better able to materially provision a woman and her offspring, and thus promote her reproductive success. Women's preferences for men with status and resources are found in many societies of very different types.

10. Women emphasize physical attractiveness less than men do, but they still consider attractiveness important. Like men, women prefer male faces that are average and symmetrical because they too are looking for mates of high genetic quality. Women are also attracted to faces that exhibit features of masculinity. Most women are attracted to highly masculine men because such men are likely to be good protectors of them and their children, and would have been especially so in ancestral environments.

11. Throughout the animal world, there is a very close association between male dominance and reproductive success, and this association is found as well in humans. Evidence in support of this association is extensive and very strong.

12. Because of their desire for sexual variety and multiple mates, men show a keen interest in looking at naked female bodies. Thus pornography of one type or another is found in virtually all societies across space and time. Women show little interest in

pornography because looking at naked male bodies gives them no reproductive advantage. Women instead show interest in romance novels, which depict relationships between women and heroic men, with whom they can enter into committed relationships based on intense romantic love.

13. Homosexuality exists in two forms, situational and preferential, both of which are found widely in human societies. Situational homosexuality mostly occurs among heterosexual men as a result of a scarcity or absence of women.

14. Preferential homosexuality means a gay sexual orientation. It is widely found in human societies, although whether it is a human universal is unknown. Studies of modern societies show that about 4 percent of men and 2 percent of women are preferentially homosexual (or bisexual). Numerous studies show that the majority of adult homosexuals exhibit gender nonconforming or atypical behavior in childhood.

15. There is controversy over whether preferential homosexuality is a choice or an innate desire. Most likely it is an innate desire. Homosexuality shows a moderate to high level of heritability, and brain studies show differences in the brains of gays and straights. The most likely explanation for homosexuality is that during the period of fetal development when the brain is being "sexed," a homosexual orientation may develop if the fetus's brain is flooded by hormones of the opposite sex.

QUESTIONS FOR DISCUSSION

✓ Explain the difference between incest avoidance and incest taboos.

✓ How have anthropologists and sociologists traditionally explained incest taboos?

✓ Explain Westermarck's theory of incest avoidance.

✓ What is some of the evidence that has accumulated to test Westermarck's theory? Does this evidence tend to support or refute the theory? Discuss.

✓ What is inbreeding depression and how does it relate to incest avoidance from an evolutionary perspective?

✓ Despite incest aversions and incest taboos, why does incest sometimes occur?

✓ What is the difference between natural selection and sexual selection? Do they work together or somehow against each other?

✓ What are the two types of sexual selection identified by Darwin and still considered valid today? Give examples of each.

✓ Discuss differences between the sexes in terms of sexual urgency, the desire for sexual variety, and the desire for casual or impersonal sex.

✓ Why should sexual jealousy be such a powerful human emotion?

✓ How do men and women differ in the types of jealousy they express?

✓ When men choose mates, what are the principal criteria by which they make their choices? Are these criteria widely found throughout the world or are they specific to modern societies?

✓ What is the relationship between physical attractiveness and overall genetic fitness for both males and females? Discuss.

✓ There are four adaptive problems that women must solve in selecting long-term mates. What are these problems and how have women solved them? In other words, what are women looking for in mates?

✓ Why do men like pornography whereas few women take an interest in it?

✓ There is a large worldwide market for romance novels. Why are these novels read almost exclusively by women?

✓ How are male and female mate choice related to potential reproductive success?

✓ What is the relationship between male dominance and reproductive success, both in humans and in other animal species?

✓ Discuss the difference between situational and preferential homosexuality. Give some examples of situational homosexuality. Under what circumstances is it most likely to occur?

✓ How do social constructionist theories explain sexual orientation?

✓ There is now extensive research on homosexuality from a biological point of view. Discuss this research and its implications for explaining preferential homosexuality.

✓ What might a good theory of preferential homosexuality look like?

References and Notes

1. Among urban Greek settlers living in Roman Egypt in the first few centuries CE, brother-sister marriage was encouraged and constituted about one-sixth of marriages (Hopkins 1980; Shaw 1992). In Iran in the sixth century BCE, some marriages occurred between brother and sister and father and daughter, and perhaps even mother and son (Scheidel 1996). And in some societies, such as the ancient Egyptians, Hawaiians, and Incas, brother-sister marriage often took place within ruling elites, a practice known as royal incest (Van den Berghe and Mesher 1980). The Iranian case is very poorly understood, the Greek case only slightly better. We know more about some of the cases of royal incest, which may have been motivated by a desire to keep wealth concentrated within family lines. In any event, in none of

these societies did incestuous unions involve more than a fraction of the population, which is why they are at best only partial exceptions.

2. Davis 1949.

3. Davis 1949, p. 403.

4. The original formulation of the theory was gradually extended in later editions of *The History of Human Marriage*, and replies to critics were added. For the latest version, see Westermarck 1922b.

5. Seemanova 1971. See also Ember 1983; Shepher 1983; Durham 1991; and Scheidel 1996.

6. Bittles and Neel 1994.

7. Saggar and Bittles 2008.

8. Spiro 1958; Talmon 1964.

9. Shepher 1969, 1983.

10. A. P. Wolf 1966, 1970, 1995.

11. A. P. Wolf 2004b.

12. McCabe 1983.

13. Fessler 2007; Kushnick and Fessler 2011.

14. Pusey 2004.

15. This felicitous phrase was borrowed from Sarah Blaffer Hrdy.

16. Weinberg 1955, as discussed in Erickson 2004.

17. Greenberg and Littlewood 1995, as discussed in Erickson 2004.

18. Cory and Masters 1963; Erickson 1989.

19. Westermarck 1922b, p.194; emphasis added.

20. A. P. Wolf 2004a, p. 14.

21. Bowlby 1969.

22. Erickson 2004, p. 174.

23. Flores, Mattos, and Salzano 1998.

24. Worling 1995.

25. See Lieberman and Lobel 2012.

26. Westermarck 1926, as discussed in Fessler and Navarrete 2004.

27. Durham 1991, 2004.

28. Unpublished research carried out by the author.

29. Coyne 2009; Alexander et al. 1979.

30. Alexander et al. 1979; Le Boeuf and Reiter 1988, as discussed in Geary 1998.

31. Alexander et al. 1979. See also Anderson and Fedak 1985; Andersson 1994.

32. Correlation coefficients for nineteen pinniped species: weight dimorphism X average harem size = .906, weight dimorphism X maximum harem size = .824.

33. Alexander et al. 1979. Correlation coefficients for seventeen ungulate species: length dimorphism X average harem size = .642, length dimorphism X maximum harem size = .665.

34. Alexander et al. 1979. Correlation coefficients for twenty-two primate species: weight dimorphism X average harem size = .570, weight dimorphism X maximum harem size = .608.

35. Petrie 1994.

36. Petrie, Halliday, and Sanders 1991.

37. Coyne 2009.

38. Coyne 2009.

39. Zahavi and Zahavi 1997, pp. 32–33.

40. Coyne 2009.

41. Trivers 1972; Gowaty 1992; Smuts 1995; Hrdy 1997.

42. Trivers 1972; Gowaty 1992; Smuts 1995; Hrdy 1997.

43. Trivers 1972; Gowaty 1992; Smuts 1995; Hrdy 1997.

44. Clark and Hatfield 1989.

45. Clark and Hatfield 1989.

46. Voracek, Hofhansl, and Fisher 2005.

47. Hald and Høgh-Olesen 2010.

48. Hald and Høgh-Olesen 2010.

49. Conley 2011.

50. Simpson and Gangestad 1991; Simpson 1998.

51. Schmitt 2005.

52. Schmitt 2005.

53. Schmitt's correlation coefficients: male-female SOI ratio X gender empowerment = -.56, male-female SOI ratio X women in parliament = -.35. My revised coefficients: male-female SOI ratio X gender empowerment = -.65, male-female SOI ratio X women in parliament = -.59, male-female SOI ratio X women in labor force = -.62.

54. Schmitt 2005.

55. Schmitt 2003.

56. Buss 2000.

57. Thornhill and Gangestad 2008.

58. Symons 1979.

59. Salmon 2005, p. 246.

60. Buss 2000.

61. Daly, Wilson, and Weghorst 1982.

62. Buss 2000; Betzig 1989.

63. Stephens 1963; Whyte 1978; Leacock 1980.

64. Daly, Wilson, and Weghorst 1982.

65. Buss 2000.

66. Buss et al. 1992.

67. Pietrzak et al. 2002.

68. Buss 2000.

69. Buss 2000.

70. Pietrzak et al. 2002.

71. Sagarin et al. 2012.

72. Symons 1979.

73. Thornhill and Gangestad 2008.

74. Thornhill and Gangestad 1993; Jones and Hill 1993; Symons 1995, pp. 97–101; Møller and Thornhill 1998.

75. N. Wolf 2002, as discussed in Gottschall et al. 2008.

76. Symons 1995.

77. Gottschall et al. 2008.

78. Gottschall et al. 2008.

79. Gangestad and Scheyd 2005.

80. Møller 2006.

81. Thornhill and Gangestad 1993; Thornhill et al. 2010.

82. Gangestad and Scheyd 2005.

83. Pflüger et al. 2012.

84. Kenrick and Keefe 1992; Kenrick, Trost, and Sheets 1996.

85. Kenrick and Keefe 1992; Kenrick, Trost, and Sheets 1996.

86. Buss 1989, 1992, 1994.

87. Buss 1989, 1992, 1994.

88. Symons 1979.

89. Bereczkei and Csanaky 1996.

90. Jones 1995.

91. G. Miller 2009.

92. G. Miller 2009, p. 137.

93. Singh 1993a.

94. Zaadstra et al. 1993.

95. See Symons 1995, p. 92.

96. Singh 1993a, 1993b, 1994; Singh and Young 1995; Singh and Luis 1995; Barber 1995; Furnham, Dias, and McClelland, 1998.

97. Singh, Frohlich, and Haywood 1999; Dixson et al. 2010; Singh et al. 2010.

98. Singh, Frohlich, and Haywood 1999.

99. Tassinary and Hansen 1998.

100. Bronstad and Singh 1999.

101. Bronstad and Singh 1999; Streeter and McBurney 2003.

102. For example, Wetsman and Marlowe 1999; Yu and Shepard 1998.

103. L. Sugiyama 2004.

104. Marlowe and Wetsman 2001.

105. Marlowe, Apicella, and Reed 2005.

106. Women are well aware that men are attracted to high lordosis. This is one of the things that is behind the otherwise puzzling practice of wearing high heels. A woman can increase the tilt of her pelvis from 25 degrees in stocking feet to 45 degrees in two-inch heels and 55 degrees in three-inch heels (E. O. Smith 1999). Walking in high heels also exaggerates the female gait, making women appear more feminine than when walking in flat shoes. Compared to men, women take shorter strides, walk at a more rapid cadence, and display more pelvic rotation, all of which are intensified when walking in heels (Morris et al. 2013). Wearing high heels over a long period of time can lead to back injuries, foot deformation, debilitation of ligaments in the lower leg and foot, and other problems. Therefore, the advantages to women of wearing heels must outweigh the disadvantages or at least be perceived to outweigh them (E. O. Smith 1999).

107. Yu and Shepard 1998.

108. Perilloux, Webster, and Gaulin 2010.

109. Singh 1993a; Thornhill and Gangestad 2008.

110. Jasieńska et al. 2004.

111. Symons 1979.

112. Quotation is from Symons 1979, p. 199.

113. Buss and Schmitt 1993.

114. Buss and Schmitt 1993.

115. Buss 1994, p. 26.

116. B. J. Ellis 1992.

117. Buss and Schmitt 1993.

118. Kenrick et al. 1990.

119. Gottschall et al. 2004.

120. See also Buss and Schmitt 1993.

121. However, there is another wrinkle with respect to intelligence. Prokosch, Yeo, and Miller (2005) found that the body symmetry of seventy-eight young males was significantly correlated with general intelligence. The authors concluded that intelligence is a good indicator of genetic fitness. In choosing more intelligent males, women are also choosing more symmetrical males and thus, in terms of the logic discussed earlier in this chapter, fitter males.

122. Møller and Thornhill 1998.

123. Thornhill and Gangestad 2008.

124. Thornhill and Gangestad 2008.

125. Coontz 2005.

126. Salmon 2005, p. 247.

127. Salmon 2005, pp. 247–248.

128. L. Ellis 1995.

129. Geary 1998.

130. Pérusse 1993. Individual studies cited in Pérusse's bibliography.

131. Low 2000. Individual studies cited in Low's bibliography.

132. Chagnon 2013.

133. Betzig 2005.

134. Betzig 2009.

135. Betzig 2009, p. 52.

136. Betzig 2009, p. 52.

137. Zerjal et al. 2003.

138. Pérusse 1993.

139. Van den Berghe and Whitmeyer 1990.

140. Weeden et al. 2006.

141. Fieder and Huber 2012.
142. Percy 1996; Cantarella 1992.
143. Percy 1996; Cantarella 1992; Posner 1992.
144. Percy 1996; Cantarella 1992.
145. Leupp 1995.
146. Cantarella 1992.
147. Kelly 1976.
148. Herdt 1984, 1987.
149. Kinsey et al. 1948.
150. Kinsey et al. 1948.
151. Laumann et al. 1994, as discussed in LeVay 2011.
152. Results of six studies reported in Berman 2003.
153. Whitam 1983; Whitam and Mathy 1986.
154. See, for example, Berman 2003.
155. Plummer 1982.
156. Seidman 2003, p. 39.
157. Rich 1980; Seidman 2003. See also Weeks 1986.
158. Ellis and Ames 1987.
159. LeVay 1991, 1996.
160. All studies reviewed in LeVay 1996.
161. Bailey and Pillard 1991.
162. Whitam 1983.
163. Bailey et al. 1993.
164. Hershberger 2001.
165. Kirk, Bailey, and Martin 2000.
166. Alanko et al. 2010.
167. Hamer and Copeland 1994.
168. Hu, Pattatucci, and Patterson 1995; Vilain 2000; Mustanski et al. 2005.
169. Swaab and Hofman 1990, as discussed in Mustanski et al. 2005.
170. LeVay 2011.
171. LeVay 2011.
172. Bailey and Zucker 1995.
173. Cardoso 2009.
174. Bartlett and Vasey 2006.
175. Rieger et al. 2008, as discussed in LeVay 2011.
176. Green 1987, as discussed in LeVay 2011.
177. Alanko et al. 2010.
178. Van Beijsterveldt, Hudziak, and Boomsma 2006.
179. Whitam 1983; Whitam and Mathy 1986.
180. Posner 1992.
181. LeVay 2011, pp. 277–278.

Family and Marriage

In the nineteenth century many anthropologists thought that humans originally lived in a state of sexual promiscuity. Marriage did not exist, and every man had unbridled sexual access to all of the women and every woman unbridled access to all of the men. The children who were born from these unions did not belong to any organized family group, but to the entire community. This view was held by almost all of the anthropologists of the day, including such luminaries as Johann Bachofen, John McLennan, Prince Peter Kropotkin, and the great American anthropologist Lewis Henry Morgan. There were few challengers.[1]

One who dared to challenge was the great Edward Westermarck, the author of the famous incest avoidance theory discussed in Chapter 5. It was the promiscuity question that Westermarck took up in his doctoral dissertation, which was expanded to become his book *The History of Human Marriage*. Westermarck pointed to a number of logical flaws in the argument. He pointed, for example, to the widespread existence of sexual jealousy throughout the world; to a sense of possession between the spouses, especially the possession of the wife by the husband; and to the demand for a bride's premarital virginity in many societies. All of these factors and several others, he contended, made it inconceivable that humans were originally promiscuous. Thus humans must always have had marriage and always organized themselves into family groups.[2]

And, indeed, Westermarck turned out to be right. Everywhere, even in simple, small-scale societies, marriage and family life exist. This chapter explores the nature of these social institutions. We begin by looking at the importance of kinship in human societies, and then to the various ways in which kinship groups are organized. From whom do people consider themselves descended, and why do they often emphasize one set of ancestors over another? This leads to a discussion of marital institutions. Are people limited to one spouse at a time, or can they have several? What determines the number they are permitted? And, not least, why does marriage exist at all?

Kith and Kin

In the ancestral environment, people spent most of their lives interacting with kin, not only parents and offspring but also aunts, uncles, and cousins of varying degrees of relatedness. Kinship enveloped everyone and was the whole basis of the structure of society. People favored kin over non-kin and close kin over more distant kin. So important was kinship in the ancestral environment that anthropologists have often called these kinds of societies "kinship-based societies," and when studying their modern offshoots they spend a great deal of time reconstructing the kinship system.

Modern hunter-gatherer societies are as enveloped in kinship relations as their ancestral counterparts. But horticultural, agrarian, and pastoral societies also pay great attention to kinship. Kin groups can be thought of in terms of three levels of kinship extension. The smallest and simplest kin group is the nuclear family, which consists of parents and offspring living together in a common household. Nuclear families are always embedded in larger or extended families, which extend kinship vertically (multiple generations) and laterally (related nuclear families that include aunts, uncles, and cousins). Sometimes these extended families can be very large, in which case anthropologists speak of *lineages* and *clans*. Lineages and clans are named groups (usually after animals, e.g., Eagle Clan, Lizard Clan), own collective title to land or animal herds, regulate marriage, and perform common religious and other rituals.[3] Nuclear families predominate in hunter-gatherer and industrial societies, lineages and clans in horticultural and some agrarian societies, and extended families in most agrarian societies.[4]

When the extended family is the basic residential unit, it can take different forms. One type of extended family is the *joint family*—three generations living under a common roof, pooling resources, and headed in most cases by the eldest male. All of the brothers live together along with their fathers, sons, and in-marrying wives, and inherit equally at the father's death. This type of family was found in Asian societies such as China and India and was also prominent for many centuries throughout much of Eastern Europe.[5] In Serbia, for example, the most common family unit was the *zadruga*, a large extended household containing three or four nuclear families controlled by a patriarch and functioning as a single economic unit. A *zadruga* could include as many as thirty people. In the Russian province of Kurland there was a similar type of extended household, the *Gesind*, whose average size was about fourteen members.[6] Where people live in joint families they are thoroughly enveloped by kin relations.

A *stem family* is a segment of a joint family; it consists of a couple, their unmarried minor children, and one married son and his wife. Under this system, only one son (usually the eldest) inherits the farm and continues to live with his parents. Other sons normally leave the household and work for others as, say, farm hands or servants, or in some cases join religious orders or the military. For centuries throughout Western Europe this type of family was the rule, although from about the sixteenth century nuclear families became increasingly prominent.[7]

A half century ago many sociologists were claiming that family and kinship had "shrunk" in modern industrial societies—that they are no longer as important in these societies as they are in nonindustrial societies. Talcott Parsons, a legendary sociologist at Harvard University, put forth the idea that the modern family is an "isolated nuclear family."[8] This nuclear family neither lives with nor pools its money with the extended kin group of either husband or wife, is economically independent, and in most cases has limited contact with extended kin. But no sooner was this thesis stated than it was challenged. The family historian Edward Shorter looked at working-class families in a section of London and found what he called a "stunning intensity of kin contacts."[9] Other studies also contradicted, or at least strongly qualified, Parsons's thesis. These studies found that extended kin networks in urban areas had seldom disintegrated, that most urban working-class couples spent much more of their leisure time with extended kin than with friends or work associates, and that the urban middle classes expressed a nearly universal desire to spend time with extended kin.[10]

In 1977 sociologists Robert Winch and Gay Kitson found that the vast majority of the people they studied were significantly involved in larger kin networks. They noted that only 13 percent of American families could be described as isolated nuclear families. By contrast, 75 percent belonged to what the authors called "embedded" nuclear families, which were nuclear families highly involved in a network of extended kin.[11]

For the past three decades an international network of social scientists has engaged in a large-scale project known as the World Values Survey. They have interviewed thousands of persons in selected nations, by now nearly one hundred. Researchers ask people questions about their values and attitudes, but the one most germane here is, "How important is family in your life?" Table 6.1 summarizes the findings for selected countries for the year 2006. The results are striking, to say the least. The overwhelming majority of people in every society say that family relations are very important to them. At the other end of the spectrum, the percentage of individuals who say that family relations are not at all important is vanishingly small, in fact barely above zero and never above 1 percent. And it makes little difference whether people live in an advanced industrial society or a very poor traditional society. Families are virtually as important for people living in the rich democracies as they are for people living in the poorest traditional societies.

Nevertheless, in recent decades the family has weakened in industrial societies as divorce has become increasingly common and single-parent households much more numerous.[12] If you think this might overturn the theory of kin selection, remember that the maximization principle is a *modified* maximization principle. Biological predispositions always interact with socioecological context, and in many cases this context can alter how predispositions function, enhancing them in

TABLE 6.1   Importance Attached to Family Life in
Selected Contemporary Societies

Society	Family Very Important	Family Not at All Important
Egypt	98	0.0
Indonesia	98	0.0
Turkey	98	0.1
Mexico	95	0.3
United States	95	0.5
Iran	94	0.3
Poland	94	0.3
Canada	93	0.1
Ethiopia	93	0.6
Italy	93	0.1
Japan	93	0.1
Mali	93	0.1
Argentina	92	0.2
Sweden	92	0.3
Zambia	92	0.2
India	91	0.1
Chile	90	0.3
Norway	90	0.0

Source: World Values Survey 1981–2008, http://www.worldvaluessurvey.org.
Numbers are percentages.

some instances but also toning them down in others. The special conditions of late industrial societies—the kind of work people do, the emergence of highly effective and widely available contraception, the massive entry of women into the labor force, and the rising status of women more generally—have had a major impact on family life. But people still favor kin over non-kin and, as Table 6.1 indisputably shows, family relations are still extremely important to people in even the most advanced industrial societies. Kin selection is still alive and well throughout the entire world in the early twenty-first century.

Father's Kin or Mother's?

All societies organize relatives into groups based on one or another principle of descent. The descent principle familiar to the members of modern industrial societies is *bilateral* descent. People trace their relatives on both the father's side and the mother's side, and the relatives on each side are, in principle at least, considered equally important. One has grandparents, uncles, aunts, and cousins who are paternal and those who are maternal. Inheritance is passed down through both sons and daughters, in many cases more or less equally. Bilateral descent is found where the nuclear family is the basic form of family life, which is the case in all industrial societies and the majority of hunter-gatherers, or where people are organized into extended families of fairly small scale.

Only about a third of the world's societies have bilateral descent, so you can see that it is not the most prominent form. That form is *patrilineal* descent. Here people are aggregated into large extended families or lineages and clans. Patrilineal means "father's line," so in a patrilineal society people emphasize the father's relatives over the mother's. The ancestors are one's father, his father, his father's father, and so on. Descendants include both sons and daughters, and the sons' offspring but not the daughters' offspring. When they marry, daughters end up belonging elsewhere—to a different patrilineal group—because they cannot marry within their own group, a nearly universal prohibition known as *exogamy*. Obviously you cannot marry your sisters or brothers, but neither can you marry cousins within your group (although you can often marry cousins belonging to some other group). Sons stay with the group and bring in wives from other groups. Daughters leave and marry into other groups. Whether daughters become lost to their natal groups (the group of their birth) often depends on how far away the husband's group is. If it is far away, as was often the case in traditional China, the daughter could be lost to her lineage, although she might still retain some ties to it. If the husband's group is nearby, which it often is, then the daughters usually maintain a close association with their natal group.

In addition to determining which relatives to emphasize, people obviously have to organize themselves into households. If husbands and wives are going to live together, because they come from different kin groups someone has to move. In patrilineal societies it is almost always the wife, in which case we say that the composition of the household is *patrilocal*. The wife moves in with her husband's group, which includes his father, brothers, father's brothers, and so on. This is the case if the residential unit is some kind of extended family. Nuclear families in some cases maintain separate households but still live close by, maybe next door or at the very least in the same village or section of a village. In this case the new wife is living only with her husband and their children.

For countless years China was a strongly patrilineal and patrilocal society. India has also been patrilineal and patrilocal for millennia, as has the Islamic world. These are the three regions of the world most likely to be patrilineal and usually intensely patrilineal. (Europe, by contrast, has a long history of bilateral descent.) But patrilineality has also been found in many horticultural and pastoral societies, being especially common among herders.

Close to half of the world's societies have had some form of patrilineality. Others, on the order of about one in seven, have adopted the practice of tracing their principal relatives through mothers. This practice, *matrilineal* descent, has some interesting features that are unfamiliar to the members of modern industrial societies and usually seem strange and perplexing. The principal ancestors are one's mother, mother's mother, mother's mother's mother, and so on. Because members of matrilineal groups have to obtain spouses from other groups, once again someone has to move—although, as we shall see, not always—and usually a man moves in with his wife's group, in which case we say that the household is *matrilocal*. But he is not and does not become part of the descent group whose members he is living with, instead keeping his affiliation with his original matrilineal group. When a couple has children they are brought up in that matrilocal household, but frequently when the sons reach puberty they move out. The household they move into is that of their mothers' brothers, their maternal uncles. This is where it gets interesting.

In patrilineal societies the key relationships are between fathers and sons and between brothers. They are the core of the lineage or clan. But in matrilineal societies things work differently. The key relationships are mother-daughter, mother-son, and brother-sister. Fathers and their children have an important relationship, but the children (sons in particular) have a more important tie to their mother's brothers. Fathers live with and rear sons when they are still young, but later the uncle more or less takes over the upbringing, disciplining, and orienting of his sister's sons. This is the reason the son may eventually move in with his mother's brother, a form of residence known as *avunculocality*. (The term is based on the Greek word *avunculus*, which means maternal uncle. The Greeks had a different word for the paternal uncle, *patruus*. The distinction between the two kinds of uncles was important for them, hence the different terms. Because we use only a single term for both sets of uncles, the distinction for us is obviously unimportant.) In matrilineal societies, the matrilineage (or matriclan) is the property-owning group. Rights to the lineage's or clan's property pass through women (mothers) but are usually controlled by men (mothers' brothers). Young men gain access to property by virtue of their membership in the matrilineage.

The most famous matrilineal society ever described is the Trobriand Islanders, a group living off the northeast coast of New Guinea. They were closely studied in the 1920s by the legendary anthropologist Bronislaw Malinowski of the London School of Economics.[13] The Trobrianders take the view that it is the mother alone who produces offspring, men not contributing in any way. It has often been said that they are the only known society not to recognize that sexual intercourse is the basis of reproduction. However, this seems very unlikely; why should there be only one society on earth not to know this? Though the Trobrianders may imply this, it seems likely that when they say the man does not contribute to the formation of children, they are simply expressing the fact that the more important *social connection* is mother to child rather than father to child.

Be that as it may, for Trobrianders, the term "father" has a social rather than a biological meaning. This "father" is thought of mainly as the mother's husband, and is known as a boy's *tama*. But as a boy matures he learns that he does not belong to the same clan as his *tama*, and the *tama* is often described as a *tomakava*—an outsider or even a stranger. Malinowski described marital residence among the Trobrianders as patrilocal, since a wife goes to live with her husband, but it is more accurately identified as avunculocal, since upon marriage a boy leaves his *tama's* household and moves into the household or village of his mother's brother, or *kada*. The relationship between a boy and his *tama* is close and affectionate and the *tama* exercises authority over him, but at the boy's maturity his *kada* takes over. He becomes the authority figure, and the authority of the *tama* declines proportionately.[14] The *kada* instructs his nephew

> in lineage and sub-clan traditions; he takes his nephew to work with him
> in the fields to which the youth has a claim. . . . The mother's brother
> introduces the youth to pride in his lineage, ambition, and promises of
> future wealth and prestige. As the boy grows older his mother's brother
> demands more work of him. The boy goes frequently to his mother's
> brother's house for ceremonies and feasts involving his own sub-clan.[15]

The term "mother's brother" is a bit of shorthand, not only in the Trobriand case but with respect to all matrilineal societies, because a boy or man usually has several mother's brothers. Usually mother's brother refers to the eldest brother, who is the primary authority figure; nevertheless, other brothers also tend to play a role.[16]

Another well-known instance of matrilineality is the Nayar of the Malabar coast of India. The Nayar have the main features of matrilineal descent, but with some interesting variations. The most important of these is the unusually weak relationship between a husband and wife. Marriage is frequently a mere formality, and a woman often ritually marries several husbands. A husband usually does not live with his wife, only visiting her from time to time in order to have sex and, in some instances, for companionship. It is considered perfectly acceptable for a woman to have sex with all of her "husbands." When a man wants to visit his wife he may make arrangements in advance with the other "husbands," or leave his weapons at the door to indicate to any other "husband" that she is occupied. A man has no responsibility to support his wife because she receives all of the basic necessities of life from her matrilineal group, which the Nayar call the *taravad*.[17]

Because a woman regularly has sexual relations with several ritual husbands (and sometimes with other men as well), the question of paternity naturally arises. The Nayar handle this problem by asking one of the husbands, or sometimes more than one, to acknowledge paternity. But this is more a social than a biological recognition of paternity, since in most cases paternity cannot be determined with any degree of certainty. What then is the nature of the relationship between the man who assumes paternity, the "father," to his "son"? The tie is usually weak, although if a man thinks a particular boy is actually his own natural son then he might feel a special affection for him. But a "father" has no obligations toward his "sons," and the "sons" have no claims on the "father" or other members of his kin group.[18]

The man with the obligations, of course, is the mother's brother, known as the *karanavan* (more precisely, the *karanavan* is the mother's eldest brother). A *karanavan* trains his nephews in literacy, military skills, and agricultural work, and he secures the land of the *taravad* for them as his heirs. Nephews owe their *karanavan* great respect. The younger uncles also take an interest in their nephews, and the nephews are taught to show respect to these uncles as well.

Matrilineality is frequently confused with *matriarchy*, the exercise of power or authority by women. In fact, in all matrilineal societies, as in every other known society, it is men who are the principal power holders even though matrilineal inheritance passes through women. Nevertheless, women generally have more influence, sometimes much more, in matrilineal societies than in patrilineal or bilateral societies. The Iroquois of upstate New York and adjacent parts of Canada were a matrilineal society in which women were considered the principal owners of property, and they wielded considerable authority over the affairs of their matrilineages. A special position held by a highly regarded woman was that of *matron*. This was a woman who had the authority to veto decisions made by men. Notice, however, that this was *veto power only*. It was the men who were really in charge. The Iroquois would have been a matriarchy only if it were the women who were mainly in charge and the men who had the veto power.

What explains these different descent patterns? Why is patrilineality more common than any other form of descent, and, given its unusual nature, why does matrilineality exist at all? Descent groups are mainly about reproduction and heirship. As we have seen, in patrilineal societies the key relationships are father-son and brother-brother. Emphasis is placed on producing more sons than daughters and on passing inheritance to these sons. Why sons? Because the reproductive potential of males is greater, often much greater, than that of females. Females can only produce so many offspring in a lifetime, but males can produce many, sometimes hundreds.[19] This is especially true when men have several wives. John Hartung looked at over four hundred societies from the *Ethnographic Atlas* for which there was information on both inheritance type and marriage type. He found that 58 percent of monogamous societies transmitted wealth primarily or only to sons compared to 80 percent of societies with limited polygyny and 97 percent of societies with more extensive polygyny.[20] (Polygyny is the marriage arrangement whereby men take more than one wife. It is discussed below.)

The widespread practice of patrilineal descent therefore makes sense as a strategy designed to maximize reproductive success. But what then of matrilineal descent? Why would a maternal uncle take precedence over a (reputed) biological father? In matrilineal societies men often spend long periods away from their home villages. The Trobrianders participate in a network of long-distance economic exchange known as the *kula ring*. Men leave in their canoes and may be gone for weeks trading with societies hundreds of miles away. Among the Nayar, men specialize in warfare—the Nayar are actually a military subcaste—and many of them are not home much at all. Among the Iroquois men traveled hundreds of miles to fight wars against other tribes and to participate in the fur trade. Like the Trobrianders and the Nayar, they were gone much of the time and the women were left at home to tend the gardens and manage their matrilineage's affairs. Among the Navaho of the American Southwest, another matrilineal society, many men were gone from their villages for long periods working for wages. And among the Mosuo, a matrilineal minority population in southwest China, men have had prolonged absences participating in the caravan trade.

Different scholars have developed contrasting views of the significance of long-term male absence, but what is likely happening is captured by the old phrase "when the cat's away the mice will play." In all societies (except under very unusual circumstances) men feel sexual jealousy and try to prevent their wives from having sexual affairs with other men. This means, at the very least, paying attention to the men the women are interacting with and women's unexpected absences from their usual tasks. If a woman is observed expressing more than a casual interest in a man other than her husband, and if both are seen to be absent from their village during a particular afternoon, suspicions arise. And actions are taken. But what if the men are away from home much of the time? There may lie the secret. When a husband is not around to watch what his wife is doing, then it is much easier for her to take an interest in a man who *is* around and to act on that interest. She is a mouse whose cat has disappeared over the horizon.

A Darwinian evolutionary explanation of matrilineality that picks up on this theme has been developed by Richard Alexander and Jeffrey Kurland.[21] Whereas patrilineality involves the investment of fathers in their sons, matrilineality involves the investment of a man in his sister's sons. Why do the latter rather than the former? *Because the boys you think are your sons may not actually be your sons*! If you invest heavily in them and they are another man's sons, then you are promoting *his* reproductive success rather than your own. When men are away much of the time, they have good reason to suspect that their wives may be unfaithful. If they are having sex with other men, there is a good chance they will be impregnated by some of those men, which means that husbands have a high degree of uncertainty about paternity. For men, paternity uncertainty is bad. Very bad.

How can men deal with this threat to their reproductive interests? Alexander and Kurland suggest that the solution is to invest in a sister's sons because men are certain they are related to them by one-quarter of their genes. This is preferable to investing in boys to whom one may have zero relatedness. In essence men are attempting to cut their losses. Matrilineality for men leads to lower levels of reproductive success than patrilineality—although this can be counteracted by being unfaithful yourself and impregnating other men's wives or unmarried women—but it will lead to greater reproductive success than being cuckolded by a wife. From this point of view, matrilineality is an anticuckoldry strategy.

There is good reason to think that this explanation may well be correct. A study that analyzed sixty nonindustrial societies found that 92 percent of matrilineal societies had low paternity certainty compared to 20 percent of bilateral societies and just 18 percent of patrilineal societies.[22] These findings are bolstered by ethnographic evidence. Among the Nayar, for example, high levels of paternity uncertainty are unavoidable when a man's wife has sex with other "husbands" (and also other lovers). Kathleen Gough quotes a saying of the Malayali, neighbors of the Nayar: "No Nayar knows his father."[23] Indeed.[24]

One Wife or Many?

Why do people marry? In modern societies, nearly everyone marries for love and lifelong companionship. Most couples intend to produce children. Yet increasingly there are people who seek love and companionship but not children, and for them marriage is love and companionship pure and simple. Nonindustrial peoples would have difficulty understanding these motives, for the fact is that in all societies up until modern times marriage was a *reproductive contract*, a way to produce and successfully rear children.[25] This makes complete sense from a Darwinian evolutionary perspective in which people are trying to promote their reproductive success. Of course, marriage is still to a large extent a reproductive contract, but it is a good deal more than that. In nonindustrial societies marriage was *only* a reproductive contract.

The question is, how to marry, whom to marry, and how many wives or husbands to have. In all modern industrial societies, indeed in the majority of societies in the contemporary world, marriage is monogamous by law. Only in sub-Saharan Africa and in parts of the Islamic world may a man take more than one wife.[26] But it has not always been this way. Throughout history, *polygyny*—the marriage of one man to two or more women—has been permitted and usually encouraged.[27] In the *Ethnographic Atlas*, fully 85 percent of the societies permit polygyny and only about 14 percent are monogamous. Since most societies have been polygynous, we begin with them.

In the majority of polygynous societies, only a small percentage of the male population, often less than 10 percent, will ever have more than one wife. But in some societies the percentage can be much higher. Anthropologists speak of *general polygyny* when 20 percent or more of the adult male population is polygynously married. General polygyny can become very general indeed. Two regions lead the world in the extent of male polygyny, aboriginal Australia and sub-Saharan Africa. In both regions, about one-third of adult males are on average polygynous, and in some societies the percentages can be astonishingly high. In Australia, among the Tiwi 70 percent of men are involved in polygynous unions, and among the Aranda the figure is 60 percent.[28] In sub-Saharan Africa, about 60 percent of men among the Otoro have multiple wives; among the Ganda, it is 55 percent, the Ashanti 49 percent, the Nyakyusa 44 percent, and the Thonga and Hausa 40 percent. But the leader among sub-Saharan African societies is clearly the Mende, among whom 90 percent of adult males are polygynous at some point in their lives. Some societies in both North and South America have had exceptionally high levels of polygyny. Among the North American Hidatsa the figure was 90 percent and among the Pawnee 54 percent. In South America, among both the Warrau and the Saramacca, 60 percent of men have more than one wife.[29]

The level of polygyny in a society can also be ascertained by looking at the number of women who are in polygynous unions, which of course will always exceed the number of men. Among the Tiwi 90 percent of women are in polygynous unions and among the Aranda it is 78 percent. Among the Otoro 77 percent of women have co-wives and among the Mende it is 97 percent. Among the Warrau and Saramacca the respective figures are 95 and 85 percent.[30]

Where only a small fraction of men have multiple wives, and where societies have significant divisions of status and wealth, it is invariably wealthy, high-status men who are the polygynists, and in direct proportion to their social standing. Laura Betzig has closely studied the relationship between social rank and the number of wives a man possesses. In societies in which differences in status and wealth are extreme, men of highest rank often have harems of hundreds of wives. In ancient Israel, for example, King Solomon is reported to have had some seven hundred. Among the Zande of Africa, the king may have had five hundred or more wives, and lesser chiefs as many as one hundred. The Inca of Peru had a graded political and economic hierarchy that closely corresponded to a graded hierarchy of polygyny. Persons of highest rank got fifty wives, leaders of vassal nations thirty, heads of large provinces twenty, and leaders of small provinces twelve to fifteen.[31]

How is it possible for so many men to have more than one wife when a society has approximately the same number of women as men? There are two basic reasons. First, not all men in a society are polygynously married at a single time. A man often starts out with a single wife and adds wives as he gets older. In addition, many men may have *no wives*. Polygynous men take women out of circulation and make them scarce as potential wives. Some men therefore will never be able to marry.

Why is polygyny so widespread? A common answer is that it enhances male prestige. This explanation, though, begs the question as to why having more than one wife would be considered prestigious. Moreover, a man needs prestige in the first place in order to obtain extra wives. As we saw in Chapter 5, in all societies women seek husbands of high status who command resources, as do women's families when seeking to arrange a marriage. Men with higher status and greater resources offer a better life for a woman and her children. Men of ordinary social status and few economic resources end up being monogamous or never marrying. Thus the causal arrows tend to point to prestige determining polygyny rather than polygyny determining prestige, although the more wives a man has the more his prestige is likely to be enhanced.

Other than status and resources, few factors show any consistent relationship with polygyny. Polygyny is related to a society's type of economy as well as to the extent to which women perform valuable agricultural labor. Polygyny is most common in societies that practice some type of horticulture or pastoralism and less common among hunter-gatherers. In agrarian societies only a small fraction of men are polygynous (almost all of them elite men), the rest being monogamous or celibate. If a man is to have several wives, he has to be able to support them, and most men in agrarian societies are poor peasants who do not have the resources to do so. Women in many of these societies perform little agricultural labor—as noted earlier, these are male-farming societies—and thus are economically costly. Women earn their keep primarily through domestic labor and bearing and rearing offspring.

Horticultural societies, though, are female-farming societies, or those in which women do the bulk of the agricultural labor. This makes women less costly economically, and thus it is easier for a man to support more than one wife. Women often become economic assets rather than liabilities; more land can be cultivated with several wives than with just one, and thus more economic resources can be obtained. Polygyny may therefore have an economic motive.

But this is not men's principal motive. To identify this motive, we once again look to the animals. Most mammals are polygynous and in many species a few dominant males may copulate with most of the females. Polygyny in nonhuman animals can be understood in terms of the differences between male and female reproductive strategies. Since eggs are expensive relative to sperm—a male can produce millions of sperm in a single ejaculate, whereas a female can only produce a small number of eggs in a reproductive lifetime—it is to any female's advantage to be selective in her choice of mate and to choose a male who can provide the best genes for her offspring. It is also natural that she would be the sex to provide most of the parental care. But since sperm is cheap it makes sense for males to attempt copulation with many females and to invest less effort in parental care. (Recall the distinction made in the last chapter between parental investment and mating effort.) These differences in reproductive strategy will, of course, have a biological substrate in the brain; males will be driven by their innate predisposition to acquire multiple mates. Just as it is with most mammals, so it is with humans. The human male is a naturally polygynous creature. His brain is telling him to seek sexual variety as an end in itself, and it is this desire that is the proximate cause of widespread polygyny (the ultimate cause being the reproductive benefits that come with multiple mates).

So polygyny exists in a society because men want it. But how do women feel about the presence of co-wives? They may resist it because they dislike sharing a husband and because conflict among co-wives is common. One might construct a thought experiment in which a number of strangers come together to establish a new society from scratch and women are given a choice of monogamy or polygyny. What will they choose? The chances are very good that they will choose monogamy.

However, in real societies men usually exercise more power than women and are more likely to get their way in marriage arrangements. Polygyny logically follows. If polygyny already exists within a society at the behest of men, what will women choose under these particular circumstances? Many of them will now choose to enter into polygynous marriages and put up with the disadvantages because polygynous men are those with status and resources, the things that women most readily seek in a husband.[32] Men with low status and few resources may be less desirable even if the marriage is monogamous. There is a saying: "Better to be the fifth wife of a wealthy man than the only wife of a poor one."

But which women choose polygyny and which reject it depends a great deal on the social position of the woman. In regions of the contemporary world where polygyny is still permitted, the women who are most likely to be in polygynous marriages are found in the traditional rural sectors of their societies. These women often have few options and polygynous marriage may be the best they can do. But better-educated women from higher-status backgrounds who work in cities generally resist polygyny. They regard it as degrading and are unwilling to put up with it. Moreover, they are more likely to find men of means with whom they can form monogamous marriages.[33]

If men so strongly desire polygyny, then why do some societies go against the grain and become monogamous? Richard Alexander has distinguished two forms of monogamy—*ecologically imposed* and *socially imposed*. Ecologically imposed monogamy results when polygyny is allowed but resources are so scarce that no man can support extra wives. It is likely that most societies classified as monogamous in cross-cultural data banks are monogamous for this reason, not because polygyny is disdained and monogamy idealized. Socially imposed monogamy, on the other hand, results when polygyny is prohibited by custom or law. All modern industrial societies and the majority of less-developed societies have socially imposed monogamy. In these societies it is against the law to be legally married to more than one woman. A man who wants to take a second wife must divorce the first.

A number of agrarian societies are thought to have had socially imposed monogamy, such as the ancient Egyptians and Babylonians, the Manchu and northern Chinese, and the ancient Greeks and Romans. However, only the Greeks and Romans (and to some extent medieval Europeans) unambiguously belong in this category, since elite polygyny clearly existed in all of the other societies.[34] And even the Greeks and Romans were not strictly monogamous, since men were permitted concubines—women who served as companions and sexual partners but did not have full rights as wives; most elite men had them. Elite men also had sexual access to large numbers of female slaves. In essence, Rome and Greece were technically monogamous but had de facto polygyny, or, as Betzig has put it, *marriage* was monogamous but *mating* was polygynous.[35]

Alexander has proposed an interesting theory of socially imposed monogamy that emphasizes what he calls reproductive opportunity leveling. The basic idea starts from the recognition that polygyny leads to conflict between men because they are competing with each other for wives. And the more widespread polygyny is in a society the more intense the conflict. In large-scale societies engaged in frequent wars of conquest, large pools of young men must be recruited as soldiers. Wars will be more successful when conflict among warriors is minimized and armies constitute highly cohesive units. The best way to ensure this, Alexander claims, is to impose monogamy on all men. Every man is thus able to marry (in principle at least), and this reduces conflict among men over women.

One attempt to test this theory examined eighty-four contemporary nation-states with socially imposed monogamy and seventy-two that permitted polygyny. If Alexander was right, then large-scale societies with monogamy would be expected to exhibit greater success than large-scale societies permitting polygyny. The results were consistent with this hypothesis. For example, the monogamous societies were much larger, averaging 52 million inhabitants compared to 20 million for the polygynous societies. The monogamous societies also had a higher level of economic development—$9,710 in per capita gross domestic product compared to $2,235—as well as greater military strength.[36] However, we do not know what the direction of causation is. Rather than monogamy coming first and leading to greater societal success, it is just as plausible to claim that societies that are already more successful are the ones that go on to develop monogamy.

The most obvious difficulty with Alexander's theory is that, as noted above, all nonindustrial states, except for ancient Rome and Greece and medieval Europe, have not had socially imposed monogamy. For Alexander's theory to be convincing, a large number of nonindustrial states should have prohibited polygyny. But they didn't. Moreover, there is no indication that the polygynous civilizations of earlier times were less successful because of it. As Kevin MacDonald has pointed out, "Classical China existed as a civilization for 3,000 years with an intensively polygynous mating system and the civilizations of India, the Moslem world, and the New World (Aztecs and Incas) were similarly long lived."[37] In large-scale states, only elite men have the means to support multiple wives. The vast majority of nonelite men do not need to have monogamy imposed on them, since many are unlikely to marry in the first place. Most warriors are recruited from outside the elite, and many of these will never even have one wife, let alone more than one.

Perhaps the most promising explanation of socially imposed monogamy is the incompatibility of polygyny with companionate marriage, a type of marriage in which husbands and wives are intimate partners and vow to remain romantically and sexually exclusive for a lifetime.[38] This would seem to account for monogamy's universality in modern industrial societies, all of which have companionate marriage. But there are still the cases of ancient Greece and Rome. Why did they have socially imposed monogamy? There is no agreed-on answer to this question, but there are some hints. Women had a higher status in Rome than in virtually all other agrarian societies. When a woman took property into a marriage in the form of a dowry, her husband claimed control of it, but the wife was entitled to a considerable inheritance upon his death. For an agrarian society, Rome also gave an unusual amount of emphasis to the husband-wife unit, and in fact Rome may have had a kind of precursor of modern companionate marriage.[39]

As Rome entered its period of decline and eventual collapse, it was overrun by the Germanic tribes that had lived on its borders for centuries. These tribes practiced elite polygyny, and thus polygyny was reestablished in the new feudal society that began to develop in medieval Europe. However, it was strongly opposed by the Catholic Church, which fought against it for centuries, and by the twelfth century (or perhaps somewhat earlier) polygyny was abolished once and for all. Monogamy became legally imposed on all men throughout Europe.

As Europe rose to world dominance after about 1500 CE and colonized many parts of the non-Western world, polygyny gradually fell by the wayside in those regions as well. This occurred either as the result of European encouragement (or insistence), the imitation of Western civilization, or both. One Asian nation after another embraced monogamy: Japan in 1880, Thailand in 1935, China in 1953, India in 1955, and Nepal in 1963. Even Islamic Turkey and Tunisia outlawed polygyny, in 1926 and 1956, respectively. And in nations where polygyny persists today, various legal restrictions have been placed on it, such as requiring a husband at the time of marriage to declare that he will take no additional wives.[40] Eventually the whole world is likely to have socially imposed monogamy. With continuing economic development and modernization, the last holdouts will eventually crumble as the status of women rises and more marriages become companionate.

One Husband or Many?

In addition to monogamy and polygyny there are two other possible ways to marry. One of these is *polyandry*, the marriage of one woman to two or more men. Polyandrous marriage is never found alone; in any society in which it is practiced, there are also some monogamous and even some polygynous marriages. Polyandrous marriages may not even constitute half of all marriages. There is also another type of marriage, polygynandry, that is found in conjunction with polyandry, but let us leave it aside for the moment.

Polyandry is a rare practice, found in only about one-half of one percent of the world's societies. From a Darwinian perspective, it is not difficult to see why. Because men compete among themselves for mates, and because they desire numerous mates, polyandry is a strategy that represents the very antithesis of male desire, especially when male sexual jealousy over females is added to the mix. How could any man tolerate sharing his wife with other men, and how could he possibly promote his own reproductive success by doing so?

Interestingly, almost all of the societies where polyandry is practiced are concentrated in one part of the world—Tibet and adjacent regions of Nepal and India. A number of Tibetan rural communities have been studied over a period of several decades by the anthropologist Melvyn Goldstein. In the village of Chimdro in south central Tibet, Goldstein found that in thirty-two of sixty-two marriages (52 percent) two or more men shared a wife, with the rest of the marriages being monogamous. The men in polyandrous unions were not just any randomly selected men, however, but were brothers, a practice known as *fraternal polyandry*. In twenty-four of the thirty-two polyandrous marriages, two brothers shared a wife, in seven others it was three brothers, and in the remaining union four brothers were sharing a wife (these are known, respectively, as bi-fraternal, tri-fraternal, and quatra-fraternal polyandry).[41]

Another Tibetan community, this one located in the Ding-ri valley of southwestern Tibet, has been studied by Barbara Aziz. She found that although the Ding-ri valley Tibetans practice polyandry, only 19 percent of all marriages were polyandrous. Most (72 percent) were monogamous, but 5 percent were polygynous, and in the majority of these the wives were sisters, a form of polygyny known to anthropologists as *sororal polygyny*. But it gets even more interesting. Aziz found that 8 of the 430 marriages she studied took a form known as bi-generational polyandry, a union in which a man whose wife has died joins with a son to take on a wife. Aziz also found ten cases of bi-generational polygyny, or unions in which a widow and her daughter undertook a marriage with one man.[42]

And there is a further wrinkle. Nancy Levine studied eighty-nine marriages in the village of Barkhang in northwestern Nepal. She discovered forty-six polyandrous marriages, or about 52 percent of the total, exactly the same rate of polyandry as found among the Chimdro Tibetans. The majority of these were either bi-fraternal or tri-fraternal unions, but there were eleven quatra-fraternal unions (4 brothers), four that were penta-fraternal (5 brothers), one that was hexa-fraternal (6 brothers), and one that was septa-fraternal (7 brothers). Thirty-eight marriages were monogamous (43 percent) and five were polygynous (6 percent).[43]

Obviously, marriage among these Tibetan and Nepalese peoples is extraordinarily varied, but there is still one more form of marriage: *polygynandry*, two instances of which were found by Levine among the Barkhang. Polygynandry exists when two or more men (usually brothers) are simultaneously married to two or more women (usually sisters). In the nineteenth century a number of anthropologists speculated that some societies practiced a kind of "group marriage." Eventually this idea was pooh-poohed and it was decided that no such thing had ever existed. But it does, and polygynandry is it! It is extremely rare, of course, but there it is among the Barkhang, and if the Barkhang have it then there is a good chance that at least one or two other communities have it as well.

What is at play here? Why does polyandry exist, and why is it found in con-junction with other marriage types, sometimes with all of the possible types? The communities just discussed all practice agriculture or animal husbandry and live in very dry environments at extremely high elevations (around 13,000 feet). Water is extremely scarce, much of the land is strewn with boulders, and cultivation is difficult. Bringing previously uncultivated land into production is an arduous task.[44] Surviving in such an environment is a real challenge because the land is not very productive, and among some groups land is scarce and the size of a family farm tends to be small. How then to manage the land so that people can do the best job of surviving and reproducing?

These polyandrous communities recognize that to divide the land among broth-ers from one generation to the next (a practice known as *partible inheritance*) would give no brother enough land to make a living. Therefore, although each brother is entitled to a share of the land, the brothers generally pool their shares in order to farm the land as a collective unit, and they bring in a wife to carry out domestic work and to give them offspring. Thus polyandry.[45]

Understanding why polyandry may range from bi-fraternal to septa-fraternal is a matter of understanding family composition. Bi-fraternal polyandry results when there are two brothers, tri-fraternal when there are three, and so on. If there is only one son, then the likely outcome is monogamy. But what if there are no sons at all but, say, two daughters? Each daughter could be separately married off to a set of brothers, but it is also possible for someone else's only son to join these sisters in a polygynous marriage. Polygyny can also result when a wife in a monogamous union has been declared infertile or has failed to produce sons, and the husband brings in a second wife to produce (male) heirs. Finally, polygynandry would be the outcome if, in a bi-fraternal polyandrous marriage, the wife was infertile or failed to produce sons and a second wife was brought in. If she happened to be a sister of the first wife, then we would have the extraordinary practice of "bi-fraternal, bi-sororal polygynandry."

The Stanford anthropologist William Durham, who has surveyed in detail all of these instances of polyandry, concludes that polyandry is an economic strategy that has evolved from the unusual nature of the environments in which the Tibetan and Nepalese populations live. Keeping brothers together prevents land from being partitioned into excessively small plots, and thus maximizes the amount of land a family can farm. It also maximizes the number of males available to work the land, because labor scarcity is another fact of life in these high-altitude communities. Durham calls his idea the "hypothesis of family property conservation."[46]

But Durham also wants to know whether polyandry could actually have reproduc-tive advantages. At first glance the answer would seem to be a clear no, since brothers can only inseminate a single woman. Indeed, a study by Goldstein and Cynthia Beall found that men in polyandrous marriages had lower levels of reproductive success than men who were monogamously married.[47] (Note that calculating reproductive success in polyandrous marriages is complicated by the fact that, regardless of who is the biological father of a given child, all of the brothers will be related to that child by at least one-quarter of their genes. In other words, all but the biological father will be the child's uncles.) However, Goldstein and Beall's study was limited to calculating reproductive success for just a single generation. Durham carried out computer simulations in which he calculated levels of reproductive success over several generations. He found that monogamy led to greater reproductive success for one or two generations, but that polyandry was superior after three generations. Moreover, monogamy generally led to reproductive disaster after several generations, with entire family lines becoming extinct.

Durham points out that these populations do not emphasize the beneficial long-term reproductive consequences of polyandry, but rather its beneficial economic consequences. Indeed, he notes that they, like humans everywhere, are generally incapable of calculating reproductive gains or losses several generations down the road. And were their focus to be on short-term reproductive benefits (one or two generations), they would be misled into favoring monogamy since it is more beneficial over the short term. The explanation for their behavior, then, is economic rather than reproductive despite the long-term reproductive benefits of that behavior. More precisely, the proximate cause of their behavior is economic but the ultimate cause is reproductive. Has natural selection, then, shaped the human brain to carefully adjust marital behavior so as to maximize reproductive success even though people may not realize that is what they are actually doing? It is a tantalizing suggestion.

Be that as it may, Durham's focus on the importance of family property conservation seems justified by an additional line of evidence that has so far not been mentioned. The practices we have been discussing have been found among people who own land and who have the right to pass their land to later generations. But there are other groups who live by working someone else's land and who consequently have no land to pass to heirs. And these groups are strictly monogamous. If there is no family property to conserve, and if that is the point of polyandry, then why practice it, especially since it goes strongly against the grain of human nature, male nature in particular?

In a paper published in 2012, Katherine Starkweather and Raymond Hames insist that polyandry is not as rare as most anthropologists think. They distinguish between what they call *classical* and *nonclassical* polyandry. Classical polyandry refers to the Tibetan and Nepalese societies discussed above. In classical systems, the frequency of polyandrous unions relative to other unions is greater than in nonclassical systems, sometimes reaching 50 percent or higher. In addition, polygynandry is sometimes found in classical systems but not in nonclassical systems.[48]

The authors have combed through the ethnographic literature and claim to have identified fifty-three instances of nonclassical polyandry. They divide this category into two subcategories, formal and informal polyandry. In formal nonclassical polyandry there is a socially recognized marriage and coresidence. Thirty-nine of the nonclassical cases were of this type. In informal nonclassical polyandry there is no actual marriage or coresidence. Rather, several men have regular sexual relations with the same woman and these relations are considered legitimate within the society. Moreover, all of the men are considered responsible for taking care of the woman and her children. Fourteen of the nonclassical cases belonged to this category.[49]

Nonclassical polyandry is a horse of a different color from classical polyandry. In addition to the differences mentioned above, nonclassical polyandry is found mostly in egalitarian bands or tribes of hunter-gatherers and horticulturalists, whereas classical polyandry is found in agricultural or agro-pastoral societies. And to be counted as having nonclassical polyandry, a society needs to have just one recorded polyandrous union. What accounts for this different type of polyandry? Starkweather and Hames find that the most critical factor is a sex ratio that is highly skewed toward males. When there are not enough marriageable women to go around, one solution is for two or more men to share a wife. Such a solution is likely to be temporary, given that sex ratios can fluctuate rapidly. A sex ratio that changes from highly male-skewed to more evenly balanced should lead to a reduction in the number of polyandrous unions, or even their elimination. And there is evidence of this happening on a number of occasions.[50]

Nonclassical polyandry therefore seems like making the best of a bad situation. It is hardly an idealized form of marriage. What then of classical polyandry? Is it an idealized marriage arrangement? Although it is a more highly institutionalized and long-term practice than nonclassical polyandry, it also seems to be something of a necessary evil.[51] One serious problem with classical polyandry is conflicts and tensions between brothers and the disruption of overall family harmony. Sexual access to the wife is in principle equal, but this is often not the case in practice and can be a major source of tension. It is common for the oldest brother (senior cohusband) to restrict the access of his younger brothers to the wife, thus leading to their dissatisfaction and resentment as well as to the likelihood of reduced reproductive success. In addition, younger brothers are sometimes much younger than the wife, perhaps as many as ten to fifteen years younger. This rubs up against the male desire for younger women; junior husbands may find less satisfaction in being married to an older woman. These difficulties often lead polyandrous unions to break up, and it is the younger brothers who are most likely to leave the unions. They may then marry a younger wife, leading to both greater sexual satisfaction and better reproductive outcomes.[52] Problems in classical polyandrous marriages are most acute when there are three or more cohusbands.[53] In their study of the Nyimba, an ethnically Tibetan group living in Nepal, Nancy Levine and Joan Silk found that 58 percent of unions with four cohusbands broke up, compared to only 10 percent of unions with two cohusbands.[54]

Because of the wide range of terms used for different marriage arrangements and the intricacies of some of these arrangements, Table 6.2 has been constructed for ease of understanding.

TABLE 6.2   Forms of Marriage in the World's Societies

Marriage Form	Description	Variants	Frequency
Monogamy	Marriage of one man to one woman	*Socially imposed*: Monogamy imposed by custom or law. *Ecologically imposed*: Environmental circumstances make it difficult to support more than one wife.	Socially imposed monogamy found in all modern industrial societies. Ecologically imposed found in some 15 percent of nonindustrial societies
Polygamy	Plural marriage	Polygyny, polyandry, polygynandry	See under polygyny and polyandry
Polygyny	Marriage of one man to two or more women	*Sororal*: Marriage of one man to two or more sisters. *Non-sororal*: Marriage of one man to two or more women who are not sisters.	85 percent of world's societies
Polyandry	Marriage of one woman to two or more men	*Fraternal*: Marriage of one woman to two or more brothers. *Non-fraternal*: Marriage of one woman to two or more men who are not brothers.	Rare; less than one percent of world's societies
Classical polyandry	As above	As above	As above
Nonclassical polyandry	A very small number of unions (marital or sexual) within a society between one woman and several men	*Formal*: Socially recognized marriage and co-residence. *Informal*: Several men have sexual relations with one woman and assume responsibility for her and her children.	Rare, but more common than classical polyandry
Polygynandry	Marriage of two or more men to two or more women	None known.	Extremely rare. Found only in societies with polyandry as the dominant mode of marriage

SUMMARY

1. Kinship is of great importance in all societies. In small-scale societies people spend most of their time interacting with kin. Hunter-gatherers often live in nuclear families, but in horticultural and agrarian societies people live in one or another type of extended kin network. Even in modern industrial societies kin ties remain extremely important.

2. Many societies, especially horticultural societies, are organized into lineages and clans. In the majority the descent pattern is patrilineal, or traced through the father's line. In some the descent pattern is matrilineal, or traced through the mother's line. In the latter a boy's father is less important than his mother's brother, or maternal uncle. In matrilineal societies the matrilineage is the property-holding group, but property is usually controlled by the men of the lineage, the mother's brothers, rather than by fathers, as is the case in patrilineal societies. The much greater frequency of patrilineal descent may be due to the greater reproductive potential of males.

3. Matrilineal descent has drawn considerable attention from anthropologists, and a variety of explanations have been proposed. In recent years there has been convergence on the role of paternity uncertainty. Men in matrilineal societies are often gone from their home villages for extended periods. This makes it more likely that their wives will have affairs with other men, who may impregnate them. Men are therefore aware that in some cases they may not be the actual fathers of their wives' offspring. Under such circumstances, men may choose to invest in their sisters' offspring, to whom they are related by one-fourth of their genes, rather than in their wives' offspring, to whom they may not be related at all.

4. The vast majority of the world's societies (85 percent) have permitted polygyny, and in some polygynous societies a high percentage of men may have multiple wives. Polygyny is highly favored by men because of their desire for multiple mates and sexual variety. When men mate with several women rather than being limited to one, they increase their level of reproductive success, which means that polygyny is a male reproductive strategy.

5. Because women prefer men with status and resources, it is dominant males who are most likely to be the polygynists. In societies with sharp distinctions of status and wealth, elite men often have many wives and the number of wives is frequently proportionate to men's place within an elite status hierarchy.

6. Monogamy may be ecologically imposed or socially imposed. Ecologically imposed monogamy occurs when resources are so scanty that no man is able to provide for more than one wife. Socially imposed monogamy occurs when polygyny is prohibited by law or custom; no man is permitted more than one wife. Small-scale bands and tribes that are monogamous practice ecologically imposed monogamy.

7. The only large-scale nonindustrial societies to have socially imposed monogamy were the ancient Greeks and Romans. With these exceptions, socially imposed monogamy is found only among societies in the contemporary era.

8. After about 1500 CE and the European colonization of much of the world, polygyny began to fall by the wayside. Many societies that had permitted polygyny adopted monogamy. Nevertheless, in today's world nearly half of the world's nation-states still permit polygyny, although they may restrict it in certain ways. Most of these societies are found in Africa and the Middle East.

9. There is no consensus concerning the reasons for socially imposed monogamy. One theory is based on the idea of reproductive opportunity leveling. Because polygyny leads to conflict between men, large-scale societies impose monogamy on men in order to reduce this conflict. The point of reducing conflict is to increase the effectiveness of military units by making them more cohesive. A serious difficulty with this theory is that all large-scale nonindustrial societies other than Greece and Rome did not have socially imposed monogamy.

10. Another theory is that polygyny is incompatible with romantic love and close companionship as the principal basis for marriage. All highly developed modern societies have companionate and love-based marriage, and all have socially imposed monogamy.

11. A few societies have adopted the unusual practice of polyandry, or the marriage of one woman to two or more men, usually brothers. Most of these societies are located in Tibet and adjacent regions of Nepal and India. In societies that practice polyandry, some marriages are polygynous and others monogamous.

12. A common explanation of polyandry is that it is a form of impartible inheritance. The regions in which it is found are located at extremely high elevations; water is scarce and the land is difficult to cultivate. If brothers inherited the land separately, no man would have enough land to support a family. Keeping the brothers together and bringing in a wife provides enough land and labor to work the land. Polyandry is not an idealized form of marriage but tries to make the best of a difficult situation. One problem is that it frequently leads to conflict among brothers over sexual access to the wife.

13. Recently some anthropologists have identified several dozen cases of so-called nonclassical polyandry. In these cases only a very small number of marriages in a society will be polyandrous. Unlike classical polyandry, nonclassical polyandry may result from sex ratios that are highly skewed toward males, leading to a shortage of marriageable females.

QUESTIONS FOR DISCUSSION

✓ Are kin ties less important to people in modern societies than to people who lived in earlier societies? Why or why not?

✓ What is bilateral descent and where is it most likely to be found?

✓ Explain the differences between patrilineal and matrilineal societies.

✓ How does matrilineality work among the Trobriand Islanders, the best-known matrilineal society that has ever been discovered?

✓ In what ways may patrilineal and matrilineal descent be reproductive strategies? How does each relate to the problem of paternity uncertainty? Discuss.

✓ Patrilineal descent is the most common type of descent in the full range of human societies. Matrilineal descent is the least common. Why should the former be more common than the latter?

✓ What are the differences between monogamy, polygyny, and polyandry?

✓ In most of the world's societies polygyny is permitted and in some societies a high percentage of men are engaged in polygynous marriage. Why should this be?

✓ In a polygynous society, which men are most likely to be engaged in polygynous unions?

✓ Under what circumstances might polygyny be beneficial to, and favored by, women?

✓ Some have recently suggested that polygyny should be relegalized in modern societies because it is a basic human right. Do you think this could ever happen? How would women react to such a proposal? How would men react?

✓ What is the difference between ecologically imposed and socially imposed monogamy?

✓ If you were involved in a scavenger hunt and told to find a society with socially imposed monogamy, where would you look first?

✓ How can socially imposed monogamy be explained? Why is it a minority type of marriage arrangement?

✓ How common is polyandry and where is it found?

✓ Why is it that in societies classified as polyandrous many marriages are monogamous and some are polygynous? Discuss.

✓ Explain the difference between classical and nonclassical polyandry. Should societies with the nonclassical version really be called polyandrous societies?

✓ What are some of the causes of classical and nonclassical polyandry?

✓ What kinds of conflicts tend to develop in polyandrous marriages? How can they be resolved?

✓ Why is polyandrous marriage so rare?

References and Notes

1. Westermarck 1922a.
2. Westermarck 1922a.
3. Fox 1983.
4. Stephens 1963; Van den Berghe 1979.
5. Therborn 2004.
6. Alderson and Sanderson 1991.
7. Van den Berghe 1979; Therborn 2004.
8. Parsons 1943.
9. Shorter 1975.
10. Studies summarized in Sussman and Burchinal 1962.
11. Winch and Kitson 1977.
12. Popenoe 1993.
13. Malinowski 1929.
14. Fathauer 1961.
15. Fathauer 1961, pp. 252–253.
16. There can also be a situation in a matrilineal society in which a mother has no brothers. In this case, a grandmother's brother may then function as the mother's brother. In the rare instance in which even the grandmother has no brothers, a man can be "adopted" from another lineage to play this role.
17. Gough 1961.
18. Gough 1961.
19. In this regard, see Betzig 2012.
20. Hartung 1976, 1982.
21. Alexander 1974, 1975; Kurland 1979.
22. Unpublished research undertaken by the author. Measures of paternity certainty have been constructed by Gaulin and Schlegel 1980; Huber, Linhartova, and Cope 2004; and Flinn 1981. Results reported here are based on Flinn's measure.
23. Gough 1961.
24. Actually, there appears to be more to the story of matrilineality than paternity uncertainty. Recent research suggests that paternity uncertainty is important but that other factors are also involved. However, this research is very technical and therefore is beyond the bounds of the current discussion. But see Holden, Sear, and Mace 2003; Mattison 2011.
25. Buckle, Gallup, and Rodd 1996.
26. Michael Price 1999 classifies eighty-four contemporary nation-states as requiring monogamy and seventy-two as permitting multiple wives. Price leaves thirteen nation-states unclassified, but virtually all of these are undoubtedly monogamous.
27. Everyone wants to call this polygamy. But technically speaking, polygamy simply means plural marriages, and there are two types. Polygyny means multiple wives. In the few instances in which there may be multiple husbands, we call this form of polygamy polyandry.
28. D. White 1988.
29. D. White 1988.
30. D. White 1988.
31. Betzig 1986.
32. Sanderson 2001.

33. Ware 1979; Welch and Glick 1981; Armstrong et al. 1993; Nasir 1994; Pitshandenge 1994.
34. MacDonald 1990; Scheidel 2008.
35. Betzig 1992a, 1992b.
36. Price 1999.
37. MacDonald 1990, p. 198.
38. Posner 1992.
39. Goody 1990.
40. Scheidel 2008.
41. Goldstein 1976, 1978, as summarized in Durham 1991.
42. Aziz 1978, as summarized in Durham 1991.
43. Levine 1988, as summarized in Durham 1991.
44. Durham 1991.
45. Durham 1991.
46. Durham 1991.
47. Beall and Goldstein 1981.
48. Starkweather and Hames 2012.
49. Starkweather and Hames 2012.
50. Starkweather and Hames 2012.
51. Durham 1991.
52. Levine and Silk 1997.
53. Goldstein 1978; Durham 1991.
54. Levine and Silk 1997.

7

Parenthood

Parental investment in offspring is a huge part of life, in a sense the very point of it. When people decide to have children, they are making what is likely the most important decision of their lives. Because there is an inverse relationship between parental investment and mating effort, the sex that produces fewer gametes (eggs for females, sperm for males) in a lifetime will be the sex that will devote more time to parental care. Conversely, the sex that produces larger numbers of gametes in a lifetime will put more effort into mating than into parental care. Women produce a single egg once a month, only twelve per year and just 360 in an entire reproductive lifetime (assuming a reproductive lifetime of about thirty years, which would be an outer limit in most societies). But men produce millions of sperm in one ejaculate. Evolutionary theory thus tells us that women should invest more in parental care than men, and indeed they do.

In this chapter we begin with motherhood and describe the dominant role of mothers the world over. But mothers' regard for their offspring sometimes fails, for reasons we will explore. We will see that women are primed to mother, but under certain conditions they fail to do so, or at least fail to do so adequately. The consequences for children can be horrendous. Many die, and those who survive frequently experience great psychological suffering and damage. We will sketch out these consequences by way of experimental studies of nonhuman primates as well as studies of children who have been abandoned and end up in institutions where they receive care that is distant and cold.

Regarding parenthood, people have two important decisions to make: how many children to have, and whether to place more emphasis on sons or daughters. These decisions are not made in a vacuum but in a socioecological context. In some contexts it makes sense to have many children, whereas in others in makes more sense to have few. A lot depends on the rate of infant and child survival. Concerning sons or daughters, because males emphasize mating effort over parental effort, they are the sex with greater reproductive potential. Evolutionarily, parents should therefore invest more in sons than in daughters, and in most societies they do. But in some societies people invest more in daughters. We will see why.

Finally, we return to the issue of the failure of parental care, in this case in its most extreme form: the practice of infanticide. Infanticide is found in all societies, but it is much more common in some than in others. What would lead parents to abandon an infant to the elements and allow it to die, or actually kill it, by suffocation or some other means? The conditions are remarkably consistent the world over and are the same basic conditions for infanticide in other animals, also a widespread practice.

Maternal Instincts

Beginning in the 1930s, a great debate arose over whether mothering is a matter of "maternal instinct" or something that women learn after giving birth. It was the classic case of "nature versus nurture." In the minds of many social scientists the debate was resolved largely in favor of nurture, and that perspective grew stronger and stronger over time. But let's see what the evidence shows today.

In every human society, mothers provide the overwhelming majority of the care of infants and very young children, usually on the order of 90–95 percent. Fathers take a larger role as their children grow older, but the asymmetry between mothers and fathers is still very large. In one study of eighty nonindustrial societies, in nearly two-thirds fathers rarely or never spent time with their infants. In the remaining one-third, fathers contributed an average of only 6 percent of direct parental care, and spent only 14 percent of their time interacting with children in any way.[1] Even in modern industrial societies with high levels of gender equality, the vast majority of child care is in the hands of mothers. And, indeed, most mothers prefer it that way.

Girls spend much more time than boys at play parenting, and of course doll play among girls in Western societies is legendary. Boys studiously avoid such behavior. The sociologist Alice Rossi has summarized evidence showing that compared to males females show greater sensitivity to touch, sound, and odor; have greater fine motor coordination and finger dexterity; pick up nuances of voice and music more readily; are more sensitive to context; and are more attracted to human faces. These are precisely the traits that contribute heavily to the successful rearing of infants and small children. Rossi notes that because of long infant and child dependency, prolonged infant care through intense attachment of the mother and the infant is critical to its survival. In hunter-gatherer societies there is extremely close contact between mother and infant, and infants are usually nursed for at least two or three years and sometimes for as many as four or five. Under such conditions, it is almost inconceivable that the female of the species would not have been selected for strong nurturing tendencies.[2]

In her brilliant book *Mother Nature: A History of Mothers, Infants, and Natural Selection*, the primatologist and cultural anthropologist Sarah Blaffer Hrdy of the University of California at Davis presents an almost encyclopedic biosocial analysis of motherhood throughout history and across societies.[3] Hrdy shows in great detail

FIGURE 7.1   Rajasthani Mother and Baby, India
(Rodger Dashow/Anthro-Photo)

how maternal behavior is the result of the complex interaction of biological predisposition and various features of the socioecological environment. Although sensitive to the concerns of many feminists (being a feminist herself), Hrdy bursts the balloon of those who claim that because mothers often mistreat and abandon their babies and allow them to die, motherhood is only a "social construction." Although there is no such thing as a "maternal instinct," she asserts, motherhood nonetheless rests on a strong biological foundation. The average human female is primed to bond to her infant and to nurture it, but the conditions for rearing must be good for that behavior to be elicited.[4]

In modern industrial societies, with high levels of affluence and low levels of infant and child mortality relative to the past, the conditions for rearing are in most cases very good. Most mothers bond to their infants shortly after they are born, but not all do. There are always individual differences between women just as there are between men. Some women do not want children. On becoming pregnant, many women choose to abort. In the days before abortion was legalized, many women who brought a baby to term did not keep it. They may have chosen to give it up for adoption, abandon it on someone's doorstep, or in rare cases kill it.

In past societies, conditions for rearing were often unfavorable. These conditions included insufficient resources to give a child adequate nourishment for good health and survival; babies spaced too close together, so that the second took away valuable resources from the first; a baby born unhealthy or defective with low probability of survival; or a lack of support from a husband or female relatives. When one or more of these conditions was present in earlier societies, a mother was likely to choose not to rear her infant.

In modern societies with high levels of affluence and advanced medical technology, all of these conditions can usually be coped with, and so infants can be successfully reared. Even babies born with serious biological defects, such as a hole in the heart or spina bifida, can often be treated successfully and grow to adulthood. But no such thing was even remotely possible in any nonindustrial society, or even in industrial societies a century ago.[5]

Hrdy summarizes the important work of historian John Boswell, who stumbled onto trial and church records that showed that from the early Christian era to the fifteenth century, an astonishingly large number of infants were abandoned throughout Europe. Boswell estimated that in Rome in the first three centuries CE, nearly half of women who had brought up one or more children had abandoned at least one. His estimates showed that 20–40 percent of all children born ended up being abandoned, and abandonment occurred in every social class.[6]

Abandonment didn't cease after the Renaissance but continued for many centuries right up through the early twentieth century. In Florence, Italy, in the 1840s, for example, 43 percent of all infants baptized had been abandoned. Between 1659 and 1900 in Milan, nearly 350,000 children were left at the doorsteps of foundling homes. In Sicily between 1783 and 1809, 72,000 were abandoned. These figures are for Italy, but similar statistics exist for other European countries.[7]

Mothers who intend to abandon their infants almost always do so within the first seventy-two hours after birth. Mothers who keep the baby longer and breast-feed it usually begin to bond with the infant and experience much greater difficulty in abandoning it. Hrdy points out that this "does not necessarily mean that there is a critical period right after birth during which mothers must bond or else. Rather, what it suggests is that close proximity between mother and infant during this period produces feelings in the mother about her baby that make abandonment unbearable."[8]

Although abandoning or killing infants is rare in modern societies, there is child abuse, a behavior that has received enormous attention from sociologists and other social scientists over the past forty years. Who abuses? Research shows that children in poor health and thus with poor future prospects are much more likely to be mistreated than healthy children. Malnourished, apathetic, anorexic, and unresponsive children, as well as children who are physically handicapped and developmentally delayed, are at substantially greater risk for mistreatment. Children are also more likely to be abused if they strain family resources too much, especially when younger children take away resources from older children in whom a great deal has already been invested.[9] Child abuse in modern societies seems to stem from the same circumstances that led mothers to abandon or kill their infants in earlier societies. Abuse, in other words, seems to have replaced these more severe measures.

But there is another cause of abuse that appears to be the most important of all: being reared by a stepparent rather than a biological parent. The pioneers of research into the role of stepparents in child abuse, the evolutionary psychologists Martin Daly and Margo Wilson of McMaster University in Ontario, Canada, have accumulated detailed statistics on child abuse from a number of Western countries that show that stepchildren are at much greater risk for abuse than children living with their biological parents. This is especially true for the more severe forms of abuse; stepchildren are between 70 and 100 times more likely than biological children to be the victims of lethal assault.[10] Stepchildren also appear to be more at risk for serious abuse when stepparents' genetic offspring are present in the household.[11] The sexual abuse of young girls is much more frequently committed by stepfathers and foster fathers than by natural fathers.

The much greater maltreatment of children by stepparents is perfectly consistent with **inclusive fitness theory**, and is in fact predicted by it. Biological parents share half of their genes with their offspring, but none with stepsons or stepdaughters. Inclusive fitness theory tells us that people invest more in kin than in non-kin and more in close kin than in distant kin. Stepchildren are not genetic kin at all.

But back to good mothering. It is not overstating the matter to say that women *need* to mother and many feel empty if they never have the chance, either because they are unable to conceive or because they choose a career over marriage and later regret it (and find themselves too old to get pregnant). There is a fascinating phenomenon that has recently been discovered called "baby fever," which is a strong, often overpowering desire to have a child. It can occur at any age, but the most interesting version of it kicks in around age thirty-five. Women who were firmly committed to never having a child suddenly begin to experience an overwhelming desire for one.[12] There are numerous examples of women in their twenties or early thirties who declare emphatically that they do not intend to have children because they want to devote themselves exclusively to their careers. But in a few years they make an about-face, become pregnant, and give birth in their mid-thirties. Often they have a second child as well. These women appear to "need to mother."

Some years ago on the television program *60 Minutes*, Lesley Stahl interviewed four women who had been educated at highly prestigious universities and had gone on to high-powered jobs that put them in the national limelight. But in their late twenties or early thirties they decided they no longer wanted to do that. They quit their jobs, began having babies, and said they were so fulfilled that they had no intention of going back to work.

There is an innate predisposition to mother and if the conditions for rearing are good, most women choose to mother and successfully bond with their children. This bonding process is extremely important, but so far we have only been looking at it from the perspective of the mother, a "mother's-eye view," as it were. There is also a "child's-eye view." What's in it for the child? An enormous amount, as it turns out.

A Child's-Eye View

In late-eighteenth-century Russia the government set up foundling homes or orphanages that accepted children who had been abandoned and later found, or had been deliberately left at the orphanage by a parent. The vast majority of these children died within two or three years. In other orphanages at other times and places the situation has been much the same. In the early twentieth century in foundling homes in the United States there was a preoccupation with making the homes as free of disease as possible. Children were kept in cribs that were placed so far apart they could not touch each other, and sheets were draped over them to isolate them further. There was a widespread belief at the time that children did not need mothering, indeed were worse off for it. Staff members were instructed to attend to the infants' needs by changing diapers and providing regular feeding, but they were not to pick the babies up or even touch them. It was thought that the babies' only needs were physical. Nonetheless, death rates were still extremely high. And there was another negative outcome: most of the babies suffered from severe emotional disturbance.[13]

In the 1940s, the psychoanalyst René Spitz closely observed children in a foundling home in Mexico. This home adhered to the same rules and practices as homes elsewhere. Children lay in cribs that had been draped with sheets so they were unable to see other children. The children had no human contact apart from feeding and diaper changing, and the staff wore gloves and masks. Children could see little but the ceiling for hours, days, weeks, and months on end. And despite the obsession with cleanliness, the children still died at an alarming rate.[14]

Spitz was more interested in how the conditions of the home affected the children psychologically than physically. What he observed were children who were far from normal in their psychological development. They showed great emotional distress and anger and were extremely disengaged and detached from their environment and from other people: "An all-pervasive gloom settled over the little form in the crib; a formerly cheerful (pre-separation) toddler was transformed into a 'frozen,' 'passive,' and 'apathetic' automaton."[15] Spitz concluded that the high death rate was due mainly to the emotional damage the children suffered. The extreme psychological stress induced by the conditions the children faced severely compromised their immune systems, facilitating death from infection or disease.[16]

Spitz concluded, against expert opinions of the day, that what the children were missing was love. He thought that a mother would be the best provider of love, but any halfway affectionate caretaker would be vastly superior to what he described as "solitary confinement."[17] About the same time that Spitz was doing his research, the University of Cambridge psychologist John Bowlby, whom we met in Chapter 5, began thinking about the process of attachment between mother and child. Although Bowlby started out using a Freudian perspective, he soon came to feel that it couldn't answer crucial questions. Gradually he turned to Darwin and Darwinism to understand the mother-child relationship.[18]

In attempting to understand mother-child attachment, Bowlby looked at the conditions mothers and their children faced in the kind of environment humans lived in for most of their history. We know this environment already as the ancestral environment of small hunter-gatherer bands; Bowlby called it the Environment of Evolutionary Adaptedness (EEA). He reasoned that in the EEA danger lurked everywhere, from predators, both animal and human, as well as from numerous vagaries of nature. Under such circumstances, the risks to an infant or small child were great. It needed protection, and who better to provide this protection than its own mother. The mother therefore had to be biologically primed to attach to her child in order to protect it. But the attachment worked both ways: just as the mother needed to bond to her child, so the child needed to bond to its mother. The responsiveness of the child to its mother was needed to elicit the maternal behavior that would keep it safe. For Bowlby, mother-child attachment was an adaptation that evolved to promote the child's survival, which would in turn promote the mother's reproductive success.[19]

Harry Harlow was a psychology professor at the University of Wisconsin–Madison at about the same time that Bowlby was a Cambridge don. Each would soon learn of the other. As a young assistant professor, Harlow was given an old abandoned university building in which he was allowed to construct a laboratory for experiments with rhesus macaque monkeys. Harlow started his career with no interest in the psychology of love, but it soon became his overriding passion and the focus of his entire career. A Yale University researcher who was studying monkeys had noticed that when blankets were put at the bottom of monkeys' cages, they seemed to develop an inordinate liking for them. They would squeeze them and rub their faces on them. In fact, they would clutch them tightly and appeared to develop an emotional dependency on them. Were they actually "bonding" to the blankets? Harlow and his research assistants wanted to find out. But how?[20]

Eventually Harlow came up with an ingenious idea for an experiment that would have revolutionary implications. He decided to construct two different kinds of artificial monkey "mothers." One surrogate mother would be made of wood but covered in sponge rubber and terrycloth. It would also have a head made of wood and provided with eyes and a smiling mouth. A lightbulb was put behind it to give off warmth like a real mother's warm body. The other surrogate mother was made of wire with nothing covering it. It also had a face, but the eyes were just dark holes and the mouth was set in a frown. Ingeniously, the wire mother was supplied with a baby bottle filled with milk. Both surrogates were put inside a monkey's cage. If all a baby monkey needed was to be fed, it should clearly prefer the wire mother. If physical contact didn't matter, then the monkey should not show a preference for either mother.[21]

But neither of these things happened. All of the monkeys clearly preferred the cloth mother and ignored the wire mother except for feeding. They would leave the cloth mother and rush up to the wire mother to feed, but drink quickly and return immediately to the cloth mother. They spent only as much time with the wire mother as necessary to obtain sustenance—no more than an hour each day— spending the rest of their time with the cloth mother. They cuddled with the cloth mother, slept on it, and burrowed into it when startled or frightened.[22]

Wire mothers, then, were obviously very poor substitutes for real mothers, but were the cloth mothers good substitutes? Indeed they were not. They were better than the wire mothers, but not nearly as good as a real mother. As the months went by and the monkeys started growing up, a number of pathologies emerged. Some mauled themselves by biting their arms and tearing out fur. Many seemed highly apathetic, sitting in the corners of their cages and appearing to see and hear nothing. Others wrapped their arms around themselves and rocked back and forth. The monkeys exposed only to wire mothers turned out to the most dysfunctional of all. They gave off an aura of utter desperation. In sum, the surrogate-reared monkeys were "like alien monkeys from the planet nowhere."[23]

Harlow reasoned that the cloth mothers could not possibly substitute for real mothers because they did not interact in any way with the infants. An artificial mother couldn't hug a little monkey, teach it anything, or steer it in any direction. The cloth mothers could do none of the things that real mothers do in preparing their charges for the world of other monkeys. All the monkeys were able to learn was isolation and separation.[24]

In time Harlow and Bowlby became aware of each other's work, and Bowlby visited Harlow's lab not long after his early studies had been finished. When Bowlby toured the lab and looked at the monkeys, he was horrified by what he saw. He told Harlow that the monkeys exhibited more psychopathology than he had ever seen in his human patients. Nevertheless, Harlow's experiments continued and became even more extreme. He wanted to see how the babies would react to mothers that were truly mean—"monster mothers." One surrogate mother was designed to shake violently. Another blasted compressed air, and yet another was constructed so that it would throw the baby off its body. Worst of all was the "spike mother," which was equipped with brass spikes that were retracted but would be thrust into the clinging monkey periodically. Yet the young monkeys' need to bond was so strong that they were undeterred by these actions. Even though they were frightened and no doubt extremely confused, they would not only return to a monster mother but cling to it more tightly than ever. Later Harlow discovered that real monkey mothers who were rejecting or abusive elicited the same responses from their infants. The infants were desperate to make contact regardless of how much abuse was doled out.[25]

Some of the surrogate-raised females later became mothers themselves. Because they were incompetent at sexual relations, they had to be strapped down in order to be inseminated. These monkeys made horrible mothers. Because they had never experienced love, they did not know how to give it. Often they just ignored their infants but could also be extremely cruel. One mother chewed off her infant's feet and fingers; another crushed her infant's head in her mouth.[26]

So we have learned that motherhood is vital—and that childhood is as well.

Many Children or Few?

Maximizing reproductive success does not mean having as many children as possible. Modern parents often complain about the cost of clothing and feeding one or two growing teenagers; those costs would be multiplied with the addition of each new child. For many people, the economic costs of having as many children as possible would be prohibitive. The key is to have an *optimal* number of children: as many as you can successfully support and who can then go on to have their own optimal reproductive careers. The number of children people have depends greatly on circumstances.

Hunter-gatherers must be especially careful. People who live from hand to mouth and move frequently would be foolish to have numerous children. Children must be balanced against resources as well as against the demands of child rearing under conditions that parents face, mothers in particular. Have too many and most will die. But have too few and you may also end up with a poor reproductive career. These points are nicely illustrated by a fascinating study carried out by Nicholas Blurton Jones on the !Kung.[27] Research that Blurton-Jones examined showed that !Kung women tended to space their children about four years apart even though there was no biological reason why they couldn't have them closer together. Some critics suggested that this birth-spacing pattern showed that !Kung women were not maximizing their reproductive success. Why were they not having more children more often?

It turns out that there was a very good reason. Mothers in hunter-gatherer societies face special demands. When they collect plants they must take their infants and young children with them as they forage. Babies and young children hang on to their mothers' backs and go with them everywhere, and infants breast-feed on demand, often for several years. This is the problem known as "backload." A mother needs to wean her baby and get it up and toddling around before she can have another. If a mother has a clinging and nursing baby, having another too soon means that she is now responsible for two—a serious burden, especially when she also has to carry what she has collected back to camp. Short birth intervals produce more children, but more will die and the number of children surviving to adolescence is likely to be fewer than otherwise.

Blurton Jones devised an ingenious way of determining the optimal birth interval for !Kung women by taking backload into consideration. He conceptualized the optimal birth interval as the one that produced the most children surviving to age ten or older. He performed a computer simulation for the !Kung that showed an optimal interval of approximately fifty months, meaning that mothers would be maximizing their reproductive success (number of surviving offspring) by spacing them fifty months apart. Birth intervals of twenty to thirty months or eighty to one hundred months produced fewer surviving offspring. If a mother spaced her children twenty-four months apart she saw a higher percentage of them die, with lowered reproductive success. If she spaced them eighty-four months apart, child mortality was reduced but fewer children were born, again leading to lower reproductive success.

The most common birth interval for !Kung mothers, forty-eight months, is almost identical to Blurton Jones's simulation results. The next most common intervals were thirty-six months and sixty months. Of all of the mothers included in Blurton Jones's study, 30 percent spaced at forty-eight months, 24 percent at thirty-six months, and 17 percent at sixty months. This means that nearly three-fourths of the mothers were using a birth interval of three to five years. But if mothers chose outside the optimal range, it was better to choose longer intervals (72 months or more) than shorter ones (24 months). The twenty-four-month interval yielded the fewest surviving offspring. Seventy-two months or more was better than twenty-four months, but it was still poorer than forty-eight. Significantly, 23 percent of mothers chose an interval of seventy months or more, whereas a minuscule 6 percent chose a twenty-four-month interval. Blurton Jones concluded that "the !Kung optimize with remarkable precision."[28]

But how do mothers bring about the optimal interval? Choosing one and making it work are not the same thing. What prevents a mother who plans a forty-eight-month interval from ending up with a twenty-four-month or even shorter interval? After all, an interval just slightly longer than nine months is biologically possible. The answer is prolonged lactation. Hunter-gatherer mothers nurse their babies longer than mothers in other types of societies, and this long lactation is effective (though by no means foolproof) in preventing ovulation and pregnancy. It is a very good birth control method in the absence of other methods.

Of course, not all hunter-gatherer societies are the same. Habitats are different, for one thing, and this can make a lot of difference. The Aché of the Paraguayan rain forest have birth intervals and total female fertility that are different. !Kung women have on average five children in their lifetime, whereas Aché women have eight. In addition, the average Aché birth interval is shorter, thirty-eight months compared to forty-eight.[29] The shorter birth interval and higher fertility for the Aché may result from greater food abundance in their environment compared to the scanty resources of the !Kung environment.

What then of societies that live by horticultural or agricultural methods? Here we usually see higher total fertility and shorter birth intervals, largely because women can be less mobile. Attending to children is not as physically demanding. The Yanomama reproductive patterns resemble the Aché, with seven children per woman per lifetime, and an average birth interval of thirty-five months.[30] The Yanomama pattern is probably similar to that in the majority of horticultural societies. An analysis of the **Standard Cross-Cultural Sample** (SCCS or Standard Sample), a subset of the *Ethnographic Atlas* containing 186 nonindustrial societies, shows that a greater number of mothers in horticultural societies (36 percent) than in forager societies (25 percent) finish weaning by twenty-four months and, as noted above, weaning usually corresponds to a woman's return to full fecundity. From this we may infer that more women in horticultural societies become pregnant again in shorter periods of time than do forager mothers.

As for agrarian societies, things are more complicated because these societies are more complex and have more social class differentiation. But let's take peasants, who make up some 80–90 percent of the population in most agrarian societies. Peasant fertility tends to be high, probably similar to fertility among horticulturalists, which means in the range of six to nine children born in a woman's reproductive lifetime. Marvin Harris points out that in agrarian societies very young children typically perform such tasks as gathering firewood, carrying water for cooking and washing, grinding and pounding grains, taking food to adults in the fields, sweeping floors, and running errands. Older children are involved in cooking meals, working full-time in the fields, hunting, herding, fishing, and making pots, containers, mats, and nets. They also spend a lot of time looking after their younger brothers and sisters. Under these conditions, he argues, it makes very good sense for people to keep their fertility high to maximize the economic benefits that children can provide.[31] (Presumably Harris intends his argument to apply to horticultural societies as well.)

Although this view seems plausible, careful thought shows that it does not work. Bobbi Low has claimed that "children's labor is never sufficient to result in a net economic gain to parents," and Paul Turke argues that in all societies "the net flow of services and resources will usually be from older to younger generations."[32] Low and Turke conclude that the economic argument is backwards: people do not use reproductive resources to acquire economic benefits, but use economic resources to gain reproductive benefits. They claim that fertility behavior is governed by considerations of reproductive success rather than the economic value of children's labor.

Anthropologist Hillard Kaplan tested the economic argument by using data from three tribal societies in South America, all of which practiced a mixture of hunting and gathering and horticulture.[33] In all three societies fertility was very high—an average of 8.15 for the three societies combined—but children in each society were producing far fewer calories than they were consuming. Kaplan concluded that benefits flowed overwhelmingly from parent to child rather than the reverse.

Another way to test the economic argument is to compare fertility levels in agrarian and modern industrial societies. It is well-known that people in industrial societies tend to have, at best, only two or three children rather than the six to nine produced by peasants or farmers. In the middle of the nineteenth century fertility levels in societies that were beginning to industrialize were still high. But around 1870 fertility levels began to drop and by about 1930 family size had been dramatically reduced. This shift from high fertility to low fertility regimes is known as the *demographic transition*. It started in the most economically developed countries, but eventually the majority of less-developed countries followed suit.

Theorists like Harris claim that the shift to low fertility stems from the changing economic value of children's labor. In highly urbanized, industrialized societies children are no longer a source of important economic benefits. Indeed, they become economic liabilities because they no longer do much work for the family, have to be educated for many years, must be dressed properly to go to school, and so on. Children become a drain on family resources. As a result, people choose to have fewer.

But there are other quite different explanations. In recent years a number of scholars have attributed high fertility in agrarian societies and low fertility in industrial societies to differences in the status of women. Where women's status is low, as it most often is in agrarian societies, fertility will be high, but as women's status improves with industrialization fertility will drop. This argument is based on the assumption that women generally wish to have fewer children than the number their husbands want because the burdens of child care fall disproportionately on mothers. Where women's status is low, their husbands can pressure them to have more children. But when women acquire a more equal status, they gain a greater voice in childbearing decisions.[34]

Empirical tests of this argument have tended to support it. One study examined the role of gender on fertility in India, specifically the effects of active gender discrimination and gender bias in the marriage system. The researchers found that gender discrimination and gender bias in the marriage system—assessed as the proportion of fifteen- to nineteen-year-old girls who were married and the extent to which girls had to leave their home villages to marry—were associated with higher fertility.[35] Another study of Indian fertility found that higher levels of female literacy and greater female labor force participation were associated with lower fertility.[36]

Yet another way to explain fertility differences between agrarian and industrial societies comes from human behavioral ecology. As suggested by Low and Turke, fertility behavior is a matter of adjusting numbers to socioecological conditions so that reproductive success is maximized. Carey and Lopreato argue that infant or child mortality is the main determinant of fertility levels.[37] Humans have evolved a "two-surviving-children psychology," they contend, in which they gear their total fertility to the frequency with which offspring survive to adulthood. When infant and child mortality are high, fertility will be high in order to replace offspring expected to die before they reach reproductive age. But when infant and child mortality is low, fertility is adjusted downward. If two children born are both very likely to survive, why have more? As Carey and Lopreato note, Darwin himself

> argued that, despite the tendency of populations to outpace the growth of their resources, a countertendency toward population stability is a characteristic of all species. The theory of natural selection suggests that, given the real or potential Malthusian [resource] scarcity and the associated struggle for existence, the fertility of individuals displays a vigorous tendency to track mortality.[38]

Carey and Lopreato's argument that people in all societies aim for two surviving offspring may be claiming too much, but their more general point that fertility should track mortality—higher rates of infant and child mortality tend to be accompanied by having more children (higher fertility), while lower rates of infant and child mortality tend to be accompanied by having fewer children (lower fertility)—can be accepted. Demographers have long thought that fertility levels should be responsive to levels of infant and child mortality, and a number of studies show this to be the case.

In an attempt to test the economic, female empowerment, and behavioral ecological theories directly against each other, Sanderson and Dubrow looked at fertility levels in forty-two contemporary societies in 1960 and sixty-three societies in 1990. Results consistently showed that infant mortality was the strongest determinant of fertility and the level of female empowerment the second strongest. When infant mortality was high, fertility was high, and when female empowerment was high, fertility was low. The economic value of children's labor was measured by using the percentage of the labor force working in agriculture along with the percentage of the population living in urban areas. Neither of these factors made any difference.[39] A follow-up analysis of fertility rates in 145 societies in 2008 obtained essentially the same results. Therefore, both the behavioral ecological theory and the female empowerment theory passed empirical scrutiny, but the economic value of children's labor theory did not.[40]

Bear in mind, however, that the decision to have fewer children is more complicated than greater female empowerment and changing levels of infant and child survival. Modern societies are organized in very different ways from past agrarian societies. One of the most dramatic changes accompanying industrialization has been the development of mass education and skill-based competitive labor markets.[41] If children are going to become successful in today's world, they have to be educated and prepared to compete with other children so they can acquire the things they need to promote their *own* reproductive success. Unless families are well-off, this becomes difficult if they have, say, seven or eight children. Better to have one or two (perhaps three) and invest intensively in each. Harris is quite right to say that children in modern societies have become economically costly. This expense is another factor requiring adjustments in childbearing. In essence, people have adapted themselves to rising costs by trading the *quantity* of children for their *quality*.[42]

Sons or Daughters?

Along with deciding how many offspring to have, another crucial decision parents must make is whether to invest more in sons, in daughters, or in sons and daughters equally. This may seem harsh to modern readers, the vast majority of whom regard investing equally in offspring of both sexes as the only appropriate thing to do. But throughout the world and throughout history parental investment has generally been sex-selective. Parents can favor one sex, for example, by giving it more time and attention than the other sex, by giving it priority in regard to nutrition and health care, or by passing most or all of their wealth to children of that sex.

How does the process in its various manifestations work? Some years ago two evolutionary biologists, Robert Trivers and Dan Willard, formulated a hypothesis that has garnered enormous research attention and eventually came to be considered one of the leading ideas in the new fields of sociobiology and evolutionary psychology. Their focus was the male-female sex ratio at birth in animal species. Under certain conditions, they said, natural selection will favor systematic deviations from a 50:50 sex ratio. One of these conditions is the health of the mother. Mothers who are in good condition tend to produce more sons, whereas mothers in poor (or at least poorer) condition tend to produce more daughters. Moreover, there will tend to be a bias in parental investment after birth such that mothers in better condition will invest more in sons than in daughters.[43]

Although Trivers and Willard were interested mainly in animals, they indicated that their hypothesis should also apply to humans. The condition of the mother could be assessed in terms of her position on a socioeconomic scale. Being at the high end of the scale would indicate good condition, being at the low end poor condition. Therefore, high-status mothers should bear more sons than daughters, and favor sons over daughters after birth, whereas low-status mothers should bear more daughters and favor them after birth. This outcome is dependent on a correlation between reproductive success and social status. As Trivers and Willard put it, "The model can be applied to humans differentiated along a socioeconomic scale as long as the RS [reproductive success] of a male at the upper end of the scale exceeds his sister's, while that of a female at the lower end of the scale exceeds her brother's."[44]

Natural selection should favor such an outcome because the reproductive potential of sons is usually greater than that of daughters. As we have seen, in many species, humans included, males compete to inseminate many females and the winning males, the dominant males, are differentially successful at doing so. But how does the process work at the biological level? What kind of physiological mechanism is involved? The basic answer is that males are the "weaker" sex and more difficult to bring to term. At conception the ratio of males to females is at least as high as 110:100, with some estimates actually running as high as 160:100.[45] Male fetuses are more likely to die than female fetuses throughout fetal development. One study of spontaneously aborted and prematurely delivered fetuses in the second trimester found a sex ratio of 136:100,[46] and it has been well established that at birth the sex ratio has been reduced to about 105:100. A mother is more likely to bring her male fetus to term when she is healthy. Unhealthy mothers spontaneously abort more male fetuses and thus on average give birth to more daughters.

It did not take long for social scientists to see if the provocative Trivers-Willard hypothesis, or TWH as it came to be known, applied to parents in human societies. Numerous studies have found support for it.[47] A fascinating study concentrating on the high end of the socioeconomic scale was one of American political leaders by anthropologist Laura Betzig and biologist Samantha Weber. Looking at various sources of biographical information, Betzig and Weber found that members of the executive branch of government during the terms of the first twenty American presidents produced seventy-four legitimate males and thirty-one legitimate females, a hugely imbalanced sex ratio of 239:100. As for the presidents themselves, the first twenty had fifty-five legitimate sons and thirty-one legitimate daughters, a sex ratio not as unbalanced as that of members of the executive branch, but still extremely high at 177:100. The authors also studied birth patterns among presidents' fathers and their sons, and similar results were obtained. Fathers of the first twenty presidents produced eighty-one legitimate sons and fifty-six legitimate daughters (sex ratio = 145:100). Sons of the first twenty presidents produced seventy-three legitimate sons and fifty-three legitimate daughters (sex ratio = 133:100). Since most of the individuals considered would have been men of very high status, the strong imbalance in favor of sons fits TWH very well.[48]

As for parental investment after birth, there is again evidence of a male bias. Betzig and Weber examined presidents' wills and found that nine of twelve demonstrated no sex bias in inheritance; of the three that did, there was a clear preference for sons as heirs. The evidence from the wills shows only a slight male bias, but evidence from investment in children's education shows a pronounced bias; many more sons than daughters were provided with expensive educations.

So much for male-biased investment at the high end of the socioeconomic scale. Is there evidence for female-biased investment at the lower end? Various studies are suggestive.[49] In one study, Betzig and Paul Turke found differential investment in sons and daughters among villagers on the Micronesian island of Ifaluk. The level of parental investment was assessed by recording the amount of time that parents spent with children of each sex. On Ifaluk, some men worked for wages and had more income and higher status than men who were not engaged in wage work. Betzig and Turke found that high-status men spent about two-thirds of their time interacting with sons, but low-status men spent about two-thirds of their time with daughters. Wives of high-status men spent about 56 percent of their time with sons, whereas wives of low-status men spent only about 34 percent of their time with sons and 66 percent of their time with daughters.[50]

By far the most fascinating case of female-biased investment after birth is the Mukogodo, a group that anthropologist Lee Cronk has spent more than twenty years studying.[51] The Mukogodo are a very poor society in Kenya whose members traditionally lived by foraging and beekeeping. More recently they have taken up pastoralism, but they are still poor and have very low status compared to neighboring pastoral societies. As with many low-status groups, Mukogodo women's marital and reproductive prospects exceed those of their brothers. Mukogodo women are in demand by men of their wealthier and high-status neighbors, especially the cattle-keeping Maasai. The reason is the widespread practice of *hypergyny*. Women desire to "marry up," that is, to marry men of higher status, which is what makes poor Mukogodo men less appealing to Mukogodo women. From the point of view of men of such high-status groups as the Maasai, attractive daughters among low-status groups are highly desired, especially where polygyny is practiced.

Based on TWH, the Mukogodo should favor daughters over sons, and indeed Cronk has found that they do. In some of his early research he found a sex ratio for children under four years of 67:100, indicating that Mukogodo daughters must be getting much better care than Mukogodo sons. One way in which daughters receive better treatment involves visits to health clinics. In 1986 Mukogodo parents took 191 daughters to a Catholic dispensary for treatment compared to only 109 sons. By 1992 there was still a daughter bias, although not as great: 104 daughters were taken compared to 99 sons. By contrast, non-Mukogodo visits to the same dispensary showed a bias in favor of sons. In 1986, 229 clinic visits were made on behalf of sons, 185 on behalf of daughters; the corresponding figures for 1992 were 112 sons and 97 daughters.[52]

Cronk also devised other indicators of Mukogodo parental investment. One assessed how close or far away a caregiver stood to sons relative to daughters. Cronk found that all caregivers taken together stood an average of 1.15 meters (about 45 inches) from sons, but only 0.38 meters (about 15 inches) from daughters. When mothers alone were considered, the son-daughter difference was even more tilted in favor of daughters: mothers stood 1.14 meters (about 44 inches) from sons compared to 0.32 meters (approximately 12 inches) from daughters. Cronk also estimated how much time caregivers spent holding children, and found that daughters were held almost twice as long as sons. In looking at nursing time, he found that sons were nursed 4 percent of the time but daughters 11 percent. Finally, Cronk looked at growth and physical development. Here he found that daughters were doing better than sons in both height and weight relative to norms for their sex and age, and thus daughters appeared to be better nourished.[53]

One of the most remarkable features of daughter bias among the Mukogodo is that most Mukogodo deny any daughter favoritism. When Cronk interviewed 121 mothers, he found only 9 who expressed a daughter preference. Fourteen actually expressed a son preference, and the remaining mothers indicated no particular preference one way or the other.[54] Why do most Mukogodo mothers deny daughter preference when there is indisputable evidence of it? The reason seems to be that the group to whom they most frequently give their daughters in marriage, the Maasai, are a high-status group and the Maasai do in fact favor sons. The world over, people of low status often imitate people of high status. For Mukogodo mothers to express daughter preference would be very "un-Maasai," and the Mukogodo do not wish to be seen as "un-Maasai." The Maasai already tend to look down their noses at the lowly Mukogodo, so why give them another reason to do so.[55]

Nearly all of the studies that find support for TWH are based on nonindustrial societies, and so the question naturally arises whether the parental behavior of high-status and low-status groups in modern industrial societies is consistent with TWH. One of the first studies designed to answer this question was carried out by the sociologists Jeremy Freese of Northwestern University and Brian Powell of Indiana University. They looked at several thousand eighth graders and their parents and assessed parental investment in several ways: how much money parents had saved for college, whether they sent their children to private or public schools, the kinds and number of educational objects in the home, parents' involvement (or lack thereof) in parent-teacher groups, whether parents enrolled their children in cultural classes and provided them with other cultural activities, and whether parents knew their children's friends and the friends' parents. Results showed no support for TWH, with high-status and low-status parents investing about equally in sons and daughters.[56]

Evolutionary social scientists Matthew Keller, Randolph Nesse, and Sandra Hofferth studied US children between six and twelve years of age. The authors' indicators of parental investment were the number of hours a week parents participated in activities with a child, the level of warmth parents were observed to display toward their children, whether or not a child was breastfed and the number of months it was breastfed, and a child's birth weight. Like Freese and Powell, Keller, Nesse, and Hofferth found no sex-selective parental investment by social status.[57]

In another investigation the sociologists Lee Ellis and Steven Bonin studied 11,000 college students in the United States and Canada. They determined the sex of each student and the sex of their siblings. Using a variety of measures of the social status of the students' parents, they found no relationship between status and the sex ratio at birth.[58] In a 2005 study, sociologist Rosemary Hopcroft used data from a huge national survey of more than 22,000 Americans and measured parental investment in terms of the years of education attained by a child. Hopcroft believes her results support TWH, but the differences in son versus daughter investment between high-status and low-status parents were very small. For example, sons of fathers at the very highest level of socioeconomic status received 16.6 years of education, daughters 16.1 years. And sons of fathers at the lowest socioeconomic level received 10.6 years of education whereas daughters received 11.0 years. These differences are too small to suggest a reliable TWH effect. Hopcroft also tested for a sex ratio effect. She found that high-status fathers had more sons than daughters (59 percent sons) and that low-status fathers had more daughters than sons (60 percent daughters). Although these results are consistent with TWH, Hopcroft's results for women point in the opposite direction. High-status mothers gave birth to more daughters than sons (56 percent daughters), whereas low-status mothers produced more sons than daughters (63 percent sons).[59]

Because of this inconsistency, Hopcroft's results are difficult to interpret. One solution is to pay attention to mothers rather than fathers because, after all, TWH posits that it is *mothers* in good condition who should have more sons. But Hopcroft finds that it is mothers in *poor* condition who have more sons, and by a nearly 2:1 ratio. This is in direct contradiction to TWH. Another way to interpret Hopcroft's findings is to take the average for fathers and mothers. If we do this, we find that 51.5 percent of the offspring of high-status parents and 51.3 percent of the offspring of low-status parents are sons. These figures are nearly identical and therefore do not support TWH.

In short, it appears that TWH effects exist in many nonindustrial societies, but not in the two industrial societies studied thus far (someone should undertake a study of other industrial societies for comparison purposes). Freese and Powell believe that their negative results overturn TWH, but my view is that they simply qualify it. TWH does not apply to industrial societies for the simple reason that in such societies the reproductive potential of males differs little from that of females. This is because industrial societies have legally imposed monogamy, whereas most nonindustrial societies are polygynous. Monogamy reduces male reproductive potential. In addition, the marital prospects of women in industrial societies, especially over the past century, have not differed significantly from the prospects of men. Therefore, it makes sense for parents of all status levels to invest equally in sons and daughters, just as empirical findings tell us they are doing.

This conclusion also helps make sense of an additional set of findings from the Betzig and Weber study. Although highly male-biased sex ratios characterized the first twenty US presidents and their fathers and sons, sex ratios became considerably more balanced over time. Men in the executive branch during the administrations of the second twenty presidents produced 262 legitimate sons and 234 legitimate daughters, for a sex ratio of 112:100. The second twenty presidents had thirty-one legitimate sons and twenty-seven legitimate daughters, a ratio of 115:100. And sons of these same presidents had thirty-five legitimate sons and thirty-six legitimate daughters, a sex ratio actually favoring daughters at 97:100.

One of the more remarkable changes that has occurred in industrial societies over the past sixty years is the shift in the male-female balance in undergraduate college enrollments. In 1950, about 60 percent of students were males, but now the situation is nearly the reverse. In many industrial societies today, between 55 and

60 percent of undergraduate students are females (the figure for the United States is about 58 percent). This does not necessarily mean that parents are deliberately investing more in the education of daughters than sons. It may simply mean that more women are choosing to attend college and more men are electing not to. However, as women receive more education relative to men, their marital and thus reproductive prospects also improve. This could mean that daughter bias will become characteristic of industrial societies in the years ahead.

Infanticidal Deeds

Unlike abortion, which is the termination of a pregnancy, infanticide is the termination of the life of a baby that has already been born. In the United States and all other industrial societies infanticide is rare but, as noted above in the discussion of motherhood, it has been quite common in nonindustrial societies. The mother may abandon the baby, smother it, or simply refuse to nurse it. In medieval Europe, mothers would sometimes end their infants' lives by what is known as *overlaying*. Because infants slept with their mothers, a mother might occasionally roll over on her infant and accidentally suffocate it. However, the rate of infant death from overlaying was often suspiciously high. Many coroners would take the mother's word that the overlaying was accidental, but some were skeptical. In London between 1855 and 1860, 3,900 infant deaths were attributed to overlaying, but further investigation by coroners and other officials concluded that at least a third of the deaths were intentional.[60]

Something like this may also occur in modern societies and thus increase the modern rate of infanticide. Sarah Blaffer Hrdy contends that many cases of Sudden Infant Death Syndrome (SIDS) may actually be deliberate smotherings, and that many of these go unrecognized by coroners and physicians; in some cases they may actually be recognized or suspected but swept under the rug. Much evidence supports Hrdy's contention. For example, several decades ago medical personnel and police secretly videotaped mothers in a London hospital whose infants were there for the purpose of discovering the causes of their sleep apnea. The videotapes revealed that many mothers in the hospital with their infants attempted to suffocate them. Hrdy also relates the extraordinary case of Waneta Hoyt, a mother from New York State who was tried for child murder in 1995. All five of her children had died, four as newborns and one somewhat older, and all of the deaths were attributed to SIDS. The cases aroused suspicion because of the extreme statistical improbability of five infants born to the same woman dying from SIDS, and also because nursing staff and other hospital personnel observed that Mrs. Hoyt displayed complete indifference to her newborn infants, refusing to hold them or interact with them in any way.[61]

What explains infanticide? Is it the result of something gone terribly wrong in the human psyche? To modern Westerners it seems like a horrible and unthinkable act that is inexplicable from the point of view of mother love. How can a mother kill her own child or allow it to die? Since it seems like an extraordinarily cruel and heartless thing to do, many people, including some well-trained scholars, refuse to believe that it actually exists except in cases of severely emotionally disturbed mothers. It also appears to utterly contradict inclusive fitness theory, since parents who kill an infant have one less child. Such behavior would seem to reduce rather than promote reproductive success.

However, as Daly and Wilson point out, infanticide makes sense from the point of view of inclusive fitness maximization if letting a child die promotes the well-being of an older child or children in whom a great deal of time, energy, and resources have already been invested, and if resources must be withdrawn from them and provided to a newborn. It also may make little sense to invest in children whose chances of survival are low regardless of whether other children are present, as well as in children who are defective and thus may die long before reaching reproductive age. Humans, like most mammals, evolved to provide good parental care as long as the conditions for rearing offspring are good. But since this is often not the case in nonindustrial societies, parental care should not be indiscriminate. Investing in offspring with a poor chance of survival, or whose existence threatens other offspring, reduces rather than promotes parents' reproductive success.[62]

Daly and Wilson examined 112 reported cases of infanticide in over three dozen preliterate societies, and discovered that 97 of them resulted from one or more of three circumstances: when the circumstances for rearing the infant were poor, such as food scarcities or a mother's lack of social support from the father or female relatives; when the infant would be taking away resources needed by an older child; and when there were doubts about paternity (this obviously applies to the father rather than to the mother).[63] In only 4 of the 112 cases could infanticide be said to be damaging to the parent's inclusive fitness.[64]

In modern industrial societies, the risk to an infant is greatest in the case of a teenage mother, and it declines as mothers move into their twenties and thirties. Mothers experiencing difficult economic circumstances are also much more likely to commit infanticide, and infanticide is more common among single than among married mothers.

Considerable evidence thus suggests that infanticide is an evolutionary adaptation. The adaptationist argument is also supported by evidence from numerous studies showing that infanticide is widespread among animal species. The most critical reasons why animals sometimes become infanticidal are much the same as those operating in the human case: defective infants; conditions such as resource scarcity that make an infant's likelihood of survival poor; and the presence of older offspring whose well-being would be harmed if resources were shared with the newborn.[65] In addition, in numerous animal species unrelated males often kill offspring sired by another male because the infanticidal male can then mate with the mother and produce offspring that carry his genes rather than his rival's.

Daly and Wilson note that the data on infanticide are consistent with the reality of maternal bonding. They delineate three stages of bonding: the mother initially assesses the quality of the child and her own circumstances; if the child is deemed to be of acceptable quality, she then begins to establish an individualized love for it; in the final stage maternal love gradually deepens over time. Thus child-specific parental love is variable and highly contingent on the extent to which rearing circumstances are favorable. Parental feeling seems to be such that the likelihood of infanticide declines progressively with the age of a child. This reflects the child's growing value to the parent, and we might say that parents have evolved to love children more as they grow because of older children's greater reproductive value.

Daly and Wilson report recent data for Canada demonstrating the effects of age. They point out that teenage children are at very low risk of being killed by their parents, even though a state of conflict often exists between the two; they are much more likely to be killed by nonrelatives than by relatives. When parents kill older children, depression or insanity are likely to be involved. This is indeed a situation in which "something has gone wrong with the psyche."[66]

Anthropologists have long known that most infanticide is female-biased. This has usually been attributed to the patriarchal or male-dominated nature of most societies; men have a preference for sons and can impose this preference on their wives. In traditional China and India, for example, the preference for sons was so strong that female infanticide could reach astonishingly high levels. Hrdy reports that in eighteenth- and nineteenth-century China the ratio of boys to girls could be as high as 154:100 in some regions. "In large cities like Beijing," she says, "wagons made scheduled rounds in the early morning to collect corpses of unwanted daughters that had been soundlessly drowned in a bucket of milk while the mother looked away."[67] In contemporary China, the law restricting families to one child has led to so much female infanticide that today there is a large shortage of marriageable women. If the first child is a daughter, parents often let her live, but any following daughters are usually disposed of until a son is born.[68] (Many parents violate the one-child law and some receive special permission to have more than one child.) In some villages of nineteenth-century India, as many as 80 percent of daughters were killed, and among some segments of the population the figure could be 100 percent. In the 1840 census taken of the Jetwa Rajputs of the Indian district of Poorbunder, there were 452 males for every 100 females.[69] And of 8,000 abortions performed at one Indian clinic in recent times, 7,997 were performed on female fetuses.[70]

Extreme patriarchy is no doubt one of the conditions responsible for the predominance of female over male infanticide, but it is not the only condition and may not even be the most important. As already noted, Darwinians have long recognized that the reproductive potential of sons is usually higher, often much higher, than that of daughters. Daughters can produce only so many children in their lifetime, but men can inseminate many women, either by having many wives or by extensive extramarital philandering.[71] Sons will therefore be more highly valued than their sisters because they can generate more reproductive success for their families, not only in their own generation but in many future generations down the line.

However, there are circumstances in which male infanticide is more common than its counterpart. The anthropologist Mildred Dickemann has found that sex-selective infanticide often varies sharply by a family's position in a society's socioeconomic hierarchy. In a fascinating study, Dickemann examined infanticide patterns in three societies with high levels of social inequality: China and India in the nineteenth century and late medieval Europe.[72] In both China and India there was extensive hypergyny, or women marrying men of higher social status. Hypergyny is common all over the world. Often it is simply a statistical tendency that results from female preferences for high-status, resource-rich men who can provide for a woman's children better than low-status, resource-poor men. But sometimes hypergyny becomes an institutionalized societal practice that is tantamount to a social norm.

Indian society is permeated by caste distinctions, and marriage is usually caste endogamous—people marry within their own caste. But most castes have subcastes that may be exogamous, meaning that people marry outside their subcaste. In some cases two or more subcastes may have established marital alliances. Among many castes in northwest India in recent centuries, there were ranked subcastes that practiced hypergyny, which was highly preferred and sometimes even required. Hypogyny (sometimes called hyperandry), women's marrying down, was highly disdained. For example, families of the high-ranking Jhareja, Jetwa, and Soomra subcastes of the Rajput caste in the region around Benares took the daughters of various subordinate subcastes as wives for their sons. This practice was clearly advantageous to the lower-ranking daughters because it got them married off to high-status men with wealth. But it imposed a severe disadvantage on higher-ranked daughters. They could not marry up because there was no "up," that is, no higher-ranked group to marry into. Theoretically, they could marry men of their own rank, but because most of these men were importing wives from lower subcastes, their marriage prospects were dismal. In essence, high-status daughters were excluded from reproduction and, since there were few other roles available to them, they were largely useless to their families.[73]

What were superordinate subcastes to do with their "excess" daughters? The most common solution was infanticide, which sometimes meant killing *all* daughters, or allowing them to die. But for the subordinate subcaste, the reverse situation prevailed: daughters had better marital and reproductive prospects than their brothers because of the superordinate families' desire for them. For subordinate families, the problem was therefore not excess females but excess *males*. As a result, male infanticide was more common, although it seldom reached the extraordinary proportions of female infanticide in superordinate subcastes. Surviving sons usually had a difficult time finding a wife because so many girls had married higher-status males. Inasmuch as bachelor sons were costly to their families, they would often leave their households to work as servants, shop clerks, artisans, or agricultural laborers. They could also join the military or go into monasteries. Sometimes their families sent them to work in the mines; a goodly number would become beggars or thieves.[74]

Another part of this complex marriage system was *dowry*, the practice whereby families of lower-status daughters were obligated to provide items of value to the groom's family. The more desirable a potential husband was deemed to be, the larger the dowry his family could demand, and families often made extreme sacrifices and incurred significant debt to provide the best dowries possible. By contrast, because of the upward flow of wealth, higher-status families stood to get even richer. This continued enrichment of the superordinate partners in the marriage arrangements may well have been the main reason for the practice of hypergyny—indeed, why the high often imposed it on the low.[75]

In China a similar situation prevailed. Hypergyny was idealized and daughters flowed upward from low-status to high-status groups. Dowries had to be provided from subordinates to superordinates or a marriage could not take place. The shortage of marriageable females for males in the subordinate groups could be extreme. In a study of Hopei County, for example, there were only five females age twenty-one or older who remained unmarried out of 5,255 lower-status families, but in these same families 1,177 males remained unmarried.[76]

Dickemann concludes that sex-selective infanticide is a strategy of inclusive fitness maximization. Even though the proximate cause of high-status groups importing lower-status women may have been the desire to accumulate wealth, such wealth would contribute to better conditions for rearing children and thus greater reproductive success over the long run. As for those of lower status, wealth could not be a motive since they were *giving up* whatever wealth they had and usually making themselves worse off economically. So in their case the aim (not necessarily conscious) was reproductive success pure and simple. Indeed, marrying off their daughters to resource-rich men, instead of to the resource-poor men of their own social status, was often essential for the survival of their lineages.[77]

SUMMARY

1. In all societies mothers provide the overwhelming majority of infant and child care. There is considerable evidence that women are primed to mother. Girls spend much more time at play parenting than boys. Compared to males, females show greater sensitivity to touch, sound, and odor; have greater fine motor coordination and finger dexterity; pick up nuances of voice and music more readily; and are more attracted to human faces. These are traits that are important in the successful rearing of infants and small children.

2. Intense bonding between mother and child is critical to the child's survival, especially in the ancestral environment. In hunter-gatherer societies infants go everywhere with their mothers; they are nursed almost continually and often for as long as four or five years.

3. Maternal behavior, however, is highly contingent on the circumstances for successfully rearing an infant. When circumstances are poor, mothers may choose not to invest in an infant. Under these conditions children are often abandoned. In Europe before the last two centuries many children were left at the doorsteps of foundling homes.

4. The quality of care provided by natural parents is usually much higher than the quality provided by stepparents. This is because stepchildren are not genetic kin whereas natural children are. This outcome is predicted by kin selection theory.

5. In the first half of the twentieth century children reared in foundling homes had an extremely high rate of early death and suffered from great emotional distress. They were reared impersonally and had little contact with their nurses or with other children. It was concluded that the children were suffering from the effects of extreme maternal deprivation.

6. These results make sense in terms of Bowlby's attachment theory. Attachment theory postulates that mother-infant bonding is an adaptation that evolved in the ancestral environment to keep infants and children safe from threats posed by both nature and other people. And without normal mother-infant bonding, infants cannot develop normally psychologically nor can they develop essential social skills.

7. Harry Harlow carried out experiments with rhesus monkeys designed to understand the effects of severe maternal deprivation. He created artificial monkeys to serve as mother surrogates. Both were made of wire, but one was wrapped in terrycloth and included large artificial eyes, whereas the other was made only of wire but was equipped with a milk bottle. Infant monkeys ignored the wire mothers except to nurse and spent virtually all of their time clinging to the terrycloth surrogates. The terrycloth mothers were more like real monkey mothers, which is why they were preferred.

8. Monkeys raised by artificial mothers all suffered severe emotional disturbance and were themselves unable to mother properly. In additional experiments some monkeys were exposed only to wire mothers, and these monkeys turned out to be even more disturbed and dysfunctional.

9. To promote their reproductive success, a crucial decision for prospective parents is how many offspring to have. In hunter-gatherer societies this is often a matter of how far apart to space the birth of children. Because resources are always limited and

must be shared by offspring, having them too close together will lead to more offspring deaths. Having them too far apart will lead to fewer offspring being born. In both cases reproductive success is not being maximized. The key is to aim for optimal birth intervals, or those that are neither too short nor too long.

10. In horticultural and agrarian societies fertility levels are much higher than in modern industrial societies (approximately 5–8 offspring born versus 2–3). In part this is the result of higher rates of infant and child mortality among farmers. When children are more likely to die before they reach reproductive age, more children must be born in order for parents to attain the desired number of surviving children. Because the vast majority of children in modern societies survive to reproductive age, parents can achieve reproductive success by having fewer children. In addition, children are much more economically costly in modern societies. They not only have to be fed and clothed, but educated so they can compete successfully in skill-based labor markets.

11. The Trivers-Willard hypothesis (TWH) states that mothers in good condition will give birth to more sons, whereas mothers in poor condition will give birth to more daughters. With respect to humans, the hypothesis states that quality of condition can be assessed by a mother's position on a socioeconomic scale. Thus high-status mothers should produce more sons, low-status mothers more daughters.

12. TWH can also be used to predict sex-biased parental investment after birth. High-status parents should invest more in sons, low-status parents more in daughters. For high-status families the marital and reproductive prospects of sons exceed the prospects of daughters, whereas for low-status families the reverse is true. Most studies of parental investment in nonindustrial societies support this argument. However, most studies of industrial societies show no differences in sex-biased parental investment by social status.

13. Infanticide has been found in all societies at all times in history. Although this practice seems to contradict kin selection theory, careful research actually supports it. Research shows that infanticide is most likely when the conditions for rearing an infant are poor. It may make sense for a mother to abandon her infant if resources are limited and the infant's chances of survival are low; if an infant is born too close to an older child from whom resources must be withdrawn to provide for the new infant; if an infant is born with a serious biological defect; or if a mother lacks essential social support for rearing her infant. If one or more of these conditions is present, a mother may decide not to rear her infant and wait until conditions improve.

14. Infanticide is usually sex-selective, there being considerably more female than male infanticide. Female infanticide is especially likely in highly patriarchal societies in which sons are highly favored over daughters. However, male infanticide does

occur and often exceeds the level of female infanticide. It is often a question of the relative marital and reproductive prospects of sons and daughters. In high-status groups where daughters' prospects are poor, female infanticide may be much more common than male infanticide. But in low-status groups where daughters' prospects exceed the prospects of sons, male infanticide may be more common. This is in essence another dimension of sex-biased parental investment.

QUESTIONS FOR DISCUSSION

✓ To what extent do mothers monopolize infant and child care in human societies? What qualities do women have that predispose them to mother?

✓ What is the nature of attachment between mothers and children and why is it so important?

✓ What does it mean to say that although women are predisposed to mother, maternal care is contingent? Discuss.

✓ What is "baby fever" and under what circumstances is it most likely to occur?

✓ Compare the quality of parental care provided by natural parents relative to step-parents.

✓ What do the experiences of abandoned infants tell us about the importance of attachment?

✓ Describe Harlow's experiments with monkeys and discuss their implications for humans. How do his research findings bear on Bowlby's theory of attachment?

✓ Why are hunter-gatherer women careful about birth spacing? What factors determine birth spacing? What does it mean to say that most mothers aim for optimal birth spacing?

✓ Discuss the variations in the number of offspring people have in different types of societies. What factors determine the number of offspring parents aim for?

✓ Discuss the Trivers-Willard hypothesis. What are the advantages and disadvantages for people in different societies, or for people in different socioeconomic positions in the same society, of having either sons or daughters? Who prefers sons, who prefers daughters, and why?

✓ The Trivers-Willard hypothesis seems to apply to nonindustrial but not to modern industrial societies. Explain why this should be. Does the failure of TWH to apply to industrial societies overturn it?

✓ What is hypergyny and what role does it play in marital and reproductive decisions?

✓ Infanticide is common in most societies. Explain the circumstances under which it is most likely.

✓ If mothers engage in infanticide, do they feel any emotional pain? Why or why not?

✓ In what ways is infanticide sex-selective? Why is it sex-selective?

References and Notes

1. Liesen 1995; Katz and Konner 1981.
2. Rossi 1977, 1984.
3. Hrdy 1999.
4. Hrdy 1999.
5. Hrdy 1999; Daly and Wilson 1988.
6. Boswell 1988, as discussed in Hrdy 1999.
7. Kertzer 1993, as discussed in Hrdy 1999.
8. Hrdy 1999, p. 316.
9. Korbin 1987; Gelles 1987.
10. Daly and Wilson 1998.
11. Harris et al. 2007.
12. Rotkirch 2008.
13. Hrdy 1999.
14. Spitz 1945, 1946; Hrdy 1999.
15. Hrdy 1999, p. 395.
16. Blum 2002.
17. Blum 2002.
18. Bowlby 1969.
19. Bowlby 1969.
20. Blum 2002.
21. Blum 2002.
22. Blum 2002.
23. Blum 2002, p. 193.
24. Blum 2002. Some of Harlow's first papers summarizing the monkey experiments are Harlow 1959a, 1959b; Harlow and Zimmerman 1959.
25. Blum 2002.
26. Blum 2002, p. 217.
27. Blurton-Jones 1986.
28. Blurton-Jones 1986.
29. Hill and Hurtado 1996.
30. Hill and Hurtado 1996.
31. Harris 1989; Harris and Ross 1987a; B. White 1973, 1982; Boserup 1981, 1986.
32. Low 1993, p. 184; Turke 1989, p. 76.
33. Kaplan 1994.
34. Dyson and Moore 1983; Malhotra, Vanneman, and Kishor 1995; Handwerker 1993.
35. Malhotra, Vanneman, and Kishor 1995.
36. Murthi, Guio, and Dreze 1995. See also Jejeebhoy 1995; Mason 2001.
37. Carey and Lopreato 1995.
38. Carey and Lopreato 1995, p. 616.
39. Sanderson and Dubrow 2000.
40. Unpublished research by the author.
41. Kaplan 1996.

42. Cleland 2001; Kaplan and Lancaster 2000.

43. Trivers and Willard 1973.

44. Trivers and Willard 1973, p. 91.

45. Shettles 1961.

46. Jakobovits 1991.

47. For example, Hartung 1982; Voland 1984; Boone 1986; Mealey and Mackey 1990; Betzig 1992b, 1993, 1995; Betzig and Turke 1986; Irons 2000. Summaries provided by Cronk 1991; Hrdy 1999.

48. Betzig and Weber 1995.

49. See Cronk 1991 for summary.

50. Betzig and Turke 1986.

51. Cronk 1989, 1991, 2000, 2004.

52. Cronk 1989, 1991, 2000, 2004.

53. Cronk 1989, 1991, 2000, 2004.

54. Cronk 1991, Table 6.

55. Cronk 1991, 2004.

56. Freese and Powell 1999.

57. Keller, Nesse, and Hofferth 2001.

58. Ellis and Bonin 2002.

59. Hopcroft 2005.

60. Langer 1972; Hrdy 1999.

61. Hrdy 1999.

62. Daly and Wilson 1988.

63. Daly and Wilson 1988.

64. Daly and Wilson 1988.

65. Hrdy 1979.

66. Daly and Wilson 1988; Hrdy 1999.

67. Hrdy 1999, pp. 320–321.

68. Hrdy 1999.

69. Dickemann 1979.

70. Hrdy 1999.

71. See Betzig 2012.

72. Dickemann 1979.

73. Dickemann 1979.

74. Dickemann 1979.

75. Dickemann 1979.

76. Gamble 1954; Dickemann 1979.

77. Hrdy 1999.

8

Gender

Sex is universal, but so is gender. What is the difference? Sex refers to distinctions between males and females in terms of biological anatomy and physiology, whereas gender involves how the sexes relate to each other, what roles each may play, who may have more social influence, and so on. It also refers to ideological conceptions of what males and females are like—whether men are deemed more suitable to lead, women more suitable for motherhood and domestic roles, and so on.

Over the past three or four decades, unfortunately, the word "gender" has almost completely replaced the word "sex." On many questionnaires, such as those at doctors' offices, not only do the forms ask for gender rather than sex, but the choices for gender are usually listed as "male" and "female." But these terms refer to sex, not gender. If the category is gender, then the choices have to be "man/boy" and "woman/girl." One even sees the occasional reference to the "gender" of mice or other animals. This is nonsensical. Only humans can have gender.

Why has the word "sex" been replaced by "gender"? Probably because many people have come to the conclusion that one's gender is entirely detached from one's sex, and that to use the word "sex" is to perpetuate the belief, now disavowed by the majority of social scientists, that gender is built mostly on the foundation of sex. But in fact gender and sex are closely intertwined. Sex by no means entirely determines gender, but neither can gender be uncoupled from sex.

This chapter explores the role of sex and gender in human societies. There are both universal and variable features of gender relations throughout the world, and we will explore each in turn. Understanding the major gender universals requires a Darwinian perspective. Variations in gender among societies have a lot to do with the kinds of economies societies have. In modern industrial societies, for example, gender relations differ dramatically in important respects from gender relations in agrarian and other nonindustrial societies. In our discussion of modern societies, we look at two topics: how gender is learned by each sex (which turns out to be more subtle than usually thought), and why men and women tend to pursue different academic and occupational options. What kinds of academic fields do men and women go into? What kinds of work do men and women do? Why are men disproportion-ately represented at the highest levels of the work world, but also concentrated in the dirtiest and most dangerous jobs?

Gender Everywhere

First let's consider the universals because they are the dimensions of gender that are most directly linked to sex and thus have a strong evolutionary foundation. At least six can be identified:

- Everywhere men display more aggressiveness.
- Everywhere men are more competitive.
- Everywhere men monopolize political leadership.
- Everywhere women do the majority of the parenting.
- Everywhere men and women display different kinds of cognitive skills.
- Everywhere men and women have a strong sense of gender identity.

Aggressiveness

Everywhere males show greater aggressiveness than females. (This means *average* aggressiveness. Some women are more aggressive than some men.) Aggression is the use of physical violence against the members of one's own community or against people in other societies. John Archer has reviewed hundreds of studies using dif-ferent research methodologies that show this to be the case.[1] These methodologies include self-report, observation, and experiment. Evidence that greater male aggres-siveness is evolutionarily selected comes from numerous sources. First we observe that greater male aggressiveness is widely found in mammals. Even early in life, males in most mammalian species are much more likely than females to engage in rough-and-tumble play and dominance-oriented behavior. There is also hormonal evidence for both mammals and humans. Experiments in which female monkeys have been injected with testosterone indicate that they display more aggression and dominance.[2] Girls with higher-than-average levels of the sex hormone androgen have been shown in numerous studies to display more aggressiveness than girls with normal androgen levels.[3] Another important line of evidence is the age at which sex differences in aggressiveness first appear. Large differences are seen as early as a year and a half to two years of age, far too early for socialization to have a significant impact.[4]

There is also the important matter of human sexual dimorphism. Men are on average about 8 percent taller than women and about 25 percent heavier.[5] One re-view of over a hundred studies showed that women's average strength was about 61 percent of men's.[6] Men have much greater upper body muscularity, with 99.9 per-cent of women actually falling below the male average in this regard.[7] Evolutionary selection for greater size and strength in human males is obviously intertwined with evolutionary selection for aggression.

Evolutionary selection for male aggression is also seen in warfare, a preserve that is almost exclusively male. No society has ever made women the principal warriors, and in the vast majority women do not participate at all. In one study of seventy nonindustrial societies, men did all of the fighting in 89 percent of them. In the remaining 11 percent, women's involvement was mostly limited to providing aid to the men. Men still did the overwhelming majority of the fighting.[8] As David Buss points out, "There exists not a single case in which women formed same-sex coalitions to kill other female coalitions for the purpose of purloining resources, territory, and mates."[9] Men's greater physical strength and aggressiveness naturally incline them to be the sex that fights wars.[10]

Competitiveness

Just as males are more aggressive, they are also more competitive. The two qualities are closely linked, and both spring from the same hormonal basis: testosterone. Whereas aggressiveness is using physical violence, competitiveness is about jostling with others to acquire status and resources, including mates. Men's greater competitiveness is clearly indicated by their enormous overrepresentation in all societies' high-status positions.[11] It does not matter what these positions are. Whatever a society regards as its most important and valued positions, these will be predominantly in the hands of men, and among the high-status positions men are most overrepresented in the highest of the high.

Consider, for example, the old Soviet Union in the years after World War II. This was a Marxist-Leninist society dedicated to greater gender equality, and indeed it appeared to achieve a good measure of it well before the Western industrial countries did. Women constituted 72 percent of physicians; 90 percent of dentists, medics, and nurses; 35 percent of lawyers; 47 percent of judges; 76 percent of accountants, statisticians, and planners; and 38 percent of scientists.[12] However, these numbers are misleading for two reasons. First, there was a dramatic shortage of male workers because millions of Soviet soldiers had been killed in World War II. Had such a shortage not existed, it is likely that these numbers would be diminished by half to two-thirds. In addition, within each of these professional fields there were large gender differences in status and responsibility. In medicine, for example, men headed the hospitals and its various departments and made up the vast majority of the highest-paid specialty, surgery; women were more likely to be nurses, midwives, and ward attendants. In the legal profession, the highest paid lawyers were mostly men, and male judges monopolized the higher courts, female judges the lower ones. In the Soviet Academy of Science, only 2 percent of full members were women. In factories and collective farms, the highest-paid and most-prestigious positions were overwhelmingly male.[13]

But what precedes what? Does a position have a higher status because it is held mostly by men, or is it the other way around? In other words, does a position that already has high status come to be monopolized by men for that reason? Evidence suggests the latter. Positions have a certain status for a variety of reasons, especially the level of technical knowledge and training the position requires. Men, on average, seek positions of higher status more vigorously than women because of their greater desire for high rank in the wider society. And when a position loses status, men tend to abandon it to women. A good example is the position of bank teller. In the 1950s, the vast majority of tellers were men. But today, most tellers are women. Because of occupational changes that have occurred in modern society, the job of bank teller has lost status, men have abandoned it for positions of higher status, and it has been taken over largely by women.

Not only are males everywhere (on average) more competitive than females; they are also more inclined toward risk and danger. We see this in both nonindustrial and industrial societies. In industrial societies men are highly overrepresented in such activities as car racing, sky diving, hang gliding, and gambling, and they also have many more automobile accidents.[14] Risk taking is another part of the adaptive complex that includes aggressiveness and competitiveness, and thus all three are closely intertwined. The best explanation for this complex is sexual selection.[15] Human males have evolved to invest more in mating than in parenting, and thus to compete with each other for the resources necessary for obtaining mates, especially high-quality mates.

Political Leadership

Political leadership is another important part of this adaptive complex. Here again, it is men who predominate. In small-scale societies lacking official positions of power and authority—where leadership is only informal—this leadership is invariably in the hands of men. The Iroquois are often cited as an exception, since some women held positions—the so-called matrons discussed earlier—in which they had the authority to veto decisions made by men. But this is not a genuine exception because the principal political positions were held only by men. In complex horticultural societies that do have positions of formal authority, which is usually invested in a hierarchy of chiefs, the chiefs are almost always men. In societies with an advanced agricultural technology, kings or emperors greatly outnumber queens and empresses. The only reason there are queens and empresses at all is to keep political power within family lines. It is not because men consider women just as suitable as political leaders, or because they happily stand aside to give women a fair chance to compete.

The sociologist Martin King Whyte examined political leadership in ninety-three of the societies in the Standard Sample and found that in sixty-five political leadership was exclusively in the hands of men. In most of the others women had some participation in political leadership but took a backseat to men. In only two societies did women hold positions that gave them political power equivalent to men, but men were much more numerous in these positions.[16] And yet Whyte may actually overstate the extent to which women participate in leadership in some societies. Further scrutiny shows that in several of the societies in which women were deemed to have "significant power," this power was limited to affairs within the household; it was not society-wide.[17]

In modern industrial societies the executive and legislative branches of government are strongly male dominated, and all modern nation-states are overwhelmingly led by men. The Dutch political scientist Vincent Falger reports that on

> June 14, 1992, at the end of the United Nations Conference on Environment and Development (UNCED) in Rio de Janeiro, pictures were taken of the largest collection of heads of state and government ever together in world history. Of the ninety-nine persons shown, only two were women. . . . The number of female foreign secretaries, ministers of defence, finance, international trade or economic affairs, to mention five other highly "international" top positions in politics, is to be counted on the fingers of two hands.[18]

Tatu Vanhanen, a Finnish political scientist, has reported on the female composition of the national parliaments of 122 contemporary nation-states.[19] In the 1980s, women constituted only 9.9 percent of the members of these parliaments. Things have changed somewhat since then. As of 2010, women occupied an average of 19 percent of the seats in parliament in all of the world's nation-states. The Scandinavian countries are far and away the leaders in women's political representation, with an average of 42 percent of parliamentary seats held by women. The rest of Europe averages 20 percent, the Americas 22 percent, and Asia and sub-Saharan Africa close behind with 18 and 19 percent, respectively. Unsurprisingly, women have the least parliamentary representation in Arab states, at only 10 percent.[20] Women are a good deal less represented as heads of state. In 2010 only twelve women held the position of president or prime minister, or about 6 percent of the total number. In general, as a leadership role increases in power and authority, it is more likely to be held by men.

Parenting

Another universal sex difference is parenting. In many animal species males contribute little parental care and often none at all. But humans are an important exception. Human fathers generally contribute a good deal more to their offspring than their nonhuman counterparts. Nevertheless, as discussed in Chapter 7, the parental care provided by fathers pales in comparison to that provided by mothers. In every human society, mothers provide the overwhelming majority of infant and child care.

The great extent to which mothers are involved in parental care helps explain many recurrent features of the sexual division of labor worldwide. Men rather than women tend to occupy roles that cannot be easily interrupted without affecting performance and that require long periods of time away from home. As noted above, men are also more likely than women to engage in dangerous and risky activities. Compared to men, women are highly averse to risk and danger, as well they should be. Dangerous and risky activities expose infants and children to a greater chance of early death. This is not going to promote a mother's reproductive success. Moreover, since infant and child care in human societies, especially ancestral human societies, is a continual activity, it is difficult for mothers to combine it with work that requires high levels of concentration and that cannot be easily interrupted. Finally, mothers cannot be lugging their babies with them for long distances for days at a time, as the consequences for those babies would be highly adverse: more danger, less reliable food supply, fewer interested adults to care for them, and so on.[21]

Cognitive Skills

A subject of much discussion in recent years is whether cognitive skills are sexually differentiated. There are good reasons to suggest that they are. Women consistently score higher than men on tests of verbal ability, as well as on tests involving remembering the locations of objects, whereas men consistently score higher on tests of spatial ability, route finding, maze running, and the mental rotation of objects. These differences have been found in the entire range of human societies and in many other mammalian species.[22] Innate sex differences in spatial skills are also suggested by hormonal evidence. These differences become pronounced at puberty, just as the male sex hormone testosterone is kicking in full blast.[23] Evidence from hormonal disorders is also highly suggestive. Males who suffer from a disease known as kwashiorkor often have elevated levels of estrogen, and these males generally exhibit poorer spatial skills than normal males.[24] Another hormone disorder, idiopathic hypogonadotrophic hypogonadism, is also associated with decreased male spatial ability. In this disorder, males have small genitalia and abnormally low levels of testosterone.[25]

If these differences are innate, why would they have evolved? How would they be adaptive for each sex? There are two main theories. Gaulin and FitzGerald theorize that these differences evolved by sexual selection throughout the mammalian line.[26] Because most mammal species are polygynous, males must navigate large territories in search of mates, and this puts a premium on good spatial skills. The researchers were able to test this claim by studying two different species of voles (field mice), one polygynous (meadow voles) and the other monogamous (pine voles). Male meadow voles ranged much farther from home than females, whereas among the pine voles no sex difference in range was found. Male meadow voles also significantly outperformed females in a maze-running task, whereas both sexes of pine voles showed the same maze-running abilities. In a follow-up study, Gaulin and FitzGerald found that male meadow voles expanded their navigational ranges only when the breeding season arrived and only after they had reached reproductive maturity. Female meadow voles' navigational ranges, by contrast, remained the same under these different conditions.[27]

Additional evidence consistent with the sexual selection hypothesis comes from a 2011 study of two carnivore species, polygynous giant pandas and monogamous small-clawed otters. As in the case of the vole studies, pandas and otters were given maze-running tasks. Male pandas made significantly fewer maze-running errors than females, whereas there was no significant sex difference in maze-running errors for otters.[28]

Can these findings be extended to humans? Evidence does suggest that in nonindustrial societies males usually have larger navigational ranges than females, and most nonindustrial societies are polygynous.[29] Larger navigational ranges have been found for the Yanomama, the Ifaluk, Trinidadians, the Kipsigis, and the Aka pygmies. Among the Aka, not only did males have a larger navigational range than females, but there was a positive correlation between the size of males' exploration ranges and the size of their mating ranges.[30]

The other theory has been proposed by Irwin Silverman and Marion Eals. They call it the hunter-gatherer theory. Their theory is based on the cognitive implications of the sexual division of labor in societies characteristic of the ancestral environment. Tracking animals and killing them require different kinds of spatial skills than plant collecting. Tracking animals requires the kinds of skills at which men have consistently been found to be superior: mental rotation of physical objects in three-dimensional space, maze learning, and map reading. By contrast, foraging for plants requires remembering the location of objects. In their original research, the authors administered several tests to students from Toronto's York University. The first test was designed to measure spatial relations and mental rotation. Men scored much higher on both measures. A second test involved measures of object location memory. As expected, women did better, although the difference was not large. A third test used a different measure of location memory. Once again, women scored higher, but in this case the difference was large: women scored 70 percent higher than men.[31]

More recent research is consistent with these findings. Silverman and five colleagues again used a student sample from York University. The most interesting part of this study was two "way finding" tests. Students were led one at a time in a roundabout manner through woods and asked to do two things. First they were stopped at certain prescribed locations and asked to place an arrow that pointed in the direction in which the walk started. Then they were asked to lead one of the experimenters back to the starting point via the most direct route. Results showed that males performed significantly better on both tasks than females.[32]

Another study, by Elizabeth Cashdan and four colleagues, examined spatial ability among the hunting and gathering Hadza. The authors administered three tests, a water level test, a targeting accuracy test, and a pointing accuracy test. The water level test was designed to measure horizontal and vertical accuracy. Two pictures of a half-filled bottle were placed at an angle atop two water levels, one horizontal and the other tipping down. Subjects were asked to indicate the correct water level (which is of course horizontal). Men significantly outperformed women at this task. The targeting task involved throwing a beanbag at a fixed target from three different distances. Once again, men performed better, demonstrating much greater targeting accuracy from all three distances. In the pointing accuracy test, subjects had twelve locations described to them and were asked to indicate, by pointing, which of the locations they had visited. This test is considered a measure of so-called dead-reckoning ability. Men scored higher on the test, but the male-female difference was relatively small.[33]

Of course, we want to know if these sex differences in spatial abilities are widespread or indeed universal. To test for this, Silverman, Choi, and Peters used data that the British Broadcasting Corporation had collected via the Internet.[34] Over 200 countries and 250,000 participants were represented in the study. The BBC researchers asked participants to respond to several tests, including tests that measured object location memory (OLM) and three-dimensional mental rotation (3DMR). Silverman and colleagues used data from forty of the countries and the seven different ethnic groups included in the BBC study. In all forty countries and seven ethnic groups, men scored higher than women at mental rotation. For thirty-five countries and all seven ethnic groups, women scored higher than men on location memory. The authors' conclusions? "This study unequivocally supported the universality of the male advantage in 3DMR across human societies. Though the same cannot be said for OLM, the data provided a strong suggestion of a universal difference."[35]

So what to conclude on the different theories? This is a very difficult question to answer because there has never been a decisive test pitting the two theories directly against each other. Until such a test is made—and that will be a very difficult test to carry out—no definitive conclusion can be drawn. Both theories may be right, at least with respect to males. Men's particular spatial abilities could be selected for by both the widespread search for mates and the demands of tracking and killing animals.

Gender Identity

In all societies men and women have a strong sense of gender identity; in fact, it is the most salient identity humans have. A major study of the influence of hormones on gender identity and gendered behavior has been carried out by J. Richard Udry, a sociologist at the University of North Carolina–Chapel Hill.[36] Udry relied on data from the Child Health and Development Study, a major research project in which blood samples were obtained from pregnant women between 1960 and 1969 and then frozen for thirty years. In 1990 and 1991 Udry and his research team interviewed many of the daughters born to these women between 1960 and 1963, who were by then in their late twenties. The respondents completed a variety of questionnaires designed to determine their degree of femininity or masculinity and their socialization experiences. Udry found that prenatal levels of sex hormone binding globulin (SHBG) had a strong effect on the daughters' levels of femininity or masculinity when they were adults. SHBG binds testosterone and transports it in the blood, and the higher the SHBG level the lower the level of testosterone. Women who had low prenatal SHBG levels (and thus high prenatal levels of testosterone) were significantly more masculine in their gender role orientation and behavior than women with high SHBG levels (and thus low prenatal levels of testosterone).

Because Udry was only studying prenatal hormone levels and masculine versus feminine orientation in females, and because there is less variation in these orientations within the female sex than between females and males, his findings have major implications for male-female differences in gender orientation. Because males have much higher levels of prenatal androgens, it is unsurprising that their highly masculine behavior contrasts sharply with that of women's feminine behavior.

A Tragic Experiment

A tragic case came to light some years ago in which a ten-month-old male infant, one of twins, had his penis destroyed in a botched circumcision. The prominent sex researcher John Money of Johns Hopkins University was consulted and recommended removing the baby's testicles and rearing him as a girl. He based this recommendation on his view that gender identity is entirely the product of learning. The parents followed Money's advice. Originally named Bruce, the baby was renamed Brenda. Unfortunately, the results for Brenda proved disastrous. Although living as a girl and being treated as a girl by her family, she always felt like a boy—in fact, insisted that she *was* a boy. She hated being dressed in frilly dresses and behaved like a highly masculine male—picking fights, roughhousing, playing in the dirt, and so on. She had severe adjustment problems at school because she did not fit in with either the girls or the boys. Both sexes rejected her and teased her mercilessly. She could not understand why she was so unlike everyone else, which caused her constant torment. What had happened to Bruce as a baby was concealed, but in early adolescence she finally learned the truth. Finally she understood what she had always felt: that she truly was a boy. At this point she decided to have sex reassignment surgery (for the second time!) and live as a male, changing her name to David. However, because these experiences were so traumatic, the restored David eventually committed suicide.[37]

Unfortunately, the medical profession had long been surgically changing genetic males with severe penile disorders—botched circumcisions, micropenis, and so on—into females and instructing their parents to rear them as girls. William Reiner, a urologist later turned child psychiatrist, followed twenty-nine such children and found that during psychosexual development all exhibited a male-typical gender shift. Many declared themselves to be male and lived as males.[38]

Physicians previously performing sex reassignment surgery have now been cautioned not to perform it at birth but to wait and see what kind of behavior the patient reveals later on.[39] In light of these and other cases, physicians have now rethought their previous orthodoxy that gender identity is entirely a matter of social learning.

Learning About Gender

The vast majority of anthropologists and sociologists contend that gender has little if any relation to human biology. Instead, it is a social construction that the members of a society arrive at and transmit to future generations via the socialization process. There are several serious problems with this claim. For one thing, there is no consistent argument concerning where any particular social construction comes from. Are social constructions arbitrary? Do they just drop down from the sky and somehow burrow into individual brains? If gender is just a social construction, it stands to reason that we should find enormous variation among societies in how people think about gender and how gender relations are structured. There are important variations in some respects, but as we have just seen there are universals that are extremely difficult to explain by the idea that "each culture constructs its own notions of gender."

If social construction and consequent socialization are the causes of gender differences, then in many societies, say about one-third, women should show more aggressiveness and competitiveness than men and men should assume primary responsibility for infant and child care; in another third there should be no significant differences between the sexes in these traits; and in the remaining third we should find the more familiar pattern of greater aggressiveness and competitiveness in men and greater nurturing tendencies in women. In other words, we should find the entire range of possible variation. But this is not what we find.

Another problem is the extent to which boys and girls are actually socialized differently. There are numerous studies indicating that in today's world they are in fact treated very similarly. Few differences show up with respect to encouragement of achievement or dependency, warmth and nurturance, restrictiveness, or sex-typed activities.[40] The most comprehensive review of these studies examined 172 published articles involving nearly 28,000 subjects.[41] The only difference that consistently emerged was fathers' discouraging boys from playing with girls' toys, especially dolls. In this case it is likely that fathers were simply responding to the fact that boys rarely play with girls' toys in the first place and, in the few instances in which they do, this is usually predictive of a later gay sexual orientation.[42] So there does appear to be differential parental encouragement of masculinity and femininity.

Yet even this has to be qualified. In most instances, boys already exhibit typical masculine behavior early in life, girls feminine behavior, and thus differential encouragement is usually not necessary. When it occurs, it is largely a matter of social reinforcement of biological tendencies. It might be argued that masculine behavior in boys and feminine behavior in girls is the result of imitating the same-sex parent.

But even this proves to be false, since boys will imitate masculine behavior and girls feminine behavior regardless of the sex of the parent.[43]

In Udry's study of hormonal influence on later gender-role orientations, he found that socialization did play a role in determining levels of masculinity and femininity, but in a very specific way inconsistent with the social constructionist explanation of gender. Socialization experiences interacted in an important way with prenatal hormone levels. Women who had low prenatal exposure to androgens were fairly responsive to their parents' socialization efforts: feminizing socialization efforts made them even more feminine. But women who had high prenatal androgen levels, and thus tended to be more masculine from the time they were young girls, resisted their parents' efforts to encourage feminine behavior. In fact, parents who worked hard to encourage femininity in less-feminine daughters were not only unsuccessful, but their efforts tended to backfire; the daughters became even less feminine in adulthood.

Udry's findings have important implications for social change efforts in the direction of greater gender equality and the possibility of a completely degendered society. These findings, as well as those discussed earlier in the chapter, clearly indicate that a completely degendered society is not possible. Achieving such an aim, as Udry points out, would require a coercive social engineering program that would necessitate a "continuous renewal of revolutionary resolve and a tolerance for conflict."[44] Even then, such a program would fail because of the recalcitrance of human nature. Moreover, very few people would want to live in such a society under any circumstances.

As for the likelihood of realizing gender equality, this depends on one's definition. If this means exact proportional representation of the sexes in every sphere of life—work, child care, and so on—this is tantamount to degendering and therefore impossible. But if gender equality means equal chances for the sexes to achieve their aims and goals, this is certainly possible. Indeed, modern industrial societies have moved a long distance along this path already, and even highly patriarchal societies like Japan are now moving in this direction.[45]

Gender Economies

Just as there are gender universals, there are also gender variations. These are especially apparent across the broad range of human societies from hunter-gatherers to modern industrial nation-states. In hunter-gatherer societies there is gender differentiation but usually little that can be called gender inequality. Men hold leadership positions, but in most cases these positions confer no real power or authority to command the actions of others, women included. Gathering is an important economic activity among most hunter-gatherers, except for those at high latitudes where growing seasons are extremely short and there is little to gather. Thus women's economic contribution is important and men depend on them for much of what they eat.

The !Kung San come about as close to a gender egalitarian society as is possible. Women have the opportunity to participate in important ways in group discussions. There are no strong stereotypes of women, taboos associated with them, or restrictions on their behavior, all of which are common in many other types of societies. Overall, women probably fare better relative to men among hunter-gatherers than in any type of nonindustrial society.

Horticultural societies are difficult to generalize about because they display a wide range of variation in the status of women. Perhaps the safest thing to say is that in the majority of horticulturalists women tend to do worse than among hunter-gatherers. At one extreme we find groups like the Yanomama. Here men control almost everything. They not only hunt but also are the principal cultivators of the land. They totally dominate political leadership and even their religious practices are heavily slanted toward men. When he began fieldwork among them in the 1960s, Napoleon Chagnon dubbed them "the fierce people" because of the very high levels of aggressive behavior he observed. Men would take insult easily and challenge other men to fights involving long poles that they would use to club each other over the head. If a pole fight did not settle a dispute, the matter could escalate to fighting with axes. But men did not restrict their violent behavior to other men. They subjected women to beatings, axe attacks, and gang rapes involving as many as fifty men. If you are a woman, the Yanomama are not a very nice bunch to be around.[46]

Much better for a woman to live among the Iroquois. Recall that the Iroquois were a matrilineal society in which women owned the land, wielded considerable influence over the affairs of their matrilineages, and even held important political positions. Although the Iroquois have been mistakenly called a matriarchy—there have never been any matriarchies—they came about as close to gender equality as any other horticultural society has.

Overall, things got a lot worse for women when horticultural societies evolved into agrarian societies. In horticultural societies women are often the primary cultivators, but when people began to cultivate the land by using plows and draft animals, the economic division of labor changed dramatically. Women lost most of their productive role outside the home; men became the primary cultivators because farming the land in this fashion is extremely demanding and difficult work, quite unlike the much lighter demands of horticulture. Agrarian cultivation also poses dangers that are absent in horticultural systems, especially to children. Children can easily be trampled by horses or oxen, or get caught under the blades of plows. Consequently it makes more sense for males to assume these activities while women tend the children elsewhere.

There is still plenty for women to do. They have primary responsibility for infant and child care, and domestic tasks also have their demands. A much sharper distinction emerges than in earlier societies between "men's work" and "women's work," a distinction that the anthropologists Kay Martin and Barbara Voorhies refer

FIGURE 8.1   Veiled Bedouin Women, Egypt
(Lila Abu-Lughod/Anthro-Photo)

to as the "inside-outside dichotomy": men work outside the home, women inside it.[47] Women thus became "domesticated" to an extent not seen in earlier societies. It is likely that it was at this point in social evolution that the stereotypes of men and women familiar to us today began to emerge in their most elaborate form.

In nearly all agrarian societies, women were social inferiors. This was true throughout both Europe and Asia, but in Asia things were worse. For thousands of years women have had very low status throughout much of south and east Asia. Throughout the broad region that includes much of north India, Pakistan, and Bangladesh, even today women are expected to follow the custom of *purdah*, which is their seclusion and veiling in the presence of men. This governs much of a woman's daily life. When she is in the presence of others, a young woman must display disinterest in her husband, not look directly at him, and not even speak to him; and of course she must be veiled. All land and other productive resources are owned by men. Women have little participation in affairs outside the home, and are thought by men to be unsuited for such activity. Even within the household, women defer to men in a wide range of ways, such as eating only after the men have been served and spending much of their time physically apart from the men. Women's sexuality is also tightly controlled, which is the main purpose of seclusion and veiling.[48] The anthropologist David Mandelbaum sums up the situation by saying that "women are everywhere undervalued in relation to men."[49]

These restrictions are especially stringent among groups of higher status. Lower-status women have more of a public presence, such as working in the fields and negotiating sales in the bazaars. A more relaxed atmosphere between men and women prevails inside the home. There are also importance differences between north and south India. In the south, purdah restrictions are less stringent and, in general, the status of women is higher. But there is no clear geographical dividing line, so that in general women's status improves gradually as one moves from north to south.[50]

Practices closely resembling purdah are also found among agrarian peoples in north Africa, the Middle East, and central Asia, where Islam is the dominant religion. But as one moves east into southeast and east Asia, even though women are still subordinate they have greater freedom.[51] In China, for example, women were not veiled or secluded. Nevertheless, they usually did not own property and had little public role. A woman was under the strict authority of her husband and other members of his kin group and was regarded as social inferiors. Especially among higher-status groups, women were subjected to the infamous custom of foot binding: a girl's feet were bound in such a way that prevented them from growing normally. This made it difficult or impossible to work in the fields or to run away. (It was also regarded as a mark of beauty.)

In pastoral societies the status of women has usually not been much better. Almost all pastoralists are strongly patrilineal, which gives men the upper hand in family arrangements. Most pastoralists assign herding entirely to men, although in some groups women engage in dairying. And among pastoralists who practice substantial cultivation, men too are dominant. Most pastoral societies resemble agrarian societies in the structure of gender relations. As Martin and Voorhies point out, "There is typically a strict dichotomization of the sexes conceptually, and the assignment of opposite and complementary behaviors. With few exceptions, males control both social and political affairs, and manage the flow of property by birthright. Women assume a position of submission or often actual avoidance in face-to-face public encounters with real or potential husbands."[52]

With the advent of industrial capitalism in the eighteenth and nineteenth centuries, the old agrarian pattern of gender relations began to change, slowly at first but then picking up steam as rural life shifted to urban and farming gave way to work in factories and offices. Women began to move back into the economic sphere. At first this was largely limited to unmarried women, approximately half of whom were employed outside the home at the beginning of the twentieth century. Only a small proportion of married women with children were engaged in gainful employment, but this too changed dramatically after midcentury. By the end of the century most married women with children were gainfully employed, although many of them worked only part-time. Many of the old gender stereotypes and male prerogatives have now declined or disappeared altogether, and women have moved progressively closer to equality with men despite important differences in the kinds of work that men and women do.

The key to understanding why gender relations differ from one type of society to another is the nature of the economy and how each sex fits into it. The sex that controls the economy tends to control both the other sex and the social and public spheres, or at least to control them more than would otherwise be the case.[53] Women make important economic contributions in both hunter-gatherer and horticultural societies, but they are largely pushed out of economic work in agrarian and pastoral societies. They therefore tend to do far better in the former two types than in the latter two.[54] The economic contribution made by women also helps explain why they do better in some agrarian societies than in others. As noted above, women do better in south India than in the north, likely because of their greater involvement in cultivation in the south. Ecology and climate make the south suitable for rice cultivation, and much of this can be carried out by women because preparing the land by plowing is not necessary. In the north, by contrast, the staple crop is wheat, and its cultivation using the plow favors male rather than female labor, and thus women are heavily excluded from agricultural work.[55]

In early industrial societies women were largely excluded from economic work, and for good reason: they had major domestic responsibilities. In the first half of the twentieth century women put in a full and hard week's work every week of the year—doing laundry, cleaning house, shopping for food, and preparing meals, as well as numerous other tasks. In homes heated by coal, walls had to be washed down regularly to remove accumulated coal dust, something unheard of today. Beginning in the 1950s, labor-saving devices began to appear, including automatic washers and dryers, self-defrosting refrigerators, and electric vacuum cleaners. They substantially reduced the amount of time and effort women had to spend on domestic tasks. Later the emergence of the fast food industry, prepackaged meals, and microwave ovens also saved time. Because of these innovations it became much easier for women to work outside the home if they were so inclined.

And many were. After World War II the expanding service and information sector of the economy created jobs that women found especially suitable, and many sought work to supplement family income.[56] As women got drawn into the work world, most discovered a whole new sphere of self-expression and gratification and wanted more of it. Staying home all day minding the children and doing domestic work seemed less interesting. These were some of the forces that stimulated the new wave of feminism that began in the early 1960s.

Men, Women, and Work

One of the more interesting features of gender relations in modern societies is the different kinds of work men and women do. To explore this topic we can start by looking at some representative studies of gender differences in expressed occupational interests.

Who Chooses What?

The most widely used and highly regarded inventory of occupational interests is the Strong Interest Inventory, or SII.[57] The SII identifies 325 occupations and asks subjects to indicate their level of interest in each by choosing "like," "dislike," or "indifferent." The occupations are grouped into six categories, each of which represents a general occupational theme:[58]

- *Realistic*: High scores indicate good physical skills, a desire to work with tools and outdoors, and working with things rather than people or ideas.
- *Investigative*: High scores demonstrate an interest in science, the physical world, and solving abstract problems.
- *Artistic*: High scores indicate an interest in self-expression, especially in artistic media. High scorers on this scale show an interest in problems that are highly structured.
- *Social*: High scorers are sociable, responsible, and humanistic, and have a strong desire for self-expression. They prefer to solve problems through discussion with others.
- *Enterprising*: High scorers are verbally skilled and show an interest in persuading others of their viewpoint. They like leadership. They are impatient with work requiring precision or sustained intellectual effort.
- *Conventional*: People with high scores like orderly verbal and numerical work in offices. They prefer tight structure and exact expectations from bosses and supervisors.

Kaufman and McLean administered this test to 936 subjects ranging in age from sixteen to sixty-five.[59] The sample was 60 percent female and 40 percent male, and the ethnic composition was 81 percent whites, 9 percent blacks, and 6 percent Hispanics, with a scattering of other groups. Males scored much higher than females on the realistic category, and significantly higher on the investigative category. Females scored somewhat higher on the social and artistic categories. On the scales measuring the enterprising and conventional categories, gender differences were minor. The results were similar to those reported in many other studies.[60] They indicate that males are more interested than females in doing work that requires good physical skills, working with tools and working outdoors, working with things rather than with people, and solving abstract problems. They also show that females are more interested than males in doing work that involves sociability, in humanistic pursuits, and in problem solving through discussion with others.

In more-detailed analyses, Kaufman and McLean found that in the realistic category the largest male-female differences pertained to mechanical work and work involving a sense of adventure. Here gender differences were large. The authors report the results in terms of standardized scores. For mechanical work the male score was 54.2, the female score 42.7. For work involving a sense of adventure the male score was 56.0, the female score 44.0. And in the investigative category, gender differences were largest for an interest in science and mathematics. On science males scored 51.3, females 45.1; on mathematics males scored 50.1, females 44.8. In the social category, the male-female difference was greatest for domestic activities (males = 45.0, females = 55.0), office practices (males = 47.8, females = 56.4), and social services (males = 47.2, females = 53.4).[61]

In another study, Aros, Henly, and Curtis administered the SII to an extremely large sample of 16,484 subjects (6,567 males and 9,917 females) between the ages of eighteen and twenty-two.[62] They obtained occupational like and dislike scores for twenty-eight white collar and professional occupations. Scores for eleven of these are listed in Table 8.1. The significance of these findings can be summarized by looking first at male-female differences in the likes scores. The occupations men liked much more than women were jet pilot, building contractor, draftsman, and architect. Twice as many men as women liked the occupation of jet pilot (62 versus 32 percent), four times as many men showed an interest in being a building contractor (32 versus 8 percent), three times as many men liked the job of draftsman (24 versus 8 percent), and 12 percent more men than women expressed an interest in being an architect.

The occupations most liked by women were social worker, flight attendant, elementary school teacher, registered nurse, and public relations specialist. Three times as many women as men expressed liking for the job of flight attendant (39 versus 13 percent) and for registered nurse (27 percent versus 8 percent). Two and a half times as many women expressed liking for the job of social worker (48 percent versus 20 percent). Compared to men, women liked an elementary school teacher's job by nearly two to one (52 to 28 percent), and women expressed more liking than men for the job of public relations specialist (48 to 32 percent).

If we look at the dislike scores, we see that men most dislike the occupations of registered nurse (71 percent) and flight attendant (61 percent), jobs that are clearly much more liked by women than by men. Women express a strong dislike for the job of draftsman (72 percent) and building contractor (69 percent), occupations that men like much more than women.

The remaining two occupations—sales manager/salesperson and high school teacher—were liked and disliked almost equally by men and women.

Column 5 of Table 8.1 summarizes the differences in the male-female like scores and the male-female dislike scores. For example, 30 percent more men than women like the occupation of jet pilot, and 31 percent more women than men express dislike for this occupation. And 28 percent more women than men like the job of social worker, but 24 percent more men than women dislike the job of social worker.

TABLE 8.1   Occupational Preferences by Gender

Occupation	Assessment	Percent Men	Percent Women	Percent Men Minus Percent Women
Jet Pilot	Like	62	32	30
	Dislike	18	49	−31
Building Contractor	Like	32	8	24
	Dislike	32	69	−37
Draftsman	Like	24	8	16
	Dislike	42	72	−30
Architect	Like	44	32	12
	Dislike	26	43	−17
Sales Manager	Like	30	29	1
	Dislike	41	45	−4
High School Teacher	Like	38	39	−1
	Dislike	38	38	0
Public Relations Specialist	Like	32	48	−16
	Dislike	37	25	12
Registered Nurse	Like	8	27	−19
	Dislike	71	48	23
Elementary School Teacher	Like	28	52	−24
	Dislike	48	26	22
Flight Attendant	Like	13	39	−26
	Dislike	61	36	25
Social Worker	Like	20	48	−28
	Dislike	50	26	24

Source: Jesse R. Aros, George A. Henly, and Nicholas T. Curtis, "Occupational sextype and sex differ-ences in vocational preference-measured interest relationships," *Journal of Vocational Behavior* 53 (1998):227–242. Occupations are listed from most male-preferred to most female-preferred.

Who Does What?

A crucial question is the extent to which these stated likes and dislikes correspond to the kinds of work men and women actually do—how men and women are sorted out in the occupational structure of modern society. In fact, they correspond re-markably well. Table 8.2 shows that the occupations whose choices are the most male-slanted are overwhelmingly performed by men, and the occupations whose choices are the most female-slanted are overwhelmingly performed by women. Those occupations whose choices are approximately equal in terms of gender are about equally performed by both men and women. We can add in this respect the job of physician. Aros, Henly, and Curtis found virtually no gender difference in expressed like or dislike of this profession.[63] Today some 34 percent of physicians

TABLE 8.2 Occupational Preferences and Occupational Representation by Gender

Occupation	Percent Male	Percent Female
Jet Pilot *(male preferred)*	95.9	4.1
Building Contractor *(male preferred)*	93.6	6.4
Draftsman *(male preferred)*	83.4	16.6
Architect *(male preferred)*	76.5	23.5
Registered Nurse *(female preferred)*	9.4	90.6
Elementary School Teacher *(female preferred)*	18.6	81.4
Social Worker *(female preferred)*	19.4	80.6
Flight Attendant *(female preferred)*	22.4	77.6
Public Relations Specialist *(female preferred)*	41.8	58.2
Sales Manager/Salesperson *(no gender preference)*	51.3	48.7
High School Teacher *(no gender preference)*	42.7	57.3

Source: Bureau of Labor Statistics, *Household Data Annual Averages*, 2012, http://bls/gov/cps/cpsaat11.pdf.

and surgeons are women, but this in part reflects the large number of older males from an earlier era who are still practicing.[64] Today women make up 50 percent of medical students. So men and women show approximately equal preference for the job of physician and today are about equally represented in that job (or at least soon will be). In short, the occupations men and women end up in are to a great extent the occupations they like or dislike the most.

Another way of summarizing the data is to calculate correlations between expressed interest scores and occupational concentration scores. This can be done by taking the male-female difference in the likes scores of Column 5 of Table 8.1 as one variable, and the percentage of an occupation that is male in Table 8.2 as the second variable. Computing the relationship between the two shows an exceptionally high correlation of .945. (Six other occupations listed by Aros and colleagues were added to increase accuracy, for a total of 17.) Also computed was the relationship between the male-female difference in the dislikes scores and the percentage of an occupation that is male. In this case an even larger correlation of -.971 was obtained. The correlations are identical if the percentage of a population that is female is used in place of the percentage that is male, except the signs are reversed (-.945 and .971, respectively).

Looking at another type of work, the specialized academic professions, we do not have data on stated likes or dislikes, but we do have data on how men and women are distributed throughout these academic fields and their various specialties. We find that although today men and women earn doctoral degrees in the United States in about equal proportions, they choose very different fields of study. The most male-concentrated fields are physics and engineering. In 2009 men earned 82 percent of the PhDs in physics and 79 percent of the degrees in engineering.[65] And there are differences among specialties within these fields. In 2012 men made up 95 percent of mechanical engineers and 91 percent of electrical and electronic engineers, but women earned 25 percent of the degrees in environmental health engineering and bioengineering. In physics, the field that is the most male-concentrated is elementary particle physics, with about 96 percent of these physicists being men.

Women are much more heavily represented in the social and behavioral sciences. In 2009, 72 percent of PhDs in psychology were awarded to women.[66] In sociology, women earned 60 percent of the PhDs in 2009 and in anthropology 61 percent.[67] There are important subfield differences in these fields too. For example, 38 percent of degrees in physiological psychology went to women compared to 80 percent of the degrees in developmental and child psychology. In sociology women are most heavily concentrated in the specialties of gender and marriage and family relations. They are highly underrepresented in sociological theory and are rare in mathematical sociology. In the anthropological subfields of biological anthropology and linguistics, men are highly overrepresented. However, the part of biological anthropology devoted to the study of primates has proven very attractive to women, and some of the leading primatologists are women.[68]

As for working class or blue collar occupations, the vast majority are performed by men. For example, in 2012, 99.9 percent of brick and stone masons were men, as were 98.5 percent of roofers, 95.4 percent of sheet metal workers, 98.5 percent of highway maintenance workers, 98.4 percent of aviation mechanics and service technicians, 98.8 percent of automotive service technicians and mechanics, and 95.2 percent of telecommunications line installers and repairers.[69] (It is noteworthy that in nonindustrial societies we find the same pattern of occupational differences. In the societies of the SCCS, men overwhelmingly dominate building activities. They do 99 percent of woodworking, 95 percent of working in bone, 92 percent of stone work, 96 percent of boat building, and 100 percent of metal working.)

Many blue-collar jobs are physically demanding, dangerous, and dirty. Using these criteria, *The Jobs Rated Almanac* identified what it considered the twenty-five worst jobs and found that the sex composition of twenty-three of them was over 90 percent male. These included firefighter (97.5 percent), construction laborer (94.5 percent), miner (98.6 percent), mechanic (96 percent), timber cutter or logger (97 percent), truck driver (94.7 percent), and welder or cutter (94.9 percent). One of the most dangerous, strenuous, and dirty kinds of work is road and bridge construction, and it is overwhelming performed by men. The few women who work in these jobs mostly hold signs and direct traffic. The people doing the really dirty, dusty, dangerous, and physically demanding work—digging, jack-hammering, paving, and so on—are exclusively men.[70]

The job of firefighter is especially interesting. In 2000 only 36 out of 11,000 New York City firefighters were women, and in Boston the number was only 12 of 1,600. In New York City during one hiring period, 850 women signed up to take the required written test, but most ended up never taking it. Of the 17,000 people who took the test, a mere 450, or 2.6 percent, were women. Of these, 354 passed, but only 105 actually went on to the next stage, the physical test. That test involved things like raising a large ladder and using a heavy fire hose filled with water. Only 11 of the 105 female test takers passed, but most of the men did.[71]

Explaining Occupational Differences

How to explain these differences? At the proximate level, they fit with the contrasting interests discussed earlier. We have seen that in the white-collar and professional occupations there is a close correspondence between stated occupational likes and dislikes and the kinds of work men and women actually do. The gender composition of an occupation reflects, to a large extent, occupational interests (although this is by no means the whole story). Men go into the fields they like most (or dislike least), and avoid those they dislike most (or like least). And the same holds for women. Differences in cognitive skills matter as well. The most male-preferred occupations shown in Table 8.2—building contractor, jet pilot, draftsman, and architect—require excellent spatial cognition, at which men excel. None of the female-preferred occupations shown in the table require such skills. However, those occupations do require good verbal skills, and most studies show that women outscore men on tests of verbal ability and acuity.

But can we say the same thing for academic and blue-collar work? Is the representation of men and women in these kinds of work closely related to their occupational preferences? It appears so. Recall that in the Kaufman and McLean study men scored significantly higher than women on the investigative subscale, especially the science and mathematics components. Men appear much more inclined than women toward abstractions. Physics is very abstract and highly mathematical, and engineering represents the application of physical and mathematical principles to building things (roads, bridges, machines, computers, electrical grids, airplanes, etc.). These are also fields that require excellent spatial cognition, and advanced mathematical skills more generally. In such intellectually demanding fields differences in ability are just as important as differences in interest level. Through high school, girls stay more or less even with boys, but fall behind as the level of mathematical difficulty increases. Once the rarefied level of the mathematically gifted is reached, males greatly outnumber females. Among mathematically gifted students in their twenties, for every gifted female who is pursuing an advanced degree there are eight males who are equally talented.[72]

Women's greater attraction to psychology, sociology, and anthropology can be understood as a reflection of their interest in human relationships. Recall that women outscored men on the social subscale of the SII. The greater emphasis that women place on human relationships can also explain why they are highly overrepresented in such occupations as social worker, registered nurse, and elementary school teacher. The last two actually have another dimension, a strong nurturant element. Women's overrepresentation in these occupations probably reflects their overwhelming predominance in parenting in the world's societies. Compared to men, women display more warmth, compassion, and empathy. Thus it should not be surprising that they are attracted to fields in which these qualities are a central and necessary part of the work being performed. Women's worldwide role as mothers may also explain why women psychologists are overrepresented in the subfields of developmental and child psychology. Men's overrepresentation in physiological psychology may reflect their expressed interest in science and mathematics, inasmuch as this branch of psychology is highly abstract and mathematical.

In the Kaufman and McLean study men also scored much higher than women on the SII's realistic scale. As already noted, they express more interest than women in doing physical work, working with tools, and building and fixing things, and they prefer these kinds of work to working with people. This interest is the likely explanation for men's overrepresentation among building or construction contractors and architects. The occupation of jet pilot is related to the adventure dimension of realistic, on which men score particularly high. Someone lacking advanced spatial and navigational skills could never pilot a large airplane.

Men's high scores on the realistic subscale can also explain, at the proximate level, why men are so highly overrepresented in blue-collar work. Most blue-collar activity involves working with things rather than people, and requires the mechanical interests and skills so characteristic of most men. Much of it involves outdoor work. Many kinds of blue-collar jobs put a premium on strength, and men have much greater upper-body strength than women. Wielding a jackhammer, for example, and lifting bundles of roofing tiles onto roofs so they can be hammered into place are physically demanding activities. Many blue-collar jobs are also dangerous—policeman, firefighter, miner, timber cutter and logger, and so on—and dirty—brick mason, highway construction worker, plasterer, plumber, earth driller, automotive repair man, and so on—and women have been shown to strongly dislike those things.[73] Men's greater interest in and willingness to do jobs that are dangerous has another proximate cause: testosterone. This male hormone is not only related to greater aggression and competitiveness, as shown earlier, but also to an orientation to danger and risk. Women's much lower testosterone levels disincline them to danger and risk.

But if modern occupational differences between men and women reflect their different interests and inclinations, then we must explain why these interests and inclinations differ. So far we have suggested proximate causes of occupational differences, but what are the ultimate causes? This, of course, is the crucial question from a Darwinian evolutionary point of view.

Looking at men first, how did selection, either natural or sexual (or both), act on them in ancestral environments to craft the occupational interests they currently display? Ancestral men were hunting game, competing with each other for mates, and fighting wars to acquire women and wealth. To hunt game successfully, especially big game, men had to spend hours tracking animals over long distances. These large ranges required good navigational abilities. If we accept the arguments of Gaulin and FitzGerald discussed earlier in this chapter, male competition for mates and polygyny also played an important role in increasing the size of men's navigational range and their need for good navigational skills.[74] These practices, either together or separately, would have selected for the kinds of spatial skills at which men excel, especially three-dimensional mental rotation of objects.[75] The main weapons for hunting game and fighting wars in the ancestral environment were the spear and the bow and arrow, the use of which created selection pressures for good throwing and aiming abilities. These abilities are tied in to spatial cognition as well because they require a capacity to understand the trajectories of moving objects.[76] And, of course, tools and weapons had to be manufactured, work that was done overwhelmingly by men.[77] This would have created selection pressures on men for good mechanical abilities.

Although women performed an important role as gatherers and processors of food in the ancestral environment, the most critical activity they performed was rearing children. This meant that there were very strong selection pressures on females for the development of traits necessary for successful motherhood, which would have been mostly a package of emotions centered on nurturant tendencies, emotional sensitivity, compassion, empathy, and good verbal and interpersonal skills. Modern women's stated occupational preferences directly reveal these kinds of traits. As for the kinds of work that women tend to avoid, such as work that is dangerous and dirty, there is also a strong connection to the rearing of young children. Women have a much lower threshold than men for danger and risk because work involving these things increases children's chances of injury or death. Engaging in dangerous work is not a prescription for women's successful promotion of their reproductive success. Women also seem to have a much lower threshold than men for dirtiness. Here again the motherhood role is critical. To keep infants healthy and free of disease, they must be kept relatively clean.

"Is" Does Not Imply "Ought"

Certain misconceptions often creep into considerations of men's and women's activities and the likely reasons for them, and these misconceptions need to be dispelled. The most common is the assumption that because people tend to do certain kinds of things, they *should* do those things. Obviously such an assumption is unsupportable and is an example of what is known as the *naturalistic fallacy*: deriving a statement about "ought" from a statement about "is." Most scholars agree that you cannot infer a moral or political judgment from a descriptive (or theoretical) statement because these are different realms of discourse. Noting that men gravitate toward careers as firefighters rather than nurses is not to suggest that men *should* be firefighters or women *should* be nurses. Or, putting it the other way around, it is not to suggest that firefighters should be men or nurses should be women.

In a related vein, women may choose to pursue careers that explore or emphasize human relationships and care work, but that cannot be taken to suggest that women are incapable of becoming abstract thinkers. Indeed, half of law students are now women, and much of law involves trying cases in court. This requires an ability to sort through evidence and draw compelling conclusions, which is obviously impossible without abstract thinking. Moreover, many university professors are now women, and the ability to manipulate abstract ideas is the most fundamental aspect of professorial work, both teaching and research.

Conclusion

When we consider the positions of men and women and their life outcomes in modern industrial societies, we need to look at the whole picture. We need, as it were, a "gender balance sheet." It seems unwise to assume automatically and uncritically that women are invariably worse off than men. If we take a broad perspective and total things up, with one column for men and another for women, then women will come out looking better than is often imagined, or at least men worse than usually imagined.

Kingsley Browne points out that even though women earn less on average than men, men die more frequently on the job, often work in less pleasant environments, and usually work longer hours. Moreover, Browne suggests that women today actually have more real choices than men. A woman can choose to devote herself entirely to a full-time career, to balance a full time career with family, to opt for part-time work, or to be a full-time housewife and mother.[78] Browne adds that the male "desire for status and tangible rewards is biologically ingrained. . . . It will be the rare man who is willing to stay home with the children and be supported by his wife for an extended period, and it will be the rarer wife who is willing to support such a husband and who finds such a man sexually attractive."[79]

SUMMARY

1. Roles and relationships based on gender are a universal feature of human societies. All societies build gender differences out of sex differences and make gender a fundamental part of all social relations. There are several aspects of gender relations that are found universally, and these are the dimensions of gender that have been selected for throughout human evolution.

2. In all known societies males display, on average, greater aggressiveness and competitiveness than females. The same pattern is found in most species of mammals. These behaviors are linked to such male hormones as testosterone. Males are also more prone to risk taking than females and more likely to engage in dangerous activities.

3. Men seek high-status positions more vigorously than women and thus are overrepresented in them. Even in societies with a strong commitment to gender equality, men predominate in high-status positions. If a position in which men are highly concentrated loses status, men tend to abandon it and it comes to be held primarily by women. Likewise, if a position held primarily by women rises in status, it will be increasingly pursued by men.

4. Throughout the world men are the predominant and in many societies the only political leaders. In modern industrial societies women have made inroads into politics, but still constitute an average of only about one-fifth of legislative bodies. As a political position increases in its level of power and authority, it is increasingly composed of men. The overwhelming majority of heads of state in modern nation-states are men.

5. War is in all likelihood the most male-dominated activity in the world. In most societies men do all of the fighting, and in the rest they do the vast majority of it. Until modern times, women's involvement in warfare was limited to providing support and assistance to men.

6. In humans fathers play a greater role in parenting than in most other animal species (birds excepted), but the vast majority of the care of infants and young children is provided by mothers. Motherhood accounts for several aspects of the sexual division of labor, such as women's absence from roles that involve considerable risk and danger.

7. Studies consistently show that men and women throughout the world have different cognitive skills. Men are better at maze running, mentally rotating three-dimensional objects, and map reading. Women generally have superior verbal skills and also tend to outperform men in tasks involving object location memory. There is debate over why these differences exist. One theory attributes males' superior spatial

skills to polygyny. To find extra wives men had to leave their own villages to obtain wives in other villages, and this requires greater navigational range. Another theory is that males need better spatial skills for hunting, especially tracking animals over long distances, and that better location memory is useful for female gathering activities.

8. A sense of gender identity is extremely important in all societies. Identifying as either boy or girl and man or woman is the most important of all human identities. The brain plays a major role in determining this identity. Boys and girls have a strong identity as one or the other sex early on. Gender identity is highly resistant to change by socialization processes. Gender engineering experiments involving infant males with damaged penises being reared as females have proved highly unsuccessful, in some cases disastrous. Most genetic males changed into anatomical females and raised as girls still have a male gender identity.

9. The Standard Social Science Model contends that gender roles and relations are produced by the different socialization experiences of boys and girls. However, a comprehensive review of nearly two hundred studies showed that today there is little difference in how boys and girls are socialized. One difference is discouragement of feminine behavior in boys and masculine behavior in girls. It is not socialization experiences but sex hormones that primarily determine feminine versus masculine outcomes. Research shows that girls with low prenatal testosterone levels who were encouraged to be feminine became even more feminine. But girls with high prenatal testosterone levels who exhibited more masculine behavior early in life were shown to be highly resistant to parental encouragement of femininity.

10. The status of women varies dramatically from one type of society to another. Women have done worst in agrarian and pastoral societies. These societies tend to be highly patriarchal and have a sharp division of gender roles. Women have little public role and their sexuality is often tightly controlled by seclusion and veiling. Women have done much better in hunter-gatherer and industrial societies, in the latter now having come close to equality with men.

11. The key factor determining women's status is the extent to which they make important economic contributions in their society. In agrarian and pastoral societies men dominate economic life. In hunter-gatherer societies women usually make an important economic contribution by gathering. In modern industrial societies women have been brought back into the economy in a dramatic way, and this has led to a substantial improvement in their status.

12. In modern societies, men and women display different occupational interests. Men show more interest in work that involves physical skills and in working with things rather than people. They also display more interest in scientific abstractions and in

work that involves mathematical skills. Women prefer work that emphasizes human relationships and problem solving through discussion with others.

13. Occupations in which men are highly concentrated include jet pilot, building contractor, draftsman, and architect. Women are heavily concentrated in such fields as registered nurse, social worker, and elementary school teacher. Academic disciplines pursued most by men are physics and engineering, whereas those pursued most by women are the social and behavioral sciences. Blue-collar work is largely male, with many blue-collar jobs being more than 95 percent male.

14. Occupational interests strongly predict the occupations men and women end up in. Men tend to end up in the kinds of jobs they indicate liking most (or disliking least), and the same holds for women. Occupational interests are also related to the kinds of cognitive skills that the sexes display. In ancestral environments selection would have honed men's spatial and navigational skills, targeting abilities, and capabilities at tool and weapon making. Women would have been under selective pressure to develop skills related to successful gathering, such as object location memory, as well as to develop the social and emotional skills related to successful child rearing.

15. A "gender balance sheet" shows that although men enjoy certain advantages over women, they also suffer substantial disadvantages. Men in all societies die younger than women. Men are greatly overrepresented in what are often rated as the worst jobs. They work longer hours and are much more likely than women to die on the job. Women have a choice between working and devoting themselves to their children, but men do not realistically have this choice. They are expected to work both because few women will respect a husband who does not work and because men who choose not to work are disdained by other men.

QUESTIONS FOR DISCUSSION

✓ What are some universal features of gender relations?

✓ Does research evidence back up claims that men are more aggressive and competitive in all societies? Explain.

✓ Men are overrepresented in every society's high-status social positions. Why should this be? From a gender point of view, what happens to a social position that loses status? What happens to a position that gains status?

✓ To what extent are men involved in political leadership in human societies?

✓ Who are the warriors, and why?

✓ Who dominates parenting in the world's societies?

✓ Discuss differing cognitive skills in men and women. Why do the sexes have these different skills?

✓ A sense of gender identity is extremely important in all societies. Why?

✓ What is the likely outcome when an infant or child of one anatomical sex is surgically reassigned to the opposite sex?

✓ What role does socialization play in gender roles and orientations in modern societies?

✓ What is the relationship between hormones and gender identity and behavior?

✓ The status of women varies dramatically in the world's societies. In what kinds of societies is women's status lowest, and in what kinds does it tend to be highest?

✓ What factors determine the status of women in any particular society? Why do women have very low status in some societies but much higher status in others?

✓ In modern societies how do men and women differ in their occupational interests?

✓ What are the differences in the kinds of work men and women do in modern societies? In which occupations do men concentrate the most, and in which are women most highly represented?

✓ What is the relationship between occupational interests and the sex composition of modern occupations?

✓ Give a Darwinian explanation for male-female differences in occupational interests and choices.

References and Notes

1. Archer 2009.

2. Parker and Parker 1979.

3. Parker and Parker 1979.

4. Bjorklund and Pellegrini 2000; Archer and Côté 2005; Baillargeon et al. 2007; Tremblay et al. 1999. All as discussed in Archer 2009.

5. Archer 2009.

6. Pheasant 1983, as discussed in Archer 2009.

7. Lassek and Gaulin 2009.

8. Whyte 1978.

9. Buss 2009, p. 272.

10. Recently in the United States women have come to serve in combat positions in the military, but their numbers are limited. And they can only do this at all because of modern sophisticated military technology—military assault weapons and the like. In nonindustrial societies where warriors use mostly spears, swords, and bows and arrows, putting women in combat positions in a military unit would place

that unit at a severe competitive disadvantage against units without women warriors. For an interesting discussion of the debate over women's role in modern combat, see Browne 2007.

11. Goldberg 1993.

12. Rosenthal 1975.

13. Rosenthal 1975.

14. Browne 1995.

15. Archer 2009.

16. Whyte 1978.

17. Low 2000.

18. Falger 1992, p. 171.

19. Vanhanen 1992.

20. http://www.ipu.org/wmn-e/world-htm.

21. J. Brown 1975; Lancaster 1991.

22. Kimura 1987, 1992, 1999; Gaulin and FitzGerald 1986, 1989; Gaulin and Hoffman 1988; Silverman and Eals 1992; James and Kimura 1997; McBurney et al. 1997; Moffat, Hampson, and Hatzipantelis 1998; Dabbs et al. 1998; Cashdan et al. 2012.

23. Gaulin and Hoffman 1988.

24. Gaulin and Hoffman 1988.

25. Kimura 1999.

26. Gaulin and FitzGerald 1986.

27. Gaulin and FitzGerald 1989.

28. Perdue et al. 2011.

29. Gaulin 1992.

30. Hewlett, van de Koppel and Cavalli-Sforza 1986, as discussed in Gaulin 1992.

31. Silverman and Eals 1992; Eals and Silverman 1994.

32. Silverman et al. 2000.

33. Cashdan et al. 2012.

34. Silverman, Choi, and Peters 2007.

35. Silverman, Choi, and Peters 2007, p. 267.

36. Udry 2000.

37. The entire episode is recounted in detail for a general audience in Colapinto 2000. Two physicians, Milton Diamond and H. Keith Sigmundson, were the first professionals to make the case public and to criticize Money for his recommendations (Diamond and Sigmundson 1997a). The authors found that Money had severely misrepresented the case by claiming that Bruce/Brenda made a good adjustment to being a girl. Money, now deceased, never accepted responsibility for his poor advice and subsequent misrepresentations.

38. Reiner 2004.

39. Diamond and Sigmundson 1997b.

40. Geary 1998.

41. Lytton and Romney 1991.

42. LeVay 2011.

43. Barkley et al. 1977, as discussed in Geary 1998.

44. Udry 2000, p. 454.

45. In this regard, see Kuhle 2012.

46. Chagnon 1983, 1992; Good 1991.

47. Martin and Voorhies 1975.

48. Mandelbaum 1988.

49. Mandelbaum 1988, p. 100.

50. Mandelbaum 1988.

51. Mandelbaum 1988.

52. Martin and Voorhies 1975, p. 348.

53. Blumberg 1984.

54. Blumberg 1984; Sanderson and Dubrow 2005.

55. Mandelbaum 1988.

56. Harris 1981.

57. Kaufman and McLean 1998.

58. Kaufman and McLean 1998.

59. Kaufman and McLean 1998.

60. For example, Aros, Henly, and Curtis 1998.

61. See Browne 2002 for further discussion.

62. Aros, Henly, and Curtis 1998.

63. Aros, Henly, and Curtis 1998.

64. Bureau of Labor Statistics 2012, www.bls.gov/cps/cpsaat11.htm.

65. http://chrisblattman.com/2011/06/24/what-of-phds-go-to-women-in-your-discipline.

66. http://www.nsf.gov/statistics/wmpd/digest/theme2_1.cfm.

67. http://chrisblattman.com/2011/06/24/what-of-phds-go-to-women-in-your-discipline.

68. Browne 2002.

69. Bureau of Labor Statistics 2012, www.bls.gov/cps/cpsaat11.htm.

70. Furchtgott-Roth and Stolba 1999; Browne 2002.

71. Browne 2002.

72. Geary 2010, citing Lubinski and Benbow 1994.

73. Browne 2002.

74. See also Geary 2010.

75. Geary 2010.

76. Geary 2010.

77. Geary 2010.

78. Browne 1998.

79. Browne 1998, p. 56.

9

Status and Wealth

Although some societies are relatively egalitarian, humans all over the world are natural status strivers. They seek high rank and want other people to look up to them and defer to them. High status has important benefits. People enjoy having high status because it makes them feel important and superior to others. And high status provides tangible benefits. As seen in earlier chapters, women prefer men with high status, and thus these men are more likely to obtain high-quality mates than men of lower status; in societies that permit polygyny they can obtain a larger number of high-quality mates. Another tangible benefit is the acquisition of wealth. People of high status are more likely to gain access to social networks that include other high-status people. Membership in these networks helps people convert status into wealth. And then wealth feeds back to create even greater status because people look up to wealthy people. Status and wealth reinforce each other.

Some societies are relatively egalitarian because the resources needed to acquire status and wealth are unavailable. But once these resources are present, innate desires for status and wealth can be given free rein. And the greater and more numerous these resources, the greater are the possibilities for status and wealth. A process of social evolution is set in motion whereby societies become increasingly divided into groups that can be called social classes.

In this chapter we examine evidence for innate status seeking, along with evidence for the evolution of inequality as more intensive modes of economic production evolve. The first part of the chapter focuses on hunter-gatherer, horticultural, and agrarian societies. The next part considers status and wealth in modern societies, looking in particular at the leveling of status distinctions in the shift from agrarian to industrial societies despite continuing inequalities in wealth, and at contemporary patterns of conspicuous consumption.

Status Striving

Numerous lines of evidence support the claim that humans are natural status strivers. Various observational studies of young children, and in some cases even infants, suggest that dominance- and rank-oriented behavior emerge before major socialization influences have had much chance to take effect.[1] One study of kindergartners through third graders in a middle-class private school queried children in regard to their perceptions of other children. Specifically, the children were asked their perceptions concerning which children were the toughest, smartest, and nicest. From the first grade on, children were in greatest agreement on which children were the toughest.[2] A related study followed two cohorts of boys between the first and ninth grades, assessing them for toughness, dominance, leadership, and popularity. In both cohorts toughness was highly correlated with the other traits, dominance in particular, and this correlation remained stable over time.[3]

Barbara Hold has attempted to determine the extent to which these findings stand up cross-culturally. Hold looked for similarities in the behavior of German and Japanese kindergartners and G/wi San children of comparable age. She found that the children in all three cultures sorted themselves into dominance hierarchies; some G/wi children, just like German and Japanese children, sought the limelight. In all three cultures a select few children were the center of attention and these children were frequently imitated by lower-ranking children. High-ranking children were much more likely to initiate activities than were lower-ranking children. There were two important differences between G/wi children on the one hand and German and Japanese children on the other: G/wi children did not try to dominate or manipulate other children, and the G/wi rank order seemed to be less rigid than the German and Japanese rank orders. These differences probably result from the fact that among the G/wi equality is stressed and strongly policed because of the particular exigencies of the G/wi economic situation (the G/wi are hunter-gatherers closely related to the !Kung).[4]

If the tendency toward status striving and hierarchy is part of our species-specific nature, then we should find biochemical indicators of such tendencies. Are there hormones or neurochemicals that are responsible for status striving? The answer is a clear yes. Testosterone has long been linked to aggressive, competitive, and dominance-oriented behavior,[5] but the neurotransmitter serotonin appears to be an equally good candidate. In an early study, Douglas Madsen found substantial correlations between men's blood serotonin levels and certain personality characteristics.[6] Men with aggressive, competitive, and hard-charging personalities had substantially higher levels of serotonin in their blood than individuals low on these personality characteristics. In a second study, this time experimental, Madsen divided his subjects into groups with high, average, and low levels of blood serotonin. His major finding was that the high serotonin group showed a different physiological response to a competitive situation than the average and low serotonin groups. The cortisol levels of the high serotonin group soared in response to the onset of actual competition, whereas no such effect was observed in the other two groups.[7]

Moreover, we know why a tendency to strive for status should be an integral part of human nature: the competition for high social rank is fundamental to mating and reproductive success. Our earlier examination of reproductive behavior showed that social rank and reproductive success are closely linked in many mammalian species and in most human societies. The evidence for this is simply overwhelming. Yet despite the link between status and reproductive success, individuals are often unaware that this is the ultimate reason for their strivings. Humans find it "pleasurable to compete successfully. Consequently, high rank and its associated privileges are often pursued for their own sake—for the sheer pleasure of success."[8]

We need to resist any tendency to overgeneralize. Not all individuals are interested in competing for high social rank, or at least not as interested as others; there is always variation among individuals in any society in people's inclinations toward status striving. But most individuals are status strivers to at least some extent, and it only takes a few to shift a highly egalitarian society to one in which social inequality is the norm.

But if status strivings are innate, then why are some societies characterized by strikingly high levels of social equality? Shouldn't all societies be hierarchical if people naturally seek status? In many hunter-gatherer societies, for example, there are no formally recognized status distinctions. Some individuals may be highly respected and their judgment trusted more than others, but this doesn't add up to elevated social rank. The answer to the question is that there are indeed individuals in highly egalitarian societies who seek to outrank others, but they are prevented from doing so by the rest of the group. James Woodburn points out that "people are well aware of the possibility that individuals or groups within their own egalitarian societies may try to acquire more wealth, to assert more power, or to claim more status than other people, and are vigilant to prevent or to limit this."[9] In other words, status-striving individuals exist but their actions are being monitored and policed continually. Were they not, then some individuals would achieve high rank and begin to lord it over others. The anthropologist Richard Lee, who has spent many years living among the !Kung, points out that in this highly egalitarian society sharing and humility are compulsory social habits. The !Kung intensely dislike any kind of stinginess or arrogance. Lee explains:

> But as seriously as they regard the fault of stinginess, the !Kung's most scathing criticisms are reserved for an even more serious shortcoming: the crime of arrogance. . . . A boasting hunter who comes into camp announcing "I have killed a big animal in the bush" is being arrogant. A woman who gives a gift and announces her great generosity to all is being arrogant. Even an anthropologist who claims to have chosen the biggest ox of the year to slaughter for Christmas is being arrogant. The !Kung perceive this behavior as a danger sign, and they have evolved elaborate devices for puncturing the bubble of conceit and enforcing humility. These leveling devices are in constant daily use, minimizing the size of others' kills, downplaying the value of others' gifts, and treating

one's own efforts in a self-deprecating way. "Please" and "thank you" are hardly ever found in their vocabulary; in their stead we find a vocabulary of rough humor, back-handed compliments, putdowns, and damning with faint praise.[10]

If individuals were not endowed with any sort of innate status-seeking tendency—in other words, if such behavior were nothing more than a social construction—then there would be no need for such tactics.

Status Striving Unleashed

Most hunter-gatherer societies produce very little and live largely from hand to mouth. They don't store food and they consume their foraged products as they acquire them. This is another reason why such societies can be egalitarian: there are few economic resources to fight over. But what happens when the situation changes? What happens when hunter-gatherers find themselves living in environments so abundant that food can be accumulated and stored?

A compelling answer to this question has been provided by the French anthropologist Alain Testart who, as we saw in Chapter 3, draws a distinction between hunter-gatherers who store food and those who don't. In a study of forty hunter-gatherer societies, Testart found that 80 percent of the food storers had significant status distinctions, often accompanied by wealth distinctions, compared to only 7 percent of the nonstoring societies.[11] The classic examples of stratified hunter-gatherers are many of the tribes inhabiting the Northwest coast region of North America, an area that stretches from northern California to northern British Columbia. This region of the world is blessed with exceptionally rich environments that have permitted high-density, complex societies to develop. Many of these societies were presided over by ruling chiefs who were obsessed with social rank and the pursuit of prestige.

What is true in recent times seems to have been true of the distant past. Archaeological evidence shows that a number of prehistoric hunter-gatherer societies in the two millennia prior to the Neolithic (about 12,000–10,000 years ago) were characterized by marked distinctions of status or rank. The archaeologist Paul Mellars has uncovered evidence of complex hunter-gatherer societies in late Upper Paleolithic southwestern France. Mellars suggests that these societies had begun to exploit a much wider range of food resources than in earlier times. The archaeological sites reveal evidence of specialized craftsmen and grave goods that suggest the presence of significant social ranking. Like the northwest coast tribes, these were densely populated societies living in regions of abundant resources that had adopted the practice of food storing.[12]

In small-scale tribal societies practicing relatively unintensive horticulture, we see some particularly interesting forms of status competition. Many of these societies, especially those in the southern Pacific island chain of Melanesia, feature highly ambitious men who spend much of their time attempting to achieve or maintain status. Known locally by terms that roughly translate as "big man," their principal objective is to hold large feasts for the members of a man's own village and some from neighboring villages. The road to high status is accumulating as many valuable foodstuffs as possible and then giving them all away on the day of the feast. At any given time several men are competing for the status of "big man," and this position goes to the man who can hold the biggest feasts.[13]

Among the Kaoka speakers, who are Melanesian horticulturalists, a candidate for bigmanship spends months making his gardens flourish and increasing the size of his pig herds and then declaring that he intends to compete for the leadership of his village by holding a big feast.[14] He spends time accumulating large amounts of dried fish, yam cakes, yam pudding, and numerous pigs. It is then his task to give these foodstuffs away to everyone assembled at the feast.[15]

When foodstuffs are distributed, everyone invited to the feast consumes them. But in some instances the competition may involve producing certain kinds of foods that have special status value. For example, among the Central Abelam of Papua New Guinea, men grow two kinds of yams—*ka*, which are relatively small yams, and *wabi*, which may be nearly ten feet long. *Ka* are grown for direct consumption; they are more efficient to cultivate in that they yield a high rate of caloric return for the amount of labor time invested in growing them.[16]

Wabi cultivation is less efficient. Not only do *wabi* take more time to grow, but they are woody and inedible. Why, then, do Abelam men spend so much time growing them? Because they are prestige items. Like other Melanesian groups, men hold feasts for the purpose of gaining or holding on to high status. Along with other foodstuffs, *ka* and *wabi* are distributed at these feasts; the former can be consumed by everyone, but the latter are presented by a man to his principal status rival. The bigger a man's *wabi*, the greater the status he can achieve. Moreover, his rival is obligated to try to match these yams with *wabi* as big as or even bigger than those he received. Otherwise, he loses status. The evolutionary anthropologists Rebecca Bliege Bird and Eric Alden Smith describe how the competition works:

> Long yams are destined for use in ceremonial yam exchanges . . . in which the best and longest yams are decorated with elaborate painted wooden masks, baskets, shell rings, feathers, and other accoutrements and given to the exchange partner of the visiting hamlet. The exchange is accompanied by a day-long feast, displays of dancing, and "bombastic" oratory. By accepting the yams, the recipient obligates himself to match the display or else lose status, and the largest, finest yams may be rejected by the recipient, fearing that he may not be able to match their size or quality. Thus . . . the fundamental dynamic is one of competitive display, as underlined by the fact that if the yam is rejected, the grower

leaves the yam on display to rot rather than using it in another exchange and yet gains immediate prestige.[17]

Since status in many societies is gained by accumulating and retaining wealth rather than giving it away, earning status through competitive giving may seem puzzling. But further reflection shows that it is not. Giving away large quantities of food or very large yams is a form of advertising or signaling that the giver is a man of special skill. People differ in their ability to accumulate enough food to hold the largest feasts, and growing large yams is difficult and demanding. In addition, yams differ in their genetic quality. A man who is able to acquire pieces of an especially good yam that he can plant as propagules has a better chance of ending up with one of the best yams. A man who does not have good propagules may be able to obtain them from other men, but this requires forming alliances with the men who have them. Men differ in their ability to negotiate these alliances, and alliance building is another highly valued skill that brings high status.[18]

An even more exaggerated form of status competition prevailed among some of the northwest coast tribes. This is the *potlatch*, a fascinating practice that reached its highest level of development among the tribe known as the Kwakiutl. The potlatch was an elaborate giveaway feast held by village chiefs as a means of validating and reinforcing their high rank. The highest status went to chiefs who could give away the most property and in so doing compel other chiefs to give away their property too.

When a chief decided to hold a potlatch he would invite another chief and his followers, usually weeks in advance so that elaborate preparations could be made by both parties. The host chief would assemble a vast array of valuables, including fish, fish oil, berries, animal skins, blankets, and other items.[19] At the appointed time the visiting group would arrive, and serious feasting would begin. After the feasting concluded, the host chief would begin presenting gifts to the visitors. The more gifts he was able to bestow, the greater he was and the more honor and respect he commanded. As the host chief gave away his valuables, he would sing and chant about his greatness, uttering such things as:

> *I search among all the invited chiefs for greatness like mine.*
> *I cannot find one chief among the guests.*
> *They never return feasts,*
> *They disgrace themselves,*
> *I am he who gives these sea otters to the chiefs, the guests, the chiefs of the tribes.*
> *I am he who gives canoes to the chiefs, the guests, the chiefs of the tribes.*[20]

The successful potlatch not only brought greatness to the host chief but heaped shame on the visiting chiefs unless they were able to reply with even greater potlatches of their own. Thus chiefs to whom much property had been given were highly motivated to organize future potlatches, at which time they would have a chance to banish their shame and reassert their own greatness.

Although the northwest coast tribes lived by hunting and gathering, their rich environments allowed them to exceed the economic productivity of most horticultural tribes, and thus accumulate greater wealth. Status competition was thus more intense than in Melanesian big-man systems because there was more to give away.

To gain a deeper Darwinian understanding of the behavior of big men and potlatching chiefs, we can turn to a new wrinkle that was introduced into Darwinian theory in the 1970s by the Israeli evolutionary biologists Amotz and Avishag Zahavi.[21] They formulated a new concept that they called the **handicap principle** or **costly signaling**. This involves an animal's signaling its own high quality to another. The signal must be costly in some way, or impose a "handicap" on the signaler. Moreover, in order to indicate quality, the signal must be genuine or honest, or one that cannot be faked. Costly signaling can be directed to conspecifics—members of the same species—or to members of other species. One of the best examples of the first kind of signaling is the peacock's tail. As noted in Chapter 5, the most elaborate tails take a lot of energy to grow, and thus the largest and most beautiful tails are grown by the fittest peacocks. But the tails also impose a handicap on the peacock by making it vulnerable to predators.

Another example of signaling to conspecifics is the heavy antlers sported by deer and elk. The heaviest antlers are costly to grow and impose a handicap by limiting mobility. Antlers originally evolved as weapons in male combat but, according to the Zahavis, in a number of species evolved in the direction of greater size and elaborateness. They then became signals of quality because of the handicap they imposed. They could still be used in fighting, but in ritualized rather than truly combative fighting. Signaling in this case was directed toward female conspecifics.

The second kind of signaling is common in predator-prey relationships. An example given by the Zahavis is what is known as gazelle "stotting." A gazelle sees a predator, say a cheetah, but instead of running away immediately it jumps high on all four legs a number of times, only then running away. This behavior signals to the cheetah that the gazelle is fast enough to escape and not to waste its time trying to catch it. Stotting appears to be an important evolutionary adaptation. An observational study of gazelles on the Serengeti plain of Africa, where gazelles were preyed on by wild dogs and hyenas, found that the predators ignored gazelles that stotted and instead pursued those that did not. Stotting gazelles, then, survived to live (and reproduce) another day.[22]

The Zahavis intend costly signaling theory to apply to humans, and numerous applications have been made. The theory is highly relevant to the status displays discussed above. Because large, inedible yams are difficult to grow and require a considerable expenditure of time and energy, the grower is signaling his quality and gaining status. And the potlatch is an even more striking status display. The competitive displays that involve giving away large amounts of property to a rival exemplify costly behavior par excellence.

Costly signaling theory becomes even more relevant in societies at later and more complex stages of social evolution. In the most-advanced horticultural societies, status competition continues but with a distinct difference: instead of giving wealth away, persons of high rank also keep much of what they accumulate. In big-man societies, some men outrank others, but they are not wealthier; everyone is living more or less at the same economic level. But in advanced horticultural societies, important wealth distinctions appear, and in many cases these become sufficiently crystallized so that we can speak of distinct social classes. Simple horticultural societies evolve into more advanced ones when people intensify their production. Land becomes scarcer and as a result competition over land ensues. Because individuals are unequally endowed for success in this competition, what tends to happen is that some individuals and their followers gain control over much of the land, leaving the majority of the population to get by with less land to cultivate.

The result of these changes is what sociologists call *social stratification*, relatively distinct social classes characterized by significant wealth differences and the hereditary transmission of wealth. Classes are distinguished by differences of social rank, dress and ornamentation, consumption patterns, involvement in economic production, availability of leisure time, and general styles of life. Stratification systems of this sort have been found among many advanced horticultural societies in sub-Saharan Africa as well as among a number of the precontact societies of Polynesia, Hawaii being the outstanding example.[23]

Before Europeans arrived in the eighteenth century, Hawaii was divided into three main classes: high-ranking chiefs and their families, stewards who managed local or regional domains of a chiefdom, and a very large class of commoners. The highest-ranking or paramount chief was thought to be divine, and contact with him was regulated by elaborate taboos. For example, it was prohibited to let one's shadow fall on the paramount's house or possessions, to pass through his door ahead of him, to put on his robe, or to touch anything used by him. In his presence, others were expected to prostrate themselves on the ground, and when he traveled people were told that he was coming so they could properly prepare themselves. High chiefs and their families took no part in the production of daily subsistence and constituted a kind of primitive "leisure class."[24] Chiefs rose to power by gaining control of land as well as by attracting allies who would support their power, militarily if needed. These accomplishments were honest signals that chiefs were men of high quality. Chiefs were usually great orators, which was another indicator of quality. Polynesian chiefs also distinguished themselves by wearing special feathered cloaks, which were difficult and time-consuming to make. Even though the chiefs seldom made these cloaks themselves, they were signaling quality by showing that they had the power to command specialists to make them.

Although they are often highly stratified, advanced horticultural societies have nonetheless had a so-called redistributive ethic, which also falls into the category of costly signaling. Chiefs maintained large storehouses of foods that could be distributed to the entire population when times were difficult. Chiefs were expected to be generous and their popularity could sharply decline if they were not.[25] Generosity itself was another sign of quality because it indicated that a chief controlled enough wealth to be able to give some of it away. But with the transition to agrarian societies, with their intensive systems of economic production, the redistributive ethic essentially disappeared and there emerged an extreme form of stratification in which most of the population was impoverished and sometimes degraded. The gap between the dominant and the subordinate classes often reached immense proportions.[26]

The social classes most basic to the functioning of agrarian societies are a small class of landlords and a large class of peasants. Landlords claimed ownership of large portions of available land, and land they didn't own directly was often under their administrative control. Some peasants owned title to land, but those who didn't fell under the control of landlords. Peasants in essence became renters, and were required to pay rent and taxes and provide labor services to landlords. The result was in most instances the impoverishment of the peasant class and the enrichment of the landlords, and it is hard to avoid the conclusion that the relationship between the two was highly exploitative. The status gap between the average landlord and the average peasant was huge.

Many landlords held noble status, but they were not the only nobles. The nobility also included, among others, government officials occupying high-ranking positions. In traditional China, for example, men could gain entry into the gentry by spending many years studying impractical subjects, such as poetry, and then passing a series of rigorous examinations. The gentry was an intensely status-conscious class in which the "emphasis was on the idle, highly-cultivated man; status markings, such as wearing long fingernails to indicate remoteness from manual work, were used. The content of Chinese high culture thus developed great subtlety of tastes. Out of this situation came the high aesthetic standards of Chinese arts, cuisine, architecture, and furnishings."[27]

Nobilities frequently imposed *sumptuary regulations*, institutionalized by custom (and sometimes by law), which prescribed different modes of dress for persons of different status. For example, in the seventeenth century Louis XIII of France issued edicts that prohibited persons who were not princes or nobles from wearing gold embroidery as well as shirts and collars that had been embroidered with lace. Puffs and bunches of ribbon were also restricted to those of high status.[28] In medieval Japan the shogun and the daimyo (nobility) imposed numerous sumptuary regulations on persons of lower status, merchants in particular. A list of prohibitions handed down in 1649, for example, specified that, among other things, merchants were not to wear wool capes or have gold lacquer on their riding saddles. Merchants' servants were not to wear silk. A law passed in 1683 forbade merchants and their families from having embroidered crests. Violation of such sumptuary regulations, though common, could be punished and sometimes was. On an occasion when the shogun observed the wife of a merchant dressing too ostentatiously, his outrage led to their property being confiscated and their banishment from the capital city.[29]

Consider also the behavior of members of elites at court in early modern Europe:

> Courts became places of considerable enforced leisure. Large numbers of ladies and gentlemen were obliged to spend a great deal of time waiting upon the king, and developed means of whiling away the hours. Conversation became an art form with elaborate emphasis on politeness and topics of respectable entertainment. It is at this time that verbal taboos began to develop, especially taboos on the vulgar language of the people. Particularly at the court of Louis XIV in the seventeenth century, great emphasis was placed on elaborate mutual bowings and curtseying, flowery greeting and farewell rituals, and polite inquiries after one's health. The correct style of conversation kept politics and other business for the backstage, while entertaining conversation came to consist of *bon mots* and flowery compliments, clever discussions of personalities and love affairs. At Versailles, the mastery of trivial details of etiquette and an elaborate secret language of hints and catch-words could make or break careers.[30]

Status and Wealth in Modern Times

Modern societies are something of an exception to the general pattern of increasing inequality over the long course of social evolution.[31] The huge social and economic gap between landlords and peasants in agrarian societies has been replaced by a situation in which the majority of the population enjoys a standard of living unimaginable to the average peasant of times past. The distribution of income and wealth is still highly unequal—there are extremely rich people and others of severely limited means—but few experience anything approaching the indignities and deprivations of peasants past.

Modern societies are, of course, organized differently from those that existed prior to modern times because they depend on an industrial and postindustrial economy. Most people work in factories or offices making consumer goods, providing services, or organizing and supervising the performance of these activities. All modern industrial societies have a similar structure: a very small class of extremely wealthy people; an upper middle class of top business managers and learned professionals; a lower middle class of small businessmen and low-level business managers; a working class; and a relatively small segment of the working class that may live below the official poverty threshold.

People in these different social classes are unequally rewarded. Upper middle class people have higher incomes than lower middle class people, who in general have higher incomes than working class people. And the working class is itself divided into higher and lower segments with unequal income levels. Modern industrial societies will always have a similar class structure with its corresponding unequal rewards.

Compared to the kinds of societies that existed prior to the emergence of industrial societies, most modern societies are much more egalitarian in terms of distinctions of *social status*. As we have seen, the preindustrial societies in the centuries before industrialization were very hierarchical societies with sharp and often highly rigid distinctions. In the eighteenth and nineteenth centuries there was a clear understanding of who was superior and who inferior. Social elites were sharply distinguished from other social classes by distinctions in dress, manners, and morals, and they expected deference from those below them. Elites performed a wide range of status displays to demonstrate their superiority, such as the sumptuary regulations mentioned above.

In the late nineteenth century, especially in the United States, this rigid status hierarchy began to break down. A general leveling of society was under way. The middle class was growing and had the means to imitate the status displays of the upper class. The middle class was split into upper and lower segments, with the former tending to look down on the latter. But this too was to change, as the lower middle class gained respectability.[32] Status distinctions between the middle and working classes lasted longer because of significant differences in lifestyles, but these distinctions were gradually reduced as well, especially after World War II. In short, what we now see are mass societies in which status distinctions for most people are minimal. There is a social and cultural atmosphere of informality and a presumption of social equality. In the United States in particular, the old habit of calling people Mr. and Mrs. has given way to most people being on a first-name basis.[33]

What accounts for this reversal of status distinctions in societies that are still very unequal in terms of income and wealth? The answer is the massive increases in the standard of living that have emerged over the past century and a half. Nearly everyone can now enjoy a living standard that dramatically exceeds that of all but the richest members of society 150 years ago. And in some ways it even exceeds the richest, since the consumer goods available to people today—luxury cars, big-screen televisions, automatic washers and dryers, personal computers, and the like—were unavailable in earlier times. When everyone is able to consume at a high level, status distinctions are difficult to maintain. People who were once of lower status acquire the economic means to imitate the lifestyles of those of higher status, and as a result status distinctions become increasingly blurred. People of higher status may not like to be imitated by those of lower status, but is there anything they can do about it?

Status Striving Run Amok

Of course, what they can do is intensify their own status strivings to try to put more distance between themselves and those creeping up on them. In his classic book *The Theory of the Leisure Class*, the Norwegian-born American economist Thorstein Veblen coined several famous terms to describe modern-day status seeking, in particular *conspicuous consumption* and its corollary, *conspicuous waste*.[34] Veblen argued that as soon as the ownership of property emerged in earlier societies, people struggled with each other for the consumption of material goods. However, the main purpose of consumption was not the utility of the goods—the degree to which they could provide comfort, and so on—but the prestige or honor they conferred. Others then sought to emulate these patterns of consumption in order to gain prestige for themselves. This is a kind of self-perpetuating and self-defeating process. Veblen noted that "as fast as a person makes new acquisitions, and becomes accustomed to the resulting new standard of wealth, the new standard forthwith ceases to afford appreciably greater satisfaction than the earlier standard did. The tendency in any case is constantly to make the present pecuniary standard the point of departure for a fresh increase of wealth."[35] Veblen added the important qualification that the consumption of wealth was not devoted purely to status ends; material comfort was also sought. But status was consumption's main aim.

Like other early sociologists, Veblen looked to the past to find evidence of such status seeking. He saw that expensive feasts and entertainments were among the first forms of status advertising. Veblen noted that for such displays to achieve their goal they must be *costly*. As he put it,

> Costly entertainments . . . are peculiarly adapted to serve this end. The competitor with whom the entertainer wishes to institute a comparison is, by this method, made to serve as a means to the end. He consumes vicariously for his host at the same time that he is witness to the consumption of that excess of good things which his host is unable to dispose of single handed, and he is also made to witness his host's facility in etiquette.[36]

In order for status displays to be successful, they must also be *conspicuous*—easily observable by others. Hence conspicuous consumption. They must also be *wasteful*, as "no merit would accrue from the consumption of the bare necessities of life."[37] Hence conspicuous waste. By waste Veblen meant that consumption be of "superfluities," or things that are unnecessary to human life or well-being. By means of wasteful consumption, the consumer indicates to others that he is a person of honor and respect because he can afford to be wasteful. Interestingly, Veblen refers to the use of dogs and horses as objects of display. Many dog breeders have produced dogs that Veblen calls "grotesque" but are nevertheless regarded as beautiful by the owners and by many others. Such dogs confer high status because of the high costs of producing them. They serve no useful purpose other than demonstrating their owners' special qualities. Horses are also expensive and thus wasteful, and may confer equal if not greater status.

It is impossible not to notice that what Veblen was describing is a type of costly signaling. Veblen was no Darwinian, but his ideas indisputably anticipated costly signaling theory.

Veblen wrote his book in 1899, during the Gilded Age. He was thinking primarily of families of great wealth such as the Vanderbilts and Astors, who built huge, ornate homes for themselves and their children. Cornelius Vanderbilt built eight huge mansions in New York City. He also built several summer estates, the largest and most elaborate of which was the famous Marble House in Newport, Rhode Island. Marble and other items of exceptional quality and expense were imported from Italy for the project. The Vanderbilts and Astors were ranking members of Veblen's leisure class. But Veblen also intended his notions of conspicuous consumption and waste to apply throughout the class structure. Everyone was seeking to emulate those above them, and to catch up with and surpass them if possible. And today we find the same behaviors. In principle, nothing has changed. The economist Robert Frank gives some striking examples of today's luxury products available for conspicuous consumption:[38]

- *Outdoor grills.* The Viking-Frontgate professional grill, with an 828-square-inch grilling surface, 5,000 BTU burner, two side burners that produce 15,000 BTUs, and built-in smoker system with a wood chip-drawer to give grilled food a woodsy flavor. It's yours for a mere $5,000.
- *Stoves.* The 15,000 BTU grill apparently did not satisfy conspicuous consumers for long. Later a stove was manufactured with a 35,000 BTU wok, a ceramic pizza oven, and halogen burners.
- *Wristwatches.* A Patek Philippe wristwatch selling for $17,500. Patek Philippe also manufactures a more expensive limited edition model for $44,500. Apparently sales have been brisk.
- *Private homes.* The average private home in the United States in the 1950s was not much more than 1,000 square feet, usually with two bedrooms and only one bathroom to be shared by all. By 1996, the average home had grown to 2,000 square feet with at least three bedrooms, and often with 2.5 baths. In the same year one in seven new homes exceeded 3,000 square feet. Today it is not uncommon to find homes of 4,000, 6,000, or 10,000 square feet, with four to ten bedrooms and four to eight baths. Meanwhile, the size of the average household has steadily declined, currently standing at about three people.[39] And more and more people now have second or even third homes that are often as luxurious as their first (and a far cry from the quaint "summer cottage" of fifty years ago).

- *Expensive wines.* Some wines now sell for several hundred dollars a bottle, even though one can get a perfectly serviceable bottle for $12. But there are much higher prices. A bottle of 1961 Chateau Petrus sold at auction for $2,696. At another auction a twelve-bottle case of 1945 Chateau Mouton-Rothschild went for $112,500, or $9,375 a bottle. The most expensive bottle of wine at a famous restaurant in Boulder, Colorado, a few years ago required the purchaser to fork over $19,550!

Some readers may object that these examples are germane only to the very wealthiest Americans. They might also find such behavior highly objectionable in light of the growing economic disparities between certain classes of Americans in recent years. However, the point of the discussion is to highlight the extremes to which status competition through costly signaling can go. Very few of us are in a position to spend close to $20,000 on a single bottle of wine—or $5,000, $500, or even $100—but obviously some people are.

The famous French sociologist Pierre Bourdieu coined a term that has gained widespread usage in sociology and to some extent in anthropology: *symbolic capital*, sometimes called *cultural capital*.[40] The more familiar form of capital is *economic capital* (usually just called capital), which consists of such material goods as money, stocks, land, buildings, machinery, and so on. Symbolic capital is more abstract. It consists of the kind of sophistication that comes from worldly knowledge, especially knowledge of little or no practical use. A person possessing great symbolic capital has been educated at a top university; likely knows a great deal about art, music, literature, and cuisine; has traveled extensively; is poised and an excellent conversationalist; speaks with an especially pleasant voice and accent and uses excellent grammar; speaks two or more languages; displays wit and the art of subtle put-downs; and so on. To the average person who has led a sheltered life, such an individual can be intimidating or even overwhelming. Bourdieu indicates the importance of symbolic capital, especially with respect to art, by saying that

> the quality of the person . . . is affirmed in the capacity to appropriate an object of quality. The objects endowed with the greatest distinctive power are those which most clearly attest the quality of the appropriation, and therefore the quality of their owner, because their possession requires time and capacities which, requiring a long investment of time, like pictorial or musical culture, cannot be acquired in haste or by proxy, and which therefore appear as the surest indications of the quality of the person. This explains the importance which the pursuit of distinction attaches to all those activities which, like artistic consumption, demand pure, pointless expenditure, especially of the rarest and most precious thing of all . . . , namely, time, time devoted to consumption or time devoted to the cultural acquisition which adequate consumption presupposes. . . .

Of all the conversion techniques designed to create and accumulate symbolic capital, the purchase of works of art, objectified evidence of "personal taste," is the one which is closest to the most irreproachable and inimitable form of accumulation, that is, the internalization of distinctive signs and symbols of power in the form of natural "distinction," personal "authority" or "culture." The exclusive appropriation of priceless works is not without analogy to the ostentatious destruction of wealth; the irreproachable exhibition of wealth which it permits is, simultaneously, a challenge thrown down to all those who cannot dissociate their "being" from their "having" and attain disinterestedness, the supreme affirmation of personal excellence. And as is shown, for example, by the primacy given to literary and artistic culture over scientific or technical culture, the exclusive possessors of a "vast culture" behave no differently when they fling into the potlatch of social encounters the time they have spent without thought for immediate profit in exercises as prestigious as they are useless.[41]

Another type of status display is philanthropy. Many wealthy individuals give millions of dollars to foundations, hospitals, universities, art museums, and many other types of institutions. Is this altruism? Well, yes, in a sense, but it is also costly signaling in the form of conspicuous waste. It's something like the potlatch: the more you give away, the more you must have. Usually the donors wish to be recognized by, say, having a hospital wing named for them, or perhaps even the entire hospital. Wealthy donors are fond of giving to business schools in universities and having the schools carry their names. Gad Saad, a pioneer in the evolutionary analysis of marketing and consumption, has studied the naming of business schools in American universities.[42] Of the business schools ranked in the top fifty, thirty-eight (76 percent) were named for their benefactors. But of the remaining 313 business schools, the majority of which were obviously undistinguished, only 29 percent were named for someone. Saad points out that it is more costly to have one's name attached to a top business school.[43]

Conclusion

This chapter is based on the premise that humans naturally strive for status and seek resources; this striving is an evolutionary adaptation that promoted the reproductive success of the most successful strivers in the ancestral environment (and continues to do so today). And yet distinctions of status and wealth have been elaborated throughout long-term social evolution far beyond anything directly relevant to successful reproduction. People do not become avaricious conspicuous consumers and wasters just to have more progeny. They do this because they want to impress others and because luxury goods are creature comforts as well as status signals.

Thus it is important to note that the steady pursuit of status and wealth has become, and continues to become, "detached" from its original evolutionary function. In other words, it has acquired a life of its own.

SUMMARY

1. Several studies of young children in very different societies show that they readily sort themselves into dominance hierarchies. This suggests a natural human tendency toward status striving. This tendency is also suggested by biochemical indicators. Testosterone levels have been linked to aggressive, competitive, and dominance-oriented behavior. The neurotransmitter serotonin has also been shown to affect individuals' levels of competitiveness and dominance-oriented behavior.

2. The competition for status is an evolved adaptation because individuals of higher status are able to acquire more resources, which has major implications for reproductive success. High-status men are more likely to acquire mates, multiple mates, and mates of high reproductive value.

3. Most small-scale societies are highly egalitarian, but this is mainly because they are unable to produce real wealth that can be distributed unequally. Small-scale societies always include highly competitive individuals who seek high status, but this behavior is strongly policed by others and not allowed to develop into significant status distinctions.

4. In societies with levels of economic productivity that yield small surpluses, status competition is more difficult to police. Such competition often takes the form of individuals trying to outdo each other by producing more foodstuffs. Costly signaling theory is one explanation of this competition. Men in Melanesia may cultivate large yams that are difficult to grow and present these yams to their rivals. Rivals who cannot respond with yams of equal or greater size lose status.

5. When economic productivity increases and economic surpluses become substantial, wealth distinctions emerge alongside status distinctions. Societies become stratified into social classes. As surpluses continue to increase, the level of stratification increases and powerful chiefs gain coercive power. In agrarian societies with large economic surpluses, a landlord class emerges and subordinates a large peasantry. Landlords usually become part of a nobility that distinguishes itself from the peasantry (and other classes) by sharp status markers.

6. In modern industrial capitalist societies there are large inequalities of wealth and status, but industrial societies are structured in such a way that the standard of living is

very high for most of the population. Beginning in the nineteenth century a process of social leveling began. Because everyday people were able to consume many goods once available only to the wealthy, it was difficult for the wealthy to distinguish themselves by status markers. Status distinctions based on ritualized deference and subordination gradually disappeared.

7. Partly in response to this leveling, high-status individuals increasingly engaged in displays of conspicuous consumption. But as wealth continued to increase, these displays could be imitated by everyday people (although on a lesser scale). Costly signaling theory is relevant here because the most elaborate forms of conspicuous consumption involve the consumption and display of items that are very expensive, of little or no utilitarian value, and wasteful.

8. Status striving often involves the acquisition and display of cultural or symbolic capital, which may include a top university education; knowledge of art, music, literature, and cuisine; extensive world travel; excellence at conversation; speaking several languages; and having wit and the art of subtle put-downs. Few individuals are able to accumulate all of these forms of symbolic capital, or even some of them.

9. Over the past ten thousand years societies have evolved in very similar ways in many parts of the world. As societies have grown in population, become more technologically advanced, and developed greater complexity, differences in status and wealth have become greater and greater. The process has never gone in the opposite direction: societies moving from inequality to increasing equality—except, to a limited extent, in the advanced capitalist societies of the past century.

10. Social inequality and stratification are biosocial phenomena in the sense that they represent the social elaboration of an innate human tendency toward displaying status and accumulating wealth.

QUESTIONS FOR DISCUSSION

✓ What do studies of young children show in terms of their tendency to sort themselves into status hierarchies?

✓ Are there biochemical indicators of status seeking in general, as well as individual differences in status seeking?

✓ Is status seeking an evolutionary adaptation? If so, why would it be?

✓ If status seeking is an innate human trait, why are there highly egalitarian societies?

✓ What is social stratification? Where can it be found?

✓ What is the relationship between increasing economic productivity and social stratification?

✓ What kinds of societies are the most stratified? What kinds are the least stratified?

✓ How does costly signaling theory explain status displays and wealth accumulation?

✓ What does it mean to say that modern industrial societies are more socially egalitarian than the agrarian societies that preceded them?

✓ What is cultural or symbolic capital? If you wanted to increase your level of symbolic capital, how would you do it?

✓ As societies have evolved they have become increasingly stratified. Has this process ever gone into reverse? Why or why not?

✓ What does it mean to say that social inequality and stratification are biosocial phenomena? Discuss.

References and Notes

1. Russon and Waite 1991.
2. Omark and Edelman 1975.
3. Weisfeld, Omark, and Cronin 1980.
4. Hold 1980.
5. See Mazur and Booth 1998 for a review of the evidence.
6. Madsen 1985.
7. Madsen 1986.
8. Green 1994, p. 197.
9. Woodburn 1982, p. 432.
10. Lee 1978, p. 888.
11. Testart 1982.
12. Mellars 1985.
13. Sahlins 1963.
14. Hogbin 1964; Harris 1974.
15. Hogbin 1964; Harris 1974.
16. Bliege Bird and Smith 2005.
17. Bliege Bird and Smith 2005, p. 228.
18. Biege Bird and Smith 2005.
19. Harris 1974; Piddocke 1965.
20. Benedict 1934, p. 191.
21. Zahavi and Zahavi 1997.
22. FitzGibbon and Fanshawe 1988, as discussed in Zahavi and Zahavi 1997.
23. Fried 1967; Sahlins 1958.
24. Sahlins 1958.
25. Lenski 1966.
26. Lenski 1966.
27. Annett and Collins 1975, p. 178.

28. Kohler 1963.
29. Shively 1964.
30. Annett and Collins 1975, p. 179.
31. Lenski 1966.
32. Collins and Sanderson 2009.
33. Collins and Sanderson 2009.
34. Veblen 2007.
35. Veblen 2007, p. 25.
36. Veblen 2007, pp. 53–54.
37. Veblen 2007, p. 67.
38. Frank 1999.
39. http://www.census.gov/prod/1/pop/p25–1129/pdf.
40. Bourdieu 1984.
41. Bourdieu 1984, pp. 281–282.
42. Saad 2007.
43. Some of the ideas discussed in this section were suggested by Bliege Bird and Smith 2005.

10

Power and Politics

Having *power* means having the ability to get your way in interactions with others even when they resist. In its more extreme forms, power allows an individual or a group to dominate others and impose severe penalties on them. Power seeking is likely less common than status seeking, but it exists in every society. People seek power because of the advantages it provides, although some seem to like it for its own sake; they simply enjoy controlling others. But most power seekers are after tangible benefits, including more land and laborers to work the land, more wealth, more leisure time, more time to enjoy high culture—and, of course, more and better mates.

This chapter traces the process of political evolution over the very long term. Except for small-scale societies, the pattern that we invariably observe in world history is one in which a few individuals rise to power and form themselves into small elites that lord it over the rest of society. Running a society passes from the hands of the many into the hands of the few. Wielding power requires resources. Power holders must be able to control people's economic resources and they also need allies. You cannot have or maintain power over everyone in your society if no one is going to back you up when those under your thumb become dissatisfied with what you are doing. In small-scale societies these resources are seldom available, and thus there are no real power holders. There are leaders, but these are people who have only informal influence; they have no capacity to boss people around when those people don't want to be bossed around. These societies can be called "societies without bosses." Societies that have prestige-seeking big men, for example, are societies without bosses because big men have no ability to command others. If they try, they will simply be ignored. If they keep on trying and try too hard, worse things can happen to them.

In political evolution big men have often turned into chiefs, who are leaders with real power. Chiefs need to be able to control economic resources, and they need allies. Usually they have these things, although often to a limited extent. Over time as societies grow larger, chiefs control more resources and gain more allies, and their power becomes more solidified. They can tell people what to do most of the time and get away with it. Later in political evolution chiefs turn into kings or emperors if the resources they control are vast and they can recruit and maintain large numbers of allies. They can also build large armies capable of putting down rebellions by the dissatisfied masses.

Before describing and trying to explain the long-term process of political evolution, we need to look at the nature of the human penchant for power seeking.

Struggling for Power

For millennia after the rise of formal government, democracy was virtually nonexistent. The political scientists Albert Somit and Steven Peterson insist that the historical rarity of democracy can be laid at the feet of human nature: people are naturally inclined to lord it over others, as well as to obey when they are in a subordinate position. They point out that virtually all of the

> great philosophers . . . have been unanimous in their hostility to democracy. The point warrants repetition: from Athenian days to the present, no major Western philosopher has endorsed the proposition that public policy should be decided either by direct popular vote or by representatives chosen on the basis of anything approximating universal suffrage. Pericles, to be sure, eulogized Athenian democracy, but Plato's and Aristotle's assessment of rule by the majority ranged from the disparaging to the acutely hostile. Nor did their fellow Greek philosophers disagree.[1]

The Roman and medieval philosophers who followed were nearly unanimous in their rejection of democracy.[2] In the non-Western world the situation was the same if not worse, such large-scale societies as China and India being even more autocratic than those in the West.

The idea that antidemocratic tendencies are a fundamental part of human nature is highly controversial. But if human nature is not at work in the formation of political systems, then we would expect to find at least some large-scale nonindustrial societies with a democratic mode of government, and at least some premodern philosophers advocating democracy. But the situation is so overwhelmingly slanted in one direction that the human nature assumption is very difficult to avoid.

When some issue commands, it is to be expected that others will obey. Under those circumstances failure to obey can be life threatening, and thus over thousands of years there should have been strong selection pressure for obedience to authority. Submissive personalities would have been favored because they would have been more likely to avoid being killed and thus would have left more offspring than those who were disobedient and rebellious.[3]

The idea that most people have a natural tendency to obey has been tested, although in a roundabout way. Several decades ago the psychologist Stanley Milgram set up a series of experiments in which subjects were told that they were partici-pating in a study of memory.[4] The subjects were asked to sit in front of a contrived machine that they were told would administer punishment in the form of electric shocks to a "learner" sitting out of view. They were told that if the learner remem-bered an item correctly they were to do nothing. But if he remembered incorrectly, they were to administer an electric shock. With each incorrect response, a more severe shock was to be administered.

Milgram found that his subjects were disturbingly willing to administer shocks when the experimenter, a scientist with authority, told them they must. Even though many of the subjects found this emotionally wrenching, the vast majority obeyed the experimenter, even when they thought the shocks were extremely painful (ac-tually reaching a dangerous level) and the "victim" they could not see screamed in apparent agony. It is interesting that Milgram, in the days before sociobiology and evolutionary psychology, interpreted his findings in evolutionary terms:

> Behavior, like any other of man's characteristics, has throughout succes-sive generations been shaped by the requirements of survival. Behav-iors that did not enhance the chances of survival were successively bred out of the organism because they led to the eventual extinction of the groups that displayed them. . . .
>
> A potential for obedience is the prerequisite of such social organi-zation, and because organization has enormous survival value for any species, such a capacity was bred into the organism through the extend-ed operation of evolutionary processes.[5]

Many people, both scholars and laypersons, have found Milgram's findings very unsettling. But some years later even more disturbing findings were presented by another psychologist, Philip Zimbardo.[6] Zimbardo carried out an experiment at Stanford University in which he created a mock prison and observed how his sub-jects interacted. Twenty-two persons from the surrounding Stanford community, who were students on summer vacation from other universities, were chosen to participate. Half were randomly assigned to be "guards," the other half "prisoners." The experiment was carried out in the basement of the psychology building. Pris-oners were held in barred cells that physically constrained them and conveyed a real sense of imprisonment. A small closet near the cells was used as a facility for solitary confinement. There were several rooms that were used by the guards for resting and relaxing and for changing in and out of uniform. The prisoners were told that they would be under surveillance and have some of their civil rights suspended. The guards were told that their main task was to maintain a level of order that would allow the prison to function effectively, but they were given few details about how this should be done.

What happened was extraordinary. Guards and prisoners could interact in any way they chose, within the constraints maintained by the guards, but their interactions were primarily negative. Guards and prisoners showed marked mutual hostility. Most of the guards behaved in controlling and dominating ways toward their charges, some exhibiting cruelty. Guards commonly harassed prisoners, and were often observed deprecating and insulting them. The most common verbal behavior of the guards was issuing commands, and the most frequent form of physical behavior was aggression. Guards used their power in arbitrary and capricious ways, and treated acts of rebellion severely: loss of privileges, solitary confinement, or humiliation. These behaviors escalated with each passing day as the guards adjusted to their roles, and when individual guards were alone with a prisoner and out of range of videotaping equipment, harassment was observed to be even greater.

Several of the guards seemed to take great satisfaction from their role. One commented that the prisoners "were fighting to keep their identity. But we were always there to show them just who was boss."[7] Another said that "acting authoritatively can be fun. Power can be a great pleasure."[8] Zimbardo and his colleagues make the point more generally:

> Being a guard carried with it social status within the prison, a group identity (when wearing the uniform), and above all, the freedom to exercise an unprecedented degree of control over the lives of other human beings. This control was invariably expressed in terms of sanctions, punishment, demands, and with the threat of manifest physical power. There was no need for the guards to rationally justify a request . . . , and merely to make a demand was sufficient to have it carried out. Many of the guards showed in their behavior and revealed in post-experimental statements that this sense of power was exhilarating.[9]

Zimbardo stresses that the guards' behavior was determined by situational forces, not by personality variables or individual dispositions. It was a matter of social forces causing "good men to turn evil." But if so, why should these situational forces produce this kind of behavior? The guards could have maintained order using methods that were far less severe. It is not a question of good versus evil. It is simply a question of what kind of species humans are, and how easy it is for dominating behavior to emerge when opportunities become available.

To return to the question of obedience, there was a strong tendency for the prisoners in the Zimbardo experiment to obey their guards. But not all did. And, more generally, the potential for people to obey those who have power or authority over them should not be exaggerated. Although most will obey, in general people dislike being dominated, and if this domination is sufficiently great it will be resisted. Somit and Peterson suggest that major collective acts of rebellion have been relatively rare in world history, but this is overstating the matter. Under the right conditions people will rebel, although in most cases their rebellions prove unsuccessful. But what is also striking is the frequency with which the dominated can turn into the dominators when circumstances permit. Lenin and the Bolsheviks, for example, fought to free the masses from czarist oppression in Russia, producing a social revolution in 1917. But the revolution did not lead to a new society free from oppression. It led instead to severe oppression by Lenin and the new Bolshevik elite and the imprisonment and murder of millions of people. The same kind of thing happened in China in 1949 after the revolutionary victory of Mao Zedong and the Communists.

Societies Without Bosses

And yet there are societies in which no one exercises power over anyone else—the "societies without bosses" mentioned earlier. How can this be possible if so many people are power seekers? The answer is that to have power over others you have to be able to back it up, and in most small-scale societies the resources needed to do so (discussed in the next section) are unavailable. Societies without bosses are most characteristic of hunter-gatherers and small-scale horticulturalists and pastoralists. These societies have leaders, but instead of real power leaders have what is most appropriately called influence—an ability to persuade and convince others that a given course of action is the best way to go.

The simplest type of political structure, the earliest stage of political evolution, is the band.[10] Bands are found only among hunter-gatherers, although not all hunter-gatherers are organized at the band level. Band leaders, or headmen, are individuals of influence who are trusted and respected. People follow their advice because it generally worked well in the past. But a headman can lose his influence if the quality of his advice deteriorates. The role of headman is often fused with another role, that of shaman. Shamans are healers who induce trances in their subjects in order to drive out the malevolent spirits thought to be causing their illnesses.

One step up in political evolution is the tribe.[11] Tribes consist of people who share a common culture and speak a common language but live in relatively autonomous villages. Members of different villages often exchange women as wives and form political alliances for such purposes as war making, but the basic unit of political control is the village. Like bands, tribes have only informal leaders. Those who gain leadership positions are men who have such qualities as good oratorical skills, magical powers, and bravery in war. In societies with big men, they are the political leaders as well as the status competitors; politics and status are inextricably intertwined. Leadership has to be earned; it cannot be inherited. As such, it has to be continually merited by decision making that inspires confidence. Leaders cannot rest on their laurels; should they become lazy or take too much for granted, they can quickly be replaced.

Tribes are usually found among simple horticulturalists and small-scale pastoralists. Among the Nuer, the cattle-raising pastoralists mentioned in Chapter 3, there are several leadership positions, but the most important one is the leopard-skin chief, so called because he has the right to wear a leopard-skin cloak as a symbol of his position.[12] One of his special duties is to end feuds, but he can only do this through persuasion. He commands no obedience.[13] The anthropologist Lucy Mair points out that among these people "certain persons are leaders in the sense that they are respected, and people will wait to see what they do and then follow suit; others have ritual powers that are not shared by all members of the community, and certain ceremonies can be performed only by them. But none of these persons can claim to give orders, nor do they even announce decisions that have been taken collectively."[14]

The situation was similar among the Comanche of the North American plains.[15] The Comanche had two types of headmen, peace chiefs and war chiefs. The peace chiefs had little to do beyond holding their group together; their influence was subtle, sometimes barely noticeable. As E. Adamson Hoebel expresses it, the peace chief

> worked through precept, advice, and good humor, expressing his wisdom through well-chosen words and persuasive common sense. He was not elected to office or even chosen. . . . In the making of any important decisions of group policy all men were free to have their say. Yet among them all, the wiser old head, whose time-tested judgment the people respected, was the leader. In matters of daily routine, such as camp moving, he merely made the decisions himself, announcing them through a camp crier. Anyone who did not like his decision simply ignored it. If in time a good many people ignored his announcements and preferred to stay behind with some other man of influence, or perhaps to move in another direction with that man, the chief had then lost his following. He was no longer the chief, and another had quietly superseded him.[16]

But things were different for the war chiefs, who had dictatorial power during times of war. A war chief determined the aims of a raid, appointed scouts, established the route the march would take, and divided the war booty. He was generally obeyed, but obedience was not obligatory. One was free to object, but if he did he had to leave the war party.[17]

In all societies there is conflict and friction, often reaching violent proportions. Acts such as killing or stealing have to be dealt with in order to maintain order within the group. There needs to be some resolution that is considered fair or just. In a very old study that is still relevant today, the British sociologists L. T. Hobhouse, G. C. Wheeler, and Morris Ginsberg distinguished four forms of conflict resolution or justice found in nonindustrial societies.[18] Where *purely private justice* prevails, there is no community-wide authority to sanction offenses, and individuals must resort to personal means of punishing the offense. If a man is murdered, for example, his kin group may seek justice by killing the murderer, or perhaps by demanding some sort of indemnity payment. In the category of *qualified private justice*, people must seek their own personal satisfaction for most offenses against them, but some offenses can be sanctioned by a leader with formal public authority or at least strong persuasive powers. Justice may also take the form of *qualified public justice*; individuals or groups who have binding authority can redress most offenses, with some offenses still being settled privately. The highest level of the administration of justice is *purely public justice*. Here most offenses are treated as matters of public concern and are sanctioned by individuals or groups with strong binding authority.

Throughout political evolution there has been a clear shift from private to public justice. Hobhouse and his colleagues did not divide the four hundred societies they studied by stage of political evolution, but they did separate them into stages of techno-economic development. They found that 97 percent of hunter-gatherers practiced purely or predominantly private justice. In societies with small-scale horticulture, the corresponding figure was 74 percent, and for intensive agriculturalists it was 58 percent. Looking at it in terms of purely public justice, the figures are 3 percent for hunter-gatherers, 26 percent for small-scale horticulturalists, and 42 percent for intensive agriculturalists.

These figures show that in political evolution societies without bosses gradually give way to societies *with* bosses. Next we look at some of these societies.[19]

Chiefs on the Horizon

Another North American tribe, the Cheyenne, lived in small camps most of the year. Like the Comanche, each group had a headman who lacked binding authority. However, all of the camps assembled during the summer into one large group. At this time, many of the headmen assumed the role of tribal chiefs, who were organized into a council numbering forty-four. The chiefs were appointed to regular offices that lasted for a specified time. After serving a number of years, a chief appointed his own successor, most often a man from his own band. But the successor could not be his son because the Cheyenne wanted to avoid hereditary dynasties. Nor could a chief succeed himself, although he could be reappointed to succeed another man. When a chief died, the surviving chiefs would collectively appoint his successor.[20]

The tribal council had a certain amount of binding authority; it had the power to make peace, banish murderers, and commute the sentence of a murderer when he was thought to have repented. Individual chiefs mediated cases of adultery and directed camp movements.[21] But even though there was a council with binding authority, the Cheyenne were not organized into a *chiefdom* as anthropologists normally use that term. Chiefdoms have chiefs who not only have binding authority but real power over others. They often use this power arbitrarily and in ways that impose severe penalties over other members of the community. They are a far cry from the Cheyenne.

Whereas tribes consist of politically autonomous villages, chiefdoms bring the individual villages under common control and the villages lose their independence. The classical chiefdom is marked by the integration of many separate villages into a centrally coordinated complex whole governed by a hierarchy of powerful chiefs. Chiefdoms were found all over the world in prehistoric times, perhaps as early as eight thousand years ago in some regions. In North America, for example, chiefdoms of varying size and scope were found in the southeastern United States when the new European settlers arrived on the scene, and the prehistory of these chiefdoms has been studied. One of the best known of the so-called Mississippian chiefdoms was located at a site named Cahokia, just outside present-day St. Louis.[22] Archaeological research shows that it predated European contact by several hundred years.

Chiefdoms vary considerably in size and complexity. The smallest and simplest may contain only one or two thousand members, whereas others approach 50,000 or even 100,000 inhabitants. Some of the simplest chiefdoms were found among the Trobriand Islanders, whom we met in the discussion of matrilineal kinship. Every Trobriand community had a man of authority, but his authority was limited unless he was a man of high rank. Rank was closely intertwined with kinship. There were four clans, each of which contained a number of subclans. At the time Bronislaw Malinowski did his fieldwork, the highest-ranking subclan was Tabulu, which had the highest-ranking chief, To'uluwa, who presided over the community of Kiriwina. To'uluwa was regarded with great respect and awe, being approached by others as if he were some sort of supreme despot. When visiting other communities he was seated on a high platform. His power was considerable. He was paid tribute by a number of villages and could call on men from other villages to work for him. He could punish those who offended him, usually by means of sorcery. If an offense was serious enough, the chief had henchmen who were charged with killing the offender.[23]

The Trobrianders were not organized into classical chiefdoms inasmuch as there were no real chiefly hierarchies and no full integration of villages into centralized political units. In many ways Trobriand political organization represented something of a halfway point between big-man systems and true chiefdoms. On a much greater scale were many of the societies of Polynesia just prior to the arrival of Captain Cook and the Europeans in the late eighteenth century. The chiefdoms found on Tonga, Tahiti, and Hawaii were the largest and most complex discovered anywhere in the world. Some of the Hawaiian chiefdoms included as many as 100,000 inhabitants and were spread over hundreds or thousands of square miles. When Cook arrived, all of the Hawaiian island chiefdoms had recently been brought under the authority of a single great chiefdom.[24]

The classical Polynesian chiefdom was a pyramidal arrangement of higher and lower chiefs. These chiefs were regular and official holders of offices and titles, and they claimed genuine authority over permanently established groups of followers. Chiefs gained access to their position through a line of hereditary succession. They extracted tribute from the people and used their large food storehouses to support a permanent administrative apparatus that carried out a variety of political functions. Such administrative officials as supervisors of the stores, talking chiefs, ceremonial attendants, and high priests, as well as specialized warrior corps, were supported from the chief's storehouse.[25]

Prior to inter-island unification, each major Hawaiian island possessed a single chiefdom, which contained three major hierarchical levels. At the very top was a paramount chief, the *ali'i-'ai-moku*. He controlled the lands throughout an entire island and could redistribute land as he saw fit once he was installed in office. Below him were a number of subchiefs, the *ali'i-'ahupua'a*. They held land distributed to them by the paramount and saw to the management of regional affairs. The day-to-day work of this management was assigned to even lower-ranking chiefs known as *konohiki*. They directly supervised household economic production, making sure that the land was being cultivated, and also controlled and supervised access to water for irrigation.[26]

At the very bottom of society was the vast majority of the population, commoners, or *maka'ainana*. Their main function was to produce surplus food that would periodically be funneled through stewards and chiefs all the way up to the paramount. It was this tribute that supported chiefly rule, since chiefs considered it demeaning to have to work in the gardens and fields themselves. The *maka'ainana* also contributed labor for communal building projects undertaken by the chiefs. Commoners often led a precarious existence. They could be dispossessed from land for such reasons as concealing surplus production, failing to contribute labor for the construction of irrigation works, or failing to make their household plots sufficiently productive. Refusing to comply with a demand for labor could spell the end of a commoner.[27]

At some point in social evolution big men and other informal leaders without binding authority turn into chiefs who can command the actions of others and punish them for failing to comply. What allows the latter to do these things when the former cannot? Essentially, chiefs control critical resources that informal leaders don't. These resources are of two main types. Chiefs control land that they claim as their own. Commoners are allowed to live on this land, but only by working it productively and producing an economic surplus. Yet this can hardly be the whole story, since we still have to explain how chiefs can get away with claiming the land as their own and preventing commoners from freely using it. Enter military power. In big-man societies men acquire allies, but these allies are limited in what they can do. But as big men gradually turn into chiefs, the chiefs' allies become their protectors, in essence a kind of permanent or semipermanent warrior corps. Warriors have two main functions: fighting wars against rival chiefdoms and policing the members of their own chiefdoms. The latter they do mainly through intimidation, but they control deadly force should intimidation be insufficient to get the message across.[28] Many of their actions closely resemble those of mafiosi and other thugs; they make the common people "offers they can't refuse."

Some social scientists point to a third type of resource that is useful in maintaining chiefly power: ideology.[29] In this case chiefs attempt to convince commoners that their rule is of divine origin and failure to obey it carries supernatural sanctions. This works to some extent but not always, and it can hardly be on the same level as military force. If people feel too exploited and oppressed, ideology can be cast aside and a popular rebellion launched. And chiefdoms experience revolts. The authority of even the most powerful chiefs is not limitless. Chiefs are still related to the common people through kinship ties and are expected to show at least moderate concern for the common good. People are willing to put up with only so much. In Polynesia, for instance, many a chief who "ate the powers of government too much"—who compelled commoners to work too hard and relinquish too much of their surplus production—found himself in the midst of a popular rebellion and was often dethroned and executed.[30]

Kings, Emperors, and Oriental Despots

States and Civilizations

Although their power may be great, chiefs rarely become true despots because they lack a military force powerful enough to stem the tide of rebellion when the people become extremely disenchanted. Some chiefdoms, however, have eventually developed a level of force sufficient to prevent such an occurrence. Once this has happened, we speak of a *state* as coming into existence.

A state is a type of political society in which the ruling powers maintain a monopoly over the means of violence. To say that a state monopolizes the means of violence does not mean that its monopoly is total—that no persons outside the state are entirely lacking in weapons. In the modern United States, for example, many people own guns, knives, crossbows, and so on, which they may use for such things as hunting and target shooting, and of course for self-defense. The Second Amendment of the US Constitution says that the people have a right to be armed, and many other contemporary societies also permit the ownership of weapons. However, were people to use their arms to attempt to overthrow the state, the likelihood of their success would be low. States possess enough force—in most instances much more than enough—to crush any rebellion or revolution. States also monopolize violence in the sense that they prohibit their members from using their weapons *against each other* and punish those who do. States thus pacify populations, another new development in political evolution.[31] In nonstate societies, there are usually no formal prohibitions on interpersonal violence, and it occurs with considerable frequency.

Archaeologists who specialize in the study of the earliest states sometimes refer to them as *civilizations*, using the terms interchangeably. However, it is a bit more accurate to say that a civilization is a type of society with a number of key characteristics, *one of which* is a state form of political rule. In addition to rule by a state, civilizations usually have large populations, intensive agriculture, a high level of economic and occupational specialization, a hereditary class structure with a large gap in wealth and living standards between rich and poor, large cities, monumental architecture, a complex system of trade and markets, a judicial apparatus (laws and courts), and writing and record keeping.[32]

The world's first states arose in Mesopotamia (what is today mostly Iraq) around 3100 BCE. The first Mesopotamian state was centered around the city of Uruk. It contained upward of 10,000 people and had several large temples, one of which was built on a ziggurat, or stepped pyramid. The civilization that developed in this region, most commonly known as the Sumerian civilization, consisted of some thirteen politically autonomous city-states. Yet despite their autonomy they belonged to the same basic cultural tradition and "had collectively developed many of the classical elements of southwest Asian civilization, including ziggurats, brick platforms, the potter's wheel, wheeled carts, metalworking, sailboats, and writing."[33] The economy was highly specialized, with palace entertainers and servants, gatekeepers, cooks, stewards, cupbearers, messengers, masons, potters, reed weavers, cloth workers, leatherworkers, carpenters, smiths, stonecutters, millers, and brewers, among many other occupations.[34] At the very top of the sociopolitical hierarchy was a god-king, and directly below him a class of nobles or princely families.[35]

Civilization and the state developed in Egypt at about the same time. But whereas Mesopotamia was characterized by a highly decentralized city-state system, Egypt had a highly centralized, bureaucratic state. Egyptian civilization was centered around a royal court, royal mortuary complexes, and, in general, on the person of the king. Like Mesopotamia, Egypt had extremely powerful political leaders. The Egyptian kings—the pharaohs—claimed divine status; the pharaoh's person was taboo, and he was thought to maintain cosmic order as well as law and order on earth.[36] Egypt was unexcelled in its monumental architecture, especially the great pyramids, the first of which was constructed around 2680 BCE. This pyramid and the others built later were grand symbols of state power. As the noted archaeologist Brian Fagan has commented, "There is something megalomaniacal about the pyramids, built as they were with an enormous expenditure of labor and energy. They reflect the culmination of centuries of gradual evolution of the Egyptian state, during which the complexity of the state and the authority of the bureaucracy grew hand in hand."[37]

States and civilizations also arose in China and India. In China the transition to civilization and the state took place around 1700 BCE. At this time the basic characteristics of civilization were present or in the process of emerging: monumental architecture, large population concentrations, occupational specialization, written records, dramatic differences in wealth and power, and major public works projects. Early Chinese civilization was highly stratified and was headed by a king who was assisted by a hierarchically arranged nobility.[38] Chinese civilization was clearly on a par with Mesopotamia and Egypt. Ceremonial centers and administrative structures during the Shang dynasty (seventeenth to eleventh centuries BCE) were not quite as impressive as the ziggurats and temples of Mesopotamia, but the Shang easily matched the Mesopotamian level of occupational specialization, the enormous wealth displayed in royal burials, and the intensity of the agricultural and economic systems.[39]

In the Indus River valley of north India (what is now Pakistan) a civilization known as the Harappan civilization emerged around 2600 BCE. Our understanding of this civilization is general and sketchy. Archaeological data are very limited and there is no historical record that can fill in the gaps.[40] In any event, at its peak, the Harappan civilization is estimated to have had a population of around 200,000. It had two cities, the larger of which, Mohenjo-daro, contained about 40,000 people. There was considerable occupational specialization at Mohenjo-daro: farmers, herdsmen, goldsmiths, potters, weavers, brick masons, and architects, for example.[41] There were apparently classes of wealthy and impoverished persons, since archaeological research has uncovered sumptuous items of personal adornment and precious metals and beads.[42] The Harappan civilization was probably organized as a state,[43] but this is by no means certain since "not a single temple or palace has been uncovered, not a single royal tomb excavated."[44]

In Europe states developed first in the Mediterranean region, especially in Greece, perhaps as early as 2000 BCE and certainly no later than 700 BCE.[45] In temperate Europe, states emerged later, around the second century BCE among the Celts. The Celtic kingdoms had a specialized ruling elite composed of a king and his retinue; supreme power was in the hands of the king, and his companions served as political and military lieutenants.[46]

In the New World, civilizations and states developed entirely independently of Old World states. The main areas of New World state formation were Mesoamerica and Peru. The pinnacle of political evolution in the Mesoamerican lowlands was achieved by the Maya, who were spread out from the northern Gulf Coast region of Mexico all the way down into what is now Guatemala, Belize, and Honduras.[47] The Maya, who achieved the peak of their development between 300 and 900 CE, constructed ceremonial centers with plazas, causeways, temple pyramids, stelae, and altars.[48] The greatest ceremonial center was the one at Tikal, which may have contained as many as 80,000 inhabitants.[49] Mayan society achieved elaborate occupational specialization, with flint and obsidian workers, potters, woodworkers, stoneworkers, textile weavers, human carriers, leatherworkers, musicians, manuscript painters, merchants, basket makers, and bark cloth makers.[50]

In the Valley of Mexico (the Mesoamerican highlands) civilization and the state had emerged by 1 CE. Here arose Teotihuacán, one of the greatest cities in pre-Hispanic Mesoamerica. It unified the entire Valley of Mexico and controlled it for hundreds of years. At its peak, the city numbered at least 125,000 inhabitants and perhaps as many as 200,000. It was planned with great care, containing two large pyramids, the Pyramid of the Sun and the Pyramid of the Moon, which were laid out along the central avenue known as the Street of the Dead. This street also

FIGURE 10.1 Mayan Temple, Palenque, Mexico
(Barry Kass/Anthro-Photo)

contained many temple complexes. Most of the political, commercial, and religious activity in the Valley of Mexico was concentrated in this great center.[51]

The most complex and elaborate civilization in all of pre-Hispanic Mesoamerica was established by the Aztecs, who achieved their peak between 1400 and 1520 CE. Had they not been conquered by Cortes in 1521, they would have gone on for many more years, perhaps centuries. The Aztecs established their capital at Tenochtitlán, on an island in the middle of a lake. Tenochtitlán covered some five square miles and had a population of 150,000 to 200,000. The city was linked by canals and causeways to outlying regions, which together with the city itself may have totaled 400,000 inhabitants. At the top of the political hierarchy was a king, and below him were nobles with their own estates. The Aztecs were a highly militaristic and imperialistic society constantly engaged in extending their range of political control.[52] They were a ruthless and bloodthirsty lot.

South American civilization began in the Andes sometime during the early first millennium CE. One of the first states in this region was the Mochica civilization, which flourished between 200 and 700 CE. The capital city, Moche, contained two massive adobe structures and an extensive plaza. One of the adobe structures, the Huaca del Sol, was a terraced platform 135 feet high.[53] Archaeologists have discovered evidence of distinctive modes of dress denoting highly specialized positions: rulers, nobles, warriors, priests, messengers, and servants. Differences in wealth shown by grave goods tell of a stratified society. Rulers are shown being carried about in chairs, sitting on thrones, and overseeing the execution of war captives.[54]

Another important Andean state was the Chimu empire, founded around 800 CE. It was a highly imperialistic conquest state that at its peak controlled valleys over a distance of more than 600 miles. The Chimu were conquered and incorporated into the Inca empire, clearly the apex of political evolution in pre-Hispanic South America. Like the Aztecs, the Inca achieved their peak in the fifteenth and sixteenth centuries CE. At the top of the Inca political system was Sapa Inca, the emperor who claimed to be descended from Inti, the sun god. The Inca empire was huge, stretching all the way from Colombia in the north to central Chile in the south. The various parts of the empire were connected by a large network of paved roads. Only the Sapa Inca's court and priests were allowed to occupy the Inca capital, Cuzco.[55]

Explaining State Origins

Why did so many chiefdoms evolve into states in so many parts of the world? A variety of explanations have been proposed, but the best-known theory, developed by the anthropologist Robert Carneiro of the American Museum of Natural History, is the so-called *circumscription theory*. This theory gives pride of place to three primary factors: population pressure, warfare, and what Carneiro calls *environmental circumscription*. Population pressure sets everything in motion. When population pressure builds up in a region, growing numbers of groups come into contact, and conflict, including warfare, eventually ensues. However, if land is relatively plentiful people have the option of moving into previously unoccupied areas. When land is not abundant or is not suited for cultivation, this option is unavailable. Enter environmental circumscription. Circumscribed environments are regions that contain fertile land, but obstacles block movement beyond the region, such as large bodies of water, mountain ranges, or inhospitable deserts. Increasing population pressure in circumscribed zones leads to escalating warfare as land becomes scarcer and people attempt to take over land held by others. Politically uncentralized societies evolve into chiefdoms, chiefdoms evolve into states, and states sometimes evolve into multistate empires.[56]

This theory has part of the story right, but there is an important omission. Population pressure and limited land are not the only reasons large-scale societies go to war. Far from it. Political conquest involves capturing land not just so it can be farmed by populations that have become more land starved. Conquerors in most instances want to capture the land of others, along with their slaves and other workers, so they can collect tribute and increase their wealth. Political conquest also leads to the direct capture of wealth in other forms, such as treasure and domesticated animals. Political evolution at its more advanced stages is at least as much a matter of the struggle for wealth as the struggle to deal with increasing population density, a process not emphasized by Carneiro. Carneiro's theory is not necessarily wrong, just incomplete.

Feudal and Centralized Bureaucratic States

Two types of states have been of persistent interest to social scientists, *feudal* and *centralized bureaucratic* states. In feudal societies there is a king or emperor at the top who claims the land within a territory, but his claim is largely a fiction. Although he is thought of as the greatest landlord, in reality he subdivides his land into parcels known as *fiefs*. These fiefs are granted to other powerful men who then become indebted to the king, and the king can call on them for military service. In a true feudal system the fiefs will be further subdivided so that greater lords acquire dependent lesser lords who owe them military service and protection. Those given a fief are known as the *vassals* of the lords who gave them land. This process can continue down through several levels, so that an entire hierarchy of greater and lesser lords is created, all of whom are bound to each other by oaths of loyalty. The relationship between a superior and an inferior lord is known as *vassalage*; an inferior lord is a vassal of a superior lord. In this type of political structure, the nobility becomes a specialized equestrian warrior class and there is no standing army.

A feudal state is highly decentralized or fragmented and a landlord's power extends only as far as his fief. He has jurisdiction and control within that realm but not beyond it. The state is thus divided into nodes of power.[57] When the state as a whole goes to war against other states, the lords call on their vassals to form a large fighting unit. Here we have, in essence, Sir Lancelot and King Arthur and the Knights of the Round Table. But not all is harmonious among the lords. They inevitably engage in internecine war, meaning that they fight each other for control. Power seeking is often a complex and multilayered process.

True feudal systems have been uncommon. At most there are three genuine examples. The prototype of feudalism prevailed in Western Europe from the ninth to the fifteenth century. In addition, a similar type of feudalism existed in Japan from the twelfth to the nineteenth century, with a peak between the fourteenth and sixteenth centuries.[58] Like late medieval Europe, medieval Japan had a specialized noble warrior class. There were great lords, the *daimyo*, and lesser lords, the *samurai*. Also like the Europeans, Japanese warriors were mounted on horseback.

Some scholars consider the Zhou dynasty in China to have had a kind of feudal system. China introduced the horse and the war chariot from the Eurasian steppes around 1200 BCE. At the time the Shang dynasty was a decentralized state with power in the hands of regional lords. The Shang were overthrown by the Zhou around 1050 BCE; the superior Zhou chariots may have been an important factor in their victory. Zhou aristocrats increasingly became mounted warriors, and the old conscript armies declined in importance.[59] The classical period of Zhou feudalism was between the eighth and fifth centuries BCE, by which time "the realm disintegrated into hundreds of practically autonomous polities, with rulers or 'dukes' who maintained only the semblance of vassal subservience to the Zhou overlord, to whom they swore allegiance."[60]

Many other states have been called feudal, but this is mostly careless use of terminology. What accounts for feudal states? Azar Gat points to three principal conditions: an agrarian economy that is rudimentary and small in scale such that the state is unable to develop the economic and bureaucratic machinery necessary to administer it; the possession of the horse; and a preference for the horse as an instrument of war.[61] European feudalism, for example, was created in the aftermath of the fall of Rome. The collapse of Roman political authority left communities vulnerable to attack by marauding Germanic tribes that preyed on much of what was formerly the Roman empire. For some time the situation bordered on anarchy, there being no central authority to administer the economy. The Germanic tribes, which were really chiefdoms, already contained a warrior aristocracy on horseback. All of the conditions for the development of a feudal state were therefore present.

Most states have been highly centralized rather than feudal. In this kind of state, power is concentrated in the hands of a tiny group of persons or in a single ruler standing at the pinnacle of society; private ownership of land may exist to some extent, but land is primarily owned by the state itself; the state involves itself intensively in directing various forms of public works affecting the entire society; and the state rules the mass of people in despotic fashion, severely punishing any activity perceived as a threat to its existence. Such states have been found in many of the great agrarian civilizations, such as China, India, and ancient Egypt. These states are far removed from the vassalage and fief systems of feudal regimes. They are all-powerful, despotic states severely repressing their subjects.[62]

Many years ago the historian Karl Wittfogel made an extensive study of such states, referring to them by the term *Oriental despotism*. Wittfogel thought that these highly despotic states developed because of the need for irrigation agriculture. The irrigation works were complex and extensive, and required an elaborate bureaucracy to build and manage them. European societies were based on rainfall farming, and thus highly centralized states were unnecessary.[63] Wittfogel's idea, though, is no longer accepted by more than a handful of scholars, Marvin Harris being the most prominent. Was Wittfogel right? Probably not. Be that as it may, Harris offers a colorful description of Oriental despotism:

> Despite the development of philosophies and religions advocating justice and mercy, the rulers of these vast realms frequently had to rely on intimidation, force, and naked terror to maintain law and order. Total submissiveness was demanded of underlings, the supreme symbol of which was the obligation to prostrate oneself and grovel in the presence of the mighty. . . . In all of these ancient empires there were ruthless systems for rooting out and punishing disobedient persons. Spies kept the rulers informed about potential troublemakers. Punishments ranged from beatings to death by torture. . . . In ancient India the magistrates condemned disobedient subjects to eighteen different kinds of torture, including beat-

ings on the soles of the feet, suspension upside down, and burning of finger joints. . . . In China the emperor punished those who expressed incautious opinions by having them castrated in a darkened cell.[64]

Wittfogel notwithstanding, states of this nature are an extreme type of what the historian John Kautsky calls *aristocratic empires*. They almost always result from political conquest, which is the main role of the state in such societies. But the term "societies" is highly misleading, because such "societies" are not really societies in the modern sense of the term. They have no clear boundaries, only frontiers,[65] and they rule over the populations they conquer without having much contact, if any, with their subjects. Most people are peasants who are exploited in various ways by the aristocracy, but collection of taxes and tribute is in the hands of lesser functionaries. For the past five thousand years conquest has been the norm and has existed on a massive scale throughout the world. But the life of empires is usually short, with a few exceptions such as the Roman empire.[66]

In the sixth century BCE Persian conquerors under Cyrus the Great created an empire that stretched from the Aegean Sea and Egypt all the way to the Indus River valley in north India. But internecine conflict set in, as it always does in empires, and within a century the empire had essentially collapsed. Within another century Alexander the Great conquered much of the old empire and united it with Greece.[67]

About the same time, the Roman republic began to evolve toward imperial status, conquering one tribe after another and then other empires. Late in the first century BCE it had created an empire that extended from northern Mesopotamia to the British Isles. Of course, the collapse of this empire is legendary. Roman decline began as early as the late first century of the Christian era, but it took another four centuries before the empire disintegrated completely, overrun by the barbarian Germanic tribes.

Rome's empire was massive, but it was not the world's largest. This "honor" belongs to the Mongols, state-organized equestrian pastoralists living on the vast steppes along the northern fringes of China. In the thirteenth and fourteenth centuries CE the Mongols repeatedly attacked China, which is why the Chinese built their Great Wall—to keep the Mongols at bay. Ultimately the Mongols conquered Persia, all of central Asia, the Mesopotamian caliphate, and the kingdoms of Georgia, Azerbaijan, and Kiev. At its peak the empire covered nearly 10 million square miles. Of course, this empire, like every other, disintegrated within a couple of centuries; it was never rebuilt.[68]

Conclusion

What can a Darwinian perspective contribute to understanding long-term sociopolitical evolution, inasmuch as it is primarily determined by socioecological circumstances? Quite a bit as it turns out. Socioecological context is the framework within which human nature plays itself out. The exercise of power requires resources, and when these resources are limited or lacking there are no persons or groups who can capture and deploy it. But throughout social evolution the resources essential for power grabbing became increasingly available, and there were always individuals who saw the new opportunities and seized them. This is precisely what a Darwinian theory of power and politics predicts.

If the human mind were a blank slate, then almost anything would be possible. Because there would be nothing natural about power seeking, we should find large-scale societies with a great deal of concentration of power at the top, but also large-scale societies with little or no power concentration. Yet there are no such large-scale societies. It is true that in modern democracies the coercive power of political leaders is neutralized to a large extent, but these types of governments have only been able to evolve in very recent times and under very special circumstances.[69] Even then, those in control of governments seek to extend the range of their power as far as they can.

Some social scientists believe that in the present era we are evolving in the direction of a world state. However, they are divided about whether such a state would be a positive or a negative outcome. Those who favor a world state believe that it would provide important social benefits, such as limiting war, evening out inequalities between nations, and controlling environmental degradation.[70] To others, however, a world state is a frightening prospect. They fear that a state with no other state to check its power would likely concentrate power on an unprecedented scale. Such critics like to invoke the famous words of Lord Acton: "Power tends to corrupt, and absolute power corrupts absolutely. Great men are almost always bad men."

SUMMARY

1. Power seeking is a pervasive feature of social life. Having power is useful for acquiring resources and maximizing reproductive success. Not everyone seeks power, but many do and power seeking plays an important role in all societies. The role it plays is heavily determined by socioecological context.

2. Power and obedience are two sides of the same coin. Experiments have shown that ordinary people can be induced to obey legitimate authority even when they believe that such obedience causes severe discomfort to others. Other experiments show that when people are given the power to control others who have little or no option but to obey, those with power frequently act like brutal tyrants.

3. Although many humans naturally seek power, in small-scale societies this tendency is held in check. In these societies power seekers lack the resources necessary to

acquire and hold power. These societies have no "bosses," only informal leaders who lack binding authority.

4. In all societies offenses against some individuals by others inevitably occur, and thus means of handling or adjudicating them must be found. Because societies without bosses have no leaders with binding authority, justice is purely or predominantly private. Throughout political evolution there is a gradual shift from private to public justice. When there is public justice, many offenses are treated as offenses against the entire community or society and are punished (often severely) by groups with strong binding authority.

5. The most important resources necessary to the development of power are military force and political allies. Once these resources develop, it becomes increasingly difficult for people to check the self-aggrandizing tendencies of power seekers. As these checks disappear, the overall tendency is for power to be increasingly concentrated in a few hands.

6. The earliest types of societies with concentrated power are chiefdoms. Here previously autonomous villages are brought under the centralized control of a chief and, if the chiefdom is sufficiently large, a retinue of subchiefs. In small chiefdoms the chief's power and authority is limited, but in large chiefdoms it can be great and in some cases nearly absolute.

7. States differ from chiefdoms in that state rulers hold a monopoly over the means of violence. States arose in prehistory in conjunction with the rise of civilizations, or societies (or networks of societies) characterized by such things as intensive agriculture, occupational specialization, a hereditary class structure, large cities, monumental architecture, trade and markets, writing and record keeping, and public justice.

8. The earliest states arose in the Old World in Mesopotamia and Egypt about five thousand years ago, and in India, China, and Europe somewhat later. In the New World states arose more recently in Mesoamerica and Peru.

9. Long-term sociopolitical evolution is mainly a product of denser populations, technological advancement, and increasing stratification. An important factor in the rise of the earliest states was natural environments that were highly circumscribed. These are areas of land from which migration was difficult or impossible because of mountain ranges, large bodies of water, or areas of adjacent land poorly suited for cultivation. If population pressure builds up in such environments, people cannot move away and may have little recourse but to try to take over the lands of others by force, thus creating a state.

10. States vary along a continuum from highly decentralized to highly centralized. The most decentralized states are feudal states, which were found in Europe during the Middle Ages and in Japan between the fourteenth and nineteenth centuries. Zhou China between the eighth and fifth centuries BCE may also have been organized along feudal lines.

11. Most states have been highly centralized. Here the state concentrates power in the hands of a single ruler, owns and administers large tracts of land, directs large-scale public works projects, and rules its subjects in despotic fashion. Ancient China and India had states of this type, as did the Persians and Romans.

12. The factors determining sociopolitical evolution are socioecological rather than biological in that new evolutionary stages do not occur as the result of genetic changes. Nevertheless, human nature is involved in a very important way, because the innate human quest for power constrains how changing conditions affecting political life will play themselves out.

QUESTIONS FOR DISCUSSION

✓ Why should so many people be natural power seekers?

✓ People don't like to be dominated but generally do not hesitate to dominate others when circumstances permit. Explain this statement with reference to the experiments of Milgram and Zimbardo.

✓ How can we reconcile humans' natural power-seeking tendencies with the fact that in many societies there are no political leaders who have actual power?

✓ Explain the difference between private and public justice and their relationship to long-term sociopolitical evolution.

✓ For political leaders to gain and hold on to power, they must control certain kinds of resources. What are some of these resources?

✓ Explain the major differences between chiefdoms and states.

✓ What is the difference between a civilization and a state?

✓ What were some of the earliest civilizations and states, and when and where did they evolve?

✓ What are some of the most important factors that have propelled long-term sociopolitical evolution?

✓ What are feudal states? Give some examples.

✓ How do highly centralized states differ from feudal states? Give some examples of highly centralized states.

✓ What role does human nature play in sociopolitical evolution?

✓ Do you think that a future world state would be a good idea? Would it solve most of the world's problems?

✓ Explain the meaning of the following statement: "Power tends to corrupt, and absolute power corrupts absolutely."

References and Notes

1. Somit and Peterson 1997, p. 88. One can accept Somit and Peterson's overall argument, but they overstate their case by using the phrase "the present." Within the past two centuries many major philosophers have endorsed democracy. If Somit and Peterson had said "from Athenian times *up until recent centuries,*" their statement would be accurate.
2. Somit and Peterson 1997.
3. Cochran and Harpending 2009.
4. Milgram 1974.
5. Milgram 1974, pp. 124–125.
6. Haney, Banks, and Zimbardo 1973; Zimbardo 2008.
7. Haney, Banks, and Zimbardo 1973, p. 86.
8. Haney, Banks, and Zimbardo 1973, p. 86.
9. Haney, Banks, and Zimbardo 1973, p. 92.
10. Service 1971.
11. Service 1971.
12. Mair 1964.
13. Mair 1964.
14. Mair 1964, p. 63.
15. Hoebel 1954.
16. Hoebel 1954, p. 132.
17. Hoebel 1954.
18. Hobhouse, Wheeler, and Ginsberg 1965.
19. There are some exceptions to the general rule that for leaders to have real power and authority they must control important resources, which are usually economic and military resources. In his discussion of the Yanomama, Napoleon Chagnon 2013 shows that in small villages headmen have no real power or authority. However, in some of the larger villages tyrannical headmen have emerged. These men are especially aggressive and violent and are feared by most village members because they can be treacherous killers. One such tyrant was Krihisiwa. One day he told Chagnon with great relish how he had killed three young men who were not enemies but rather innocent visitors in his village. He killed them by driving his steel axe into their skulls. He planned his killings in a particularly deceptive way, taking the three of them by complete surprise. An even crueler headman in another village was Moawa, who had killed twenty-one men. Moawa was extremely fierce and intimidating in everyday face-to-face interaction. He was also extremely possessive. When Chagnon brought steel axes to Moawa's village, he would demand them all for himself. One day Chagnon brought ointment to cure the eye infections of many of the villagers and their children. Moawa demanded all of it for himself, even though he scarcely needed more than a small amount.

Why don't other people band together to drive these headmen out of their village or even kill them? Chagnon's answer is that these cruel tyrants' kinsmen were important allies who could keep the tyrant in power. Moawa, for example, had attracted a large following. Chagnon points out that these despots are found only in the largest villages. He speculates that they are able to use their power to hold their villages together, which gives them a clear advantage over their enemies (most Yanomama villages are small). This may be another reason why such men are tolerated.

Chagnon suggests that the emergence of Yanomama despotic headmen marks an evolutionary step in the direction of chiefdoms and states. However, this is debatable because it is not clear how much one can generalize to other societies from the Yanomama case.

20. Hoebel 1954.
21. Hoebel 1954.
22. Muller 1997; Cobb 2003.
23. Malinowski 1950.
24. Sahlins 1963; Kirch 1984, 2000; Earle 1997.
25. Sahlins 1963; Kirch 1984.
26. Sahlins 1963.
27. Sahlins 1963.
28. Earle 1997.
29. See Earle 1997.
30. Sahlins 1963.
31. Frost 2010.
32. Sanders and Webster 1978; R. Cohen 1978; Johnson and Earle 2000; Fagan 2009.
33. Wenke 1999.
34. R. McC. Adams 1966; Wenke 1999.
35. R. McC. Adams 1966; Wenke 1999.
36. Janssen 1978; Trigger 1982.
37. Fagan 2009, p. 421.
38. Wenke 1999.
39. Wenke 1999.
40. Possehl 1990.
41. Wenke 1999.
42. Possehl 1990.
43. Possehl 1990.
44. Lamberg-Karlovsky and Sabloff 1979, p. 203.
45. Fagan 2009; Milisauskas 2010; Champion et al. 1984.
46. Champion et al. 1984, p. 316.
47. R. E. W. Adams 1991.
48. Blanton et al. 1981, pp. 195–196.
49. Blanton et al. 1981.
50. Blanton et al. 1981.
51. R. E. W. Adams 1991.
52. R. E. W. Adams 1991; Fiedel 1992.
53. Fiedel 1992.
54. Fiedel 1992, p. 326.
55. Fiedel 1992.
56. Carneiro 1970, 1981, 1987.
57. P. Anderson 1974.
58. Gat 2006.
59. Gat 2006.
60. Gat 2006, p. 337.
61. Gat 2006.
62. Wittfogel 1957.
63. Wittfogel 1957.
64. M. Harris 1977, p. 157.
65. Giddens 1985.
66. Kautsky 1982.
67. Kautsky 1982.
68. Kautsky 1982.
69. Rueschemeyer, Stephens, and Stephens 1992; Sanderson and Alderson 2005.
70. See, for example, Chase-Dunn 2003.

11

Violence

Violence is a pervasive feature of human social life. It has existed throughout history and prehistory and is found in all societies, from hunter-gatherer bands to modern industrial societies. Violence comes in various forms and various degrees of intensity. At one end of the continuum there is simple slapping, at the other all-out war destroying enormous amounts of property and killing millions of people. In between we find simple assault; lethal assault; intentional homicide (or attempted homicide); small-scale war; riots motivated by race, ethnicity, or religion; and revolutions.

This chapter is about violence, specifically murder and war. How common is murder in the world's societies and who are the people most likely to commit it? Who are its principal victims? Why does it occur? Are there similarities between human violence and the violence observed in chimpanzees—our nearest relatives? Do chimpanzees commit murder? These are the questions we will address in the first part of this chapter.

Murder is mostly one-on-one violence, but war involves groups from one society or village attacking groups in another. Like murder, it has been widespread throughout human history and prehistory and in most known societies of all types. In small-scale societies war involves the use of very simple military weapons, mostly spears, knives, and bows and arrows. In large-scale nonindustrial societies the military technology is much more advanced and thus the killing power of weapons far greater. As a result, wars become much more deadly and devastating to property. A critical question, of course, is why people go to war. What do people expect to gain from it, in light of the severe costs it imposes on human populations? Why is it that human societies cannot live in peace with one another? We will take up these questions in the second part of this chapter.

Murder, He Wrote

It is well-known that most homicides occur between people who know each other—family members, friends, or close acquaintances. In a study of 690 homicides in

Detroit, Michigan, in 1972, Martin Daly and Margo Wilson found that 25 percent occurred between relatives, 48 percent between acquaintances, and only 27 percent between strangers.[1]

At first glance these results seem to suggest that there is something wrong with inclusive fitness theory. Surely something must be amiss if relatives are killing each other this frequently. However, a closer look at the findings tells a different story. Most of these killings involved spouses, who obviously are not genetically related to their killers, and only 6 percent of the overall total involved genetic relatives. These were mostly cases in which parents killed children, children killed parents, or brothers killed brothers.[2] Homicide rates for other large American cities tell basically the same story. A study of 550 homicides committed in Philadelphia between 1948 and 1952 found that only about 5 percent were between genetic relatives, and an analysis of 574 homicides committed in Miami in 1980 found that only 2 percent occurred between genetic relatives.[3]

Killings that involve a genetic relative are worth further consideration. In Canadian homicides between 1974 and 1983 involving adult genetic relatives, offspring were much more likely to kill parents than the reverse; 84 percent of the killings were committed by offspring. This is the pattern predicted by inclusive fitness theory, since the reproductive value of offspring is much greater than that of parents. Parents have already reproduced, whereas offspring either have not reproduced or have not yet achieved their lifetime reproductive potential. However, inclusive fitness theory is only part of the story, because the motives for killings in these cases are very different from the motives in killings generally. For example, in many instances in which sons kill fathers, the fathers are alcoholics who severely abuse their sons' mothers and often the sons themselves. Psychiatric disturbance also plays an important role in offspring killing parents and in parents killing offspring. And the psychiatric disturbance is frequently intertwined with domestic abuse, since victims of abuse are more likely to develop psychiatric disorders than the offspring of parents who are not abusive.[4]

Also consistent with inclusive fitness theory is the finding that parents who kill offspring usually kill the very young. For example, in parent-offspring killings in Canada between 1974 and 1983, the homicide rate was thirty-four children killed per million population when the child was one year old or younger (most of these were infanticides attributable to the factors mentioned in earlier discussions). The rate dropped to about four per million by age four, and steadily declined to zero by age seventeen. Killing younger rather than older children makes sense from a Darwinian perspective because little parental investment has been made. But as children grow older, parents have invested a great deal of time and energy in rearing them and are reluctant to waste this investment. When older children are killed by parents, psychiatric disturbances tend to be involved, such as maternal depression. Stepparents also kill children at a much higher rate than natural parents.[5]

But most homicides spring from causes that are now well understood. Age, sex, and a community's level of economic inequality are the top three. Age is one of the

FIGURE 11.1   Male Homicide Rates by Age for Two Populations

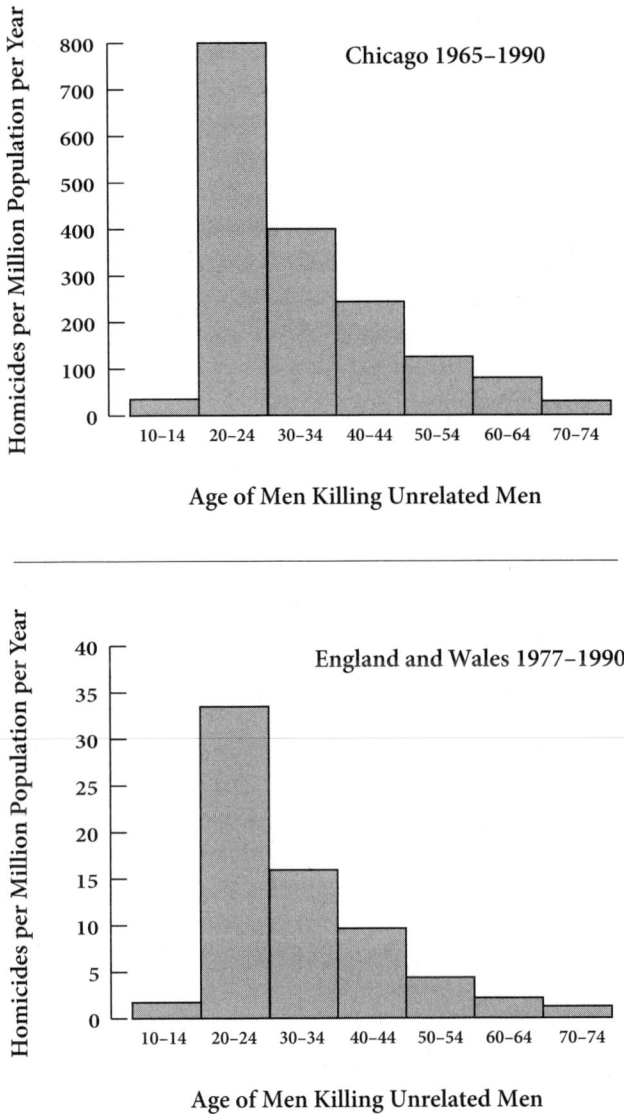

Chicago 1965–1990

(y-axis: Homicides per Million Population per Year; values 0, 100, 200, 300, 400, 500, 600, 700, 800)

(x-axis: 10–14, 20–24, 30–34, 40–44, 50–54, 60–64, 70–74)

Age of Men Killing Unrelated Men

England and Wales 1977–1990

(y-axis: Homicides per Million Population per Year; values 0, 5, 10, 15, 20, 25, 30, 35, 40)

(x-axis: 10–14, 20–24, 30–34, 40–44, 50–54, 60–64, 70–74)

Age of Men Killing Unrelated Men

Source: Adapted from data in Martin Daly and Margo Wilson, "Crime and conflict: Homicide in evolutionary psychological perspective," *Crime and Justice* 22 (1997):51–100.

two most powerful predictors of homicide. Homicide is most common in the 20–24 age-group, after which it steadily drops off. The pattern is everywhere the same: in all known industrial and nonindustrial societies, killing is heavily concentrated in the 20–24 age-group.[6] Figure 11.1 shows the age distribution of homicide rates for Chicago between 1965 and 1990, and England and Wales between 1977 and 1990. As can

TABLE 11.1   Male-on-Male and Female-on-Female Homicides in Selected Communities and Societies

Society/ Community	Time Period	Number of Male-on-Male Homicides	Number of Female-on-Female Homicides	Percentage Male-on-Male Homicides
Iceland	1946–70	7	0	100
!Kung (Botswana)	1920–55	12	0	100
Mayan village (Mexico)	1938–65	15	0	100
Tiv (Nigeria)	1931–49	74	1	98.7
Bhil (India)	1971–75	50	1	98.0
Canada	1974–83	2,387	59	97.6
Chicago	1965–81	7,439	195	97.4
Alur (Uganda)	1945–54	33	1	97.1
Detroit	1972	316	11	96.6
England and Wales	1977–86	2,195	95	95.9
Baluyia (Kenya)	1949–54	65	3	95.6

Source: Martin Daly and Margo Wilson, "Killing the competition: Female/female and male/male homicide," *Human Nature* 1 (1990):81–107.

easily be seen, the age distribution of homicides in Chicago and in England/Wales is almost identical. After peaking in the 20–24 age-group, the homicide rate drops off sharply in stair-step fashion so that by age 70 it is only a tiny fraction of what it was at its peak. In Chicago the rate of the 20–24 group was twenty-seven times the rate of the 70–74 group. In England/Wales, the peak rate was thirty-three times the rate of the 70–74 group. The only real difference between Chicago and England/Wales is that the rate of homicide in Chicago is much higher. In the peak age-group, there were nearly twenty-five times as many homicides in Chicago as in England/Wales.

Sex is an equally powerful determinant, the vast majority of homicides being committed by males. Age and sex are inextricably intertwined, with most homicides being perpetrated by males in their early reproductive years. (The numbers in Figure 11.1 obviously pertain only to males.) This has been reported for every known society, and it is a virtual certainty that it is a human universal. Who are the victims? Overwhelmingly, they are other young males. Men sometimes kill women, and women occasionally kill other women, but the vast majority of same-sex homicides are male-on-male homicides. Table 11.1, which includes a wide range of industrial and nonindustrial societies, shows that between 95.6 and 100 percent of killings are male-on-male killings, with an average per society of 97.9.

Poverty or economic deprivation is also correlated with homicide rates. In Detroit in 1972, 41 percent of adult male homicide perpetrators were unemployed, as were 43 percent of adult male homicide victims, but the overall unemployment rate for adult men in the city was only 11 percent.[7] However, poverty per se does not appear to be an actual cause of homicide. The real culprit is economic inequality, or the range of incomes within a community or society. In an early study, the sociologists Judith and Peter Blau examined 1970 homicide rates in 125 US metropolitan areas. They found that the percentage of people living in poverty was moderately correlated with the homicide rate, but that the degree of income inequality was very strongly correlated with the homicide rate.[8] Several other studies have found a strong correlation between income inequality and homicide. One of these used a sample of contemporary nation-states; a second looked at all fifty US states for 1990; and a third studied seventy-seven Chicago neighborhoods between 1988 and 1992.[9] A 2001 study carried out by Daly, Wilson, and Vasdev examined the ten Canadian provinces between 1981 and 1996 and found an extremely high correlation.[10]

However, since the level of poverty and the degree of inequality are correlated with each other, Blau and Blau examined the effect of inequality on homicide by controlling for (factoring out) the effect of poverty. They found that the effect of poverty disappeared whereas the effect of inequality remained strong.[11] Similarly, Daly, Wilson, and Vasdev found that most of the extremely large correlation between inequality and homicide in the Canadian provinces remained when average household income was factored out.[12]

Why is economic inequality so closely tied to homicide rates? And if young males are mostly killing other young males, what is the conflict about? The most plausible answer from an evolutionary point of view is conflict over women.[13] One of the most common forms of urban homicide in the United States and other industrial societies is the result of what Daly and Wilson call "seemingly trivial altercations." These are conflicts in which one man kills another in, say, a bar fight that has escalated out of control. The most common provocation in such fights is an insult (or series of insults) to a man's honor. One man may question another's manhood, or the fight may be over a woman for whom the two men are competing. A man may have stolen, or is threatening to steal, another man's girlfriend or wife, or there may have been an adulterous affair.[14]

Daly and Wilson point out that although these situations often look trivial to outsiders, they are anything but. Men are fighting for status, and status means access to females, which means reproductive success. In an evolutionary sense, men are fighting about fitness, or at least that is the way selection (sexual selection in this case) has wired the male psyche.

The age distribution of homicide as shown in Figure 11.1 offers strong support for this argument. Homicide rates begin to escalate after males reach fourteen or fifteen years of age and peak at the time when competition for mates is at its height. Data on the relationship between marital status and homicide also support the argument. In Detroit in 1972, unmarried men in the age category 25–34 committed

2.6 times as many murders as married men of the same age; for men in the age category 35–44, the corresponding figure was 3.6. In Canada in the period 1974–1983, the discrepancy was even greater: unmarried men ages 25–34 committed 3.4 times as many murders as married men in this age-group, and unmarried men ages 35–44, 6.8 times as many.[15] Married men age 24 and older have achieved success in the mating game, whereas unmarried men of the same age have yet to achieve it. Of course, not all men wish to be married by age 24, but many do. It is often said that marriage "civilizes" men. Indeed, it does. They become more settled and less unruly because they have attained one of their most important goals in life.[16]

Interestingly, these differences persist throughout men's lifetimes. Older men who become widowed or divorced display the same elevated rate of homicide as never-married men. Most widowed and divorced men reenter the mating market, and thus become subject to its same pressures and constraints as are never-married men.[17]

Another line of evidence supporting the evolutionary psychological interpretation of homicide comes from a seemingly unlikely source: the relationship between homicide and life expectancy. Wilson and Daly found an extremely strong negative correlation (-.880) between life expectancy and homicide rates in the seventy-seven Chicago neighborhoods they studied. (Life expectancy varied between 54.3 and 77.4 years, homicide rates between 1.3 and 156 murders per year per 100,000 population. Life expectancy rates were calculated with the effects of homicide mortality removed.) Neighborhoods with the lowest life expectancy were those with the highest homicide rates. Wilson and Daly argue that young men with low life expectancy "discount the future." When they see men around them dying young, they readily infer that they also have a good chance of dying young; under such circumstances, they are more likely to engage in risky, including homicidal, behavior. These findings and their interpretation do not displace those for the role of economic inequality, because inequality itself is closely related to life expectancy. Life expectancy shortens as economic inequality increases.[18]

All of this tells us why it is inequality (and low life expectancy) rather than poverty that is at the root of homicide. It is relative rather than absolute deprivation that is critical. High levels of income inequality and low life expectancy mean that male competition for status and mates at the bottom of the social hierarchy is intensified, which invariably leads to more homicide in the most extreme cases. Another way of thinking about this is to imagine an industrial society in which everyone is poor but all have the same income. (There is no such society on earth, but this is just a thought experiment.) Imagine also that the society has socially imposed monogamy. In such a hypothetical society, in which both income and life expectancy are the same for all men, we would predict that violent male-male conflict would be dramatically reduced. There would still be some male-male conflict because not all males would be considered equally desirable as mates. Women do look for physical attractiveness in males, and they also look for "niceness." And, of course, males are still looking for physical attractiveness, youth, and so on, and thus will be competing for the most desirable women.

Moreover, in this imaginary society many men and quite a few women are apt to become sexually unfaithful at least once in their lives. In this respect there is nothing hypothetical about the society, since infidelity is universal. Here we find another major motive for homicide: sexual jealousy. When men discover that their wives are sexually involved with other men, they often fly into a jealous rage that occasionally ends with one of the offending parties being killed. Sexual jealousy and infidelity in our imaginary society, as in all real ones, will drive up the homicide rate. The person most likely to be killed is the man who is poaching, and the person most likely to kill him is his lover's husband. Daly and Wilson have summarized data on so-called love-triangle homicides for two American cities (Detroit and Miami) and one English city (Birmingham) and found that of a total of ninety-three homicides, 88 percent involved the husband killing his wife's lover. Similarly, for five nonindustrial societies (the Bhil, Bison-horn Maria, Munda, and Oraon of India, and the Basoga of Uganda), the authors found that out of fifty-four love-triangle homicides a whopping 98 percent involved the husband killing the wife's lover.[19] In other words, men are much more likely to kill when they are being cheated on than women are when they are the victims of infidelity.

Sometimes, of course, men do kill their philandering wives. And the wife doesn't have to be caught philandering, or actually be philandering at all; the mere suspicion of infidelity is sometimes enough to do her in. In every society infidelity is regarded as a violation, but it is usually regarded as more serious if it is the wife rather than the husband who is being unfaithful. In all societies wives are killed, at least occasionally, for actual or suspected infidelity. One man's wife said to him, "You are so damned stupid that you don't even know she is someone else's child and not yours." The man later told the authorities, "I was shocked! I became so mad I took the rifle and shot her."[20]

We know that in many Muslim countries unfaithful wives are sometimes stoned to death. Among the Yapese of Oceania, a man who caught his wife having sex with another man was entitled to kill both of them, even by burning them to death in the house they were in at the time. Japan and China, along with several other Asian countries, have historically given similar rights to the husband. Closer to home, in New Mexico, Utah, and Texas until the 1970s if a man caught his wife in flagrante delicto—in the very act of sexual intercourse with another man—he was legally permitted to kill them both. (Although he had to do it immediately as an act of uncontrollable rage; he couldn't go away for an hour or two to think about it and then come back and shoot them.) Even now, juries are often more lenient with a man who has killed his wife and her lover when catching them in bed together; a certain sympathy is displayed for the husband.[21] Wilson and Daly describe the situation in more detail:

A minority of wife-killers are found "unfit to stand trial" or "not guilty by reason of insanity," and these are often diagnosed as psychiatric cases of "morbid jealousy" . . . on the basis of obsessive concern with suspected infidelity and a tendency to invoke bizarre "evidence" in support. However, most jealous wife-killers are not considered insane. Quite the contrary: Anglo-American law specifically deems killing upon the discovery of a wife's adultery to be the act of a "reasonable man" and deserving of reduced penalty. . . . Other legal traditions—European, Oriental, Native American, African, Melanesian—all concur. . . . Not only is jealousy deemed "normal," but so even is lethal reaction, at least if perpetrated by a man and in the heat of passion.

Moreover, violent sexual jealousy is deemed normal or at least unsurprising both in societies in which the cuckold's violence is seen as a reprehensible loss of control, . . . and in those where it is seen as a praiseworthy redemption of honor. . . . The cross-cultural familiarity of jealous rages supports the view that the psychological links between sexual proprietariness and violent inclinations are not arbitrary aspects of particular cultures, but are evolved aspects of human male psychology.[22]

The unfaithfulness of wives is taken more seriously than the unfaithfulness of husbands in all societies because infidelity can impose a much greater reproductive cost on men. They can be cuckolded by a wife, but there is no such thing as a woman being cuckolded by her husband. Killing a wife for infidelity is an act of imposing the ultimate punishment for potential cuckoldry. Of course, the punishment is usually less severe—violence short of murder—but it is punishment nonetheless.

As noted in the discussion of sexual strategies in Chapter 5, cuckoldry is bad, very bad indeed. Not only does being cuckolded impose a severe reproductive cost on a man; it is also extremely harmful to his reputation. Cuckolded men are mocked, laughed at, ridiculed, and often held in contempt. The damage to a man's reputation is very likely to lower his position in a social hierarchy, or at the least interfere with his ability to rise higher within it, and thus harms his ability to attract future mates, should he desire them. Therefore, the male psyche has evolved strong anti-cuckoldry tactics to combat this, and killing the woman doing the cuckolding is one of them. In this way a man can protect both his reproductive interests and his reputation in the community.[23]

The specifics of violence against women for real or suspected infidelity also make sense from a Darwinian point of view. Men are more likely to engage in violence toward younger rather than older wives because younger wives have greater reproductive potential. Similarly, marriages in which a man is much older than his wife—a fifty-year-old man, say, married to a twenty-five-year-old woman—are characterized by much higher levels of violence.[24] Here again we have a situation in which the wife's reproductive potential is high, but in addition a much younger wife is more likely to be unfaithful than a wife closer to her husband's age. Violence toward women also appears to be more common where women are scarcer and thus male competition for mates more severe. Among the Yanomama, for example, many males attempt to lure other men's wives into sexual affairs, and gang rape of young unmarried girls or women is common. The Yanomama have one of the world's highest reported rates of violence toward wives and women in general.[25]

Occasionally wives also kill unfaithful husbands. A celebrated case occurred some years ago in Dallas, Texas. When a woman discovered that her husband was cheating on her, she made a decision to kill him. But she didn't take out a gun and shoot him or a knife and stab him, nor did she try to poison him. She drove her car to a parking lot and when he appeared in sight she ran him down. And not once, but several times. Tires were squealing all over the place. She was actually caught on videotape, and so evidence of her rage was right there for everyone to see (and the video was shown on television news throughout the country).

Wilson and Daly have assembled evidence to show that women seem much more likely to kill husbands in modern industrial than in nonindustrial societies. In Detroit in 1982–1983, two-thirds of spousal homicides were committed by wives, and slightly more than half were committed by wives in Chicago between 1965 and 1989 and in Houston in 1969. In Miami in 1980, Philadelphia between 1948 and 1952, and the United States between 1976 and 1985, slightly less than half were committed by wives. However, in some other industrial societies wives have committed fewer spousal homicides than husbands. In Australia, Canada, Denmark, England/Wales, and Scotland between 1933 and 1987 (years vary by country), an average of only 22 percent of spousal homicides were committed by wives.[26]

Nevertheless, the industrial/nonindustrial divide still holds, since data from the mid-twentieth century for six African societies (Tiv, Luo, Basoga, Gisu, Banyoro, and Baluyia) show that only 5 percent of the killers were wives, and for four tribal societies in India (Bison-horn Maria, Munda, Oraon, and Bhil) none of the killers were wives.[27] These differences likely reflect the higher status of women in industrial societies as well as the much greater degree to which men control female sexuality in nonindustrial societies. Many wives everywhere may feel the urge to kill unfaithful husbands, but in societies in which men's control over women is very great, they are usually unable to do so.

But as strong as the homicidal reaction to infidelity may sometimes be, husbands are most likely to kill their wives when the wives leave them or threaten to leave them. In a study of a Canadian city that examined data on wife killings over a period of twenty-two years, 63 percent of the wife killings resulted from the wife's leaving her husband. A study of 293 North Carolina women who had been killed by their boyfriends or husbands in 1991–1993 showed that 43 percent of the killings occurred after the women left their mates or threatened to leave them. A corresponding figure of 32 percent was obtained in a study of over five hundred murders of intimate partners in Ontario, Canada. These figures may actually understate the real numbers, which could be as high as 70 percent.[28]

David Buss has extended the Darwinian analysis of homicide in some interesting ways. Buss contends that the mind, especially the male mind, evolved in the ancestral environment to kill under certain circumstances because such killing had many potential benefits: eliminating an important antagonist; acquiring a rival's resources or territory; gaining access to a rival's mate; preventing a rival from encroaching upon one's own mate; protecting resources needed for reproduction; eliminating an entire lineage of reproductive competitors; and cultivating a fierce reputation that is effective in deterring enemies.[29] For Buss, the tendency to murder is an evolutionary adaptation. In his words,

> It may seem coldhearted to talk about killing as adaptive or murder as advantageous, but if we consider the nature of reproductive competition humans have faced over the long time spans of our evolution, then we can appreciate just what an edge in that evolutionary competition killing would have provided. The benefits of killing, in an evolutionary sense, must be momentous and manifold, because, on the other side, the negative reproductive consequences of being killed are so profound.[30]

Of course, killing can have profoundly negative consequences as well, since in modern societies with police, laws, and courts, people can be apprehended, convicted, and sentenced to life in prison or executed. But the human brain did not evolve in modern societies. It evolved in ancient environments where there were no police, no laws, and no courts, and thus murderers could act with relative impunity.

Drawing on extensive interviews of nearly a thousand people from five different cultures, Buss also shows that even though the overwhelming majority of people never commit murder, most have thought of it at least once, and many of these thoughts are extremely graphic and display marked hostility toward the potential victim. Buss relates the story of a friend who kept talking about killing his wife because she flirted with other men and showed him disrespect. Buss at first made light of these remarks, but as time went on he began to realize that his friend was serious. One evening at a party the wife was flirting again. When her husband pulled her aside and she showed him more disrespect, a bad argument ensued. Before the night was over the woman had packed her bags and left her husband. Did she leave because she feared her life might be in danger? Buss thinks so.[31]

Getting in Touch with Our Inner Chimp

In the late 1960s there was a popular idea that humans were the only species who killed members of their own kind. In the 1968 movie *Planet of the Apes*, an American space traveler, played by Charlton Heston, ends up on a planet that is ruled by apes who have enslaved humans. All three great ape species—chimpanzees, gorillas, and orangutans—"star" in the movie. What is most pertinent about the film for the present discussion is the portrayal of the chimps as nonviolent, peace-loving animals. The two other ape species in the film are depicted more negatively. Gorillas are the really bad guys. They lord it over everyone, are mean and nasty, and are extremely militaristic. The orangutans are sort of in between. Unfortunately, the movie's portrayal of chimps and gorillas was not only wrong but completely backwards. Yet the depictions reflected the common understandings of the day. Few people had observed violence among chimps, and gorillas were generally seen as menacing because of their huge size and fierce appearance.

What we have learned about chimps in the meantime is that they are a violent species. Many adult males are power hungry and engage in aggression to achieve and hang on to the rank of alpha male. Primatologists have discussed chimp dominance behavior at length, but no one has done it better than Frans de Waal, a primatologist originally from the Netherlands but now at Emory University in Atlanta.[32] De Waal tells the fascinating story of three male chimps at the Arnhem Zoo in the Netherlands: Nikkie, Yeroen, and Luit. At one point Luit became the alpha male in a contest with Yeroen that lasted three months. Yeroen became intensely hostile toward Luit and, with Nikkie's assistance, eventually overthrew him. Subsequently Nikkie became the alpha male, with Yeroen acting as his ally. Yet this coalition crumbled when Nikkie started to interfere with Yeroen's access to the most desirable females. After months of conflict, Yeroen had had enough and walked away from Nikkie, who was unable to patch up the relationship. Chimps tend to reconcile after a conflict, but in this case Yeroen refused to make up. A power vacuum was created, and Luit quickly stepped into it.

Nikkie and Yeroen became despondent, which is normal when dominant males are dethroned, and eventually decided to team up again in order to get even. One night they attacked Luit viciously. He was found by his keepers the next morning with puncture wounds all over his body from Nikkie's and Yeroen's bites. Some fingers and toes had been bitten off, and he was missing his testicles (it was later discovered that they had literally been squeezed out of his scrotal sac). He was rushed into surgery but the effort to save his life failed. In describing this incident, de Waal noted, "Power is the prime mover of the male chimpanzee. It's a constant obsession, offering great benefits if obtained and intense bitterness if lost."[33] The main benefits are more and better food and more and better mates. This is the usual situation in the struggle for dominance among primates, and among mammals in general for that matter.

In addition to violent struggles for power among individual male chimps, there is another type of violence that has even more severe consequences. Small groups of males often canvass their territories looking for outsiders who might be potential trouble. The Harvard University anthropologist Richard Wrangham calls these "border patrols." The patrols make good sense, because chimp communities attacking other communities is pretty common. Actually, it is not an entire community attacking another, but several males of one community attacking a few males of the other. Groups of males, sometimes as many as twenty, will move into the territory of a rival community looking for adult males or juveniles who are alone. The intruders will attack and kill males and juveniles, although females are usually spared.[34] John Mitani, David Watts, and Sylvia Amsler studied a community over a ten-year period between 1999 and 2008.[35] This community was located at Ngogo, Kibale National Park, Uganda, and numbered about 150. The territory they occupied was about 29 square kilometers (11 square miles). Over the entire period, there were eighteen lethal attacks and another three deaths that were thought to be due to violence. Most of the attacks were made in a region to the northeast, and eventually the Ngogo chimps annexed the rival territory, which covered 6.4 square kilometers, or about 2.5 square miles. The authors note that whether the chimps were seeking food or mates was unclear, but tentatively concluded it was food.[36] Nevertheless, because the Ngogo community had access to more fruit trees, the females could eat more fruit and thus reproduce more rapidly. This would not only be promoting reproductive success but enabling the group to grow in size and become stronger.[37]

Wrangham finds major implications in such behavior for humans, especially human warfare. The parallels seem to him quite striking. Not only are the tactics similar—stealthy raids in both chimps and small-scale human bands and tribes—but the number of male deaths is astonishingly similar. About 30 percent of male chimps die through violence, and figures closely approximating this have been reported for many human tribes. Wrangham contends that it is only chimpanzees and humans who engage in this kind of intercommunity violence, and he dubs the males of both species *demonic males*. Not a very nice appellation, but seemingly true nonetheless. In the following section we tease out the implications.

Killing Enemies: The Small Scale

The Frequency of War in Small-Scale Societies

Homicide is usually one-on-one killing, whereas war involves teams of combatants who attack and attempt to kill other teams. The idea has often prevailed that war is relatively infrequent in nonindustrial societies, but most recent research refutes this claim. The evidence comes both from studies of band and tribal societies as well as from archaeological investigations. Just as we have learned that chimps are pretty violent, we have learned that humans are pretty violent as well.[38]

In a study of fifty bands and tribes, 90 percent were unquestionably engaged in warfare, and the remainder engaged in violent conflict to some extent.[39] In another study, also of fifty small-scale societies (not the same ones), only 13 percent seldom or never engaged in war, but nearly all of these were ethnic groups or tribes that either had been pacified by modern nation-states or were living in such geographical isolation that there were virtually no neighbors to attack.[40] A third study looked at

157 North American Indian societies. It found that less than 5 percent were truly peaceful, and these were all small bands living in isolation.[41] In a study of ninety hunter-gatherer societies, only three could be classified as relatively peaceful and, once again, these societies were isolated.[42] Two things are clear from these studies: most small-scale societies engage in war, and those that do not usually inhabit environments that make war unfeasible.

The archaeological evidence also indicates that war is common. Lawrence Keeley reviews evidence showing that violent conflict between small-scale societies seems to have been frequent in many regions of the world between 35 and 5 Kya. This evidence comes from Czechoslovakian cemeteries (dating between 35 and 24 Kya), Egyptian Nubia (between 14 and 12 Kya), hunter-gatherer societies in western Europe (between 10 and 5 Kya), and prehistoric North America. Keeley also shows that many villages in early agricultural tribes and simple chiefdoms in Neolithic Europe were surrounded by ditches and palisades designed to keep enemies out. In Britain, and possibly elsewhere, there is clear evidence that palisades were attacked and burned.[43]

So most small-scale societies, from the distant prehistoric past down to the present, have fought wars. But how often have they done so? One study found that 66 percent of prestate societies engaged in war at least once a year.[44] Another reported a figure of 62 percent.[45] Of 160 societies in the Standard Sample for which data are available, 42 percent engaged in war at least once a year, and most of these fought almost continually.

Another way of thinking about the extent of war is to look at the percentage of male deaths that result from violence. Figures are available from numerous studies. Over a period of twenty years, about 30 percent of men among the Murngin of Australia died from violence, and a figure of 24 percent has been reported for the Yanomama. In New Guinea war has often been extremely intense. Figures for the Enga and the Gebusi indicate about 35 percent of men dying from violence. Other studies show similar figures, and a reasonable overall estimate for tribal societies may be about 25–30 percent of men suffering violent deaths.[46] (It is striking that about 30 percent of male chimpanzees die from violence in their natural habitats.)

In some societies many women also die violent deaths. When these deaths are added to male deaths, the number of violent deaths can become staggeringly high. Among the Achuar, Aché, and Waorani, all lowland South American tribes, the combined male-female percentage of deaths from violence has been recorded at 42, 43, and 56 percent, respectively.[47]

Not all violent deaths result from war; some are the product of interpersonal homicide. But it is likely that most violent deaths result from war.[48] Almost all violent deaths of women are the result of war.

Richard Wrangham, Michael Wilson, and Martin Muller have assembled data on the number of deaths from intercommunity violence for both chimps and humans.[49] Table 11.2 shows their data for several human communities. The figures represent

TABLE 11.2 Annual Rates of Intercommunity Violence for Selected Human Societies

Group	Region	Subsistence Mode	Deaths/100,000/year
Gidjingali	Australia	Hunter-Gatherer	148
Yorok	California	Hunter-Gatherer	240
Modoc	California/Oregon	Hunter-Gatherer	450
Piegan	North America	Hunter-Gatherer	1,000
Yanomama	Venezuela	Horticultural	290
Mtetwa	South Africa	Horticultural	590
Kalinga	Philippines	Horticultural	600
Hewa	New Guinea	Horticultural	778
Kato	California	Horticultural	1,450

Source: Richard W. Wrangham, Michael L. Wilson, and Martin N. Muller, "Comparative rates of violence in chimpanzees and humans," *Primates* 47 (2006):14–26.

the number of deaths from intercommunity violence for both hunter-gatherer and horticultural communities, standardized in terms of 100,000 people. There is a lot of variation among communities, so obviously various features of the socioecological environment matter a great deal, especially the mode of subsistence. Horticulturalists experience much more intercommunity violence than hunter-gatherers. The authors have calculated the average rates of intercommunity violence for hunter-gatherers and horticulturalists separately. The average for hunter-gatherers is 249 deaths per 100,000 population per year, for horticulturalists 580. (Calculations are based on 12 hunter-gatherer groups and 20 horticultural groups, many of which do not appear in Table 11.2.) Initially these numbers might not appear terribly high, but in fact they are very high. For example, the average of 249 for hunter-gatherers is just for one year. In ten years 2,490 violent deaths would occur, in twenty years 4,980, and in thirty years 7,470. That is a lot of killing. But it is only the average. If we take the rate for the Piegan, there are 1,000 deaths in one year, 10,000 in ten years, 20,000 in twenty years, and 30,000 in thirty years. The twenty horticultural groups average 580 deaths per 100,000 per year. That computes to 5,800 in ten years, 11,600 in twenty years, and 17,400 in thirty years. If we take the number of deaths for the Kato of 1,450 per 100,000 per year, we end up with 14,500 in ten years, 29,000 in twenty years, and 43,500 in thirty years.[50] Obviously this is killing on a very large scale.

However, one qualification must be entered. Very few horticultural tribes number 100,000 people, and hunter-gatherer bands and tribes are even smaller. Take the Yanomama, for example. In the 1960s they numbered about 20,000. Their rate of death from intercommunity violence is listed in Table 11.2 as 290 deaths per 100,000 per year, which would be 2,900 in ten years, 5,800 in twenty years, and 8,700 in thirty years. But to get the actual number of people killed in thirty years in this particular tribe of 20,000 people, we would have to multiply by 0.20 (20,000 ÷ 100,000), which would give us 1,740 violent deaths in thirty years. That is still a great deal of killing.

What then of the human-chimp comparison? Wrangham, Wilson, and Muller calculated the chimp rate of death by intercommunity violence for several different communities as 271 deaths per 100,000 per year. This is close to the average for hunter-gatherers (249), which seems the most appropriate comparison because hunter-gatherers are the closest representatives of the human ancestral environment. Chimps and ancestral humans, then, are about equally violent.

The pattern of fighting among hunter-gatherer bands and horticultural tribes is almost always the same. Large confrontations are usually avoided because they are too risky. Too many people on both sides would be killed. In some cases the combatants may confront each other in an open space but at a considerable distance. They shake their spears, yell insults, and boast about their ability to defeat the other. Consequently some anthropologists call this a social ritual that has nothing to do with war. But although the behavior may appear ritualized, it is not a social ritual as such but often a prelude to war. Often opponents size each other up to see which side may be stronger.[51]

The classic case of war that many anthropologists deem a social ritual and little else is found among the Dugum Dani of New Guinea. Men on each side assemble in an open area and hurl spears and shoot arrows at each other, but few people are killed. One side may call another to fight, but the other side has the right to refuse and often does so. Then nothing happens. When combatants do confront each other, they appear casual about what they are doing. A lot of the action involves insults and banter.[52] If it is a particularly hot day, "both sides simply withdraw and sit in groups, smoking, talking, and resting for a while before resuming hostilities."[53] Many of the warriors are not involved in any fighting at all even though others are. If it rains, participants likely go home.

Although the Dani don't seem to be particularly interested in killing each other, in fact they are. The problem they face is the unusual nature of their terrain. Much of it is muddy water and swampland, a condition that prevents one group from directly attacking another. There are areas of dry land, but much of it consists of narrow corridors. One group could use a corridor to attack another, but this is usually unsuccessful and, besides, the attacking group would often be left with no means of escaping if it became necessary. And thus the peculiar type of war that the Dani fight.[54] We know it is atypical because "the onset of battle elsewhere in the highlands did not depend on the prior agreement of both parties. Instead of being prearranged, battles typically began with one side invading or otherwise forcing a confrontation on the other."[55] These battles often led to high mortality rates and, when victors pursued their victims to their villages, gardens and houses would be destroyed.[56]

In any event, the most common method of fighting is a village or band raiding another, usually by surprise and preferably at night.[57] Among the Yanomama, for example, a group of warriors might travel for two or three days to attack a neighboring village. They wait through the night and attack just before dawn, while people are still sleeping or only beginning to stir. The objective is to kill as many men as possible, although women and children are sometimes killed as well. Younger women in their prime reproductive years are captured and dragged back to the at-tackers' village, where they become wives. This pattern has been found in band and tribal societies all over the world.[58]

But the Yanomama also have another tactic, the "treacherous feast." One village may invite another for a feast, the idea being to discuss a possible alliance. However, once the visitors are settled in the host village and plied with food and drink, they are attacked and many are killed. Treacherous feasts are also known from other parts of the tribal world.[59]

Explaining Small-Scale War

Because of the extraordinary frequency of war, as well as the striking similarities between tribal warfare and chimpanzee lethal raiding, it is difficult to avoid the con-clusion that violent aggression is an innate human predisposition. But if this is so, what are people fighting about? Do they just like being mean and nasty, or do they do it for sport? Surely not. We know that throughout the animal world, aggression is closely linked to competition for resources, and the scarcer resources are the more aggressively they are fought for. But what resources? In animals it is territory, food, and mates. Is it the same for humans?

Several decades ago Marvin Harris proposed the well-known "protein theory." Harris argued that in tropical forests game animals are not abundant, and people inhabiting these environments are therefore unable to eat as much meat as they would like. Among groups such as the Yanomama, violent conflict results from pro-tein scarcity, which grows worse when numbers increase and populations become denser. War leads to the creation of "no-man's-lands," uninhabited areas where game animals can be protected from overexploitation.[60]

This is an interesting theory, but Napoleon Chagnon figured out a way to test it. Over a month's time he weighed the meat the Yanomama brought back from a hunt. He found that they were eating more animal protein than the members of several industrial societies, and nearly as much as the world leaders in animal consump-tion—Australia and New Zealand.[61] Nevertheless, the discovery that the Yanomama seem to be consuming adequate amounts of animal protein is not necessarily a fatal blow to Harris's theory. Brian Ferguson, an anthropologist at Rutgers University, points out that the protein hypothesis does not predict an actual deficiency of an-imal protein in the diet; rather, it simply predicts that war will stop declining con-sumption of animal protein before it has a chance to reach unhealthy levels.[62] This is presumably the significance of Harris's point about war creating no-man's-lands. So Harris's theory could still be correct. However, if correct, it can be only part of the story. Surely there must be more to fight about than just meat.

Ferguson has proposed an alternative theory that emphasizes a broader set of factors. He suggests that band and tribal peoples evaluate the costs and benefits of war and will only go to war when they think the benefits will outweigh the costs.

Ferguson points to six possible benefits that can be obtained through warfare: increasing access to fixed resources by eliminating competitors; capturing movable goods; imposing an exploitative relationship on previously independent groups; conquering and incorporating other groups; enhancing the power and status of war leaders; and defending against attacks by other groups.[63]

Most of these factors have limited relevance to explaining war in bands and tribes. Such groups are seldom able to conquer and incorporate other groups or impose exploitative relationships on them because they lack the necessary power and force. Such war motives are largely limited to societies at greater levels of political complexity—chiefdoms and states. War does enhance the status of war leaders, but this is more a consequence than a cause of war. Capturing movable goods may be a motive, but only if there are such goods to capture. Defending against attacks by other groups is certainly a good reason for war, but it begs the question why there are attacks to defend against in the first place. Someone has to go on the offense before someone else needs to put up a defense. Ferguson's first factor, increasing access to resources by eliminating competitors, is highly pertinent, but it still leaves open the question of what the most important resources are (Ferguson presumably means land and the plants and animals on it).

Ferguson frames his list of causal factors in the context of a more general point, namely, that warfare among tribal peoples has resulted mainly from Western contact.[64] Native populations, he notes, have often been drawn into colonial rivalries between European powers and engaged in war as a result. Europeans have often introduced epidemic diseases that have created severe population imbalances and led to warfare designed to capture women and children in order to redress these imbalances. Most significantly, Ferguson emphasizes conflict over the allocation and control of Western manufactured goods. Steel axes, which the Yanomama and other indigenous groups acquired many years ago from missionaries, are especially valued because they are superior to stone axes in terms of dramatically reducing expenditures of time and energy. The Yanomama can clear forest seven to ten times faster using steel instead of stone axes. Many native Amazonian peoples have also become dependent on such manufactured goods as shotguns, machetes, knives, fishhooks, pots, manioc griddles, matches, tobacco, kerosene, beads, and clothing. Throughout Amazonia, and in all historical periods, Ferguson claims, native groups have gone to war to gain access to these and other highly desired goods.[65]

Ferguson is not implying that there was no war in Amazonia prior to European intrusion, since there was. But he does see the introduction of Western goods as greatly intensifying war. This argument is not compelling. There is much evidence that many bands and tribes that have had very little contact with Westerners still have very high levels of warfare. For example, Lyle Steadman, an anthropologist at Arizona State University, studied the Hewa, a very isolated group in New Guinea who had never seen a Westerner until he arrived. (Because of his light skin, they were not even sure what kind of human being he was—or if he was one at all!)

Steadman reports that the Hewa have one of the highest levels of violent conflict of any known tribal group.[66] Referring to the tribes of the northwest coast of North America, the Israeli political scientist Azar Gat points out that the first European explorers in the late eighteenth century found some of these tribes using body armor made from hide or wooden slats.[67] Moreover, war has been recorded for these tribes for the past four thousand years. And, as already noted, there is extensive archaeological evidence for war from all over the world for thousands if not tens of thousands of years.

The most recent theory to attract wide attention starts from the assumption that women constitute the main scarce resource in bands and tribes. Donald Symons of the University of California at Santa Barbara has pointed out that women are always scarce to at least some extent in all societies, and that men therefore are always in competition for them.[68] This claim may surprise most readers, but remember that men are competing not just for any women but for the most desirable women— those who are young, attractive, and most likely to bear healthy offspring. Moreover, given the widespread practice of polygyny, which can reach very high levels in some tribal societies, a large percentage of men may have to endure enforced bachelorhood, or else resort to rape or to luring other men's wives into adulterous affairs.

One of the first anthropologists to follow up on the theoretical significance of Symons's point was Napoleon Chagnon. Focusing on the Yanomama, Chagnon has argued that they fight primarily over women and that blood revenge is a major motive for war once it has started. Chagnon reports that most fights begin over infidelity and suspicions of infidelity, attempts to seduce other men's wives, stealing women from visiting groups, and sexual jealousy. Many of the fights that arise over sexual matters culminate in killings both within and between villages.[69]

As noted in Chapter 5, the most important status among Yanomama men is that of *unokai*—a man who has killed another man—and Chagnon has shown that *unokais* have more wives than non-*unokais*. Analyzing several hundred Yanomama men, Chagnon calculated that the *unokais* had an average of 1.63 wives per man, whereas the non-*unokais* averaged only 0.63 wives per man. The gap was particularly wide among men ages 20–24. In this age-group, five *unokais* had a total of four wives, but seventy-eight non-*unokais* had a total of only ten wives. The figures for the 20–24-year-old non-*unokais* are especially striking, because if the ten wives were equally apportioned to ten men—in other words, if each man had a single wife—then sixty-eight non-*unokais* had no wives at all![70] These numbers graphically illustrate Symons's point about female scarcity.

The Yanomama are only one case, but there is a great deal of evidence from other bands and tribes that conflict over women is a major cause of war. Laura Betzig has pointed out that 90 percent of disputes among the Tiwi of Australia involved women. Betzig also reports that among the Kapauku of Melanesia most wars are the result of violations of a husband's exclusive sexual rights; that sexual jealousy was a major motive for killings among the Marquesans of Polynesia; and that quarrels over women were the most frequent kind of dispute among the Saramacca of the upper Surinam river basin.[71]

The female scarcity theory of war seems compelling, but it is not necessary to assume that this is the only thing band and tribal peoples are fighting about. In general, they are fighting over those most critical resources that are scarce, and the greater their scarcity the greater the frequency and intensity of war. People need territory and the plant and animal resources on it to survive and reproduce. Economic resources and mates are thus inextricably intertwined. Azar Gat expresses it very well:

> After all, what was the reason that more resources and more prestigious goods were desired and accumulated, most successfully by the chiefs and "big men"? For somatic reasons, to be sure—that is, above all, in order to feed, clothe, and dwell as well as they could, but also to feed, clothe, and house larger families, with more wives and more children, and to demonstrate their ability to do so in advance, in order to rank as worthy of the extra wives. Competition over resources was at least partly conflict over the ability to acquire and support women and children.[72]

Another reason war is so common among bands and tribes is that these societies lack individuals or groups with the authority to prevent violent conflict from occurring. In state-level societies, the state monopolizes the means of violence, which means that violent interpersonal conflict, as well as intervillage conflict, can be prevented (or at least minimized) by law or custom. Chagnon relates the story of a Yanomama man who had learned Spanish from missionaries and was sent to the territorial capital in Venezuela to receive instruction in practical nursing. While there, he was amazed to discover the existence of police and laws. When he returned to his village, he told Chagnon in excited terms that he had spoken to the territorial governor and pled with him to make police and law available to his tribe so they no longer had to live in constant fear of wars of revenge.[73]

People in bands and tribes are living in what the English philosopher Thomas Hobbes called a state of nature, a condition in which there is no overarching political authority. Once war gets started under such conditions, it is extremely difficult to stop. And, as we have seen, it seems to get started with remarkable ease. The threshold for initiating war in a state of nature is extremely low.

Killing Enemies: The Large Scale

The nature and causes of war have changed dramatically throughout human history.[74] Broch and Galtung have shown that what they call "economic war"—war fought for land or other economic valuables—and "political war"—war to conquer and subordinate other societies—are closely intertwined with the overall evolution of society. They examined over six hundred societies representing all stages of social evolution. Only 14 percent of bands and simple tribes had economic or political war compared to 46 percent of larger tribes and chiefdoms and 95 percent of states.[75]

While some of the motives for war found among bands and tribes appear to continue in the transition to chiefdoms, a new motive—political conquest—comes hurtling onto the scene. Tribal populations can put together, at most, teams of a few dozen warriors, but chiefdoms are capable of establishing fighting forces that may number into the hundreds and sometimes into the thousands.[76] Chiefdoms are expansionary societies, and the larger they are the more they expand. They can eat up a great deal of land in a short time, especially in circumscribed environments. The most circumscribed of all environments are islands, and it is in many of the societies of Oceania, especially Polynesia, that some of the most impressive and interesting chiefdoms have been found. Large chiefdoms on small islands can suffer from population pressure and environmental degradation, and such forces play a role in chiefdom-level warfare.

But acquiring more land just to feed more people is only one of the motives for war. Ruling chiefs are extremely ambitious men who achieved their position by defeating their rivals. They seek power both as an end in itself and as a means of acquiring other resources, especially wealth (and to some extent access to young, desirable women). Warfare in chiefdoms is driven more by these motives than by the need to acquire more land to feed more people.

Robert Carneiro has studied chiefdom-level warfare in the Cauca valley of Colombia and in Fiji. Warfare among chiefdoms in these regions, Carneiro says, was nearly constant. Fiji was seldom without war, and in the Cauca valley warfare was acute and incessant.[77] As to the causes of warfare among these chiefdoms, Carneiro notes that the "sorts of grievances that provoked warfare between autonomous villages continued to provoke it at the chiefdom level. But in addition, such things as offenses against the dignity of persons of rank, especially the paramount chief, began to play a role."[78] A common motive for hostilities was the self-aggrandizement that a paramount of one chiefdom was seeking at the expense of his counterparts in other chiefdoms. In the Cauca valley, chiefs went to war to gain control of gold mines, salt deposits, and other natural resources. "Territorial conquest was a particular incentive for Guaca and Popayan, two chiefdoms of the valley which, when the Spaniards arrived in the early 1500s, were actively expanding their territory and apparently well on their way to becoming states."[79]

Patrick Kirch sounds the same theme with respect to warfare among Polynesian chiefdoms. Population pressure was one motive for war, but most war had predominantly political motives. In Mangaia, Tahiti, and Hawaii, chiefdoms had become highly militarized, and powerful chiefs sought to capture the territories of other chiefs for their own political purposes. In Mangaia the god of war, Rongo, was surrounded by a cult of human sacrifice. In Hawaii huge stone temples were constructed for worship of the war god Ku. Each island in the chain contained a major chiefdom, and when Captain Cook arrived in 1779 a single inter-island chiefdom (or possibly small state) was in the process of forming.[80]

In states, as in chiefdoms, economic and political factors are also at the forefront of war. Historically, many state-level societies have been organized as large empires. Empires are extremely predatory political entities in which war is both massive and seemingly unending. Killing was often carried out on an enormous scale. It is impossible to improve on the descriptions of warfare that Laura Betzig has located in numerous passages from the Old Testament:

> Even before they made Othniel the first of their judges, the Judahites killed ten thousand at a battle in Canaan. Ehud, who came after Othniel, eliminated ten thousand in Moab; then Gideon used trumpets and broken pots to defeat one hundred thirty thousand Midianites. Shamgar leveled six hundred Philistines with an ox goad, Samson crushed a thousand with an ass's jawbone. . . . When Samuel was a boy, the Philistines eliminated thirty-four thousand Israelites.
>
> But Saul slew thousands of Philistines, and David ten thousand. David went on to slaughter twenty-two thousand Syrians at Zobah, eighteen thousand Edomites in the Valley of Salt, and another forty-seven thousand Syrians across the Jordan. Judah's king Asa put one million three hundred thousand Ethiopians to death. When Israel's king Ahad went to war with Ben-hadad, one hundred thousand Syrians died on the battlefield. . . . Amaziah took out another twenty thousand Edomites, and when Sennacherib set siege to Jerusalem under "strong, proud" Hezekiah, one hundred eighty-five thousand Assyrians were left dead by "the angel of the Lord."[81]

Some of these figures are undoubtedly exaggerations, but the world of biblical times was still a very violent world.

The agrarian states and empires that have dominated history were gigantic war machines. Indeed, war was their very reason for existence; the aim of war was political conquest, and the aim of conquest was wealth. By conquering other states, the conquerors could acquire "additional agricultural land; additional labour in the form of slaves and soldiers; additional fixed capital in the form of captured military equipment, irrigation systems, buildings, transport facilities, etc.; treasure; and additional tax revenue."[82] According to the Australian economic historian Graeme Donald Snooks, this strategy of economic gain was preferred to all others because it was the most cost-efficient and produced the greatest return on investment. In order to achieve this return, ancient civilizations had to give more emphasis to advancing their level of military technology than their level of subsistence technology. The advance of military technology in the ancient world occurred, Snooks says, because war was not a game but a business, and in fact a very big business.[83]

One of the great conquest states of the ancient world was the Assyrian empire, located on the northeastern edge of the Mediterranean. It began as a kingdom in the fourteenth century BCE and later grew to imperial status, achieving its heyday between the ninth and seventh centuries BCE. The Assyrians had iron-armored archers, armored spearmen, mounted troops with bows, and heavy two-wheeled chariots used as fighting platforms by bow-wielding aristocrats. These made up an incredibly powerful and successful fighting force. The Assyrians were not content with merely winning battles; they wanted to leave their opponents utterly destroyed and claim all of their wealth. In order to obtain all of the land, goods, slaves, metals, and treasure they sought, they had to destroy not only opposing armies but entire cities. They invented siege machines capable of bringing down city walls. Once the walls were down, systematic slaughter and looting began in earnest. The aim was total annihilation.[84]

The Roman republic, forming in the sixth century BCE, began expanding toward imperial status in the middle of the third century BCE and continued to expand for another three or four hundred years. The Romans had a well-organized professional army that moved on Rome's excellent roads. At its peak the army may have numbered close to 300,000 soldiers. Rome was so committed to militarism that 40–70 percent of state income was allocated to the military.[85] Even more than in Assyria, in Rome war was a business and a very expensive business. But it paid handsome dividends, bringing in enormous amounts of land, booty, taxes, and slaves. Slaves were particularly critical since they formed a vital part of the economy. Military expansion was essential in order to meet the constantly increasing demand for slaves.[86]

In the twenty-four centuries between 3000 and 600 BCE, the number of war deaths throughout the Old World remained fairly steady, but in the next six centuries war exploded in scale. During this period the number of war deaths increased seventy-fold.[87] War was clearly becoming much more deadly, and for two principal reasons. For one thing, empires were growing much larger, and larger empires meant more war against other, also larger, empires. In 1000 BCE, China had the world's largest empire, which extended over some 175,000 square miles, and all of the world's empires together covered approximately 400,000 square miles. Four hundred years later things had changed dramatically. In 600 BCE Persia had the largest empire at slightly more than 2 million square miles, and all of the world's empires combined extended over approximately 3 million square miles. And imperial growth continued. By 200 BCE the world's largest empire, which was located in central Asia, was about the same size as the earlier Persian empire, but the world's empires collectively covered nearly 6 million square miles.[88]

The increasing scale and deadliness of war also resulted from the development of iron weapons, which became more widely disseminated after 1200 BCE. Assyrian battering rams were equipped with an iron head, and Greek hoplite soldiers had bronze shields and helmets but iron swords and iron-tipped spears. The Chinese were also developing iron weapons during this time. They were much more effective than earlier bronze weapons, increasing the killing power of combatants dramatically.[89]

The vast majority of empires have been built on an agrarian base. This has usually been necessary in order to produce enough food to maintain a large state administrative complex and feed the armies that empires fielded. A few empires, such as the Aztec and Inca empires of the New World, were built on a horticultural base, but the horticulture was very intensive. Rarely could empires be constructed on a pastoral foundation, but the few that were are among the most fascinating in history. On the northern steppes of central Asia lived pastoral peoples who used horses for both food and riding. The horse was the central focus of economic and political life. These groups varied in political structure from tribes to chiefdoms to states to empires.

Most pastoralists large and small raid their sedentary agricultural neighbors for animals and other valuables. The states of the central Asian steppes developed their raiding strategy into a finely tuned art that was the key to their often enormous wealth. The earliest of the steppe empires, the Xiongnu, emerged in the third century BCE. The Xiongnu were extremely predatory, and their main victim was the great civilization to their immediate south, China. The Xiongnu would strike deep into China, looting, raping, burning, and capturing women, and then flee back to the steppes. As skilled horsemen and great marksmen, they acted with impunity because it was nearly impossible for the Chinese to pursue them successfully. Xiongnu society was puny compared to China. There were more than 50 million Chinese, whereas the Xiongnu numbered only a million. And yet the Chinese were relatively helpless.[90]

The Xiongnu terrorized China for several centuries. About the only recourse China had was to negotiate treaties. These would always be to the Xiongnu's advantage but at least they could produce a relative, if temporary, peace.[91] The other recourse was to erect fortifications to keep the Xiongnu out. Earthen walls were built in the third century BCE, and eventually these were integrated into what became the Great Wall. But even this massive structure was only partially effective in holding the raiders at bay.[92]

Like all empires, the Xiongnu eventually disintegrated and was replaced by others. Pastoral empires waxed and waned for nearly a thousand years until the greatest of all the steppe empires arose in the twelfth century. This was the Mongol empire of the infamous Chinggis Khan. At its peak the empire stretched as far west as Turkey and eastern Europe, as far east as the Pacific, and as far south as the northern edges of India and southeast Asia; it covered a territory of nearly 10 million square miles.[93]

The Mongol strategy was in broad outlines the same as that of the Xiongnu and other steppe empires: raid, loot, kill, burn, destroy, capture, and then ride back to the steppes. The Mongols and their predecessors sought not only economic valuables but women as well. Sometimes they went with their captors voluntarily because this resulted in greater safety and security.[94] The Mongols were so militarily powerful that their raids were great successes. But, ironically, they ended up being *too* successful. Their blitzkrieg style of warfare, still studied today by military strategists, ended up destroying almost everything and thus nearly killing the goose that laid the golden eggs.[95] What then to do? Earlier steppe empires did not attempt to conquer China, preferring to raid, loot, and escape. Conquering China would have meant administering it, and that could have changed everything.[96]

Yet the Mongols ultimately had little choice but to take over and rule what was left of China. A new dynasty, the Yuan dynasty, came to power in 1206, but Chinggis and his cohorts knew little about administering a state resting on sedentary agriculture. Fifty years of misrule ensued, especially with respect to the management of peasant agriculture. Like state administration, agriculture was alien to the Mongols and all of their predecessors. In time Chinggis was succeeded by Khubilai Khan, who turned out to be a much better administrator. He thought of himself as a Chinese emperor in a way that Chinggis did not and could not. The Yuan dynasty lasted until 1368, when it was finally conquered by Ming Chinese from the south. The Mongols then returned to their original home on the steppes.[97]

SUMMARY

1. Most homicides occur between members of the same family or between people who know each other. But killing within families seldom involves killing genetic relatives. The vast majority of intra-family killing occurs between spouses, most commonly husbands killing wives.

2. When a genetic relative is killed, it is most often children killing parents, usually because of severe abuse. Except for cases of infanticide, parents rarely kill children, especially older children. Usually parent-child killing springs from psychiatric disturbance.

3. In all known societies most homicide is committed by young males, especially those in the 20–24 age-group. The homicide rate begins to escalate rapidly for males around 14–15 and peaks at around 25. It then begins a sharp decline that continues throughout life.

4. Evolutionary psychologists consider conflict over women to be the leading cause of homicide in all societies. When young males kill, they kill mostly other young males. In order to promote their reproductive success, young males must acquire mates, and often the competition for mates is acute. A young unmarried male may kill to gain access to a mate, and a married young male may kill a young male who is attempting to poach the married male's wife. A married man may also kill his wife (and her lover) if he discovers them in an adulterous liaison.

5. Economic inequality in modern societies is highly correlated with homicide rates. As levels of inequality rise, more men are left at the bottom of the socioeconomic scale. Many of these men have poor prospects of obtaining a mate and thus the competition between them is greater than for men of higher status. Such competition increases the likelihood of homicide.

6. Like humans, chimpanzees are prone to violence. There are two main forms of violence in chimpanzee societies. Male chimpanzees compete fiercely for dominance, which invariably leads to high levels of conflict. In some cases the conflict ends in a killing. Chimps also engage in a collective form of violence that resembles human warfare. Males of one community may raid the territory of rival communities and kill some of the males. The principal motivation of the invading chimps apparently is to take over the territory of their rivals.

7. The similarities between humans and chimpanzees in their violent behavior suggests to some scholars that both species may have acquired their violent tendencies from their last common ancestor several million years ago.

8. Ethnographic and archaeological evidence shows that human warfare has been found everywhere at all times. In small-scale societies the most common form of war is the stealthy raid. In any particular raid only a few people may be killed, but frequent raids may produce a high death toll over time. In some societies a third of the male population will die from violence, most of it intercommunity violence.

9. Various theories of war in small-scale societies have been proposed. Some theorists have argued in favor of the scarcity of material resources. One idea is that groups like the Yanomama have few game animals and thus meat is scarce. Warfare causes villages to move farther apart, which leads to the formation of so-called no-man's-lands, or areas conducive to the replenishment of game. This theory is lacking in supporting evidence.

10. Another line of theorizing about small-scale war is that people weigh the costs and benefits of going to war and do so when there are important benefits to be gained and the likely costs are low. Some of the benefits of war include increasing access to scarce resources by eliminating competitors, capturing movable goods introduced through Western contact, imposing exploitative relationships on other groups, conquering and incorporating other groups, enhancing the power and status of war leaders, and defending against attacks by other groups. The first two of these suggested benefits seem reasonable enough, but the others are dubious.

11. Evolutionary psychologists stress that warfare in small-scale societies is primarily the result of competition for and conflict over women. This theory assumes that women

are a scarce resource in all small-scale societies for a variety of reasons. One of these is the practice of polygyny, which if widespread takes many women out of circulation and leaves many men without access to a wife. Evidence has accumulated from many societies that women figure importantly in both intra- and intercommunity violence.

12. War is easy to start and hard to stop in most small-scale societies because there is no centralized authority capable of preventing it. Such societies have no laws, police, or courts to prevent violence from getting out of hand.

13. In chiefdoms the motivations for war are different. Chiefdoms in circumscribed environments often suffer from land scarcity as population pressure builds up. Going to war against other chiefdoms may therefore be motivated by the need to acquire more land. But chiefdoms are also conquest societies in which the aim of war is to conquer rival chiefdoms for political and economic ends. Defeating rivals can be valuable in and of itself, but conquest can also bring valuable resources other than land, such as precious metals, valuable minerals, and treasure.

14. Nonindustrial states are the most predatory of conquest societies, and warfare has been waged between and among them for thousands of years. Nonindustrial states have more advanced military technology than chiefdoms and thus can wage deadlier wars. War is often the principal means of acquiring wealth and, indeed, a kind of highly lucrative business. The conquest of one or more nonindustrial states by another led to the formation of multinational empires in which the scale of war became even greater. Sometimes the goal of imperial conquest was the total annihilation of enemies.

QUESTIONS FOR DISCUSSION

- ✓ Homicides often occur between relatives. Opponents of evolutionary psychology contend that this fact shows that kin selection theory is flawed. How do evolutionary psychologists respond to this contention?

- ✓ Using evolutionary principles, explain why the vast majority of homicides throughout the world involve young males killing other young males.

- ✓ It is sometimes said that women "civilize" young men. What does this mean from a Darwinian point of view?

- ✓ There is a close relationship between the level of income inequality in a community and its homicide rate. Why should this be?

- ✓ Why is there a close relationship between rates of life expectancy and homicide rates in different American neighborhoods? What sense does this make in Darwinian terms?

✓ In so-called love-triangle homicides, who tends to kill whom and why?

✓ It has been claimed that the human mind is designed to kill. Is this an outrageous statement lacking factual evidence, or is there something to it? Discuss.

✓ In the movie *Planet of the Apes*, chimpanzees are portrayed as peace-loving animals. Is this a realistic portrayal? Discuss by comparing chimpanzees and humans.

✓ Many anthropologists have claimed for decades that war is relatively uncommon in small-scale societies. Will this claim hold up to scrutiny?

✓ What are some of the reasons why war may occur in small-scale societies? Discuss by comparing evolutionary and nonevolutionary theories.

✓ Once war starts in small-scale societies, it is hard to stop. Why should this be?

✓ How do the motives for war differ between large-scale societies (chiefdoms and states) and small-scale societies?

✓ Give examples of some of the most predatory empires in world history. On what kind of economic foundation did these empires rest?

✓ In the second half of the first millennium BCE, the scale and deadliness of war increased dramatically. Why should this have happened?

✓ Pastoral societies on the Eurasian steppes frequently raided and looted China. Since the Chinese had much greater numbers, how could the raiders get away with this nefarious behavior?

✓ Why did the Chinese build their Great Wall?

References and Notes

1. Daly and Wilson 1988.
2. Daly and Wilson 1988.
3. Wolfgang 1958; Wilbanks 1984. Both as summarized in Daly and Wilson 1988.
4. Studies reviewed in Daly and Wilson 1988.
5. Daly and Wilson 1988.
6. Hirschi and Gottfredson 1983.
7. Daly and Wilson 1988.
8. Blau and Blau 1982.
9. Krohn 1976, correlation coefficient = .600; Kennedy, Kawachi, and Prothrow-Stith 1996, correlation coefficient = .725; Daly and Wilson 1997, correlation coefficient = .811. Results summarized in Daly, Wilson, and Vasdev 2001.
10. Daly, Wilson, and Vasdev 2001, correlation coefficient = .845.
11. Blau and Blau 1982.
12. Daly, Wilson, and Vasdev 2001.

13. Many readers will be inclined to ask, "But isn't much violence about gangs and drugs?" Yes, gangs and drugs are part of the equation, but we have to consider why gangs and drugs exist in the first place. They are mainly about lower-status males gaining access to resources, which is necessary to attract women.

14. Daly and Wilson 1988.

15. Daly and Wilson 1990.

16. As is well-known, the American West in the nineteenth century was an especially violent place. In many areas the sex ratios were extremely imbalanced, which was one of the reasons there was so much violence. In Nevada County, California, in 1851–1856, the homicide rate was 83 per 100,000 population; for Leadville, Colorado, in 1880 the figure was 105; and for Bodie, California, during the period 1878–1882 it was 116. Compare these rates to eastern US cities during the same period: 5.8 per 100,000 for Boston and 3.2 for Philadelphia. As for sex ratios, in Dodge City, Kansas, in 1875, there were nearly five times as many men as women in the 20–29 age range; and in Wells County, Dakota Territory, in 1885 there were nine times as many men as women in the 20–29 age range. Women were often reluctant to accompany their husbands (or prospective husbands) to the frontier West, but in time more did. And women also began to go west on their own in search of husbands. Thus sex ratios became more balanced, and as they did homicide rates dropped. The women were civilizing the men. (These figures come from David Courtwright's extraordinarily interesting book, *Violent Land: Single Men and Social Disorder from the Frontier to the Inner City*, 1996.)

17. Daly and Wilson 1997.

18. Wilson and Daly 1997.

19. Daly and Wilson 1988.

20. Buss 2000.

21. Buss 2000.

22. Wilson and Daly 1993.

23. Wilson and Daly 1993. See also Wilson, Johnson, and Daly 1995.

24. Daly and Wilson 1988.

25. Chagnon 1983.

26. Wilson and Daly 1993.

27. Wilson and Daly 1993.

28. Research summarized in Buss 2005.

29. Buss 2005.

30. Buss 2005, p. 37.

31. Buss 2005.

32. De Waal 1982, 2005.

33. De Waal 2005, p. 45.

34. Wrangham and Peterson 1996; De Waal 2005; Wade 2010.

35. Mitani, Watts, and Amsler 2010.

36. Mitani, Watts, and Amsler 2010.

37. Wade 2010.

38. McCauley 1990; Keeley 1996; LeBlanc 2003.

39. Otterbein 1989.

40. M. H. Ross 1983.

41. Jorgensen 1980.

42. Shaw and Wong 1989.

43. Keeley 1996.

44. Otterbein 1989.

45. M. H. Ross 1983.

46. The figures are summarized in Gat 2006.

47. Walker and Bailey 2013.

48. Walker and Bailey 2013.

49. Wrangham, Wilson, and Muller 2006.

50. Thirty years is chosen as an upper limit because it approximates the length of time over which a

man would have opportunities for killing. It might be slightly too high, which is why the number twenty is also given.

51. Shankman 1991; Roscoe 2011.
52. Roscoe 2011.
53. Heider 1970, p. 111; cited in Roscoe 2011, p. 60.
54. Roscoe 2011.
55. Roscoe 2011, p. 66.
56. Roscoe 2011.
57. Gat 1999, 2006.
58. Gat 1999.
59. Chagnon 1983, 2013; Gat 1999.
60. Harris 1984; Divale and Harris 1976.
61. Chagnon 1983; Chagnon, Flinn, and Melancon 1979.
62. Ferguson 1989.
63. Ferguson 1984, 1990a.
64. Ferguson 1990b, 1995; Ferguson and Whitehead 1992.
65. Ferguson 1990b.
66. Steadman, personal communication.
67. Gat 2006.
68. Symons 1979.
69. Chagnon 1988, 2013.
70. Chagnon 2013.
71. Betzig 1986.
72. Gat 2006.
73. Chagnon 1988.
74. Ferguson 1990a.
75. Broch and Galtung 1966.
76. Carneiro 1990.
77. Carneiro 1990.
78. Carneiro 1990, p. 193.
79. Carneiro 1990, pp. 193–194.
80. Kirch 1984.
81. Betzig 2009, p. 52.
82. Snooks 1996, p. 276.
83. Snooks 1996.
84. Snooks 1996.
85. Mann 1986.
86. Snooks 1996; Gat 2006.
87. Eckhardt 1992.
88. Taagepera 1978; Eckhardt 1992.
89. Derry and Williams 1961; Mann 1986; Runciman 1998.
90. Barfield 1989.
91. Barfield 1989.
92. Barfield 1989; Gat 2006.
93. Eckhardt 1992.
94. This is a good point at which to emphasize that the motive of acquiring women does not disappear in warfare conducted by chiefdoms, states, and empires. Women are never completely out of the picture, even if the main aim is political and economic conquest. In some instances women may become the main motive. In his fascinating book *The Rape of Troy* (2008), Jonathan Gottschall discusses the Trojan War during the time of Homer in ancient Greece (about 1000 BCE). Homeric society was primarily organized into chiefdoms. Gottschall finds in Homer's *Iliad* constant references to women as the leading cause of war. Gottschall explains that in Homeric society sex ratios were highly imbalanced: there were many more males than females of marriageable age. This was probably because of extensive polygyny in which elite men took many women out of circulation, and also because of preferential female infanticide

in a highly patriarchal society. In most societies organized at the chiefdom level or above, women will not be the principal cause of war, but all warriors in these societies know that women will be part of the benefits of the successful side. Indeed, note that a constant in warfare in societies of all types is rape of enemy women. This has probably occurred in virtually every war that has ever been fought, including wars in modern industrial societies. And the scale of rape is often extensive.

95. Barfield 1989; Gat 2006.
96. Barfield 1989.
97. Barfield 1989; Gat 2006.

12

Race and Ethnicity

Race is a volatile subject, especially in the United States—one of the most racially divided and racially tinged societies the world has ever seen. This chapter seeks to shed light on this subject from an evolutionary perspective. Physical differences between anatomically modern human populations were probably small before humans left Africa some fifty thousand years ago. But as the exodus from Africa occurred, and as humans spread throughout the world, they encountered a wide range of climates very different from the ones they left behind. Many climates were colder, had different types of flora and fauna, and so on. New physical adaptations became necessary if humans were to thrive in these environments. Racial differences were the outcome of migrations into new environments.

The chapter first discusses the current debate between those who argue for the traditional view that races are biological categories and those who adopt the more recent perspective that racial distinctions are social constructions having little to do with biology. Then we turn to the all-important question of racism. Is racism largely a product of the plantation slavery that emerged in Western civilization several hundred years ago? Or is it much more widely found? Does racism exist in non-Western societies? And is it modern or ancient? Did ancient societies such as Greece and Rome exhibit racism?

Finally we consider ethnicity, the close cousin of race. People's attachments to their own ethnic groups, or those usually defined primarily by culture and language, are worldwide and often very intense. Is this because people have an innate tendency to attach to such groups and favor them over other groups? And if so, what accounts for such a tendency? Is ethnic attachment an evolutionary adaptation?

The Origins of Races

Fifty years ago anthropologists and sociologists, and nearly everyone else, thought of races as objective biological categories and of three main racial groups. They classified races according to skin color, nose and head shape, stature, presence or absence of an epicanthic fold (extra eyelid), and so on. The basic classification identified three main groups, sometimes called racial "stocks"—Caucasoid, Mongoloid, and Negroid—each of which was further subdivided.

For some time this terminology has been considered highly objectionable, and around 1960 began to disappear from the textbooks. By the 1980s the idea emerged that races are not objective biological categories at all but merely *social constructs*, or imagined categories that were originally invented by Europeans and Americans to justify the subordination of blacks, and to some extent other groups (e.g., American Indians, Japanese Americans, Chinese Americans). An entire academic industry grew up called "whiteness studies." The basic idea was that the concept of "whiteness" did not exist until the last three or four centuries, when it became socially and politically useful. Until then no one ever thought of themselves as "white." The idea of whiteness became something of a buzzword and was often accompanied by another buzzword, "white privilege." The two terms fit together hand in glove since the basic contention was that whiteness was invented for the purpose of gaining and hanging on to privilege.

In his introductory anthropology textbook, University of Michigan anthropologist Conrad Kottak succinctly states the constructionist perspective: "Races are culturally constructed categories," he says, "that may have little to do with actual biological differences."[1] He concedes that biological diversity is obvious, but assigning people to distinct groups is difficult. Races are not biologically distinct categories, Kottak avers, ultimately concluding that in anthropology race is a "discredited concept."[2]

Thinking about race has changed dramatically in less than half a century. However, human variation is studied in many countries throughout the world, and some do not follow the current American perspective. In a survey of Polish biological anthropologists conducted in 1999, only 25 percent rejected the race concept, a dramatic contrast with the 76 percent of American biological anthropologists who rejected it.[3] Even more interesting are the findings from a survey of articles on human variation published in the journal *Acta Anthropologica Sinica*, the only Chinese journal of biological anthropology. Rather than asking anthropologists questions about what they thought, the authors, Qian Wang, Goran Strakalj, and Li Sun, examined all of the articles on human variation ever published in this journal between 1982 (the year it was founded) and 2001, 324 articles in all. Every article used the race concept and it was not questioned even once.[4]

Why would all Chinese biological anthropologists and three-quarters of Polish biological anthropologists accept the race concept, while only 24 percent of American biological anthropologists accept it?[5] The answer is not hard to find: the United States has a long history of divisive relations between blacks and whites going all the way back to slavery in the eighteenth century. It has been the second-most racially divided society in modern history (after South Africa) and much of its "race problem" remains to be solved. But Poland never imported slaves from Africa to work on plantations, and only a tiny number of people of African descent have ever lived there. The same is true for China—a non-Western society with a very different historical and cultural tradition extending back thousands of years. Race is not a central issue, or even a minor one, in Polish or Chinese social life. As a result, scholars in these countries are able to do research and formulate theories of human variation unencumbered by the highly politicized racial environment found in the United States. Polish and Chinese biological anthropologists have the luxury of studying human variation without worrying about what political implications someone might draw from their research. The Chinese probably don't give it a second thought.[6]

The idea that race is not real except as a social construct and an ideology leaves a lot to be desired, but it does contain an important grain of truth. Racial distinctions are not always thought of in the same way in all societies. The United States has a two-category system of racial classification that is based on a mental calculus that Marvin Harris calls the rule of hypodescent, more commonly known as the "one drop rule."[7] There are only two groups, whites and blacks, and a person must belong to one or the other. There is no middle ground. To be placed in the white category, once must be, or at least appear to be, unambiguously white. If there is any degree of blackness—just "one drop" of blackness, either objectively or as a matter of perception—then one is classified as black. Of course, perception doesn't always line up with biological reality so that a person with some African ancestry who has no apparent African traits can pass as white.

The one drop rule, however, has not always been applied consistently. Many decades ago, for example, it was common to speak of "mulattoes," people known to be of mixed race. This term has long since disappeared and has been replaced by "biracial." Still, blacks continue to apply the one drop rule to themselves even more vigorously now than they ever did. The vast majority of people who know they have black ancestry consider themselves black. The one drop rule originated among whites and is still used by them, but its most ardent proponents today are black nationalists and so-called Afro-centrists. They strongly identify with being black and want blacks to maintain a separate identity. The one drop rule actually serves their interests because it increases the number of blacks in the country.

After the United States, the world's most racially divided societies are South Africa and Brazil. South Africa's system includes three categories—whites, blacks, and mixed-race persons called "coloureds." But since this system does not differ significantly from the US system, we can pass over it. It is traditionally understood that the Brazilian system comprises a wide range of racial categories that shade into each other based on various combinations of skin color, eye color, hair color, and hair texture. But people do not necessarily belong to just one category. In fieldwork conducted in Brazil in the late 1950s and early 1960s, Marvin Harris showed subjects photographs of people of widely varying physical appearance. He asked them to name the category to which the person in the photograph belonged. There was widespread disagreement among the people Harris questioned; any given person could be assigned to a range of different categories by different people. To complicate matters even more, Brazilians classify people in terms of income and wealth in addition to physical appearance. There is a famous Brazilian saying: "Money whitens the skin." This means that people who look almost exactly alike can be assigned to different categories if they are of different economic means, with the better-off person in a lighter category. This makes it possible for people to change their racial identity simply by becoming richer.[8]

However, not everyone accepts this view of how Brazilians think about race. Francisco Gil-White contends that it confuses race with color. When Harris and his colleagues asked Brazilians to identify the race of the person in the photograph, the respondents were really thinking of color differences, which are, of course, extremely diverse in Brazil. But color is only one dimension of race, which is why so many respondents could identify full siblings as belonging to different categories. Slight variations in skin tone among full siblings could be picked out and different labels attached. In the minds of Brazilians racial categories are deeper, broader, and more fundamental than color labels, and focusing on the latter confuses the former. Gil-White concludes that Brazilian racial categories are not as fuzzy and flexible as Harris and others have suggested, and thus that the Brazilian and US systems are not as different as traditionally thought.[9]

A recent study by Ricardo Ventura Santos and six collaborators provides evidence that seems to support Gil-White's contention.[10] They interviewed 425 Brazilian students between the ages of thirteen and twenty-one and asked them to indicate the color/race category to which they belonged. Eighteen different categories were identified, but just four categories made up 94 percent of the responses. These were: 42.4 percent *branca* (white), 32.2 percent *parda* (brown), 11.8 percent *negra* (black), and 7.1 percent *morena* (mulatto, but also used to indicate brown). Several of the categories were named by only 0.2 percent of the respondents, and none of these other categories was named by more than 1.6 percent. Apparently the Brazilian system is not so fuzzy and complex after all.

Nevertheless, it still differs from the US system in that there is no rule of hypodescent. Moreover, Santos and colleagues found that some 20 percent of their respondents placed themselves into a different category when they were reinterviewed four months later. So the system is certainly more flexible than the US system. This greater flexibility suggests that the constructionists are not completely wrong. And yet constructionism is a rather odd perspective. The traditional view that races are objective biological categories continues to have numerous advocates, and this position is bolstered by new research in molecular genetics. Several studies come to extremely similar conclusions about how races can be categorized based on genetic similarities and differences between populations worldwide. One study looked at the genomes of 354 individuals from eight different populations representing every major world region. It found four distinct racial clusters: Africans, Caucasians, Asians, and Pacific Islanders.[11] A second study looked at 1,056 individuals from fifty-two different world populations and found six clusters, five of which correspond to major geographical regions.[12] The Stanford University geneticist Neil Risch and his colleagues summarized the results of these studies and several others by identifying five basic racial groups: Africans, Caucasians, East Asians, Pacific Islanders, and Amerindians.[13] As Risch notes, these groups correspond remarkably well to "the classical definition of races based on continental ancestry."[14] Moreover, the groups were so similar to people's subjective perception of their own racial category that self-reported ancestry could reliably be used as a proxy for genetic race.

The classification above is organized from the oldest to the most recent human populations, Africans being the oldest and Amerindians being the youngest. Thus the classification provides additional support for the Out of Africa theory of modern human origins. As we saw in Chapter 2, humans left Africa 50 to 60 Kya and then fanned out into Europe and southwest, central, south, southeast, and east Asia. From extreme northeast Asia (Siberia) some crossed the Bering land bridge into Alaska about 20 Kya and quickly populated the Americas.

Risch points out that skin color is usually given too much significance as a racial marker. Indeed, the studies summarized by Risch did not even use genetic markers for skin pigmentation. To quote Risch, "none of the population genetic studies [that were examined] used skin pigment of the study subjects, or genetic loci related to skin pigment, as predictive variables. Yet the various racial groups were easily distinguishable on the basis of even a modest number of random genetic markers."[15]

Constructionists frequently point out that there are no "pure" races.[16] True, but the argument is a red herring. Given the enormous amount of migration throughout human history and prehistory, how could there be? Moreover, no serious scholar has ever claimed that there are pure races, only genetically related individuals who tend to cluster together despite being genetically related to other clustered populations. This, of course, is precisely what Risch and other population geneticists are now showing. Yet if we wish we can also think of race differences as varying along a fine-grained continuum. This can be a useful exercise as long as we do not use it to speak of "endless variation" and "meaningless" or "arbitrary" clusters. Racial traits vary along a continuum, but the continuum is "lumpy"—very lumpy.

Where then did racial variation come from? Why does it exist? The obvious answer is migration into different environments with different climates. As people moved out of Africa, they had to adapt to the new conditions they faced. One important adaptation involved skin color. Dark skin is highly adaptive in extremely hot and sunny climates where ultraviolet radiation (UVR) reaches its highest levels. Table 12.1 shows skin tones for a wide range of human populations along with the latitudes at which these populations live and the levels of UVR they receive.[17] The correlations between skin color and latitude and skin color and UVR are extremely high, in fact nearly perfect.[18] Skin color is darkest at the lowest latitudes with the highest levels of UVR, lightest at the highest latitudes with the lowest levels of UVR.

Hominins living in Africa were once rather hairy with pinkish skin. As these hominins gradually lost most of their body hair, there had to be selection for darker

TABLE 12.1   Skin Color, Latitude, and Ultraviolet Radiation for Selected Societies

Country	Skin Color	Latitude	Ultraviolet Radiation
Uganda	7.67	0.2	350
Rwanda	7	2.0	350
Zaire	7	4.2	350
Ghana	7	5.3	350
Kenya	6.67	1.2	350
Saudi Arabia	4	24.4	350
Egypt	4	28.8	250
Thailand	3.67	14.7	300
Lebanon	3.67	33.5	250
Jordan	3	31.6	250
Syria	3	33.3	250
Cyprus	2	35.1	250
Greece	2	37.6	200
Spain	2	40.2	200
Japan	2	40.3	200
China	2	41.2	200
Hungary	1	47.4	150
Germany	1	52.3	150
Denmark	1	55.4	100
Finland	1	60.1	50

Source: William H. Durham, *Coevolution: Genes, Culture, and Human Diversity* (Stanford, CA: Stanford University Press, 1991); Gabrielle Bloom and Paul W. Sherman, "Dairying barriers affect the distribution of lactose malabsorption," *Evolution and Human Behavior* 26 (2005):301e1–301e33; R. Biasutti, *Le Razze e Popoli della Terra* (Torino, Italy: Unione Pipografiza-Editrice Torinese, 1967).

Skin color is measured using the 1–8 scale devised by Renato Biasutti, where higher numbers represent darker skin. Latitude is distance from the equator north or south. Ultraviolet radiation is measured in standardized units of UV-A radiation, which can penetrate the dermis of the skin.

skin. Without dark skin, people living under such conditions would be highly vulnerable to a number of serious negative effects. It was once thought that the main function of dark skin in climates with high UVR was to protect against skin cancer, but new research suggests a different answer. In a major study, Nina Jablonski and George Chaplin point out that even though dark skin in areas of high UVR does protect against skin cancer, skin cancers such as basal cell and squamous cell carcinomas have little effect on fitness because they usually occur later in life after individuals have finished reproducing.[19] High UVR damages light skin in numerous ways, but the most important seems to be its effect on the body's metabolism of folic acid. Folic acid is necessary for DNA biosynthesis. The body converts folic acid to folate, which is necessary for normal human development. High UVR acting on light skin causes folate photolysis (decomposition), and has severe consequences for health and reproductive success. One of the most severe consequences is neural tube defects in developing embryos. The embryos may become anencephalic, meaning that the brain remains a mass of undifferentiated cells. Anencephalic embryos sometimes survive to term but almost always die shortly after birth. The disease spina bifida is another common result of insufficient folate. It is also a critical factor in spermatogenesis, and decomposition of folate may cause infertility. Jablonski and Chaplin conclude that

> regulation of folate levels appears to be critical to individual reproductive success. Folate levels in humans are influenced by dietary intake of folic acid and by destructive, exogenous factors, such as UV radiation. Therefore, the solution to the evolutionary problem of maintaining adequate folate levels in areas of high UV radiation involved the ingestion of adequate amounts of folic acid in the diet and protection against UV radiation-induced folate photolysis. The latter was accomplished by increasing the concentration of the natural sunscreen, melanin, in the skin.[20]

But why did skin lighten as people moved from low to high latitudes? We encountered this question in Chapter 4 in the discussion of lactose absorption, skin color, and milk drinking among northern European populations. The lightening of the skin wasn't just a matter of the skin losing its melanin because it was no longer needed, much as a rodent with eyes loses them as it evolves into a mole and lives underground. Lighter skin was *adaptive* under the new conditions. As we saw in the earlier discussion, very light skin helped pull in ultraviolet radiation so that the body could make more vitamin D to enhance calcium absorption.[21]

Outside of Europeans, the populations that experienced the greatest degree of skin depigmentation were in northeast Asia. As shown in Table 12.1, northern Europeans (Hungarians, Germans, Danes, and Finns) score a 1 on the Biasutti skin color scale, whereas northeast Asians (Japanese and Chinese) score 2. Why did skin color lighten more in Europe than in northeast Asia? Because of lower levels of UVR in northern Europe, northern Europeans were under more selective pressure for synthesizing vitamin D from sunlight, and greater lightening of the skin facilitated this. In this regard, note from Table 12.1 that southern Europeans (Spaniards and Greeks) have the same skin color score as northeast Asians, 2. In southern Europe there are higher levels of UVR than in northern Europe, and thus there was less need for the skin to become extremely light.

Interestingly, several genes involved in skin pigmentation have now been identified, and it appears that the genes responsible for depigmentation in European populations are not the same as those responsible for depigmentation in northeast Asians.[22] This is another example of what evolutionary biologists call *convergent evolution*: similar traits emerging independently from different starting points. (The first example was the evolution of lactase persistence in Europe and Africa discussed in Chapter 4.) Unfortunately, the genetic analyses that have demonstrated this are so technical and complex that they fall beyond the limits of this discussion.

Racism Then and Now

No concept has been more thoroughly debased and emptied of meaning than the concept of *racism*. Not so very long ago it had a precise meaning, but lately it has come to mean almost everything having to do with race, and therefore nothing at all. "Racism" is a word used so freely and carelessly that it has become not only useless but insidious and dangerous. The term has come to stand for anger, hostility, or discrimination against the members of another racial group, or even for taking note of such obvious racial differences as variations in skin color. Moreover, the definition of racism has been expanded to include a power dimension. Being a racist requires belonging to a racial group that is deemed to hold social power, and thus members of racial groups presumed to have less power cannot by definition be racists. In addition, the concept has become partially detached from individuals and reattached to social entities, such as corporations, schools, and governments. Even if the individual members of these entities are not themselves racists, the entity itself is said to be racist if any inequalities exist between its racially diverse members.[23]

What does the term "racism" mean in its undebased form? The definition of the eminent race-relations specialist Pierre van den Berghe cannot be improved on. He says that racism "is the belief that certain physical attributes, such as skin pigmentation or facial features, are linked to attributes of intellect, morality, or behavior, and thus establish a hierarchy of quality or worth between sub-groups of our species. The core of racism is thus the belief that inherited, visible phenotypes of physical appearance are causally linked to abilities or behaviors by biological inheritance."[24] It is often added that members of different racial groups deserve their positions in society and that no special provisions should be made to change such arrangements. Indeed, because race differences are ineluctably biological, racial differences in social outcomes are essentially uncorrectable.

We need to recapture this original meaning in order to determine who or what is racist, whether racism is the main cause of racial inequality in societies like the United States, and whether racism has declined, persisted, or worsened. Here a sense of historical perspective is useful. How old is racism and what societies or civilizations have exhibited it?

The standard view is that racism is a unique product of the past few hundred years and was not exhibited in any of the ancient civilizations.[25] Oliver Cromwell Cox, an eminent African American sociologist of the mid-twentieth century, claims for example that there is "no basis for imputing racial antagonism to the Egyptians, Babylonians, or Persians," adding that "we do not find race prejudice even in the great [Greek] Hellenistic empire which extended deeper into the territories of colored people than any other European empire up to the end of the fifteenth century."[26] Nor did the Romans express racism, Cox contends, because they made invidious distinctions on the basis of cultural rather than physical differences. Since they drew slaves from provinces occupied by people of different races, they made no connection between slavery and race. Slaves were regarded as inferior beings, but no race was thought to have a "monopoly on stupidity." Audrey Smedley takes essentially the same view, criticizing scholars who naively assume that humans have an innate tendency toward racism and race prejudice. Smedley sees racism as a unique product of Western European and North American capitalist expansion between the sixteenth and nineteenth centuries.[27]

But not everyone agrees. Thomas Gossett, for example, contends that racism is widespread and perhaps even universal, finding racism or race prejudice in ancient India, in early Chinese thought, and among the ancient Jews.[28] In India, he says, race prejudice was evident as long as five thousand years ago because in-migrating Aryans made disparaging remarks about darker-skinned Indians. Chinese historians of the Han dynasty in the third century BCE spoke "of a yellow-haired and green-eyed barbarian people in a distant province 'who greatly resemble monkeys from whom they are descended.'"[29] And among the Jews, "the prophet Ezra preached the abomination of mixing the seed of Israel with that of the Ammonite and the Moabite."[30]

In fact there is growing evidence for the historical antiquity of racism. In the great ancient civilizations there was certainly an awareness of race differences. Royal tombs in ancient Egypt suggest that the Egyptians marked off four main races: the Egyptians themselves, who were painted red; Asiatics, painted yellow; Negroes, painted black; and westerners or northerners, who were painted white with blue eyes and fair beards. The Egyptians saw blacks in negative terms. For example, Pharaoh Sesostris III ridiculed Africans, calling them weak and faint-hearted.[31]

In ancient Rome there is evidence of "racialized thinking," or racial stereotyping. For example, the Romans thought that Africans—they were most familiar with Ethiopians—were hypersexual and highly musical, stereotypes similar to those found today. In ancient Greek and Roman art blacks were often shown with especially large penises, sometimes erect. Whether or not the Romans developed an ideology of racial superiority is unclear. As noted above, Cox argues that the Roman sense of superiority over everyone was based on cultural rather than racial differences.[32] And yet the Romans referred to blacks as "monkeylike," which is certainly a reference to more than their culture and is more than a mere stereotype.[33]

Be that as it may, the "prize" for ancient racism goes to Islamic civilization. Like the Egyptians, Arabs and Muslims regarded blacks as having great sexual appetites and abilities. The ninth-century Islamic poet and satirist Janiz of Basra wrote that they had boundless stupidity and nasty dispositions. They were derided as cannibals and as not knowing their own fathers. In the tenth century a certain Maqdisi said that their minds were so defective that learned men were virtually unknown among them. In the thirteenth century the geographer Nasir al-Din Tusi declared that the only difference between blacks and other animals was that blacks walked on two feet. Others thought apes were more intelligent and educable than blacks, and that blacks were carefree, happy, and possessed a natural rhythm.[34] There is great irony here, since a substantial number of black Americans have adopted Islam as a religion, and some have even declared that Islamic civilization consisted of blacks.

So racism is clearly very old and frequently took a form resembling modern racism. And yet the racism that developed after about 1500 became a much more pervasive feature of social life than earlier forms of racism. This date marks the beginnings of Europe's exploration of the New World and its establishment of slave plantation colonies in the United States, the Caribbean, and parts of Central and South America, especially Brazil. The labor for these plantations was drawn from Africa, and Africans were sold into slavery by other Africans in exchange for European goods. The entire European adventure marked the first sustained and large-scale contact between peoples of European and African descent.

Why then a highly developed racism beginning in the sixteenth and seventeenth centuries? A very popular argument is that it arose as an ideological justification for the enslavement of millions of Africans.[35] If the people who are enslaved are biologically inferior or perhaps even subhuman, then there is no reason they should be deserving of the same rights as others. This argument depends on the assumption that because England, France, and the United States had moved significantly in the direction of concepts of the rights of man, then stripping black Africans of freedom required special justification to avoid moral contradiction. The contradiction could be avoided if blacks were defined as something other than fully human. After all, such leading founders of the newly formed United States as George Washington and Thomas Jefferson were strongly devoted to human rights yet owned slaves.

One difficulty with this argument is that racism did not end when slavery was abolished. Indeed, it picked up steam in the second half of the nineteenth century and peaked around 1920.[36] If racism was merely an ideological prop of slavery, then it should have disappeared or at least declined once slavery ended. A second problem is that this theory cannot tell us why racism against blacks was much stronger than racism against American Indians, nor can it explain racism in Brazil, by far the largest slave plantation society in the New World. Brazilian slave owners were under no particular pressure to justify slavery on moral grounds because neither Brazil nor the society from which the slave owners hailed, Portugal, had any democratic principles at all. There was thus no unsettling sense of moral contradiction between stealing the freedom of some groups and maintaining an abstract notion of human rights.[37]

A further difficulty is that slavery was not really a racial institution but an economic one. Europeans did not choose Africans as slaves because they considered them biologically inferior, but rather because Africa provided a huge supply of labor that could be transported to the New World more cheaply than slaves drawn from, say, India or China, which were much farther away.[38] Slavery has an extremely long history and until modern times never had a close connection with race. Indeed, it will no doubt come as a shock to most readers to learn that there were actually *black* slave owners in the United States.[39] Some of them inherited their plantations and slaves from their white masters, who may have developed affection for them, felt guilty about enslaving them, or may have had no other heirs. Yet most of the black slave owners were free blacks who actually purchased their properties.[40] And these slave owners ran their plantations in the same way as white slave owners. The plantations were capitalist institutions devoted to making a profit.[41]

A final problem is that racism was found among many of Europe's leading intellectuals. Leading thinkers of the Enlightenment, such as Hume, Voltaire, Montesquieu, and Kant, were among the most prominent racists. None of these men owned slaves or participated in the institution of slavery. The classic description of European racism is found in the book *The Inequality of Human Races*, written in 1853 by Joseph Arthur de Gobineau, a French diplomat and scholar who had a close tie to the celebrated theorist of American democracy, Alexis de Tocqueville.[42] Even Karl Marx uttered racial slurs on a number of occasions. In the United States, the great emancipator, Abraham Lincoln, although opposed to slavery, believed that blacks were intellectually inferior, worrying that they could never compete on equal terms with whites once they were free citizens. In fact, it is probably fair to say that racism was the standard view of Europeans and North Americans throughout these centuries, regardless of the position they occupied in society. It probably would have been hard to find someone who was *not* a racist.

Is there, then, another serious theory of racism? One possibility is that racism is the most intense form of ethnic animosity. As we will see later in the chapter, there seems to be a natural tendency for people to sort themselves into groups based on language and cultural differences, and these groups often take dim views of each other. Under various circumstances, antagonism emerges between them and sometimes reaches severe levels. People look for markers of group identity and can seize on relatively small things. But physical differences are in many ways the most prominent markers, especially if they are conspicuous. Europeans have the lightest skin of all of the world's populations, whereas people of African descent have the darkest (although Dravidians in south India and aboriginal Australians also have very dark skin). And these populations differ in other readily observable ways as well (e.g., hair texture, nose shape). However, this view remains highly controversial and has not really been tested empirically. Whether there is anything to it is difficult to say.

In any event, whither racism? Has it declined? Yes, certainly, and not only in the public sphere but also in the private. As recently as 1960 the United States was an overtly racist society. It was considered perfectly acceptable to make racist remarks either in public or in private, to tell racist jokes, to invoke racial stereotypes, and so on, and all of these things occurred with considerable frequency. But that is no longer true. This does not mean that racism has disappeared. Of course racists still exist, but most of them hide their beliefs because about the worst thing you can call someone in the United States today is a racist. Racism has become completely delegitimized, especially in the public sphere.

However, many sociologists continue to insist that the United States is still a fundamentally racist society; it is just that racism has gone underground and become much more subtle. Moreover, it is charged that racism continues to be the main reason for the ongoing plight of blacks. The existence of economic inequality between blacks and whites is taken to be indisputable evidence of persistent racism and its behavioral counterpart, racial discrimination. Study after study and book after book by sociologists make such a claim over and over again. For example, in his book on contemporary Brazilian race relations, Princeton University sociologist Edward Telles shows that the Brazilian pattern of racial inequality is very similar to the American pattern. People of dark skin earn less and stand lower on the socioeconomic ladder than people of light skin. And black-white differences fit neatly along a continuum; the darker their skin, the worse off people are. Telles automatically assumes that this is evidence of a pattern of racial discrimination mimicking the US pattern. Unfortunately, he does not present any evidence that discrimination is the actual cause of racial disparities; he simply infers it from the disparities themselves.

Is there anything else that might account for these patterns? A reasonable suggestion has been offered by George Farkas and Keven Vicknair, sociologists at the University of Texas–Dallas. Farkas and Vicknair hypothesized that differences in cognitive skills might explain persistent wage gaps between blacks and whites, a hypothesis they tested by using data from a large national sample of male workers between the ages of twenty-six and thirty-three for the year 1991. Their findings strongly supported the hypothesis. Once differences in cognitive skills were taken into account, the wage gap not only disappeared but actually shifted slightly in favor of blacks. In other words, when blacks and whites were compared at the same level of cognitive skill, *blacks actually out-earned whites!*[43] (In referring to cognitive skills Farkas and Vicknair are not talking about IQ. They are talking about the kinds of cognitive skills taught in schools, such as reading, mathematics, and analytical reasoning.)

The authors conclude that blacks are not lagging behind whites because of discrimination, but because of the abysmal quality of the majority of the schools they attend. Because their schools are so poor, they are not developing the cognitive skills needed to compete with other groups on an equal basis. Of course, this leaves unanswered the question of why schools attended largely by blacks are so poor. Farkas and Vicknair do not seem to be entirely sure of the answer but ponder the matter by asking a series of questions:

> Why have real expenditures for public schools soared without showing commensurate increases in student achievement? . . . What sociological factors have affected the public schools so that even as African-American mayors and school administrators have become increasingly prominent during the 1980s and 1990s, the school performance of inner-city African-American students has failed to significantly improve? . . . What programs will help inner-city children to read at grade level and achieve the cognitive skills necessary for employment in good-paying jobs? Which of the many current school reform proposals will significantly improve the school performance of the hundreds of thousands of at-risk students in our nation's cities?[44]

Although Farkas and Vicknair are not sure why so many predominantly black schools are failing, they do insist that school failure, rather than alleged discrimination and racism, must be the focus of efforts to change the situation.

There is an additional wrinkle on the racism theme that merits attention. Several studies have shown that the relationship between skin color differences and differences in social outcomes is more fine-grained than any simple white-black distinction can capture. Among blacks themselves skin tone variations are correlated with income level and socioeconomic status. Two studies published just a year apart drew on the National Survey of Black Americans, a sample of over two thousand American blacks. Both found that lighter-skinned blacks had better outcomes than darker-skinned blacks, and the differences were substantial. Using a five-point scale of skin color ranging from very light to very dark, the authors of the second study, Verna Keith and Cedric Herring, found that 31 percent of very light blacks held professional and technical occupations compared to only 11 percent of very dark blacks. With respect to income, the average annual income for very light blacks was $10,600 compared to only $6,500 for very dark blacks.[45] The authors of the first study, Michael Hughes and Bradley Hertel of Virginia Tech, obtained very similar results despite a cruder indicator of skin color, a three-point rather than a five-point scale. But Hughes and Hertel went a step beyond Keith and Herring in comparing differences among blacks to differences between blacks and whites. They found that the light black–dark black differences in social outcomes were nearly as great as the black-white differences. For example, 26 percent of light or very light blacks were employed in professional or technical occupations compared to only 14 percent of dark or very dark blacks. This was almost identical to the difference between blacks and whites: 28 percent of whites were in professional or technical occupations compared to 15 percent of blacks. With respect to income, light or very light blacks were earning $12,600 a year compared to only $9,150 for dark or very dark blacks; whites were earning $17,250 a year, blacks $10,150.

Hughes and Hertel do not offer an explicit explanation of their findings, simply stating that "skin color is an important factor in the life chances of black Americans."[46]

However, Keith and Herring do, attributing their findings to discrimination against darker-skinned blacks by lighter-skinned blacks. They note that skin tone differences within the black community have always been important: "During slavery, advantages went to mulattoes and other fair-skinned blacks. Through the years, the offspring of these lighter-skinned blacks have also realized relative advantage."[47] Unfortunately, this explanation leaves unanswered the question of why blacks of lighter skin would look down on blacks of darker skin. Why is there not some sort of black solidarity? Is there some sort of human tendency, expressed both across and within racial groups, to regard light skin as somehow "better" or "superior"? If so, that itself would need explaining.

Ethnic Primordialism

Closely related to race is ethnicity. The two are usually distinguished on the grounds that racial groups are based on physical differences, ethnic groups on culture and language. Now that many anthropologists and sociologists have decided that race is social rather than biological, this distinction is more problematic for them than it used to be. However, for those who subscribe to the notion that races are objective biological categories, the distinction presents no problem.

Ethnic groups, or *ethnies*, are groups like the Dutch, the Italians, the East Indians, the Turks, and the Japanese. In earlier days we would have spoken of the Egyptians, the Assyrians, the Persians, the Mongols, the Romans, the Gauls, the Chinese, and the Aryans (of course, we can still speak of the Chinese, the world's oldest continuous civilization). But race and ethnicity often overlap, as in distinguishing the Chinese and the Japanese from the Dutch and the Italians, or Ethiopians and Nigerians from Moroccans and Algerians.

The question arises as to how ethnies view themselves. Do they think of themselves *only* in terms of culture and language, *primarily* in terms of culture and language but *secondarily* in terms of physical traits, or in terms of a more *equal mixture* of culture, language, and physical traits? This varies from one group to another. European ethnies, for example, think of themselves primarily in terms of culture and language because the physical differences between them are not very large. The Dutch speak Dutch, grow tulips, have an extensive system of canals, and have a distinctive type of architecture. They also have certain important social norms, such as not closing your curtains or drapes in the evening until you are ready for bed (their reasoning is that people who close their drapes have something to hide). The French, by contrast, speak French and love fine cuisine, art, and philosophy. Their architecture is also distinctive. So it is likely that the Dutch and the French distinguish themselves primarily in terms of these cultural traits.

However, the Dutch and the French can be distinguished physically, although the differences are subtle. It is difficult to distinguish a Dutchman from a German, but it is possible to recognize a Frenchman on the basis of a narrow face, close-set eyes, and a long, pointed nose. (Not all French people have these traits, of course. It's just that they are more common among the French than among other groups.) It is even easier to distinguish the French from, say, the Norwegians. The Norwegians have much rounder faces, a trait common in very cold climates because rounder faces help retain heat, and usually much lighter hair. And it is still easier to distinguish northern Europeans from such southern Europeans as Italians and Spaniards. Italians and Spaniards have slightly darker skin and there is less variation in hair and eye color.

This can be taken further. Francisco Gil-White once asked a Mixtec Indian from Oaxaca, Mexico, if someone could become a Mixtec if his parents were not Mixtec. The Mixtec reacted with incredulity, wondering what on earth the question could mean. His response was that you can only be Mixtec if your parents are Mixtec.[48] This is ethnicity as genetic ancestry, not simply culture and language. Gil-White also studied groups of Kazakhs and Mongols in Mongolia. He asked the Kazakhs the following question: "Let's say that a child's father is Kazakh and his mother is Mongol, but everybody around the family is Mongol and the child has never seen any Kazakhs, other than his father. The child will learn Mongol customs and language. What is the ethnicity of the child?" Eighty-three percent said the child would be Kazakh. For them, it was genetic ancestry that mattered, not culture. Since the Kazakhs were patrilineal, ethnicity was identified in terms of the ancestry of the child's biological father.[49]

Gil-White posed a follow-up question: "A Kazakh couple gives up their child to a Mongol family. The child is completely absorbed into Mongol culture, never sees a Kazakh, and does not know that he was adopted. What is this child's ethnicity?" The majority of Kazakhs still said that he was Kazakh, and many were extremely insistent. Gil-White then asked them, "Do you mean that culture and language don't matter at all?" A frequent response was something like, "That's right, the only thing that matters is the ethnicity of the *törcönaav* [birth father]. The kid may not know it, but he's still Kazakh."[50]

Sometimes one ethnic group will be absorbed into another. In Kenya, some Turkana were absorbed into Samburu and intermarried with them, but it took time for them to actually *become* Samburu. Only after at least two generations could they be accepted as Samburu. Similarly, in Malaysia some Arabs were assimilated into a Malay identity, but only after several generations of intermarriage. If multigenerational intermarriage is required, obviously these ethnic groups are thinking of themselves in biological terms.[51]

Gil-White's research suggests to him that most people think of ethnicity in terms of the same type of category they use for biological species.[52] This shows beyond any real doubt that ethnicity has a large genetic component in the minds of the ethnies themselves. But this is also true objectively speaking. Because ethnies have a bias toward endogamy, or in-marrying, the members of an ethny will be more genetically similar to each other than to other ethnies. Of course, in many instances the genetic differences will be very small (English vs. Danes, Dutch vs. Germans, Japanese vs. Koreans, etc.). So technically perhaps these groups might more accurately be called "ethnogenetic" or even "ethnoracial" groups.

The geneticists L. Luca Cavalli-Sforza, Paolo Menozzi, and Alberto Piazza, in their celebrated book *The History and Geography of Human Genes*, provide detailed data on the genetic distances between forty-two ethnic populations from all over the globe.[53] Representative numbers for twelve of the populations are shown in Table 12.2. Low scores in the table indicate close genetic relatedness between two populations, whereas high scores indicate genetically distant populations. It can easily be seen that the Danish, English, and Italians are closely related to each other, only moderately related to Uralic peoples, Inuit, and Japanese, and very distantly related to African Bantus and Mbuti. Similarly, Japanese, Koreans, and Mongols are closely related but are quite distant from Bantus and Mbuti. Iranians and East Indians are close, which is to be expected since it was the so-called Aryans from Iran and surrounding areas who migrated into India several thousand years ago bringing with them their religious ideas and their languages (and as we now know, their genes). Polynesians are most closely related to the southern Chinese and Micronesians. This also makes sense in light of the fact that it was peoples from southern China and southeast Asia who first colonized the Pacific islands, first the nearby Micronesian islands and later the more distant Polynesian islands. And note especially that the Mbuti are the population that is most distant from every other population, followed by the Bantu. This is to be expected, considering that Africans are the oldest human populations on earth.

Why is ethnicity so important, and why does it have a significant biological component in the minds of most of the members of ethnic groups? Some students of ethnic relations adhere to a theory known as *primordialism*.[54] For evolutionists, the basic idea is that ethnic affiliation is an evolutionary adaptation. In early times ethnicity took the form of tribalism. Under the conditions in which tribes lived, the way things were done in one's own tribe was seen as the right way; other tribes were not only denigrated but were often seen as less than human. Indeed, the usual meaning of a tribe's name for itself is "humans." Ethnic groups in today's world are in a very real sense extremely large tribes.

But why would a tendency toward strong tribalism and ethnic identity be an evolutionary adaptation? What would be adaptive about it? Pierre van den Berghe points out that ethnies are a lot like kin groups because the people in them are more closely related to one another than to the members of other ethnies. People who favor their own ethny are in essence practicing an extended form of kin selection. Although people's genetic relationship to the members of their own ethny is less close than to the members of their kin group, they still share many genes in common with co-ethnics. And to identify with co-ethnics means to act cooperatively toward them and aid and assist them. In the most extreme case, it means going to war to defend their ethny against other ethnies.

TABLE 12.2 Genetic Relationships Among Selected World Ethnic Populations

Population	Genetically Closest	Genetically Intermediate	Genetically Most Distant
African Bantu	African San (94), Nilo-Saharan (118)	Basques (1474), Greeks (1479)	New Guineans (3372), Melanesians (3375)
East Indians	Iranians (154), Near Eastern (229)	Malaysian (1130), African San (1246)	Bantu (2202), African Mbuti Pygmies (2663)
Iranians	Greeks (70), Indians (154)	Indonesians (1246), Mon Khmer (1282)	Bantu (2241), Mbuti Pygmies (2588)
Japanese	Koreans (137), Mongols (218)	English (1244), East Africans (1345)	Bantu (2361), Mbuti Pygmies (3089)
Koreans	Japanese (137), Mongols (170)	Filipinos (1218), Sardinians (1327)	Bantu (2668), Mbuti Pygmies (2996)
Thai	Mon Khmer (99), Southern Chinese (105)	Northern Turkic (1225), Inuit (1417)	Bantu (3364), Mbuti Pygmies (3872)
Southern Chinese	Thai (105), Mon Khmer (254)	Danish (1306), New Guineans (1503)	Bantu (2963), Mbuti Pygmies (3384)
Danish	English (21), Italians (72)	Uralic (828), North American Indians (948)	Bantu (1708), Nilo-Saharans (1723)
English	Danish (21), Italians (51)	Uralic (1023), Mon Khmer (1100)	Bantu (2288), Mbuti Pygmies (2373)
Italians	Iranians (133), Basques (141)	Inuit (1135), Japanese (1145)	Bantu (2292), Mbuti Pygmies (2931)
Central Amerindians	South American Indians (159), North American Indians (291)	Polynesians (1313), Filipinos (1527)	Nilo-Saharans (2701), Mbuti Pygmies (3499)
Polynesians	Southern Chinese (508), Micronesians (512)	Chukchi (1575), African San (1940)	Bantu (2649), Mbuti Pygmies (3136)

Source: L. Luca Cavalli-Sforza, Paolo Menozzi, and Alberto Piazza, *The History and Geography of Human Genes,* abr. ed. (Princeton, NJ: Princeton University Press, 1994).

Favorable action toward co-ethnics can thus promote one's "extended inclusive fitness."[55] This means that people have not only economic and political interests but *genetic* interests as well; ethnic genetic interests are reproductive interests writ large.[56] As one scholar of the problem has put it, "Ethnies are indeed superfamilies. . . . Although being more dilute stores of genetic interest than families, ethnies can number in the millions and so are often orders of magnitude more precious."[57] This is what lies at the root of ethnic identification and, ultimately, the various forms of ethnic conflict. The great Darwin himself weighed in on this:

> A tribe including many members who, from possessing in high degree the spirit of patriotism, fidelity, obedience, courage and sympathy, were always ready to aid one another, and to sacrifice themselves for the common good, would be victorious over most other tribes; and this would be natural selection.[58]

SUMMARY

1. Until recently race was conceptualized in biological terms. Races were seen as populations that could be distinguished on the basis of physical characteristics, both observable and unobservable. But in recent years many anthropologists and sociologists have rejected the notion that race is biological. They claim that race is really a social category. It is a social construction that attempts to "naturalize" race.

2. The social constructionist view has become dominant among contemporary anthropologists and sociologists. A linchpin of the constructionist argument is that there are no pure races, and that human populations shade into each other gradually. However, recent genetic research is showing that although there are no "pure" races, it is possible to divide the world's populations into reasonably discrete categories on the basis of genetic markers, even ignoring skin color as one of the markers. One classification identifies five main groups: Africans, Caucasians, East Asians, Pacific Islanders, and Amerindians.

3. Racial variation has arisen over the past 50,000 years as anatomically modern humans left Africa and migrated into the other major regions of the world. Racial differences emerged primarily because of climate differences. For example, dark skin is highly adaptive in regions of low latitude that have very high levels of ultraviolet radiation. Without dark skin, people living in these regions would suffer skin damage and some of its serious biological consequences, which would reduce both survival and reproductive success. As people moved to higher latitudes with lower ultraviolet radiation, their skin lightened. When ultraviolet radiation is low, light skin is adaptive be-

cause more radiation can penetrate the skin and allow the body to make more vitamin D to enhance calcium absorption.

4. The social constructionist view is not necessarily completely wrong because different multiracial societies think about races and classify them in somewhat different ways. For example, Brazilians think about race in a more complex and nuanced way than Americans do. The American system is based on a rule of hypodescent in which there are only two groups, whites and blacks, and all people belong to one or the other. The Brazilian system has no such rule. It is more complex and flexible, with a wider range of racial categories.

5. The term racism is used with great frequency in the modern world, especially in multiracial societies like the United States. But the concept is now used so broadly and to refer to so many things regarding race that it has become useless if not dangerous.

6. The original meaning of the term racism is a set of beliefs that link racial differences to attributes of intellect, morality, or behavior, and that create a hierarchy of superiority and inferiority among different racial populations. Those who hold racist beliefs usually think that different races deserve the positions they hold in society because of unchangeable genetic differences.

7. Some students of race contend that racism did not exist until Europeans began to conquer parts of the world, especially the New World, in the sixteenth century. Other scholars hold that racism existed in many ancient civilizations. They point to racial beliefs and stereotypes that are similar to beliefs and stereotypes held today.

8. The evidence suggests that racism in one form or another preceded modern racism by several millennia. Nevertheless, modern racism has been more intense and pervasive than earlier forms of racism and has had much greater consequences for the racial structure of modern societies.

9. It is often argued that modern racism arose as a justification for slavery. It was considered acceptable to deny certain groups full human rights and enslave them if they were genetically inferior to those doing the enslaving. However, racism did not end after slavery was abolished, and in fact grew stronger, which suggests that this argument for the origins of racism is likely wrong. There are other problems as well. The theory cannot explain why racism against blacks was stronger than against American Indians. It would also be hard-pressed to explain why many leading European intellectuals, who had no involvement with slavery, held racist beliefs.

10. Whether racism persists or has declined is hotly debated by both scholars and laypersons. There is also extensive debate over whether persistent racial inequality is

the product of racism and its behavioral correlate, discrimination. Some say that persistent racial inequality is the product of differences in cognitive skills between whites and blacks. In this view, many blacks are held back by the poor development of the kinds of cognitive skills taught in schools, and this is the result of the very poor schools that the majority of blacks attend. One difficulty in assessing these arguments is that there are inequalities among blacks themselves. Lighter-skinned blacks tend to outperform darker-skinned blacks, a difference that has a long history in the United States.

11. Ethnic groups, or ethnies, differ in terms of language and culture. But they also differ genetically. For example, the English, Danes, and Italians are very closely related, as are Japanese and Koreans. Greeks, Indians, and Iranians are closely related, as are African Bantu, African San, and Nilo-Saharans. Most ethnies recognize that they are distinctive genetically and use genetic criteria as well as language and culture as an important dimension of group identity.

12. People throughout the world are most closely attached to kin, but after kin their most important attachments are ethnic. Some Darwinians contend that ethnic attachments are evolutionary adaptations, a variant of a view known as ethnic primordialism.

13. A Darwinian explanation for people's strong sense of ethnic identity is that ethnicity is an extended form of kin selection. People are obviously less closely related to members of their own ethny than to their kin, but they are more closely related to members of their ethny than to the members of other ethnies. Ethnicity is a diluted form of genetic relatedness relative to kinship, but people have a very small number of kin compared to perhaps many millions of co-ethnics. Favoring millions of co-ethnics therefore has important inclusive fitness consequences.

QUESTIONS FOR DISCUSSION

✓ What does it mean to say that race is a social construction rather than a set of biological categories?

✓ Why do you think the social constructionists oppose the traditional idea that race is biological?

✓ Evaluate the position of those who continue to say that race consists of objective biological categories. What kind of evidence do they use? If there are biological races, how many of them are there?

✓ Assuming for the sake of argument that race is biological, why are there race differences among peoples throughout the world? How old might race differences be?

✓ How do the American and Brazilian systems of racial categorization differ? Are they completely different systems or are there important similarities?

✓ What is the original meaning of the term racism? In what ways has this meaning changed in recent decades?

✓ Where and when has racism existed?

✓ What is the relationship between racism and slavery, both in recent centuries and in ancient times?

✓ Why is there racism in the world? Discuss.

✓ Evaluate the claim that persistent inequality between whites and blacks in the United States is attributable to racism and racial discrimination.

✓ Are ethnies just groups distinguished by culture and language, or is there something more that differentiates them? Discuss.

✓ What is the degree of genetic relatedness between English and Danes? Between Greeks and Iranians? Between Danes and Nilo-Saharans? Between Japanese and Bantu?

✓ In what way may a strong sense of ethnic attachment be an evolutionary adaptation?

✓ Explain what it means to say that strong ethnic identity is a form of extended kin selection.

References and Notes

1. Kottak 2000, pp. 148–149.

2. For other representative statements of the constructionist viewpoint, see Cartmill 1999 and Smedley 1999. See also the official statement on race put out by the American Anthropological Association, published in the *American Anthropologist* 100 (1998): 712–713.

3. Kaszycka and Strzalko 2003.

4. Wang, Strakalj, and Li 2003.

5. Lieberman and Kirk 2002.

6. Strakalj 2007.

7. Harris 1964.

8. Harris 1964.

9. Gil-White 2001b.

10. Santos et al. 2009.

11. J. F. Wilson et al. 2001, as discussed in Risch et al. 2002.

12. Rosenberg et al. 2002.

13. Risch et al. 2002. And see Wade 2006.

14. Risch et al. 2002, p. 3.

15. Risch et al. 2002, p. 4.

16. Templeton 1999.

17. The skin color scores are based on the eight-point scale devised by Biasutti 1967. Jablonski and

Chaplin 2000 have computed an alternative measure of skin color for forty-five societies. They use skin reflectance as an indicator of skin color. Lighter skin reflects more sunlight than darker skin. Of the forty-five societies, the highest skin reflectance score is for the Netherlands at 67.37, the lowest is for Mozambique at 19.45. For the forty-five societies, the Biasutti scores correlate at -.918 with the Jablonski-Chaplin scores, which suggests that both are very good measures of skin tone.

18. Correlation coefficients: skin color X latitude = -.941, skin color X ultraviolet radiation = .943. The coefficients are based on a larger group of fifty-five societies.

19. Jablonski and Chaplin 2000.
20. Jablonski and Chaplin 2000, p. 63.
21. Jablonski and Chaplin 2000.
22. Norton et al. 2007.
23. Van den Berghe 1996.
24. Van den Berghe 1996, p. 1055.
25. Cox 1948. See also Smedley 1993; D'Souza 1995.
26. Cox 1948, p. 323.
27. Smedley 1993.
28. Gossett 1963. See also Kovel 1984; Todorov 1993.
29. Gossett 1963, p. 3.
30. Gossett 1963, p. 4.
31. Sarich and Miele 2004.
32. Cox 1948; Thompson 1989.
33. Sarich and Miele 2004.
34. Sarich and Miele 2004.
35. Cox 1948; Noel 1972; Foner 1975.
36. Van den Berghe 1967.
37. D'Souza 1995.
38. Wallerstein 1974.
39. Halliburton 1975.
40. Oakes 1982.
41. Fogel and Engerman 1974.
42. D'Souza 1995.
43. Farkas and Vicknair 1996. See also Farkas et al. 1997.
44. Farkas and Vicknair 1996, p. 559.
45. Hughes and Hertel 1990; Keith and Herring 1991.
46. Hughes and Hertel 1990, p. 1116.
47. Keith and Herring 1991, p. 775.
48. Gil-White 1999.
49. Gil-White 1999.
50. Gil-White 1999, p. 797.
51. Hjort 1981; Nagata 1981. Both as discussed in Gil-White 1999.
52. Gil-White 2001a.
53. Cavalli-Sforza, Menozzi, and Piazza 1994.
54. Van den Berghe 1981; Vanhanen 1999; Reynolds, Falger, and Vine 1987.
55. Salter 2002, 2003.
56. Salter 2002, 2003.
57. Salter 2002, p. 123.
58. Darwin 1871.

13

Religion

Religion consists of beliefs and practices devoted to postulated supernatural agents. The beings may be gods or certain types of spirits. Numerous religions have many gods that are much like humans: some do good and thus are considered useful to humans, whereas others do evil and need to be avoided, or at least not antagonized. In other religions there is One True God who is not human-like, but rather a transcendent God who is outside the universe and brought it into existence. In many societies there may be no real gods at all, but simply an array of greater and lesser spirits. In many small-scale societies there are witches, which are thought to be capable of great harm. Some societies, especially those in Oceania, have religions that contain *mana*—an abstract supernatural force rather than a specific god or spirit.[1]

In this chapter we will consider the wide range of religious phenomena. We begin by looking at some examples of spirits, gods, and ritual specialists in small-scale societies. Then the focus shifts to the primordial religious practitioners, shamans, and the important role they play in hunter-gatherer societies. In the following section, we examine the nature of religion in advanced horticultural and agrarian societies organized into chiefdoms and states. For several millennia these societies had polytheistic religions, or pantheons of gods with specialized roles to play in the lives of humans. In time monotheistic societies, or societies with one very powerful God, evolved. We ask why polytheism persisted so long but eventually gave way to monotheism (without, however, disappearing). Having surveyed these forms of religious life, we ask why there are so many differences, but also why there are important similarities and why people in all societies have religious beliefs and practices. The chapter concludes by looking at recent critiques of the human religious experience and efforts to abolish it.

Spirits, Gods, and Ritual Specialists

Many years ago the sociologist Guy Swanson attempted to survey the types of gods that nonindustrial societies have. He came up with a category that he called "high gods."[2] A high god is a deity who is "the ultimate source of events in nature and supernature."[3] If a society has a high god, this god must be the only god, although there can still be other supernatural beings and forces of lesser scope. High gods are often thought to have created the universe. They may or may not be worshiped, and may or may not be interested in human affairs. Some high gods simply withdraw after the act of creation. Others may take an interest in only some human activities.

Swanson was careful to point out that the high gods of the vast majority of non-industrial societies, especially very small-scale societies, are very different from the gods of the great world religions, such as Judaism, Christianity, and Islam. Unfortunately, he then contradicted himself by sliding back into calling any society with a high god "monotheistic." This term should be reserved for the world religions that emerged in the second half of the first millennium BCE, which we discuss later in the chapter.

Many small-scale societies don't have a high god of any type. Of the hunter-gatherer societies in the SCCS, 13 percent have an active high god, 31 percent an inactive high god, and 56 percent no high god at all. Among horticulturalists, 22 percent have an active high god, 42 percent an inactive high god, and 36 percent no high god. Among intensive agricultural or agrarian societies, 46 percent have an active high god, 27 percent a high god that is inactive, and 27 percent no high god. There is a clear evolutionary trend: societies at more-advanced stages of social evolution are more likely to have a high god, especially one who takes an interest in human affairs. If we add modern industrial societies to the picture, nearly all have an active high god, but this god will be quite different from earlier high gods.

Among the Santal of India, there are some 150 spirits or deities known as *bongas*, which are associated with various clans or subclans. Most *bongas* are benevolent, but there are malicious ones. These are the forest *bongas*, which include the souls of people who died under unnatural or suspicious circumstances.[4] The Ojibwa Indians of North America conceived of many spirits and forces, some benevolent (or at least benign) and some malicious. The benevolent ones were largely forces of nature, such as the sun, moon, four winds, thunder, and lightning, whereas the malicious ones were ghosts, witches, and a supernatural cannibalistic giant, Windigo. There was also a great spirit, Kiccimanito, that presided over all the others.[5]

Religion is much more than beliefs. It also consists of a range of important rituals, and rituals require certain types of religious practitioners or specialists. The simplest rituals are individualistic. Here individuals perform their own rites, which often involve going out into the wilderness on vision quests. This is "do-it-yourself" religion.[6] Shamanic rituals are extremely widespread and involve intense interaction between a shaman and one or more clients, or sometimes the entire community. There are also collective rituals in which segments of a community, or perhaps the entire community, perform rites associated with agriculture or puberty. Ancestor worship is another type of collective ritual. It is extremely widespread, and some scholars think it universal.[7]

The Gond of India had shamans who performed classic shamanic rituals. They believed that illness and other misfortune were caused by evil spirits or by deities who had been offended. Diviners and soothsayers were charged with determining what kinds of supernatural agents were responsible and trying to appease them.[8] The Santal had healer-diviners who functioned in the same manner as the Gond diviners. The Santal also performed life cycle rituals—those involving initiation, marriage, and death—and collective agricultural rituals, especially in regard to sowing, transplanting, and harvesting crops.[9] Among the Comanche of North America, individualistic practices dominated, the male vision quest being the most important.[10]

The religious specialists of bands and tribes are usually informal and perform part-time. In more-complex societies we find priests who monopolize religious knowledge and may be full-time specialists. Priests perform rituals for laypersons, who largely function as an audience. The Maori, an advanced horticultural society in New Zealand, had priests who received specialized training. The polytheistic and monotheistic religions of the ancient world all had priests as their leading specialists.

Another important type of religious practitioner is the prophet. Prophets proclaim new religious ideas and seek a following for them. In essence, they found new religions and help them spread. The best-known prophets, of course, have been the Jewish prophets, Zoroaster of ancient Iran, Jesus, Muhammad, the Buddha, and, in very recent times, Joseph Smith, the founder of the Mormons.

Shamans and Healers

Shamans have been found throughout the world and are nearly universal in hunter-gatherer societies. This type of religious specialist would have been the principal religious practitioner in the vast majority of societies in the human ancestral environment. Shamanic religion is thus the primordial religion, and shamans the primordial religious specialists. But shamans continue to be found in religions at more-advanced evolutionary stages.[11]

The shaman performs a variety of activities: healing and curing illness, divination, protecting and finding game animals, communicating with the dead, recovering lost souls, and protecting people from evil spirits and malevolent magic. Shamans also go on "soul flights" and "vision quests." Shamanic rituals typically involve rhythmic repetition, especially drumming, dancing, singing, and chanting, activities that are thought to induce an altered state of consciousness. There are striking similarities among shamanic practices all over the world, which suggests that they have been independently developed time and again on a common psychobiological basis.[12]

The key shamanic ritual is the curing ceremony. The shaman involves the local community in activities imbued with a variety of emotional experiences, especially fear and awe. Shamans enact struggles involving animals and spirits and summon their spirit allies who accompany them on their vision quests. They typically chant, sing, beat drums, and dance in violent and excited ways. After collapsing from exhaustion, shamans begin their magical flight into the spirit world, which normally involves ascending to the upper world and then descending to the lower in order to communicate with spirits and try to obtain their cooperation in earthly matters.[13]

Shamans claim to be able to control spirits, and their communities agree that they can. Shamanic curing assumes that illness results when people have lost their souls, or when they are under the influence of ghosts, spirits, witches, or malevolent acts performed by other shamans. The altered states of consciousness that shamans undergo are trance-induced by means of hallucinogens or opiates and other drugs; through hunger, thirst, loss of sleep, or other forms of sensory deprivation; or by extreme forms of sensory stimulation.[14]

The Sakha are a people of northeast Siberia, the region of the world where shamans were first discovered centuries ago. The word *shaman*, in fact, is borrowed from a Siberian language. The Sakha live through hunting, fishing, and herding. They exhibit the classical form of shamanism. Shamans fall into trances as community members beat drums, sing, dance, and recite. In a state of ecstasy, the shaman travels to other worlds to retrieve souls that evil spirits have abducted, to pacify angry spirits, and to approach good spirits with requests from members of the community.[15] Shamans among the !Kung enter into trances for the purpose of curing illness and protecting people from malevolent spirits. A trance state is thought to occur when a shaman pleases a spirit and is temporarily absorbed into it. This absorption allows the shaman to locate the source of a person's illness and then to heal him by using such ritual devices as tortoise shell rattles, herb bundles, charms, and beads. Then the shaman tries to pull the illness out of his body. !Kung shamans also play an important role in attempting to prevent food shortages. In a trance a shaman summons animal spirits and attempts to mediate between them and the animals.[16]

Although shamans dominate most religious activity among hunter-gatherers, they continue to be important in horticultural societies. They persist, at least in the slightly altered forms that Michael Winkelman, an anthropologist specializing in shamanism, calls shaman-healers, healers, sorcerer-witches, and mediums.[17] These new types of practitioners are not all that different from shamans, however; they engage in many of the same activities, especially healing. Moreover, shamans continue to be found even in societies where religions with formal doctrines and full-time priesthoods have developed. Indeed, in affluent industrial societies a religious practitioner strikingly reminiscent of the ancient shaman is found in the form of the "faith healer." Modern faith healers, like many of their shamanic counterparts, lay their hands on a person and try to pull his illness out of him. In the 1950s and 1960s there was a famous faith healer in the United States by the name of Oral Roberts. He held large evangelical meetings during which he invited people to come up to the stage and be healed. He would lay his hands on the person and actually show them flesh that he claimed he had extracted from them. Apparently the person believed it, but later it was discovered that he was actually showing things like pieces of liver that he hid behind his back while performing his rite. Or at least so it was claimed by skeptics.

Many Gods or One?

As noted above, in the vast majority of small-scale societies there is no high god or, if there is, this god is usually not active in human affairs. Many kinds of spirits are present, and there may be gods other than high gods, but in most cases these will be gods of limited scope. With the transition to some large-scale chiefdoms, as well as to most states, gods become more numerous, more active, and more powerful. This brings us to the polytheistic religions of the ancient world.

Polytheistic religions have pantheons of highly specialized gods and professional priesthoods that monopolize religious knowledge and lead elaborate rituals for a lay audience. A striking feature of the gods is their anthropomorphic character: they are very much like humans. Some are considered good, others evil; some are highly competent at what they do, whereas others are considered fools; the gods usually eat and drink and often have great banquets; they usually like sex and often have orgies; they marry and have offspring; they also fight and go to war. Like humans, anthropomorphic gods are finite and mortal; they can be killed and even eaten.

The most famous polytheistic religions were those of the ancient Sumerians and Egyptians, the ancient Greeks and Romans, and the Maya, Aztecs, and Incas in the New World. The Aryans who invaded India around 1500 BCE brought with them a polytheistic religion, and some Polynesian and African chiefdoms and states have had early forms of polytheism. The Inca of ancient Peru worshiped a creator god known as Viracocha, who was thought to have created the other supernatural beings. These included the sun, the weather god, and the moon, stars, earth, and sea. There was a specialized priestly class that was organized into a hierarchy that paralleled the political hierarchy.[18] The Egyptians believed in a supreme power, or *neter*, who created the universe and a number of lesser gods, or *neteru*.[19] These included Horus, the falcon god; Re, the sun god; and Osiris, the god of vegetation. Each god had its own priesthood.[20] The ancient Greeks worshiped a pantheon that included Zeus at the top; Phoebus, the god of light; Poseidon, the sea god; Aphrodite, the goddess of love; and Dionysus, the god of vegetation.[21] Among the Egyptians and the Greeks each city or city-state tended to focus its religious activity around one particular god. The Egyptian god Amon, for example, was the god of Thebes in Upper Egypt, and the Greek goddess Athena was the patron god of Athens.

During the historical period known as the Axial Age, between about 600 BCE and 1 CE, there was an important shift from the polytheistic religions of the ancient world to the so-called world religions, several of which were monotheistic.[22] The first monotheism was Zoroastrianism, which arose in Iran sometime in the sixth century BCE. Judaism had already existed for several hundred years, but it was polytheistic until around 600 BCE, when it evolved into its more familiar monotheistic form. Its most prominent god, Yahweh, was elevated to the position of the One True God. Several hundred years later Christianity emerged out of Judaism, the result of messianic movements that had been occurring within Judaism for some two centuries. The Near Eastern peoples who developed Judaism and Christianity were all intensive agriculturalists or pastoralists or practiced some combination of the two.[23]

There were many important novelties in the new world religions: the shift from an anthropomorphic god to a *transcendent* god that was little like humans and was omnipresent, omniscient, and omnipotent; an emphasis on salvation from this world and on God's love and mercy; increasingly elaborate religious doctrines; and increasingly powerful priesthoods. As noted earlier, Swanson applies the term "monotheism" to small-scale religions with a high god, but this is a serious error. The single high god of the new monotheisms had little in common with the high gods of small-scale societies. He was much more powerful in many ways, always took great interest in human affairs, was always worshiped, and was never identified with such natural phenomena as the sun or moon. He was indescribable in ordinary terms because he transcended all physical reality. As God spoke to Moses, "I am that I am."

Why Are People Religious?

In the evolutionary study of religion, there are two central questions. First, why are people religious everywhere we find them, and second, given that they are religious, why are there so many different types of religion? We have sketched out various types of religious beliefs, rituals, and religious practitioners, but have made little attempt to explain these differences. Before doing that, we must try to answer the more general question: why is there religion at all? A variety of theories have been offered to explain religion,[24] but our concern here is with the new Darwinian approaches. In the last fifteen or twenty years there has been an explosion of scholarly work on religion by evolutionary psychologists and anthropologists.[25] There have been two main evolutionary approaches, *by-product theories* and *adaptationist theories*.

By-Product Theories

The best-known evolutionary by-product theories of religion are those of Pascal Boyer and Scott Atran.[26] They contend that the key feature of religion is *counterintuitive beliefs* in supernatural agents, and that these agents are for the most part structured by our natural intuitions. Humans have cognitive modules for agency in the sense that they recognize that persons have goals and pursue various means to reach them. One of humans' most important cognitive modules is an *agency-detection module*, which is biased toward overdetection. Because of our evolutionary heritage, we need to be able to detect both predators and prey, and it is far better to overdetect than to underdetect because the costs of not detecting agents when they are around are much greater than the costs of detecting them when they are not around. In the ancestral environment it was highly adaptive for humans to know what animals or other humans might be around and capable of doing them harm.

Religious beliefs emerge from agent-based interpretations of complex events. Human brains are programmed to look for agents as the causes of complex and uncertain happenings. In social interaction, people manipulate this hypersensitive cognitive aptitude so as to create the agents who order and unite the culture and the cosmos. People in all religions believe that the world has been purposefully created by unseen agents, that humans have souls that live on after their bodies die, and that through rituals they can persuade gods or spirits to change the world for human betterment. A central focus of the supernatural agents that the human brain constructs involves dealing with people's existential anxieties—death, disease, pain, catastrophe, loneliness, injustice, want, loss, and so on.

For by-product theory, in the evolution of the human brain there was no specific selection for religious concepts. Thus there is no specialized "religious module" in the brain, no network of neurons that is specifically designed for handling thoughts about supernatural entities. Religious concepts have "piggybacked" on the extremely adaptive evolutionary imperative to look out for predators and other sources of danger. In sum, for by-product theorists, religion is an evolutionary phenomenon but only in an indirect way.

Adaptationist Theories

Although by-product theory is currently the more widely adopted approach, some interesting adaptationist theories have been developed. Richard Sosis uses costly signaling theory to explain why religious rituals are so important in all religions.[27] According to Sosis, ritual is the primary mechanism through which religious communities maintain beliefs among their members. Since relaxed rituals are not especially costly to perform, they are "easy to fake." Consequently these religious communities are easily invaded by free riders who seek to reap the benefits of religious membership while paying low costs. Demanding rituals, on the other hand, are costly and thus more difficult to fake.

When religious communities ask their members (or prospective members) to pay such costs, they are asking for clear signs of commitment. Continued participation in costly rituals actually serves to create or intensify religious belief. At the same time, strong believers come to evaluate ritual performances as less costly than those whose beliefs are weaker. Strong believers see ritual performance as less of a burden, and moreover, the opportunity costs of engaging in other behaviors are lower. Strong believers therefore receive a large payoff in religious group membership, whereas people who cannot muster a sufficient level of belief and commitment tend to drop out. Thus, in enhancing belief and commitment, costly, hard-to-fake rituals contribute to interpersonal trust and social cohesion. The key benefit of religion is that it enhances group cooperation, and this in turn has individual fitness benefits.[28]

Sosis and his colleague Candace Alcorta are at pains to stress that religion is not a "functionless by-product," and they see this as one of the main differences between their position and that of the by-product theorists. However, by-product theorists do not assume that all elements of religion are functionless; on the contrary, both Boyer and Atran have stressed that a central element of religion is how frequently it is invoked in dealing with existential anxiety.[29]

A different kind of adaptationist argument has been made by Michael Winkelman and James McClenon, who invoke brain neurochemistry and focus on the nature of shamanism.[30] Winkelman gives particular attention to the striking similarities among shamanic practices throughout the world, suggesting that they have developed from a common psychobiological basis. The universal characteristics of shamans "reflect biosocial and neurophenomenological structures that constitute the primordial basis for religion."[31] McClenon adds the point that shamans induce altered states of consciousness that can produce high levels of relaxation and benefits for physical and psychological health. He points to research indicating the existence of a "shamanic syndrome," which is "characterized by hypnotizability, dissociative ability, propensity for anomalous experience, fantasy proneness, temporal-lobe lability (measured by EEG), and thinness of cognitive boundaries."[32]

This book takes the position that the adaptationist line of theorizing is better supported by the evidence than the by-product position. There are several lines of evidence to be considered, but we limit ourselves here to only two, the impact of religion on health, and religion's contribution to reproductive success.[33]

Religion and Health

A great deal of research has been carried out on the relationship between religiosity and both physical and mental health. A comprehensive survey has been conducted by Koenig, McCullough, and Larson, who looked at literally hundreds of studies.[34] In terms of physical health, 75 percent of sixteen studies found lower levels of heart disease and cardiovascular mortality among persons assessed as more religious, and 88 percent of sixteen studies found lower blood pressure among the more religious. In terms of longevity, 75 percent of fifty-two studies reported that more religious people lived longer. In terms of mental health, the authors examined ninety-three studies of religiosity and depression and found that 65 percent reported significant correlations between religiosity and lower levels of depression. Similarly, out of sixty-eight studies of suicide, 84 percent found lower suicide rates among the more-religious. Half of sixty-nine studies of anxiety found that the more religious reported lower anxiety levels; only ten studies (14 percent) reported higher levels of anxiety in more religious individuals. The authors also surveyed studies that related religiosity to alcohol and drug abuse. The vast majority of eighty-six studies of alcohol abuse (88 percent) and fifty-two studies of drug abuse (92 percent) reported significantly lower levels of these addictions among the more religious.

The positive effect of religiosity on health is not limited to modern societies. Shamanic curing and healing rituals have been shown to be surprisingly effective in the absence of anything remotely resembling modern medicine. Generally the rituals are most effective in producing results in illnesses that have at least a partial psychological basis. The altered states of consciousness induced by shamans seem to produce their effects primarily through improving physiological relaxation and reducing tension and anxiety, both of which have positive effects on overall immune system functioning.

Religion and Reproductive Success

Reproductive success, not health and longevity, is the ultimate currency of Darwinian adaptationism, but we know from earlier discussions of human mate choice that people in better health have on average greater reproductive success than those in poorer health. People in better health are more likely to find mates, and to find mates of high genetic quality, and thus to leave more offspring as a result. Religion can therefore promote reproductive success by means of promoting health.

However, considerable evidence suggests that religion also promotes reproductive success directly. One important study used data from the European Values Survey conducted in 2000 to assess religion's impact on childbearing rates of women age 18–44 in the United States and Western Europe.[35] The investigators found a significant impact of religiosity on fertility. In the United States, women who attended religious services more than once a Week had an average fertility rate of 1.65 children compared to 1.18 for women who never attended services. In terms of religious belief, women who regarded religion as very important in their lives had a fertility rate of 1.61, whereas women who regarded religion as unimportant had a fertility rate of 1.04. For Western Europe, women who attended church more than once a week had an average of 2.66 offspring compared to 1.10 for women who never attended. Western European women who regarded religion as very important in their lives averaged 2.07 offspring compared to 1.15 for women who regarded religion as unimportant.

To explain why religion seems to promote reproductive success directly, we can invoke the biblical injunction "be fruitful and multiply." Mormons in the United States, for example, often have four to six children, which is far above the average for the society as a whole (about two children per couple). American Jews, many of whom are secular and Jewish by ethnic identification only, have an average fertility of 1.86. But Orthodox Jewish women in the United States have an average fertility of 3.3 children, and among American Orthodox Haredim, who are perhaps the most devoutly religious of all Jews, fertility is an extremely high 6.6.[36] The Hutterites, a devout religious sect found in the western United States and Canada, had in the recent past an average of some ten children per family.

Religion in Its Socioecological Context

Even though we cannot say exactly why, it seems clear that humans have a natural religious sense. But why does it produce such variety: spirits or gods; one god or several; active or inactive gods; benevolent or malevolent gods; anthropomorphic or transcendent gods; intensely emotional rituals or highly stylized and mechanical rituals; shamans, priests, or prophets? The short answer is that it is a matter of an evolved human religious sense interacting with the entire socioecological context in which people find themselves.[37]

When people were still living as hunter-gatherers, shamans were the principal religious practitioners. Once agriculture developed people began to add rituals devoted to bringing rain and helping the crops grow, as well as worshiping their ancestors. When people began to live in more-intensive agricultural societies organized into complex chiefdoms and early states, the gods of earlier and simpler times were elevated to higher status. Then we got polytheism and its anthropomorphic gods. These gods differed from most earlier ones in taking a much greater interest in human affairs. Indeed, this interest was often very great, which was why their worshipers were so interested in appeasing them through elaborate rituals. Appeasement could prevent harm—many of the gods could do mean and nasty things—and could also help promote rulers' most important goals, such as preserving or expanding their own power and achieving success in war. And with the new gods came priests, who formed themselves into religious monopolies that often stood sharply apart from ordinary people.

The anthropomorphic gods seemed to meet the religious needs of people, both elites and commoners, for thousands of years. But during the Axial Age anthropomorphic gods began to fall to the side, and people in some parts of the world began to worship a transcendent and omnipotent God who was considered the One True God. Apparently people's religious needs were changing as a result of social, economic, and political upheavals that were occurring during this time. There were two changes that were especially important.

One was large-scale urbanization. Many more people were tightly packed into large, squalid cities and living amid strangers and alien ethnic groups. The other was a dramatic increase in the scale of war. Advances in military technology, such as the introduction of iron weapons, increased war's killing power, and there was a tremendous increase in both the frequency of war and the number of people who were being killed. These changes, especially when occurring together, would have disrupted people's lives and would have created chronic anxiety—in short, much greater human misery and suffering. Under such circumstances, people would have become highly receptive to the teachings of prophets who promised release from suffering.[38]

Of the major world religions, Christianity may have been the one that was most responsive to suffering, and this may help account for its enormous success throughout the two millennia since it was founded. It spread rapidly throughout the Roman empire in the first three and a half centuries after the birth of Christ, with the number of Christians reaching some 34 million by 350 CE, over half the population of the entire empire.[39] Christianity spread throughout Europe during the Middle Ages and was carried to many of Europe's colonies between the sixteenth and twentieth centuries. It has grown enormously in recent times, penetrating sub-Saharan Africa in particular, and is currently the world's predominant religion. Some 2.1 billion people, nearly a third of the world's population, call themselves Christians. (Islam is second in line with 1.5 billion adherents, Hinduism third with 900 million.)

People everywhere seem to have an innate religious sense and innate religious needs, but these needs vary. The religious needs of egalitarian hunter-gatherers or small-scale horticulturalists are very different from those of people living in highly stratified societies organized into large chiefdoms and states. This is why shamans are especially prominent in the former and priests and prophets become much more prominent in the latter. Changing socioecological context produces new challenges, including new religious challenges. And thus do the varieties of religious experience proliferate.

The New Atheism

In the last decade there has emerged something called the new atheism. Promoted by numerous scholars, especially Richard Dawkins, Daniel Dennett, Christopher Hitchens, and Sam Harris, it attacks religion as a form of irrationality that is harmful to both societies and individuals.[40] The new atheists' strongest objection to religion is that it undermines rational thinking and science. They also believe that it does psychological harm. Hitchens says that religion "poisons everything," and suggests that parents' teaching their children religious beliefs might even qualify as child abuse, a point seconded by Dawkins. Dawkins calls the God of the Old Testament a "cruel ogre," and Hitchens suggests that much of the Old Testament is a "nightmare." The new atheists also emphasize the enormous amount of violence that has been carried out under the banner of religion.

The new atheists' main objective is to remove religion from the life of society. Dawkins, who is an evolutionary biologist at Oxford University in England and one of the world's most brilliant thinkers, has even formed a group that actively works to abolish religion, the Richard Dawkins Foundation for Reason and Science. The foundation has placed a large sign on some double-decker buses in England that proclaims, "There probably is no God. So relax and enjoy your life." As an evolutionist Dawkins is obviously aware of the new evolutionary theories of religion, including adaptationist theories, but this cuts no mustard with him. And yet it seems reasonable to ask, If religion is adaptive for people in terms of promoting health and longevity, do we really want to remove it from organized social life? Of course, one has to draw the line in those cases where religion actively interferes with science by insisting that creationist theories of life be taught alongside Darwinian natural selection in science classes. (If creationism is to be taught in public institutions, it has to be in a nonscientific context—in world religions courses, for example—and, in a religiously pluralistic society, taught along with other religious cosmologies.) Moreover, if religion is an evolutionary adaptation, *can* it be removed? It is true that there has been a certain amount of secularization in modern societies, but most people in these societies still have religious beliefs of one kind or another, and most actually pray.

And secularization can probably go only so far. Religion is not going away. Indeed, there is a good chance that secularization will be at least partially reversed. Because people who are more religious have higher levels of reproductive success than less religious people, and because religion is at least partly heritable,[41] it may be revived in Western societies and continue in full force in the less-developed world (which is currently a lot more religious than the developed world). Atheists tend to have the lowest reproductive success of any segment of modern society. They are at a demographic disadvantage in comparison to the religious, especially the devoutly religious.[42]

SUMMARY

1. Religion consists of beliefs and practices about postulated supernatural agents: spirits, gods, witches, and the like. All societies have religion, and in all religions there are both benevolent and malevolent supernatural agents.

2. Some small-scale societies have high gods who take an active interest in human affairs, but most do not. Such societies either have no high god at all, or a high god who is inactive. Such gods may or may not be worshiped.

3. All societies have religious rituals and ritual specialists. In hunter-gatherer societies the principal religious specialist is the shaman, whose main function is healing and curing. Two other types of religious specialists are prophets and priests. Prophets formulate new ideas and attempt to gain a following for them. If successful, they become the founders of a new religion. Priests acquire knowledge of formal religious doctrines, which they often monopolize, and perform rituals for a lay audience.

4. Shamans are the primordial religious specialists. They are found in nearly all hunter-gatherer societies and continue to be found in societies at more-advanced stages of social evolution. Shamans undergo trance-induced altered states of consciousness during which they seek to cure illness, recover lost souls, communicate with the dead, and protect people from evil spirits and malevolent magic.

5. The agrarian states of the ancient world were characterized by polytheistic religions in which there were pantheons of highly specialized gods. These gods were anthropomorphic in nature. Some were benevolent, others malevolent, and some both. People propitiated benevolent gods for help in the attainment of human goals, such as success in war, good crops, or success in love. Gods capable of malevolence were feared

and usually appeased by rituals involving animal sacrifice. Since the gods were like humans, they needed to eat and thus had to be "fed" by their subjects.

6. During the Axial Age, in some parts of the world new kinds of religions evolved. In the Near East Zoroastrianism, Judaism, and Christianity were founded on the basis of an omniscient and omnipotent God. This God was not anthropomorphic but transcendent. He was outside the universe and brought it into existence. A major theme in the new monotheistic religions was salvation from the miseries and sufferings of life.

7. Two central questions in the evolutionary study of religion are why people are religious, and why there are so many different kinds of religious beliefs and practices.

8. Some evolutionists advocate a by-product theory to explain why people are religious. They claim that there is no religious module in the brain. Religion is not itself an evolutionary adaptation but is hitching a ride or piggybacking on other cognitive modules that are evolutionary adaptations. Especially important is a module for thinking about agency, or actions that are caused by persons. People extend this agency module beyond persons to supernatural agents. Events that are not clearly the result of human action are attributed to unseen agents with supernatural powers.

9. Other evolutionists contend that religion is indeed an evolutionary adaptation. Some adaptationists use costly signaling theory to explain religion. Many religious groups ask their members to perform demanding rituals and follow a long list of religious prescriptions and proscriptions. This is costly to individuals, but it will increase the commitment of those who are willing to pay such costs and strengthen the religious organization. It will also increase the strength of religious belief.

10. Another type of adaptationism focuses on the psychobiological basis for shamanic rituals. It explains the widespread existence of shamanism, and the strikingly similar behavior of shamans wherever they are found, in terms of brain neurochemistry that evolved in the ancestral environment. Shamanic rituals apparently provide benefits for physical and mental health.

11. The adaptationist position is supported by numerous lines of evidence, especially religion's positive impact on both health and reproductive success. People who strongly believe in God and attend worship services regularly have better physical and mental health, and generally live longer. They also have lower rates of alcoholism and drug use. A variety of studies based on different societies and cultures show that people who report themselves to be more religious generally have more offspring.

12. Religion is highly sensitive to socioecological context. As this context changed throughout social evolution, new forms of religious belief and practice developed.

Shamans gave way to polytheistic pantheons of gods, and later monotheism began to replace polytheism. Prior to the emergence of the monotheistic religions, most religions were primarily concerned with earthly rewards. With the evolution of monotheism the focus shifted to otherworldly rewards, especially release from suffering.

13. There are numerous explanations of the rise of the Axial Age religions, but the timing is highly suggestive. The Axial Age was a time of great social disruption brought on by large-scale urbanization and the intensification of warfare. These changes increased the amount of human misery and suffering, and the new religions arose in order to help people cope with this suffering.

14. In recent years a social movement of new atheists has arisen. The new atheists attack religion as irrational superstition that inhibits a rational and scientific understanding of the world. They also claim that religion does psychological and social harm. Many of the new atheists are actively working to eliminate religion from organized social life. However, if there is an innate human religious sense, such an attempt is unlikely to succeed.

QUESTIONS FOR DISCUSSION

✓ What is religion? How old is it? Where can it be found?

✓ What does Swanson mean by a high god? What kinds of high gods are there?

✓ What is the relationship between the presence or absence of high gods and the stages of social evolution?

✓ What do shamans do and how do they do it? Why are they sometimes referred to as the primordial religious specialists?

✓ Discuss the nature of the gods in polytheistic religions.

✓ What was the Axial Age? Discuss.

✓ What is the difference between anthropomorphic and transcendent gods?

✓ Compare and contrast the by-product and adaptationist evolutionary theories of religion.

✓ How might costly signaling theory apply to religion?

✓ Is there a relationship between religiosity (religious commitment) and health? Between religiosity and reproductive success?

✓ In what ways is religion influenced by socioecological context? Discuss.

✓ What are some of the views of the so-called new atheists? Do you think their arguments are sound? Why or why not? If you happened to meet one of them, what would you say?

References and Notes

1. Swanson 1960.
2. Swanson 1960.
3. Swanson 1960, p. 56.
4. O'Leary and Levinson 1990, vol. 3
5. O'Leary and Levinson 1990, vol. 1.
6. Wallace 1966.
7. Steadman and Palmer 2008.
8. O'Leary and Levinson 1990, vol. 3.
9. O'Leary and Levinson 1990, vol. 3.
10. O'Leary and Levinson 1990, vol. 1.
11. Eliade 1964.
12. McClenon 2002.
13. Eliade 1964; Winkelman 1990, 2000.
14. Eliade 1964; Winkelman 1990, 2000.
15. Kosko 2004.
16. Butler and Salamone 2004.
17. Winkelman 1990, 2000.
18. D'Altroy 2002.
19. Zeitlin 1984.
20. McNeill 1963.
21. Smart 1976.
22. Jaspers 1953.
23. The Axial Age was also marked by the emergence of world religions in India and China, especially Hinduism, Buddhism, Confucianism, and Daoism. However, since these were not monotheistic religions, or at least not strict monotheisms in the manner of the Near Eastern religions, they are left aside in this discussion.
24. A brief but very useful summary of the most important theories of religion can be found in Zeitlin 2004.
25. See, for example, Boyer 2001; Atran 2002; Sosis 2003; Atran and Norenzayan 2004; Whitehouse 2004; Barrett 2004; Kirkpatrick 2005; Alcorta and Sosis 2005; Liénard and Boyer 2006; Bulbulia et al. 2008; Steadman and Palmer 2008; Feierman 2009; Pyysiäinen 2009; and Wright 2009.
26. Boyer 2001; Liénard and Boyer 2006; Atran 2002; Atran and Norenzayan 2004.
27. Sosis 2003.
28. Alcorta and Sosis 2005.
29. Alcorta and Sosis 2005.
30. Winkelman 1990, 2000; McClenon 2002.
31. Winkelman 2000, p. 71.
32. McClenon 2002, p. 134.
33. Additional lines of evidence are discussed in Sanderson 2008b.
34. Koenig, McCullough, and Larson 2001.
35. Frejka and Westoff 2006.
36. Singer 2006.
37. Sanderson and Roberts 2008.
38. Sanderson 2008a.
39. Stark 1996.
40. Dawkins 2006; Dennett 2006; Hitchens 2007; S. Harris 2004. The new atheism has generated an

enormous amount of intellectual discussion. Amarasingam 2010 is a collection of essays both defending and criticizing the new atheism. The book also provides many references to other relevant books and articles.

41. Harris and McNamara 2008.

42. There has been a parallel tendency in recent years for authors of books on scientific topics to slip in a few words of their own criticizing religion (e.g., E. O. Wilson 2012; Pinker 2011; Carroll 2005). These critiques are usually far less hostile than the attacks of the new atheists, but the authors clearly believe that religion poses a serious threat to science and think that the world would be a better place if there was no religion it in. One wonders about the need for such criticism. Why not just present the scientific arguments and the evidence for them? Religion is not a serious threat to science. We live in a science-based civilization, and science is not going to go away. It will continue to be highly influential and increase its range of influence.

These "soft" critics of religion, along with the "hard" critics (the new atheists), also condemn religion for contributing to bloody violence that kills millions. It is true that conflict between rival religions has led to the deaths of millions of people in human history, but there is nothing unique about religion in this respect. In all likelihood different ethnic groups have engaged in more violence against each other than have religious groups. And what of World War II? Sixty million people died in that war, but it had nothing to do with religion. (Of course, the war involved Nazi persecution of the Jews, but this persecution was primarily on ethnic rather than religious grounds. It was not a war based on rival religions. Indeed, Hitler was an atheist.) Throughout human history most wars have not been about religion at all, as was demonstrated in the chapter on violence.

14

Arts

Humans are artistic animals, and the arts are human universals. The arts comprise three principal activities: visual art, such as painting and sculpture; literature, or the telling of stories; and music, the playing of instruments and the singing of songs. This chapter explores all three arts with a special focus on their evolution: why do humans have them? Did the arts evolve as adaptations? Some scholars think so and suggest various useful functions that they have for survival and reproductive success. There are three versions of the idea of the arts as adaptations: they evolved by natural selection, they evolved by sexual selection, or they evolved by another form of selection known as group selection (explained below). A fourth point of view is that the arts aren't adaptations at all, but by-products of other adaptations. This perspective says that the arts are not necessary or useful, but merely pleasing experiences. Any society that did not have arts would not be in any danger of collapsing into a heap of individuals, nor do the arts help people survive or leave more offspring. In this chapter we explore these perspectives on the arts and try to adjudicate among them.

What Are the Arts?

To begin, we need to understand what constitutes the objects, performances, and experiences that qualify as art. What do visual art, literature, and music have in common? Surely there must be something, or we couldn't group them together under a common heading. The philosopher of art Denis Dutton has identified twelve central features of the arts that apply cross-culturally and cross-historically:[1]

1. *Direct pleasure.* Art objects are pleasing to look at, stories are interesting to read, and music is pleasant to listen to. Arts are valued in and of themselves without regard to any usefulness.
2. *Skill and virtuosity.* The object or performance shows a high level of specialized skill.

3. *Style*. Objects and performances have recognizable styles that reflect modes of form, composition, and expression.

4. *Novelty and creativity*. An art should show originality, imagination, and the capability of surprise.

5. *Criticism*. Forms of art evoke critical judgments of appreciation, both by their audience and by other artists.

6. *Representation*. Arts imitate or represent real or imaginary objects or experiences occurring in the world.

7. *Special focus*. Artistic works and performances tend to be separated from everyday life and given a special significance.

8. *Expressive individuality*. Arts express the unique personality of the artist.

9. *Emotional saturation*. Works of art are permeated by emotion, on both the part of the artists and of their audiences.

10. *Intellectual challenge*. Works of art are intended to make use of artists' perceptual and intellectual capabilities, and ideally the full use of these capabilities.

11. *Traditions and institutions*. The arts gain much of their significance by virtue of their place in history and the kinds of traditions they represent. Arts exist within a world of other artists, both contemporaneously and historically.

12. *Imaginative experience*. Art objects and performances spring from the imagination of artists, but also evoke imaginative experience for their audiences.

Dutton's characterization of the arts raises a question: For something to be called art, must it have all of these characteristics? For example, when second graders do finger painting, their teachers call it art. But it does not fit into any kind of historical tradition. Are there "art worlds" of finger painters? Not likely. And do finger paintings evoke emotions from the parents of the wee tots who paint them? Probably not, at least not strong emotions. In fact, finger painting seems to lack most of the twelve characteristics Dutton identifies. Yet nearly all of us would say that it is art even if only in a very rudimentary sense. Let's say you write a short story that is dull, unimaginative, utterly lacking in creativity, painful to read, and so on. Is it an art form? Is it literature? It qualifies technically, despite a complete absence of merit. And what if you sing in the shower just making up the tune and the words as you go. Is this music? It's hard to say it isn't.

So then, either Dutton's criteria are much too demanding, or these simple acts don't deserve to be called art. Which is it? It would seem to depend on whether an object or performance is of sufficient quality to make it worthy of critical evaluation and appreciation by its intended or potential audiences, both elite and mass. Dutton specifically mentions that an art must give pleasure, show skill, exhibit creativity, and so on. In short, it must be meritorious. Therefore, your dull, unimaginative short story that is painful even for your own parents to read doesn't count. Nor does my attempt at painting with acrylics if all I've produced is an unsightly mess.

Dutton's characterization may seem elitist, but he would likely reject such a charge. He has spent time in New Guinea observing the artistic creations of native artists, which are mostly wood carvings produced by ordinary people. He sees in these carvings his cluster of characteristics, or at least most of them. And he fully recognizes that the arts are universal and acknowledges that in all societies there are artistic productions that can legitimately be called such. So let's accept his characterization as a starting point for analysis.

Unfortunately, the problem is more complicated than that. Colin Martindale claims that most aestheticians reject the idea that art can be defined by a list of specific characteristics.[2] This would seem to be true with respect to the examples of finger painting, unimaginative stories, and singing in the shower. But take an even more dramatic example. The famous early-twentieth-century artist Marcel Duchamp's most famous artwork was an ordinary urinal placed on a platform, signed "R. Mutt 1917," and named *Fountain*. In 2004 five hundred of the most influential people in the art world—not only artists, but critics, curators, and dealers—were given a list of twenty of the twentieth century's best-known art works and asked to identify which of them they thought was the most influential. Lo and behold, *Fountain* came out on top, garnering 64 percent of the first-place votes.[3]

And yet most people who are not art critics or experts would say that *Fountain* is not art. It can't be because it doesn't give pleasure—it is actually ugly to look at—and shows no skill or virtuosity. How then can it be art, let alone high art? But note that it does have many of the other traits listed by Dutton: novelty and creativity, criticism, representation, special focus, expressive individuality, and intellectual challenge. Dutton has actually said that despite the extraordinary ease of its creation, many art aficionados regard *Fountain* as a work of genius because it demonstrated Duchamp's skill "in knowing exactly what unusual, however minimal, art will be admired by a sophisticated art-world audience."[4] Duchamp was famous for his use of "readymades," ordinary objects such as shovels or combs. These too are considered art by the critics. But if Duchamp had conceptual skill, did he also have *technical* skill? This is a matter of debate. One of his most famous paintings was *Nu descendant un escalier* (Nude Descending a Staircase), a work of highly abstract art that some would regard as skillful.[5] However, Duchamp was not particularly respected as a painter.[6]

What are we left with? Martindale says art is whatever you say it is (or at least whatever art experts say it is). But this seems too general. Why not say that the arts are objects or performances that contain *many* if not *most* (and in some cases *all*) of Dutton's criteria. This seems to be a reasonable compromise. In any event, most people recognize the arts when they see them, so perhaps they don't even need to be defined. People know that when they read a Dickens novel or a Robert Frost poem that these things are literature, that when they listen to Mozart or Elvis Presley they are hearing music, and that when they look at a painting by Rembrandt or van Gogh or a sculpture by Rodin *(The Thinker)* they are experiencing works of art.

Visual Art

Visual art—painting, sculpting, carving, and so on—goes back at least 50,000 years. In Chapter 2 we considered the famous cave paintings at Lascaux, Altamira, and Chauvet, and carvings made of ivory or bone. In many small-scale societies, body decoration using striking colors has been common, including tattooing, scarification, and applying paint-like substances on special occasions. The northwest coast Indians produced elaborately carved totem poles, and the Aztecs and Maya of Mesoamerica produced elaborate statues designed to represent their gods and to intimidate the masses. The famous Easter Islanders of Polynesia also produced statues in the form of huge heads.

Mass Versus Elite Art

The distinction between mass and elite art is important. Mass art is produced for large segments of a population. (The paintings of Norman Rockwell and Thomas Hart Benton certainly fit here.) It is visually pleasing to most people, mass produced, and displayed widely, not just in art museums. Japanese artists made beautiful prints that were mass produced. Elite art is produced primarily for other artists. The extremely abstract cubist paintings of Picasso belong here, as do the paintings of Impressionists like Monet, Degas, and Renoir, and certainly the ready-mades of Duchamp. True elite artists don't care what the mass of the population thinks about their products; their only concern is what other artists think, or at most other members of the elite art community (critics, curators, etc.).

And yet the mass-elite distinction should not be overplayed. Elite art is *intended* for other artists or a social elite audience. A new style of elite art is often rejected by other artists and social elites when it first appears, but in time it catches on and comes to be appreciated. It can also trickle down to large segments of the population. Original paintings are made into prints, which can be sold by the tens or hundreds of thousands in art museum stores. Large numbers of people now buy prints of paintings by Rembrandt, Breughel, Monet, Cézanne, Gauguin, van Gogh, Picasso, and many other famous artists.

In the early 1990s two Russian émigré artists, Vitaly Komar and Alexander Melamid, carried out a famous study.[7] They wanted to know what kind of paintings the average person liked best and liked least, so they commissioned a poll of American tastes. They discovered that people liked realistic paintings, especially landscapes, with a lot of blue to represent water and the sky and green to represent grass and trees. They liked to see people in the landscapes, especially women and children, and they liked to see animals. After these initial results, Komar and Melamid wanted to know whether the tastes of Americans were unique or widespread, so they had polls conducted in nine other countries: China, Denmark, Finland, France, Iceland, Kenya, Russia, Turkey, and Ukraine. Several million people were queried. The results showed that there was nothing unique about American taste. People liked the same things not only in other Western countries but also in Asian and African countries. What accounts for this high level of consensus on artistic preferences throughout the world?

The most common answer is that people want to look at the kind of natural environment in which early humans evolved. There is now wide agreement among biological anthropologists that this environment was the savanna of east Africa. This has led Gordon Orians and Judith Heerwagen to formulate what they call the "savanna hypothesis."[8] In savannas there is a lot of open grassland, but also some trees. There is a lot of biomass and thus plenty of meat available. Orians and Heerwagen note that such an environment would have been evolutionarily adaptive in the sense that it "should have favored individuals who were motivated to explore and settle in environments likely to afford the necessities of life but to avoid environments with poorer resources or posing higher risks."[9] And those individuals who were motivated to live in this type of environment should have developed a keen visual sense of it, which eventually would have evolved into an aesthetic preference. This preference would have become part of human nature and been retained down to the present day.[10] (Incidentally, humans show a strong liking for public parks and golf courses, most of which resemble savannas and in all likelihood have been designed with that in mind.)[11]

This is a plausible hypothesis, except for the fact that modern people like landscape paintings depicting water, and water is relatively scarce in savannas, as Orians and Heerwagen themselves note. This suggests a role for social experience. Throughout human evolution people migrated extensively and lived in other types of environments, especially those containing trees and water. Aesthetic preferences for these features could then have been selected for. There also appears to be a role for human development. Two studies have explored the possibility of age differences in landscape preferences. Eight-year-old children consistently favor the savanna type of environment, but after age fifteen they like environments with mountains and forests equally well. So there appears to be a social experience effect when individuals are exposed to a wider range of environments.[12]

Komar and Melamid also asked people what kind of painting they most *disliked*. Again there was uniformity. Most people disliked modern twentieth-century abstract art. And why? Because most people don't understand it and it is extremely far removed from their natural tastes. Picasso's paintings of women in extremely distorted shapes bear no relationship at all to the world of humans that other humans recognize. Salvador Dali's Surrealist paintings in which limpid clocks hang from tree branches violate deep ontological categories of human experience: such things simply don't exist. And of course there is Duchamp's *Fountain* as well as another one of his ready-mades, a snow shovel titled *In Advance of a Broken Arm,* which was actually placed in a museum alongside masterpieces by Picasso and van Gogh. This is art, people say? And some of the most recent art—such as Chris Ofili's liberal use of elephant dung in paintings, or Andres Serrano's photograph of a crucifix in a jar of urine—can be deeply offensive to most people's sensibilities. Moreover, Geoffrey Miller makes the point that the average person not only finds modern art abhorrent, but ridiculous. People say things like "my five-year-old could have done that," "a monkey could have done that," or "it was done by an idiot." Miller adds that another major reason such artwork is rejected is that it does not tell the audience anything about the abilities of the artist.[13]

Here is the way the comedians Mason and Felder describe their reaction to Picasso:

> Phonies point to a Picasso painting and explain why the bull's head is on top of the smokestack, why the lampshade is on the side of the goat, why the woman's leg is coming out of the salami, and most notably, why Picasso named the painting *Enchanted Sunset in Sevilla.* . . .
>
> If your brother-in-law painted a picture like Picasso, he would be locked away in a sanitarium. If we showed you a painting of a banana under a suspension bridge, a spoon protruding from a pig's head, and the moon shining under a sewer grating, you would say, "Who painted this? A serial killer?" . . .
>
> True story: We have a wealthy friend who owned a Picasso and only when an art expert came to dinner last year did our friend learn that for the past 30 years he had been hanging the Picasso upside down.[14]

Steven Pinker doesn't like modern art either. In his chapter on the arts in his book *The Blank Slate*, he bemoans the current state of the arts in general and of visual art in particular.[15] By the first decade of the twentieth century, art had already begun to be taken over by so-called modernism. The turning point was the year 1910, which marked a London exhibition of the postimpressionist paintings of Van Gogh, Cézanne, and Gauguin. Pinker castigates modernism for its "freakish distortions of shape and color" and its "abstract grids, shapes, dribbles, and splashes." He charges that it glorified pure form and disdained beauty. This castigation of modernism is also extended to postmodern art. Postmodernism in art, such as Cindy Sherman's photographs of "grotesquely assembled bi-gendered mannequins," is held in considerable contempt.[16]

Modernists and postmodernists have lost touch, Pinker says, with innate human aesthetic desires. The vast majority of people can no longer understand or appreciate art "without a support team of critics and theoreticians." "The dominant theories of elite art and criticism in the twentieth century," he says, "grew out of a militant denial of human nature. One legacy is ugly, baffling, and insulting art. The other is pretentious and unintelligible scholarship."[17]

If the problem is that modern and postmodern art deny human nature and its role in the appreciation of art, then for Pinker the solution is for artists to regain an understanding of human nature and a respect for "the minds and senses of human beings." And fortunately, he says, this is beginning to occur. A revolt has begun and a new philosophy of art is emerging. He mentions various new artistic movements that stress the return to beauty and technique in art, such as Derrière Guard, Natural Classicism, The Return of Beauty, and No Mo Po Mo.

Pinker has many interesting and valid points to make. However, despite what Pinker says, modernism was never really opposed to beauty in art. It was opposed to commonly received opinions of beauty, as well as to making beauty the paramount (or the only) goal of art, but it was not against beauty per se. Most if not all of the Abstract Expressionists (a school of modernism), for example, were looking for very specific and personal kinds of beauty in their art. And the art of one of the greatest of the early modernists, Matisse, was primarily about beauty. One of the most famous Abstract Expressionists, Jackson Pollock, used an extremely innovative technique in which he placed large canvases on the floor and dripped and threw paint onto them, sometimes even using a can of paint (rather than a brush) to do so. Despite their abstract nature, many regard Pollock's paintings as extremely beautiful.[18] And they do not contain any of the distortions or grotesque features of a Picasso or a Dali. Moreover, a five-year-old or a monkey could not do what Pollock did, not even remotely. Pollock's paintings were the product of enormous skill. If you don't believe it, try it yourself and see what happens. Make sure someone is nearby to clean up the ungodly mess.

Pinker, not being an artist himself, is not in an ideal position to appreciate the world of the artist, especially elite artists. Artistic styles cannot remain static because people would become bored with them and their significance would wane. Novelty is essential for art to survive. Artists must demonstrate *creativity* or *originality* or they will not be taken seriously by fellow artists; they cannot simply copy what others have been doing. Elite artists, or at least those who aspire to be, have no interest in what the general public wants in art, indeed usually have nothing but disdain or outright contempt for the public. These artists create their works primarily for each other.

Pinker wants to see artists return to producing works that the public likes. Yet there are still many artists outside the artistic elite who paint the kinds of things most people want. Most artists lack the skill and imagination needed to become part of the elite. If they want to produce art and make a living from it, then they must give the public what it wants in the sense that their works of art must *sell*. The public is not being deprived of the kind of art it prefers—unless, of course, people spend all of their time in museums of modern art instead of your average art shop.

Art and Evolution

Evolutionary psychologists agree that art is a product of evolution, but not on how evolution produced it. Most evolutionists who have studied art—and only a very few have—divide into one of two camps: art either evolved as a by-product of selection for something else, or it evolved by sexual selection. The first camp contends that art is not an adaptation at all; it's an important part of human experience, but it doesn't do anything that promotes either survival or reproductive success. The second camp sees art as an adaptation, but for mating rather than survival.

The best-known by-product theory is Pinker's. He finds it puzzling that people should give so much attention to art because art seems pointless in Darwinian terms. Even though Pinker is a thoroughgoing adaptationist with respect to most of the features of the brain, with respect to art he says that "it is wrong to invent functions for activities that lack . . . design merely because we want to ennoble them with the imprimatur of biological adaptedness."[19] Art is merely a by-product of other adaptations that stimulate the pleasure centers of the brain. It "is a pleasure technology, like drugs, erotica, or fine cuisine."[20] Art is most likely a spin-off of such things as the desire to look at objects and environments that are adaptively relevant, the ability to design useful artifacts (such as pottery and tools), and the desire for status.[21] For example, as noted earlier, even though what people like most are landscapes that resemble the kind of savanna environment in which humans first evolved, and even though this preference seems to be an evolutionary adaptation, paintings of landscapes are only a small part of art. Most of van Gogh's paintings are not landscapes. His famous painting *Starry Night* is a bit like a landscape, but only in a very modernist sense. Two other famous van Gogh paintings, *The Potato Eaters* and *Sunflowers,* are not landscapes at all. Renoir's *The Fisherman* and *Le Moulin de la Galette* are far removed from landscapes, as is Monet's *Le Palais Contarini.* Yet these are among the most famous artists and paintings of all time, and widely consumed. Surely these paintings are by-products, elaborations of an original, innate preference—which would explain why many people do not like them.

Denis Dutton and Geoffrey Miller have formulated interesting sexual selectionist theories of art.[22] Dutton concedes that the worldwide preferences for landscape painting evolved by natural selection. But most art, he contends, has evolved by sexual selection. It makes little sense to think of art as contributing to survival, he says, because "artistic objects and performances are typically among the most opulent, extravagant, glittering, and profligate creations of the human mind. The arts squander brain power, physical effort, time, and precious resources. Natural selection on the other hand, is economical and abstemious: it weeds out inefficiency and waste."[23]

Body decoration was probably the first form of visual art.[24] Darwin noted the many forms of body decoration around the world and believed they were the product of sexual selection. We even see something like art in other animal species. Recall the Australian bowerbirds, which construct aesthetic displays in order to attract mates. And then, of course, there are the elaborate tails and colors of such birds as peacocks and birds of paradise. We now know that these are products of sexual selection.

Miller refers to his theory as *fitness indicator theory*: the artist is using his art to signal his fitness. "We find attractive," he says, "those things that could have been produced only by people with attractive, high-fitness qualities, such as health, energy, endurance, hand-eye coordination, fine motor control, intelligence, creativity, access to rare materials, the ability to learn difficult skills, and lots of free time."[25] Fitness indicator theory is in essence an application of costly signaling theory. As Miller points out, throughout history

> the perceived beauty of an object has depended very much on its cost. That cost could be measured in time, energy, skill, or money. Objects that were cheap and easy to produce were almost never considered beautiful. . . . Our sense of beauty was shaped by evolution to embody an awareness of what is difficult as opposed to easy, rare as opposed to common, costly as opposed to cheap, skillful as opposed to talentless, and fit as opposed to unfit.[26]

Dutton also uses costly signaling theory along with Veblen's notion of conspicuous waste. As in the case of Miller, for Dutton art is a fitness indicator. He delineates a number of ways in which art is associated with costliness and waste:[27]

- Art objects are often made of materials that are both rare and expensive, such as gold, jade, marble, rare dyes, jewels, and fine hardwoods.
- Works of art take a lot of time to create, and thus demonstrate conspicuous leisure.
- Artworks usually require high intelligence and creativity.
- Intelligence and creativity must be turned into specific artistic skills, and these skills can take a lot of time to acquire.
- Artworks are often most impressive when they are utterly useless.
- Most works of art are fleeting. They are ignored; the relative few that inspire interest lose attention over time, usually quickly. Most works of art are confined to attics or thrown into the trash. This is waste par excellence, and certainly costly when considerable resources have been put into creating the art object.

Miller notes that art does not have to be directly about sex to have evolved by sexual selection. Nevertheless, it has long been observed that many of the greatest artists have had enormous sexual appetites and many sexual partners—Picasso, Diego Rivera, and Gauguin, for example. Modigliani sought to have sex with hundreds of his models.[28] Moreover, it is males who are producing most of the art. This leads Miller to predict that men's artistic production should show a dramatic increase after sexual maturity, hit a peak in young adulthood (because sexual competition is greatest at that time in life), and then decline thereafter, sharply at first (because males now have mates) and then more slowly throughout the rest of life.[29]

To test this prediction, Miller sampled 3,374 modern paintings from the *Tate Gallery Collections*.[30] The Tate Gallery in London is one of the world's greatest art museums and displays some of the world's greatest art. Miller's predictions were confirmed. Males constituted 87 percent of the artists (644 men and 95 women), and produced 88 percent of the paintings (2,979 vs. 395). The histogram presented in Figure 14.1 summarizes Miller's findings. Here we see a sharp rise in the number of paintings produced by men after age 20–25. The number of paintings peaks between ages 31 and 45, and then begins a sharp decline throughout the remainder of life. The age distribution for women is somewhat different. It shows a substantial rise in the number of paintings after age 20–25, with the number of paintings peaking between the ages of 31 and 40. In this respect the distribution is similar to that for men. However, the decline in women's painting production beginning at age 41 is much less precipitous than that of men. From age 46 on, the number of paintings produced by women remains essentially flat. But the big story, of course, is the far greater number of paintings produced by men of all ages.

Literature

The simplest definition of literature is that it tells fictional stories. The word itself implies that the stories are written down, but storytelling is ancient. Ever since the advent of behaviorally modern humans, people have told stories around campfires at night, as well as on other occasions. When alphabetic writing was invented some three thousand years ago, stories could be written down and made much more elaborate; thus Homer's *Iliad* and *Odyssey*.[31] Storytelling is an extremely large part of human life. As Dutton points out, "Human beings across the globe expend staggering amounts of time and resources on creating and experiencing fantasies and fictions."[32]

Miller sticks to his sexual selection argument for literature as well as visual art. There is no need to recapitulate that argument. We can simply mention his quantitative test. Here he examined 2,837 books of fiction written in the English language and listed in *The Writers Directory*. Men constituted 79 percent of the authors and wrote 78 percent of the books. The age distribution of men's works of fiction is much like the age distribution of their paintings, but the age distribution of women's literary works is slightly different from their distribution of paintings. For literature, there is a sharper rise in women's productivity between the ages of twenty and fifty, and then a gradual decline after this age. Women thus contribute more to literature than to painting (or to music). But why should women contribute more to literature than to the other arts? The answer may lie in what was shown in the chapter on gender: women have a keen interest in social relationships, especially of the type portrayed in many novels, such as those written by Jane Austen (*Pride and Prejudice*, *Sense and Sensibility*) and Charlotte Brontë (*Jane Eyre*). And then of course there are the very popular romance novels, all written by women.

Although taking a sexual selectionist view of visual art, with respect to literature Dutton shifts to a natural selectionist argument. Literature, he contends, gives us the

FIGURE 14.1   Output of Modern Paintings by Age and Sex

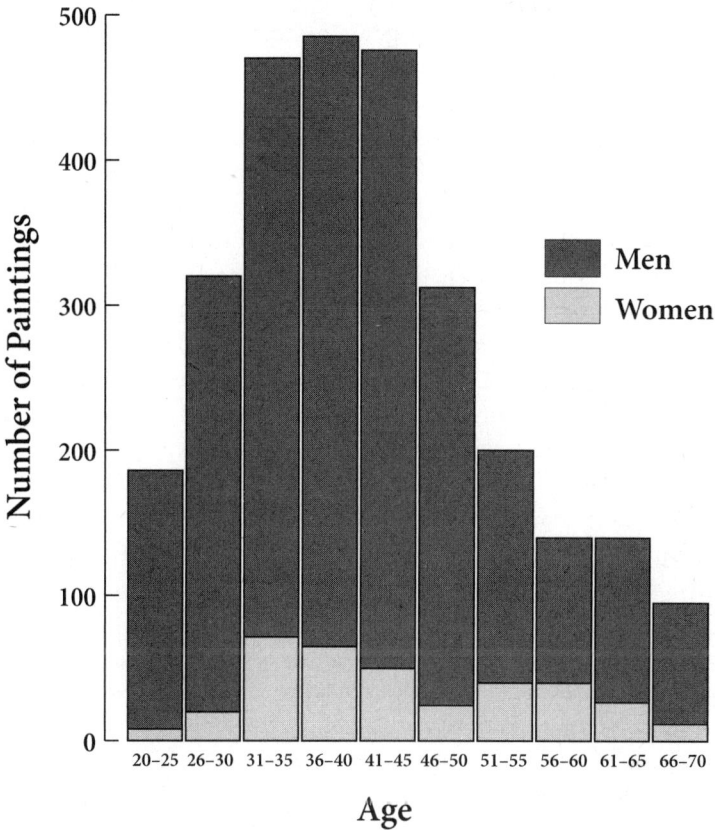

Source: Adapted from data in Geoffrey F. Miller, "Sexual selection for cultural displays," in Robin Dunbar, Chris Knight, and Camilla Power, eds., *The Evolution of Culture: An Interdisciplinary View* (New Brunswick, NJ: Rutgers University Press, 1999).

useful cognitive abilities to be "supposition-makers" and "thought-experimenters." He lists three main adaptive advantages of fiction:

- It provides low-cost, low-risk surrogate experiences giving us the capacity to work out in advance strategies for dealing with the problems, threats, and opportunities that we may have to confront in real life.
- It provides highly useful sources of factual information.
- It allows us to explore the points of view, motives, and beliefs of other people, thereby offering us interpersonal abilities that may be highly adaptive in negotiating social life. Stories enhance mind-reading capabilities.

In short,

> The adaptive value of storytelling in the ancestral environment would
> lie . . . in the capacity of the human mind to build a store of experience
> in terms of individual, concrete cases—not just the actual lived and
> self-described life experiences of an individual but the narratives accu-
> mulated in memory that make up storytelling traditions: vivid gossip,
> mythologies, technical know-how, and moral fables—in general what
> would have been the lore of a hunter-gatherer society. Whatever the
> brain processes that enable it, the human mind acquires and organizes a
> vast knowledge-store in terms of dramatic episodes of clan history, war
> stories, hunting anecdotes, near misses, tales of forbidden love, fool-
> hardy actions with tragic outcomes, and so forth. These cases are used
> analogically and in terms of shared and differentiated features to make
> sense of new situations and to interpret past experience.[33]

To illustrate his main argument, Dutton draws on several characters from famous literature. In Dickens's novel *Hard Times*, Tom and Louisa Gradgrind's father
prevents them from reading literature, and as a result they are emotionally stunted.
There is also the example of Esther Summerson in Dickens's novel *Bleak House*. As a
child growing up, Esther receives no affection but is able to overcome her situation
by creating an imaginary world in which she talks with her doll. Finally there is David Copperfield. Abused and deprived, David discovers books that belonged to his
dead father and this changes his life. Dutton quotes Joseph Carroll concerning the
significance of David's discovery:

> What David gets from these books is lively and powerful images of hu-
> man life suffused with the feeling and understanding of the astonish-
> ingly capable and complete human beings who wrote them. . . . He is
> not escaping reality; he is escaping from an impoverished reality into
> the larger world of healthy human possibility. . . . He directly enhances
> his own fitness as a human being, and in doing so he demonstrates the
> kind of adaptive advantage that can be conferred by literature.[34]

Jonathan Gottschall's argument is similar to Dutton's.[35] Noting that stories everywhere focus on the "great predicaments of the human condition," Gottschall contends that literature provides us with a means to practice and work out in advance
the most important social skills of human life. Gottschall depends on an analogy
between literature and learning difficult piloting skills. Pilots who land planes on
aircraft carriers, a very difficult task, first undergo months of training in flight sim-
ulators. Literature provides people with a kind of flight simulator, Gottschall believes.[36] It is therefore adaptive. As he puts it, "If the evolutionary function of fiction

is—at least in part—to simulate the big dilemmas of life, people who consume a lot of fiction should be more capable social operators than people who don't."[37]

This kind of argument leaves a lot to be desired. Much of modern literature contains themes that are the themes of most gossip, and in fact literature itself contains a great deal of gossip. Gossip is an adaptation because it is a very good way for people to acquire all kinds of information about what other people are up to, information that can be used to good effect. Say John gossips with Mary about Bill's interest in Jill. John is interested in Jill and doesn't want anyone else to be. If he is complacent and thinks no one else has an interest in Jill, he may not pursue her too aggressively and, if so, Bill captures Jill's heart before John can. But if Mary tells John that Bill is interested in Jill, then John can move more quickly and win Jill for himself. Or suppose Mort gossips with Jane about Mort's friend Jake. Jane tells Mort that Jake is in fact deceitful; he pretends to be Mort's friend, but only does so to advance himself at Mort's expense. This is very useful information for Mort, since he may be able to use it to thwart Jake's devious plans. The point is this: why do people need stories to help them negotiate life? Do most people take away moral lessons or useful information from stories? It seems unlikely. Moral lessons and useful information can be acquired directly from parents, friends, and other members of society. Stories are designed for enjoyment and entertainment. That's why people listen to them or read them. In oral societies, people sit around the campfire at night telling stories as a way of passing the time. What else is there to do? You can't hunt, gather, or plow because it's too dark and dangerous.

Consider also that many stories are fantasies. Fantasies have no adaptive function. They are amusements, or ways of escaping from real life for a while. There is also science fiction. This allows us to imagine other worlds that may intrigue us or offer better worlds than the one we currently inhabit. They are fascinating purely and simply and there is no other reason for their existence. Then there are fairy tales. These often contain useful suggestions about how children should try to live the right kind of life. Children may get the point—or they may not. They may see a story as just a story. Besides, you don't need the story to get young people to lead the right kind of life. Parents can just instruct their children directly without the use of stories. Or they can give them real life examples, not stories, of what bad things happened to so-and-so when he didn't follow certain rules.

Michele Sugiyama relates the Yanomama folktale of Jaguar and Millipede.[38] Millipede criticizes Jaguar for walking too noisily through the jungle, then shows him how to walk more softly so as not to attract unwanted attention from predators or enemies. Dutton says that this story is filled with useful information and good advice. No doubt that is true, but the same result can be obtained without reliance on any story. Parents and tribal members can simply say to children, "Don't make too much noise when you walk in the forest. You might be attacked by an enemy or a dangerous animal." In fact, people say things like this to their children all of the time in all societies.

Moreover, the examples given above of the central characters in *Hard Times*, *Bleak House*, and *David Copperfield* are inadequate to show that literature is an evolutionary adaptation. Literature may have been very beneficial for these particular characters, but that hardly means it is equally useful for everyone else. The examples only show the adaptive value of literature for abused and deprived children. Most children are not abused or deprived, and thus they don't need literature to overcome their deprivation. And the characters are themselves fiction, not real people. They represent the point of view of the author (Dickens), who very likely has a strong bias in favor of the importance of literature. We can all agree that literature is important and valuable without making it essential to human survival or psychological well-being. People just like stories and that's about it.

Theories like Dutton's and Gottschall's are very difficult if not impossible to test. If something is an adaptation in Darwinian terms, it must promote differential survival and reproductive success. Imagine a hypothetical experimental test of the Dutton/Gottschall theory in which six-year-old children are randomly assigned to one of two groups. The first group reads literature until the end of the experiment, at age thirty, say, whereas the second group has no contact with literature at all during the same period. Then we could check to see if more members of the first group survived and left more offspring than members of the second group. That might constitute a reasonable test. Of course, the experiment is impossible to perform because it is totally unethical. Imagine another test in which we look at the consequences for societies that have stories and compare them to societies that do not. But that test is impossible as well because all known societies have stories. There is no comparison that can be made.

Nevertheless, some scholars have attempted to test the kind of natural selection theory favored by Dutton and Gottschall. Unfortunately, the tests are very weak. Raymond Mar and colleagues carried out two studies. In the first they asked ninety-four subjects to take an author recognition test in which they indicated how many authors of fiction they recognized out of a list of fifty and how many authors of non-fiction they recognized out of a list of fifty.[39] This test operates on the assumption that the number of authors people recognize can serve as a proxy for how many books they have read. The researchers then gave the subjects tests to measure such abilities as perspective taking, empathic concern, and reading the mental states of others by attending to their eye regions. In relating subjects' average author recognition scores to their interpersonal skills, the authors claim that their results show that more fiction reading leads to better interpersonal sensitivity and social skills but that more nonfiction reading does not. However, the results of this study do not support what the authors claim. Their correlations are so low as to be meaningless, and in one case the relationship is negative rather than positive. A second study using 252 subjects attempted to replicate the findings of the first study. Results were basically the same.[40]

Music

The Nature of Music

Evidence suggests that music is very old. Archaeologists have recovered numerous objects that were very likely musical instruments. Some seventeen flutes made of bone have been found at the site of Isturitz in the Pyrenees dated to about 20 Kya. The oldest bone flutes come from the site of Geissenklosterle in Germany. Made from the wing bones of a swan, they are dated to about 37 Kya.[41] Some other artifacts have been discovered that may have been percussion instruments. It is likely that flutes were also made from hollow sticks or reeds, since it is much easier to bore holes in them than in bone, but sticks and reeds cannot be preserved. Stick and reed flutes, if they existed, may be even older than bone flutes.[42]

Steven Brown points out that there is a very wide range of musical forms and musical performances throughout the world.[43] In small-scale societies music is highly social, and in fact is almost exclusively performed in groups. Most of this music involves singing and is usually associated with group rituals. Very little music in the world's societies has involved people singing alone. Solo singing did not become prominent until the rise of the Old World civilizations, and functioned largely to entertain and glorify ruling classes.[44] Music involving a distinction between performers and an audience listening to them is a relatively recent development in the evolution of music.

Brown contends that there are important relationships between social structure and "musical structure." He provides important insight into how musical structure has evolved socially:

> As cultures expand in size and become stratified, many functional properties, including musical performance style, change in a dramatic way. At a fundamental level, a shift in social focus from the group to the individual occurs, as symbolized by the status of the ruling class of the culture. Musical strata evolve in a corresponding fashion through a progressive process whereby new strata are added onto pre-existing ones. The core stratum, ritual music, is present in some form in every culture. It is accompanied by a stratum of non-ritual music, something we can refer to as folk music. The next layer in the progression is the formation of classical music, which is the private music of the ruling class and aristocracy in a hierarchical society. This development is accompanied by a simultaneous expansion of folk music as an opposition not only to ritual music but to classical music as well. The last layer, which is added onto ritual, folk, and classical musics, is commercial or popular music, which is a stratum found only in the technologically advanced societies of the 20th century.[45]

Music as a By-Product

We are back once more to the question of evolutionary origins. Pinker again takes a by-product view: "As far as biological cause and effect are concerned, music is useless. It shows no signs of design . . . ; music could vanish from our species and the rest of our lifestyle would be virtually unchanged. Music appears to be a pure pleasure technology, a cocktail of recreational drugs that we ingest through the ear to stimulate a mass of pleasure circuits at once."[46] Pinker contends, as have numerous others, that music probably borrows much of its structure from language. As we saw in Chapter 2, for Pinker language is an adaptation shaped by natural selection, and it is incontestable that children quickly learn to speak and understand language. In terms of music, however, Pinker notes that most people cannot play an instrument and cannot carry a tune (or at least carry one very well). And except for musical geniuses like Mozart and Beethoven, people can only become good at performing music by undergoing long periods of training and constant practice.[47]

Tecumseh Fitch criticizes the by-product argument, contending that it is contradicted by music's ancient history, by the universality of music, and by the enormous quantities of music produced by humans. He says that music attracts attention from potential predators or enemies because so much of it is loud, and it is energetically costly (in some societies people may sing and dance until they are completely exhausted).[48] Another potential problem with the by-product argument as presented by Pinker is that in many societies, especially those that resemble the ancestral environment, musical instruments are often easy to learn to play. And since in such societies most music is group singing, those whose voices are not very good can be compensated for by those with good voices. The stronger voices drown out the weaker ones.

Music as a Product of Sexual Selection

Those who favor sexual selection as the basis of music's origins often look to birdsong as an analogy because most birds sing to attract mates. (They also sing as a means of territorial defense, but this is in the service of attracting mates.)[49] Slater points out that many male birds stop singing after they have mated; moreover, if a male loses his mate, his singing picks up again.[50]

Miller, unsurprisingly, favors the sexual selection argument. In this regard he examined a sample of 1,892 jazz albums and found that jazz is almost exclusively a "male thing." Men constituted 95 percent of the composers and produced 95 percent of the albums. For men, the age distribution is almost the same as their distribution for painting and books, whereas for women there is virtually no distribution; production is basically flat across all age-groups.[51] Miller also looked at over 1,500 rock albums and more than 3,800 works of classical music and found basically the same pattern as for jazz albums.[52] Again Miller invokes costly signaling, claiming that music is used conspicuously in courtship and serves as an indicator of strength, coordination, and high aerobic capacity. Top performers show an ability to put together complex learned behaviors.

Miller also points out that music is found in all societies and at all times in history; that it develops according to a standard schedule in individual ontogeny (development); that, contrary to by-product theory, almost all individuals have musical ability, being able to carry a tune, learn melody, and enjoy musical performances; that it involves a specialized memory such that normal adults can reproduce thousands of melodies; and that it has clear analogs in the acoustic signals of other species, especially birds.[53]

Steven Brown has strongly criticized the sexual selection argument. He makes the following points:[54]

1. Because the sexual selection argument views music as a largely competitive activity among men, it is unable to explain why so much of it is highly group-oriented and cooperative.
2. In songbirds, males are the main singers, but females also sing, and there is duetting.
3. Men do not sing to women in any face-to-face sense, as would be expected in a courtship display.
4. In most societies, women make musical contributions that are equal to those of men. Music is not a sexually dimorphic trait.
5. Once music evolved, it could be co-opted for courtship displays, but this does not mean it evolved for that reason.
6. Miller's evidence is limited to top musical performers in Western societies, but music in most societies is engaged in by all members of society.
7. Miller limits himself to the highly commercialized musical culture of the contemporary Western world, with its emphasis on "sexy superstars" and the theme of love. However, this is only a tiny part of the world's music, both cross-culturally and historically.[55]
8. Throughout the world love is not a particularly common musical theme. This theme is largely limited to modern popular music. The Aka pygmies, for example, have more than twenty different categories of music, but just one is about love.

To Brown's criticisms several more can be added. Miller's findings showing the predominance of young males in modern music probably apply to more than music or any of the other arts. For example, if we graphed contributions to physics or mathematics by the leading contributors to these fields, the graph would probably look basically the same. We know that these fields are overwhelmingly male dominated at the highest levels, and also that the main contributions come at a young age, usually by age thirty. For example, Einstein's leading contributions came when he was young, the special theory of relativity when he was twenty-six and the general theory at age thirty-six. He made no major contributions after that time. But surely mathematics and physics did not evolve by sexual selection.

In addition, much music in modern times (outside of popular music) suggests nothing like sexual selection. How would music performed by modern orchestras, choruses, church choirs, and so on, be about sexual selection? Moreover, national anthems have nothing to do with sexual selection, nor do military marches. Many other musical forms could be added to the list.

Music as a Product of Group Selection

Brown's alternative is that music is a product of **group selection**.[56] This is a special form of Darwinian selection in which the units of selection are not genes or individual organisms, but entire social groups. In the 1960s and 1970s the idea was severely criticized and embraced by only a tiny handful of evolutionists. Recently, however, it has been revived and is given more serious consideration,[57] although it is still a minority position. Most Darwinians continue to regard individual organisms or genes as the principal (if not the only) units of selection.[58] Nevertheless, Brown wishes to pursue this kind of argument. He contends that theorists who have attempted to understand the origins of music have made a major mistake in focusing excessively on music in large-scale societies, because much of this music is very different from the nature of music in societies characteristic of the ancestral environment. A focus on small-scale societies is therefore critical. Brown says that if

> we use large cultures as our starting point, with their many [musical] strata and mixed musical forms, we have great difficulties in determining which features of music reflect ancestral functions. However, when we examine small-scale cultures, *in which ritual music is the major stratum of the music culture*, we see that the structural properties, contexts, contents, and performance practices of music are overwhelmingly groupish and cooperative rather than individualist and competitive. . . . In such cultures, sexual display is secondary to the process of group assembly, not a primary motivation for musical expression.[59]

For Brown, it then follows that music evolved because of its ability to promote cooperation, coordination, and cohesion within social groups or entire societies. It is a major source of group identity and is able to accomplish this because it is an "emotive enhancer." For example, music promotes coordinated action as people work, which we know has been a major feature of African societies. Musical rituals also help to coordinate preparation for action, not just the action itself. In short, music promotes relative group fitness. In support of his argument, Brown points out the following:[60]

- In classless societies characteristic of the ancestral environment, the distinction between musicians and nonmusicians—performers and audiences—does not exist. Everyone is a musician. Children begin singing at the earliest possible age, and teaching them to sing is an important part of their upbringing. The oldest members of society continue to sing as long as it is physically possible for them to do so. The whole society is musical. (To Brown's point it can be added that in modern societies children are taught music early. Even in kindergarten they are taught rudimentary forms of music, such as banging sticks together or striking tambourines, and of course singing.)

- The content of ritual music is heavily group oriented. It often focuses on honoring and obeying spirits and gods, showing respect for the ancestors, celebrating core beliefs and values of the society, and so on.
- Music involves the blending and patterning of pitch. Good blending is especially prominent in the societies of sub-Saharan Africa and the Pacific Islands, where it is highly valued culturally and where individual showiness is disdained.
- Because of the importance of blending, musical performance requires a great deal of teamwork. This is clearly shown by the very elaborate group dancing and choral singing styles found throughout the world.

Music and Language

Many observers have drawn connections between music and language.[61] Brown points out that because music and language share phonological (sound) and syntactic (unit combination) structures, they are obviously related and thus could have evolved in tandem. He suggests five possible scenarios: (1) each could have arisen independently but evolved along parallel lines; (2) each could have arisen independently but evolved together by mutual interaction; (3) music could have been derived from language; (4) language could have been derived from music; and (5) both had a common ancestor, "musilanguage," from which each diverged at some later point although continuing to share a number of common features.[62]

Brown favors the last scenario. He suggests that language and music can be arranged along a continuum, language at one end and music at the other. Language is about "sound reference" and conveys *symbolic meaning*: the meanings of words, phrases, sentences, and so on. Music is about "sound emotion," which conveys *emotional meaning*. Language and music differ primarily in emphasis, not in kind, and "are essentially reciprocal specializations of a dual-natured precursor that used both sound emotion and sound reference in creating communication sounds."[63] After they diverged, language specialized in specifying relationships between subjects and objects and in the capability of assessing truth and falsity through the use of reason. This is because language became freed from music's acoustic modality. Music specialized in the formation of an acoustical (sound) modality, which permitted a dramatic expansion of the repertoire of acoustic range and pitch relative to its musilanguage progenitor. Music could therefore develop into "a complex and hierarchical syntax system based on pitch patterning and multipart blending."[64]

And of course, for Brown, music's divergence was a result of group selection.

However, even if Brown is right about musilanguage, the divergence of music and language can in principle be explained by any form of selection.

Conclusion

So what are we left with? Clearly natural selection theories don't work for the arts because the arts have no pragmatic utility in promoting survival. We have already extensively criticized the natural selection theory of literature, and there is no need to say more on that. But visual art and music don't promote survival either. Or at least it is very difficult to see how, which is probably why few people have proposed such an interpretation.

As for sexual selection, we have already seen that there are many features of music that do not fit this theory well at all. Brown's critique of sexual selection theory is highly compelling, although he does not dismiss sexual selection entirely. He concedes that there are musical styles that are soloist, competitive, poorly blended, and restricted by age and sex; but these are a minority of musical forms and not typical of ancestral forms.

Can sexual selection explain visual art or literature? Perhaps visual art originated in sexual selection in very early times, but the enormous elaboration of visual art through the ages makes little sense in terms of sexual selection. So what if some of the greatest painters were voracious womanizers who had many sexual partners and thus potentially very high reproductive success? For every one of these, there are probably hundreds whose reproductive success was no higher than average and many who had no reproductive success at all. Van Gogh, for example, had no children and virtually no success at attracting women (the best he could do was live for a few months with a Dutch prostitute). As for literature, it is even less likely to be about sexual selection. Many writers have been women who were hardly using their works as courtship displays.

What then of group selection? As Fitch points out, it is important to distinguish group *functions* from group *selection*. The fact that music functions to bind individuals into groups does not necessarily mean that it was evolutionarily selected in order to do that.[65] Group selectionist arguments have difficulty separating cause and consequence. Something may contribute to social cohesion, but only as an unintended consequence, not as an actual cause. Miller makes a similar point by saying that although music is performed *in* groups, this does not mean that it is performed *for* groups.[66]

Is there a grand conclusion that can be drawn? Natural selection can be dismissed. Group selection is dubious, and in any event arguments relying on this concept are very difficult to test empirically. That leaves only by-product and sexual selection arguments. It may be best to go with the by-product argument, although very provisionally. Much more research has to be done before any definitive conclusions can be drawn (if they ever can be). The evolutionary study of the arts is still in its infancy.

SUMMARY

1. The arts include visual art, literature, and music. They are universal and extend far back into prehistory. Arts are not always easy to define. Some contend that art is whatever people say it is, but such a definition is unsatisfying. Another approach is to list some of the leading characteristics of the arts. One list suggests that arts give pleasure, demonstrate virtuosity, can be critically evaluated, express the individuality and imagination of the artist, are permeated by emotion, and are intellectually challenging.

2. This characterization of the arts seems to apply to arts that are of high quality. Arts such as finger painting or singing in the shower lack most of the characteristics listed above, but it is difficult to deny that they are arts in some general sense.

3. Two of the most important forms of visual art are painting and sculpture. There is an important distinction between mass art and elite art, at least in early modern and modern societies. Mass art is produced for large segments of a population, whereas elite art is produced mainly for other artists or art aficionados. Artists who produce for the masses care what they think of this art, but elite artists tend to disdain mass taste, sometimes in the extreme.

4. Recently several million people in ten societies worldwide were queried about their artistic tastes. People consistently preferred landscape paintings with lots of blue and green and containing people and animals. Evolutionists claim that these preferences correspond to the natural environment in which humans first evolved. People worldwide most dislike modern abstract art. They dislike abstract squares and angles, and abstract paintings in which people and objects are depicted in distorted ways. Most people cannot relate to this sort of art because it is outside the realm of normal human experience.

5. Evolutionists do not agree on the origins of art. Some say it is simply a by-product of other adaptations and does not contribute to survival or reproductive success. Others contend that art evolved by sexual selection. One sexual selection theory, fitness indicator theory, holds that artists are signaling their fitness to potential mates. Good art can only be produced by people who have such high-fitness qualities as energy, endurance, hand-eye coordination, fine motor control, intelligence, and creativity. Fitness indicator theory is actually a type of costly signaling theory combined with Veblen's concept of conspicuous waste.

6. Artistic production is highly male dominated. Men produce most of the paintings. It is also highly age related. The number of paintings produced by men rises sharply after age twenty and peaks around age forty, after which production declines throughout the rest of life.

7. Literature is about telling stories, either orally or in written form. Here we find sexual selection theories, natural selection theories, and by-product theories. Theories based on sexual selection rely on the age and sex distribution of literature. Most literature is produced by relatively young men whose literary production declines sharply with age. Literature is regarded as a courtship display.

8. Natural selection theories of literature contend that literature provides people with important insights into social relationships that can be used to negotiate real life effectively. It is argued that people who are more effective than others in negotiating social life have better survival skills. But it is by no means clear that literature provides these benefits, nor is it likely that people need literature to help them negotiate social life.

9. Stories are in all likelihood nothing more than evolutionary by-products of adaptations that evolved to facilitate successful human interaction; they are mental projections or representations of these adaptations. In all probability people tell stories simply because they like them, and they like them because they like thinking about the problems and opportunities presented by interacting with other people. Stories are forms of enjoyment that have no evolutionary function.

10. Music is universal and very old. Archaeologists have discovered flutes made of bone that date back as far as 37 Kya. A wide variety of musical forms have socially evolved in a cumulative fashion throughout human history. In the earliest societies most music consisted of group singing in the context of rituals. Later on, folk music was added. Then followed classical music, which was the music of elites in highly stratified societies. As classical music developed, folk music expanded in opposition to classical music. Last to evolve was the commercial or popular music of the twentieth century.

11. Sexual selection theorists conceive of music as a courtship display. They usually draw an analogy between music and birdsong because the latter is used by males to attract females. There are several difficulties with the sexual selection argument: human males seldom sing to females face to face; although love is a major theme in modern popular music, it does not figure prominently in earlier music; and many musical genres, such as classical music, military marches, or national anthems, have no connection at all to love or courtship.

12. Another theory is that music evolved for the benefit of entire groups rather than individuals. In this view music promotes group cooperation and cohesion, and that is its adaptive function. Those who take this position rely heavily on the group-oriented focus of music in small-scale societies, and also on the fact that many musical performances involve a great deal of teamwork. This kind of argument is hard to test because of the difficulty of disentangling causes and consequences. Just because music requires

coordination and teamwork, and just because it may enhance group cohesion, does not mean that it evolved for that purpose.

13. Some argue that music is a by-product of other pleasure-enhancing brain modules. Like visual art and literature, music produces pleasure but there is no indication that it is useful for survival or that it promotes reproductive success.

14. It is generally accepted that music and language are related, but there is no widespread agreement as to how. Language could have been an outgrowth of music, or music could have been derived from language. Another possibility is that both music and language had a common ancestor, musilanguage, from which they diverged at some point in the evolution of the brain.

QUESTIONS FOR DISCUSSION

✓ How common are the arts? How far back into prehistory do they extend?

✓ What are the arts? How can they be defined or characterized?

✓ Is finger painting art? Singing in the shower?

✓ What is the difference between mass art and elite art?

✓ Why do elite artists disdain mass art? Discuss.

✓ What kinds of paintings do people worldwide prefer? What kinds of paintings do they dislike? Why do they like or dislike these painting styles?

✓ What can account for art movements like modernism or postmodernism?

✓ Have the arts evolved by natural selection? Why or why not?

✓ Is it possible that the arts evolved by sexual selection rather than natural selection?

✓ By-product theorists of the arts rely on the claim that they are evolutionarily useless. Explain the meaning of this.

✓ Discuss the relationship between artistic production and age and sex.

✓ Is there elite and mass music in much the same sense that there is elite and mass art? Discuss.

✓ Discuss the evolution of musical forms over the past few thousand years.

✓ How may music and language be related?

References and Notes

1. Dutton 2009.

2. Martindale 1990.

3. Dutton 2009.

4. Dutton 2009, p. 197.

5. The author of this book likes it and it is hanging in his home. To him it looks like a work of considerable technical skill.

6. Derek Sanderson, personal communication. The cool reception to Duchamp's paintings was the reason he turned to the ready-mades.

7. Wypijewski 1997.

8. Orians and Heerwagen 1992; Dutton 2009.

9. Orians and Heerwagen 1992, p. 557.

10. Orians and Heerwagen 1992; Dutton 2009.

11. Dutton 2009.

12. Balling and Falk 1982; Synek and Grammer, undated online version. Both as discussed in Orians and Heerwagen 1992; Dutton 2009.

13. Miller 2000a.

14. Mason and Felder 2007, pp. 140–141.

15. Pinker 2002.

16. Pinker 2002.

17. Pinker 2002, p. 416.

18. The present author does, for example.

19. Pinker 1997, p. 525.

20. Pinker 2002, p. 405.

21. Pinker 2002.

22. Miller 1999, 2000a; Dutton 2009.

23. Dutton 2009, p. 136.

24. Miller 2000a.

25. Miller 2000a, p. 281.

26. Miller 2000a, p. 281.

27. Dutton 2009.

28. Miller 2000a.

29. Miller 1999.

30. Miller 1999.

31. Homer did not write these down himself. In his lifetime they were told orally. They were not written down until several generations after his death. Derek Sanderson, personal communication.

32. Dutton 2009, p. 109.

33. Dutton 2009, p. 113.

34. Carroll 2004, p. 68, as quoted in Dutton 2009, p. 123.

35. Gottschall 2012.

36. Gottschall is expanding on a simulation analogy originally developed by Mar and Oatley 2008.

37. Gottschall 2012, p. 66.

38. M. Sugiyama 2005, as discussed in Dutton 2009.

39. Mar et al. 2006.

40. Mar, Oatley, and Peterson 2009.

41. Fitch 2006; Kunej and Turk 2000.

42. Fitch 2006; Kunej and Turk 2000.

43. S. Brown 2000b.

44. Lomax 1968, as discussed in S. Brown 2000b.

45. S. Brown 2000b, p. 263.

46. Pinker 1997, p. 528.

47. Pinker 1997.

48. Fitch 2006.

49. Fitch 2006.

50. Slater 2000.

51. Miller 1999.

52. Miller 2000b.

53. Miller 2000b.

54. S. Brown 2000b.

55. Anyone who listens to popular music even casually will have noted that love—being in love, losing love, betrayal in love, and so on—is a very prominent theme. But it may be helpful to document it. A study by Ostlund and Kinnier 1997 analyzed the twenty-five most popular American songs for each of four decades (the 1950s, 1960s, 1970s, and 1980s) and found that across all of these decades an average of 73 percent contained lyrics that were predominantly about love. These findings are consistent with those from an earlier study that found that love and/or sex was the predominant theme in 71 percent of the most popular American songs of the 1960s (Cole 1971).

56. S. Brown 2000b.

57. Sober and Wilson 1998; D. S. Wilson 2007; Wilson and Wilson 2007.

58. An excellent critique of group selection and defense of traditional natural selection theory can be found in Pinker 2012.

59. S. Brown 2000b, p. 264; emphasis in original.

60. S. Brown 2000b.

61. Jackendoff 2009; Jackendoff and Lerdahl 2006.

62. S. Brown 2000a.

63. S. Brown 2000a, p. 278.

64. S. Brown 2000a, p. 293.

65. Fitch 2006.

66. Miller 2000b.

Epilogue

Evolution and Existence

There are two really big questions: why is there a universe, and why are we in it? Putting it slightly differently, why is there something rather than nothing, and what is the meaning of human existence?

Hardly anyone has the slightest idea how to answer the first question, and only cosmologists are qualified even to speculate on an answer. But they don't really know the answer either, or at least cannot agree on an answer.[1]

Traditionally philosophers and theologians have addressed the second question. Jean-Paul Sartre said that the main point of life is to live authentically, which apparently means being true to yourself. This sounds okay until you realize that perhaps Hitler was being true to himself, and Stalin too. Sartre also said that life is absurd, which is itself pretty absurd. As for modern theologians, they say a variety of things, such as knowing the mind of God or becoming one with the universe.

But it is possible to use a scientific perspective to try to formulate an answer to the second question. Here are four possibilities (the list is not exhaustive):

1. The meaning of human existence is simply what people define it to be at any given place or time. Sartre and other existentialist philosophers said something like this when they said that "existence precedes essence." We find ourselves in the world and we have to figure out for ourselves what we are doing here. A lot of anthropologists and sociologists also like this kind of answer, especially the social constructionists. Since society is just a matter of people collectively defining social reality, a group of people can simply get together and decide how to organize things so that life is good and makes sense. Often they like to add, and so it is "fair" and "just."

2. Human existence has no meaning or purpose, or at least any absolute or ultimate meaning. Like other organisms, humans evolved bodies and brains by natural selection, and just "are." We are here because natural selection working over hundreds of millions of years produced us, and that's about it.

3. The meaning of human existence is simply to make more copies of your genes

than your rivals are making of theirs. The basic meaning of human life is to make more human life.

4. The meaning of human existence is to achieve satisfaction with respect to the basic goals and desires that are a part of human nature. Since in real life these goals and desires are often in conflict, they must be harmonized or balanced in some way.

The first answer seems pretty obviously false. The social constructionists, or at least the more extreme ones, seem to think that people can just make up social life any way they wish. Nothing constrains what they do. But a deep and wide understanding of human society throughout time and space easily shows this answer to be fanciful if not nonsensical, as this book has attempted to show.

The second answer is true in the sense that there is no ultimate meaning or purpose, and also in the sense that evolution by natural and sexual selection is how we got here. But it is bleak and unsatisfying. If there isn't any meaning or purpose to what we are doing, then why are we spending time doing it?

The third answer is a little better. It's a lot like the second, but it says that we can get a lot of satisfaction in life if we have children and grandchildren and watch them grow up. But the fourth answer may be the best because it is grounded in what is true in the second and third answers. Does this mean, then, that we can use a Darwinian perspective to answer this age-old question of the meaning of life? Yes.

The evolutionary anthropologists Eric Alden Smith and Bruce Winterhalder have suggested that "some significant portion of the preferences . . . exhibited by humans in diverse times and places has been shaped directly or indirectly by natural selection."[2] The following can be suggested as the most fundamental human preferences that have been shaped by selection, both natural and sexual (the preferences will already be familiar from previous discussions):[3]

1. A complete and long life
2. Health
3. Reproduction and parental care
4. Sexual mating
5. Familial bonding
6. Gender identity
7. Social ranking
8. Wealth
9. Political rule
10. Reciprocal exchange
11. Ethnic identity
12. Beauty
13. Aesthetic pleasure
14. Religious understanding

From a Darwinian perspective, what gives life meaning is the ability of people to satisfy all or at least most of these preferences or desires. And life is meaningful *only* if people are able to satisfy them. This is the meaning of human existence. Of course, the desires cannot all be satisfied at the same time, or perhaps even in an entire lifetime. People have to decide which ones are most important to them as individuals and work on satisfying those. There are always trade-offs.

There are also individual differences in how people will rank these preferences. Albert Einstein said that he had no interest in money, power, or fame (he therefore had little concern for preferences 7, 8, and 9). He won a Nobel Prize, but he didn't need it to be happy. All he needed, he said, were three things: his sailboat, his violin, and physics. The last was clearly the most important since he spent most of his time on it. He therefore sought to satisfy a human preference not on the list, intellectual understanding. (There are some other preferences that could be added to the list, such as friendship, a sense of justice, or respect for cultural traditions.) Einstein, though, was unusual. Most people do want money, fame, power, awards, and the like.

Even if they find Darwinian explanations of human behavior persuasive, many people will object to the conclusions drawn above. Their main objection will be that the concept of purpose has been eradicated. Everything happens for a purpose, they will say, and where is that in your analysis? At first blush they appear to be stating the obvious: all effects have causes. But this is not what they mean. What they mean is that everything that happens is the product of some deep *cosmic* purpose embedded in the universe or, more likely, in the mind of God. Evolutionary and cognitive psychologists have been able to identify a number of cognitive biases imbedded in the human brain. One of these is a *teleological* bias. Teleological means having to do with purpose. Teleological thinking is a fundamental part of all religions, but it can exist apart from religion. The floor collapsed and the woman died not simply because the floor was weak, but because someone or something made the floor weak so that the woman would fall through it and die. There was a purpose or plan for this woman that was carried out. The trees rustle because the wind is blowing, but why is the wind blowing at that particular time and place and who or what is making the wind blow? What purpose is being served by the wind blowing? God has a purpose for everything that happens, including a purpose for your life. What happens to you is determined by God—with your cooperation, of course.

This kind of thinking is pervasive. The human brain has evolved to think that way and it is extremely difficult to break free from it. Scientists have only given up teleological thinking in the past century or two. Physicists were the first to abandon it, but biologists were clinging to it as recently as a century ago. Not long after Darwin first proposed it, biologists came to accept the idea that evolution had occurred, but there was great resistance for many years to the mechanism Darwin proposed to explain *how* evolution occurred, natural selection.[4] If variation was random and evolution just a matter of environments retaining favorable traits and purging unfavorable ones, what room was left for purpose? It wasn't until a new field of biology developed in the early twentieth century, population genetics, that it could finally be shown how natural selection could work in the absence of some larger purpose inherent in nature.

Teleological thinking dies hard—very hard. And it is making a comeback in the most unlikely of places, physics, the most rigorous of all the sciences and the first to abandon teleology. Some years ago a new idea was introduced called the Anthropic Principle.[5] It was based on the recognition that for intelligent life to exist on earth a very specific combination of conditions must exist. These are the constants we observe in the universe and in our solar system. For example, the universe has to be a certain age in order for stars to form and carbon to be produced, since life is carbon based. And the temperatures found on earth have to stay within a fairly narrow range. If it gets too cold the oceans will freeze permanently, too hot and they will boil away. Life will then be impossible because it requires water. Therefore, the earth has to be about the distance from the sun that we observe, about 93 million miles. There also has to be a precise ratio of the mass of the proton to the mass of the neutron. The Anthropic Principle says that these features and many others have been fine-tuned to such a degree that even a tiny variation in any one would make intelligent life impossible. The probability of all of this occurring is thought by adherents of the Anthropic Principle to be so infinitesimal that it could not have occurred by chance. If not by chance, then how? By some sort of plan or design (Plan or Design).[6]

The Anthropic Principle is related to another idea that emerged in physics in the 1920s as part of an overarching theory called quantum mechanics. It was shown that if one wanted to measure the properties of an elementary particle, such as an electron, this could only be done in a probabilistic manner. If you ascertained an electron's location in space, you could only ascertain its momentum within a certain range of probability. Conversely, if you determined with precision an electron's momentum, then you could only determine its location probabilistically. This was because the experimenter doing the measuring, that is, observing the electron, actually influenced it. This quickly led to a very radical idea: an electron doesn't really exist as an independent reality, but is brought into existence by the very act of observation. Since the universe is made up of electrons and other elementary particles, then it doesn't exist until it is observed.

If we try to connect the two—the specific values of the constants and the notion that the universe is brought into existence through observation—we end up with a huge conundrum. Since the universe is around 14 billion years old, and since humans have been around for only a tiny fraction of that time, no one could have been there to observe anything 14 billion years ago. Therefore, the universe should not exist. But it does. The solution must be that there was some other type of observer, an Observer with a capital "O," that brought the universe into existence and gave it the specific combination of precise values needed for intelligent life to exist.

All of this seems to force the conclusion that the evolution of intelligent life must be the reason for the universe's existence: the universe exists *in order to produce us*. This is its purpose (perhaps better called its Purpose with a capital "P"). What kind of observer could have done this? In essence, some sort of Mind (capital "M"), or what the great nineteenth-century German philosopher G. W. F. Hegel called the Absolute Spirit. As we saw in the discussion of religion in Chapter 13, another fundamental cognitive bias in the human brain is that of *agency*, the idea that there has to be some sort of agent that causes things to happen. This agent can be a conscious person or a type of supernatural being. Whatever kind of agent it is, there is meaning and purpose behind what it does.

The Anthropic Principle takes us right back to philosophy and theology, but by way of science. Can the Anthropic Principle be correct? There are a lot of skeptics, among them some of today's greatest physicists. The eminent physicist Roger Penrose of Oxford University says that

> with a spatially infinite and essentially uniform universe . . . the strong anthropic principle is almost useless for tuning physical parameters, beyond demanding that the physical laws be such that sentience [intelligence] is possible (which is itself fairly unusable, since we do not know the prerequisites for sentience). For if sentient life is possible at all, then we expect that, in a spatially infinite universe, it will occur. This will happen even if the conditions for sentience are extraordinarily unlikely to come about in any given finite region in the universe. In a spatially infinite universe, our expectation is that there should be *somewhere* in its infinite reaches where sentience does happen, if only by the mere chance coming together of all the necessary ingredients. This would indeed occur just by chance, even if extraordinarily infrequently.[7]

There are other difficulties involved in positing an Observer outside the universe who brought it into existence. For one thing, it is a statement not subject to any sort of scientific verification or falsification. We cannot see this Observer or measure anything about it. Moreover, even if there was an Original Observer who brought the universe into existence, shouldn't there logically have been a prior Observer— some sort of "Pre-Original Observer"—who brought the Original Observer into existence? You see the problem. We inevitably end up with an infinite regression—an infinite chain of Observers and Observed—and therefore have made no progress at all in answering the question why there is something rather than nothing.

A sensible conclusion is that the universe just *is* and doesn't exist for any actual reason or purpose. Intelligent life doesn't exist for any reason or purpose either. It just evolved from less-intelligent forms of life, and the first life-forms popped into existence by way of a certain fortuitous combination of chemical conditions.[8] Most people find conclusions like this distressing. If there is no ultimate purpose to our lives, life is emptied of all meaning. Why then bother to live at all? The reason to bother is to fulfill the desires that emanate from our species-specific human nature. This is sufficient. There doesn't need to be anything else for life to be meaningful.

References and Notes

1. In his book *Why Does the World Exist?* Jim Holt discusses some of the best-known answers to the question of why there is something and not nothing. None of the answers are especially illuminating. But evolution did not sculpt our brains for answering such a deep question. It only sculpted them to cope with the things we find ourselves surrounded by and to which we must adapt. Evolution can only recognize something; it cannot recognize nothing.

2. Smith and Winterhalder 1992a, pp. 49–50.

3. These preferences are drawn from a longer list proposed by the Darwinian political philosopher Larry Arnhart 1998.

4. Bowler 1983.

5. Barrow and Tipler 1986.

6. Barrow and Tipler 1986.

7. Penrose 2005.

8. In a recent book, Addy Pross 2012 outlines some of the latest thinking on the transition from the chemical (inorganic) to the biological (organic). The transition from nonlife to life is another of the great questions, not only of our own time but of much earlier times as well. Progress is being made in this area of science.

BIBLIOGRAPHY

Abrams, H. Leon Jr. 1987. "The preference for animal protein and fat: A cross-cultural survey." In Marvin Harris and Eric B. Ross, eds. *Food and Evolution: Toward a Theory of Human Food Habits*. Philadelphia: Temple University Press.

Adams, Richard E. W. 1991. *Prehistoric Mesoamerica*. 2nd ed. Norman: University of Oklahoma Press.

Adams, Robert McC. 1966. *The Evolution of Urban Society*. Chicago: Aldine.

Alanko, Katarina, Pekka Santtila, Nicole Harlaar, Katarina Witting, Markus Varjonen, Patrik Jern, Ada Johansson, Bettina von der Pahlen, and N. Kenneth Sandnabba. 2010. "Common genetic effects of gender atypical behavior in childhood and sexual orientation in adulthood: A study of Finnish twins." *Archives of Sexual Behavior* 39:81–92.

Alcorta, Candace S., and Richard Sosis. 2005. "Ritual, emotion, and sacred symbols: The evolution of religion as an adaptive complex." *Human Nature* 16:323–359.

Alderson, Arthur S., and Stephen K. Sanderson. 1991. "Historical European household structures and the capitalist world-economy." *Journal of Family History* 16:419–432.

Alexander, Richard D. 1974. "The evolution of social behavior." *Annual Review of Ecology and Systematics* 5:325–383.

Alexander, Richard D. 1975. "The search for a general theory of behavior." *Behavioral Science* 20:77–100.

Alexander, Richard D. 1989. "Evolution of the human psyche." In Paul Mellars and Christopher Stringer, eds. *The Human Revolution: Behavioural and Biological Perspectives on the Origins of Modern Humans*. Princeton, NJ: Princeton University Press.

Alexander, Richard D. 1990. "Epigenetic rules and Darwinian algorithms." *Ethology and Sociobiology* 11:241–303.

Alexander, Richard D., John H. Hoogland, Richard D. Howard, Katharine M. Noonan, and Paul W. Sherman. 1979. "Sexual dimorphisms and breeding systems in pinnipeds, ungulates, primates, and humans." In Napoleon A. Chagnon and William Irons, eds. *Evolutionary Biology and Human Social Behavior*. North Scituate, MA: Duxbury Press.

Amarasingam, Amarnath, ed. 2010. *Religion and the New Atheism: A Critical Appraisal*. Leiden: Brill.

American Anthropological Association. 1998. "AAA Statement on Race." *American Anthropologist* 100:712–713.

Anderson, Perry. 1974. *Passages from Antiquity to Feudalism.* London: New Left Books.

Anderson, S. S., and M. F. Fedak. 1985. "Grey seal males: Energetic and behavioural links between size and sexual success." *Animal Behaviour* 33:829–838.

Andersson, Malte. 1994. *Sexual Selection.* Princeton, NJ: Princeton University Press.

Annett, Joan, and Randall Collins. 1975. "A short history of deference and demeanor." In Randall Collins, *Conflict Sociology: Toward an Explanatory Science.* New York: Academic Press.

Archer, John. 2009. "Does sexual selection explain human sex differences in aggression?" *Behavioral and Brain Sciences* 32:249–311.

Archer, John, and S. Côté. 2005. "Sex differences in aggressive behavior: A developmental and evolutionary perspective." In R. Tremblay, W. W. Hartup, and John Archer, eds. *Developmental Origins of Aggression.* New York: Guilford Press.

Armstrong, Alice, Chaloka Beyani, and Chuma Himonga. 1993. "Uncovering reality: Excavating women's rights in African family law." *International Journal of Law and the Family* 7:314–369.

Arnhart, Larry. 1998. *Darwinian Natural Right: The Biological Ethics of Human Nature.* Albany: State University of New York Press.

Aros, Jesse R., George A. Henly, and Nicholas T. Curtis. 1998. "Occupational sextype and sex differences in vocational preference-measured interest relationships." *Journal of Vocational Behavior* 53:227–242.

Arrighi, Giovanni. 2007. *Adam Smith in Beijing: Lineages of the Twenty-First Century.* London: Verso.

Ash, Jessica, and Gordon G. Gallup Jr. 2007. "Paleoclimatic variation and brain expansion during human evolution." *Human Nature* 18:109–124.

Atran, Scott. 2002. *In Gods We Trust: The Evolutionary Landscape of Religion.* New York: Oxford University Press.

Atran, Scott, and Ara Norenzayan. 2004. "Religion's evolutionary landscape: Counterintuition, commitment, compassion, communion." *Behavioral and Brain Sciences* 27:713–770.

Aubet, Maria Eugenia. 1993. *The Phoenicians and the West.* Cambridge, UK: Cambridge University Press.

Aziz, Barbara N. 1978. *Tibetan Frontier Families: Reflections of Three Generations from Dingri.* Durham, NC: Duke University Press.

Badcock, Christopher R. 1991. *Evolution and Individual Behavior: An Introduction to Human Sociobiology.* Oxford: Blackwell.

Bailey, Drew H., and David C. Geary. 2009. "Hominid brain evolution: Testing climatic, ecological, and social competition models." *Human Nature* 20:67–79.

Bailey, J. Michael, and R. C. Pillard. 1991. "A genetic study of male sexual orientation." *Archives of General Psychiatry* 48:1089–1096.

Bailey, J. Michael, R. C. Pillard, M. C. Neale, and Y. Agyei. 1993. "Heritable factors influence sexual orientation in women." *Archives of General Psychiatry* 50:217–223.

Bailey, J. Michael, and Kenneth J. Zucker. 1995. "Childhood sex-typed behavior and sexual orientation: A conceptual analysis and quantitative review." *Developmental Psychology* 31:43–55.

Baillargeon, Raymond H., Mark Zoccolillo, Kate Keenan, Sylvana Côté, Daniel Pérusse,

Hong-Xing Wu, Michel Boivin, and Richard E. Tremblay. 2007. "Gender differences in physical aggression: A prospective population-based survey of children before and after 2 years of age." *Developmental Psychology* 43:13–26.

Balling, J. D., and J. H. Falk. 1982. "Development of visual preference for natural environments." *Environment and Behavior* 14:5–28.

Barber, Nigel. 1995. "The evolutionary psychology of physical attractiveness: Sexual selection and human morphology." *Ethology and Sociobiology* 16:395–424.

Barfield, Thomas J. 1989. *The Perilous Frontier: Nomadic Empires and China.* Oxford: Blackwell.

Barfield, Thomas J. 1993. *The Nomadic Alternative.* Upper Saddle River, NJ: Prentice Hall.

Bar-Josef, Ofer. 1998. "On the nature of transitions: The Middle to Upper Paleolithic and the Neolithic Revolution." *Cambridge Archaeological Journal* 8:141–163.

Bar-Josef, Ofer. 2002. "The Upper Paleolithic revolution." *Annual Review of Anthropology* 31:363–393.

Barkley, R. A., D. G. Ullmann, L. Otto, and J. M. Brecht. 1977. "The effects of sex typing and sex appropriateness of modeled behavior on children's imitation." *Child Development* 48:721–725.

Barkow, Jerome H., Leda Cosmides, and John Tooby, eds. 1992. *The Adapted Mind: Evolutionary Psychology and the Generation of Culture.* New York: Oxford University Press.

Barrett, Justin L. 2004. *Why Would Anyone Believe in God?* Lanham, MD: AltaMira Press.

Barrow, John D., and Frank J. Tipler. 1986. *The Anthropic Cosmological Principle.* Oxford: Clarendon Press.

Barth, Frederik. 1961. *Nomads of South Persia.* New York: Humanities Press.

Barth, Frederik, ed. 1969. *Ethnic Groups and Boundaries.* Boston: Little, Brown.

Bartlett, Nancy H., and Paul L. Vasey. 2006. "A retrospective study of childhood gender-atypical behavior in Samoan *fa'afafine.*" *Archives of Sexual Behavior* 35:659–666.

Beall, Cynthia M., and Melvyn C. Goldstein. 1981. "Tibetan fraternal polyandry: A test of sociobiological theory." *American Anthropologist* 83:5–12.

Beals, Ralph L., and Harry Hoijer. 1971. *An Introduction to Anthropology.* 4th ed. New York: Macmillan.

Beaud, Michel. 1983. *A History of Capitalism: 1500–1980.* New York: Monthly Review Press.

Beckerman, Stephen. 1989. "Hunting and fishing in Amazonia." Paper presented at Wenner-Gren Symposium 109, Nova Friburgo, Brazil.

Bell, Daniel. 1973. *The Coming of Post-Industrial Society.* New York: Basic Books.

Bellwood, Peter. 2005. *First Farmers: The Origins of Agricultural Societies.* Oxford: Blackwell.

Benedict, Ruth. 1934. *Patterns of Culture.* Boston: Houghton Mifflin.

Bennett, H. S. 1937. *Life on the English Manor: A Study of Peasant Conditions, 1150–1400.* Cambridge, UK: Cambridge University Press.

Bereczkei, Tamas, and Andras Csanaky. 1996. "Mate choice, marital success, and reproduction in a modern society." *Ethology and Sociobiology* 17:17–35.

Berman, Louis A. 2003. *The Puzzle: Exploring the Evolutionary Puzzle of Male Homosexuality.* Wilmette, IL: Godot Press.

Bettinger, Robert, Peter Richerson, and Robert Boyd. 2009. "Constraints on the development of agriculture." *Current Anthropology* 50:627–631.

Betzig, Laura L. 1986. *Despotism and Differential Reproduction.* New York: Aldine de Gruyter.

Betzig, Laura L. 1989. "Causes of conjugal dissolution: A cross-cultural study." *Current Anthropology* 30:654–676.

Betzig, Laura L. 1992a. "Roman polygyny." *Ethology and Sociobiology* 13:309–349.

Betzig, Laura L. 1992b. "Roman monogamy." *Ethology and Sociobiology* 13:351–383.

Betzig, Laura L. 1993. "Sex, succession, and stratification in the first six civilizations." In Lee Ellis, ed. *Social Stratification and Socioeconomic Inequality.* Vol. 1. Westport, CT: Praeger.

Betzig, Laura L. 1995. "Medieval monogamy." *Journal of Family History* 20:181–216.

Betzig, Laura L., ed. 1997. *Human Nature: A Critical Reader.* New York: Oxford University Press.

Betzig, Laura L. 2005. "Politics as sex: The Old Testament case." *Evolutionary Psychology* 3:326–346.

Betzig, Laura L. 2009. "The fertility of prominent men in the Bible and Ancient Middle East." In Rick Goldberg, ed. *Judaism in Biological Perspective: Biblical Lore and Judaic Practices.* Boulder, CO: Paradigm Publishers.

Betzig, Laura L. 2012. "Means, variances, and ranges in reproductive success: Comparative evidence." *Evolution and Human Behavior* 33:309–317.

Betzig, Laura, and Paul Turke. 1986. "Parental investment by sex on Ifaluk." *Ethology and Sociobiology* 7:29–37.

Betzig, Laura, and Samantha Weber. 1995. "Presidents preferred sons." *Politics and the Life Sciences* 14:61–64.

Biasutti, Renato. 1967. *Le Razze e Popoli della Terra.* Torino, Italy: Unione Pipografiza-Editrice Torinese.

Bickerton, Derek. 1990. *Language and Species.* Chicago: University of Chicago Press.

Billing, Jennifer, and Paul W. Sherman. 1998. "Antimicrobial functions of spices: Why some like it hot." *Quarterly Review of Biology* 73:3–49.

Binford, Lewis R. 2001. *Constructing Frames of Reference: An Analytical Method for Archaeological Theory Building Using Hunter-Gatherer and Environmental Data Sets.* Berkeley: University of California Press.

Bittles, Alan H., and James V. Neel. 1994. "The costs of human inbreeding and their implications for variations at the DNA level." *Nature Genetics* 8:117–121.

Bjorklund, D. J., and A. D. Pellegrini. 2000. "Child development and evolutionary psychology." *Child Development* 71:1687–1708.

Blanton, Richard E., Stephen A. Kowalewski, Gary Feinman, and Jill Appel. 1981. *Ancient Mesoamerica.* New York: Cambridge University Press.

Blau, Judith R., and Peter M. Blau. 1982. "The cost of inequality: Metropolitan structure and violent crime." *American Sociological Review* 47:114–129.

Bliege Bird, Rebecca, and Eric Alden Smith. 2005. "Signaling theory, strategic interaction, and symbolic capital." *Current Anthropology* 46:221–248.

Bliege Bird, Rebecca, Eric Alden Smith, and D. W. Bird. 2001. "The hunting handicap: Costly signaling in male foraging strategies." *Behavioral Ecology and Sociobiology* 50:9–19.

Bloom, Gabrielle, and Paul W. Sherman. 2005. "Dairying barriers affect the distribution of lactose malabsorption." *Evolution and Human Behavior* 26:301e1–301e33.

Blum, Deborah. 2002. *Love at Goon Park: Harry Harlow and the Science of Affection.* New York: Berkley Books.

Blumberg, Rae Lesser. 1984. "A general theory of gender stratification." In Randall Collins, ed. *Sociological Theory 1984.* San Francisco: Jossey-Bass.

Blurton Jones, Nicholas G. 1986. "Bushman birth spacing: A test for optimal interbirth intervals." *Ethology and Sociobiology* 7:91–105.

Boas, Franz. 1940. *Race, Language, and Culture.* New York: Macmillan.

Boone, James L. III. 1986. "Parental investment and elite family structure in preindustrial states: A case study of late medieval–early modern Portuguese genealogies." *American Anthropologist* 88:859–878.

Boserup, Ester. 1965. *The Conditions of Agricultural Growth.* Chicago: Aldine.

Boserup, Ester. 1970. *Women's Role in Economic Development.* New York: St. Martin's Press.

Boserup, Ester. 1981. *Population and Technological Change.* Chicago: University of Chicago Press.

Boserup, Ester. 1986. "Shifts in the determinants of fertility in the developing world: Environmental, technical, economic, and cultural factors." In David Coleman and Roger Schofield, eds. *The State of Population Theory.* Oxford: Blackwell.

Boswell, John. 1988. *The Kindness of Strangers: The Abandonment of Children in Western Europe from Late Antiquity to the Renaissance.* New York: Pantheon.

Bourdieu, Pierre. 1984. *Distinction: A Social Critique of the Judgement of Taste.* Trans. Richard Nice. Cambridge, MA: Harvard University Press.

Bowlby, John. 1969. *Attachment.* London: Tavistock.

Bowler, Peter J. 1983. *The Eclipse of Darwinism: Anti-Darwinian Evolution Theories in the Decades Around 1900.* Baltimore: Johns Hopkins University Press.

Boyd, Robert, and Peter J. Richerson. 1985. *Culture and the Evolutionary Process.* Chicago: University of Chicago Press.

Boyd, Robert, and Peter J. Richerson. 2005. *The Origin and Evolution of Cultures.* New York: Oxford University Press.

Boyer, Pascal. 2001. *Religion Explained: The Evolutionary Origins of Religious Thought.* New York: Basic Books.

Brass, Paul. 1976. "Ethnicity and nationality formation." *Ethnicity* 3(3):225–241.

Braudel, Fernand. 1984. *The Perspective of the World: Civilization and Capitalism 15th–18th Century.* Vol. 3. Trans. Sian Reynolds. New York: Harper & Row.

Broch, Tom, and Johan Galtung. 1966. "Belligerence among the primitives." *Journal of Peace Research* 3:33–45.

Bronstad, P. M., and Devendra Singh. 1999. "Why did Tassinary and Hansen fail to replicate the relationship between WHR and female attractiveness?" Paper presented at the annual meetings of the Human Behavior and Evolution Society, University of Utah, Salt Lake City, June 2–6.

Brown, Judith K. 1975. "Iroquois women: An ethnohistoric note." In Rayna R. Reiter, ed. *Toward an Anthropology of Women.* New York: Monthly Review Press.

Brown, Steven. 2000a. "The 'musilanguage' model of music evolution." In Nils L. Wallin, Bjorn Merker, and Steven Brown, eds. *The Origins of Music.* Cambridge, MA: MIT Press.

Brown, Steven. 2000b. "Evolutionary models of music: From sexual selection to group selection." *Perspectives in Ethology* 13:231–281.

Browne, Kingsley. 1995. "Sex and temperament in modern society: A Darwinian view of the glass ceiling and the gender gap." *Arizona Law Review* 37:970–1106.

Browne, Kingsley. 1998. *Divided Labours: An Evolutionary View of Women at Work*. New Haven, CT: Yale University Press.

Browne, Kingsley. 2002. *Biology at Work: Rethinking Sexual Equality*. New Brunswick, NJ: Rutgers University Press.

Browne, Kingsley. 2007. *Co-Ed Combat: The New Evidence That Women Shouldn't Fight the Nation's Wars*. New York: Sentinel.

Buckle, Leslie, Gordon G. Gallup Jr., and Zachary A. Rodd. 1996. "Marriage as a reproductive contract: Patterns of marriage, divorce, and remarriage." *Ethology and Sociobiology* 17:363–377.

Bulbulia, Joseph, Richard Sosis, Erica Harris, Russell Genet, Cheryl Genet, and Karen Wyman, eds. 2008. *The Evolution of Religion: Studies, Theories, and Critiques*. Santa Margarita, CA: Collins Foundation Press.

Bureau of Labor Statistics. 2012. *Household Data Annual Averages*. http://www.bls.gov/cps/cpsaat11.pdf.

Buss, David M. 1989. "Sex differences in human mate preferences: Evolutionary hypotheses tested in 37 cultures." *Behavioral and Brain Sciences* 12:1–49.

Buss, David M. 1992. "Mate preference mechanisms: Consequences for partner choice and intrasexual competition." In Jerome H. Barkow, Leda Cosmides, and John Tooby, eds. *The Adapted Mind: Evolutionary Psychology and the Generation of Culture*. New York: Oxford University Press.

Buss, David M. 1994. *The Evolution of Desire: Strategies of Human Mating*. New York: Basic Books.

Buss, David M. 2000. *The Dangerous Passion: Why Jealousy Is As Necessary As Love and Sex*. New York: Free Press.

Buss, David M. 2005. *The Murderer Next Door: Why the Mind Is Designed to Kill*. New York: Penguin Press.

Buss, David M. 2007. *Evolutionary Psychology: The New Science of the Mind*. 3rd ed. Boston: Allyn & Bacon.

Buss, David M. 2009. "The multiple adaptive problems solved by human aggression." *Behavioral and Brain Sciences* 32:271–272.

Buss, David M., Randy J. Larsen, Drew Westen, and Jennifer Semmelroth. 1992. "Sex differences in jealousy: Evolution, physiology, and psychology." *Psychological Science* 3:251–255.

Buss, David M., and David P. Schmitt. 1993. "Sexual strategies theory: An evolutionary perspective on human mating." *Psychological Review* 100:204–232.

Butler, Noah, and Frank Salamone. 2004. "!Kung healing, ritual, and possession." In Mariko Namba Walter and Eva Jane Neumann Fridman, eds. *Shamanism: An Encyclopedia of World Beliefs, Practices, and Cultures*. Vol. 2. Santa Barbara, CA: ABC-CLIO.

Call, Josep, and Michael Tomasello. 2008. "Does the chimpanzee have a theory of mind? 30 years later." *Trends in Cognitive Sciences* 12:187–192.

Cann, R. L. 1987. "In search of Eve." *The Sciences* 27:30–37.

Cann, R. L., M. Stoneking, and A. C. Wilson. 1987. "Mitochondrial DNA and human evolution." *Nature* 325:31–36.

Cantarella, Eva. 1992. *Bisexuality in the Ancient World.* Trans. Cormac O'Cuilleanain. New Haven, CT: Yale University Press.

Cardoso, Fernando Luiz. 2009. "Recalled sex-typed behavior in childhood and sports preferences in adulthood of heterosexual, bisexual, and homosexual men from Brazil, Turkey, and Thailand." *Archives of Sexual Behavior* 38:726–736.

Carey, Arlen D., and Joseph Lopreato. 1995. "The evolutionary demography of the fertility-mortality quasi-equilibrium." *Population and Development Review* 21:613–630.

Carneiro, Robert L. 1970. "A theory of the origin of the state." *Science* 169:733–738.

Carneiro, Robert L. 1981. "The chiefdom: Precursor of the state." In Grant D. Jones and Robert R. Kautz, eds. *The Transition to Statehood in the New World.* New York: Cambridge University Press.

Carneiro, Robert L. 1987. "Further reflections on resource concentration and its role in the rise of the state." In Linda Manzanilla, ed. *Studies in the Neolithic and Urban Revolutions.* Oxford: British Archaeological Reports. International Series, no. 349.

Carneiro, Robert L. 1990. "Chiefdom-level warfare as exemplified in Fiji and the Cauca Valley." In Jonathan Haas, ed. *The Anthropology of War.* New York: Cambridge University Press.

Carroll, Joseph. 2004. *Literary Darwinism: Evolution, Human Nature, and Literature.* New York: Routledge.

Carroll, Sean B. 2005. *Endless Forms Most Beautiful: The New Science of Evo Devo.* New York: Norton.

Cartmill, Matt. 1999. "The status of the race concept in physical anthropology." *American Anthropologist* 100:651–660.

Cartwright, John. 2008. *Evolution and Human Behavior: Darwinian Perspectives on Human Nature.* 2nd ed. Cambridge, MA: MIT Press.

Cashdan, Elizabeth A. 1994. "A sensitive period for learning about food." *Human Nature* 5:279–291.

Cashdan, Elizabeth A., Frank W. Marlowe, Alyssa Crittenden, Claire Porter, and Brian M. Wood. 2012. "Sex differences in spatial cognition among Hadza foragers." *Evolution and Human Behavior* 33:274–284.

Cavalli-Sforza, L. Luca, Paolo Menozzi, and Alberto Piazza. 1994. *The History and Geography of Human Genes.* Abr. ed. Princeton, NJ: Princeton University Press.

Chagnon, Napoleon A. 1983. *Yanomamö: The Fierce People.* 3rd ed. New York: Holt, Rinehart & Winston.

Chagnon, Napoleon A. 1988. "Life histories, blood revenge, and warfare in a tribal population." *Science* 239:985–992.

Chagnon, Napoleon A. 1992. *Yanomamö: The Last Days of Eden.* San Diego: Harcourt Brace Jovanovich.

Chagnon, Napoleon A. 2013. *Noble Savages: My Life Among Two Dangerous Tribes—The Yanomamo and the Anthropologists.* New York: Simon & Schuster.

Chagnon, Napoleon A., Mark V. Flinn, and Thomas F. Melancon. 1979. "Sex-ratio variation among the Yanomamö Indians." In Napoleon A. Chagnon and William Irons, eds. *Evolutionary Biology and Human Social Behavior.* North Scituate, MA: Duxbury Press.

Chagnon, Napoleon A., and William Irons, eds. 1979. *Evolutionary Biology and Human Social Behavior: An Anthropological Perspective.* North Scituate, MA: Duxbury Press.

Champion, Timothy, Clive Gamble, Stephen Shennan, and Alasdair Whittle. 1984. *Prehistoric Europe*. New York: Academic Press.

Chandler, Tertius. 1987. *Four Thousand Years of Urban Growth*. Lewiston, NY: St. David's University Press.

Chang, Kwang-chih. 1986. *The Archaeology of Ancient China*. 4th ed. New Haven, CT: Yale University Press.

Chase-Dunn, Christopher. 2003. "Globalization from below: Toward a collectively rational and democratic global commonwealth." In Gernot Köhler and Emilio José Chaves, eds. *Globalization: Critical Perspectives*. New York: Nova Science.

Chomsky, Noam. 1965. *Aspects of the Theory of Syntax*. Cambridge, MA: MIT Press.

Chomsky, Noam. 1988. *Language and Problems of Knowledge*. Cambridge, MA: MIT Press.

Cipolla, Carlo. 1993. *Before the Industrial Revolution: European Society and Economy, 1000–1700*. New York: Norton.

Clark, Russell D., and Elaine Hatfield. 1989. "Gender differences in receptivity to sexual offers." *Journal of Psychology and Human Sexuality* 2:39–55.

Cleland, John. 2001. "The effects of improved survival on fertility: A reassessment." *Population and Development Review* 27(Supplement): 60–92.

Cobb, Charles R. 2003. "Mississippian chiefdoms: How complex?" *Annual Review of Anthropology* 32:63–84.

Cochran, Gregory, and Henry Harpending. 2009. *The 10,000 Year Explosion: How Civilization Accelerated Human Evolution*. New York: Basic Books.

Cohen, Jere. 1980. "Rational capitalism in Renaissance Italy." *American Journal of Sociology* 85:1340–1355.

Cohen, Mark N. 1977. *The Food Crisis in Prehistory*. New Haven, CT: Yale University Press.

Cohen, Mark N. 1985. "Prehistoric hunter-gatherers: The meaning of social complexity." In T. Douglas Price and James A. Brown, eds. *Prehistoric Hunter-Gatherers*. New York: Academic Press.

Cohen, Mark N. 1989. *Health and the Rise of Civilization*. New Haven, CT: Yale University Press.

Cohen, Mark N. 2009. "Rethinking the origins of agriculture." *Current Anthropology* 50:591–595.

Cohen, Mark N., and George J. Armelagos. 1984. "Paleopathology at the origins of agriculture: Editors' summation." In Mark N. Cohen and George J. Armelagos, eds. *Paleopathology at the Origins of Agriculture*. New York: Academic Press.

Cohen, Ronald. 1978. "State origins: A reappraisal." In Henri J. M. Claessen and Peter Skalnik, eds. *The Early State*. The Hague: Mouton.

Colapinto, John. 2000. *As Nature Made Him: The Boy Who Was Raised as a Girl*. New York: Harper Perennial.

Cole, R. R. 1971. "Top songs of the sixties: A content analysis of popular lyrics." *American Behavioral Scientist* 4:389–399.

Collins, Randall, with abridgement and update by Stephen K. Sanderson. 2009. *Conflict Sociology: A Sociological Classic Updated*. Boulder, CO: Paradigm Publishers.

Conley, Terri D. 2011. "Perceived proposer personality characteristics and gender differences in acceptance of casual sex offers." *Journal of Personality and Social Psychology* 100:309–329.

Coon, Carleton. 1951. *Caravan*. New York: Holt.

Coontz, Stephanie. 2005. *Marriage, A History: How Love Conquered Marriage*. New York: Penguin Books.

Cory, Donald W., and R. E. L. Masters. 1963. *Violation of Taboo: Incest of the Great Literature of the Past and the Present*. New York: Julian Press.

Cosmides, Leda, and John Tooby. 1992. "Cognitive adaptations for social exchange." In Jerome H. Barkow, Leda Cosmides, and John Tooby, eds. *The Adapted Mind: Evolutionary Psychology and the Generation of Culture*. New York: Oxford University Press.

Courtwright, David T. 1996. *Violent Land: Single Men and Social Disorder from the Frontier to the Inner City*. Cambridge, MA: Harvard University Press.

Cox, Oliver C. 1948. *Caste, Class, and Race*. New York: Monthly Review Press.

Coyne, Jerry A. 2009. *Why Evolution Is True*. New York: Penguin.

Crawford, Charles, and Dennis L. Krebs, eds. 1998. *Handbook of Evolutionary Psychology*. Mahwah, NJ: Lawrence Erlbaum.

Cribb, Roger. 1991. *Nomads in Archaeology*. Cambridge, UK: Cambridge University Press.

Cronk, Lee. 1989. "Low socioeconomic status and female-biased parental investment: The Mukogodo example." *American Anthropologist* 91:414–429.

Cronk, Lee. 1991. "Preferential parental investment in daughters over sons." *Human Nature* 2:387–417.

Cronk, Lee. 1999. *That Complex Whole: Culture and the Evolution of Human Behavior*. Boulder, CO: Westview Press.

Cronk, Lee. 2000. "Female-biased parental investment and growth performance among the Mukogodo." In Lee Cronk, Napoleon Chagnon, and William Irons, eds. *Adaptation and Human Behavior: An Anthropological Perspective*. New York: Aldine de Gruyter.

Cronk, Lee. 2004. *From Mukogodo to Maasai: Ethnicity and Cultural Change in Kenya*. Boulder, CO: Westview Press.

Cronk, Lee, Napoleon Chagnon, and William Irons, eds. 2000. *Adaptation and Human Behavior: An Anthropological Perspective*. New York: Aldine de Gruyter.

Dabbs, James M. Jr., et al. 1998. "Spatial ability, navigation strategy, and geographic knowledge among men and women." *Evolution and Human Behavior* 19:89–98.

Dahlberg, Frances. 1981. *Woman the Gatherer*. New Haven, CT: Yale University Press.

Dalton, George. 1969. "Theoretical issues in economic anthropology." *Current Anthropology* 10:63–102.

D'Altroy, T. N. 2002. *The Incas*. Oxford: Blackwell.

Daly, Martin, and Margo Wilson. 1978. *Sex, Evolution, and Behavior*. North Scituate, MA: Duxbury Press.

Daly, Martin, and Margo Wilson. 1988. *Homicide*. New York: Aldine de Gruyter.

Daly, Martin, and Margo Wilson. 1990. "Killing the competition: Female/female and male/male homicide." *Human Nature* 1:81–107.

Daly, Martin, and Margo Wilson. 1997. "Crime and conflict: Homicide in evolutionary psychological perspective." *Crime and Justice* 22:51–100.

Daly, Martin, and Margo Wilson. 1998. *The Truth About Cinderella: A Darwinian View of Parental Love*. New Haven, CT: Yale University Press.

Daly, Martin, Margo Wilson, and Shawn Vasdev. 2001. "Income inequality and homicide rates in Canada and the United States." *Canadian Journal of Criminology* 43:219–236.

Daly, Martin, Margo Wilson, and Suzanne J. Weghorst. 1982. "Male sexual jealousy." *Ethology and Sociobiology* 3:11–27.

Darwin, Charles. 1859. *On the Origin of Species by Means of Natural Selection, or The Preservation of the Favoured Races in the Struggle for Life*. London: John Murray.

Darwin, Charles. 1871. *The Descent of Man and Selection in Relation to Sex*. London: John Murray.

Davis, Kingsley. 1949. *Human Society*. New York: Macmillan.

Dawkins, Richard. 2006. *The God Delusion*. Boston: Houghton Mifflin.

Degler, Carl N. 1991. *In Search of Human Nature: The Decline and Revival of Darwinism in American Social Thought*. New York: Oxford University Press.

Dennett, Daniel C. 2006. *Breaking the Spell: Religion as a Natural Phenomenon*. New York: Viking.

Derry, T. K., and Trevor I. Williams. 1961. *A Short History of Technology: From the Earliest Times to AD 1900*. New York: Oxford University Press.

De Waal, Frans. 1982. *Chimpanzee Politics: Power and Sex Among Apes*. New York: Harper & Row.

De Waal, Frans. 2005. *Our Inner Ape*. New York: Riverhead Books.

Diamond, Milton, and H. Keith Sigmundson. 1997a. "Sex reassignment at birth: A long-term review and clinical implications." *Archives of Pediatrics and Adolescent Medicine* 151:298–304.

Diamond, Milton, and H. Keith Sigmundson. 1997b. "Management of intersexuality: Guidelines for dealing with individuals with ambiguous genitalia." *Archives of Pediatrics and Adolescent Medicine* 151:1046–1050.

Dickemann, Mildred. 1979. "Female infanticide, reproductive strategies, and social stratification: A preliminary model." In Napoleon A. Chagnon and William Irons, eds. *Evolutionary Biology and Human Social Behavior*. North Scituate, MA: Duxbury Press.

Divale, William Tulio, and Marvin Harris. 1976. "Population, warfare, and the male supremacist complex." *American Anthropologist* 78:521–538.

Dixson, Barnaby J., Katayo Sagata, Wayne L. Linklater, and Alan F. Dixson. 2010. "Male preferences for female waist-to-hip ratio and body mass index in the highlands of Papua New Guinea." *American Journal of Physical Anthropology* 141:620–625.

Dobb, Maurice. 1963. *Studies in the Development of Capitalism*. Rev. ed. New York: International Publishers.

D'Souza, Dinesh. 1995. *The End of Racism*. New York: Free Press.

Duffy, David L., Grant W. Montgomery, Wei Chen, Zhen Zhen Zhao, Lien Le, Michael R. James, Nicholas K. Hayward, Nicholas G. Martin, and Richard A. Sturm. 2007. "A three-single-nucleotide polymorphism haplotype in intron 1 of OCA2 explains most human eye-color variation." *American Journal of Human Genetics* 80(2):241–252.

Dunbar, Robin I. M. 1998. "The social brain hypothesis." *Evolutionary Anthropology* 6:178–190.

Dunbar, Robin I. M. 2003. "The social brain: Mind, language, and society in evolutionary perspective." *Annual Review of Anthropology* 32:163–181.

Dunbar, Robin I. M., and S. Shultz. 2007. "Evolution in the social brain." *Science* 317:1344–1347.

Durham, William H. 1991. *Coevolution: Genes, Culture, and Human Diversity*. Stanford, CA: Stanford University Press.

Durham, William H. 2004. "Assessing the gaps in Westermarck's theory." In Arthur P. Wolf and William H. Durham, eds. *Inbreeding, Incest, and the Incest Taboo*. Stanford, CA: Stanford University Press.

Dutton, Denis. 2009. *The Art Instinct: Beauty, Pleasure, and Human Evolution*. New York: Bloomsbury Press.

Dyson, Tim, and Mick Moore. 1983. "On kinship structure, female autonomy, and demographic behavior in India." *Population and Development Review* 9:35–60.

Eals, Marion, and Irwin Silverman. 1994. "The hunter-gatherer theory of spatial sex differences: Proximate factors mediating the female advantage in recall of object arrays." *Ethology and Sociobiology* 15:95–105.

Earle, Timothy. 1997. *How Chiefs Come to Power: The Political Economy in Prehistory*. Stanford, CA: Stanford University Press.

Eckhardt, William. 1992. *Civilizations, Empires, and Wars*. Jefferson, NC: McFarland.

Eliade, Mircea. 1964. *Shamanism: Archaic Techniques of Ecstasy*. Princeton, NJ: Princeton University Press.

Ellis, Bruce J. 1992. "The evolution of sexual attraction: Evaluative mechanisms in women." In Jerome H. Barkow, Leda Cosmides, and John Tooby, eds. *The Adapted Mind: Evolutionary Psychology and the Generation of Culture*. New York: Oxford University Press.

Ellis, Lee. 1995. "Dominance and reproductive success among non-human animals: A cross-species comparison." *Ethology and Sociobiology* 16:257–333.

Ellis, Lee, and M. Ashley Ames. 1987. "Neurohormonal functioning and sexual orientation: A theory of homosexuality-heterosexuality." *Psychological Bulletin* 101:233–258.

Ellis, Lee, and Steven Bonin. 2002. "Social status and the secondary sex ratio: New evidence on a lingering controversy." *Social Biology* 49:35–43.

Ember, Carol. 1978. "Myths about hunter-gatherers." *Ethnology* 17:439–448.

Ember, Melvin. 1983. "On the origin and extension of the incest taboo." In Melvin Ember and Carol R. Ember, eds. *Marriage, Family, and Kinship*. New Haven, CT: HRAF Press.

Enard, Wolfgang, Molly Przeworski, Simon E. Fisher, Cecilia S. L. Lai, Victor Wiebe, Takashi Kitano, Anthony P. Monaco, and Svante Paabo. 2002. "Molecular evolution of FOXP2, a gene involved in speech and language." *Nature* 418:869–872.

Erickson, Mark. 1989. "Incest avoidance and familial bonding." *Journal of Anthropological Research* 45:267–291.

Erickson, Mark. 2004. "Evolutionary thought and the current clinical understanding of incest." In Arthur P. Wolf and William H. Durham, eds. *Inbreeding, Incest, and the Incest Taboo*. Stanford, CA: Stanford University Press.

Evans, Nicholas, and Stephen C. Levinson. 2009. "The myth of language universals: Language diversity and its importance for cognitive science." *Behavioral and Brain Sciences* 32:429–492.

Evans-Pritchard, E. E. 1940. *The Nuer: A Description of the Modes of Livelihood and Political Institutions of a Nilotic People*. Oxford, UK: Clarendon Press.

Fagan, Brian M. 2009. *People of the Earth: An Introduction to World Prehistory*. 13th ed. Upper Saddle River, NJ: Prentice Hall.

Falger, Vincent S. E. 1992. "Sex differences in international politics: An exploratory study of coalitional behaviour in biopolitical perspective." In Johan M. G. van der Dennen, ed.

The Nature of the Sexes: The Sociobiology of Sex Differences and the "Battle of the Sexes." Groningen, Netherlands: Origin Press.

Farkas, George, Paula England, Keven Vicknair, and Barbara Stanek Kilbourne. 1997. "Cognitive skill, skill demands of jobs, and earnings among young European American, African American, and Mexican American workers." *Social Forces* 75:913–940.

Farkas, George, and Keven Vicknair. 1996. "Appropriate tests of racial wage discrimination require controls for cognitive skill." *American Sociological Review* 61:557–560.

Fathauer, George H. 1961. "Trobriand." In David M. Schneider and Kathleen Gough, eds. *Matrilineal Kinship.* Berkeley: University of California Press.

Feierman, Jay R., ed. 2009. *The Biology of Religious Behavior: The Evolutionary Origins of Faith and Religion.* Santa Barbara, CA: Praeger.

Ferguson, R. Brian. 1984. "Introduction: Studying war." In *Warfare, Culture, and Environment.* New York: Academic Press.

Ferguson, R. Brian. 1989. "Game wars? Ecology and conflict in Amazonia." *Journal of Anthropological Research* 45:179–206.

Ferguson, R. Brian. 1990a. "Explaining war." In Jonathan Haas, ed. *The Anthropology of War.* New York: Cambridge University Press.

Ferguson, R. Brian. 1990b. "Blood of the Leviathan: Western contact and warfare in Amazonia." *American Ethnologist* 17:237–257.

Ferguson, R. Brian. 1995. *Yanomami Warfare: A Political History.* Santa Fe, NM: School of American Research Press.

Ferguson, R. Brian, and Neil L. Whitehead. 1992. *War in the Tribal Zone: Expanding States and Indigenous Warfare.* Santa Fe, NM: School of American Research Press.

Fessler, Daniel M. T. 2007. "Neglected natural experiments germane to the Westermarck hypothesis: The Karo Batak and the Oneida community." *Human Nature* 18:355–364.

Fessler, Daniel M. T., and Carlos David Navarrete. 2003. "Meat is good to taboo: Dietary prescriptions as a product of the interaction of psychological mechanisms and social processes." *Journal of Cognition and Culture* 3:1–40.

Fessler, Daniel M. T., and Carlos David Navarrete. 2004. "Third-party attitudes toward sibling incest: Evidence for Westermarck's hypotheses." *Evolution and Human Behavior* 25:277–294.

Fiedel, Stuart J. 1992. *Prehistory of the Americas.* 2nd ed. New York: Cambridge University Press.

Fieder, Martin, and Susanne Huber. 2012. "An evolutionary account of status, power, and career in modern societies." *Human Nature* 23:191–207.

Fisher, Simon E., and Constance Scharff. 2009. "FOXP2 as a molecular window into speech and language." *Trends in Genetics* 25(4):166–177.

Fitch, W. Tecumseh. 2006. "The biology and evolution of music: A comparative perspective." *Cognition* 100:173–215.

Fitch, W. Tecumseh, Marc D. Hauser, and Noam Chomsky. 2005. "The evolution of the language faculty: Clarifications and implications." *Cognition* 97:179–210.

FitzGibbon, C. D., and J. H. Fanshawe. 1988. "Stotting in Thompson's gazelles: An honest signal of condition." *Behavioral Ecology and Sociobiology* 23:69–74.

Flatz, Gebhard, and Hans Werner Rotthauwe. 1973. "Lactose nutrition and natural selection." *Lancet* 2(7820):76–77.

Flinn, Mark V. 1981. "Uterine vs. agnatic kinship variability and associated cousin marriage preferences: An evolutionary biological analysis." In R. D. Alexander and D. W. Tinkle, eds. *Natural Selection and Social Behavior: Recent Research and New Theory*. New York: Chiron Press.

Flinn, Mark V., David C. Geary, and Carol V. Ward. 2005. "Ecological dominance, social competition, and evolutionary arms races: Why humans evolved extraordinary intelligence." *Evolution and Human Behavior* 26:10–46.

Flores, Renato Z., Luiz F. C. Mattos, and Francisco M. Salzano. 1998. "Incest: Frequency, predisposing factors, and effects in a Brazilian population." *Current Anthropology* 39:554–558.

Fogel, Robert William. 2004. *The Escape from Hunger and Premature Death, 1700–2100: Europe, America, and the Third World*. New York: Cambridge University Press.

Fogel, Robert William, and Stanley L. Engerman. 1974. *Time on the Cross: The Economics of American Negro Slavery*. Boston: Little, Brown.

Foner, Philip S. 1975. *A History of Black Americans*. Westport, CT: Greenwood Press.

Fox, Robin. 1983. *Kinship and Marriage: An Anthropological Perspective*. Cambridge, UK: Cambridge University Press.

Frachetti, Michael D. 2012. "Multiregional emergence of mobile pastoralism and nonuniform institutional complexity across Eurasia." *Current Anthropology* 53:2–38.

Frank, Andre Gunder. 1998. *ReOrient: Global Economy in the Asian Age*. Berkeley: University of California Press.

Frank, Robert H. 1999. *Luxury Fever: Money and Happiness in an Era of Excess*. Princeton, NJ: Princeton University Press.

Freese, Jeremy, and Brian Powell. 1999. "Sociobiology, status, and parental investment in sons and daughters." *American Journal of Sociology* 106:1704–1743.

Frejka, Tomas, and Charles F. Westoff. 2006. "Religion, religiousness, and fertility in the U.S. and Europe." Working paper WP 2006–013. Rostock, Germany: Max Planck Institute for Demographic Research.

Fried, Morton H. 1967. *The Evolution of Political Society*. New York: Random House.

Frost, Peter. 2010. "The Roman state and genetic pacification." *Evolutionary Psychology* 8:376–389.

Fujimoto, Giichi. 2003. "History of dairy farming in Japan: From ante-Nara period to the Edo period." *Animal Husbandry* 57:1339–1342.

Furchtgott-Roth, Diana, and Christine Stolba. 1999. *Women's Figures: An Illustrated Guide to the Progress of Women in America*. Washington, DC: American Enterprise Institute Press.

Furnham, Adrian, Melanie Dias, and Alastair McClelland. 1998. "The role of body weight, waist-to-hip ratio, and breast size in judgments of female attractiveness." *Sex Roles* 39:311–326.

Gamble, S. D. 1954. *Ting Hsien: A North China Rural Community*. Stanford, CA: Stanford University Press.

Gangestad, Steven W., and Glenn J. Scheyd. 2005. "The evolution of human physical attractiveness." *Annual Review of Anthropology* 34:523–548.

Gat, Azar. 1999. "The pattern of fighting in simple, small-scale prestate societies." *Journal of Anthropological Research* 55:563–583.

Gat, Azar. 2006. *War in Human Civilization.* Oxford: Oxford University Press.

Gaulin, Steven J. C. 1992. "Evolution of sex differences in spatial ability." *Yearbook of Physical Anthropology* 35:125–151.

Gaulin, Steven J. C., and R. W. FitzGerald. 1986. "Sex differences in spatial ability: An evolutionary hypothesis and test." *American Naturalist* 127:74–88.

Gaulin, Steven J. C., and R. W. FitzGerald. 1989. "Sexual selection for spatial-learning ability." *Animal Behavior* 37:322–331.

Gaulin, Steven J. C., and Carol A. Hoffman. 1988. "Evolution and development of sex differences in spatial ability." In Laura A. Betzig, Monique Borgerhoff Mulder, and Paul W. Turke, eds. *Human Reproductive Behavior: A Darwinian Perspective.* New York: Cambridge University Press.

Gaulin, Steven J. C., and Donald McBurney. 2003. *Psychology: An Evolutionary Approach.* 2nd ed. Upper Saddle River, NJ: Prentice Hall.

Gaulin, Steven J. C., and Alice Schlegel. 1980. "Paternal confidence and paternal investment: A cross-cultural test of a sociobiological hypothesis." *Ethology and Sociobiology* 1:301–309.

Geary, David C. 1998. *Male, Female: The Evolution of Human Sex Differences.* Washington, DC: American Psychological Association.

Geary, David C. 2010. *Male, Female: The Evolution of Human Sex Differences.* 2nd ed. Washington, DC: American Psychological Association.

Gelles, Richard J. 1987. "What to learn from cross-cultural and historical research on child abuse and neglect: An overview." In Richard J. Gelles and Jane B. Lancaster, eds. *Child Abuse and Neglect: Biosocial Dimensions.* New York: Aldine de Gruyter.

Giddens, Anthony. 1985. *The Nation-State and Violence.* Berkeley: University of California Press.

Gil-White, Francisco. 1999. "How thick is blood? The plot thickens . . . : If ethnic actors are primordialists, what remains of the circumstantialist/primordialist controversy?" *Ethnic and Racial Studies* 22:789–820.

Gil-White, Francisco. 2001a. "Are ethnic groups biological 'species' to the human brain? Essentialism in our cognition of some social categories." *Current Anthropology* 42:515–554.

Gil-White, Francisco. 2001b. "Sorting is not categorization: A critique of the claim that Brazilians have fuzzy racial categories." *Journal of Cognition and Culture* 1:219–249.

Goldberg, Steven. 1993. *Why Men Rule: A Theory of Male Dominance.* Chicago: Open Court.

Goldstein, Melvyn C. 1976. "Fraternal polyandry and fertility in a high Himalayan valley in northwest Nepal." *Human Ecology* 4:223–233.

Goldstein, Melvyn C. 1978. "Pahari and Tibetan polyandry revisited." *Ethnology* 17:325–337.

Good, Kenneth. 1991. *Into the Heart: An Amazonian Love Story.* London: Hamish Hamilton.

Goody, Jack. 1990. *The Oriental, the Ancient, and the Primitive: Systems of Marriage and the Family in the Pre-Industrial Societies of Eurasia.* Cambridge, UK: Cambridge University Press.

Gossett, Thomas F. 1963. *Race: The History of an Idea in America.* Dallas: Southern Methodist University Press.

Gottschall, Jonathan. 2008. *The Rape of Troy: Evolution, Violence, and the World of Homer.* New York: Cambridge University Press.

Gottschall, Jonathan. 2012. *The Storytelling Animal: How Stories Make Us Human.* Boston: Houghton Mifflin.

Gottschall, Jonathan, Johanna Martin, Hadley Quish, and Jon Rea. 2004. "Sex differences in mate choice criteria are reflected in folktales from around the world and in historical European literature." *Evolution and Human Behavior* 25:102–112.

Gottschall, Jonathan, et al. 2008. "The 'beauty myth' is no myth: Emphasis on male-female attractiveness in world folktales." *Human Nature* 19:174–188.

Gough, Kathleen. 1961. "Nayar: Central Kerala." In David M. Schneider and Kathleen Gough, eds. *Matrilineal Kinship.* Berkeley: University of California Press.

Gowaty, Patricia. 1992. "Evolutionary biology and feminism." *Human Nature* 3:217–249.

Gowlett, John, Clive Gamble, and Robin Dunbar. 2012. "Human evolution and the archaeology of the social brain." *Current Anthropology* 53:693–722.

Green, Penny Anthon. 1994. "Toward a biocultural theory of class circulation: An application of Joseph Lopreato's sociology." *Revue européenne des sciences sociales* 32:195–214.

Green, Richard. 1987. *The "Sissy-Boy Syndrome" and the Development of Homosexuality.* New Haven, CT: Yale University Press.

Greenberg, Maurice, and Roland Littlewood. 1995. "Post-adoption incest and phenotypic matching: Experience, personal meanings, and biosocial implications." *British Journal of Medical Psychology* 68:29–44.

Gurven, Michael, and Kim Hill. 2009. "Why do men hunt? A reevaluation of 'man the hunter' and the sexual division of labor." *Current Anthropology* 50:51–74.

Hald, Gert Martin, and Henrik Høgh-Olesen. 2010. "Receptivity to sexual invitations from strangers of the opposite gender." *Evolution and Human Behavior* 31:453–458.

Halliburton, Rudia Jr. 1975. "Free black owners of slaves: A reappraisal of the Woodson thesis." *South Carolina Historical Magazine* 76:129–142.

Hamer, Dean, and Peter Copeland. 1994. *The Science of Desire: The Search for the Gay Gene and the Biology of Behavior.* New York: Simon & Schuster Touchstone.

Hames, Raymond B. 1988. "The allocation of parental care among the Ye'kwana." In Laura L. Betzig, Monique Borgerhoff Mulder, and Paul W. Turke, eds. *Human Reproductive Behavior: A Darwinian Perspective.* New York: Cambridge University Press.

Hames, Raymond B. 2001. "Human behavioral ecology." *International Encyclopedia of the Social and Behavioral Sciences,* 6946–6951.

Hames, Raymond B., and William T. Vickers. 1982. "Optimal foraging theory as a model to explain variability in Amazonian hunting." *American Ethnologist* 9:358–378.

Hamilton, William D. 1964. "The genetical evolution of social behavior, parts 1 and 2." *Journal of Theoretical Biology* 7:1–52.

Handwerker, W. Penn. 1993. "Empowerment and fertility transition on Antigua, WI: Education, employment, and the moral economy of childbearing." *Human Organization* 52:41–52.

Haney, Craig, Chris Banks, and Philip Zimbardo. 1973. "Interpersonal dynamics in a simulated prison." *International Journal of Criminology and Penology* 1:69–97.

Harlow, Harry F. 1959a. "The development of affectional patterns in infant monkeys." In B. M. Foss, ed. *Determinants of Infant Behavior.* New York: Wiley.

Harlow, Harry F. 1959b. "Love in infant monkeys." *Scientific American* 6, no. 200.

Harlow, Harry F., and R. R. Zimmerman. 1959. "Affectional responses in the infant monkey." *Science* 130:3373.

Harris, Erica, and Patrick McNamara. 2008. "Is religiousness a biocultural adaptation?" In Joseph Bulbulia et al., eds. *The Evolution of Religion: Studies, Theories, and Critiques.* Santa Margarita, CA: Collins Foundation Press.

Harris, Grant T., N. Zoe Hilton, Marnie E. Rice, and Angela W. Eke. 2007. "Children killed by genetic parents versus stepparents." *Evolution and Human Behavior* 28:85–95.

Harris, Marvin. 1964. *Patterns of Race in the Americas.* New York: Norton.

Harris, Marvin. 1966. "The cultural ecology of India's sacred cattle." *Current Anthropology* 7:51–66.

Harris, Marvin. 1974. *Cows, Pigs, Wars, and Witches: The Riddles of Culture.* New York: Random House.

Harris, Marvin. 1977. *Cannibals and Kings: The Origins of Cultures.* New York: Random House.

Harris, Marvin. 1981. *America Now: The Anthropology of a Changing Culture.* New York: Simon & Schuster.

Harris, Marvin. 1984. "A cultural materialist theory of band and village warfare: The Yanomamö test." In R. Brian Ferguson, ed. *Warfare, Culture, and Environment.* New York: Academic Press.

Harris, Marvin. 1985. *Good to Eat: Riddles of Food and Culture.* New York: Simon & Schuster.

Harris, Marvin. 1987. "Foodways: Historical overview and theoretical prolegomenon." In Marvin Harris and Eric B. Ross, eds. *Food and Evolution: Toward a Theory of Human Food Habits.* Philadelphia: Temple University Press.

Harris, Marvin. 1989. *Our Kind.* New York: Harper & Row.

Harris, Marvin, and Eric B. Ross. 1987a. *Death, Sex, and Fertility: Population Regulation in Preindustrial and Developing Societies.* New York: Columbia University Press.

Harris, Marvin, and Eric B. Ross, eds. 1987b. *Food and Evolution: Toward a Theory of Human Food Habits.* Philadelphia: Temple University Press.

Harris, Sam. 2004. *The End of Faith: Religion, Terror, and the Future of Reason.* New York: Norton.

Hartung, John. 1976. "On natural selection and the inheritance of wealth." *Current Anthropology* 17:607–622.

Hartung, John. 1982. "Polygyny and inheritance of wealth." *Current Anthropology* 23:1–12.

Hassig, Ross. 1985. *Trade, Tribute, and Transportation: The Sixteenth-Century Political Economy of the Valley of Mexico.* Norman: University of Oklahoma Press.

Hauser, Marc D., Noam Chomsky, and W. Tecumseh Fitch. 2002. "The faculty of language: What is it, who has it, and how did it evolve?" *Science* 298:1569–1579.

Hawkes, Kristen, Kim Hill, and James F. O'Connell. 1982. "Why hunters gather: Optimal foraging and the Aché of eastern Paraguay." *American Ethnologist* 9:379–398.

Hawkes, Kristen, and James F. O'Connell. 1985. "Optimal foraging models and the case of the !Kung." *American Anthropologist* 87:401–405.

Heider, Karl G. 1970. *The Dugum Dani: A Papuan Culture in the Highland of West New Guinea.* New York: Wenner-Gren.

Herdt, Gilbert H. 1984. *Ritualized Homosexuality in Melanesia.* Berkeley: University of California Press.

Herdt, Gilbert H. 1987. *The Sambia: Ritual and Gender in New Guinea*. New York: Holt, Rinehart & Winston.

Hershberger, Scott. 2001. "Biological factors in the development of sexual orientation." In Anthony R. D'Augelli and Charlotte J. Patterson, eds. *Lesbian, Gay, and Bisexual Identities and Youth: Psychological Perspectives*. New York: Oxford University Press.

Hewlett, B. S., J. M. H. van de Koppel, and L. L. Cavalli-Sforza. 1986. "Exploration and mating ranges of Aka Pygmies of the Central African Republic." In L. L. Cavalli-Sforza, ed. *African Pygmies*. New York: Academic Press.

Hill, Kim. 1988. "Macronutrient modifications of optimal foraging theory: An approach using indifference curves applied to some modern foragers." *Human Ecology* 16:157–197.

Hill, Kim, and A. Magdalena Hurtado. 1996. *Aché Life History: The Ecology and Demography of a Foraging People*. New York: Aldine de Gruyter.

Hill, Kim, and Hillard S. Kaplan. 1989. "Population description and dry season subsistence among the newly contacted Yora (Yaminahua) of Manu National Park, Peru." *National Geographic Research* 5:317–334.

Hill, Kim, Hillard S. Kaplan, Kristen Hawkes, and Ana Magdalena Hurtado. 1985. "Men's time allocation to activities among Aché hunter-gatherers." *Human Ecology* 13:29–47.

Hirschi, Travis, and Michael Gottfredson. 1983. "Age and the explanation of crime." *American Journal of Sociology* 89:552–584.

Hitchens, Christopher. 2007. *God Is Not Great: How Religion Poisons Everything*. New York: Twelve.

Hjort, A. 1981. "Ethnic transformation, dependency, and change: The Ilgira Samburu of Northern Kenya." In J. G. Galaty and P. C. Salzman, eds. *Change and Development in Nomadic and Pastoral Societies*. Leiden: E. J. Brill.

Hobhouse, L. T., G. C. Wheeler, and Morris Ginsberg. 1965. *The Material Culture and Social Institutions of the Simpler Peoples*. London: Routledge & Kegan Paul. Originally published in 1915.

Hoebel, E. Adamson. 1954. *The Law of Primitive Man*. Cambridge, MA: Harvard University Press.

Hogbin, H. Ian. 1964. *A Guadalcanal Society: The Kaoka Speakers*. New York: Holt, Rinehart & Winston.

Hold, Barbara C. L. 1980. "Attention structure and behavior in G/wi San children." *Ethology and Sociobiology* 1:275–290.

Holden, Clare Janaki, Rebecca Sear, and Ruth Mace. 2003. "Matriliny as daughter-biased investment." *Evolution and Human Behavior* 24:99–112.

Hole, Frank. 1977. *Studies in the Archaeological History of the Deh Luran Plain*. Ann Arbor: University of Michigan Museum of Anthropology, Memoir no. 9.

Holt, Jim. 2012. *Why Does the World Exist? An Existential Detective Story*. New York: Liveright.

Hopcroft, Rosemary L. 2005. "Parental status and differential investment in sons and daughters: Trivers-Willard revisited." *Social Forces* 83:1111–1136.

Hopkins, Keith. 1980. "Brother-sister marriage in Roman Egypt." *Comparative Studies in Society and History* 22:303–354.

Howell, Nancy. 1986. "Feedback and buffers in relation to scarcity and abundance: Studies of hunter-gatherer populations." In D. Coleman and R. Schofield, eds. *The State of Population Theory*. New York: Basil Blackwell.

Hrdy, Sarah Blaffer. **1979**. "Infanticide in animals." *Ethology and Sociobiology* 1:13–40.

Hrdy, Sarah Blaffer. **1997**. "Raising Darwin's consciousness: Female sexuality and the prehominid origins of patriarchy." *Human Nature* 8:1–49.

Hrdy, Sarah Blaffer. **1999**. *Mother Nature: A History of Mothers, Infants, and Natural Selection*. New York: Pantheon.

Hu, S., A. M. Pattatucci, and C. Patterson. **1995**. "Linkage between sexual orientation and chromosome Xq28 in males but not in females." *Nature Genetics* 11(3):248–256.

Huber, Brad R., Vendula Linhartova, and Dana Cope. **2004**. "Measuring paternal certainty using cross-cultural data." *World Cultures* 15(1):48–59.

Hughes, Michael, and Bradley Hertel. **1990**. "The significance of skin color remains: A study of life chances, mate selection, and ethnic consciousness among black Americans." *Social Forces* 68:1105–1120.

Irons, William. **2000**. "Why do the Yomut raise more sons than daughters." In Lee Cronk, Napoleon Chagnon, and William Irons, eds. *Adaptation and Human Behavior: An Anthropological Perspective*. New York: Aldine de Gruyter.

Irons, William, and Lee Cronk. **2000**. "Two decades of a new paradigm." In Lee Cronk, Napoleon Chagnon, and William Irons, eds. *Adaptation and Human Behavior: An Anthropological Perspective*. New York: Aldine de Gruyter.

Jablonski, Nina G., and George Chaplin. **2000**. "The evolution of human skin coloration." *Journal of Human Evolution* 39:57–106.

Jackendoff, Ray. **2009**. "Parallels and nonparallels between language and music." *Music Perception* 26:195–204.

Jackendoff, Ray, and Fred Lerdahl. **2006**. "The capacity for music: What is it, and what's special about it?" *Cognition* 100:33–72.

Jackendoff, Ray, and Steven Pinker. **2005**. "The nature of the language faculty and its implications for evolution of language (Reply to Fitch, Hauser, and Chomsky)." *Cognition* 97:211–225.

Jakobovits, A. A. **1991**. "Sex ratio of spontaneously aborted fetuses and delivered neonates in the second trimester." *European Journal of Obstetrics, Gynecology, and Reproductive Biology* 40(3):211–213.

James, Thomas W., and Doreen Kimura. **1997**. "Sex differences in remembering the locations of objects in an array: Location-shifts versus location-exchanges." *Evolution and Human Behavior* 18:155–163.

Janssen, Jac. J. **1978**. "The early state in ancient Egypt." In Henri J. M. Claessen and Peter Skalnik, eds. *The Early State*. The Hague: Mouton.

Jasieńska, Grażyna, et al. **2004**. "Large breasts and narrow waists indicate high reproductive potential in women." *Proceedings of the Royal Society of London B*: 271:1213–1217.

Jaspers, Karl. **1953**. *The Origin and Goal of History*. Trans. Michael Bullock. New Haven, CT: Yale University Press.

Jejeebhoy, Shireen J. **1995**. *Women's Education, Autonomy, and Reproductive Behaviour: Experience from Developing Countries*. Oxford: Oxford University Press (Clarendon Press).

Johanson, Donald C., and Timothy D. White. **1979**. "A systematic assessment of early African hominids." *Science* 203:321–330.

Johnson, Allen W., and Timothy Earle. 2000. *The Evolution of Human Societies: From Foraging Group to Agrarian State*. 2nd ed. Stanford, CA: Stanford University Press.

Jones, Doug. 1995. "Sexual selection, physical attractiveness, and facial neoteny: Cross-cultural evidence and implications." *Current Anthropology* 36:723–748.

Jones, Doug, and Kim Hill. 1993. "Criteria of facial attractiveness in five populations." *Human Nature* 4:271–296.

Jorgensen, J. 1980. *Western Indians*. San Francisco: Freeman.

Kaplan, David. 2000. "The darker side of the 'original affluent society.'" *Journal of Anthropological Research* 56:301–324.

Kaplan, Hillard S. 1994. "Evolutionary and wealth flows theories of fertility: Empirical tests and new models." *Population and Development Review* 20:753–791.

Kaplan, Hillard S. 1996. "A theory of fertility and parental investment in traditional and modern human societies." *Yearbook of Physical Anthropology* 39:91–135.

Kaplan, Hillard S., and Kim Hill. 1992. "The evolutionary ecology of food acquisition." In Eric Alden Smith and Bruce Winterhalder, eds. *Evolutionary Ecology and Human Behavior*. New York: Aldine de Gruyter.

Kaplan, Hillard S., and Jane B. Lancaster. 2000. "The evolutionary economics and psychology of the demographic transition to low fertility." In Lee Cronk, Napoleon Chagnon, and William Irons, eds. *Adaptation and Human Behavior: An Anthropological Perspective*. New York: Aldine de Gruyter.

Kaszycka, Katarzyna, and Jan Strzalko. 2003. "'Race'—still an issue for physical anthropology? Results of Polish studies seen in the light of U.S. findings." *American Anthropologist* 105:116–124.

Katz, Mary Maxwell, and Melvin J. Konner. 1981. "The role of the father: An anthropological perspective." In Michael E. Lamb, ed. *The Role of the Father in Child Development*. New York: Wiley.

Kaufman, Alan S., and James E. McLean. 1998. "An investigation into the relationship between interests and intelligence." *Journal of Clinical Psychology* 54:279–295.

Kautsky, John H. 1982. *The Politics of Aristocratic Empires*. Chapel Hill: University of North Carolina Press.

Keegan, William F. 1986. "The optimal foraging analysis of horticultural production." *American Anthropologist* 88:92–107.

Keeley, Lawrence H. 1996. *War Before Civilization: The Myth of the Peaceful Savage*. New York: Oxford University Press.

Keith, Verna M., and Cedric Herring. 1991. "Skin tone and stratification in the black community." *American Journal of Sociology* 97:760–778.

Keller, Matthew C., Randolph M. Nesse, and Sandra Hofferth. 2001. "The Trivers-Willard hypothesis of parental investment: No effect in the contemporary United States." *Evolution and Human Behavior* 22:343–360.

Kelly, Raymond C. 1976. "Witchcraft and sexual relations." In P. Brown and G. Buchbinder, eds. *Man and Woman in the New Guinea Highlands*. American Anthropological Association Special Publication 8.

Kelly, Robert L. 1995. *The Foraging Spectrum: Diversity in Hunter-Gatherer Lifeways*. Washington, DC: Smithsonian Institution Press.

Kennedy, Bruce P., Ichiro Kawachi, and Deborah Prothrow-Stith. 1996. "Income distribution and mortality: Cross-sectional ecological study of the Robin Hood index in the United States." *British Medical Journal* 312:1004, 1007, 1194.

Kennett, Douglas J. 2005. *The Island Chumash: Behavioral Ecology of a Maritime Society.* Berkeley: University of California Press.

Kenrick, Douglas T., and Richard C. Keefe. 1992. "Age preferences in mates reflect sex differences in human reproductive strategies." *Behavioral and Brain Sciences* 15:75–133.

Kenrick, Douglas T., Edward K. Sadalla, Gary Groth, and Melanie R. Trost. 1990. "Evolution, traits, and the stages of human courtship: Qualifying the parental investment model." *Journal of Personality* 58:97–116.

Kenrick, Douglas T., Melanie R. Trost, and Virgil L. Sheets. 1996. "Power, harassment, and trophy mates: The feminist advantages of an evolutionary perspective." In David M. Buss and Neil M. Malamuth, eds. *Sex, Power, Conflict: Evolutionary and Feminist Perspectives.* New York: Oxford University Press.

Kertzer, David I. 1993. *Sacrificed for Honor: Italian Infant Abandonment and the Politics of Reproductive Control.* Boston: Beacon Press.

Kimura, Doreen. 1987. "Are men's and women's brains really different?" *Canadian Psychology* 28:133–147.

Kimura, Doreen. 1992. "Sex differences in the brain." *Scientific American* 267(3):119–125.

Kimura, Doreen. 1999. *Sex and Cognition.* Cambridge, MA: MIT Press.

Kinsey, Alfred C., Wardell B. Pomeroy, Clyde E. Martin, and Sam Sloan. 1948. *Sexual Behavior in the Human Male.* Philadelphia: Saunders.

Kirch, Patrick Vinton. 1984. *The Evolution of the Polynesian Chiefdoms.* New York: Cambridge University Press.

Kirch, Patrick Vinton. 2000. *On the Road of the Winds: An Archaeological History of the Pacific Islands Before European Contact.* Berkeley: University of California Press.

Kirk, K. M., J. M. Bailey, and N. G. Martin. 2000. "Measurement models for sexual orientation in a community twin sample." *Behavior Genetics* 30:345–356.

Kirkpatrick, Lee A. 2005. *Attachment, Evolution, and the Psychology of Religion.* New York: Guildford Press.

Klein, Richard G. 2009. *The Human Career: Human Biological and Cultural Origins.* 3rd ed. Chicago: University of Chicago Press.

Klein, Richard G., and Blake Edgar. 2002. *The Dawn of Human Culture.* New York: Wiley.

Koenig, Harold C., Michael E. McCullough, and David B. Larson. 2001. *Handbook of Religion and Health.* New York: Oxford University Press.

Kohl, Philip. 1987. "The ancient economy, transferable technologies, and the Bronze Age world-system: A view from the northeastern frontier of the ancient Near East." In Michael Rowlands, Mogens Larsen, and Kristian Kristiansen, eds. *Centre and Periphery in the Ancient World.* Cambridge, UK: Cambridge University Press.

Kohler, Carl. 1963. *A History of Costume.* New York: Dover Publications.

Korbin, Jill. 1987. "Child maltreatment in cross-cultural perspective: Vulnerable children and circumstances." In Richard J. Gelles and Jane B. Lancaster, eds. *Child Abuse and Neglect: Biosocial Dimensions.* New York: Aldine de Gruyter.

Kosko, Maria. 2004. "Sakha (Yakut) shamanism." In Mariko Namba Walter and Eva Jane

Neumann Fridman, eds. *Shamanism: An Encyclopedia of World Beliefs, Practices, and Cultures.* Vol. 2. Santa Barbara, CA: ABC-CLIO.

Koster, Jeremy. 2008. "The impact of hunting with dogs on wildlife harvests in the Bosawas Reserve, Nicaragua." *Environmental Conservation* 35:211–220.

Koster, Jeremy, Jennie Hogden, Maria D. Venegas, and Toni J. Copeland. 2010. "Is meat flavor a factor in hunter's prey choice decisions?" *Human Nature* 21:219–242.

Kottak, Conrad Philip. 2000. *Anthropology: The Exploration of Human Diversity.* 8th ed. New York: McGraw-Hill.

Kovel, Joel. 1984. *White Racism: A Psychohistory.* New York: Columbia University Press.

Krohn, Marvin D. 1976. "Inequality, employment, and crime: A cross-national analysis." *Sociological Quarterly* 17:303–313.

Kuhle, Barry X. 2012. "Evolutionary psychology is compatible with equity feminism but not with gender feminism." *Evolutionary Psychology* 10(1):39–43.

Kunej, Drago, and Ivan Turk. 2000. "New perspectives on the beginnings of music: Archaeological and musicological analysis of a Middle Paleolithic bone 'flute.'" In Nils L. Wallin, Bjorn Merker, and Steven Brown, eds. *The Origins of Music.* Cambridge, MA: MIT Press.

Kurland, Jeffrey A. 1979. "Paternity, mother's brother, and human sociality." In Napoleon A. Chagnon and William Irons, eds. *Evolutionary Biology and Human Social Behavior.* North Scituate, MA: Duxbury Press.

Kushnick, Geoff, and Daniel M. T. Fessler. 2011. "Karo Batak cousin marriage, cosocialization, and the Westermarck hypothesis." *Current Anthropology* 52:443–448.

Lai, C. S. L., S. E. Fisher, J. A. Hurst, F. Vargha-Khadem, and A. P. Monaco. 2001. "A novel forkhead-domain gene is mutated in a severe speech and language disorder." *Nature* 413 (6855):519–523.

Lamberg-Karlovsky, C. C., and Jeremy A. Sabloff. 1979. *Ancient Civilizations.* Prospect Heights, IL. Waveland Press.

Lancaster, Jane. 1991. "A feminist and evolutionary biologist looks at women." *Yearbook of Physical Anthropology* 34:1–11.

Landes, David S. 1969. *The Unbound Prometheus: Technological Change and Industrial Development in Western Europe from 1750 to the Present.* New York: Cambridge University Press.

Langer, William L. 1972. "Checks on population growth: 1750–1850." *Scientific American* 226:92–99.

Lassek, William D., and Steven J. C. Gaulin. 2009. "Costs and benefits of fat-free muscle mass in men: Relationship to mating success, dietary requirements, and native immunity." *Evolution and Human Behavior* 30:322–328.

Laumann, Edward O., John H. Gagnon, Robert T. Michael, and Stuart Michaels. 1994. *The Social Organization of Sexuality: Sexual Practices in the United States.* Chicago: University of Chicago Press.

Leacock, Eleanor. 1980. "Social behavior, biology, and the double standard." In George W. Barlow and James Silverberg, eds. *Sociobiology: Beyond Nature/Nurture?* Boulder, CO: Westview Press.

LeBlanc, Steven A. 2003. *Constant Battles: Why We Fight.* New York: St. Martin's Griffin.

Le Boeuf, B. J., and J. Reiter. 1988. "Lifetime reproductive success in northern elephant seals." In T. H. Clutton-Brock, ed. *Reproductive Success: Studies of Individual Variation in Contrasting Breeding Systems*. Chicago: University of Chicago Press.

Lee, Richard B. 1968. "What hunters do for a living, or, how to make out on scarce resources." In Richard B. Lee and Irven DeVore, eds. *Man the Hunter*. Chicago: Aldine.

Lee, Richard B. 1978. "Politics, sexual and nonsexual, in an egalitarian society." *Social Science Information* 17:871–895.

Lee, Richard B., and Richard H. Daly. 1999. *The Cambridge Encyclopedia of Hunters and Gatherers*. Cambridge, UK: Cambridge University Press.

Lenski, Gerhard E. 1966. *Power and Privilege: A Theory of Social Stratification*. New York: McGraw-Hill.

Lenski, Gerhard E. 1970. *Human Societies: An Introduction to Macro-Level Sociology*. New York: McGraw-Hill.

Leupp, Gary P. 1995. *Male Colors: The Construction of Homosexuality in Tokugawa Japan*. Berkeley: University of California Press.

LeVay, Simon. 1991. "A difference in the hypothalamic structure between heterosexual and homosexual men." *Science* 253:1034–1037.

LeVay, Simon. 1996. *Queer Science: The Use and Abuse of Research into Homosexuality*. Cambridge, MA: MIT Press.

LeVay, Simon. 2011. *Gay, Straight, and the Reason Why: The Science of Sexual Orientation*. New York: Oxford University Press.

Levine, Nancy E. 1988. *The Dynamics of Polyandry: Kinship, Domesticity, and Population on the Tibetan Border*. Chicago: University of Chicago Press.

Levine, Nancy E., and Joan B. Silk. 1997. "Why polyandry fails: Sources of instability in polyandrous marriages." *Current Anthropology* 38:375–398.

Lieberman, Debra, and Thalma Lobel. 2012. "Kinship on the kibbutz: Coresidence duration predicts altruism, personal sexual aversions, and moral attitudes among communally reared peers." *Evolution and Human Behavior* 33:26–34.

Lieberman, Leonard, and R. C. Kirk. 2002. "The 1999 status of the race concept in physical anthropology: Two studies converge." *American Journal of Physical Anthropology* 102: Supplement 34.

Lieberman, Leslie Sue. 1987. "Biocultural consequences of animals versus plants as sources of fats, proteins, and other nutrients." In Marvin Harris and Eric B. Ross, eds. *Food and Evolution: Toward a Theory of Human Food Habits*. Philadelphia: Temple University Press.

Liénard, Pierre, and Pascal Boyer. 2006. "Whence collective rituals? A cultural selection model of ritualized behavior." *American Anthropologist* 108:814–827.

Liesen, Laurette T. 1995. "Feminism and the politics of reproductive strategies." *Politics and the Life Sciences* 14:145–197.

Lomax, Alan. 1968. *Folk Song Style and Culture*. New Brunswick, NJ: Transaction.

Lopreato, Joseph. 1984. *Human Nature and Biocultural Evolution*. Winchester, MA: Allen & Unwin.

Lopreato, Joseph. 1989. "The maximization principle: A cause in search of conditions." In Robert W. Bell and Nancy J. Bell, eds. *Sociobiology and the Social Sciences*. Lubbock, TX: Texas Tech University Press.

Lopreato, Joseph, and Timothy Crippen. 1999. *Crisis in Sociology: The Need for Darwin*. New Brunswick, NJ: Transaction.

Low, Bobbi S. 1993. "Ecological demography: A synthetic focus in evolutionary anthropology." *Evolutionary Anthropology* 1:177–187.

Low, Bobbi S. 2000. *Why Sex Matters: A Darwinian Look at Human Behavior.* Princeton, NJ: Princeton University Press.

Lowie, Robert. 1966. *Culture and Ethnology.* New York: Basic Books. Originally published in 1917.

Lubinski, D., and C. P. Benbow. 1994. "The study of mathematically precocious youth: The first three decades of a planned 50-year study of intellectual talent." In R. F. Subotnik and K. D. Arnold, eds. *Beyond Terman: Contemporary Longitudinal Studies of Giftedness and Talent.* Norwood, NJ: Ablex.

Lytton, Hugh, and David M. Romney. 1991. "Parents' differential socialization of boys and girls: A meta-analysis." *Psychological Bulletin* 109:267–296.

MacAndrew, Alec. 2003. "FOXP2 and the evolution of language." http://www.evolution pages.com/FOXP2_language.htm.

MacDermot, Kay D., Elena Bonora, Nuala Sykes, Anne-Marie Coupe, Cecilia S. L. Lai, Sonja C. Vernes, Faraneh Vargha-Khadem, Fiona McKenzie, Robert L. Smith, Anthony P. Monaco, and Simon E. Fisher. 2005. "Identification of FOXP2 truncation as a novel cause of developmental speech and language deficits." *American Journal of Human Genetics* 76:1074–1080.

MacDonald, Kevin. 1990. "Mechanisms of sexual egalitarianism in Western Europe." *Ethology and Sociobiology* 11:195–238.

MacNeish, Richard. 1978. *The Science of Archaeology.* North Scituate, MA: Duxbury Press.

Madsen, Douglas. 1985. "A biochemical property relating to power seeking in humans." *American Political Science Review* 79:448–457.

Madsen, Douglas. 1986. "Power seekers are different: Further biochemical evidence." *American Political Science Review* 80:261–269.

Mair, Lucy. 1964. *Primitive Government.* Baltimore: Penguin Books.

Mair, Lucy. 1974. *African Societies.* Cambridge, UK: Cambridge University Press.

Malhotra, Anju, Reeve Vanneman, and Sunita Kishor. 1995. "Fertility, dimensions of patriarchy, and development in India." *Population and Development Review* 21:281–305.

Malinowski, Bronislaw. 1927. *Sex and Repression in Savage Society.* London: Kegan Paul.

Malinowski, Bronislaw. 1929. *The Sexual Life of Savages in North-western Melanesia; An Ethnographic Account of Courtship, Marriage, and Family Life Among the Natives of Trobriand Islands, British New Guinea.* New York: Harcourt, Brace.

Malinowski, Bronislaw. 1950. *Argonauts of the Western Pacific.* New York: E. P. Dutton.

Mandelbaum, David G. 1988. *Women's Seclusion and Men's Honor: Sex Roles in North India, Bangladesh, and Pakistan.* Tucson: University of Arizona Press.

Mann, Michael. 1986. *The Sources of Social Power.* Vol. 1, *A History of Power from the Beginning to AD 1760.* Cambridge, UK: Cambridge University Press.

Mar, Raymond A., and Keith Oatley. 2008. "The function of fiction is the abstraction and simulation of social experience." *Perspectives on Psychological Science* 3:173–192.

Mar, Raymond A., Keith Oatley, Jacob Hirsch, Jennifer dela Paz, and Jordan B. Peterson. 2006. "Bookworms versus nerds: Exposure to fiction versus non-fiction, divergent associations with social ability, and the simulation of fictional social worlds." *Journal of Research in Personality* 40:694–712.

Mar, Raymond A., Keith Oatley, and Jordan B. Peterson. 2009. "Exploring the link between reading fiction and empathy: Ruling out individual differences and examining outcomes." *Communications* 34:407–428.

Marcus, Gary F., and Simon E. Fisher. 2003. "FOXP2 in focus: What can genes tell us about speech and language?" *Trends in Cognitive Sciences* 7:257–262.

Marlowe, Frank W. 2010. *The Hadza: Hunter-Gatherers of Tanzania.* Berkeley: University of California Press.

Marlowe, Frank W., Coren Apicella, and Dorian Reed. 2005. "Men's preferences for women's profile waist-to-hip ratio in two societies." *Evolution and Human Behavior* 26:458–468.

Marlowe, Frank W., and A. Wetsman. 2001. "Preferred waist-to-hip ratio and ecology." *Personality and Individual Differences* 30:481–489.

Marshall, Lorna. 1968. "Comment." In Richard B. Lee and Irven DeVore, eds. *Man the Hunter.* Chicago: Aldine.

Martin, M. Kay, and Barbara Voorhies. 1975. *Female of the Species.* New York: Columbia University Press.

Martindale, Colin. 1990. *The Clockwork Muse: The Predictability of Artistic Change.* New York: Basic Books.

Mason, Jackie, and Raoul Felder. 2007. *Schmucks! Our Favorite Fakes, Frauds, Lowlifes, Liars, the Armed and Dangerous, and Good Guys Gone Bad.* New York: Collins.

Mason, Karen Oppenheim. 2001. "Gender and family systems in the fertility transition." *Population and Development Review* 27(Supplement):160–176.

Mattison, Siobhan M. 2011. "Evolutionary contributions to solving the 'matrilineal puzzle': A test of Holden, Sear, and Mace's model." *Human Nature* 22:64–88.

Maynard Smith, John. 1964. "Group selection and kin selection." *Nature* 20(4924):1145–1147.

Maynard Smith, John. 1974. "The theory of games and the evolution of animal conflict." *Journal of Theoretical Biology* 47:209–221.

Maynard Smith, John. 1978. "The evolution of behavior." *Scientific American* 239:176–192.

Mazur, Allan, and Alan Booth. 1998. "Testosterone and dominance in men." *Behavioral and Brain Sciences* 21:353–397.

McBrearty, Sally, and Alison S. Brooks. 2000. "The revolution that wasn't: A new interpretation of the origin of modern human behavior." *Journal of Human Evolution* 39:453–563.

McBurney, Donald H., et al. 1997. "Superior spatial memory of women: Stronger evidence for the gathering hypothesis." *Evolution and Human Behavior* 18:165–174.

McCabe, Justine. 1983. "FBD marriage: Further support for the Westermarck hypothesis of the incest taboo?" *American Anthropologist* 85:50–69.

McCauley, Clark. 1990. "Conference overview." In Jonathan Haas, ed. *The Anthropology of War.* New York: Cambridge University Press.

McClenon, James. 2002. *Wondrous Healing: Shamanism, Human Evolution, and the Origin of Religion.* DeKalb: Northern Illinois University Press.

McNeill, William H. 1963. *The Rise of the West: A History of the Human Community.* Chicago: University of Chicago Press.

McNeill, William H. 1986. *Polyethnicity and National Unity in World History.* Toronto: University of Toronto Press.

Mealey, Linda, and Wade Mackey. 1990. "Variation in offspring sex ratio in women of differing social status." *Ethology and Sociobiology* 11:83–95.

Mellars, Paul A. 1985. "The ecological basis of social complexity in the Upper Paleolithic of southwestern France." In T. Douglas Price and James A. Brown, eds. *Prehistoric Hunter-Gatherers*. New York: Academic Press.

Milgram, Stanley. 1974. *Obedience to Authority: An Experimental View*. New York: Harper & Row.

Milisauskas, Sarunas. 2010. *European Prehistory*. 2nd ed. Berlin: Springer-Verlag.

Miller, Geoffrey F. 1999. "Sexual selection for cultural displays." In Robin Dunbar, Chris Knight, and Camilla Power, eds. *The Evolution of Culture: An Interdisciplinary View*. New Brunswick, NJ: Rutgers University Press.

Miller, Geoffrey F. 2000a. *The Mating Mind: How Sexual Choice Shaped the Evolution of Human Nature*. New York: Doubleday.

Miller, Geoffrey F. 2000b. "Evolution of human music through sexual selection." In Nils L. Wallin, Bjorn Merker, and Steven Brown, eds. *The Origins of Music*. Cambridge, MA: MIT Press.

Miller, Geoffrey F. 2009. *Spent: Sex, Evolution, and Consumer Behavior*. New York: Viking.

Mintz, Sydney. 1985. *Sweetness and Power*. New York: Viking.

Mitani, John C., David P. Watts, and Sylvia J. Amsler. 2010. "Lethal intergroup aggression leads to territorial expansion in wild chimpanzees." *Current Biology* 20:R507–R508.

Moffat, Scott D., Elizabeth Hampson, and Maria Hatzipantelis. 1998. "Navigation in a 'virtual' maze: Sex differences and correlation with psychometric measures of spatial ability in humans." *Evolution and Human Behavior* 19:73–87.

Møller, Anders Pape. 2006. "A review of developmental instability, parasitism, and disease: Infection, genetics, and evolution." *Infection, Genetics, and Evolution* 6:133–140.

Møller, A. P., and Randy Thornhill. 1998. "Bilateral symmetry and sexual selection: A meta-analysis." *American Naturalist* 151.174–192.

Morris, Paul H., Jenny White, Edward R. Morrison, and Kayleigh Fisher. 2013. "High heels as supernormal stimuli: How wearing high heels affects judgments of female attractiveness." *Evolution and Human Behavior* 34:176–181.

Muller, Jon. 1997. *Mississippian Political Economy*. New York: Plenum.

Murdock, George Peter. 1967. *Ethnographic Atlas*. Pittsburgh: University of Pittsburgh Press.

Murthi, Mamta, Anne-Catherine Guio, and Jean Dreze. 1995. "Mortality, fertility, and gender bias in India: A district-level analysis." *Population and Development Review* 21:745–782.

Mustanski, Brian S., Meredith L. Chivers, and J. Michael Bailey. 2002. "A critical review of recent biological research on human sexual orientation." *Annual Review of Sex Research* 13:89–140.

Mustanski, Brian S., Michael G. DuPree, Caroline M. Nievergelt, Sven Bocklandt, Nicholas J. Schork, and Dean H. Hamer. 2005. "A genome-wide scan of male sexual orientation." *Human Genetics* 116(4):272–278.

Nagata, J. 1981. "In defense of ethnic boundaries: The changing myths and charters of Malay identity." In F. C. Keyes, ed. *Ethnic Change*. Seattle: University of Washington Press.

Nasir, Jamal J. 1994. *The Status of Women Under Islamic Law and Under Modern Islamic Legislation*. London: Graham & Trotman.

Nelson, Harry, and Robert Jurmain. 1985. *Introduction to Physical Anthropology*. 3rd ed. St. Paul, MN: West.

Nielsen, François. 1994. "Sociobiology and sociology." *Annual Review of Sociology* 20:267–303.

Noel, Donald L. 1972. "Slavery and the rise of racism." In Donald L. Noel, ed. *The Origins of American Slavery and Racism*. Columbus, OH: Merrill.

Norton, Heather L., Rick A. Kittles, Esteban Parra, Paul McKeigue, Xianyun Mao, Keith Cheng, Victor A. Canfield, Daniel G. Bradley, Brian McEvoy, and Mark D. Shriver. 2007. "Genetic evidence for the convergent evolution of light skin in Europeans and East Asians." *Molecular Biology and Evolution* 24:710–722.

Oakes, James. 1982. *The Ruling Race: A History of American Slaveholders*. New York: Random House.

O'Connell, James F., and Kristen Hawkes. 1981. "Alyawara plant use and optimal foraging theory." In Eric Alden Smith and Bruce Winterhalder, eds. *Hunter-Gatherer Foraging Strategies*. Chicago: University of Chicago Press.

O'Leary, Timothy J., and David Levinson, eds. 1990. *Encyclopedia of World Cultures*. 9 vols. Boston: G. K. Hall.

Omark, Donald R., and Murray S. Edelman. 1975. "A comparison of status hierarchies in young children: An ethological approach." *Social Science Information* 14:87–107.

Orians, Gordon H., and Judith H. Heerwagen. 1992. "Evolved responses to landscapes." In Jerome H. Barkow, Leda Cosmides, and John Tooby, eds. *The Adapted Mind: Evolutionary Psychology and the Generation of Culture*. New York: Oxford University Press.

Ostlund, Deborah R., and Richard T. Kinnier. 1997. "Values of youth: Messages from the most popular songs of four decades." *Journal of Humanistic Education and Development* 36:83–91.

Otterbein, Keith F. 1989. *The Evolution of War: A Cross-Cultural Study*. 3rd ed. New Haven, CT: Human Relations Area Files Press.

Parker, Seymour, and Hilda Parker. 1979. "The myth of male superiority: Rise and demise." *American Anthropologist* 81:289–309.

Parsons, Talcott. 1937. *The Structure of Social Action*. Glencoe, IL: Free Press.

Parsons, Talcott. 1943. "The kinship system of the contemporary United States." *American Anthropologist* 45:22–38.

Penn, Derek C., and Daniel J. Povinelli. 2007. "On the lack of evidence that non-human animals possess anything remotely resembling a 'theory of mind.'" *Philosophical Transactions of the Royal Society B* 362:731–744.

Penrose, Roger. 2005. *The Road to Reality: A Complete Guide to the Laws of the Universe*. New York: Knopf.

Percy, William Armstrong III. 1996. *Pederasty and Pedagogy in Archaic Greece*. Urbana: University of Illinois Press.

Perdue, Bonnie M., Rebecca J. Snyder, Zhang Zhihe, M. Jackson Marr, and Terry L. Maple. 2011. "Sex differences in spatial ability: A test of the range size hypothesis in the order Carnivora." *Biology Letters* 7:380–383.

Perilloux, Helen K., Gregory D. Webster, and Steven J. C. Gaulin. 2010. "Signals of genetic quality and maternal investment capacity: The dynamic effects of fluctuating asymmetry and waist-to-hip ratio on men's ratings of women's attractiveness." *Social Psychological and Personality Science* 1:34–42.

Pérusse, Daniel. 1993. "Cultural and reproductive success in industrial societies: Testing the relationship at the proximate and ultimate levels." *Behavioral and Brain Sciences* 16:267–322.

Petrie, Marion. 1994. "Improved growth and survival of offspring of peacocks with more elaborate trains." *Nature* 371:598–599.

Petrie, Marion, Tim Halliday, and Carolyn Sanders. 1991. "Peahens prefer peacocks with elaborate trains." *Animal Behavior* 41:323–331.

Pflüger, Lena S., Elisabeth Oberzaucher, Stanislav Katina, Iris J. Holzleitner, and Karl Grammer. 2012. "Cues to fertility: Perceived attractiveness and facial shape predict reproductive success." *Evolution and Human Behavior* 33:708–714.

Pheasant, S. T. 1983. "Sex differences in strength—some observations on their variability." *Applied Economics* 14:205–211.

Phillipson, David W. 1985. *African Archaeology.* Cambridge, UK: Cambridge University Press.

Piatelli-Palmarini, Massimo. 1989. "Evolution, selection, and cognition: From 'learning' to parameter setting in biology and in the study of language." *Cognition* 31:1–44.

Piddocke, Stuart. 1965. "The potlatch system of the southern Kwakiutl: A new perspective." *Southwestern Journal of Anthropology* 21:244–264.

Pietrzak, Robert H., et al. 2002. "Sex differences in human jealousy: A coordinated study of forced-choice, continuous rating-scale, and physiological responses on the same subjects." *Evolution and Human Behavior* 23:83–94.

Pinker, Steven. 1994. *The Language Instinct: How the Mind Creates Language.* New York: Morrow.

Pinker, Steven. 1997. *How the Mind Works.* New York: Norton.

Pinker, Steven. 2002. *The Blank Slate: The Modern Denial of Human Nature.* New York: Viking.

Pinker, Steven. 2011. *The Better Angels of Our Nature: Why Violence Has Declined.* New York: Viking.

Pinker, Steven. 2012. "The false allure of group selection." http://edge.org/conversation/the-false-allure-of-group-selection.

Pinker, Steven, and Paul Bloom. 1990. "Natural language and natural selection." *Behavioral and Brain Sciences* 13:707–784.

Pinker, Steven, and Ray Jackendoff. 2005. "The faculty of language: What's special about it?" *Cognition* 95:201–236.

Pitshandenge, Iman Ngondo. 1994. "Marriage law in sub-Saharan Africa." In Caroline Bledsoe and Gilles Pison, eds. *Nuptiality in Sub-Saharan Africa.* Oxford: Clarendon Press.

Plummer, Ken. 1982. "Symbolic interactionism and sexual conduct: An emergent perspective." In M. Brake, ed. *Human Sexual Relations.* New York: Pantheon.

Polanyi, Karl. 1957. "The economy as instituted process." In Karl Polanyi, Conrad M. Arensburg, and Harry W. Pearson, eds. *Trade and Market in the Early Empires.* Glencoe, IL: Free Press.

Pomeranz, Kenneth. 2000. *The Great Divergence: China, Europe, and the Making of the Modern World Economy.* Princeton, NJ: Princeton University Press.

Popenoe, David. 1993. "American family decline, 1960–1990: A review and appraisal." *Journal of Marriage and the Family* 55:527–542.

Posner, Richard A. 1992. *Sex and Reason.* Cambridge, MA: Harvard University Press.

Pospisil, Leopold. 1963. *The Kapauku Papuans of West New Guinea.* New York: Holt, Rinehart & Winston.

Possehl, Gregory L. 1990. "Revolution in the urban revolution: The emergence of Indus urbanization." *Annual Review of Anthropology* 19:261–282.

Price, Michael. 1999. "The political advantages of monogamy." Manuscript, University of California, Santa Barbara.

Prokosch, Mark D., Ronald A. Yeo, and Geoffrey F. Miller. 2005. "Intelligence tests with higher *g*-loadings show higher correlations with body symmetry: Evidence for a general fitness factor mediated by developmental stability." *Intelligence* 33:203–213.

Pross, Addy. 2012. *What Is Life? How Chemistry Becomes Biology.* Oxford, UK: Oxford University Press.

Pryor, Frederic L. 1985. "The invention of the plow." *Comparative Studies in Society and History* 27:727–743.

Pusey, Anne. 2004. "Inbreeding avoidance in primates." In Arthur P. Wolf and William H. Durham, eds. *Inbreeding, Incest, and the Incest Taboo.* Stanford, CA: Stanford University Press.

Pyysiäinen, Ilkka. 2009. *Supernatural Agents: Why We Believe in Souls, Gods, and Buddhas.* New York: Oxford University Press.

Reiner, William G. 2004. "Psychosexual development in genetic males assigned female: The cloacal exstrophy experience." *Child and Adolescent Psychiatric Clinic of North America* 13:657–674.

Reynolds, Vernon, Vincent S. E. Falger, and Ian Vine, eds. 1987. *The Sociobiology of Ethnocentrism.* Athens: University of Georgia Press.

Rich, Adrienne. 1980. "Compulsory heterosexuality and lesbian experience." *Signs: Journal of Women in Culture and Society* 5:631–660.

Rieger, Gerulf, Joan A. W. Linsenmeier, Lorenz Gygax, and J. Michael Bailey. 2008. "Sexual orientation and childhood gender nonconformity: Evidence from home videos." *Developmental Psychology* 44:46–58.

Risch, Neil, Esteban Burchard, Elad Ziv, and Hua Tang. 2002. "Categorization of humans in biomedical research: Genes, race, and disease." *Genome Biology* 3(7). http://genomebiology.com/2002/3/7/comment/2007.

Robinson, George. 2000. *Essential Judaism: A Complete Guide to Beliefs, Customs, and Rituals.* New York: Simon & Schuster.

Roscoe, Paul. 2011. "*Dead Birds*: The 'theater' of war among the Dugum Dani." *American Anthropologist* 113:56–70.

Rosenberg, Noah A., Jonathan K. Pritchard, James L. Weber, Howard M. Cann, Kenneth K. Kidd, Lev A. Zhivotovsky, and Marcus W. Feldman. 2002. "Genetic structure of human populations." *Science* 298:2381–2385.

Rosenthal, Bernice Glatzer. 1975. "The role and status of women in the Soviet Union: 1917 to the present." In Ruby Rohrlich-Leavitt, ed. *Women Cross-Culturally.* The Hague: Mouton.

Ross, Eric B. 1980. "Patterns of diet and forces of production: An economic and ecological history of the ascendancy of beef in the United States diet." In Eric B. Ross, ed. *Beyond the Myths of Culture: Essays in Cultural Materialism*. New York: Academic Press.

Ross, Marc Howard. 1983. "Political decision making and conflict: Additional cross-cultural codes and scales." *Ethnology* 22:169–192.

Rossi, Alice S. 1977. "A biosocial perspective on parenting." *Daedalus* 106:1–31.

Rossi, Alice S. 1984. "Gender and parenthood." *American Sociological Review* 49:1–19.

Rotkirch, Anna. 2008. "What is 'Baby Fever'? Contrasting evolutionary explanations of proceptive behavior." In Heinz-Jürgen Niedenzu, Tamás Meleghy, and Peter Meyer, eds. *The New Evolutionary Social Science: Human Nature, Social Behavior, and Social Change*. Boulder, CO: Paradigm Publishers.

Rozin, Paul. 1987. "Psychobiological perspectives on food preferences and avoidances." In Marvin Harris and Eric B. Ross, eds. *Food and Evolution: Toward a Theory of Human Food Habits*. Philadelphia: Temple University Press.

Rozin, Paul, Larry Hammer, Harriett Oster, Talia Horowitz, and Veronica Marmora. 1986. "The child's conception of food: Differentiation of categories of rejected substances in the 16 months to 5 year age range." *Appetite* 7:141–151.

Rueschemeyer, Dietrich, Evelyne Huber Stephens, and John D. Stephens. 1992. *Capitalist Development and Democracy*. Chicago: University of Chicago Press.

Runciman, W. G. 1998. "Greek hoplites, warrior culture, and indirect bias." *Journal of the Royal Anthropological Institute* 4:731–751.

Runciman, W. G. 2009. *The Theory of Cultural and Social Selection*. Cambridge, UK: Cambridge University Press.

Russon, A. E., and B. E. Waite. 1991. "Patterns of dominance and imitation in an infant peer group." *Ethology and Sociobiology* 12:55–73.

Saad, Gad. 2007. *The Evolutionary Bases of Consumption*. Mahwah, NJ: Lawrence Erlbaum.

Saad, Gad. 2011. *The Consuming Instinct: What Juicy Burgers, Ferraris, Pornography, and Gift Giving Reveal About Human Nature*. Amherst, NY: Prometheus Books.

Sagarin, Brad J., Amy L. Martin, Savia A. Coutinho, John E. Edlund, Lily Patel, John Skowronski, and Bettina Zengel. 2012. "Sex differences in jealousy: A meta-analytic examination." *Evolution and Human Behavior* 33:595–614.

Saggar, Anand K., and Alan H. Bittles. 2008. "Consanguinity and child health." *Paedatrics and Child Health* 18:244–249.

Sahlins, Marshall. 1958. *Social Stratification in Polynesia*. Seattle: University of Washington Press.

Sahlins, Marshall. 1963. "Poor man, rich man, big man, chief: Political types in Melanesia and Polynesia." *Comparative Studies in Society and History* 5:285–303.

Sahlins, Marshall. 1968. *Tribesmen*. Englewood Cliffs, NJ: Prentice-Hall.

Sahlins, Marshall. 1972. *Stone Age Economics*. Chicago: Aldine.

Salmon, Catherine. 2005. "Crossing the abyss: Erotica and the intersection of evolutionary psychology and literary studies." In Jonathan Gottschall and David Sloan Wilson, eds. *The Literary Animal: Evolution and the Nature of Narrative*. Evanston, IL: Northwestern University Press.

Salter, Frank. 2002. "Estimating ethnic genetic interests." *Population and Environment* 24(2):111–140.

Salter, Frank. 2003. *On Genetic Interests: Family, Ethnicity, and Humanity in an Age of Mass Migration.* Frankfurt am Main: Peter Lang.

Salzman, Philip Carl. 2004. *Pastoralists: Equality, Hierarchy, and the State.* Boulder, CO: Westview Press.

Sanders, William T., and David Webster. 1978. "Unilinealism, multilinealism, and the evolution of complex societies." In Charles L. Redman et al., eds. *Social Archaeology: Beyond Subsistence and Dating.* New York: Academic Press.

Sanderson, Stephen K. 1994. "The transition from feudalism to capitalism: The theoretical significance of the Japanese case." *Review (Fernand Braudel Center)* 17:15–55.

Sanderson, Stephen K. 1995. *Social Transformations: A General Theory of Historical Development.* Oxford: Blackwell.

Sanderson, Stephen K. 2001. "Explaining monogamy and polygyny in human societies." *Social Forces* 80:329–336.

Sanderson, Stephen K. 2008a. "Religious attachment theory and the biosocial evolution of the major world religions." In Joseph Bulbulia et al., eds. *The Evolution of Religion: Studies, Theories, and Critiques.* Santa Margarita, CA: Collins Foundation Press.

Sanderson, Stephen K. 2008b. "Adaptation, evolution, and religion." *Religion* 38:141–156.

Sanderson, Stephen K., and Arthur S. Alderson. 2005. *World Societies: The Evolution of Human Social Life.* Boston: Pearson Allyn & Bacon.

Sanderson, Stephen K., and Joshua Dubrow. 2000. "Fertility decline in the modern world and in the original demographic transition: Testing three theories with cross-national data." *Population and Environment* 21:511–537.

Sanderson, Stephen K., and Joshua Dubrow. 2005. "Militarist, Marxian, and non-Marxian theories of gender inequality: A cross-cultural test." *Social Forces* 83:1425–1442.

Sanderson, Stephen K., and Wesley W. Roberts. 2008. "The evolutionary forms of the religious life: A cross-cultural, quantitative study." *American Anthropologist* 110:454–466.

Santos, Ricardo Ventura, Peter H. Fry, Simone Monteiro, Marcos Chor Maio, José Carlos Rodrigues, Luciana Bastos Rodrigues, and Sergio D. J. Pena. 2009. "Color, race, and genomic ancestry in Brazil: Dialogues between anthropology and genetics." *Current Anthropology* 50:787–819.

Sarich, Vincent, and Frank Miele. 2004. *Race: The Reality of Human Differences.* Boulder, CO: Westview Press.

Savage-Rumbaugh, E. Sue. 1986. *Ape Language: From Conditioned Response to Symbol.* New York: Columbia University Press.

Savage-Rumbaugh, E. Sue, Duane M. Rumbaugh, and Kelly McDonald. 1985. "Language learning in two species of apes." *Neuroscience and Biobehavioral Reviews* 9:653–665.

Scheidel, Walter. 1996. "Brother-sister and parent-child marriage outside royal families in Ancient Egypt and Iran: A challenge to the sociobiological view of incest avoidance." *Ethology and Sociobiology* 17:319–340.

Scheidel, Walter. 2008. "Monogamy and polygyny in Greece, Rome, and world history." Princeton/Stanford Working Papers in Classics.

Schmitt, David P. 2003. "Universal sex differences in the desire for sexual variety: Tests from 52 nations, 6 continents, and 13 islands." *Journal of Personality and Social Psychology* 85:85–104.

Schmitt, David P. 2005. "Sociosexuality from Argentina to Zimbabwe: A 48-nation study of sex, culture, and strategies of human mating." *Behavioral and Brain Sciences* 28:247–311.

Schwabe, Calvin W. 1979. *Unmentionable Cuisine.* Charlottesville: University Press of Virginia.

Seemanova, Eva. 1971. "A study of children of incestuous matings." *Human Heredity* 21:108–128.

Segerstråle, Ullica. 2000. *Defenders of the Truth: The Battle for Science in the Sociobiology Debate and Beyond.* New York: Oxford University Press.

Seidman, Steven. 2003. *The Social Construction of Sexuality.* New York: Norton.

Seldon, Arthur. 1990. *Capitalism.* Oxford: Basil Blackwell.

Service, Elman R. 1963. *Profiles in Ethnology.* New York: Harper & Row.

Service, Elman R. 1971. *Primitive Social Organization: An Evolutionary Perspective.* 2nd ed. New York: Random House.

Shankman, Paul. 1991. "Culture contact, cultural ecology, and Dani warfare." *Man.* N.S. 26:299–321.

Shaw, Brent D. 1992. "Explaining incest: Brother-sister marriage in Graeco-Roman Egypt." *Man* 27:267–299.

Shaw, R. Paul, and Yuwa Wong. 1989. *Genetic Seeds of Warfare: Evolution, Nationalism, and Patriotism.* Boston: Unwin Hyman.

Shepher, Joseph. 1969. "Mate selection among second generation kibbutz adolescents and adults: Incest avoidance and negative imprinting." *Archives of Sexual Behavior* 1:293–307.

Shepher, Joseph. 1983. *Incest: A Biosocial View.* New York: Academic Press.

Sherman, Paul W., and Geoffrey A. Hash. 2001. "Why vegetable recipes are not very spicy." *Evolution and Human Behavior* 22:147–163.

Shettles, Landrum B. 1961. "Conception and birth sex ratios." *Obstetrics and Gynecology* 18:122–130.

Shively, Donald H. 1964. "Sumptuary regulation and status in early Tokugawa Japan." *Harvard Journal of Asiatic Studies* 25:123–164.

Shorter, Edward. 1975. *The Making of the Modern Family.* New York: Basic Books.

Silver, Morris. 1995. *Economic Structures of Antiquity.* Westport, CT: Greenwood Press.

Silverman, Irwin, Jean Choi, Angie Mackewn, Maryanne Fisher, Judy Moro, and Ester Olshansky. 2000. "Evolved mechanisms underlying wayfinding: Further studies on the hunter-gatherer theory of spatial sex differences." *Evolution and Human Behavior* 21:201–213.

Silverman, Irwin, Jean Choi, and Michael Peters. 2007. "The hunter-gatherer theory of sex differences in spatial abilities: Data from 40 countries." *Archives of Sexual Behavior* 36:261–268.

Silverman, Irwin, and Marion Eals. 1992. "Sex differences in spatial abilities: Evolutionary theory and data." In Jerome H. Barkow, Leda Cosmides, and John Tooby, eds. *The Adapted Mind: Evolutionary Psychology and the Generation of Culture.* New York: Oxford University Press.

Simoons, Frederick J. 1970. "The traditional limits of milking and milk use in Southern Asia." *Anthropos* 65:547–593.

Simoons, Frederick J. 1971. "The antiquity of dairying in Asia and Africa." *Geographical Review* 61:431–439.

Simoons, Frederick J. 1980. "The determinants of dairying and milk use in the Old World: Ecological, physiological, and cultural." In J. R. K. Robson, ed. *Food, Ecology, and Culture.* New York: Gordon & Breach.

Simoons, Frederick J. 1994. *Eat Not This Flesh: Food Avoidances from Prehistory to the Present.* 2nd ed. Madison: University of Wisconsin Press.

Simpson, J. A. 1998. "Sociosexual Orientation Inventory." In C. M. Davis et al., eds. *Handbook of Sexuality-Related Measures.* Thousand Oaks, CA: Sage.

Simpson, J. A., and Steven W. Gangestad. 1991. "Individual differences in sociosexuality: Evidence for convergent and discriminant validity." *Journal of Personality and Social Psychology* 60:870–883.

Singer, Saul. 2006. "The Jewish state is happily bucking the demographic trends of the rest of the world." www.clevelandjewishnews.com/articles/2006/11/23/news/israel/akids1124.prt.

Singh, Devendra. 1993a. "Adaptive significance of female physical attractiveness: Role of waist-to-hip ratio." *Journal of Personality and Social Psychology* 65:293–307.

Singh, Devendra. 1993b. "Body shape and women's sexual attractiveness." *Human Nature* 4:297–321.

Singh, Devendra. 1994. "Body fat distribution and perception of desirable female body shape by young black men and women." *International Journal of Eating Disorders* 16:289–294.

Singh, Devendra, B. J. Dixson, T. S. Jessop, B. Morgan, and A. F. Dixson. 2010. "Cross-cultural consensus for waist-to-hip ratio and women's attractiveness." *Evolution and Human Behavior* 31:176–181.

Singh, Devendra, C. Frohlich, and M. Haywood. 1999. "Waist-to-hip ratio representation in ancient sculptures from four cultures." Paper presented at the annual meeting of the Human Behavior and Evolution Society, University of Utah, June 2–6.

Singh, Devendra, and Suwardi Luis. 1995. "Ethnic and gender consensus for the effect of waist-to-hip ratio on judgment of women's attractiveness." *Human Nature* 6:51–65.

Singh, Devendra, and Robert K. Young. 1995. "Body weight, waist-to-hip ratio, breasts, and hips: Role in judgments of female attractiveness and desirability for relationships." *Ethology and Sociobiology* 16:483–507.

Sjoberg, Gideon. 1960. *The Preindustrial City.* New York: Free Press.

Slater, Peter J. B. 2000. "Birdsong repertoires: Their origins and use." In Nils L. Wallin, Bjorn Merker, and Steven Brown, eds. *The Origins of Music.* Cambridge, MA: MIT Press.

Smart, Ninian. 1976. *The Religious Experience of Mankind.* 2nd ed. New York: Scribner's.

Smedley, Audrey. 1993. *Race in North America: Origin and Evolution of a Worldview.* Boulder, CO: Westview Press.

Smedley, Audrey. 1999. "'Race' and the construction of human identity." *American Anthropologist* 100:690–702.

Smil, Vaclav. 1994. *Energy in World History.* Boulder, CO: Westview Press.

Smith, David Livingstone. 2004. *Why We Lie: The Evolutionary Roots of Deception and the Unconscious Mind.* New York: St. Martin's.

Smith, E. O. 1999. "High heels and evolution." *Psychology, Evolution, and Gender* 1:245–277.

Smith, Eric Alden. 1983. "Anthropological applications of optimal foraging theory: A critical review." *Current Anthropology* 24:625–651.

Smith, Eric Alden. 1991. *Inujjuamiut Foraging Strategies: Evolutionary Ecology of an Arctic Hunting Economy.* New York: Aldine de Gruyter.

Smith, Eric Alden. 2000. "Three styles in the evolutionary analysis of human behavior." In Lee Cronk, Napoleon Chagnon, and William Irons, eds. *Adaptation and Human Behavior: An Anthropological Perspective*. New York: Aldine de Gruyter.

Smith, Eric Alden, and Rebecca L. Bliege Bird. 2000. "Turtle hunting and tombstone opening: Public generosity as costly signaling." *Evolution and Human Behavior* 21:245–261.

Smith, Eric Alden, and Bruce Winterhalder. 1992a. "Natural selection and decision making: Some fundamental principles." In Eric Alden Smith and Bruce Winterhalder, eds. *Evolutionary Ecology and Human Behavior*. New York: Aldine de Gruyter.

Smith, Eric Alden, and Bruce Winterhalder, eds. 1992b. *Evolutionary Ecology and Human Behavior*. New York: Aldine de Gruyter.

Smuts, Barbara. 1995. "The evolutionary origins of patriarchy." *Human Nature* 6:1–32.

Snooks, Graeme Donald. 1996. *The Dynamic Society: Exploring the Sources of Global Change*. London: Routledge.

Snooks, Graeme Donald. 1997. *The Ephemeral Civilization: Exploding the Myth of Social Evolution*. London: Routledge.

Sober, Elliott, and David Sloan Wilson. 1998. *Unto Others: The Evolution and Psychology of Unselfish Behavior*. Cambridge, MA: Harvard University Press.

Somit, Albert, and Steven A. Peterson. 1997. *Darwinism, Dominance, and Democracy: The Biological Bases of Authoritarianism*. Westport, CT: Praeger.

Sosis, Richard. 2000. "Costly signaling and torch fishing on Ifaluk Atoll." *Evolution and Human Behavior* 21:223–244.

Sosis, Richard. 2003. "Why aren't we all Hutterites? Costly signaling theory and religious behavior." *Human Nature* 14:91–127.

Speth, J. D. 1990. "Seasonality, resource stress, and food sharing in so-called 'egalitarian' foraging societies." *Journal of Anthropological Archaeology* 9:148–188.

Spiro, Melford. 1958. *Children of the Kibbutz*. Cambridge, MA: Harvard University Press.

Spitz, René. 1945. "Hospitalism: An inquiry into the genesis of psychiatric conditions in early childhood." *Psychoanalytic Study of the Child* 1:53–74.

Spitz, René. 1946. "Anaclitic depression." *Psychoanalytic Study of the Child* 2:313–343.

Stark, Rodney. 1996. *The Rise of Christianity: A Sociologist Reconsiders History*. Princeton, NJ: Princeton University Press.

Starkweather, Katherine E., and Raymond Hames. 2012. "A survey of non-classical polyandry." *Human Nature* 23:149–172.

Steadman, Lyle B., and Craig T. Palmer. 2008. *The Supernatural and Natural Selection: The Evolution of Religion*. Boulder, CO: Paradigm Publishers.

Stearns, Peter N. 1993. *The Industrial Revolution in World History*. Boulder, CO: Westview Press.

Stephens, William N. 1963. *The Family in Cross-Cultural Perspective*. New York: Holt, Rinehart & Winston.

Strakalj, Goran. 2007. "The status of the race concept in contemporary biological anthropology: A review." *Anthropologist* 9:73–78.

Streeter, S. A., and Donald H. McBurney. 2003. "Waist-hip ratio and attractiveness: New evidence and a critique of 'a critical test.'" *Evolution and Human Behavior* 24:88–98.

Stringer, Chris. 2012. *Lone Survivors: How We Came to Be the Only Humans on Earth*. New York: Henry Holt.

Stringer, Christopher, and Peter Andrews. 1988. "Genetics and the fossil evidence for the origin of modern humans." *Science* 239:1263–1268.

Stringer, Christopher, and Peter Andrews. 2005. *The Complete World of Human Evolution.* London: Thames & Hudson.

Stringer, Christopher, and Robin McKie. 1996. *African Exodus: The Origins of Modern Humanity.* New York: Henry Holt.

Sugiyama, Lawrence S. 2004. "Is beauty in the context-sensitive adaptations of the beholder? Shiwiar use of waist-to-hip ratio in assessments of female mate value." *Evolution and Human Behavior* 25:51–62.

Sugiyama, Michelle Scalise. 2005. "Reverse-engineering narrative: Evidence of special design." In Jonathan Gottschall and David Sloan Wilson, eds. *The Literary Animal: Evolution and the Nature of Narrative.* Evanston, IL: Northwestern University Press.

Sussman, Marvin B., and Lee Burchinal. 1962. "Kin family network: Unheralded structure in current conceptualizations of family functioning." *Marriage and Family Living* 24:231–240.

Swaab, D. F., and M. A. Hofman. 1990. "An enlarged suprachiasmatic nucleus in homosexual men." *Brain Research* 24:141–148.

Swallow, Dallas M. 2003. "Genetics of lactase persistence and lactose intolerance." *Annual Review of Genetics* 37:197–219.

Swallow, Dallas M., and E. J. Hollox. 2000. "The genetic polymorphism of intestinal lactase activity in human adults." In C. R. Shriver et al., eds. *The Metabolic and Molecular Basis of Inherited Disease.* New York: McGraw-Hill.

Swanson, Guy E. 1960. *The Birth of the Gods: The Origin of Primitive Beliefs.* Ann Arbor: University of Michigan Press.

Symons, Donald. 1979. *The Evolution of Human Sexuality.* New York: Oxford University Press.

Symons, Donald. 1987. "If we're all Darwinians, what's the fuss about?" In Charles Crawford et al., eds. *Sociobiology and Psychology.* Mahwah, NJ: Lawrence Erlbaum.

Symons, Donald. 1989. "A critique of Darwinian anthropology." *Ethology and Sociobiology* 10:131–144.

Symons, Donald. 1995. "Beauty is in the adaptations of the beholder: The evolutionary psychology of human female sexual attractiveness." In Paul R. Abramson and Steven D. Pinkerton, eds. *Sexual Nature, Sexual Culture.* Chicago: University of Chicago Press.

Synek, Erich, and Karl Grammer. N.d. "Evolutionary aesthetics: Visual complexity and the development of human landscape preferences." http://evolution.anthro.univie.ac.at /institutes/urbanethology/projects/urbanisation/landscapes/indexland.html.

Taagepera, Rein. 1978. "Size and duration of empires: Systematics of size." *Social Science Research* 7:108–127.

Talmon, Yonina. 1964. "Mate selection in collective settlements." *American Sociological Review* 29:491–508.

Tassinary, Louis G., and Kristi A. Hansen. 1998. "A critical test of the waist-to-hip ratio hypothesis of female physical attractiveness." *Psychological Science* 9:150–155.

Telles, Edward E. 2004. *Race in Another America: The Significance of Skin Color in Brazil.* Princeton, NJ: Princeton University Press.

Templeton, Alan R. 1999. "Human races: A genetic and evolutionary perspective." *American Anthropologist* 100:632–650.

Testart, Alain. 1982. "The significance of food storage among hunter-gatherers: Residence patterns, population densities, and social inequalities." *Current Anthropology* 23:523–537.

Testart, Alain. 1988. "Some major problems in the social anthropology of hunter-gatherers." *Current Anthropology* 29:1–32.

Therborn, Göran. 2004. *Between Sex and Power: Family in the World, 1900–2000.* London: Routledge.

Thompson, Lloyd A. 1989. *Romans and Blacks.* London: Routledge.

Thornhill, Randy, Corey L. Fincher, Damian R. Murray, and Mark Schaller. 2010. "Zoonotic and non-zoonotic diseases in relation to human personality and societal values: Support for the parasite stress model." *Evolutionary Psychology* 8:151–169.

Thornhill, Randy, and Steven W. Gangestad. 1993. "Human facial beauty: Averageness, symmetry, and parasite resistance." *Human Nature* 4:237–269.

Thornhill, Randy, and Steven W. Gangestad. 2008. *The Evolutionary Biology of Human Female Sexuality.* New York: Oxford University Press.

Thornhill, Randy, and Craig T. Palmer. 2000. *A Natural History of Rape: Biological Bases of Sexual Coercion.* Cambridge, MA: MIT Press.

Tilly, Charles. 1990. *Coercion, Capital, and European States, 990–1990.* Oxford: Blackwell.

Tishkoff, Sarah A., et al. 2007. "Convergent adaptation of human lactase persistence in Africa and Europe." *Nature Genetics* 39:31–40.

Todorov, Tzvetan. 1993. *On Human Diversity: Nationalism, Racism, and Exoticism in French Thought.* Cambridge, MA: Harvard University Press.

Tooby, John, and Leda Cosmides. 1990. "The past explains the present: Emotional adaptations and the structure of ancestral environments." *Ethology and Sociobiology* 11:375–424.

Tooby, John, and Leda Cosmides. 1992. "The psychological foundations of culture." In Jerome H. Barkow, Leda Cosmides, and John Tooby, eds. *The Adapted Mind: Evolutionary Psychology and the Generation of Culture.* New York: Oxford University Press.

Tremblay, Richard E., C. Japel, Daniel Pérusse, P. McDuff, M. Boivin, M. Zoccolillo, and J. Montplaisir. 1999. "The search for the age of 'onset' of physical aggression: Rousseau and Bandura revisited." *Criminal Behavior and Mental Health* 9:8–23.

Trigger, Bruce. 1982. "The rise of civilization in Egypt." In J. D. Clark, ed. *The Cambridge History of Africa.* Vol. 1. Cambridge, UK: Cambridge University Press.

Trinkaus, Erik. 2005. "Early modern humans." *Annual Review of Anthropology* 34:207–230.

Trivers, Robert L. 1971. "The evolution of reciprocal altruism." *Quarterly Review of Biology* 46:35–57.

Trivers, Robert L. 1972. "Parental investment and sexual selection." In Bernard Campbell, ed. *Sexual Selection and the Descent of Man, 1871–1971.* Chicago: Aldine.

Trivers, Robert L. 1974. "Parent-offspring conflict." *American Zoologist* 14:249–264.

Trivers, Robert L. 2011. *The Folly of Fools: The Logic of Deceit and Self-Deception in Human Life.* New York: Basic Books.

Trivers, Robert L., and Dan Willard. 1973. "Natural selection of parental ability to vary the sex ratio of offspring." *Science* 179:90–92.

Truswell, A. S., and J. D. L. Hansen. 1976. "Medical research among the !Kung." In Richard B. Lee, ed. *Kalahari Hunters and Gatherers*. Cambridge, MA: Harvard University Press.

Turke, Paul W. 1989. "Evolution and the demand for children." *Population and Development Review* 15:61–90.

Turke, Paul W. 1990. "Which humans behave adaptively, and why does it matter?" *Ethology and Sociobiology* 11:305-339.

Udry, J. Richard. 2000. "Biological limits of gender construction." *American Sociological Review* 65:443–457.

Vaesen, Krist. 2012. "The cognitive bases of human tool use." *Behavioral and Brain Sciences* 35:203–262.

Van Beijsterveldt, C. E. M., James J. Hudziak, and Dorret J. Boomsma. 2006. "Genetic and environmental influences on cross-gender behavior and relation to behavior problems: A study of Dutch twins at ages 7 and 10 years." *Archives of Sexual Behavior* 35:647–658.

Van den Berghe, Pierre L. 1967. *Race and Racism: A Comparative Perspective*. New York: Wiley.

Van den Berghe, Pierre L. 1978. *Man in Society: A Biosocial View*. 2nd ed. New York: Elsevier.

Van den Berghe, Pierre L. 1979. *Human Family Systems: An Evolutionary View*. New York: Elsevier.

Van den Berghe, Pierre L. 1981. *The Ethnic Phenomenon*. New York: Elsevier.

Van den Berghe, Pierre L. 1990. "South Africa after thirty years." *Social Dynamics* 16(2): 16–37.

Van den Berghe, Pierre L. 1996. "Racism." *Encyclopedia of Cultural Anthropology* 3:1054–1057. New York: Holt.

Van den Berghe, Pierre L., and Gene M. Mesher. 1980. "Royal incest and inclusive fitness." *American Ethnologist* 7:300–317.

Van den Berghe, Pierre L., and Joseph Whitmeyer. 1990. "Social class and reproductive success." *International Journal of Contemporary Sociology* 27:29–48.

Vanhanen, Tatu. 1992. *On the Evolutionary Roots of Politics*. New Delhi: Sterling.

Vanhanen, Tatu. 1999. *Ethnic Conflicts Explained by Ethnic Nepotism*. Stamford, CT: JAI Press.

Veblen, Thorstein. 2007. *The Theory of the Leisure Class*. New York: Oxford University Press. Originally published in 1899.

Vilain, Eric. 2000. "Genetics of sexual development." *Annual Review of Sex Research* 11:1–25.

Voland, Eckart. 1984. "Human sex-ratio manipulation: Historical data from a German parish." *Journal of Human Evolution* 13:99–107.

Von Hippel, William, and Robert Trivers. 2011. "The evolution and psychology of self-deception." *Behavioral and Brain Sciences* 34:1–56.

Voracek, M., A. Hofhansl, and M. L. Fisher. 2005. "Clark and Hatfield's evidence of women's low receptivity to male strangers' sexual offers revisited." *Psychological Reports* 97:11–20.

Wade, Nicholas. 2006. *Before the Dawn: Recovering the Lost History of Our Ancestors*. New York: Penguin Press.

Wade, Nicholas. 2010. "Chimps, too, wage war and annex rival territory." *New York Times*. www.nytimes.com/2010/06/22/science/22chimp.html?_r=1. Print version in *New York Times*, June 22, 2010, p. D1.

Walker, Robert S., and Drew H. Bailey. 2013. "Body counts in lowland South American violence." *Evolution and Human Behavior* 34:29–34.

Wallace, Anthony F. C. 1966. *Religion: An Anthropological View.* New York: Random House.

Wallerstein, Immanuel. 1974. *The Modern World-System: Capitalist Agriculture and the Origins of the European World-Economy in the Sixteenth Century.* New York: Academic Press.

Wallerstein, Immanuel. 1989. *The Modern World-System III: The Second Era of Great Expansion of the Capitalist World-Economy, 1730–1840s.* San Diego: Academic Press.

Wang, Qian, Goran Strakalj, and Li Sun. 2003. "On the concept of race in Chinese biological anthropology: Alive and well." *Current Anthropology* 44:403.

Ware, Helen. 1979. "Polygyny: Women's views in a transitional society, Nigeria 1975." *Journal of Marriage and the Family* 41:185–195.

Weeden, Jason, Michael J. Abrams, Melanie C. Green, and John Sabatini. 2006. "Do high-status people really have fewer children?" *Human Nature* 17:377–392.

Weeks, Jeffrey. 1986. *Sexuality.* London: Routledge.

Weinberg, S. Kirson. 1955. *Incest Behavior.* New York: Citadel.

Weisfeld, Glenn E., Donald R. Omark, and Carol L. Cronin. 1980. "A longitudinal and cross-sectional study of dominance in boys." In Donald R. Omark, Fred F. Strayer, and Daniel G. Freedman, eds. *Dominance Relations: An Ethological View of Human Conflict and Social Interaction.* New York: Garland.

Welch, Charles E. III, and Paul C. Glick. 1981. "The incidence of polygamy in contemporary Africa: A research note." *Journal of Marriage and the Family* 43:191–193.

Wenke, Robert J. 1999. *Patterns in Prehistory: Mankind's First Three Million Years.* 4th ed. New York: Oxford University Press.

Westermarck, Edward. 1906–1908. *The Origin and Development of the Moral Ideas.* 2 vols. London: Macmillan.

Westermarck, Edward. 1922a. *The History of Human Marriage.* Vol. 1. 5th ed. London: Macmillan.

Westermarck, Edward. 1922b. *The History of Human Marriage.* Vol. 2. 5th ed. London: Macmillan.

Westermarck, Edward. 1922c. *The History of Human Marriage.* Vol. 3. 5th ed. London: Macmillan.

Westermarck, Edward. 1926. *A Short History of Marriage.* New York: Macmillan.

Wetsman, A., and Frank Marlowe. 1999. "How universal are preferences for female waist-to-hip ratios? Evidence from the Hadza of Tanzania." *Evolution and Human Behavior* 20:219–228.

Whitam, Frederick L. 1983. "Culturally invariable properties of male homosexuality: Tentative conclusions from cross-cultural research." *Archives of Sexual Behavior* 12:207–226.

Whitam, Frederick L., and Robin M. Mathy. 1986. *Male Homosexuality in Four Societies: Brazil, Guatemala, the Philippines, and the United States.* Westport, CT: Praeger.

White, Benjamin. 1973. "Demand for labor and population growth in colonial Java." *Human Ecology* 2:217–236.

White, Benjamin. 1982. "Child labor and population growth in rural Asia." *Development and Change* 13:587–610.

White, Douglas R. 1988. "Rethinking polygyny: Co-wives, codes, and cultural systems." *Current Anthropology* 29:529–572.

White, Lynn Jr. 1962. *Medieval Technology and Social Change*. New York: Oxford University Press.

White, Randall. 1992. "Beyond art: Toward an understanding of the origins of material representation in Europe." *Annual Review of Anthropology* 21:537–564.

White, Randall. 1993. "The dawn of adornment." *Natural History* 102:61–67.

Whitehouse, Harvey. 2004. *Modes of Religiosity: A Cognitive Theory of Religious Transmission*. Lanham, MD: AltaMira Press.

Whyte, Martin King. 1978. *The Status of Women in Preindustrial Societies*. Princeton, NJ: Princeton University Press.

Wiessner, Polly. 1982. "Risk, reciprocity, and social influence on !Kung San economies." In Eleanor Leacock and Richard B. Lee, eds. *Politics and History in Band Societies*. Cambridge, UK: Cambridge University Press.

Wilbanks, W. 1984. *Murder in Miami*. Lanham, MD: University Press of America.

Wild, Oliver. 1992. "The Silk Road." www.ess.uci.edu/~oliver/silk.html.

Wilkinson, David. 1992. "Cities, civilizations, and oikumenes: I." *Comparative Civilizations Review* 27:51–87.

Wilkinson, David. 1993. "Cities, civilizations, and oikumenes: II." *Comparative Civilizations Review* 28:41–72.

Wilkinson, Richard G. 1973. *Poverty and Progress: An Ecological Perspective on Economic Development*. New York: Praeger.

Wilmsen, Edward N. 1982. "Studies in diet, nutrition, and fertility among a group of Kalahari bushmen in Botswana." *Social Science Information* 21:95–125.

Wilson, David Sloan. 2007. "Human groups as adaptive units: Toward a permanent consensus." In Peter Carruthers, Stephen Laurence, and Stephen Stich, eds. *The Innate Mind: Culture and Cognition*. New York: Oxford University Press.

Wilson, David Sloan, and Edward O. Wilson. 2007. "Rethinking the theoretical foundation of sociobiology." *Quarterly Review of Biology* 82:327–348.

Wilson, Edward O. 1975. *Sociobiology: The New Synthesis*. Cambridge, MA: Harvard University Press.

Wilson, Edward O. 2012. *The Social Conquest of Earth*. New York: Liveright.

Wilson, James F., Michael E. Weale, Alice C. Smith, Fiona Gratrix, Benjamin Fletcher, Mark G. Thomas, Neil Bradman, and David B. Goldstein. 2001. "Population genetic structure of variable drug response." *Nature Genetics* 29:265–269.

Wilson, Margo, and Martin Daly. 1993. "An evolutionary psychological perspective on male sexual proprietariness and violence against wives." *Violence and Victims* 8:271–294.

Wilson, Margo, and Martin Daly. 1997. "Life expectancy, economic inequality, homicide, and reproductive timing in Chicago neighborhoods." *British Medical Journal* 314:1271–1274.

Wilson, Margo, Holly Johnson, and Martin Daly. 1995. "Lethal and nonlethal violence against wives." *Canadian Journal of Criminology* 37:331–361.

Winch, Robert F., and Gay C. Kitson. 1977. "Types of American families: An unsatisfactory classification." In Robert F. Winch, ed. *Familial Organization*. New York: Free Press.

Winkelman, Michael J. 1990. "Shamans and other 'magico-religious' healers: A cross-cultural study of their origins, nature, and social transformations." *Ethos* 18:308–352.

Winkelman, Michael J. 2000. *Shamanism: The Neural Ecology of Consciousness and Healing.* Westport, CT: Bergin & Garvey.

Winterhalder, Bruce. 1981. "Foraging strategies in the boreal environment: An analysis of Cree hunting and gathering." In Bruce Winterhalder and Eric Alden Smith, eds. *Hunter-Gatherer Foraging Strategies.* Chicago: University of Chicago Press.

Winterhalder, Bruce. 1987. "The analysis of hunter-gatherer diets: Stalking an optimal foraging model." In Marvin Harris and Eric B. Ross, eds. *Food and Evolution: Toward a Theory of Human Food Habits.* Philadelphia: Temple University Press.

Winterhalder, Bruce, and Eric Alden Smith, eds. 1981. *Hunter-Gatherer Foraging Strategies: Ethnographic and Archaeological Analyses.* Chicago: University of Chicago Press.

Winterhalder, Bruce, and Eric Alden Smith. 2000. "Analyzing adaptive strategies: Human behavioral ecology at twenty-five." *Evolutionary Anthropology* 7:51–72.

Wittfogel, Karl. 1957. *Oriental Despotism.* New Haven, CT: Yale University Press.

Wolf, Arthur P. 1966. "Childhood association, sexual attraction, and the incest taboo: A Chinese case." *American Anthropologist* 68:883–898.

Wolf, Arthur P. 1970. "Childhood association and sexual attraction: A further test of the Westermarck hypothesis." *American Anthropologist* 72:503–515.

Wolf, Arthur P. 1995. *Sexual Attraction and Childhood Association: A Chinese Brief for Edward Westermarck.* Stanford, CA: Stanford University Press.

Wolf, Arthur P. 2004a. "Introduction." In Arthur P. Wolf and William H. Durham, eds. *Inbreeding, Incest, and the Incest Taboo.* Stanford, CA: Stanford University Press.

Wolf, Arthur P. 2004b. "Explaining the Westermarck effect, or, what did natural selection select for?" In Arthur P. Wolf and William H. Durham, eds. *Inbreeding, Incest, and the Incest Taboo.* Stanford, CA: Stanford University Press.

Wolf, Naomi. 2002. *The Beauty Myth: How Images of Female Beauty Are Used Against Women.* New York: Harper Perennial.

Wolfgang, Marvin E. 1958. *Patterns in Criminal Homicide.* Philadelphia: University of Pennsylvania Press.

Woodburn, James. 1968. "An introduction to Hadza ecology." In Richard B. Lee and Irven DeVore, eds. *Man the Hunter.* Chicago: Aldine.

Woodburn, James. 1982. "Egalitarian societies." *Man* 27:431–451.

Wooding, Stephen P. 2007. "Following the herd." *Nature Genetics* 39:7–8.

Worling, James R. 1995. "Adolescent sibling-incest offenders: Differences in family and individual functioning when compared to adolescent nonsibling sex offenders." *Child Abuse and Neglect* 19:633–643.

Wrangham, Richard W., and Dale Peterson. 1996. *Demonic Males: Apes and the Origins of Human Violence.* Boston: Houghton Mifflin.

Wrangham, Richard W., Michael L. Wilson, and Martin N. Muller. 2006. "Comparative rates of violence in chimpanzees and humans." *Primates* 47:14–26.

Wright, Robert. 2009. *The Evolution of God.* New York: Little, Brown.

Wypijewski, JoAnn, ed. 1997. *Painting by Numbers: Komar and Melamid's Scientific Guide to Art.* New York: Farrar Straus Giroux.

Yellen, J. E. 1977. *Archaeological Approaches to the Present: Models for Reconstructing the Past.* New York: Academic Press.

Yu, D., and G. H. Shepard. 1998. "Is beauty in the eyes of the beholder?" *Nature* 396:321–322.

Zaadstra, Boukje M., Jacob C. Seidell, Paul A. H. van Noord, Egbert R. te Velde, J. D. F. Habbema, Baukje Vrieswijk, and Jan Karbatt. 1993. "Fat and female fecundity: Prospective study of effect of body fat distribution on conception rates." *British Medical Journal* 306:484–487.

Zahavi, Amotz, and Avishag Zahavi. 1997. *The Handicap Principle: A Missing Piece of Darwin's Puzzle.* New York: Oxford University Press.

Zeitlin, Irving M. 1984. *Ancient Judaism: Biblical Criticism from Max Weber to the Present.* Cambridge, UK: Polity Press.

Zeitlin, Irving M. 2004. *The Religious Experience: Classical Philosophical and Social Theories.* Upper Saddle River, NJ: Pearson Prentice Hall.

Zerjal, Tatiana, et al. 2003. "The genetic legacy of the Mongols." *American Journal of Human Genetics* 72:717–721.

Zimbardo, Philip. 2008. *The Lucifer Effect: Understanding How Good People Turn Evil.* New York: Random House.

TECHNICAL TERMS

adaptation The adjustment of an organism to its environment so that it can survive and reproduce effectively. See also **adaptive design** and **evolutionary adaptation**.

adaptive design The structure or character of a biological feature, such as an organ or a mental module, that has been crafted by natural or sexual selection over long periods of time. For example, the vertebrate eye reveals evidence not only of adaptive design but of complex, precise, and finely tuned adaptive design.

allele A variant of a gene, such as the brown, blue, and green variants of the gene or genes for eye color.

ancestral environment The environment in which humans lived, and in some cases still live, in small local groups devoted to hunting and gathering. It was in this type of environment, between approximately 10,000 and 150,000 years ago, that the modern human brain evolved as a complex set of specialized adaptations. Also known as the **Environment of Evolutionary Adaptedness (EEA)**.

biological determinism The view that human behavior and social life are determined by human biology with little or no input from the environment. Rarely endorsed by anyone.

biological evolution See **evolution, biological.**

co-evolution The simultaneous evolution of genes and cultural practices.

correlation coefficient A statistical measure of the degree of relationship between two variables. There are several kinds of coefficients, but the most common one is the Pearson coefficient, symbolized by r. It may take any value between 1.0 and -1.0. The first value indicates a perfect positive relationship—as one variable increases, the other variable increases in the same proportion. The second indicates a perfect negative relationship—as one variable increases, the other variable decreases in the same proportion. Coefficients of 1.0, whether positive or negative, are virtually never achieved. A coefficient of 0 indicates no relationship, of .20 to .30 a weak relationship, of .31 to .50 a moderate relationship, of .51 to .65 a strong relationship, of .66 to .80 a very strong relationship, and of .81 to 1.0 an extremely strong relationship. However, what counts as a strong or weak relationship can vary by both the type of investigation and the judgment of the investigator.

costly signaling An animal's signaling to another that it is of high quality. The signal is costly if it imposes some sort of handicap on the signaler. Costly signals must be honest in the sense that they cannot be faked. Costly signaling can be directed to conspecifics (members of one's own species) or to members of other species. The peacock's tail is a costly signal directed to peahens. Gazelle stotting is a costly signal directed to other species, usually predators. Also known as the **handicap principle**.

culture The sum total of learned traditions, beliefs, values, and norms created and acquired by people as members of a particular group or society. Theories that emphasize culture as the principal determinant of human behavior are versions of the SSSM.

Darwininian explanations Explanations based on theories of natural and sexual selection. Also known as **evolutionary explanations**. See also **evolutionary psychology, sociobiology,** and **human behavioral ecology**.

differential reproductive success The unequal contribution to the gene pool of organisms within a population.

domain-general mechanisms Mental mechanisms that are assumed to be all-purpose, that is, to solve a wide range of adaptive problems. Darwinian approaches assume that the brain contains few if any domain-general mechanisms. See also **domain-specific mechanisms**.

domain-specific mechanisms Mental modules that are devoted to highly specialized adaptive problems. For example, a module that is specialized for assessing the reliability of people's stated intentions from their facial expressions. Darwinian approaches assume that the brain is a complex network of domain-specific mechanisms. See also **domain-general mechanisms**.

essentialism The idea that such social categories as race, gender, and sexual orientation have a kind of fixed essence that transcends social and cultural boundaries.

Ethnographic Atlas A large compendium of information on 1,267 nonindustrial societies. Occasionally referenced in this book to show similarities and differences among societies in various social patterns.

evolution, biological The process whereby organisms acquire those biological traits and social behaviors that are adaptive. Also, the process whereby new traits and behaviors arise because of adaptation to changed environmental circumstances.

evolution, social Long-term directional changes in the structure of societies, especially in population size, level of technological advance, and mode of economic production. Often characterized as long-term changes in the direction of greater social complexity.

evolutionary adaptation A mental module or behavioral trait that evolved by natural or sexual selection because it promotes the survival and reproductive success of its bearers, or at least promoted survival and reproductive success in the ancestral environment.

evolutionary psychology Very similar to, and an outgrowth of, sociobiology. Sociobiology rests on the principle of inclusive fitness maximization as the ultimate driving force of human behavior. Evolutionary psychology stresses that evolutionary adaptations that arose in the ancestral environment because they maximized inclusive fitness under those conditions may no longer maximize inclusive fitness in more recent or modern environments. Therefore, the theoretical goal should be to elucidate the mental modules that give rise to behavior regardless of whether they maximize inclusive fitness. Sociobiologists agree that evolutionary adaptations arose in the ancestral environment, but they still regard the study of inclusive fitness maximization as appropriate for modern environments. See also **sociobiology** and **human behavioral ecology.**

facultative adaptation An evolutionary adaptation in which people's assessment (conscious or unconscious) of socioecological context determines how the adaptation is expressed in behavior. Most adaptations are facultative.

fitness The degree to which an organism is suited for survival and reproduction in a specific environment. In Darwinian terms, fitness is measured by **differential reproductive success.**

genes Units of biochemical information that direct the construction of proteins. See also **alleles**.

group selection A postulated form of natural selection in which selection acts on entire social groups rather than individual organisms or genes. There is much controversy over whether and to what extent such a form of selection can be invoked as an evolutionary mechanism.

handicap principle See **costly signaling.**

human behavioral ecology A subtype of evolutionary theory that concentrates on how behavioral differences in human populations arise as the result of evolved adaptations interacting with ecological variation. See also **evolutionary psychology** and **sociobiology.**

human nature The inborn predispositions of humans everywhere as the result of the universal structure of the human brain. Human nature is the product of how natural and sexual selection designed the brain for survival and reproductive success.

inclusive fitness The sum total of an organism's fitness as represented by all of the genes it shares in common with kin.

inclusive fitness theory The key theoretical principle that laid the foundation for sociobiology and evolutionary psychology. It holds that human behavior is driven by efforts to maximize inclusive fitness or reproductive success.

kin selection The tendency to favor kin over non-kin and close kin over distant kin because such behavior is inclusive-fitness promoting.

maximization principle Holds that the most-fundamental human biological predisposition is to maximize reproductive success.

modified maximization principle Holds that the predisposition to maximize reproductive success can be deflected by specific socioecological conditions, especially those that differ from the ancestral environment.

natural selection The process whereby genes that best adapt an organism to its environment have a competitive advantage over other genes and tend to spread in a population.

proximate causes The more immediate and direct causes of a biological trait or behavior. For example, aggressive behavior has a close link to the hormone testosterone, and therefore high levels of testosterone can be identified as one of the proximate causes of high levels of aggression. Contrast with **ultimate causes**.

reproductive success The extent to which an organism has left copies of its genes in future generations.

role theory The idea that society provides social scripts for the occupants of social positions, which they enact as members of a group or society. A version of the SSSM.

sexual selection Evolutionary selection for traits that directly promote successful mating rather than survival.

socialization The acquisition of the culture of a group or society through direct teaching of juniors by elders or by imitation.

social evolution. See **evolution, social**.

sociobiology The study of human behavior from a Darwinian evolutionary perspective, with special emphasis on evolutionary selection for behaviors that promote reproductive success. See also **evolutionary psychology** and **human behavioral ecology**.

social constructionism The view that the features of human societies are relatively unconstrained creations of the human mind and that there are no innate mechanisms that shape human behavior. The most recent version of the SSSM.

socioecological context The entire set of environmental conditions that constrain or enable people's enactment of their biological predispositions. It includes features of the natural or physical environment as well as components of the economic, political, social, and cultural environments.

Standard Cross-Cultural Sample (SCCS) A subset of 186 societies drawn from the 1,267 societies of the *Ethnographic Atlas*. These societies represent all of the major types of non-industrial societies and every world region and microregion. Used to show similarities and differences among societies and to test specific hypotheses. It is more suitable than the *Ethnographic Atlas* for hypothesis testing because it is a representative sample of nonindustrial societies.

Standard Social Science Model (SSSM) The dominant viewpoint in the social sciences that human behavior and organized social life are entirely or at least primarily the product of people's social and cultural environments. Opposed to the idea that there is a universal human nature that plays a major role in behavior and society.

ultimate causes The deep, underlying causes of behavior that derive from mechanisms or processes that have been crafted by natural or sexual selection to promote survival and reproductive success. Explanations in terms of ultimate causes are true Darwinian evolutionary explanations. For example, if higher levels of testosterone are one of the proximate causes of higher levels of aggression in males relative to females, an explanation in terms of ultimate causes would focus on why evolutionary selection has produced higher testosterone levels in males so as to make them more aggressive than females. Contrast with **proximate causes**.

INDEX

A

Abortion, 205
Adaptations. *See* Evolutionary adaptations.
Adaptive behavior, 7, 8, 10, 12, 123, 218, 220, 296, 332, 344, 349, 365, 366, 367, 368
Adaptive design, 6, 7
Adaptive problems, 7, 137
Aggression, 20, 124, 137, 140, 216
Aggressiveness
  male-female differences in, 216–217
Agrarian societies, 53, 55
  as male-farming societies, 55
  China, 56, 57
  Egypt, 57
  Europe, 57
  Greeks, 56, 57
  India, 57
  Japan, 57
  medieval England, 57
  Mesopotamia, 57
  peasants in, 57
  plow and, 55–56, 57, 58, 82, 88, 89, 97, 98, 218, 226, 229
  plow-negative crops and, 56–57
  plow-positive crops and, 56–57
  Romans, 56
  traction animals and, 88, 218
Agriculture
  intensification of, 58–59
  irrigation, 57
  rainfall, 57
  vs. horticulture, 53
Agricultural origins, 49–53
  causes of, 51–53
  in American southwest, 51
  in central Asia, 50
  in China, 50

in eastern woodlands of US, 51
in Egypt, 50
in Europe, 50
in Greece, 50
in Indian subcontinent, 50
in Mesoamerica, 51
in Mesopotamia, 49–50
in South America, 51
in southeast Asia, 50
independent development of, 50
population pressure and, 58
spread of, 50–51
worldwide nature of, 52–53
Alanko, Katarina, 149, 150
Alcorta, Candace S., 345–346
Alexander, Richard D., 7, 169, 174
Allele, 93, 99–100
Altamira cave, 33, 358
Ames, M. Ashley, 147–148, 152
Amino acids, 32, 82
Amsler, Sylvia J., 298
Anatomically modern humans, 22, 24, 25, 32, 33, 51, 317
  exodus from Africa, 22
Ancestral environment, 6, 10, 81, 123, 126, 162, 193, 221, 237, 259, 296, 301, 341, 344, 366, 370, 372
Animal protein. *See* Meat.
Anthropic Principle, 384–385
  origin of universe and, 384–386
  quantum mechanics and, 384
  ultimate plan or design and, 384–386
Apicella, Coren, 134
Archer, John, 216
Aros, Jesse R., 231, 232
Arrighi, Giovanni, 66
Art, 356

Arts. *See also* Visual art, Literature, Music.
  as human universals, 355
  central features of, 355–356
Ash, Jessica, 26
Atran, Scott, 344, 346
Attractiveness
  facial averageness and, 127, 128
  facial symmetry and, 128
  male desire for, 10, 119, 127–129, 132, 138
  sexual, 119, 133, 134
  worldwide emphasis on, 127–128
Australopithecines, 20, 24
Australopithecus, 20, 24
Authority
  obedience to, 266–277
Avunculocal households
  among Trobriand Islanders, 166–167
Axial Age
  emergence of Near Eastern world religions and, 343–344
  emergence of South and East Asian world religions and, 353n23
  increasing scale of war and, 348
  urbanization and, 348
Aziz, Barbara N., 176

B
Baby fever, 191
Bachofen, Johann, 161
Bailey, Drew, 26
Bailey, J. Michael, 149, 150
Bands
  among hunter-gatherers, 269
  politics in, 269, 271
Barfield, Thomas J., 59
Bartlett, Nancy H., 150
Beall, Cynthia M., 177, 178
Beauty Myth, The (N. Wolf), 127
Beef
  Hindu taboo on, 87–89
Behavioral plasticity, 7
Behavioral ecology, 77
Behaviorally modern humans, 33–34
Bellwood, Peter, 59
Betzig, Laura L., 142, 171, 174, 201, 204, 304, 307
Bickerton, Derek, 28
Big men
  as political leaders, 269, 272–273
  status strivings of, 249, 251, 252, 265

Bilateral descent, 164–165
Binford, Lewis R., 43
Biological anthropology, 20, 24, 27, 234, 318–319, 359
Biological determinism, 8
Biological evolution, 3–5, 10, 69
  vs. social evolution, 69–70
Birth intervals
  among Aché, 196–197
  among hunter-gatherers, 196
  among !Kung, 195–197
  optimal, 195–196
  prolonged lactation and, 196
  reproductive success and, 196
Bittles, Alan H., 110
Blank Slate, The (Pinker), 360
Blau, Judith R., 291
Blau, Peter M., 291
Bleak House (Dickens), 366, 368
Bliege Bird, Rebecca, 86, 249
Bloom, Paul, 31
Blurton Jones, Nicholas, 195, 196
Boas, Franz, 1
Body Mass Index (BMI), 136
Bonin, Steven, 203
Bonobos, 27–28,
Boomsma, Dorret J., 151
Boserup, Ester, 58
Boswell, John, 190
Bourdieu, Pierre, 258–259
Bowlby, John, 114, 103
Boyer, Pascal, 344, 346
Brain
  as general purpose organ, 7
  domain-specificity and, 6
  encephalization quotient and, 24
  high energy cost of, 24
  increasing size of, 21, 24, 25, 26, 27
    ecological hypothesis, 26
    social brain hypothesis, 26, 27
  modular nature of, 6, 7
Broch, Tom, 305
Brooks, Alison S., 39n59
Brown, Steven, 369, 371–372, 373
Browne, Kingsley R., 238
Buss, David M., 123, 129–130, 137, 138, 217, 296

C
Calcium
  role in healthy bones and teeth, 96

Capitalism, 63–69
  causes of development of, 64–65
  in Italian city-states, 63
  in Japan, 64
  in northwest Europe, 63
  mercantilist trading companies and, 63
Cardoso, Fernando Luis, 150
Carey, Arlen D., 198–199
Carneiro, Robert L., 278, 306
Carroll, Joseph, 366
Cashdan, Elizabeth A., 80, 221
Cattle
  among pastoralists, 59–60, 87–88
  economic necessity of in India, 88–89
  Hindu taboo on consumption of, 87–89
  widespread reverence for, 87
  worldwide raising of, 87–89
Cavalli-Sforza, L. Luca, 332
Cave paintings
  at Altamira, 33
  at Chauvet, 33
  at Lascaux, 33
  at Niaux, 33
Chagnon, Napoleon A., 141, 226, 285n19,
    302, 304, 305
Chaplin, George, 322–323
Chiefdoms, 271–274
  among Cheyenne, 271
  complex, 272–274
  conditions necessary for formation of,
    273–274
  in Hawaii, 272–273
  in Polynesia, 272, 274
  in Trobriand Islands, 272
  Mississippian, 272
  political hierarchies in, 272–273
  prehistoric, 272
  simple, 272
Children, 192–193
  effects of parental deprivation on, 193
  need for parental bonding of, 193
Child abuse
  family resource strain and, 191
  future prospects of child and, 190
  poor conditions for rearing and, 190
  stepparents and, 191
  unhealthy children and, 190
Child mortality, 48, 189, 196, 198–199
Chimpanzees, 19, 24, 27–28, 38n23, 112
  annexation of rivals' territory, 298
  as demonic males, 298

border patrols among, 297–298
competition for alpha male among, 297
erroneous characterization as nonviolent,
    297
female dispersal and, 112
in Arnhem Zoo, 297
in Kibele National Park, 298
lethal raids among, 302
violence among, 297–298
Chinggis Khan
  as Mongol leader, 309–310
  extraordinary reproductive success of,
    142
Choi, Jean, 222
Chomsky, Noam, 30
Christianity, 89, 340, 343–344, 348–349
Civilizations, 274–278. *See also* States.
  common characteristics of, 274–275
  in China, 275–276
  in Egypt, 275
  in Europe, 176
  in India, 275–276
  in Mesoamerica, 276–277
  in Mesopotamia, 275
  in South America, 277–278
Clans
  as kinship groups, 115, 162, 165–167 (*see
    also* Lineages)
Clark, Russell D., 119
Cognitive biases
  for teleological thinking, 383–384
  for agency-based explanations, 385
Cognitive skills
  male-female differences in, 220–222
Cohen, Mark N., 51, 53
Competition
  for mates, 237, 291–292, 304
  for status and resources, 11–12, 246, 248,
    250–254, 256–259
Competitiveness
  male-female differences in, 217–218
Convergent evolution, 99–100
Cooperation, 11, 12, 27, 42, 57, 118, 332,
    345, 371, 372
Correlation coefficient, 26, 104n34, 105n60,
    156n32, 156n33, 156n34, 157n53,
    313n9, 338n18
Cosmides, Leda, 7, 68
Costly signaling
  in mating strategies, 251
  status seeking and, 251–252, 253, 257

Costly signaling (*continued*)
  to conspecifics, 251
  to predators, 251
Courtwright, David T., 314n16
Cox, Oliver Cromwell, 325
Critical period
  for acquisition of food tastes, 80
  for incest avoidance, 112
  for language learning, 29
Cronk, Lee, 17n18, 202–203
Cuckoldry, 123, 137, 170, 294
Cultural capital, 258–259
Culture, 1, 19, 32, 34, 127, 253, 258, 265,
    269, 317, 325, 330, 331
  acquisition of, 2, 12, 19 (*see also* Social
    learning)
Curtis, Nicholas T., 231, 232

D
Dairying, 93, 96
  coevolution of genes for lactose
    absorption and, 93, 96
  convergent evolution of lactose
    absorption genes in Europe and Africa
    and, 99–100
  historical origins of, 93
  in pastoral societies, 93
  in Western and Northern Europe, 93
Daly, Martin, 191, 206–207, 288, 291, 292,
    293, 295
Darwin, Charles, 1 (facing page), 107, 115,
    193, 199, 334, 362, 383
Darwinian evolutionary explanations, 2,
    3, 4, 5, 8, 10, 109, 118, 125–126, 169,
    170–180, 187, 193, 237, 374, 383
Darwinian evolutionism, 3, 4, 5, 10
Darwinian social science, 2, 3
David Copperfield (Dickens), 368
Davis, Kingsley, 108–109
Dawkins, Richard, 349
de Waal, Frans, 297
Deception, 26. *See also* Self-deception.
Degler, Carl N., 2
Demographic transition, 198
Dennett, Daniel C., 349
Descent principle. *See* Bilateral descent,
    Matrilineal descent, Patrilineal descent.
Diamond, Milton, 243n37
Dickemann, Mildred, 208–209
Disgust
  food and, 79, 80, 91, 92, 98

Dogs
  as food source, 78–79
  as pets, 78
  as sentry animals, 78
  domestication of, 78
Domain-specific brain mechanisms, 6
Dominant males, 141–144
  among men in Old Testament, 142
  among Yanomama, 141–142
  reproductive success of, 141–144
    among nonhuman animals, 141
    among humans, 141–144
  women's preferences for, 137–139
Dowry, 175
  hypergynous marriage and, 209
Dubrow, Joshua K., 199
Duchamp, Marcel, 357, 358
Durham, William H., 96, 177, 178
Dutton, Denis, 355–357, 362, 363, 364, 365,
    366, 367, 368

E
Eals, Marion, 221
Egalitarian societies, 179, 245
  status leveling in, 247–248
Egalitarianism, 2
Einstein, Albert, 371, 383
Ellis, Lee, 147–148, 152, 203
Ember, Carol R., 42–43
Enard, Wolfgang, 32
Environment of Evolutionary Adaptedness
    (EEA). *See* Ancestral environment.
Erickson, Mark, 113–114
Essentialist explanations, 2
Ethnic affiliation, 12, 332
  as evolutionary adaptation, 332, 334
Ethnic populations
  worldwide genetic relationships among,
    333 (table)
Ethnic primordialism, 330–334
  Arabs and, 331
  Kazakhs and, 331
  Malays and, 331
  Mixtecs and, 331
  Mongols and, 331
  Samburu and, 331
  Turkana and, 331
Ethnicity
  cognitive conceptualizations of, 331
  race and, 330
Ethnies, 330

Ethnographic Atlas, 43, 87, 115, 168, 170, 197

Evolution. *See* Biological evolution, Social evolution.

Evolution, convergent. *See* Convergent evolution.

Evolutionary adaptations, 4, 6, 7, 9, 10, 28, 30, 123, 126, 131, 206, 251, 259, 296, 317, 332, 349, 362, 368
complex design as indicator of, 30
facultative, 9

Evolutionary arms race, 25, 38n21

Evolutionary biology, 3, 7, 69, 77, 173, 200, 251, 324, 349

Evolutionary explanations. *See* Darwinian evolutionary explanations.

Evolutionary psychology, 3, 5, 6, 7, 8, 9, 12–13, 28, 68, 77, 109, 120, 122, 123, 191, 200, 267, 292, 344, 361

Exogamy, 165

Extended inclusive fitness, 334

Extended kin selection, 332

Extrapair copulation, 122, 126

F
Faʻafafine, 150
gender atypical behavior of, 150

Facial asymmetry. *See* Fluctuating asymmetry.

Facial symmetry
as indicator of genetic quality, 128
judgments of attractiveness and, 128

Facultative adaptation. *See* Adaptation, facultative.

Fagan, Brian M., 275

Falger, Vincent S. E., 219

Familial bonding, 114
vs. sexual bonding, 114

Family, 11, 162–164
embedded nuclear, 163
extended, 162
isolated nuclear, 163
joint, 162
nuclear, 162, 165
stem, 162–163
worldwide importance of, 163–164

Farkas, George, 328–329

Fat deposition
android, 136
gynoid, 136

Feasts
meat and, 81
status displays and, 86, 249–250, 256

Felder, Raoul, 360

Female sexuality
extrapair copulations and, 122, 126
reticence for casual sex, 119–120

Female mate choice, 137–141
adaptive problems involving, 137
as product of sexual selection, 115
for emotional commitment, 140
for high-status males, 137–139
for intelligence, 139
for masculinity, 139–140
for older men, 138–139
minimum standards for, 138–139
romance novel and, 140–141

Ferguson, R. Brian, 302–303

Fertile Crescent
origins of agriculture and, 49

Fertility. *See also* Birth intervals, Birth spacing.
among horticulturalists, 197
among hunter-gatherers, 195–197
among Yanomama, 197
demographic transition and, 198
economic benefits of children's labor and, 197
economic costs of children and, 198
human behavioral ecology and, 198, 199
in agrarian societies, 197
in industrial societies, 198
infant mortality and, 198–199
maximization of reproductive success and, 197, 199
quantity vs. quality of children and, 200
theories of differences in, 197–200
women's status and, 198, 199

Fessler, Daniel M. T., 91, 112

Fieder, Martin, 143

Fisher, Sir Ronald, 117

Fisherman, The (painting), 362

Fitch, W. Tecumseh, 370, 374

Fitness
as differential reproductive success, 4, 6, 34
in biological vs. social evolution, 69

FitzGerald, R. W., 220, 237

Flatz, Gebhard, 95

Flinn, Mark V., 25

Flores, Renato Z., 114

Fluctuating asymmetry, 128, 136
   parasites and, 128
   trauma and, 128
Food
   avoidances and preferences, 77–100
      individual acquisition of, 80–81
   taboos, 87–92
Foraging behavior. *See* Optimal foraging theory.
Foundling homes
   negative impact on children in, 192
Fountain (Duchamp), 357, 359
FOXP2 gene
   as language gene, 31–32, 34
Frank, Robert H., 257
Freese, Jeremy, 203
Freud, Sigmund, 9, 108

G
Gallup, Gordon G. Jr., 26
Galtung, Johan, 305
Gat, Azar, 280, 304, 305
Gaulin, Steven J. C., 136, 220, 237
Geary, David C., 25, 26
Gender. *See also* Male-female differences.
   among horticulturalists, 226
   among hunter-gatherers, 225
   among Iroquois, 226
   among !Kung, 226
   among pastoralists, 228
   among Yanomama, 226
   economic contribution of women and, 229
   in agrarian societies, 226–227
   in industrial societies, 228–238
   in Islamic world, 228
   in matrilineal societies, 226
   in south and east Asia, 227–228
   in Soviet Union, 217
   learning of, 224–225
   modern changes in, 229
   purdah and, 227–228
   vs. sex, 215
   socialization theory of, 224
   as social construction, 224
Gender atypical behavior (GAB), 149–151
Gender identity, 11, 222–224
   implications for degendered society, 225
   limited socialization influences on, 224–225
   prenatal hormone levels and, 222–223

sex reassignment surgery and, 223–224
   social constructionist arguments for, 224
Genes, 3, 4
   for lactose absorption, 93, 95, 99–100
   for language, 31–32
   for sexual orientation, 149
   for skin color, 324
Genetic interests, 334
Genetic mutations, 3, 31, 34, 146
   beneficial, 4
   harmful, 4
   role in natural selection, 3–4
Genetic quality
   mate choice and, 128
Genetic recombination, 3
Genetic variation, 3
Gil-White, Francisco, 320, 331
Ginsberg, Morris, 270
Goldstein, Melvyn C., 176, 177, 178
Gossett, Thomas F., 325
Gottschall, Jonathan, 127–129, 138, 366, 368
Gough, Kathleen, 170
Green, Richard, 150
Groth, Gary, 138
Gygax, Lorenz, 150

H
Hald, Gert Martin, 119, 120
Hamer, Dean, 149
Hames, Raymond B., 178–179
Hamilton, William D., 3
Handicap principle. *See* Costly signaling.
Hansen, Kristi A., 132, 134
Hard Times (Dickens), 366, 368
Harlow, Harry F., 193–194
Harris, Marvin, 82, 88–89, 90, 96, 197–198, 280–281, 302, 319
Harris, Sam, 349
Hartung, John, 168
Hatfield, Elaine, 119
Hawkes, Kristen, 84
Hcerwagen, Judith H., 359
Hegel, G. W. F., 385
Henly, George A., 231, 232
Heritability coefficients, 149
Herring, Cedric, 329–330
Hershberger, Scott, 149
Hertel, Bradley, 329
Heston, Charlton, 296
High gods, 339–340
   active, 340

among horticulturalists, 340
among hunter-gatherers, 340
concerned with human morality, 340
in agrarian societies, 340
inactive, 340
Hill, Kim, 84
*History and Geography of Human Genes,
The* (Cavalli-Sforza, Menozzi, and
Piazza), 332
History of Human Marriage, The
(Westermarck), 109, 161
Hitchens, Christopher, 349
Hobbes, Thomas, 305
Hobhouse, L. T., 270–271
Hoebel, E. Adamson, 270
Hofferth, Sandra, 203
Høgh-Olesen, Henrik, 119, 120
Hold, Barbara C. L., 246
Homicide, 287–296
    age and, 288–290
    among Alur, 290
    among Baluyia, 290, 295
    among Banyoro, 295
    among Basoga, 293, 295
    among Bhil, 290, 293, 295
    among Bison-horn Maria, 293, 295
    among genetic relatives, 288
    among Gisu, 295
    among !Kung, 290
    among Luo, 295
    among Maya, 290
    among Munda, 293, 295
    among Oraon, 293, 295
    among Tiv, 290, 295
    as anti-cuckoldry tactic, 294
    as evolutionary adaptation, 296
    conflict over women and, 291
    cuckoldry and, 294 (*see also* Cuckoldry)
    Darwinian evolutionary analysis of,
        291–292, 296
    economic deprivation and, 290–291
    female-on-female, 290
    in American West, 314n16
    in Australia, 295
    in Canada, 288, 291, 292, 295, 296
    in Chicago, 289–291, 292, 295
    in Denmark, 295
    in Detroit, 288, 290–291, 293, 295
    in England/Wales, 289–290, 293, 295
    in Houston, 295
    in Iceland, 290

    in Miami, 293, 295
    in Philadelphia, 295
    in Scotland, 295
    in United States, 295
    inclusive fitness theory and, 288
    income inequality and, 291
    infidelity and, 293
    life expectancy and, 292
    love triangle, 293
    male-on-male, 290
    marital status and, 291–292
    sex and, 290
    sexual jealousy and, 293
    young males and, 290–293
Hominids, 19, 38n1
Hominins, 19, 24, 27, 38n1, 321
Homo erectus, 21, 25
Homo habilis, 20, 21, 24, 25
Homo heidelbergensis, 21, 24
Homo neanderthalensis. See Neanderthals.
Homo sapiens, 21, 22, 23
Homosexuality, 144–152. *See also*
        Preferential homosexuality, Situational
        homosexuality.
Hopcroft, Rosemary L., 203–204
Horticultural societies
    as female-farming societies, 54
    in Hawaii, 54–55
    in Melanesia, 54–55
    in Micronesia, 54
    in Polynesia, 54–55
    Kapauku, 54–55
    Tahiti, 55
    Trobriand Islanders, 54
    Yanomama, 54, 55
Horticulture
    fallowing of land and, 54–55
    slash-and-burn cultivation and, 54
    vs. agriculture, 53
Households. *See* Avunculocal households,
        Matrilocal households, Patrilocal
        households.
Hrdy, Sarah Blaffer, 188–190, 205, 207
Huber, Susanne, 143
Hudziak, James J., 151
Hughes, Michael, 329
Human behavioral ecology (HBE), 17n18,
        83, 198
    and food habits, 77
    and reproductive behavior, 198
Human evolution, 20–27

Human existence. *See* Meaning of human existence.
Human nature, 1, 2, 5, 6, 9, 11, 13, 68, 69, 178, 225, 246, 266, 282, 359, 360, 382, 386
Hunter-gatherer societies, 41–49
  Aché, 42, 45, 47
  as original affluent society, 46–49
  food storing vs. non-storing, 45–46
  Hadza, 42, 46, 47
  !Kung, 42, 46, 47, 48
  meat vs. plant foods in diet, 42–44
  nomadism and, 42
  prehistoric, 42
  sexual division of labor in, 44–45
  standard of living in, 46–49
  technology in, 42
  workload in, 47–48
Hypergyny, 202, 208, 209
Hypothalamus
  INAH3 portion of, 148
  role in sexual orientation, 148–149

I

Iliad (Homer), 315n94, 364
In Advance of a Broken Arm (Duchamp), 359
Inbreeding depression, 109–110, 113, 115
Incest, 113–114
  familial vs. sexual bonding and, 114
  family dysfunction and, 114
  father-daughter, 113
Incest avoidance, 108–115
  among nonhuman animals, 112
  close childhood contact and, 109
  Israeli kibbutzim outmarriage and, 110–111
  Karo Batak marriage practices and, 112
  Lebanese cousin marriages and, 112
  one-generation vs. two-generation inhibitions and, 113
  Taiwanese *sim-pua* marriages and, 111–112
  Westermarck's familiarity breeds aversion theory of, 109–113
Incest taboos, 108, 114–115
  as recognition of harmful effects of inbreeding, 115
  social cohesion theory of, 108–109
Inclusive fitness, 4–5, 146, 191, 206, 209, 334

Inclusive fitness theory, 4–5, 146, 191, 206, 288
Industrial capitalism, 66
Industrial Revolution, 66–67
Industrial society, 66
Inequality of Human Races, The (de Gobineau), 327
Infant mortality, 9, 199
Infanticide, 205–209
  as evolutionary adaptation, 206
  birth spacing and, 206
  defective infants and, 206
  doubts about paternity and, 206
  in Canada, 207
  in medieval Europe, 205, 208
  in nonhuman animals, 206
  in traditional China, 207–209
  in traditional India, 207–208
  inclusive fitness maximization and, 206, 209
  lack of social support and, 206
  maternal bonding and, 207
  poor circumstances for rearing and, 206
  sex selectivity of, 207–209
  Sudden Infant Death Syndrome (SIDS) and, 205
Infidelity, 123–125, 293–294, 304
Innate tastes, 81–83
  for meat, 81–83 (*see also* Meat)
  for sweet foods, 81
Insects
  as food source, 79–80
Intelligence
  selection for in human evolution, 22, 24, 25, 26
Intensive agricultural societies. *See* Agrarian societies.
Irons, William, 17n18

J

Jablonski, Nina G., 322–323
Jackendoff, Ray, 32
Jane Eyre (Brontë), 364
Jasieńska, Grażyna, 136
Jealousy, 123–125
  male-female differences in, 124–125
Justice
  purely private, 270
  purely public, 271
  qualified private, 271
  qualified public, 271

K

Kaplan, David, 47, 48
Kaplan, Hillard, 197–198
Kaufman, Alan S., 230, 235, 236
Kautsky, John H., 281
Keeley, Lawrence H., 299
Keith, Verna M., 329–330
Keller, Matthew C., 203
Kelly, Robert L., 47
Kenrick, Douglas J., 138
Khan, Chinggiss. *See* Chinggis Khan.
Khan, Khubilai. *See* Khubilai Khan.
Kibbutzim
    incest avoidance and, 110–111
Kinnier, Richard T., 379n55
Kinsey, Alfred C., 146
Kinship, 11, 162–170
    clans, 115, 162, 165–167
    lineages, 162, 165–167
    worldwide importance of, 163–164
Kinship-based societies, 162
Kin selection, 4, 163–164
Kirch, Patrick Vinton, 306
Kitson, Gay C., 163
Klein, Richard G., 24, 34
Koenig, Harold C., 346
Komar, Vitaly, 358, 359
Kottak, Conrad Philip, 318
Kropotkin, Prince Peter, 161
Khubilai Khan, 310
Kurland, Jeffrey A., 169

L

Lactose
    absorbers, 93, 98
    malabsorbers, 93, 97
Landlords
    disdain for merchants and, 61
    in agrarian societies, 61, 63, 65, 253
    peasants and, 61, 253
Language, 27–32
    apes and, 27–28
    as evolutionary adaptation, 27–32
    grammatical rules in, 27, 29, 31
    language processing device and, 30
    rapid learning of, 29
    role in communication, 30
    role in internal thought, 30
    syntax in, 29, 31
Large-scale war, 305–310
    among Assyrians, 308
    among Mongols, 309–310
    among Xiongnu, 309
    in ancient Hawaii, 306–307
    in ancient Rome, 308
    in Cauca valley, 306
    in chiefdoms, 306
    in empires, 307–310
    in Fiji, 306
    in Old Testament, 307
    in Polynesian chiefdoms, 306
    in states, 307–310
    increasing historical deadliness of, 308
    military technology and, 308–309
    political conquest and, 305–310
    search for wealth and, 305–310
    self-aggrandizement of rulers and,
        306
Larson, David B., 346
Laumann, Edward O., 146
Learning. *See* Social learning.
Le Moulin de la Galette (painting), 362
Le Palais Contarini (painting), 362
Lee, Richard B., 42, 46, 247–248
LeVay, Simon, 148, 149, 151–152
Levine, Nancy E., 176, 179
Lineages
    as kinship groups, 162, 165–167 (*see also*
        Clans)
Linsenmeier, Joan A. W., 150
Literature, 364–368
    age and production of, 364–365
    as evolutionary by-product, 374
    male vs. female production of,
        364–365
    natural selection theories of, 365–368
    sexual selection theories of, 364
Lopreato, Joseph, 9, 198–199
Lordosis, 134–136, 158n106
Love
    Bowlby on, 193–194
    Harlow on, 193–194
    importance for child development,
        192–195
    maternal, 188–192
Low, Bobbi S., 197–198

M

MacDonald, Kevin, 174
Madsen, Douglas, 246
Mair, Lucy, 270
Male dominance. *See* Dominant males.

Male mate choice, 126–137
  for body size and shape (*see* Waist-to-hip
    ratio, Body mass index)
  for breasts, 136
  for physical attractiveness, 127–129
    as cultural universal, 127–129
    as indicator of genetic quality, 128
    facial averageness and, 127
    facial symmetry and, 127
  for thinness vs. plumpness, 134, 136–137
  for youth, 129–131
Male sexuality
  arousal by visual sexual stimuli and, 122
  desire for multiple partners and, 121–122
  desire for young partners and, 129
  extrapair copulations and, 122, 126
  interest in casual sex and, 119
  interest in pornography and, 122
  urgency of sex drive and, 119
Male-female sex differences, 216–224
  among mammalian species, 216
  Darwinian evolutionary theory and,
    215–224
  in aggressiveness, 216–217
  in cognitive skills, 220–222
  in competitiveness, 217–218
  in mathematical aptitude, 231, 234, 236
  in occupancy of high-status positions,
    217–218
  in occupational preferences (*see*
    Occupational interests)
  in parental behavior, 219–220
  in political leadership, 218–219
  in tolerance of risk and danger, 218
  in warfare, 217
  sexual dimorphism and, 216–217
  sexual selection and, 218
Malinowski, Bronislaw, 166–167, 272
Mandelbaum, David G., 228
Mar, Raymond A., 368
Markets, 60 63
  capitalist, 60–69
  early origins of, 60–61
Marlowe, Frank W., 134–135
Marriage, 170–180. *See also* Monogamy,
  Polyandry, Polygyny.
  as reproductive contract, 170
  companionate, 174–175
Marshall, Lorna, 48
Martin, M. Kay, 226, 228

Martindale, Colin, 357
Mason, Jackie, 360
Mate choice, 126–141. *See also* Female mate
  choice, Male mate choice.
  for long-term mates, 120, 121, 123, 137,
    140
  for short-term mates, 121, 122, 125
  high genetic quality and, 122, 128, 139
Mate guarding, 118
Maternal deprivation
  psychopathological effects of, 192–195
Mating effort
  vs. parental investment, 118, 187
Matrilineal descent, 165–170
  among Iroquois, 168, 169
  among Navaho, 169
  among Nayar, 167, 168, 169, 170
  among Trobriand Islanders, 166–169
  as anticuckoldry strategy, 169–170
  paternity uncertainty and, 169–170
  role of mother's brother and, 166–167
  vs. matriarchy, 168
Matrilocal households, 166
Mattos, Luiz F. C., 114
Maximization principle, 9, 163
Maynard Smith, John, 3
McBrearty, Sally, 39n59
McCabe, Justine, 112
McClenon, James, 346
McCullough, Michael E., 346
McLean, James E., 230, 235, 236
McLennan, John, 161
Meaning of human existence, 381–386
  as realization of natural human
    preferences, 382–383
  Darwinian evolutionary approach to,
    382–383
  philosophy and, 381
  science and, 381
  theology and, 381
Meat
  as universally preferred food, 81
  innate taste for, 82–83
  nutritional benefits of, 82
  special hunger for, 81–82
Melamid, Alexander, 358
Mellars, Paul A., 248
Menozzi, Paolo, 332
Merchants, 60–63
Milgram, Stanley, 266–267

Milk. *See also* Dairying, Lactose.
  aversion to, 92, 98
  consumption of, 92, 94–95 (table)
  lactose absorption and, 92–93 (table), 95,
    97, 98
  lactose malabsorption and, 92–93 (table)
  nutritional benefits of, 92, 95–96
Miller, Geoffrey F., 130–131, 360, 362–364,
  370–371
Mitani, John C., 298
Modified maximization principle, 9, 163
Modular brain, 6
Money, John, 223, 243n37
Monkey experiments
  cloth mothers and, 193–194
  effects of maternal deprivation and,
    194–195
  monster mothers and, 194
  spike mothers and, 194
  surrogate mothers and, 193, 195
  wire mothers and, 193–194
Monogamy, 173–175, 180
  among ancient Greeks and Romans, 173,
    175
  companionate marriage and, 174
  ecologically imposed, 173
  in contemporary world, 173
  in late medieval Europe, 173
  reproductive opportunity leveling and,
    174
  socially imposed, 173–175
Monogamous species, 118–119
Monotheism
  Christianity and, 340, 343–344
  God's love and mercy and, 344
  Judaism and, 340, 343–344
  One True God and, 339, 343, 348
  transcendent God and, 339, 344, 348
  Zoroastrianism and, 87, 343
Morgan, Lewis Henry, 161
Mother Nature: A History of Mothers,
  Infants, and Natural Selection (Hrdy),
  188
Motherhood, 188–192. *See also* Children,
  Child abuse, Monkey experiments.
  abandonment of infants and, 190
  among hunter-gatherers, 188
  as social construction, 189
  baby fever and, 191
  conditions for child rearing and, 189–190
  mother-child attachment, 193

  in nonindustrial societies, 190
  natural predisposition for, 189, 192
Muller, Martin, 299–300
Murdock, George Peter, 43
Music, 369–374
  age and production of, 370
  by-product theories of, 370
  classical, 369, 370
  commercial/popular, 369
  folk, 369
  group selection theories of, 372–373, 374
  in prehistory, 369
  in small-scale societies, 369–370
  jazz, 370
  language and, 370
  love and, 379n55
  male vs. female production of, 370
  natural selection theories of, 374
  progressive accumulation of styles and,
    369
  ritual, 369
  rock, 370
  sexual selection theories of, 370–371, 374
Musilanguage, 373
Mutations. *See* Genetic mutations.

N
Natural selection, 3, 5
Naturalistic fallacy, 238
Navarrete, Carlos David, 91
Neanderthals, 21, 22, 23, 24, 33
  extinction of, 22
Neolithic Revolution. *See* Agricultural
  origins.
Neel, James, 110
Neoteny
  male attraction to, 130
Nesse, Randolph M., 203
New Atheism, The, 349–350
  abolition of religion and, 349
  hard version of, 354n42
  irrationality of religion and, 349
  Richard Dawkins Foundation for Reason
    and Science and, 349
  soft version of, 354n42
Nobilities
  status displays of, 253–254
  sumptuary regulations and, 253–254
Nu descendant un escalier (Nude
  Descending a Staircase) (painting),
  357

O

On the Origin of Species by Means of Natural Selection (Darwin), 3
Out of Africa theory, 24, 231
Original affluent society, thesis of, 46–49
Optimal foraging theory (OFT), 83–87
    empirical status of, 104n22
    handling time in, 83
    opportunity costs in, 83
    potential exceptions to, 86
    search time in, 83
O'Connell, James F., 84
Osteomalacia
    as calcium-deficient bone disease, 96
Object Location Memory (OLM)
    female superiority at, 221
Occupational interests
    cognitive skills and, 235–236
    evolutionary selection for, 237
    male-female differences in, 230–232, 234, 235–236
    occupational representation and, 232
Odyssey (Homer), 364
Orians, Gordon H., 359
Ostlund, Deborah R., 379n55

P

Paleopathological studies, 52
Paramount chiefs
    in ancient Hawaii, 252
Parasites. *See* Fluctuating asymmetry.
Parental investment, 118, 187
    in sons vs. daughters, 200–205
    vs. mating effort, 118, 187
Parenthood, 11, 187–212
Parsons, Talcott, 1, 163
Partible inheritance, 162–163, 177
Pastoralism, 59–60
    in Africa, 59–60
    in central Eurasia, 60
    in Iran, 60
    in Saharan and Arabian deserts, 60
    in Turkey, 60
    on the Asian steppes, 60
    on the Tibetan plateau, 60
Patrilineal descent, 165, 166, 168
    in Islamic world, 165
    in traditional China, 165
    in traditional India, 165
    reproductive potential of males and, 168
Patrilocal households

    in Islamic world, 165
    in traditional China, 165
    in traditional India, 165
Peacocks
    sexual selection and, 30, 116–117, 362
Peasants, 57, 61, 64, 67, 172
    landlords and, 61, 253
Penrose, Roger, 385
Perilloux, Helen K., 136
Pérusse, Daniel, 143
Peters, Michael, 222
Peterson, Steven, 266, 268
Pflüger, Lena, 129
Piatelli-Palmarini, Massimo, 30
Piazza, Alberto, 332
Pigs
    as food avoidance, 89–92
        in Islam, 89, 90–91
        in Judaism, 89–92
    as forest creatures, 78, 90
    as worldwide food source, 89
Pillard, R. C., 149
Pinker, Steven, 28, 31, 32, 354, 360, 361, 370
Planet of the Apes (film), 296
Plant foods
    as proportion of hunter-gatherer diets, 42, 43, 44 (table)
    latitude and abundance of, 43, 44 (table)
Plummer, Ken, 147
Political evolution, 269–281
Political leadership. *See also* Chiefdoms, States.
    among Cheyenne, 271
    among Comanche, 270
    among Nuer, 269–270
    in bands and tribes, 269–271
    in chiefdoms, 271–274
    in states, 274–281
    male monopolization of, 218–219
Polyandry, 175–180
    among Barkhang, 176
    among Chimdro, 176
    among Nyimba, 179
    classical, 178–179, 180
    conflict among brothers and, 179
    family property conservation and, 177–178
    fraternal, 176
    impartible inheritance and, 177–178
    in Ding-ri valley, 176
    in India, 176

in Nepal, 176
in Tibet, 176
nonclassical, 178–179, 180
rarity of, 175
reproductive success and, 178
Polygamy, 180, 184n27
Polygynandry, 175, 177, 180
Polygyny, 170–175, 180
  among Germanic tribes, 175
  among horticulturalists, 172
  among hunter-gatherers, 172
  among Incas, 171
  among nonhuman animals, 172
  among pastoralists, 172
  attitude of women toward, 172–173
  general, 170
  high-status men and, 171
  in aboriginal Australia, 170–171
  in agrarian societies, 172
  in ancient Israel, 171
  in contemporary world, 175
  in North America, 171
  in South America, 171
  in sub-Saharan Africa, 170–171
  incompatibility with companionate
    marriage, 174–175
  male desire for multiple mates and, 172
  male prestige and, 171
  male reproductive success and, 172
  opposition of Catholic Church to, 175
  outlawing of in contemporary world, 175
  sororal, 176
  widespread practice of, 170
Polygynous species, 118–119
Polytheism
  among Aryans, 343
  among Egyptians, 343
  among Greeks and Romans, 343
  among Maya, Aztecs, and Inca, 343
  among Sumerians, 343
  anthropomorphic gods and, 343
  highly specialized gods and, 343
Population pressure
  agricultural intensification and, 58–59
  origins of the state and, 278
Pork. *See* Pigs.
Pornography
  female disinterest in, 122–123
  male interest in, 122–123
Pospisil, Leopold, 54–55
Postindustrial society, 67–68

Potato Eaters, The (painting), 362
Powell, Brian, 203
Power, 265–282. *See also* Political
    leadership.
  competition for, 11, 265–269
  human antidemocratic tendencies and,
    266
  natural tendency for obedience and,
    266–267, 268
  vs. influence, 269
  Zimbardo prison experiments and,
    267–268
Preferential homosexuality, 144, 146–152
  among nonhuman animals, 148
  biological theories of, 147–152
  causes of, 146–152
  frequency of, 146, 151
  gender atypical behavior (GAB) and,
    149–151
  heritability of, 149–150
  prenatal hormones and, 151–152
  role of hypothalamus in, 148, 149
  social constructionist theories of,
    146–147
Pride and Prejudice (Austen), 364
Prolonged lactation
  as birth spacing mechanism, 196
Prophets
  Buddha, 341
  Jesus, 341
  Jewish, 341
  Joseph Smith, 341
  Muhammad, 341
  Zoroaster, 341
Pross, Addy, 386
Protolanguage, 28
Proximate causes, 10, 126, 172, 178, 237. *See
    also* Ultimate causes.
Purdah, 227–228

R
Race. *See also* Racism, Skin color.
  as biological category, 320–321
  as social construct, 318, 320, 321
  ethnicity and, 330
  in American anthropology, 318–319
  in Brazil, 319–320, 328
  in Chinese biological anthropology,
    318–319
  in Polish biological anthropology,
    318–319

Race (*continued*)
  in South Africa, 319
  in United States, 319
  origins of, 317–324
  Out of Africa theory and, 321
  scientific classifications of, 320–321
Racism
  as ideological justification for slavery, 326
  as source of racial inequalities, 324, 328
  classical meaning of concept, 324
  explanations of, 326–327
  among ancient Egyptians, 325
  among ancient Greeks and Romans, 325
  in Islamic civilization, 325–326
  in United States, 327–328
  Joseph Arthur de Gobineau and, 327
  leading European intellectuals and, 327
  modern, 325, 326–328
  slavery and, 326–327
Rape of Troy, The (Gottschall), 315n94
Reciprocity, 68–69
Reed, Dorian, 134
Reiner, William G., 223
Religion, 12, 339–354
  adaptationist theories of, 345–347
  among Gond, 340
  among Maori, 341
  among Ojibwa, 340
  among Santal, 340–341
  as beliefs, 339
  as rituals, 339
  atheism and (*see* New Atheism)
  Axial Age and (*see* Axial Age)
  brain neurochemistry and, 346
  by-product theories of, 344–345
  costly signaling and, 345
  Darwinian evolutionary approaches to,
    344–347, 349
  evolution of, 348
  health and, 346
  high gods and (*see* High gods)
  in Polynesia, 339
  individualistic practices and, 341
  Islam and, 340
  mana and, 339
  monotheism and (*see* Monotheism)
  polytheism and (*see* Polytheism)
  priesthoods and, 341, 342
  prophets and (*see* Prophets)
  reproductive success and, 347, 350
  ritual specialists and, 340–341
    secularization and, 350
    shamans and (*see* Shamans)
    socioecological context and, 347–349
    spirits and, 340–341, 342, 345, 347
    witches and, 340, 342
Reproductive potential, 45, 288, 294–295
  male-female differences in, 168, 187, 200,
    202, 204, 207, 208
Reproductive success, 4, 6, 7, 8, 10, 25, 27,
    45, 69, 77, 83, 107, 123, 125, 126, 129,
    132, 141–143, 168, 169, 170, 176,
    177–178, 179, 193, 195, 196, 197,
    198, 200, 206, 208, 209, 220, 237, 247,
    259, 291, 298, 323, 347, 350, 362, 368,
    374
Rickets
  as calcium-deficiency disease, 96
Rieger, Gerulf, 150
Risch, Neil, 321
Role theory, 1
Rossi, Alice S., 188
Rotthauwe, Hans Werner, 95
Rule of hypo-descent. *See* One drop rule.

S
Saad, Gad, 259
Sadalla, Edward K., 138
Sagarin, Brad J., 125
Saggar, Anand K., 110
Sahlins, Marshall, 46, 47, 48
Salmon, Catherine, 122–123, 140–141
Salzano, Francisco M., 114
Sanderson, Derek S., 378n6, 378n31
Sanderson, Stephen K., 199
Santos, Ricardo Ventura, 320
Sartre, Jean-Paul, 381
Savage-Rumbaugh, E. Sue, 27
Schmitt, David P., 120–121, 122, 125–126,
    138
Schwabe, Calvin W., 78
Seemanova, Eva, 110
Seidman, Steven, 147
Self-deception, 26. *See also* Deception.
Self-interest, 11
Sense and Sensibility (Austen), 364
Sex Hormone Binding Globulin (SHBG)
  female masculinization and, 223
Sex. *See* Male sexuality, Female sexuality.
Sex ratios, 201–202, 204, 207
Sexual bonding
  vs. familial bonding, 114

Sexual dimorphism, 21, 116, 118, 216
Sexual jealousy. *See* Jealousy.
Sexual promiscuity, 161
Sexual selection, 17n9, 115–119
    among birds, 116–117
    among bowerbirds, 117
    among nonhuman primates, 116
    among peacocks, 116–117
    among pinnipeds, 115–116
    among ungulates, 116
    as female choice, 115–116
    as male combat, 115–116
    genetic fitness and, 117–118
    mating strategies and, 107, 118–121
    natural selection and, 118
Sexual variety
    male desire for, 107, 121, 172
Shamans, 341–342
    altered states of consciousness and, 342,
        347
    among Gond, 340–341
    among !Kung, 342
    among Sakha, 342
    communicating with the dead and, 341
    curing ceremonies and, 341–342
    protecting and finding game animals
        and, 341
    protecting people from evil spirits and, 341
    recovering lost souls and, 341
    trances and, 342
    vision quests and, 341
Shepher, Joseph, 111
Shorter, Edward, 163
Sigmundson, H. Keith, 243n37
Silk, Joan B., 179
Silverman, Irwin, 221, 222
Sim-pua marriage
    incest avoidance and, 111–112
Situational homosexuality, 144–146
    among ancient Greeks, 144–145
    among ancient Romans, 145
    among Etoro, 145
    among Sambia, 145
    among Siwans, 145
    among Zande, 145
    in traditional China, 145
    in traditional Japan, 145
Skin color
    Biasutti measurement scale of, 323
    convergent evolution in Europeans and
        Asians, 324

    dark skin as skin protectant, 323
    human migration and lightening of,
        323–324
    latitude and, 321–322
    skin reflectance as indicator of, 337n17
    ultraviolet radiation and, 321–322
    variations among American blacks,
        329–330
Small-scale war, 298–305
    among Aché, 299
    among Achuar, 299
    among Dugum Dani, 301
    among Gebusi, 299
    among Gidjingali, 300
    among Hewa, 300, 303–304
    among horticulturalists, 300–302
    among hunter-gatherers, 300–302
    among Kalinga, 300
    among Kapauku, 304
    among Kato, 300
    among Marquesans, 304
    among Modoc, 300
    among Mtetwa, 300
    among Murgin, 299
    among North American Indians, 299
    among Piegan, 300
    among Saramacca, 305
    among Tiwi, 304
    among Waorani, 299
    among Yanomama, 299, 301, 302, 303,
        304, 305
    among Yorok, 300
    competition for tangible resources and,
        303
    conflict over women and, 304–305
    fighting tactics and, 301–302
    frequency of, 298–299, 306
    in prehistory, 299
    male monopolization of, 217
    male mortality rates and, 299–300
    population pressure and, 306
    protein scarcity and, 302
Smedley, Audrey, 325
Smith, Adam, 68
Smith, Eric Alden, 86, 249, 382
Snooks, Graeme Donald, 307–308
Social constructionism
    as version of SSSM, 1
    gender and, 224
    race and, 318, 321
    sexual orientation and, 146–147

Social evolution, 69–70, 227, 245, 252, 254,
    259, 273, 282, 306, 340
  guiding forces of, 69
  vs. biological evolution, 69–70
Social learning
  direct teaching and, 12
  imitation and, 12
Social stratification
  in advanced horticultural societies, 252
  in agrarian societies, 253–254
  in ancient Hawaii, 252
  in modern societies, 254–256
  in traditional China, 253
  landlords and, 253
  nobles and, 253
  peasants and, 253
  sumptuary regulations and, 253–254
Socialization, 2, 216, 223, 224–225, 246
Sociobiology, 3, 5, 6, 8, 77, 109, 200, 267
Sociobiology: The New Synthesis (E. O.
    Wilson), 5
Socioecological context, 9, 12, 68, 107, 121,
    126, 136, 163, 187, 189, 198, 281–282,
    300, 347–349
Sociosexuality, 119, 121
  male-female differences in, 119 121
  restricted, 120
  socioecological context and, 121
  unrestricted, 120
Sociosexuality Inventory (SOI), 120–121
  male vs. female scores on, 120–121, 122
Somit, Albert, 266, 268
Sosis, Richard, 86, 345–346
Spices
  role in meat preservation, 80
Spitz, René, 192
Stahl, Lesley, 191
Standard Cross-Cultural Sample (SCCS),
    197, 218, 234, 299, 340
Standard Social Science Model (SSSM), 1,
    2, 6, 240
Starkweather, Katherine E., 178–179
Starry Night (painting), 362
States, 274–281. *See also* Civilizations.
  among Mongols, 281
  as aristocratic empires, 281
  as conquest societies, 278
  as war machines, 307
  centralized bureaucratic, 280–281
  circumscription theory of, 278
  feudal, 279–280

in ancient Rome, 281
in Persia, 281
Oriental despotism and, 280–281
pacification of large populations by, 274
Status striving. *See also* Social stratification,
    Wealth.
  among Central Abelam, 249
  among Kaoka Speakers, 249
  as innate predisposition, 245–248
  big men and, 249–250, 251, 252
  biochemical indicators of, 246
  conspicuous consumption and, 256–257
  conspicuous waste and, 256–257
  costly signaling and, 251–252, 256
  in young children, 245–246
  individual variation in, 247
  northwest coast tribes and, 250–251
  paramount chiefs and, 252
  philanthropic giving and, 259
  potlatch and, 250–251
  pursuit of wealth and, 252
  reproductive success and, 246–247
  suppression of among hunter-gatherers,
      247–248
Steadman, Lyle B., 303–304
Strakalj, Goran, 318
Sugiyama, Lawrence S., 134–135
Sugiyama, Michelle Scalise, 367
Sun, Li, 318
Sunflowers (painting), 362
Swanson, Guy, 339–340, 344
Sweet foods
  innate taste for, 81
Symbolic capital. *See* Cultural capital.
Symmetry. *See* Facial symmetry. *See also*
      Fluctuating asymmetry.
Symons, Donald, 7, 304

T
Tassinary, Louis G., 132, 134
Tastes
  for meat, 81–83
  for sweet foods, 81
  innate, 81–83
Teleological thinking. *See* Cognitive biases.
Telles, Edward E., 328
Testart, Alain, 45, 248
Testosterone, 17, 140, 220, 223
  aggressiveness and, 17, 119, 216, 237, 246
  competitiveness and, 217, 237, 246
  sexual orientation and, 148, 151

Theory of Mind (ToM), 25, 38n23
Theory of the Leisure Class, The (Veblen), 256
Thinker, The (sculpture), 357
Three-dimensional mental rotation (3DMR)
   male vs. female abilities at, 222
Tishkoff, Sarah A., 99
Tooby, John, 7, 68
Tool use
   in hominin evolution, 24, 25, 32
Trade networks, 62
   historical expansion of, 62
   Silk Road and, 62
   worldwide, 62
Tribes
   politics in, 269–270
Trivers, Robert L., 3, 118, 200
Trivers-Willard Hypothesis (TWH),
   200–205. *See also* Parental investment,
   Sex ratios.
   hypergyny and, 202
   Ifaluk and, 201–202
   in industrial societies, 203–204
   in nonindustrial societies, 201–203
   Maasai and, 202
   Mukugodo and, 202–203
   polygyny and, 204
Trost, Melanie R., 138
Turke, Paul W., 197–198, 201
Twin studies
   role in genetic research, 149, 151

U
Udry, J. Richard, 222–223, 225
Ultimate causes, 10, 126, 172, 178, 237. *See also* Proximate causes.
Ultraviolet radiation, 97
   skin color and, 96, 105n60, 321, 322 (table)
   skin damage and, 21, 95, 323
   vitamin D synthesis and, 95–97, 323
Unmentionable Cuisine (Schwabe), 78–79
unokais
   among Yanomama, 304
   multiple wives and, 304
   reproductive success of, 141–142
Upper Paleolithic
   cultural revolution during, 32–34

V
Vaesen, Krist, 25
Van Beijsterveldt, C. E. M., 151

Van den Berghe, Pierre L., 143, 324, 332
Vanhanen, Tatu, 219
Vasdev, Shawn, 291
Vasey, Paul L., 150
Veblen, Thorstein, 256–257
Vegetarianism, 82
Vicknair, Keven, 328–329
Violence. *See also* Homicide, War.
   chimpanzee-human similarities in, 301, 302
Violent Land: Single Men and Social Disorder from the Frontier to the Inner City (Courtwright), 314n16
Visual art, 358–364
   Abstract Expressionism and, 361
   age and production of, 364
   body decoration as, 362
   by-product theories of, 361–362
   Easter Island sculpted heads as, 358
   male vs. female production of, 363–364
   mass vs. elite, 358–361
   Maya and Aztec statues as, 358
   Modernism and, 360
   New Guinea wood carvings as, 357
   northwest coast totem poles as, 358
   Postimpressionism and, 360
   postmodernism and, 360
   sexual selection theories of, 361–364
   Upper Paleolithic cave paintings as, 32–33, 358
   widespread dislikes for, 359
   widespread preferences for, 358–359
Vitamin D
   role in calcium metabolism, 95–96
Voorhies, Barbara, 226, 228

W
Waist-to-hip ratio (WHR)
   as indicator of female attractiveness, 131–137
   as indicator of female health, 132
   as indicator of female reproductive potential, 132
   worldwide emphasis on, 132
Wang, Qian, 318
War, 298–310. *See also* Large-scale war, Small-scale war.
Ward, Carol V., 25
Watts, David P., 298
Wealth
   capitalists and, 63–68

Wealth (*continued*)
  inheritance of, 200
  landlords and, 61
  merchants and, 61
  polygyny and, 171, 173
  power and, 265, 278, 306, 307, 309
  social stratification and, 252–255, 275,
      276, 277–278
  status and, 171, 208, 256–258, 259
Weber, Samantha, 201, 204
Webster, Gregory D., 136
Weeden, Jason, 143
Weinberg, S. Kirson, 112–113
Westermarck, Edward, 2, 109, 115, 161
Wheeler, G. C., 270
Whitam, Frederick L., 149
Whitmeyer, Joseph, 143
Why Does the World Exist? (Holt), 386n1
Whyte, Martin King, 218–219
Willard, Dan, 200
Wilson, Edward O., 5, 354
Wilson, Margo, 191, 206–207, 288, 291, 292,
      293, 295
Wilson, Michael L., 299–300
Winch, Robert F., 163

Winkelman, Michael J., 346
Winterhalder, Bruce, 17n18, 382
Wittfogel, Karl, 280
Wolf, Arthur P., 111–112, 113
Wolf, Naomi, 127
Woman the Gatherer (Dahlberg), 42
Woodburn, James, 46, 47
World commercialization, 64
World Values Survey, 163
Wrangham, Richard W., 298, 299–300

X
Xq28
  as possible sexual orientation gene, 149

Y
Yellen, John E., 47

Z
Zahavi, Amotz, 117–118, 251
Zahavi, Avishag, 117–118, 251
Zerjal, Tatiana, 142
Zimbardo, Philip, 267–268
Zoroastrianism, 87
Zucker, Kenneth J., 150